Samch'ŏk

P'yongch'ang

Yŏngwol

Sunhŭng

Yean

Andong

KYŎNGSANG

Kyŏngju

Yŏngil

Tsushima

Wŏnju

Chungnyŏng

Taegu

Miryang

Masan

Chinhae

Ch'angwŏn Tongnae

Pusan

Kadŏk Island

Kŏje Island

Ich'ŏn

Chuksan

Ch'ungju

Ch'oryŏng

Sangju

Naktong River

Kyŏngsang Straits

Hansan Island

Namhan River

Yŏju

KYŎNGGI

Suwŏn

P'yŏngt'aek

Sŏnghwan

Chiksan

Ch'ŏnan

Ch'ŏngju

Konggŏmji

Sŏngju

Anŭi

Noryang-jin

Asan

CH'UNGCH'ŎNG

Kongju

Kŭm River

Poryŏng

Puyŏ

Ŭnjin

Iksan

Chŏnju

Chiri Hills

Kwangyang

Yŏsu

CHŎLLA

Naju

Mokp'o

CHEJU

JAMES SCARTH GALE
and his
HISTORY OF THE KOREAN PEOPLE

JAMES SCARTH GALE
and his

HISTORY OF THE
KOREAN PEOPLE

韓國民族史

A new edition of the HISTORY
together with a biography
and annotated bibliographies

by

RICHARD RUTT

Published for the Royal Asiatic Society
Korea Branch
by Seoul Computer Press

by the same author:

KOREAN WORKS AND DAYS (1964)

P'UNGNYU HAN'GUK (1965)

AN ANTHOLOGY OF KOREAN *SIJO* (1970)

THE BAMBOO GROVE (An introduction to *sijo*) (1971)

Copyright © 1972 by the Royal Asiatic Society, Korea Branch
Published for the RAS-KB
By Seoul Computer Press
Registration No. 15-21
Seoul, Korea

First Printing 1972
Second Printing 1982

for Roddy, Wendy, and Rosemary

CONTENTS

Illustrations

after page viii

Acknowledgements 1 Mr George J. M. Gale; 2 Dr S. H. Moffett; 3, 5, 9, 10 Carlo Rosseffi *Corea e i Coreani* Bergamo 1904; 4, 6, 7, 8, 11, 12, 13 'The Gale Portfolio' in Yonsei University Library (by permission of the librarian and Mrs E. M. Gale)

James Scarth Gale. A painting by Paek Ch'ŏlgu from a photograph.

Yi Ch'angjik, Gale's principal literary assistant.

Koreans of the middle class playing chess in the street, about 1903.

Korean sedan chair and retinue. Carlo Rossetti, Italian consul-general in Seoul 1902-3.

The Heron residence in Chŏng-dong, Seoul, about 1890. Harriet is holding Jessie and has Annie beside her.

American presbyterian missionaries at Namhan Sansŏng during the summer of 1891. *Standing:* J. S. Gale, W. M. Baird and his wife; *seated:* S. A. Moffett, Harriet Heron, Susan Doty, C. C. Vinton and his wife, D. L. Gifford and his wife; *children:* Jessie Heron (standing), Annie Heron (seated).

浚明堂

李正魯　沈相漢　金允植　金聲根　李容元　　　金炳翊　閔種默　徐正淳　李胄榮　金永典

The Emperor Kojong with officials, probably the Kiroso, a group honoured because they were more than seventy years old. Taken about 1908 outside the emperor's apartment in the Tŏksu Palace. *Left to right:* Yi Chŏngno, Sim Sanghan, Kim Yunsik *(see p. 320)* Kim Sŏnggŭn, Yi Yongwŏn, Kim Pyŏngik, Min Chongmuk, Sŏ Chŏngsun, Yi Wiyŏng, Kim Yŏngjŏn.

Kwanghwa-mun, great gate of the Kyŏngbok Palace, in the 1890s. Rebuilt by Hŭngsŏn Taewŏn'gun 1865-8.

Nam-daemun, the Great South Gate of Seoul 1902.

The abbot and monks of Sŏgwang-sa, about 1895.

James Gale and Samuel Moffett at Namhan Sansŏng, probably in 1891, soon after their journey to Mukden.

A view of Seoul looking north from the South Mountain in 1902. The tall
buildings in the left middle-distance are the Altar of Heaven built after the
Korean empire was proclaimed in 1897, and the Roman catholic cathedral (1897).

Yŏnmot-kol church 1907.

Preface

I have been helped in collecting information about James Gale's life by his son, George J. M. Gale of Montreal; his daughter, Mrs John Lloyd-Kirk of Bristol; his two stepdaughters, Mrs Esson M. Gale and Mrs George Carroll; Dr Samuel H. Moffett of Seoul; Dr Allen D. Clark; Pastor O Yunt'ae; Ryu Tongsik of the Korean Christian Literature Society; Kim Chubyŏng, general secretary of the Korean Bible Society; the late professor Kim Yangsŏn; Ko Ch'unsŏp, historian of Kyŏngsin School; Mrs Pilley Kim Choi; Song Taeam (Pierre Song); Miss Dorothy Sivyer; Dr William Scott; Miss Anne Davison, who obtained material from the office of Statistics and Records of Toronto University; Mr and Mrs Albert Krabbe,the present owners of the Gale farmhouse at Alma; the research department of the Commission on Ecumenical Mission and Relations of the Presbyterian Church in the USA; Dr George L. Paik; Dr Kim Myungsun; Mr Key P. Yang and Miss Marion Steele of the Library of Congress, Washington DC; Mr Malcolm Shields, the stated clerk of the New Albany Presbytery,Indiana; Miss Margaret Brown; the Revd Cyril Powles; the Revd Theodore Hard; Dr R. K. Anderson of the Presbyterian Church of Canada; Miss Catherine Mackenzie of the Australian Presbyterian Mission in Korea; Mr Robert Gale of Elora (Dr Gale's nephew); Mrs John Purdon; Mr Harold Stough, secretary of the British Israel Federation; the Presbyterian Historical Society, Philadelphia; the Municipal Library, Bath; the British and Foreign Bible Society, London; the American Bible Society; the Missionary Research Library of New York; the Historical Foundation of the Presbyterian and Reformed Churches, Montreat, North Carolina; and the Fédération Protestante de France.

The original publication of the *History* has many defects. There are mistakes of spelling, punctuation and grammar. Some errors are plainly due to misreading or miscopying Chinese characters and failure to read proofs; some are due to misinformation or to limited knowledge in the period at which Gale wrote. I have overhauled the punctuation, corrected the misprints and re-arranged the order of clauses within many sentences, because Gale's habit of inverting predicates, though typical of his style when he wrote the *History,* is highly irritating when indulged too many times on one page. I have retained and unified Gale's British spelling, and removed the mistakes in grammar and usage which disfigure the pages of the first edition. I have altered his vocabulary where it was misleading or ir-ritatingly mannered. (He constantly wrote *glass* for *cup* — glass drinking-vessels were all but unknown in Korea — and *pen* for *writing-brush, writing* for both *literary composition* and *calligraphy;* he overworked *master* for *expert* or *great man, soul* for *mind, round* for *routine* or *course, thought* for *meaning, ever* for *always, but* for *only* and *back of* for *behind.)* This means that I have made changes that depend on my own taste, but I believe it shows greater respect for Gale to present him without his superficial blemishes of style.

Where I have detected simple errors of fact or translation I have corrected them without annotation, but I have not tampered with Gale's opinions. If his account differs from what is now accepted as true because of advances in historical study, I have said so in the notes. I believe I have clarified his meaning without adding or deleting anything significant.

There is justification for altering his verse translations because in his later letters he wrote of them as drafts with which he was not satisfied. He usually aimed at writing iambics, most often blank verse pentameters. The paratactic nature of Chinese verse led him to ignore the possibilities of enjambement and at times to write verses of impossible length. Some of his poems fall readily into regular blank verse when the verses are rearranged with enjambement. I have therefore freely rearranged the verses. To improve the metre I have sometimes omitted words from his text (he was lavish with unnecessary words), but I have not added anything except where I have said so in the notes and given the reason. The only alterations I have made in vocabulary are those for which there was justification in his manuscripts.

The chapters of the book were the instalments of the original serial publication in the *Korea Mission Field*. They had no titles, but up to chapter xxxiii the paragraphs had cut-in headings. These may have been inserted by the editor, A. F. DeCamp, for they stop after Ellasue Wagner took over the editorship of the magazine. I have omitted these paragraph headings, but added chapter headings, and indicated the topical sections within chapters by wider spacing between the paragraphs.

Gale romanized Korean, Chinese, Sanskrit and other languages according to their Korean pronunciation in his own 'popular' style—Li Tai-paik for Li Po, Soopoori for Subhuti, Nak-yang for Lo-yang, Kooma for Kumarajiva, and so on. What would be gained by keeping the period flavour of his spellings would not offset the loss in clarity for the modern reader, so I have standardized all romanizations according to the conventions most widely accepted for this type of writing: Wade-Giles for Chinese and McCune-Reischauer for Korean. Gale gave Chinese characters in brackets after most proper names. These I have omitted.

He rarely indicated his sources, and never gave precise references for his statements and quotations. I have given references to sources known to have been available to him. Where I have identified no source, it means that I have been unable to trace one.

In editing the *History* I have been helped by many people, especially: Bishop James Pong Tak-ming of Taiwan; Chung Yung-min of Chung-chi College, Hong Kong; Kim Chihŏn, the well-known Seoul bookseller; Kwŏn Yŏngwŏn, keeper of old books at Ch'ungnam University, Taejŏn; Dr Kim Chaewŏn and Dr Kim Wŏnyong; Professor Burton Watson; Dr Harold Cook; Dr Yun Sŏngbŏm; Fr Clarence Herbst SJ; Miss Susan Buckwell; Dr W. E. Skillend; Fr John Lee Sŏkhyŏng; the late Fr Joseph P. Gibbons, MM; Brother George Every, SSM; Mr Edward Adams; the archivist of Cambridgeshire and the Isle of Ely; and the librarians of the British Museum, the city of Ayr, the Society for Psychical Research in London, the Royal Commonwealth Society, Sophia University in Tokyo, Yonsei University (where Mr Horace Underwood and his staff were untiringly helpful and where many of the books used by Gale are now kept), Seoul National University, Koryŏ University, and Tongguk University.

In the notes and bibliographies, references to western books and periodicals use upper case roman figures to indicate volumes; lower case roman figures indicate chapters of books or numbers of periodicals; arabic figures indicate page numbers. In references to old Korean books upper case roman figures indicate book (*kwŏn*) numbers, arabic figures indicate page numbers. These are sometimes followed by *a* for obverse and *b* for reverse, and further arabic figures showing the column of characters. Lower case roman figures indicate chapters. When references are given to modern reprints of books without *kwŏn* numbers, upper case roman figures denote volume numbers. In references to *Namhun t'aep'yŏng ka,* arabic numerals in brackets indicate the serial numbers of the songs.

I owe special debts to Miss Sunshine Murphy and her staff at the US Eighth Army Library in Yongsan, Seoul, for their generous help; to Mrs Sandra Mattielli, for her technical advice and painstaking work on design and production; and to Mr Robert A. Kinney, the publications chairman of the Korea Branch of the Royal Asiatic Society, who first suggested that I should undertake this book.

Joan, my wife, has shared in the research and the writing of this book to such a degree that she must be regarded as co-author. We take pleasure in dedicating it to three charming young people: Dr Gale's grandson and granddaughters.

Taejŏn   Richard Rutt
Candlemas 1972

A BIOGRAPHY OF
JAMES SCARTH GALE

i Scottish Canadian boy 1863 – 1884

Korean writers count James Scarth Gale as an Englishman, though his father
was a Scot and his mother came of an American Dutch family. He regarded
himself as a Canadian. The colophons of the books published under his name in
Korea always describe him as English because Canadians were British subjects
and the Korean and Japanese languages do not distinguish the English from the
British. He died in England and his second wife was English; but his first wife
was American and he worked most of his life for an American mission. The
final touch to his cosmopolitanism was given by his student days in Paris, so that
his fellow-missionary, William M. Baird, was to describe him in an early letter
as 'half Scotch, half Dutch, half French, yet completely English, and somewhat
"bohemian" '.

His ancestry was solidly Scots and Presbyterian. His father, John George
Gale, was born in 1819 at the Mill of Logie, by the foot of Mount Morven on
Deeside. James's grandfather, oppressed by money worries, died soon after
John's birth, leaving his wife, Jane Esson, in severe poverty. So in 1823 John's elder
brother Alexander, having graduated from Marischal College, Aberdeen, went
to Canada to join his uncle, Henry Esson, who was then a presbyterian
minister in Montreal. Alexander also became a minister and was living near
Montreal at Lachine when thirteen-year-old John and his mother and sisters
joined him in 1832. James Gale was later to recall with pleasure that his
father had crossed the ocean to live at a place called 'China', for Lachine was
the name wistfully given to the place by the sixteenth-century Breton voyager
Jacques Cartier when he was looking for a water route to the Orient and had his
hopes finally dashed by the turbulent rapids of Hochelaga.

The Gales and the Essons were part of the mass migration from the British
Isles to North America during the post-Napoleonic depression and unrest of
1815-1850. They were also among the founding families of Canadian presbyterianism. They were conservative, they favoured established religion, and were
passionately devoted to education. Both Alexander Gale and Henry Esson were
among those who struggled to achieve the foundation of Knox College, after the
families had moved from Montreal to Ontario in 1833, a year after John's arrival.
John started work in an office of the Hudson's Bay Company.

Canada was a land of promise for the Scots immigrants, who were prepared
to work hard. They had little sense of political grievance. In the summer of 1837
there was a crop failure in Ontario, and William Lyon Mackenzie, the radical
mayor of Toronto, seized the opportunity to lead a rebellion, but it failed because

the majority of the settlers feared Mackenzie's extremism. Many of them were discontented with the way in which the government and wealth of Canada were concentrated in too few hands, but he favoured independence of Britain and the joining of Canada to the United States. Even the more liberal settlers had an essential conservatism which made them volunteer against the rebels. Although John Gale was only eighteen, he found himself for a short while wearing a volunteer's uniform. Loyalism was part of the Gales' way of life, and John and his kind had no interest in struggling for radical solutions to Canada's development problems.

In 1848 John became a farmer, and took a hundred acres of land in Wellington County. A year or two later he married Miami Bradt, who was ten years younger than he was. She came of a Dutch family who had arrived in Ontario from New York State as United Empire Loyalists. In the autumn of 1829, when she was only six months old, the whole family had set out to visit relatives still living on the American side of the Niagara river, and found the ferry at the Burlington Canal was unmanned. Miami's father tried to get the horse and buggy over by himself, and they were nearing the further side when the horse shied, and all aboard the ferry were flung into the water. Death by drowning in river water took enormous toll of Canadian life at that time. On this occasion only the baby was rescued. She was sent to live with her uncle by marriage, Alexander Maclaren, and so in the course of church and family life came to meet John Gale and joined him on his new farm.

The Gale farm was registered as 'Pilkington Township, Second Concession, Lot 4'. The 'Pilkington Tract', about eighty miles north-west of Toronto, had been acquired in 1799 by Major-General Robert Pilkington of the British Royal Engineers, who was then serving in Ontario. It was a wooded area with nothing but an Iroquois trail running through it from the Grand River valley (where some Iroquois had settled after the American revolution) to the shores of Lake Huron. Pilkington took no measures for settling it till about 1820. The first settlers were loyalists from the United States; Scots began arriving before 1830.

John Gale was a latecomer to Pilkington, but he still had virgin forest growing on his hundred-acre strip rolling over the hills. Most of the land he cleared to make pasture, leaving a screen of woods in the marshy hollow at the far end. At the end nearest the road he built his house of red brick with neatly-painted white woodwork, adding to it as the years went by and the family increased. He put up rail fences of split logs round the pastures. There was a building bee in which local men came to help him raise the great barn which is the sole outbuilding and indispensable heart of an Ontario farm, where the animals live on the ground floor and fodder is stored in the enormous loft.

There were many Scots in the area. Place-names like Bon Accord (the motto of Aberdeen) and Aboyne Oatmeal Mill were typical. About a mile from the Gale farm, at the edge of the township, a Scot named Alexander McCrea settled in the same year that John Gale started clearing his land. McCrea built a farm, a store and a post-office, around which grew the village of McCrea's Corner. Five years later McCrea's holding was taken over by another Scot, John Isaacs of Aberdeen, and soon afterwards the victory of Alma in the Crimean War provided an excuse for changing the name of the village to Alma, in November 1854. Alma was the social focus of the Gales' life. Three inns there catered for teamsters from Lake Huron on their way to and from Guelph and Elora. A schoolhouse was built and a Scottish schoolmaster installed. Eventually three churches, presbyterian, Wesleyan methodist and anglican, were organized. Life was rugged but friendly. Neighbours gathered in working parties, called bees, for building, quilting, rug-hooking, or peeling apples to make apple butter. Household necessities such as cider vinegar, tallow candles and hop yeast were all homemade. There was plenty of trout in the local streams, there was still game in the woods. Alma had a tailor, a shoemaker, a carpenter, a grist-mill and a sawmill. The pedlar's wagon came to trade tinware for hardwood ashes to be used in making soap.

John Gale became a prominent citizen. He was an elder of Knox Church in the town of Elora, five miles to the south, and became one of the first trustees of Alma Presbyterian Church. His farming was mixed. He kept pigs, but his chief business was grazing cattle and raising them for export. In Canadian political terms he was a liberal, which meant no more than that he was a Scottish individualist, chary of the anglican establishment, and suspicious of the French in Lower Canada. His household seems to have been less solemn than that of his brother Alexander. This may have been because Miami brought gaiety with her, but John Gale himself loved books and read to his family by the fireside on winter evenings; and in summer they played croquet on the front lawn. By the time the children were growing up they hardly thought of themselves as pioneers.

James Scarth Gale was born on 19 February 1863, the fifth of six children: Alexander, who in later life continued the family farm; Sophia Jane, called Jenny, who became Mrs Cleghorn, of Kitchener, Ontario, and had one daughter who was named Corea; Hugh, who studied medicine at McGill University, Montreal, and became a general practitioner in Bay City, Michigan; John, who went to work on railways in the western USA; James Scarth; and Robert, who became a presbyterian minister and finished his days as pastor of the United Church at Bayfield, Ontario.

When James was living in retirement, about 1933, he wrote an explanation of his christian names:

> My name of Scarth links up with my uncle Alex in a very interesting way. It happened that while he was a student at college he became acquainted with a young lady from the Orkneys, Margaret Scarth, also studying in Aberdeen. Their mutual esteem increased as their acquaintance grew, till suddenly, just after he had taken ship for Canada, all communication was cut off. A letter of inquiry found no answer, and a silent ten years went on.
>
> One day, quite unexpectedly, a letter arrived in Canada from Margaret Scarth with this explanation: 'My aunt has passed away. In looking over her effects, I find she intercepted letters you sent me, and so you never received an answer. This is simply to make explanation. Please accept my sincere regrets.'

3

This put a new light on this dull world, and my uncle wrote asking if her heart was free and she would come to him in Canada. Her answer was: 'Delighted!' She came, and they were married in Boston. A year later a son was born to them, named James Scarth Gale. He grew up to be a fine young man, but fell under the fatal blight of tuberculosis just when all high hopes were centred on him. . . . I was born shortly after, and was called in memory of this beloved son and nephew, James Scarth Gale.

By the time James was old enough to take notice, life in Alma was changing. He was only seven years old when the Wellington, Grey and Bruce Railway was opened and put an end to the passage of the teamsters up and down the gravel road through the village. A year later Alma had its own railway station and the city of Toronto was within easy reach. Upper Canada was developing fast. The whole country had recently been disturbed by the Red River Rebellion in Manitoba, when the catholic Métis, Louis Riel, struck at the Ottawa government. The rebellion was put down, and the strongly protestant ambience of western Ontario was reinforced, but the building of the railways was opening the west in the last great pioneer efforts. The excitement of national expansion was felt even in the established farmlands of Alma.

Young James grew up in a peaceful but demanding atmosphere. As soon as he could, he helped his father and brothers with the pigs and horses. He attended the public school of No. 1 Section, Pilkington, a log-house in Alma where boys and girls were taught together. In winter they burned cordwood sticks in the stove. In the corner was a tin pail full of water, with a dipper for drinking. The schoolmaster was a Scot with a baroque nose and three quaint tufts of hair on his otherwise bald head. His name was Sanderson, and he ruled his charges with a wooden paddle called Solomon, because it was used 'for imparting wisdom'. Solomon came into action when Jim was caught drawing on his slate a well-practised caricature of Mr Sanderson's nose and three tufts; but Sanderson's corrective punishments were varied. He had a religious reverence for bread, and when he caught another boy flicking bread pellets, he made him gather up and eat the grimy little balls. When Jim was drowsy in school one day, Sanderson's cure for sleepiness was to make him lie down to sleep on a bench in front of the class. The children remembered these sardonic tricks, but they represented only one side of Sanderson's character. He taught them the elements of responsible farming by such means as giving a penny to any child who brought him a hundred thistles complete with roots; and he nourished their minds with readings from *Gulliver's Travels* and *Sindbad,* from Burns, Campbell, Coleridge, Wordsworth, Longfellow and others. They studied the Ontario Public School Books produced by the energetic Methodist educator Egerton Ryerson on lines similar to the more famous *Eclectic Readers* edited in the USA at about the same time by William Holmes McGuffey. McGuffey's blend of Hamiltonian democracy and calvinistic ethic, which did so much to form the mentality of the Middle West, differed from the pabulum of the Scots children in Ontario only in so far as the latter had a distinctly British tinge. James Gale kept some of his schoolbooks till he died, and they had a profound effect on his adult literary taste and intellectual predilections.

He was probably frequently in trouble with Sanderson, because he was the scamp of the family, bright and mischievous, full of pranks that were often blamed on his younger brother Robert, who looked very much like him. In due time he went on to High School at Elora, a charming little tree-filled town set on the Grand River where it runs through beautiful gorges. The school stood a little way above the grey cliffs at the riverside, next to the elegant new pinnacled building of Knox Presbyterian Church, dedicated when Jim was ten years old.

Again his teacher was a Scot, David Boyle. Boyle collected birds and animals, and accumulated historical and Indian relics. He contributed humorous articles to the *Elora Express,* writing in Scottish dialect under the name of Sandy McTocher. A Canadian critic has noted that the belles-lettres published in Canadian newspapers at the time were probably the worst ever published anywhere, and Sandy McTocher is probably responsible for the archness of some of James Gale's own writing for periodicals in later years.

Jim enjoyed his schooling, but he did not enjoy going to church. Every Sunday, the family would leave home at seven in the morning and drive in the buggy down the straight road over the undulating hills to Elora. During the service the horse was tied under the cedar-shingled roof of the long shed behind the church. The singing of the Scottish psalm tunes was so bad and doleful that if the precentor broke down the children enjoyed the relief from solemn monotony. Mr Duff's sermons were intolerably long, with their 'firstly . . . secondly . . . thirdly . . . and lastly . . .', after which young Jim waited anxiously for the blessed announcement: 'And in conclusion . . .' Then there was the return home in either very hot or very cold weather, and at about twenty to two they passed the croquet lawn in front of the farm with stomachs aching for the first food since early morning.

There were also sermons to be memorized. Jim did not enjoy religion; it worried and depressed him. Sometimes on Sunday evenings he was allowed by his parents to go to the red-brick Wesleyan chapel which opened in Alma village when he was twelve. Cheerful candles burned in tin sconces round the walls, and a choir which included pretty girls sat behind the minister, facing the congregation. The singing was in four parts; the sermons were inspirational rather than dogmatic. This sort of religion was more to Jim's taste, and he enjoyed seeing the girls.

His nature was essentially sunny. The radiance of the methodists appealed to a boy who liked to go chasing chipmunks and squirrels in the woods with his dog Rover. In the pine-woods and willow-meadows, along the trout-streams and by the swamps, he played among the trees: sugar-maple, birch, hemlock and tamarack, with hazel, honeysuckle and skunk-currant growing between. They met foxes, raccoons, and marmots. There was an unpleasant encounter with a skunk, and sometimes they saw a bear lumbering through the thicket. Jim loved to watch the beavers as they worked on their lodges and dams in the swamp, or slapped their tails on the mud to give warning of the approach of boy or dog.

But even in the woods he was not entirely carefree. Mr Duff's brand of christianity made Jim live in terror of judgment, and produced nightmares. With the onset of adolescence a deep gloom took over his mind and he was unable to unburden himself even to his mother. He would go into the woods and brood there in misery. The problem was a genuinely religious one, for it had a religious solution. One Sunday afternoon when he was fourteen, his eldest brother Alexander suggested, most unusually, that the two of them drive to Elora church for evening service. They went, and a Mr Macdonald preached the sermon. His text and subject were soon forgotten, but in the course of the sermon he told of a boy worried about the horrors of divine judgment, unable to unburden his heart, brooding alone in the woods. Jim recognized himself in this story, and suddenly experienced for the first time in his life a sensation of flooding light, a 'sight of that heaven to come' that was several times repeated in later years, and gave him a comfort which never deserted him. He was at peace.

At that time the family was subject to the risk of typhoid. Jim's mother had enteric fever in 1876, and her son Hugh, then a twenty-year-old medical student, nursed her and prescribed her medicines. She was strictly teetotal (though her husband was not) and Hugh and the impish Jim took great delight in making her drink whisky in her medicine without telling her what the active ingredient was. She recovered. Then Jim fell sick with typhoid, and a lugubrious pastor visited the farm to prepare the boy for impending doom. Jim was quite ready to die, because his experience during Mr Macdonald's sermon had given him unshakable peace. The minister was impressed, and suggested that if he recovered he should make his public profession of faith and become a fully-fledged member of the church. In those days this was a severe ordeal for a fifteen-year-old, and meant much teasing from his schoolfellows, but after his recovery he went through with it. He was now slightly precocious in religion, and the experience of light confirmed the romantic bent of his soul.

When he was eighteen he went for three years to St Catharines Institute in the town of St Catharines on the coast of Lake Ontario. This was milder, peach-growing country, far south of Toronto. In the quiet hours the students thought they could hear the boom of Niagara Falls only a dozen miles away. In Ontario a collegiate institute is a senior high school, and Jim was there to prepare for matriculation to the university. Once again his headmaster was a Scot, John Seath, who declaimed Shakespeare with unforgettable verve. James was deeply impressed and continued to enjoy his studies. Not surprisingly, however, he made a poor showing in examinations: he did not always bother about details. His ebullient character grew in charm. A photograph of him in his last year at St Catharines shows him at his most handsome, in the bloom of youth, with luxuriant dark hair and the high cheekbones, sloping jaw and large grey eyes that characterized him for the rest of his life.

At St Catharines Institute he first met Robert Harkness, another Canadian-born Scot, four years older than himself and much more serious. They became friends, though Harkness did not hide his opinion that Gale was frivolous; they had no idea how far they were to travel together.

ii Missionary volunteer 1884 – 1888

Gale and Harkness matriculated in 1884. Gale went to University College, Toronto. During his first year he served in the militia; and was deeply impressed by a preaching visit from Dwight L. Moody, the famous evangelist. His religious and literary orientations were stabilizing: his classmates included Jonathan Goforth, the future missionary leader in China, and J. A. MacDonald, who was to become editor of the *Toronto Globe*. By special permission of the university senate, Gale spent several months of his second year in France, where he was supposed to study French at the Collège de France and work in a protestant mission.

His family persuaded him to keep a diary of this adventure. He set off from Toronto in good spirits on 22 May 1885 by train to Montreal. The sight of the St Lawrence River made him think of Addison's *Vision of Mirza,* a piece of literature from the Ontario Public School Books that haunted him for the rest of his life. Two days later he boarded the *Circassian* at Rimouski, travelling steerage in great discomfort with uncongenial companions through the cold Atlantic fogs.

On 2 June he disembarked at Liverpool, where he saw prostitutes for the first time, and was deeply shocked, because such people had not come into his ken before. Late the same night he boarded the train for London. The English countryside looked lovely in the moonlight, and the sight of the sun rising over Bedford made him rejoice to be travelling through John Bunyan's native land. St Albans thrilled him with thoughts of the Wars of the Roses. England was the romantic land of the history he had learnt.

He arrived in London at five o'clock in the morning. The sense of romance soon evaporated, but he found cheap lodgings at 3 Wallgrave Terrace, Kensington, and started off on a full week of sightseeing in the world's greatest capital. He was excited to think that he was in Paul Dombey's town (Paul Dombey was always a favourite character of his: the fey boy was a mirror to part of his own soul). He went to weekday evensong in Westminster Abbey and was more overcome by the emotion of sitting near Poets' Corner than he was impressed by the old dean's reading of Hebrews x; but he was feeling lonely when he saw Mr Gladstone's carriage standing outside 10 Downing Street, and shortage of money added to his depression.

He called at the office of the *Toronto Globe* in Fleet Street to assuage his homesickness, visited Kew Gardens and the Zoo, and saw the South Kensington museums on a rainy Saturday morning. Seeing the prostitutes, and the down-and-outs sleeping in the open on the Thames Embankment, made him more melancholy. He felt miserable and provincial as he tramped the hard streets alone. Wishing that his sister Jenny were with him, he went to hear the Strauss orchestra in the Albert Hall, but found that music 'too high-falutin', and went out to listen to the band of the Coldstream Guards playing *Scots wha hae* in Kensington Gardens. This was Scottish and wholehearted, much more to his taste. As he sat alone on a park bench, an old cannon-maker from Woolwich

Arsenal, out for the afternoon with his wife, chatted with him, praised his courage and solaced his loneliness.

On Sunday morning he went to Kensington Presbyterian Church. It was utterly unlike his Canadian churches, and he was not pleased. 'High-church presbyterianism needs another Reformation, it seems to me,' he wrote in his diary. He was much happier in the evening among the great crowd that heard Spurgeon preach on John iii 16 at the Metropolitan Tabernacle. This was the sort of religion he had acquired a taste for in the methodist church at Alma; but the dandy in him noted that Spurgeon 'dresses very plain. I notice he wears a black tie.'

The social inequality of London—'lordism', he called it—distressed him greatly. He felt hungry on tuppenny breakfasts, and was torn between depression and the excitements of historical sightseeing. On Wednesday 10 June, he was due to leave Victoria Station by the evening train, and, having stowed his luggage at the station, he went in the afternoon to attend evensong in St Paul's Cathedral. Sitting at the back of the church he confided to his diary: 'There is something grand about it, I must confess, but can God be honoured by such mummery . . . ? The flickering candlelight and white-robed boys remind me of the dark days of Rome. Heart service from the poorest hovel, it seems to me, is worth more than all the unintelligible groanings of St Paul's Cathedral.' He was very much out of his element.

He caught the night train and left Newhaven by boat at eleven o'clock next morning. A lad from Birmingham and a Turk had become his travelling companions. The English Channel did what the Atlantic could not, and made him seasick. He disembarked at Dieppe, which looked ruinous, and took the train to Paris. At eleven o'clock at night they pulled into the Gare St Lazare, where Gale and the Turk were bilked by a guide before they found hotel-room together.

The following day the Turk departed, and Gale went to present his letter of introduction to the Reverend William Newell, a minister from New York and a director of the McAll Mission, who recommended him to Lorado Taft, a 25-year-old American sculptor from Chicago who lived on the left bank of the Seine near Montparnasse. Taft, who later had a distinguished career in America, found him a hotel room in the Rue Denfert for thirty francs a month, and he planned to get his meals at a nearby *crêmerie*. That evening Taft took him to the McAll Mission at Belleville.

Belleville had been the first preaching-place of the McAll Mission, a protestant mission to France founded in 1872 by the enthusiasm of Robert Whitaker McAll, an English congregationalist minister. It is now known as the *Mission Populaire Evangélique de France,* and has several centres in Paris as well as a dozen or more in provincial cities. The emphasis of the Mission was on preaching the gospel to the unchurched urban poor, by means of dispensaries and rural vacation plans for children as well as conventional preaching-halls, usually located in shops, which the bands of workers visited in turn. The work was carried on in fraternal co-operation with the French protestant churches. 22-year-old James Gale could not preach in French, but he frequently worked as a pavement advertiser for the services, encouraging passers-by to come in. He revelled in a christianity that was little interested in sectarian dogmatism, and his idealism was kindled by the practical approach of the McAll Mission. He conceived the idea of a vocation to work as a missioner in France.

However, he was not really happy in Paris. He toured the sights of the city. Moonlight on the Seine impressed him most; the heat of June was oppressive, and he was surprised to find himself longing for the Canadian winter. He had long talks with a free-thinking Dane, which only increased his misery. Most of his friends were American artists, whom he found boring because they talked of nothing but art. He visited the Morgue, but was far more shocked at the Ecole des Beaux Arts, where he saw a model strip herself naked for a life class: nude art passed his understanding. There were bed-bugs, the food was poor, he slept badly. Everywhere there were down-and-outs and prostitutes. At the end of July the weather turned suddenly cold, and he grew nostalgic for the Ontario harvest, but at the same time was dogged by memories of the typhoid he had had four years before. He was shocked again when he saw the can-can. Faith was his anchor.

There were some bright intervals. He received his examination results by post on 16 June, and they were as good as a tonic. A picnic party at Fontainebleau left a vivid impression, and the fête in the Champ de Mars on 14 July was exhilarating. He often had tea with the Moores, American ladies living in the Rue de Lille. Miss Moore liked his good looks and pitied his poverty, so, to the astonishment of the passing soldiers, she had him dress as a goatherd and stand on a balcony while she painted pictures of him.

His depression was made worse by a bad conscience about his studies. At the end of June he ventured to write two pages of his diary in French. It was fluent, but incorrect. Several times he went to hear French spoken at the Palais de Justice, but only twice did he attend the Collège de France. The first time he happened on an algebra lecture and was not interested enough to stay to the end. He tried reading: Balzac's *Eugénie Grandet,* Hugo's *Notre-Dame de Paris,* and Ponsard's tragedy *Charlotte Corday;* then listlessly turned to Goethe's *Iphigenie auf Tauris,* in German. The French he wrote at the end of July shows little improvement.

French catholicism both attracted and repelled him. He found nothing but 'the customary catholic gloom' in the Père Lachaise cemetery, yet a painting of the crucifixion in St Sulpice held him spellbound, and he was drawn back to that church in spite of himself. At an evening service—it was probably benediction of the Blessed Sacrament—he was 'almost struck breathless' by the blaze of lighted candles, but insisted that the clergy were comic and the laity pathetic. For the protestant from Upper Canada, the French and their religion were a dangerous combination whose charms were to be resisted as much as possible.

Early in August he moved to Taft's studio, for companionship and for economy's sake. Within four days Taft was ill with mumps, and Gale nursed him. On the feast of the Assumption Gale attended the solemn mass at Notre Dame and was moved by it. A fortnight later he was in bed with mumps himself, unable to sleep because of the many visitors to the studio. By mid-September he had recovered, but soon after this point the diary peters out. There was 'nothing in France but unbelief and monks'. He ached to be back in Ontario, scarcely realizing how much he had benefited by his experience in Paris. He was disappointed with his progress in spoken French, but his confident presbyterianism had assumed a new dimension.

Later that autumn he was back in Toronto, living among the grey towers and busy black squirrels of the university quarter. He studied at University College, but lived at Knox—not the present Knox College, but the spired and towered building in Spadina Avenue which has become the Connaught Medical Research Laboratories. He read arts for his BA, and kept alive the spirit of his hours with the McAll Mission by taking charge for two years of the Elizabeth Street Mission, in one of the poorer parts of the city, then largely Jewish, but now part of Toronto's Chinatown. It was expected that presbyterian city churches would maintain missions run by students in underprivileged neighbourhoods, and Gale's work at 180 Elizabeth Street was a mission of Central Presbyterian Church, which stood on St Vincent Street at the corner of Grosvenor. No record remains of his work at the mission beyond the fact that he was there.

He was due to graduate in 1888, and had registered to enter Knox College as a theological student, but in 1887 Robert Parmelee Wilder and John N. Forman came to preach in Toronto. Although Wilder was only twenty-five years old, he had been present, as a delegate from Princeton, at the great Mount Hermon Conference of 1886, which was the beginning of the Student Volunteer Movement for Foreign Missions. A hundred volunteers were recruited at the conference, whose most famous member was John R. Mott, then a student delegate. Wilder was chosen to visit the colleges and seminaries of Canada and the United States to arouse missionary vocations. He was joined by Forman, another Princeton man, and they usually worked together. They were impressive speakers, for in the course of a year's preaching they persuaded 2,100 more students to volunteer as missionaries. Toronto was already in the throes of a great wave of missionary volunteer enthusiasm, and the mission boards were financially hard-pressed. The two young preachers fired the students with enthusiasm for a mission to Korea, the enigmatic Hermit Kingdom, which had been opened to christian missionaries only four years before.

University College Young Men's Christian Association wanted to send its own missionaries. There was a large group of presbyterian students in the college who would have preferred to co-operate with Knox College in supporting a missionary to China, but they were won over to the idea of University College having its own missionary. It seemed obvious to many, though not at first to James Gale himself, that he was the man who should go. Before accepting the call, he went up the tower of the Varsity building and spent the night there in prayer. Then, reluctantly, he consented. There were those who questioned the wisdom of sending a man who was neither an ordained minister nor theologically trained; and there were many who questioned the rightness of sending missionaries to the far east at a time when the Canadian west was just opening up. It says a great deal for James Gale that the objections to his appointment were overcome. He was guaranteed a salary of $500 a year for eight years, by annual subscription of students and graduates of the college, and appointed, not to establish an independent mission, but to co-operate with other evangelical denominations.

When the Easter vacation came, he went home to the farm at Alma and found his brother Alexander blasting a big stone. He immediately told him the great decision. The Gales were astounded. This was the last thing they had expected of Jim.

He took his BA degree on 12 June 1888. That year Hudson Taylor, founder of the China Inland Mission, was in Ontario. Gale met him and was greatly encouraged when Taylor prayed with him. Robert Harkness graduated at the same time and was also to go to Korea, sent out by the Toronto city YMCA. Early in October he married. On 18 October both men were given rousing farewell meetings, attended largely by presbyterians. The mission, however, was elaborately non-sectarian. Gale's standard of christian doctrine was the *Doctrinal Basis* of the Evangelical Alliance, which had been formed in London in 1846 with vigorous anglican participation by anti-Puseyite churchmen. This *Doctrinal Basis* defined evangelical doctrine as:

(1) The divine inspiration, authority and sufficiency of the Holy Scriptures;
(2) The right and duty of private judgment in the interpretation of the Holy Scriptures;
(3) The unity of the Godhead, and the Trinity of Persons therein;
(4) The utter depravity of human nature, in consequence of the Fall;
(5) The Incarnation of the Son of God, his work of atonement for sinners of mankind, and his mediatorial intercession and reign;
(6) The justification of the sinner by faith alone;
(7) The work of the Holy Spirit in the conversion and sanctification of the sinner;
(8) The immortality of the soul, the resurrection of the body, the judgment of the world by our Lord Jesus Christ, with the eternal blessedness of the righteous and the eternal punishment of the wicked;
(9) The divine institution of the christian ministry, and the obligation and perpetuity of the ordinances of Baptism and the Lord's Supper.

Riders to this statement made it clear that it was not intended as a definitive creed. It satisfied the Toronto YMCA committees, and it satisfied young Gale, who later described himself in *Canadian Men and Women of the Time* (1912) as belonging to the presbyterian church but being 'in entire sympathy with all other denominations'. Since some of the denominations were violently opposed to each other, he was indicating his ideal rather than his achievement, but in the context of Korean missions that ideal was not entirely quixotic. Most of the early protestant missionaries to Korea had minimal interest in denominational loyalties, and it is ironic that the churches they founded have turned out to be so notoriously fissiparous. Even towards Roman catholicism the attitude of the missionaries was often kindly, and they all admired the heroism of Korea's Roman catholic martyrs. Gale later became a prominent presbyterian missionary, but he never lost the supra-denominational attitudes of his first commission from the young men of Toronto.

At that farewell meeting the chairman was Sir Daniel Wilson, President of Toronto University. The convener of the Harkness Committee was the architect H. B. Gordon, who later designed the first building for Severance Hospital in Seoul. The same night, after the meeting was over, Gale left Toronto by the Canadian Pacific Railway to travel through Vancouver to Korea. By strange chance, in the train across Canada, he met William Rockhill, who had been US Minister in Peking and Seoul, and was then in North America preparing to lead a Smithsonian expedition to Tibet. Rockhill was only 34, but already a distinguished orientalist. He told Gale what to expect in Seoul, and described in particular the Korean passion for smoking tobacco.

In Vancouver Gale again met Moody, who was conducting evangelistic meetings in the town. Moody gave the young missionary his blessing and promised to pray for him. Gale always treasured the memory, and never tired of telling Moody's life-story to Korean christians.

So the farmer's son, second-generation immigrant, educated decently and broadly, though not aristocratically, became a missionary. That vocation was still open to the upper as well as to the middle classes; it has lost esteem on the American continent during the last eighty years. Some of Gale's fellow missionaries claimed higher social backgrounds, but many of them shared in the pioneer tradition to which his family belonged. He was twenty-five years old, a layman, without the backing of a great mission board or society, an adventurer for Christ, and an adventurer in cultures, a scion of pioneer stock assailing the last remaining frontier.

His self-offering had an effect on China too. In September 1888 Donald MacGillivray offered to go there as a missionary of the Canadian Presbyterian Church on $500 a year 'like Gale'. Gale had set the rate. The astonished presbyterians were all but blackmailed by MacGillivray into sending him to start their Honan mission. Oddly enough, as Gale was to become a lexicographer and literature worker in Korea, MacGillivray became a lexicographer and literature worker in China. He left Toronto for China four days after Gale left for Korea.

The quality of their $500 adventure can be estimated from the fact that in the same year the Presbyterian Church in the USA increased the stipends of unmarried male missionaries in Korea to $1,000, because it had been discovered that $800 was not enough for a man to live on.

iii Pioneer missionary in Korea 1888 – 1891

Gale was joined at Nagasaki by another new missionary, the American presbyterian Daniel Lyman Gifford. They first trod Korean soil on 15 December 1888, at Pusan. Then the ship sailed round the dangerous island-studded south and west coasts of the peninsula to Chemulp'o, the harbour for entry to Seoul. They landed in the midst of a smallpox epidemic. The journey to the capital was a scene of misery in all the villages, and corpses were piled high outside the gates of the city. This was the common custom of the times, but the plague made the stench worse and more dangerous. Gale entered the capital through the Great West Gate and obtained a room in a simple earth-walled house, where he had to bar the door against inquisitive crowds. There were smallpox sufferers in the same house, but the bed-bugs tried him most. He turned again and again to Psalm xci for comfort and assurance.

They were welcomed by G. H. Underwood, the pioneer presbyterian evangelistic missionary to Seoul, who had already been living there for three years. On Sunday 23 December at two o'clock in the afternoon Gale attended a service taken by Underwood in the small Korean building in Chŏng-dong that served as a church. About fifty men were present, and when the proceedings opened with a hymn to the *Old Hundredth* tune, Gale was surprised at the vigour of the singing. During the service 'eleven dusky young Koreans' were baptized. Gale reported: 'Mr Underwood translated their replies into English, and such a succession of testimonies I have never heard before.'

The missionaries had been able to do very little work outside the capital. King Kojong had been on the throne since 1864, and was now a troubled man, thirty-six years old. Though far from stupid, he was perplexed by the course of history, and frustrated by the machinations of the factions in his court. Some of these, including the group centred on the queen, were conservative and wished to maintain Korea's traditional dependence on China; others were progressive, anxious to see the country modernized, and therefore more or less envious of Japan's modernization, more or less inclined to favour drawing Korea closer to Japan. During the king's reign there had been several rebellions, but the conservative forces were now in control and the most powerful man in Seoul was Yüan Shih-k'ai, the Resident of the Imperial Chinese Government. Outside the capital the life of the country was agricultural. The merchant class was small, and society consisted of aristocrats and peasants. Education was limited to a few, and even they studied nothing but Chinese grammar and literature. There were no railways and no factories; the roads were little more than tracks.

Roman catholic missionaries had worked clandestinely, though with great success, for fifty years. They had many martyrs, and the last persecution had been as recent as 1866. Protestant missionaries from America began to arrive in 1884 on the heels of the first western diplomatic missions. Seoul had an eager group of foreigners, all anxious to learn more about the little-known country, most of them anxious to influence its politics and open up the country to western ideas and progress.

For the first year, Gale intended to study the Korean language, and like all missionaries in the country at that time, he took a Korean name. It was socially necessary to write one's name in Chinese characters, and if possible the characters were chosen to approximate in sound to one's foreign name, yet look and sound like a genuine Korean personal name. Gale was called Ki Il. Ki is a Korean surname which literally means 'strange' or 'wonderful'; *il* means 'one'. A story is told of how once when he was travelling a Korean asked him which clan of the Ki family he belonged to. Gale replied that he belonged to no clan: surely his interlocutor knew that all foreigners were *ssangnom*—men of low caste without genealogy?

Gale determined not to stay in the capital with its small but distracting foreign community, and as soon as the bitterest winter weather was over he left Harkness and his wife in Seoul while he went and tried to buy a house in Haeju, capital of Hwanghae province. Haeju was nearly a hundred miles north-west of Seoul, but Gale's account of the journey describes it as being two hundred miles, presumably because it was so uncomfortable. It took four days. He set out early one morning with nothing but a can of milk, some coffee, a fifteen-year-old horse-boy, and a guide, both of whom were drunkards. The pony was indifferent to weather and blows, and the boy trotted alongside, laughing and singing. There were still many corpses along the roads, some of them beheaded cadavers of convicted criminals. Magistrates along the route provided Gale with an escort, so that when he entered the walled city of Haeju on the afternoon of Sunday 17 March 1889, he had two outriders clearing the streets ahead of him and a troop of seven horses and fifteen men following behind. The governor of the city was condescending when Gale said he was British, and gave him to understand that since the people of Haeju had not heard of Britain its citizenship was contemptible. He showered Gale with presents, but kept him virtually a prisoner for a fortnight. It was impossible for him to buy a house in Haeju.

Fortunately he was found by a christian named An, who offered him a welcome in his native village. So Gale left Haeju riding on a pack-pony, again escorted by two runners in blue coats and wide hats with red tassels, all guided by An to the village of Sollae, on the coast to the west in the township of Chang-yŏn. There he stayed in the house of the An family till June. Sorae, as the village's name is more commonly spelt, was the home of Sŏ Sangyun, the first Korean bible translator, who had been converted in Manchuria by Scottish missionaries. His younger brother, Sŏ Kyongjŏ, had been baptized by Underwood in Seoul in 1886, and Underwood had paid two visits to the village, where the first protestant church in Korea was later built.

Gale spent the spring days on lessons in the Korean language and making his first attempts with Korean food, accustoming himself to octopus and sea-slugs, pickled cabbage and seaweed. He learned to bear the hot Korean floor, and went through the painful business of learning to sit cross-legged without a chair, endured Korean indifference to lack of ventilation and to vermin, and grew used to living in a thatched village whose streets were muddy alleys full of scruffy dogs and naked children; made friends with Mun the acupuncturist herb-doctor and Kwak the jiggy-man; and learned about the place of women in Korean life, for he never set eyes on the women of the household where he stayed. He also learned to put up with naïve curiosity about a foreigner and his strange clothes. The villagers kept him conscious of the presence of dangerous tigers in the vicinity. And he was desperately lonely.

One day, however, in a little house by the seashore, he met a young man, twenty-three years old, named Yi Ch'angjik. Yi was of good, though hardly noble, family from Haeju, not without means, and well-educated in Chinese literature. According to the custom of his class and period, he had been married at the age of twelve to a woman older than himself. He and Gale, being nearly of an age, struck up a friendship which encouraged Gale to take Yi as his teacher. People in Sorae knitted their brows. They told Gale that Ch'angjik was unreliable, and easily influenced, but Gale relied on his intuition, for the young man's attractive manner took his fancy. He was not disappointed. Yi proved a loyal friend and able helper, who later became almost part of the Gale family.

In June Gale returned to Seoul. After prolonged and affecting farewells, he and Yi Ch'angjik, accompanied by An and Sŏ, boarded a junk and set out for Chemulp'o. The distance was only a hundred and thirty miles, but owing to strong winds the sea journey took six days. Each night they put in at an island village, and when Gale thankfully disembarked at last with Yi at Chemulp'o, An and Sŏ returned immediately to Sorae in the same boat.

Gale spent two months of the summer in Seoul, helping Underwood with the preparation of a small Korean-English dictionary. His contribution must have consisted chiefly in translating from the dictionary compiled by the French Roman catholic missionaries. He and Underwood worked in a riverside pavilion by the Han at Yanghwa-jin, battling with the soporific heat and occasionally relaxing to watch the steamers passing to and from Chemulp'o.

In August Gale left Seoul again to live in Pusan. He travelled there from Chemulp'o on the Japanese steamship *Higo Maru,* taking with him Yi Ch'angjik and a Japanese boy called Kusaba Kasutaro. Within a week or two of his departure Harkness, whose health was poor, took his wife to Japan, where they worked for the Presbyterian Church USA, first at Kanazawa, then at Osaka. (In 1895 Harkness returned to north America, where he died in 1938 as a noted minister of the Canadian United Church.)

Gale intended to stay permanently in Pusan. It was one of the three treaty ports of Korea, and no western missionaries had yet settled there. The town was still undeveloped. Bishop Charles Corfe, landing there a year later, described it as looking 'more like a heap of ruins . . . nothing more than a hamlet composed of mud-huts and mat-sheds', set between the sandy beach and the surrounding hills, which were partly wooded with pines, partly barren and treeless. The old fort of Pusan-jin dominated it from the north. There were few Chinese in the place, and no European or American merchants, though two Englishmen were employed by the Korean Customs. The Koreans were chiefly occupied in fishery, but the Japanese had begun to develop the magnificent harbour, which was then much bigger than it is today after extensive land reclamation along the waterfront. They had started their trading settlement at the southern end of the bay. Gale and Ch'angjik lodged on the hillside above the Korean town, halfway between the port and the Japanese settlement, in the area now called Ch'oryang.

About Christmas Gale made a visit from Pusan to Taegu and the historic sites of the ancient capital at Kyŏngju, travelling by government pony service, changing mounts at post-stations every five miles. He wrote a vivid description of his reception by the inquisitive crowd that escorted him to the yamen at Taegu, where he gained privacy only by deliberately playing on Korean admiration for filial piety. It was 31 December, and he persuaded the previously unsympathetic mayor that he needed a quiet place to write a letter to his parents reporting the state of his affairs at the end of the year.

No record remains of Gale's activities in Pusan. In spring a 33-year-old Australian presbyterian missionary, J. Henry Davies, sent word from Seoul that he intended visiting Pusan with a view to settling there. He journeyed overland, through Ch'ungch'ŏng and Chŏlla provinces, with Chinese bibles and books for distribution, and some quinine for sale. (Exchanging Korean *cash* was so unreliable and so inconvenient that westerners often took quinine instead of currency.) Because he was unable to speak Korean he ran into difficulties, and was treated in an unfriendly way. Three or four days before reaching Pusan he realized he was ill, but did not know what was the matter. On the rainy afternoon of 14 April 1890 Gale received a card on which was written: 'Come at once! J. H. Davies.' The coolie who brought the message took Gale and Yi Ch'angjik to a poor house about a mile away, where Davies was waiting. The Australian was weatherbeaten and weary but did not look ill. He asked Gale to deal with the coolies, who were pestering him for more pay.

Gale and Yi helped him walk to Gale's house, where he lay down on the cot, sure he would soon get better. But he could not eat, so Gale called a Japanese doctor, who diagnosed smallpox. Gale and Yi watched by turns throughout the night, and Yi proved a kind nurse. Towards noon the next day pneumonia set in. 'Er wird bald sterben,' said the Japanese doctor; and less than an hour later Davies died. Gale and a few Koreans buried him on a nearby hillside. It was Davies's death that moved Australian presbyterians to make their great efforts in the Pusan area.

Soon afterwards, in May, the daughter of J. H. Hunt, the Commissioner of Customs in Pusan, fell ill, and he sent to Seoul for Dr Heron, the king's American physician, who came overland by fast courier service, accompanied by Malcolm Fenwick. Fenwick was a zealous independent Canadian baptist missionary, who had arrived in Korea late in the previous year, and was to continue working in the country, despite various interruptions, until his death in 1936. John William Heron was born in Derbyshire, England, the son of a congregationalist minister who removed his family to Knoxville, Tennessee, when John was fourteen. John became a gold medallist of the medical school of Tennessee University, and came to Korea in June 1885 at the age of 29, less than a year after his marriage. He was the first presbyterian missionary appointed to Korea after the opening of official relations between Korea and the USA by the treaty of 1883, though another doctor, Horace Allen, arrived first. Heron held the official Korean mandarin rank of *kasŏn taebu,* the second highest grade at Court, next after the royal family. According to the theory of government and kingship then in use in Korea, a physician, because of his intimate personal association with the monarch, could not have been given lower rank.

At first he had been given the white jade headband rings and breastpiece embroidered with a single crane proper to a civil official of the third rank, but in December 1886 the king bestowed the gold headband rings and double crane breastpiece of the highest rank possible. Dr Heron was known among Koreans as Hye Ch'amp'an, 'Counsellor Hye', from the Sino-Korean form of his name, Hyeron ('orchid discourse'). He moved in the highest circles, and entertained the great Yüan Shih-k'ai at his house in Chŏng-dong. The job was not, however, a matter of honours and high living. The king entrusted diplomatic chores to him. At Underwood's wedding some palace ladies were kept waiting in a chilly summerhouse, and the queen was angry: Dr Heron was called upon to smooth things over. More delicate was the problem created by the wife of a foreign diplomat who needed extra soup-bowls for a formal dinner. She sought in the Korean market and chose some attractive brass bowls with neat little lids. High-ranking courtiers attended her supper as the king's deputies, and were astounded to be served with typical Korean chamber-pots full of clear consommé. This was taken as a studied insult, and Dr Heron had another night call to the palace.

Many of the missionaries in Seoul at this time were dazzled by the possibility of becoming known, even honoured, at court. Heron and Allen were bitterly jealous of honours received from the king, and one letter from the board in New York told them in courteous but firm tones that they had not been sent out to become mandarins. Practically every woman in the mission had friendship with the queen as one of her chief objects. In fairness to them it must be recalled that they were severely restricted by law in their missionary enterprises, and that although even in later years the missionaries who lived in Seoul were always regarded as social butterflies by those who worked in the provinces, from the middle nineties onwards much less attention was paid to the palace.

The Herons were among the few who had legitimate reason for attending at court. When the family was called to audience the doctor rode in a green palanquin and his wife in a red one, with a retinue of guards. Their four-year-old daughter Annie was taken once and delighted the king with her unabashedly colloquial Korean. He took her into his apartments and brought her back loaded with toys and sweetmeats. Mrs Heron delighted in describing the royal family:

> the king in his red satin robe, all embroidered in gold . . . and . . . the pleasant voice of the little queen as she talked to the prince through the bamboo screen which hid her from sight. . . .
>
> The little prince was actually seen bundling himself over a back balcony all undignified, and scampering through the long verandah until he came to the door of the king's audience chamber, where he solemnly took his place beside his majesty and looked as much as ever like a very pretty, proper wax figure, while all the old grey-headed officials and time-worn eunuchs bowed down before him, bumping their heads on the stone floor again and again.
>
> The little herons could also see the army of attendants and maids in long blue silk skirts and yellow jackets hovering about his little kingship all day long, powdering his face, painting his lips and finger-tips, shaving the top of his head, pulling out his eyebrows, cutting his food into the daintiest of morsels, fanning him with monstrous long-handled fans, never leaving him alone a moment, even at night guarding and watching by his bedside, singing him to sleep with a queer little lullaby that has been sung to baby kings in the Land of Morning Calm

17

for the past three hundred years. A kind 'gale' once whispered a translation of this lullaby into the little herons' ears. Here it is:

Aga, aga, don't you cry,
All my heart, my blessed boy,
My unbridled coltish baby,
Yet so wise and yet so steady,
Can your like be bought for gold?
For a silver sum be sold?
Stronger than the highest mountains,
Deeper than the deepest fountains,
Keeping all the laws of *un,*
Trusty as the monarch Shun,
All the people's lasting gain,
O'er the wide world born to reign.

The identity of the prince presents a problem. Can this have been Ch'ŏk, the prince who later became the impotent emperor Sunjong? He was eleven when the Herons arrived in Korea and seventeen by the time this description was written. His mother doted on him and Mrs Heron's account may suggest part of the reason for his incapacity. Her husband undoubtedly knew the royal family better than any other missionary.

While in Pusan Heron visited Gale, who referred to him later as 'my first and most intimate friend on the mission field'. Heron was distressed about Gale's mode of life, and persuaded Gale to return with him by steamer to Seoul and stay in the Heron household in Chŏng-dong, close behind the present US Embassy residence. It was a delightful house, surrounded by jessamine bushes and jujube trees. Only a month later, in June, Dr Heron himself fell ill with dysentery while staying at the mountain fortress, Namhan Sansŏng, where the king had provided summer quarters for the missionaries. He returned to Seoul and might have recovered, had he not been told of a sick woman who was likely to die if left unattended. He got up immediately, dressed, and rode sixteen miles on horseback in the sweltering heat to see her. She lived; but he returned to Seoul and died while Gale was watching at his bedside on 26 July. He was thirty-four years old. No foreigner had died in Seoul before, and there was no cemetery available. Heron's death compelled the government to grant the Yanghwa-jin cemetery for foreigners. His daughters were befriended by Samuel Austin Moffett, a Northern Presbyterian minister from Indiana, who had arrived in January.

Gale continued to work at the language. In June he joined H. G. Underwood, the American teacher Homer Hulbert, and others in founding the Korean Tract Society (*Han'guk Sŏnggyo Sŏhoe*), forerunner of the Christian Literature Society of Korea. In February 1891 he was appointed to the Permanent Executive Bible Committee of Korea, which had been organized in 1887 with Dr Heron as one of its five members. Gale took his place and began revising the translation of the Acts of the Apostles done by Sŏ Sangyun and John Ross in Manchuria in 1883. In the same year, 1891, his name appeared with Hulbert's as an assistant to Underwood when the Korean-English part of the dictionary on which they had worked together two years before was at last published.

Samuel Moffett had replaced Heron as Gale's closest friend. They were both still bachelors, and planned a journey to Mukden to visit the Koreans who had been baptized in Manchuria by the Scottish presbyterian missionaries, and to see the missionaries themselves, especially John Ross. Ross had not only made the first translation of the New Testament into Korean, but his *History of Corea Ancient and Modern* (1880) was the first book on the subject in English.

At noon on 27 February 1891 Gale and Moffett set off from Seoul. They had two packhorses heavily laden with strings of brass cash, and Gale's foxterrier Nip bounded alongside—named, in spite of his sex, after Susan Nipper, the sharp-tongued maid in Gale's favourite *Dombey and Son*. Gale's pock-faced boy, Ch'oe Yŏnhwa (Kŭmdori) was with them, and their guide was the dignified Sŏ Sangyun of Sorae, now forty-one years old, who had been Ross's helper for bible translation in Mukden. They spent the first night at the town of Koyang. The next morning they passed the two huge rock-hewn Maitreyas at P'aju, and on the afternoon of 1 March they reached the Imjin River. The weather was balmy, but the great stream was jammed with pack-ice. With some difficulty they got the horses ferried across, and a few miles the other side found an inn with the usual overheated floor, where they stayed the night.

The following day they entered the crumbling city of Kaesŏng in the rain. Kaesŏng was the old Songdo, capital of the Koryŏ dynasty. They stayed in an inn outside the south gate, and spent some time visiting the local sights: the famous ginseng fields; the site of the great palace of Koryŏ; and the Sŏnjuk bridge, where the stones were said still to show the bloodstains of Chŏng Mongju, assassinated there five hundred years before. A few days later they rested again, this time for a fortnight, in the then pagan and, as Gale described it, filthy city of P'yŏngyang, which Moffett had visited six months earlier because it was the centre of the area allotted to him for evangelism.

Walking on through the snow, they passed Anju and Pakch'ŏn. At Kasan they spent a pleasant day in the little town, but stones were hurled after them as they left. Then on through Yongch'ŏn till they arrived at the frontier town of Ŭiju on 24 March, having walked three hundred and fifty miles from Seoul. Gale described the town as 'a poor little Asiatic Antwerp, surrounded by brown hills', and 'a wilderness of demons, rags, dogs, unburied dead, vermin, squalor, filth and what not' — an inversion of Bunyan's description of Vanity Fair.

The two missionaries were standing on a hill behind the town, looking over the Yalu river to the mountains of Manchuria, when a smiling young Korean approached and talked with them about the historic movement of culture from China through Ŭiju into Korea. Then he accompanied them to their lodgings, and they spoke of christianity. The Scottish missionaries from Newchwang and Mukden had baptized a small group of some twenty Koreans who lived in the town. This young man was baptized when Moffett returned to Ŭiju the following year. His name was Han Sŏkchin. He remained a great friend of Gale's, and later became moderator of the Korean Presbyterian Church.

Gale and Moffett stayed in Ŭiju for twelve days. The second Sunday was Easter Day, and Moffett celebrated the Lord's Supper. On the Wednesday they crossed the triple stream of the Yalu delta and entered Manchuria, accompanied now by Paek Hongch'ŏn, an evangelist who had been baptized at Newchwang. From Ŭiju to Mukden they rode in Chinese carts with wooden wheels, no springs, and luggage in place of upholstery: 'an awful ride, bumped beyond words into insensibility'. They found the Chinese inns noisome—full of blue smoke and razor-back pigs — and the oily food repellent. 'Great, porky, greasy, oily China', Gale called it. Chinese children shouted after them: *'Yang-kuei-tzŭ!'* (foreign devils). They had to present passports at the frontier yamen, where they were provided with an armed escort of six mounted soldiers under a muslim captain. There was snow in the mountains, rain in the valleys, more often than not a knife-edged wind. Towns like Liao-yang were grotesque and dirty, but they noticed that the people were more industrious than the Koreans. They entered Mukden in a typical Manchurian dust-storm, and spent four days there with Ross, visiting the Temple of the Fox, the mosques, and the other sights of the city.

Leaving Mukden by cart in another dust-storm, they went east towards Tung-hua-hsien, looking for the Korean christian communities. From the second day onwards they were travelling through beautiful wooded mountain scenery. After two days in Tung-hua-hsien they set off south towards the Korean border sixty-five miles away, still travelling by cart. They intended to climb Paektu-san, but the spring thaws made the roads impassable, so they came down through the immense Yalu forests. On 19 April they entered the Yalu valley, and Gale wrote of it: 'We found traces of Ross's New Testament. It was talked of, it had been seen; we too had seen it, papering the mud-huts, sometimes upside-down, and sometimes inside-out. . . .' There were still seven or eight feet of ice in the ravines, and they came across a pathetic Chinese family whose pony had slipped and been killed on a precipice. Within ten miles of the Yalu some Korean squatters delighted Gale and Moffett by letting them taste Korean kimch'i (vegetables pickled in brine) again. After some hard bargaining at a Chinese lumber-camp, they were scowed across the river and arrived back in Korea by way of Chasŏng, north of Kanggye (where Korea's northernmost presbyterian mission station was later founded). They then walked over the mountain backbone of the peninsula, through Huch'ang to Changjin. For two weeks they lived on millet and dandelion soup, with two eggs and two small fishes, before they gratefully descended to the fertile rice valleys round Hamhŭng on the east coast. Following the coast they arrived at the treaty port of Wŏnsan on 9 May. From Wŏnsan they came over the Ch'ŏrwŏn pass to Seoul, where they arrived in June. In three months they had travelled 1,400 miles, 700 of them on foot, 400 by cart and 300 on horseback.

Gale was by this time probably more widely acquainted with the various parts of Korea than any other foreigner, and had an admirable background for the study of Korean history. As a result of their adventure, the two young bachelors were forming pro-Korean prejudices. Gale extolled the superiority of Korean ponies over Chinese and Manchu breeds, and enthusiastically preferred kimch'i to Chinese cooking. He was not in the least squeamish. If a Korean were offensive, he would trounce the man with his stick, and he once compelled an unwilling peasant to carry him over a stream by taking a running leap on to the man's back. In his late twenties he was still a prankster.

Before he left on the Manchurian trip he had applied to the Board of Foreign Missions of the Presbyterian Church, USA, asking to be transferred from the YMCA to the Presbyterian Mission. He was undoubtedly encouraged to do this by Moffett and other friends. Daniel Gifford and William Baird supported his application warmly. The principal reason for the transfer was financial. The YMCA in Toronto was facing a crisis, and Gale was likely to lose his support. He was in any case underpaid, and his lack of expertise with money was handicapping him further; he doubtless also felt the need of belonging to an historic church rather than continuing as a freelance worker. After some demurring by the board in New York, his application was accepted and he was officially transferred to the Presbyterian Mission on 31 August 1891.

The presbyterians stationed him at Kondang-gol, in the area where the Bando Hotel now stands in Seoul. Kondang-gol was a corruption of Koun-dam-gol, 'the village of the pretty wall', because there had been a famous wall there in the sixteenth century, painted with large Chinese characters: *hyo-je-ch'ung-sin* (filial piety, brotherly love, loyalty, sincerity). The Korean church opened there in 1893 attracted many butchers and others of the lowest castes. It was one of the cradles of Korean protestantism, but was later absorbed into the Sung-dong church. The embassy area was very close, and not far off was the Chinese community. British and American products (Cherry Blossom boot polish and Huntley and Palmers biscuits) were on sale in the Chinese shops, most foreign houses could serve iced drinks in the summer-time, there was ice-cream for parties, and lunch was called 'tiffin' by everybody. A fair degree of middle-class comfort could be maintained.

The Presbyterian Mission maintained an 'orphanage-school' called the Yesugyo Haktang in Chŏng-dong. It was hoped that this school would turn into a christian college or theological seminary, but the boys were of the lowest class, unpromising material, and there were never more than twenty-five. Moffett was put in charge almost as soon as he arrived, and Gale helped him teach the boys after he returned to Seoul from Pusan. From July to December 1891, Gale was in charge of the school.

He was spending much time in preparing a book on the language, called *Korean Grammatical Forms* (*Sagwa chinam*), though it was not published until 1894, when it was welcomed by foreign connoisseurs of things Korean. Its virtue lay in the cultural content of its material, which included proverbial matter and folk wisdom. The sentences were reportage of what Gale heard rather than deliberately-constructed examples. There was more emphasis on authenticity than on comprehensiveness or pedagogy. It thus set the tone for all Gale's subsequent work on the language and literature. A few words are mistranslated, such as 'porpoise' for globe-fish, and 'silver apricot' for ginkgo nut, but these show no more than the lack of adequate dictionaries. A few examples will indicate the quality of the whole:

58. *P'ogyange kim maeni yagyakhaoeda.* (It is hard pulling weeds in the scorching heat.)
159. *Unhaengi pakkat kŏpchirŭn samyŏni tungguna, sok almaenginŭn moga isso.*

21

(Although the outside skin of the silver apricot is round on every side, the kernel inside has corners.)

251. *Kyejibege hyanghayŏnŭn yŏngung-hogŏri ŏpta hadŏra.* (Speaking in reference to women they say that there is no such thing as a lofty and noble character.)

372. *Pŏlt'ong pajinŭn nondaniga ipso.* (Beehive-shaped trousers are worn by fast people.)

460. *Chŏttaenŭn ulgo, saltaenŭn kago, pŭttaenŭn kŭrinŭnira.* (The flute bamboo cries, the arrow bamboo flies, the pen bamboo writes.)

758. *Changgi tunŭnde hunsu mara.* (Do not prompt when we are playing chess.)

iv Wŏnsan 1892–1897

Dr Heron's widow, Harriet Elizabeth Gibson, was still living in Seoul. She was three years older than Gale, and had come to Korea in 1885 very shortly after her marriage, a southern belle from Jonesborough, Tennessee, whose slave-owning family had suffered in the American Civil war. Now she had two little daughters, Sarah Anne aged six, and Jessie Elizabeth aged four. Missionaries are inveterate matchmakers, and there was much gossip as to whether Samuel Moffett or James Gale would marry Hattie Heron, yet many expressed surprise when it was announced in autumn 1891 that the Canadian was to marry her. The marriage made him solvent again. Hattie had the benefit from John Heron's life insurance, and a gift of five hundred dollars from Queen Min. She was also prepared to sell her handwork. Transferring to the presbyterian mission had not solved Gale's financial problems; he was always impetuously generous and never learned to manage his accounts properly. The mission board in New York disapproved of the match, and took the opportunity to express disapproval of Gale's missionary methods too. He was accused of tickling trout when he should have been trawling a seine. He was hurt, but not discouraged.

The wedding took place on 7 April 1892 at the British Consulate in Seoul, before the consul, W.C.Hillier, and was followed by a religious service in Daniel Gifford's house, conducted by the methodist Frank Ohlinger, assisted by Gifford. Horace Allen, now US vice-consul, was present.

Gale's new family moved in at Kondang-gol. He was now in a feminine household, and his bachelor habits were soon corrected. Poor Nip, the fox-terrier, was banished from his sleeping-place on the bed. Gale took to the two little girls as though they were his own daughters, but did not adopt them because he did not want to change their native American citizenship. They grew up with the name of Heron, and retained their pride at being John Heron's daughters undiminished by the place which 'Papa Gale' and his achievements naturally took in their lives.

In June the family left Seoul for Wŏnsan, the new mission station on the east coast to which the local committee had appointed them. They sent the furniture round the south coast by boat, and themselves travelled across the peninsula for seven days by pony and sedan chair. Gale, who left vivid descriptions of Korean ponies and the fleas in Korean inns, boasted in 1915 that he had crossed the country in this fashion twenty-five times. The two children regarded the journey as a magnificent adventure. When they found themselves sleeping with donkeys below them, they had excited thoughts of Bethlehem; and they were equally thrilled one night when a tiger took a pig from the yard of the inn where they were staying, and the whole village turned out with flares and gongs to scare the tiger off. The fastidious Harriet did not share their feelings, though she wrote that 'the roadsides were in bloom with hawthorn and sweet white honeysuckle, and the air was full of skylarks' song'. She travelled in a palace chair provided by the queen, which was uncomfortable even though it was attended by a bannerman wearing a blue coat and a black felt hat with a scarlet oxtail attached. Harriet was sure they had been posted to the back of beyond because Mrs Underwood was jealous of the queen's friendship for her. The queen had given her jewels, headdresses and lengths of expensive dress material, as well as the five hundred dollars. The letters of missionaries at this time show that the wives were bitterly jealous of one another. Mrs Gale was the senior member of her mission by appointment, and more gifted than most, but others gave her her share of the blame.

Wŏnsan was a quiet spot for foreigners, of whom there were never more than a dozen resident adults while the Gales lived there. The Korean customs service was under the direction of a Dane, J. F. Oiesen, assisted by L. Ahrendts, the Englishman M. Knott, and others, all of whom had Chinese or Japanese wives or common-law wives. These people maintained well-laden European diningtables, and were the social centre of the community. There was a Japanese consulate, a Japanese business community and a telegraph office. Two Japanese steamers, *Tokyo maru* and *Satsuma maru*, plying between Pusan and Vladivostok, called once or twice a month. The Gales were not cut off from the world, but they suffered hardships they had never known in Seoul. At first they lived in a flimsy Japanese-style house, so badly heated that during the bitter winter weather Mrs Gale and the children went to bed every afternoon to keep warm. Snowdrifts rose above the windowsills, the inefficient stoves would not draw, and filled the rooms with smoke. Harriet caught a severe chill which developed into tuberculosis. In the following year Harriet's mother came to live with them after her own husband's death. About the same time Mr Oiesen had a new house built by Chinese workmen. Harriet copied it, and in 1894 herself supervised the work of building a more substantial Gale home on a point overlooking the magnificent scenery of the bay. It was known as 'Grandma's house', though Harriet paid for it.

Grandma was reckoned a beauty; she was certainly strong-minded. She bullied coolies into making a vegetable garden; she got money from the fashionable Church of the Covenant in Washington DC to build two extra rooms for use as a church and school, and taught Korean boys in the school, though she was already busy teaching her two granddaughters and Mr Oiesen's family; she also taught Oiesen's Chinese wife to sew western clothes. Either she or Hattie persuaded Gale to buy a cow in hope of drinking fresh milk. Korean cows are not milch cattle, and with difficulty the Gales expressed only a single cupful of beestings before the Korean christians came and begged them not to be cruel to the calf. So the cow was sold again and the children's nourishment remained deficient; Jessie got malaria, and contracted night-blindness which proved incurable.

There were hazards from lepers, who might at any time seek the traditional cure for their complaint, the flesh of children; from the tigers; and from typhoid and hydrophobia (in a hydrophobia scare Harriet killed the puppy). Life was risky, but not so dangerous as it was for Gale's Toronto friends in China who had their houses destroyed about them and their own persons attacked. Koreans were on the whole courteous and friendly to missionaries, and the hazards in life came from nature rather than from man. The family's only casualty was poor Nip, the fox-terrier who had walked and skipped to Mukden and back. A Korean who had bad legs was told by a doctor that the trouble was caused by rats in his bones, and he should send a dog after them. So Nip was stolen for medicine.

For their first Christmas in Wŏnsan the Gales gave a party to some Koreans at which they presented every guest with a tin basin, a towel and a cake of soap. This may have been a deliberate effort to improve hygiene, or may have been, for some practical reason, a convenient solution to the gift problem. It gave rise to a story sometimes discredited, though Gale averred it in writing: one of the guests told a friend that at the 'Jesus house' he had been given a rice-bowl and a head-scarf, but the cake had been hard to eat because it made his mouth foam.

In 1894 the Gales were still busy building their new house when the Sino-Japanese war broke out. Food became scarce and expensive, and money lost half its value. In August Japanese troops landed at Wŏnsan on their way to Seoul, frightening the Gales and the Chinese builders (most bricklaying for foreigners in Korea at that time was done by Chinese workmen), but the Gales declined the opportunity of evacuation on a Russian ship, and discovered that the Japanese troops, who drilled in the mission compound, were disciplined and courteous. One old Chinese took refuge for a time in the Gales' house, hiding behind the furniture, and the two children crept in with titbits to feed him, until he could escape safely. Soon it became obvious that the war was not being fought in Korea, and the Gales were glad they had stayed, although the building of their house was much delayed.

They were not the only missionaries in the place. Malcolm Fenwick claimed to have been living there before Gale. He too was a Toronto man, and still a bachelor. In November 1892 Dr Hardie, yet another Toronto missionary, arrived. W. B. McGill, an ordained medical doctor, arrived in the same year and opened a dispensary. He was a methodist, but W. S. Swallen, who arrived in 1894, was an American presbyterian pastor. Vignettes of life in Wŏnsan appear in Gale's novel, *The Vanguard,* where the mischievous portraits of Puffsnauber, the German merchant with a Japanese common-law wife, and the quarrelsome English Wintershines are based on personalities in the customs service. These portraits, however, are wholly without malice, and the real Puffsnaubers and Wintershines were much liked by the Heron girls. There were differences of opinion with the Swallens. Gale, who praised Swallen as a missionary and approved of the family as 'good, plain, earnest folk', would not teach western hymntunes to Koreans, and allowed them to chant christian lyrics in their own style. Sally Swallen said, 'The way the Koreans sing is dreadful grating on our ears,' and set about removing this inconvenience by teaching hymn-tunes to the boys in Mrs Gibson's school. Mrs Gibson was pointed in expressing her opinion that the Swallens were wasting the boys' time. The Swallens had narrower horizons than the Gales. They were hard-working fundamentalists who had little patience with Korean culture, and Sally, who was even nervous of going to dine with the Oiesens lest wine should be served, wrote her opinion of Roman catholic Koreans explicitly: 'Satan has agents everywhere.' When the Gales left Wŏnsan the Swallens took over their house, Susanna (Hattie's biblewoman) and the school. They closed the school after a few months, in March 1896, and never ceased to grumble about the bad design of the Gale house—practical efficiency was never a hallmark of the Gale family—but they approved of the strawberries and raspberries from Grandma Gibson's garden.

Annie and Jessie enjoyed Wŏnsan. It did not worry them that the potatoes froze in winter, and they liked eating Japanese tangerines with ice-crystals in the juice. They were spoiled by Yi Ch'angjik, who told them how when he had been married as a little boy his bride had at first dressed him as though he were her little brother. Occasionally they went on evangelistic visits with their mother when she was taken in her sedan chair to Kaemal (which they translated as 'dog-town'), the hamlet of thatched houses by the seashore. They often shivered to think of tigers in the hills behind their home—Nip had been chased by a tiger one night, and on a winter morning a tiger strolled through their yard at ten o'clock. One day word came that a tigress had been killed and the carcase was in a house in Kaemal with the cubs, which were still alive. Eager for copy for her articles in Washington papers, Grandma set off to the seashore with the little girls, who could barely squeeze into the small room, almost filled with the great striped body of the tiger. The cubs, alas, proved far too wild for the children to handle, but the sight of these terrors of the night at close quarters was a sufficient thrill in itself.

Children brought up in such conditions took all their adventures as normal. The girls' nearest companions were the score of olive-skinned boys of grandma's school, who wore white baggy trousers and cherry-coloured jackets, had their hair tied into big horse-tails with navy-blue ribbon at the nape of the neck, and bore such homely names as Kŏbugi ('turtle'). Korean was as easy as English. When Grandma arrived and used new idioms they began to savour exotic Americanisms and such arcana as multiplication-tables. Annie once used a multiplication table to good effect when a buddhist monk was visiting her father and had to wait. She told him it was her own type of sutra, intended to be recited very fast, and astonished him with a demonstration.

The three years during which they lived in Wŏnsan were crowded with activity for Gale. He was establishing the mission. At the first baptism on 5 April 1894, four women were christened. By the end of 1894 there were 34 baptized and 24 inquirers, with an average Sunday attendance of 80. By December 1895 he had built up a church of 64 regular members, with the women meeting separately in his dining-room. He settled the problem of what to do about ancestor-worship by circulating a questionnaire to his neophytes. They were unanimous in rejecting the traditional sacrifices, and the new church grew up in harmony with the other presbyterian churches in Korea. Nevertheless, Gale's initiative in the matter was indicative of the breadth of his theological outlook.

Together with the other missionaries of Wŏnsan, Gale explored Hamgyŏng province. He had charge of the church in Anbyŏn, from which he opened up missions in the hinterland. One of his converts was Chŏn Kyeŭn who founded the church at Munsan, near the great buddhist temple of Sŏgwangsa, and later became a distinguished pastor.

Gale's spare time was devoted to literary work. When at home, he worked at his desk every day from six in the morning to four in the afternoon. He translated *Pilgrim's Progress*, wrote his dictionary, and did sundry translations from Korean. The *Korean Repository* for December 1892 contains an account of an *ŏnmun panjŏl* found by Gale and Ohlinger at what Ohlinger called the 'noted monastery of Sayŏg-wŏn near Wŏnsan'. Sayŏg-wŏn means 'office of translators' and was probably the name of part of the temple of Sŏgwang-sa. The *panjŏl* was a woodblock for printing the Korean alphabet with an explanation in Chinese by the *panjŏl* method, which uses two characters to indicate the pronunciation of each syllable. The block also contained a Sanskrit alphabet. The missionaries described the *panjŏl*, the only part that interested them, as a 'primer'. The incident was an early stage in Gale's discovery of the language, and is now of little interest, except in so far as it illustrates the opening stages of his studies.

He had already taken his share in bible translation work by revising Ross's version of Acts in 1892. In 1893 the name Permanent Executive Bible Committee was changed to Board of Official Translators. It consisted of Gale, the presbyterians Horace Underwood and William D. Reynolds, the methodists Henry G. Appenzeller and William B. Scranton, and the anglican Mark Trollope (later bishop). They worked under the auspices of the British and Foreign Bible Society, which had taken over the work begun by Ross and continued by the locally-organized committee of 1887. During the three years at Wŏnsan, bible translation work took Gale to Seoul for long periods during which he left his wife and step-daughters at home. By 1895 he had finished a new version of St John's Gospel, and completed new drafts of Galatians, Ephesians, and both the Epistles to the Corinthians. The books that were published show the difficulty the missionaries had in deciding which word to use for the Godhead. After having tried a transliteration of the Latin *Deus* (*Teusŭ*), and the Chinese term *Ch'ŏnju* used by the roman catholics and anglicans, they finally settled on the term *Hanŭnim*, which eventually became the accepted christian word for God.

The arguments on this subject were bitter. At one point Underwood alone stood out for *Ch'ŏnju*. Then Gifford returned from furlough and joined him. Moffett and Gale were for *hanŭnim*, though they pronounced it as *hananim*, a dialectal variant. Ostensibly the problem was whether to use a Chinese-derived or a Korean-derived word. The anglicans decided to use *Ch'ŏnju* because it was used in the neighbouring anglican missions of North China. They probably also favoured it because the highly successful Roman catholic missions had adopted it. It is hard to avoid the suspicion that this was the very reason why most protestant missionaries were determined not to use it. (The story has a happy ending: seventy years later, after the Second Vatican Council, the Roman catholics decided to accept the protestant term.)

During her widowhood Harriet had begun to translate Part I of John Bun-
yan's *Pilgrim's Progress* into Korean. Gale completed this with the help of Yi
Ch'angjik, and the book was published in Seoul by the presbyterian mission in
1895. It was a woodblock edition printed on Korean paper by the Trilingual
Press at the methodist Paejae School, in two handsome old-style Korean volumes.
Another edition, in metal type, was printed on modern Chinese paper in Shang-
hai, where Gale had taken the whole family for a visit in the summer of 1893.
Both editions were illustrated with charming line-drawings by a Wŏnsan artist,
Kim Chun'gŭn, which continued to be used in succeeding editions until 1926.
The book is a landmark in the history of Korean culture, because it was the first
Korean translation of a western literary work. For this reason if for no other,
Gale's name would be remembered.

It is hard to be sure how far the credit for this translation should be shared
with Hattie and Yi Ch'angjik. There is no doubt that Hattie helped Gale in his
literary work, and when writing with her assistance he produced better work than
he did after her death. Gale himself gave her credit for the initiative in translating
Pilgrim's Progress, and it was either a remarkable inspiration or a piece of unusually sound literary judgment, because the book stimulates the visual imagination and slips easily into a vigorous Korean narrative style. So far as one can
gather from the notes left by Gale, however, he and Ch'angjik worked on it
without Hattie's co-operation. Ch'angjik, who had already fallen from grace
once or twice since he had been with Gale, several times looked up from the work
and ruefully identified himself with Pliable, whose name was translated in Korean
as Ich'ŏn, 'easily moved'. His failings had been brought home to him by a devout
old convert named Kim, a man of much lower class than himself, a friend of
potters and writing-brush makers, who loved Ch'angjik very much and recognized
his difficulty in withstanding those who tempted him. The 25-year-old scapegrace
was deeply touched by the old man's admonitions, and wrote a song for Kim's
funeral when he died early in 1894. Gale's translation of the song reads like
a typical piece of Victorian pious verse, but the original must have shown
clear evidence of the Chinese tradition of songs about parting from which
it undoubtedly stems:

> God has not, unkind in heart,
> Left us thus to meet and part;
> But our fathers' sins require
> That our bodies pay the hire:
> Then we'll meet again on high,
> Sons of immortality.

The old man also admonished Gale himself, who wrote: 'One of the last
days I saw him, when we were sitting together on the mat, he put his hand on
mine and said, "Brother, you have told me the Gospel. Be careful lest translation
work and the like should take you away from telling others also." How true and
wise this was! There are so many calls on a missionary's time that he often needs

a voice to say, "Remember the Gospel".'

Gale's *Korean-English Dictionary* (*Han-yŏng chajŏn*), was based on the 1880 *Dictionnaire Coréen-français* of the French fathers. It was the first full-scale work of modern lexicography in Korean, much more ambitious than Underwood's stop-gap book of 1890. In its three editions it remained the standard bilingual dictionary for half a century, and subsequent dictionary-makers have built on the foundations laid by it.

The Korean-English section contained 35,000 words arranged in the bizarre alphabetical order devised by the French fathers, vaguely approximating to the Roman alphabet. The Chinese section was arranged according to the Korean pronunciation of the characters, again in the French missionaries' alphabetical order, but with an index by radicals. It contained all the characters in the traditional Korean dictionary of Chinese characters, the eighteenth-century *Chŏnun okp'yŏn*, with meanings copied from Giles's *Chinese-English Dictionary* of 1892. These meanings, though a great improvement on some earlier nineteenth-century work, are often quaint, because they are inadequately translated from the definitions given in native Chinese dictionaries. Gale repeats such definitions as:

Hyŏn (33): a dark blue horse. (It really means a dark grey horse.)
Sa (9): a tree from which vermicelli is obtained. (Really a kind of chestnut.)
Kŏn (21): a call of barbarians to children. (Really a Fukienese word for 'child'.)

Multiple definitions must often have puzzled those who were not familiar with the history of Chinese writing:

Ch'ŏk (11): to pity. Angry. A battleaxe. A hunchback.
Pi (107): a white fox; also described as a tiger.
Kŏn (10): to speak out boldly. To stammer.
Chong (8): a horse's mane. The back part of a lady's hair.

Some entries amaze the western reader by their sheer reconditeness:

Kan (44): remains of straw or hay eaten by horses.
Ong (22): a term for quadrumanous animals like the spider-monkey.
P'o (23): to dig up a field instead of ploughing it.
Koek (6): to cut off the left ears of prisoners or the slain.
Man (31): a pair of birds that fly side by side, and are closely joined.
Maek (9): the offspring of an ass and a cow.

Gale must have chuckled over these, but it was fundamentally honest work, and nobody was equipped to do better at the time.

The weakest aspect of the dictionary, as of many other dictionaries of Chinese and related languages, was the treatment of botanical and zoological names. According to Bishop Trollope's *Arboretum Coreense*, Gale frankly admitted in 1918 that many of his identifications of trees and shrubs were incorrect.

One reason for this was the lack of precision in the use of Chinese characters to denote botanical species. The problem has not been entirely resolved three quarters of a century later, when the most recent dictionaries still have vagaries about biological names.

On 8 October 1895, the day Queen Min was murdered by Japanese agents, Gale was in Seoul for the decennial celebrations of the founding of protestant missions in Korea, held from 9 to 11 October. On the night after the assassination the frightened king had Gale and George Heber Jones stay near him in the palace with Generals Dye and Legendre, his foreign military advisers.

Two months later, in December 1895, the Gale family left Wŏnsan and went to Yokohama, taking Yi Ch'angjik with them. They lived there till March 1897, while Gale and Ch'angjik supervised the printing of the dictionary, which was financed to the sum of 1,200 yen by the Northern and Southern Presbyterian Missions. In Japan, Gale met a number of Koreans, including political exiles. At various parties, and once on a climb to the top of Fuji, he met Prince Ŭihwa (Yi Kang) the king's third living son. He had left Korea a month before Gale, with whom he originally intended to travel, and stayed in Japan before visiting Europe and going to America for study. Although he was not the Crown Prince, but the son of a concubine named Chang, Kojong had great hopes for him. At the time of this voyage he was twenty-one years old. Gale held him in great respect, but both Kojong and Gale were to be disappointed. The young prince enjoyed America, and especially the company of American women, to such an extent that the London *Daily Mail,* slightly muddling its information, reported that the King of Korea was to marry an American named Miss Emily Brown. Prince Ŭihwa, however, was already married in Korea, whither he returned in 1905. He came into the news again in 1920, when he attempted to escape from Korea and join the Korean independence workers in China, declaring that he would gladly accept the status of a commoner if he could live as a free Korean. The Japanese intercepted him and brought him back to Seoul, where they encouraged him to pass his days in pleasure. When he died in 1955 he was said to have twenty-eight children living.

Gale's long stay in Japan and subsequent year of furlough in America scarcely interrupted his literary output. In 1892 he had written three articles for *The Korean Repository,* a monthly review produced by missionaries in Seoul during that year. When it was revived in 1895 he wrote for it again, including what are undoubtedly the first English translations of *sijo* verse ever published. *Sijo* is a three-verse stanza which was the principal form of Korean-language lyric from the fifteenth century onwards. Gale discovered it through his friends Yang Kit'aek and his father, Yang Siyŏng, who had helped in compiling the dictionary. Kit'aek, who was eight years younger than Gale, later worked with the Englishman S. L. Bethell, and became a distinguished journalist and independence fighter. Some time before 1894 he obtained from a friend of his father's an offprint from the woodblocks of the *Namhun t'aep'yŏng ka,* a singer's word-book edited in 1863. Gale eventually published thirty-four English translations of *sijo* from this text. The translations are interesting in that they accurately reflect the peculiarities of the *Namhun t'aep'yŏng ka* versions of the poems, but, partly because they are constricted by the demands of Victorian versification, and partly because Gale had not fully understood the *sijo's* mode of expression, they do not convey the real nature of the originals. Three of the first four to be published were entitled *Love Songs*. One of them is essentially an elaboration of the old Chinese symbol of clouds and rain for sexual congress, but this is not apparent from Gale's version:

> *Thunder*-clothed he did appear,
> Chained me like the *lightning* air,
> Came as comes the summer *rain,*
> Melted like the *cloud* again.
> Now in mists from tears and crying,
> I am left forsaken, dying. (NTK 16a (174))

He recognized the Chinese proper names in Korean poetry, but transliterated them as though they were Korean words, and then allowed the exigencies of rhyme to lure him into bathos where there should have been romantic impressionism. In the following poem the Hsiao-hsiang river and the Tung-t'ing lake appear in Korean disguise:

> Frosty moon and cold winds blowing,
> Clanging by are wild geese going.
> 'Is it to the Sosang River,
> Or the Tongchung? Tell me whither.
> Through the midnight hours this crying
> Is so trying!'   (NTK 2b (18))

He wrote articles at fairly regular intervals till the magazine ceased publication in 1898, including some translations about the early history of the Three Kingdoms period from the *Tongguk t'onggam*. They contain a number of minor errors, most likely because Gale relied heavily on Yi Ch'angjik's Korean rendering of the Chinese text, and he had as yet no reliable tools for establishing Korean chronology. Hulbert hastened to correct some of the mistakes. He was the same age as Gale, but had lived in Korea two years longer, and assumed a proprietory attitude to all things Korean. He was at this time business manager of the Methodist Mission Press, which published *The Korean Repository*.

When the printing of the dictionary was finished Gale and his family went to America. Two months after leaving Japan, he was ordained minister by the presbytery of New Albany, Indiana, on 13 May 1897. This ordination was due to the efforts of Samuel Moffett, who was a member of the New Albany presbytery, and persuaded the presbytery to waive the normal canonical regulation which required an ordinand to have had presbyterian seminary training. Gale was ordained on the basis of his record in Korea. He stayed with the Moffett family in their house at Madison, Indiana, and Moffett took part in the examination of the candidate and gave the charge at the ordination service.

After this the Gales went to stay in Washington DC, where Harriet's relatives were living. The family became the designated missionaries of the Washington Sunday Schools, and Gale remained their special correspondent till he left Korea in 1927. In Washington he again met Prince Ŭihwa. Early in 1898, in New York, he spoke at the international convention of the Student Volunteer Movement for Foreign Missions, the organization which had been responsible for his own missionary vocation, and told the delegates of the conditions of missionary work in Korea. He also visited Toronto and his native district in Ontario.

During the same furlough he prepared a book of essays called *Korean Sketches,* giving his first impressions of Korea. Some of them had previously appeared in *The Korean Repository* and elsewhere. He speaks resignedly of the discomforts caused by fleas in inns, and the curiosity of the town rabbles; his humour bubbles over in describing the tantrums of Korean ponies and the relationships between foreign residents and their Korean servants; he frankly recognizes that petticoat government is normal in Korean households; he shows how deeply he had already penetrated the apparent illogicality of the Korean mind. He was unusually perspicacious about religion when he wrote: 'Because Korea has no religion apart from her national life—her whole existence, from king to coolie, being one complicated system of ancestor-worship—one may easily fail to notice what enters so subtly into every detail of her life.' He also wrote a telling paragraph on a coolie's disregard for wages reckoned as a measure of work done. He tells of community stone-fights, of tigers and ghosts, of prayer-drums on Korean junks, of a royal procession in Seoul, and of men who lived in squalid huts but wore silken clothes. He includes a conversation at Washington in 1898 with Yi Pŏmjin, Korean Minister to the USA, evidently approving Yi's prophetic recommendation of the abolition of Chinese characters and the exclusive use of Korean alphabetic script as a help towards the modernization of his country. In a chapter on special friends, Gale includes H.H. the Prince Ŭihwa, as well as a rascally boatman, an old ex-slave woman and the buddhist abbot of Sŏgwang-sa, a charming old man named Ŭmsŏrha, who discussed religion with Gale and coveted one of the family's cut-glass bonbon dishes. The book gives a catholic sampling of contemporary Korean life, but contains one sentence Gale must have regretted later: 'Literature', he writes on page 61, 'in Korea is a dead letter':

By the time he was thirty-four, James Gale had established a flourishing new mission station, compiled a major dictionary, written a pioneer work on the grammar of Korean, published the first Korean translation from occidental literature, and made fresh drafts of nearly half the New Testament in Korean. He had thus laid the foundation for his own studies in Korean culture and created essential tools for several generations of missionaries.

v Educator 1898 – 1910

The Korea to which Gale and his family returned in April 1898 was subtly changed from the Korea in which he had worked before. The Sino-Japanese war of 1895 had put an end to Chinese suzerainty over the country and Yüan Shih-k'ai had gone; the king was now styled Emperor of Korea, and had issued proclamations which ensured that modernization would proceed. Outwardly, the life of most Koreans changed only in a few details, but the process of change was irrevocably started. The political struggles of the next decade centred on the rivalry of Japan and Russia for dominance over Korea. The king tried to use Russia against Japan; meanwhile progressive Korean groups were beginning to link the idea of independence with republicanism. The uncertainties of the times made many Koreans ready to listen to the comforting message of christian missionaries, and the first ten years of the twentieth century were a period of marked growth in the churches.

The Gale family returned for a short time to Wŏnsan. The whole province was being handed over to the Canadian Presbyterian Mission, whose first missionary arrived there in November 1898. Though James Gale was a Canadian, he was employed by an American church, so he had to leave. Negotiations for the hand-over of the property began early in 1899. Swallen left in April, but Gale stayed on till the transfer was complete. Meanwhile he helped the newly-arrived Canadians with their language studies. The Canadian mission agreed to buy the property at the valuation of the American missionary committee on the field, US $1650, but the American home board raised the price to $4000 Mexican—Maria Theresa dollars then being the stablest currency in China and Korea. The Canadians on the field not only refused to pay more than the original price bargained for, but made a new condition of purchase: they must be guaranteed a right-of-way to the public thoroughfare. If that was done they were ready to purchase Mrs Gibson's property as well for US $350. It took over a year to complete the transaction. In the spring of 1900 Yun Ch'iho, who was to be an important friend of Gale's for the rest of his missionary career, went to the Wŏnsan area as governor of Tŏgwŏn, and assisted in the compilation of the deeds of sale. Gale finally handed the title deeds of the property to Dr Grierson of the Canadian Mission in September of that year. The Canadians paid 3,650 yen for the mission property and US$350 for Mrs Gibson's property.

In the midst of these negotiations the Gales had one of their most distinguished visitors: early in August Prince Henry of Prussia arrived in Wŏnsan harbour on the SMS *Deutschland,* and came ashore to walk his dachshund. On the 8th the ship's band came as well, and played at a party given for the Prince in the Gales' garden.

On 9 September 1899 the Gale family left Wŏnsan for Seoul and went to live at Yŏnmot-kol, 'Lotus-pond Hollow', now called Yŏnji-dong. Here Gale was to spend all his remaining years in Korea. He lived in a house facing south, with a path leading up from the street gate past the big ginkgo-tree that still stands there. Most of the building was a single-storey Korean house, but the west end by the front door was two-storied. Gale's spacious study was just inside the front door on the left, and the family living quarters were upstairs. It was over-furnished, in the manner of the day, with dry palm-leaves in vases, opulent hangings, Korean screens and knick-knacks, a Bellini madonna and Fra Angelico angels in the bedroom—heavy in taste, but comfortable. The style of living was ample and the house was hospitable. Korean food was often served, especially for foreign guests. Nip was replaced by Petite.

At the mission meeting of 1899 Gale reported that he had spent three months of the year at Wŏnsan, and then six months on translation projects and the correction of his *Korean Grammatical Forms*. This book was re-issued in 1903 by the Methodist Press in Seoul, better printed than the first edition, with a smaller typeface. The material was slightly rearranged, and the Korean spelling brought up to date, in line with a recent spelling reform promulgated by the government in the first official encouragement of Korean script in modern times. The script was now described as *kungmun*, 'national script', instead of *ŏnmun*, 'vulgar script', which had been the name used previously and in practice remained the colloquial term for another forty years.

In 1900 Gale became pastor of the Yŏnmot-kol church (predecessor of the present Yŏndong church) which stood very close to the missionaries' houses, half a mile inside the Great East Gate, and had been started nearly a decade earlier by his friend Daniel Gifford. Gifford's sudden death in April 1900 caused the vacancy filled by Gale. In 1903 the buildings had to be enlarged. In 1904 Gale reported a normal Sunday congregation of 163 people, and had baptized 35 and admitted 36 catechumens during the year. His sermons were remembered as uncomplicated and forceful. He never used notes when preaching, and none of his sermons were ever published, but some of his sermon notes survive, and together with his articles and essays, suggest what his preaching must have been like. The outlines are compact and logical, highly scriptural, with fewer anecdotes than one might expect, but with a simple subject and a direct message. At this period he and Underwood preached several missions together. On one occasion in 1900 they addressed a crowd of 1,500 in P'yŏngyang.

The first years of his pastorate in Seoul were the last of the Yi dynasty. Even apart from the Russo-Japanese War, 1904–5, it was a turbulent and bloody period in Korean politics. Gale, like most westerners in Korea, knew some of the progressive leaders. In May 1900 he boarded a Japanese steamer at Pusan to travel to Chemulp'o. Among the passengers was a man with a pockmarked face who appeared to be Japanese. This man spoke to Gale and reminded him that they had met five years earlier in Prince Ŭihwa's rooms in Tokyo. He was Kwŏn Yŏngjin, a former statesman who had been exiled for his implication with Japanese policies in Korea and was now returning of his own accord in response to the proclamation of an amnesty. Gale said that Kwŏn knew he would be murdered in Seoul, and spoke as though his death would be redemptive. On arrival in Seoul he surrendered himself, and he was assassinated in prison on 27 May. It was one of the last outrageous acts done in the name of the Yi dynasty. Hulbert saw it politically as part of a Russian plot, but Gale reflected on the mind of Kwŏn, who deliberately returned to certain death.

On 27 December 1901 more of Gale's acquaintances from the Tokyo days were beheaded after they landed in southern Korea and began extorting funds from the local gentry on behalf of the exiled progressive, Pak Yŏnghyo; but soon Gale was to make friends with political progressives who made a more positive contribution to the development of modern Korea. The Yŏnmot-kol church became a centre for twelve converted members of the Independence Club *(Tongnip Hyŏphoe)* after they were released from prison, where they had been under sentence because of their radical politics. Most of them had been converted during their imprisonment, when Gale, Bunker and others made special visits to the gaols. Gale was especially interested in Yi Wŏn'gŭng, a scholar and distinguished servant of the Korean Empire, father of the even more famous scholar, Yi Nŭnghwa; Kim Chŏngsik, former chief of police; and Yi Sangjae, Korea's first Postmaster-general, who played a leading part in the early stages of modernizing Korean education, and in founding the Independence Club. The most famous member of the group was Syngman Rhee, who half a century later was to be the Republic of Korea's first President. After his release from prison he went to Gale for advice and baptism. Gale declined to baptize him, because he had studied at the Paejae school, which belonged to the methodist mission, and Gale thought the methodists had a prior claim to him. Nevertheless it was Gale who helped Rhee to write a short autobigraphy in 1904, and encouraged him to go to America. Gale thought that Rhee was 'called to a higher service' than that of a political reformer—which is an indication of the relative importance of politics and the christian ministry in Gale's thinking.

These progressive leaders were the first significant group of well-born Koreans to become protestant christians. Some of them remained members of the Yŏnmot-kol church for many years, but the attraction that Gale and his faith offered them was as much educational as religious. The social implications of protestant christianity as taught by Gale and his companions represented exactly the kind of enlightenment which these men wished for their country, and the time for the awakening of Korea to modern scientific and social ideas was already overdue.

With some of them—Yi Wŏn'gŭng, Yu Sŏngjun, and Kim Chŏngsik—Gale in 1904 founded an educational association, the *Kyoyuk Hyŏphoe,* and during the same period he had other work of the same kind in hand. As early as 1900 he had been encouraging David Yer (Yŏ Pyŏnghyŏn) and others to establish a Korean YMCA. It was only to be expected that he would want to see the society that originally sent him to Korea become a permanent part of the country's christianity. At last in January 1903 he was able to join David Yer, Yun Ch'iho, Homer Hulbert, the anglican bishop Arthur Turner, the commissioner of customs Sir John McLeavy-Brown, the American consul-general Horace Allen, and others, in founding the Seoul YMCA *(Hwangsŏng Kidok Ch'ŏngnyŏn-hoe),* thus contributing to one of the most influential movements in the modernization of Korea. In 1905 he was president of the branch, and when the YMCA building in Chong-no, the main street of Seoul, given by the American businessman Sam Wanamaker, was dedicated in 1908, Gale as chairman of the board of directors took a leading part in the ceremony. In the same year Bishop Turner, who was then president of the Seoul YMCA, and others were anxious that the YMCA should develop a large-scale programme of christian literature, and that Gale should be released from his mission to undertake this as a full-time job. Nothing came of their efforts, but the plan gave recognition to Gale's deepening concern about providing modern literature for Korea. His friend Yi Sangjae, of the former Independence Club, became secretary of the YMCA in 1907 and played an important role in its development.

From the time that he arrived in Seoul to live, and felt himself at the centre of Korean affairs again, Gale, like most missionaries, began to express his opinions about political developments. He not only had a ready pen, he had two special advantages: his friendship with the Independence Club and other progressive thinkers, and his unusual ability with the Korean language. This ability occasionally led diplomats to call on his services. In December 1900 Queen Victoria made the Emperor of Korea an Honorary Knight Grand Commander of the Eminent Order of the Indian Empire, and the British Minister in Seoul asked Gale to accompany him when he went to the palace to deliver the insignia. There was some embarrassment as to how to get the collar and sash put on without offence to Kojong's imperial dignity. The solution was found when the emperor and his son retired for a while, then re-appeared with the emperor wearing the sash, and the elephant emblem dangling happily on his breast. Shortly afterwards a wily Russian told his majesty that the Order of the Indian Empire was of no more than insignificant glory, so the emperor never wore it again. The Russian was not entirely unjustified.

With such experiences to reinforce his second-hand news-gathering, and with his penchant for writing and passing judgment, Gale became a correspondent for the *North China Daily News* of Shanghai. He wrote for that paper intermittently from the end of October 1899 until August 1905, except for the months during which he was absent from Korea in 1903. After 1905 he may have felt that the Japanese take-over of the Korean government in all but name made it unwise to continue his journalism; at all events, the Shanghai paper began to draw instead on the Japanese-controlled *Seoul Press* and other correspondents.

It is practically impossible to trace with certainty all the articles Gale wrote for the Shanghai paper, because complete files of the *North China Daily News* no longer exist outside Peking. Some of the articles were unsigned, but most were signed 'Esson Third' in honour of his Scottish grandmother's maiden name. In 1901 he recorded that he was in danger because the identity of the writer of his columns was being sought by a group in Seoul; but that hazard did not cramp his style. Occasionally he wrote on cultural topics such as literature, tobacco or eunuchs, and sometimes he wrote a story, usually humorous and heavily satirical. A charming piece of November 1900 entitled 'A new coinage for Korea' tells of the proposition made by a Korean that he and Gale should co-operate in counterfeiting. In 1904 shortly before the Russo-Japanese War broke out, he reported that Seoul was uneasy and the community stone-fights had begun a month earlier than usual. One article gave a scathing pen-portrait of the emperor; another described a Korean attempt to destroy Japan by boiling a map of the island empire. The general tenor of the pieces was that Korea was asleep and unheeding, with a hopelessly corrupt court and short-sighted government, the whole country riddled with superstition, while Japan, though despised by Korea, was superficially and technically superior to Korea, and could help Korea—if she would. He clearly had distaste for Japan, and felt strong loyalty to Korea, but his loyalty was tempered with exasperation.

It was entirely consonant with this attitude that he should be active teaching young people in school. Both presbyterians and methodists had made attempts to open schools in Seoul. The methodist schools, Paejae for boys, Paehwa and Ihwa (Ewha) for girls, have been important in modern Korean education, but the presbyterians laid less stress on education than the methodists, and the early history of their schools was chequered. Miss Annie J. Ellers had started a school for girls in Chŏng-dong in 1887, which was moved to Yŏnmot-kol in 1895. This was Chŏngsin Girls' School, which still occupies the same site. Gale was naturally interested in a school so close to his own house, and helped with the teaching there. Among the pupils were Yi Ch'angjik's two daughters, and Gale taught such prominent leaders of the modern Korean education movement as the second of these sisters, Yi Hyegyŏng, and Kim P'illye (Pilley Kim Choi). They remembered him as a courteous gentleman and enthralling teacher, with astonishingly good spoken Korean. In 1909 when the reorganization of the Korean government under Japanese influence necessitated the registration of schools, and Chŏngsin became a recognized institution for the first time, Gale was named as the official founder of the school. This was because its previous history was ignored by the government, and the documents required a legal fiction. Thus Gale's name was recorded as founder of a school whose history dates back before his arrival in Korea.

He was more directly concerned with the education of boys and youths. The early presbyterian attempt at a boys' school in Chŏng-dong, where he had helped Moffett, had not done well. In 1902 Gale started again, giving lessons in rooms of his own house and the church buildings at Yŏnmot-kol. At first six boys attended, aged between 14 and 20. It was called the Intermediate School (*Yesu-gyo Chung-hakkyo*). Later, in 1905, when a brick building was erected on a site specially acquired beside the church compound, the school became known in English as 'The John D. Wells Training School for Christian Workers', after the President of the Board of Foreign Missions of the Presbyterian Church in the USA during the early years of the Korean mission, who had died at the age of 88 in 1903. Gale himself insisted in 1905 on a suitable Korean name being devised for the school, and with the help of his friends, Yi Ch'angjik, Kim Chŏngsik and Yu Sŏngjun, chose *Kyŏngsin,* 'to arouse to what is new'. In the same year Gale handed the school over to Edward H. Miller, but for some years he continued to teach the boys astronomy and christian history. Certain lessons and functions were conducted together with the Chŏngsin girls, with a curtain down the middle of the room to screen the sexes from each other. Gale's school still exists as Kyŏngsin Middle and High School in Hyehwa-dong, Seoul.

Gale produced a series of four *Korean Readers (Yumong ch'ŏnja),* owing much to the Ontario Public School Books, for use in these schools. The first three books were written in contemporary Korean book-language, combining Chinese and Korean scripts. They contain information about science (especially astronomy) and world history, health and modernization, stories from English and American literature, all with suitable moral reflections. The last book was written entirely in Chinese, and consisted of selected passages from Korean writers, which show that by 1904 Gale had formed a discriminating acquaintance with Korean literature. The language of the books is now dated. The vocabulary not only includes such things as *chongsaek* (coir colour) for 'brown', *samu* for 'work' of all kinds (now restricted to office work), *wasa,* from the Japanese *gasu,* for 'gas', and Sino-Korean *sisa* for 'Caesar', but was designed to train readers in the book-language of the day, literary Chinese. There was no attempt to improve the use of the Korean vernacular, and the forms of the Chinese characters were often recondite. Two examples translated from the first volume show the fusion of poetry, elementary science, and presbyterian morality that gives these books their peculiar cachet. The students were warned against eating raw fruit, encouraged to adopt capitalism (with bookkeeping), to trust paper money, to be punctual by using modern timepieces; and they were taught some meteorology:

> Children, do you know what those white masses are that flock together in the sky in the daytime and colour it pink in the twilight? They encircle the mountains and cover the trees, they settle on the great crags. They are like smoke or snow, or like mountain peaks, so that in olden days men of leisure who passed their time composing poetry about nature took them as a subject for impromptu verse; but they never discussed their real nature.
>
> Now, because the earth is always warmed by the sun, vapours rise into the air from the surface of the sea and land, and become clouds. If, as they pass through the sky, they suddenly meet cool air, rain is formed, and if the rain meets colder air as it falls, it turns to hail, or in winter-time to snow that flutters gently down. The reddening of the western sky at evening is clouds reflecting the light of the sun.

The calvinistic ethic is clearest in the lesson on trading:

> No human occupation is superior to trading . . . Trade is a peaceful warfare. As supplies have to be prepared for the battlefield, capital is needed for trading; as weapons are needed on the battlefield, a good reputation is needed in trading; as strategy is needed in battle, so it is necessary to know the qualities and prices of goods. The unprepared will be defeated in trade as they are in battle. Truth and honesty create goodwill and fairness. Honesty means more than not stealing another man's goods, it means behaving conscientiously in all matters . . . Koreans who intend to go into business should attend a commercial school to study goods, prices, and book-keeping.

The stories in the third *Reader* include 'The Diffident Man'. The diffident man was a clumsy fellow who overcame his shyness and accepted an invitation to dine out, but upset a bottle of ink in the ante-room before dinner. Desperately, he mopped it up with his handkerchief. Later, at table, he burned his mouth with hot pudding and wiped his sweating face with the inky handkerchief. The humour of this tale must have appealed to the young Koreans who used the textbook. Their own jokes are often intrinsically similar.

Some of the other western stories used in the *Readers* were: Addison's *Vision of Mirza,* the discovery of America by Columbus, Leonidas and the three hundred Spartans, the death of little Paul (from *Dombey and Son*), the death of Pliny at Vesuvius, an extract about Man Friday from *Robinson Crusoe,* and accounts of the Boston Teaparty, the Battle of the Nile, Beethoven's 'Moonlight Sonata', Alfred the Great, Richard Coeur-de-Lion, Grace Darling, Thomas à Becket, and Cincinnatus. The influence of the Ontario Public School Books is evident. Most of the stories convey some useful lesson, such as Columbus's teaching that the world is round, the patriotism of Leonidas, Pliny's thirst for scientific knowledge, and the hope of after-life in the story of little Paul's death.

The Korean texts in Chinese in Volume IV *(Yumong sokp'yŏn)* included the *Hung fan* from the *Shu ching,* which was regarded as Korean because Ch'i Tzŭ (Kija) was supposed to have written it. The remainder were prose extracts from such writers as King Sejong (a decree on abstinence from wine, taken from the *Kukcho pogam*), Yi Saek, Chŏng Mongju, Yi Kyubo, Chŏng Tojŏn, Kwŏn Kŭn, Yi Yulgok, and Hong Yangho. Gale's chief sources were the *Tongguk yŏji sŭngnam* and the *Tongmun-sŏn.* It is significant that he also included the preface to *Hunmin chŏngŭm,* the original publication of the Korean vernacular alphabet.

A story from his days as principal of the school illuminates Gale's approach to some Korean customs. He deplored the use of the old-style mourner's hat, a huge beehive-shaped affair of straw, which completely hid the wearer's face, and was supposed to prevent him looking up to heaven because he was guilty of the death of his parent. For some years christians debated discarding it because of its superstitious meaning, but they never plucked up enough courage to brave the accusations of filial impiety which would be hurled at them if they forsook it. In September 1904 the mother of Kim Pyŏnghŭi, one of the schoolboys, died. She had become a christian as a result of her son's encouragement. Gale seized his chance: 'Your mother is in heaven, and you did not kill her, but were the means of her salvation. You are not condemned before God and unable to look up, but are a happy boy.' The boy attended the funeral wearing a small white hat, and was severely criticized. 'Beads of perspiration gathered on Pyŏnghŭi's nose, but he went through it like a man', and other christians decided to follow his example. Gale's attitude may seem severe, but he was clearly doing what the Korean christians wanted him to do.

The Korea Branch of the Royal Asiatic Society fostered scholarship of a different kind. It was founded at a meeting held in the Seoul Union on 11 June 1900, and Gale was elected Corresponding Secretary. In the first year of the Society's existence he presented two papers of which in many ways the more interesting was an account of the city of Seoul, called 'Hanyang', published in 1901. It was based on the study of Chinese-language texts which were not then available in modern reprints, and is still a quarry for information about the city.

Some of the best writing in 'Hanyang' is a translation from the *Ch'ao-hsien fu,* written by the Ming envoy Tung Yüeh in 1488, and printed at the beginning of the *Yŏji sŭngnam.* These two extracts are typical:

When there is a message from the emperor, the king comes out to meet his envoy here (at the Mohwa kwan). The *kwan* is used as a rest-house for the envoy, and also as a gathering place for the officers of state. When the message arrives, the king puts on his ceremonial robes and crown, and comes out to meet the ambassador. The ministers, with pins in their headgear, stand like ibises in attendance, while old and young gather on the hills to see, and towers and gates are filled with people in gaudy dress. Houses are decorated and music is wafted on the breeze, drums beat, flags fly, incense goes up like mist in the morning; peach and plum blossoms give colour, and noise of moving horses and chairs is heard. The stone 'sea-lions' bask in the sun that rises from the sea: in front of the Kwanghwa Gate they sit east and west, high as towers, wonderfully hammered out. Like monkeys of Wu-shan, acrobats perform: with boys high on their shoulders they dance and cut capers, walking the tightrope like sons of fairies—with boots on too—same as mountain spirits crossing stepping-stones. They are masked, in horse-skins, as lions and elephants, and they dance as fabled birds, decorated with pheasant tails. Nothing was seen in Songdo or P'yŏngyang that compared with this. (YJSN I 6a4–b3)

There were five layers of honeyed bread and other things piled up a foot or more above the tables; the several dishes of bamboo, brass, etc., were arranged in order, and a border of hanging gems was fastened round the table. Silk cut into pieces formed flowers, and painted pictures of the phoenix were used as ornamentation. There was an absence of fruit upon the tables. Round cakes made of honey and flour and cooked in oil were placed in a circle on the dishes in different layers and in various colours, piled up until they were a foot high and more. There were also silver and white metal dishes having eight-horned borders, ornamented with blue gems, over which were laid four kinds of silk flower-leaves. Along each border there were nails of white metal made like to pearl flowers of China. Green silk decorations were embroidered with peacocks, their tails beautifully spread and their wings lifelike, all with heads down as though bowing to the guests. Koreans like to make a display when they set a table, piling up in front and leaving less at the rear. One table was arranged like the character 'one' (—). There were dainties and rice soup, like Chinese *mi-kao* and *liao-hua,* pickled relish and soy. Their fermented spirit is made of glutinous rice, and not of millet as ours, and yet it was if anything superior. The aroma spread through the room in a way that surpasses even that of Chinese drink. The flavour was of the finest, like the 'Autumn Dew' of Shantung. The wine-cups were lined out like the figure one and covered with a silk spread.

As we were seated on the mat, his majesty suddenly arose, stepped out and looked at the tables. I did not know what he meant to do until he picked up one himself and brought it forward, desiring thus to show honour. Beef, mutton and pork were among the dishes. When these were cut, the minister first tasted. Last of all there was a large table of *man-t'ou,* with a cover of silver on the dish. One official with a knife, who had cut the meat, also divided the *man-t'ou.* There were in the *man-t'ou* walnuts, dates and other things prepared and seasoned suitably. The meat used in it was all of well-fed animals. There were mutton sausages strung on sticks and broiled. Various kinds of fruits were mixed up in the preparation of them.

Dainties and soup were brought in a second time, till there was no place to put them, and so dishes were removed from the tables and put on the mats in order to make way. After eating fish and fishy food, they brought us lotus roots to sweeten the breath. (YJSN I 8a7-9a5)

This account of the reception of the imperial envoy by King Sŏngjong shows the translator's lack of experience, but gives a vivid picture of Korean manners in the fifteenth century. The other paper, 'The Influence of China upon Korea', the first ever given before the Society, throws more light on Gale's times and on personalities. He read it in the Seoul Union at four o'clock in the afternoon on 24 October 1900 in the presence of the US Minister, Horace Allen, and others, with HBM Chargé d'Affaires, J. H. Gubbins, in the chair. The paper gave a fair picture of the way in which Korean culture had been overshadowed by China. It provoked strong objections from Homer Hulbert. On 29 November he read a paper to disprove Gale's contentions and establish the importance of native Korean culture. His paper failed to make the most important points that might have been made in favour of his position. Gale's thesis required some modification, but his devastating rebuttal of Hulbert, and the suave remarks by the president of the Society, the methodist George Heber Jones, still make good reading. Jones quietly made the points that Hulbert ought to have made but did not.

History has so far dealt gently with Hulbert because, though belatedly, he vigorously espoused Korea's cause against Japanese imperialism. He was always in competition with others as a Koreanologist; in fact George Jones, Mark Trollope, and Gale were by far his superiors. He was unable to read Chinese, and bitterly sarcastic about those who could, so although he wrote excellent accounts of things he had seen for himself, he made serious misjudgments on some aspects of Korean culture. From 1901 to 1905 he produced his own magazine, *The Korea Review,* writing it almost entirely himself. Only three articles by Gale were published in it, all during its first year.

After a sparkling beginning, the Royal Asiatic Society in Seoul was active for three years. Then it went into eclipse and was not revived until 1911, when Bishop Trollope returned to Korea after ten years in England. From 1902 onwards, Gale was too busy with bible translation to do serious work for the Society. He, the methodist Appenzeller, and the presbyterian William Davies Reynolds, were appointed to form a translation committee small enough to make reasonably fast progress. In March 1902 they met at Reynolds's house in Mokp'o. During a month of meetings there they standardized the Korean forms of three thousand scriptural proper names. These forms survive in common protestant use to this day. The three men then arranged to meet again in Mokp'o for a further month's work before the rainy season. Gale arrived on time, but Appenzeller was detained in Seoul because of injuries received at the hands of some Japanese when visiting a country church. While they were waiting for him to arrive in Mokp'o, Gale and Reynolds worked on I Corinthians. Then news came that on 11 June Appenzeller and his Korean helper had been drowned in a shipwreck when the Japanese steamer in which they were travelling to Mokp'o had collided with another in a fog eighty-six miles south of Chemulp'o. As a result of this tragedy, H. G. Underwood was appointed to replace Appenzeller, and the committee moved to Seoul, where between October 1902 and March 1906 they met in 555 sessions from 8.30 to 12.30 in the mornings and from 2 to 4 in the afternoons. Their plan was only to complete the New Testament, but Gale made drafts of Proverbs and both books of Samuel in addition.

There was a six-month break in the committee's schedule from April to October, 1903, while Gale visited his wife and stepdaughters in Switzerland. They had gone to Lausanne in 1900 because of Hattie's health and the children's schooling, and remained there for six years. The girls went to a French school and Grandma Gibson taught them English at home. In the vacations they went as far afield as Holland and Germany: they were being 'finished' as nearly as possible. Keeping one's family in Switzerland strikes today's missionary as expensive, but one of the reasons for the plan was economy: life in Switzerland was simple and inexpensive. Mr Oiesen's Chinese wife and three children, one of whom was deaf, went with the Gales. Hattie received no missionary stipend while in Switzerland, and lived by boarding these children, together with Kuai-sun, the son of a wealthy Chinese from Tientsin.

Gale kept a diary of his journey across Asia by the Trans-Siberian Railway. He sailed from Chemulp'o on Saturday 18 April 1903 in the Russian ship *Argun*. The captain, a Russian of English descent, made a friend of Gale and talked to him at length. The following day was Russian Easter, and the crew had received the *antidoron* from the chaplain of a Russian man-o'-war, so they felt free to get drunk during the night. When Gale rose to a Sunday breakfast of caviare, cold meat and coffee, he found the decks strewn with drunken sailors busily kissing each other.

On Monday morning the *Argun* put in at Port Arthur, then under Russian control. The harbour was magnificent, but the town, with its streets full of Cossack police and patchwork mules, was a dreary fortress relieved only by the gorgeous dress of the Tsarist officers and their ladies. Gale scented war in the air and saw the Russo-Japanese conflict coming. The ship sailed on to Dalny, a half-finished place where armies of coolies were blasting for railway works, and the waterfront was still under construction. The part already finished was piled with mountainous heaps of coal, and the whole town was subject to the famous dust-storms of the Liaotung peninsula. Here one boarded the train for Moscow, but it left every Sunday night at eleven, and Gale had arrived on a Monday. He proposed to fill out the week with a visit to the missionaries in Mukden, and board the train there a week later. He found that this was not possible: he had to return to Dalny to buy his ticket to Siberia on the day the train left.

On Sunday morning 26 April he was back at Dalny from Mukden, but still could not buy his ticket till the evening. He went to church and attended a Russian liturgy, which he thought 'simple and naïve'. Late in the evening he managed to buy a ticket as far as the Russian-Manchurian frontier. It cost 55 dollars, first class, for the 1300-mile, three-day journey. The train was plush and comfortable, with electric lights and ornamental mirrors, spacious and smoothly-running because of its five-foot gauge. It was very different from his first journey across Manchuria in a cart, twelve years before. Next morning as they sped northwards along the South Manchurian Railway, he saw again the life of the Liaotung countryside, with pigtailed peasants dressed in blue, coffins above ground, a Chinese farmer pushing his pig and his wife in the same wheelbarrow; but Cossack cavalry drilling in the old town of Liao-yang was a reminder that the Russians were in control of Manchuria. He passed through Mukden again, and hours later crossed the long iron bridge over the Sungari river into the station at Harbin. Harbin was the junction for Vladivostok, and they had to wait an hour and a half. Gale heard Cossack soldiers singing, and toured the town before the train went on, now westwards along the Chinese Eastern Railway. Another day brought them to the walled city of Tsitsihar before they began to climb the Great Khingan Mountains, where three thousand coolies were making a tunnel. Meanwhile the train had engines front and rear which pulled and shunted it up the mountains in four great zigzags. At the top they met the eastbound express and both trains stopped while the conductors got down and kissed each other. It was very cold now; when they got out at the stations to promenade, a German lady paraded her dog in several changes of coloured coat, and some of the passengers played snowballs.

At seven o'clock on Thursday morning they reached the Siberian frontier at Manchou-li, where Gale bought a ticket to Warsaw, 5555 miles away, for 85 dollars. Ice and snow were everywhere; it was bitterly cold. The train went on to join the Trans-Siberian railway at Tarski. Mounted tribesmen watched over great herds of cattle, sheep and camels in this 'land of lamas', where the shaggy people lived in dug-out houses. At one of the halts Admiral Kuzmich, retiring at the end of a commission in the East, impressed Gale by talking kindly to an old Buryat camel-driver. So they passed along the Shilka River, through Chita, and over the Yablonovyy Mountains.

Next day, 1 May, they came down to Mysovsk on the east shore of Lake Baikal. The lake was frozen hard and covered with snow. The railway round the south end of it was still not finished, and passengers had to leave the train to board the ferry. The famous *Baikal,* white and ungainly, with two funnels set athwartships, went first and broke the ice, while the passengers followed in the *Angara*. The twenty-mile crossing took four hours. Gale went down to the second-class dining-saloon, where great quantities of Russian tea were being drunk, and the thunderous din of the ice-breaking made conversation difficult. Nevertheless he managed to chat in French and German with Pavel Valesuk, military post agent from Dalny, who was travelling to central Asia to drink *kumis,* the fermented mare's-milk of the steppes that proved such a good remedy for tuberculosis; with a Russian agent for American agricultural machinery; and a Siberian university student who was intensely proud of his homeland.

They came ashore on the west side of the lake in a snowstorm, but boys were running up and down the platform selling oranges and lemons. A forty-mile run brought the train to Irkutsk. Gale spoke of its 'scintillating domes and towers' and the rich fur coats he saw in the streets of that flourishing centre of trade, where there was an average of three murders a week. It was the wildest city in Siberia, a huge dirty frontier town, like the American wild west with a tsarist veneer of churches, museums and expensive hotels. The stationmaster politely informed the passengers that there would be no Moscow express leaving for three days. Admiral Kuzmich did not take the news easily, and it was found possible for the passengers to leave next morning at six on the ordinary train. They received back one third of the fare from Irkutsk to Moscow. It was paid, much to Gale's astonishment, in gold coin.

After Irkutsk the architecture of the stations was more splendid, but Siberia appeared to be one vast military camp, with tsarist authority making itself felt everywhere. Besides the naval officers in their dark blue and the army in their light blue-grey, there were the ubiquitous railway police. The train trundled on through the evergreen forests of the taiga for about 650 miles till it crossed the Yenisei River at Krasnoyarsk. Krasnoyarsk too was full of onion-domed churches, but looked like 'an exiled Pittsburgh'. On 6 May they crossed the Ob River and saw the sled road still visible on the ice. Coming out into the Siberian Plain through a landscape dotted with wooden windmills, the train approached Omsk, where Dostoyevsky had lived and suffered, and where there was a *kumis* sanatorium. From here till Moscow, as he looked out of the train windows over the steppes where the Kirghiz herdsmen rode, Gale saw the marmots sitting on their haunches, like the prairie dogs of his Canadian home.

The next day they were at Chelyabinsk, among the birchwoods, with its nearby Monument of Tears built by Siberian convicts. When the sun rose, the train clocks pointed to 2.30 a.m. as the time in St Petersburg. Gale had to change cars and wait for an hour and a half. He visited the town and saw more gilded churches, many warehouses, and huge piles of American-made agricultural implements, but no bookshop.

When the train left Chelyabinsk it began to climb the foothills of the Urals, which it crossed the next day. At last they were in a land of spring: the ploughing had started and birds were singing in the trees when Gale drank Russian tea with lemon in it for fifteen kopeks a glass at Miass. Later they stopped at Zlatoust, the iron town, where, only a month before, a strike by the iron-workers had been cruelly crushed by the military. The passengers bought souvenirs. Gale bought a pie-knife. Very soon afterwards they must have passed the stone pyramid at Urzhumka that marked the boundary between Asia and Europe, but Gale made no record of it.

The Ufa valley was deep in spring floods. Beyond the next range of hills was the Volga valley, and the line crossed the great river just before Syzran. Soon they were at Tula, where they had to change again. Gale noted the chapels built into the station. Admiral Kuzmich was off to Sebastopol for his health's sake, and at Tula he bade his fellow-passengers goodbye with profuse kisses. He even kissed the stiff English infantry captain who had worn a summer suit as they crossed Lake Baikal in the snow.

The train for Moscow left at midnight. Gale had trouble because he had put his case on top of a lady's hat and could not understand her Slavic expostulations. They rattled northwards through the dark and arrived at Moscow on the morning of 10 May, fifteen days and six hours after leaving Dalny. Gale called Moscow 'a golden city', and stopped keeping his travel journal. He had found the trip a great pleasure: 'I like the Russians,' he wrote, 'and with mingled hopes and fears . . . await the progress of their empire.' The Russians were important for Korea, and Gale was in their country for the first time. If Poland and central Europe made any impression on him, no record of it survives. He must have been growing impatient for his reunion with his wife and the two girls.

While he was with them in Switzerland that summer he wrote, with assistance from Hattie, his only novel, *The Vanguard*. (The title was the publisher's idea.) It is a spirited, entertaining and sentimental account of the presbyterian mission in northern and eastern Korea, chiefly P'yŏngyang and Wŏnsan. The core of the book, according to Gale, was the autobiography of Ko Ch'anik, a Wŏnsan man who became an elder of Yŏnmot-kol church; but the most vivid characters are thinly-disguised portraits of missionaries: Samuel Moffett as the hero; Malcolm Fenwick as the maverick Fireblower; Graham Lee, the ebullient bachelor, called Plum by a Korean pun on his surname; and Gale himself blended with Mr Duff of Elora and caricatured as a literary Scot, McKechern. The doctor, Sir James, is a composite portrait of Dr Heron and Dr Hall; Appenzeller appears as Foster, and Underwood as Gilbert. The portraits of Koreans, mostly lower-class converts, include, apart from Ko, Gale's 'boy' (called the Dragon), and Pang and Kim of P'yŏngyang. They are warm and unvarnished. There is a good description of the *General Sherman* incident of 1866, when an American ship of that name was destroyed at P'yŏngyang and all aboard her were massacred, including the British missionary, Robert Thomas. There is also an account of the troubles with Korean Roman catholics, who forced some protestants to contribute money for building a Roman church at Sinhwan-p'o, in Chaeryŏng prefecture of Hwanghae province in 1902. It is substantially true, and is one of the few examples of Gale's adverse reporting on christians not of his own denomination.

He took the manuscript back to Korea with him. On the return journey across Siberia, he was pestered by the Russian police, who were especially inquisitive about documents, so he concealed the pages somehow inside his trousers. The book was published in 1904 by Fleming Revell in New York, and was given an enthusiastic notice in the *Korea Review*. H. H. Underwood, in his bibliography of western writings on Korea (1930) wrote coolly that it was 'as accurate a picture as is found in most such fiction', but included it in his list of fifty basic titles on Korea. Though it would be absurd to overestimate the book's virtues, it would be equally so to overlook the abundant sincerity and enthusiasm it demonstrates for Korea and the gospel.

In March 1906 Gale again left Seoul to join his family in Switzerland, and travelled by rail across Siberia. It must have been a colder journey this time, though he was spared the ferry across Lake Baikal, for the railway round the south end of the lake had been completed. Tsarist Russia was still a militant state, but the Russo-Japanese war of 1904 had put an end for the time being to her oriental designs. Korea itself was now firmly under Japanese tutelage; Russian influence in south Manchuria had been broken. Gale cannot have failed to notice the difference.

After a short holiday in Switzerland the family visited England in early July before going to the United States for the main part of the furlough, which was only the second in Gale's eighteen years of missionary service. They did not visit Canada, but were again based on Washington DC. There was a tremendous welcome meeting, with Henry B. F. Macfarland, mayor of the city, in the chair, and Justice Harlan of the Supreme Court, and Chief Justice Peele of the Court of Claims, among the speakers. Also in the welcome committee were Dr Teunis Hamlin and other directors of Howard University, then a university attended chiefly by negro students. The directors of Howard had prepared for the visit by awarding Gale an honorary doctorate of divinity on 31 May 1904, and sent the certificate to him in Korea. The degree honoured his literary work and especially his contribution to bible translation.

During this furlough President Roosevelt asked Gale to call on him to report on the personal character of the US Minister in Seoul. Since foreign legations in Seoul had been abolished a year previously when Japan assumed direction of Korea's foreign relations, it looks as though Roosevelt was still pursuing Horace Allen, whom he had recalled in 1905; but no record is available of Gale's conversation at the White House.

Between 1900 and 1906 his intense activity in bible translation had no doubt helped to compensate for his separation from Harriet. He was overjoyed when she and the girls returned with him to Seoul from America in August 1907. The event was made even more moving by the enthusiastic party given for them by elder Ko Ch'anik and other members of the Yŏnmot-kol church. Grandma Gibson remained in America, but Annie was now an official missionary of the Presbyterian Church, teaching in the Chŏngsin School. Gale returned to his routines of teaching, preaching and literary work. Almost immediately he was elected pastor of the English-language Union Church of Seoul for 1908, and in the same year he was elected second moderator of the Presbyterian Church of Korea, a position held by only six westerners.

During 1907 the Korean presbyterian and methodist churches were rocked by a revival movement that became the wonder of the christian world, though it sometimes shocked the missionaries by its fervour. No mention of it remains in Gale's writings. Its peak was reached before his return from furlough, and he was doubtless preoccupied with Harriet's poor health, but it would be typical of his Scottish tradition if he distrusted the ecstatic signs of the outpouring of the Holy Spirit that were reported from so many Korean churches. His own congregation at Yŏnmot-kol seems not to have been affected, though it was growing fast. Between May and November 1905 the building was enlarged three times, but it was still too small. The swelling congregation included the famous royal court sorceress, Chillyŏng-gun. By 1907 the average attendance was 550, with two Sunday schools, one for boys and one for girls, whose membership totalled 800. The year's contributions from the congregation amounted to $1610.24, slightly less than $3 per capita of average attendance, at a time when the price of unskilled labour was from 15 to 25 cents a day. In 1907 they contributed two-thirds of the construction costs of a completely new wooden church, seating 1200 people, which was dedicated after Gale's return.

About the same time Ko Ch'anik entered the seminary at P'yŏngyang; but he died early in 1908. The seminary had been opened in 1901 under Moffett's direction, and was intended to serve the whole Korean presbyterian church. At the beginning there was a single three-month semester each year, and Gale used to go for a six-week lecture stint. On 19 May 1908 he laid the foundation stone of the new building of the seminary. The first class had graduated in 1907, with Han Sŏkchin as one of its members.

Little remains, apart from the four *Readers*, to show what Gale did in literature between his first and second furloughs, or immediately after his return in 1907. Work on the bible and Korean-language christian newspapers occupied most of his time. As early as 1901 he had temporarily relieved H. G. Underwood as editor of *The Christian News (Kŭrisŭdo sinmun)*, a joint methodist and presbyterian enterprise. He undertook the same job again in July 1905 and continued it, apart from his furlough, for five years. In December 1907 the name of the paper was changed to *The Church Herald (Yesu-gyo sinbo)*. The name was changed again in February 1910 to *The Christian News (Yesu-gyo hoebo)*, when the ownership was taken over by the Korean presbytery, and Gale relinquished the editorship to his old friend Han Sŏkchin. These papers appeared fortnightly. The *Herald* had contained general and political news, in line with Gale's educational concern, but the new paper was more strictly evangelistic in content.

Meanwhile Gale had been an indefatigable proofreader for the bible translation committee, and after his return from furlough, in the course of four or five months, he reviewed the translations of Leviticus, Numbers and Deuteronomy. In 1906 his collaborator Yi Ch'angjik was nominated as one of the first three Koreans officially appointed to the bible translation committee.

In 1906 Gale published a Korean translation of the *Shorter Catechism* of the presbyterian church (*Sŏnggyŏng yori mundap*). His version of Robert's *Rules of Order (Ŭihoe t'ongyong kyuch'ik)*, based on Yun Ch'iho's translation, probably also dates from this period. His life of Martin Luther in Korean, *Rut'ŏ kaegyo kiryak*, was published in 1908 as one of a series of modern educational books. In 1909 he classified christian literature work under three headings. Among work for Korean readers he gave pride of place to the bible, commenting on the impetus it had given in making a nation of readers out of a nation of non-readers. This was chiefly due to the use of the native phonetic alphabet. Other christian books had followed the bible, he said, and had 'contributed to bring about a simple form of composition, unknown before, but now employed by novel-writers, newspaper editors, and literary people in general'. His second category was literature for missionaries, chiefly dictionaries and language aids. New books of this kind were needed, but not likely to be written because potential writers were fully occupied by the great demands for direct evangelistic work. His third category was missionary information for the church at home, of which he recorded an adequate supply in print, including his own *Korean Sketches* and *The Vanguard*.

The political and cultural background of Korean life was now changing more rapidly. The Russo-Japanese War of 1904-5 had eliminated Russian influence. Railways and mails were functioning under Japanese direction, banks were operating, Seoul had telephones. On 18 November 1905 the Japanese had engineered the signing of a 'protectorate treaty'. Hulbert, who up to this time had favoured Japanese policies, suddenly began making efforts as an amateur diplomat to stop their progress. In July 1907 he was present at the second International Peace Conference at The Hague, trying to fight for Korea behind the scenes, but on 19 July the Japanese forced the Korean king to abdicate in favour of his impotent son, who became a puppet emperor. The Korea to which Gale returned was already under *de facto* Japanese rule, and it was merely a matter of time before it became a colony in the Japanese empire. It was impossible for Hulbert to return to Korea to live.

During August and September 1908, Gale was writing *Korea in Transition*, a book to be used by young presbyterians in America for study courses in 1909 and 1910. The book was translated into Danish almost immediately, along with *The Vanguard* — a sign of widespread interest in Korea at a crucial point in her history.

In 1909, when Gale's entry for *Canadian Men and Women of the Time* was written, he was described as 'the foremost literary interpreter of the Korean mind to the occidental world'. It might have been added that he had also done great things in introducing occidental ideas to Korea. That part of his work was now to be of much less importance, because Japan had taken control of Korean education, and foreigners were strictly limited in the contribution they were allowed to make. Gale's four *Readers* were eventually banned. When he protested, he was told by the censor that his inclusion of Kipling's story 'Moti Guj-Mutineer' in the third volume was inflammatory, because in that story the elephant refused to serve his second master, and Koreans might understand this as a suggestion that they should refuse to serve their new master, the emperor of Japan. The pretext was silly, but the Japanese were entirely serious: their aim was to standardize all educational materials according to their own norms. This incident and the later brutalities of 1919 destroyed the last traces of Gale's confidence in Japan's ability to lead Korea. In the Korea of the Japanese his work had to change.

His family life changed too, and tragically. Harriet had been cured of tuberculosis in Switzerland, but her physical strength had never matched the robustness of her will. Barely six months after her return to Seoul, on 29 March 1908, she died in a room filled by mourning Koreans. She declared that for the last eight nights of her life her soul had been taken from her body and rapt into heaven. Gale wrote: 'The resultant impression made by her last days is one impossible to express. Words do not touch it at all. Out of the world, yet in it; up in heaven, and still here suffering; beautifully victorious, and yet helplessly dying. We look back upon it as the most tender, most solemn, most real moment of life, never to be forgotten.' She was forty-eight years old; he was forty-five. They had been married for sixteen years, but had spent less than ten of those years together, and little more than five of them together in Korea. They had no children—they had travelled a great deal and her health had never been good. She is buried in Yanghwa-jin cemetery for foreigners, in the same grave as her first husband.

For the next two years his stepdaughters kept house for Gale: Annie taught at Chŏngsin Girls' School; Jessie was the practical one. On 15 December 1908 Tz'ŭ-hsi, the Empress Dowager of China, died, and the two Heron girls were soon afterwards invited by an English friend to stay in Peking and see the spectacular funeral. There Annie again met Esson M. Gale, son of Dr Gale's physician brother, Hugh. Esson had gone to China as a student interpreter of the United States consular service. In November 1909 he became engaged to Annie. who prepared to marry him and leave the Seoul household.

Dr Gale's parents both died during the same year.

vi Korean studies 1910 – 1920

On 7 April 1910 Dr Gale married Ada Louisa Sale, eighteen years to the day after his wedding with Harriet. He was now forty-seven and wore spectacles, but was still slim, and his wavy hair had neither greyed nor thinned noticeably. Ada was thirty-five.

She was born at Strines, Marple, Cheshire, on 25 October 1875 and educated in England and Japan. She attended the exclusive Peeresses' School Joshi Gakushuin in Tokyo while she lived at Yokohama, where her father was a partner in Sale, Frazar and Company, shipping agents and merchant bankers. George Sale had been born in 1841, and trained in the silk trade, travelling through Europe and Russia. In the 1880's, being in financial low water, he made a fresh start by moving his family to Japan. He spoke several European languages, and soon added Japanese to his repertoire. His family was prominent in the English-dominated international community of Yokohama, enthusiastic about its tennis, its singing in the church choir, and its chamber music. There was a piano quartet in the family, and Lilian spoke Italian. The Gales had formed a friendship with the Sales while Dr Gale was in Yokohama working on his Korean dictionary in 1896. When the Gales visited England in the summer of 1906, they again met the Sale family, who were living at Beckenham in Kent after their father's retirement. Harriet Gale told her little daughters that she would be happy if they were to grow up as attractive and gifted as Marie and Ada Sale; so when their beloved foster-father planned to marry Ada, who returned to the Orient for the purpose, the Heron girls gave their delighted approval. Indeed, Jessie said that Annie had engineered the whole affair.

The wedding took place in Yokohama. There was a civil ceremony at the British Consulate in the morning, and a service at the Union Church in the afternoon, conducted by T. R. Good of the Reformed Church of America, minister of the Union Church. Lilian Sale was bridesmaid, and Kim Chŏngsik, the former Independence Club member, who had also helped at Kyŏngsin School but was now doing YMCA work in Tokyo , was best man. The new Mrs Gale arrived in Seoul with her husband, accompanied by her mother and sister and Annie Heron, on 16 April. Six months later Annie married Esson and went to live in Peking. Jessie for the next nine years divided her time between the two households.

Ada provided James Gale with the comradeship that circumstances had deprived him of in his first marriage. He was always inclined to be dependent on his womenfolk. Ada did her best to join in his missionary work; her musical ability was a great help, and doubtless encouraged him in his efforts to promote a society for the study of Korean music, Chosŏn Ŭmak Yŏn'gu-hoe, in 1917–1919. Her fluency in Japanese helped to foster good relations between the missionaries and the Japanese residents in Korea, whom she visited assiduously. She never forgot that Japan had been her first love, and she had great difficulty in learning Korean. In 1918 she was still officially studying that language. It was said of her later, by way of a family joke, that she only learned three words of Korean: *moksu* (carpenter), which she confused with *moksa* (pastor); *sat'ang* (sugar), which she used for *sokt'an* (coal); and *chigŭm* (now), which she used as a universal imperative.

Japanese, however, was becoming more and more used in Korea, which had been finally annexed to the empire of Japan in October 1910. The Korean monarchy had been abolished, and both Kojong and his son lived in retirement. Few missionaries lifted their voice in protest at the time. Some Koreans regret that Dr Gale was not an independence fighter, but he was no more a political creature than he was a sectarian. His vision was far from impractical, as is amply shown by the energy he put into his work, by his enthusiasm for education, and by his brief contribution in 1907 to a symposium on Korea's greatest need: while many contributors were pious, Gale urged the need for industrial training. Nonetheless, his deepest concern was to understand the Korean mind, and much of his energy between his second marriage and his next furlough was spent in studying Korea and translating her old books.

One of the greatest fillips he received in the prosecution of these studies was a direct result of Japanese involvement in Korea. He was enthusiastic about the editions produced by the Chosen Kosho Kanko-kai, the Society for the Publication of Old Korean Books. It began to issue its volumes in the autumn of 1909, and continued to produce a book a month for seven years. The series contained a haphazard collection of texts, because it depended on the manuscripts and printed editions that happened to be in the possession of members of the society. Some of the geographical works supported old Korean claims about the northern boundaries which China had never recognized, but Japan was interested in maintaining. Gale's interest, however, was early gripped by the volumes of the *Taedong yasŭng,* a miscellany of Korean records written at various times between 1450 and 1650, some important and some merely anecdotal. There were thirteen volumes in this set, published by the Chosen Kosho Kanko-kai between November 1909 and April 1911. The second volume contained a fifteenth-century collection of anecdotes by Yi Yuk, called *Ch'ŏngp'a kŭktam,* whose weird and occult themes appealed strongly to Gale. In 1911 he had come into possession of a manuscript collection of similar anecdotes attributed to Im Pang (1640–1724). Adding three stories from sources which he never identified in print, Gale translated a selection of these tales and submitted them for publication to J.M. Dent of London. His own title for the manuscript was *Korean Imps, Ghosts and Fairies,* and in his letter to Dent he wrote: 'After a residence in Korea of over twenty-four years, I am struck by the oddity and yet the faithfulness of these stories to the world that I have lived in, but have never been able to find so marked and definite an expression for.' In an article in the *Korea Magazine* in August 1917 Gale admitted that he had no inkling of the Korean tradition of fairies and goblins until he had been in the country for twenty years, then, when he first read of such things, he discovered that his helpers had taken his knowledge of such things for granted. It must have been the *Taedong yasŭng* that opened his eyes. For the rest of his time in Korea he delighted in choosing fairy material for translation. Dent accepted the book, gave it the title *Korean Folk Tales* (which, as Arthur Ransome pointed out in an enthusiastic review, was inaccurate, for they were not true folk-tales) and used *Imps, Ghosts and Fairies* as the sub-title. The charming little work was published in London in 1913, and at the same time by Dutton in New York.

Yi Yuk's story, *The Propitious Magpie,* suggests the flavour of the whole collection:

> People say that when a magpie builds its house directly south of a home, the master of the house will be promoted in office. King T'aejong had a friend once who was very poor and had failed in all his projects. After various fruitless attempts he decided to wait until the king went out in procession and then to send a servant to build an imitation magpie's nest in some propitious place before him. The king saw it, and asked the man what he was doing. He said in reply that when a magpie builds its nest straight south of a home, the master of the house instantly gets promotion. His master, he said, had waited so long and nothing had come, that he was building an imitation nest to bring it about. The king took pity on him and ordered his promotion at once.
>
> When I was young myself a magpie built its nest before our home, but I, along with other boys, cut off the branch so that the whole nest fell to the ground, and there were the young with their pitiful yellow mouths. I felt sorry and afraid they would die, so on a propitious site to the south I had the nest hung up on a *nŭt'i* tree (zelkowa), where the young all lived and flourished and flew away. In that very winter my father was promoted three degrees in rank and was attached to the office of the prime minister.
>
> Afterwards I built a summerhouse at Ch'ŏngp'a, and before the house, directly facing south, magpies built a nest in a date tree. I had a woman slave and she pulled it down and used the nest for fuel, but

they came again the next year and built once more. The year following was 1469, when Yejong came to the throne. That year again I was promoted. In the spring of 1471 magpies came and built their nest in a tree just south of my office. I laughed and said: 'There is a spiritual power in the magpie surely, as men have said from olden times, and as I myself have proven.' (TDYS II 21)

Korean Folk Tales was dedicated to Gale's first child, George James Morley, who was born in April 1911, and baptized by pastor Kil Sŏnju, the great missioner and educator from P'yŏngyang, who became an intrepid independence leader. George was given the Korean name Cho-se ('Help the world') by his father's Korean scholar-friends, and instead of being sent to day-school with the American missionary children, was educated at home in English style. For a few months when he was eight he went for French lessons to the Sisters of St Paul of Chartres, near the Cathedral of the Immaculate Conception in Myŏng-dong. By that time Dr Gale was a good friend of the French archbishop of Seoul, Monseigneur Auguste Mutel. The Gales might belong to an American mission, but the education of the family was to be European.

When the second child was born on St Valentine's day 1916, he was named Vivian Scarth, after his mother's younger brother, Vivian, and when he was baptized in the Yŏnmot-kol church on 30 April by a Japanese pastor, Ino Kuchi, the Japanese name Masao was added. Masao, 'upright man', can also be read as an acceptable Korean name, Chŏngnam, but Masao was convenient for his Japanese amah, Otori. Ada found it easier to communicate with Otori than she had with George's Korean amah.

Gale continued his work on the Korean language. The second edition of his dictionary was published in Yokohama in 1911. It was much expanded, and contained about 50,000 entries. Several thousand historical and geographical proper names were included, setting a fashion which has been kept by most large native Korean dictionaries up to the present day. The order of the words was changed to the Korean alphabetical order. The second part, the dictionary of Chinese characters, was not re-issued till 1914. This part too was considerably revised, and slightly enlarged to include modern meanings for some characters such as 'nitrogen' for the character *chil*, 'suffocate'.

Korean Grammatical Forms appeared in an entirely rewritten version and much smaller format in 1916, remaining in general use until the second world war. It now contained 240 grammatical word-endings and 1,000 sentences and phrases. The material was updated, more christian sentences were included, and the whole book greatly improved. There is plenty of humour in the examples, especially among the proverbs:

Ch'ŏga chip malttugedo chŏrhagenne (He would bow to the horse-post of his wife's family).
Kosumtoch'ido che saekkinŭn hamhamhada handa (Even a hedgehog thinks his young soft and sleek).
159 *Unhaengi pakkat kkŏpchirŭn semoga china, sok almaenginŭn tunggŭmnida*

(The outside of the apricot is cornered, but the kernel is round). Gale had second thoughts about the way he had treated this subject in 1894, because the ginkgo nut has three layers: the fleshy outside encloses a ridged shell, inside which is the round edible part.

367 *Haesamŭn mŏkkido haryŏniwa, pidane p'urhanŭnde ssŭnŭnira* (Sea-slugs can be eaten, and are also used as starch for silk).

Old sentences were improved and mistakes corrected:

58 *P'ogyange kim maegich'ŏrŏm yagyakhan kŏsŭn ŏpso* (Nothing is harder than pulling weeds in the scorching heat).

Errors such as 'porpoise' for 'globefish' were corrected, and there were signs of the changing times:

I pŏne yebaedange tŭngŭl tarasso (We have now hung up electric lights in the church).

Dr Gale was president of the Korea Branch of the Royal Asiatic Society from 1911 to 1916. One of his best monographs was his study of the Korean alphabet, published in 1912. It was first announced for public reading in April 1911, but not delivered until December of that year—which shows the pressure under which he was working. Since 1945 research into this subject has been pushed much further, but Gale's main conclusions are still valid. They were far sounder than the speculations of Hulbert and others, and the paper is an invaluable introduction to the bases of traditional Korean thought, as well as a notable appreciation of the outstanding qualities of the Korean alphabet. Gari Ledyard in his *The Korean Language Reform of 1446* (1965) says: 'Gale's study was, for its time, a great achievement. He examined all the theories critically, and investigated as many Korean sources as he knew about or were available to him.'

Gale's next paper, 'Selection and Divorce', was less thorough. It is the least satisfying of his studies: the subject-matter—the occult considerations affecting the selection and rejection of spouses—was closely in harmony with his interest in the preternatural, but the material was unwieldy and difficult to summarize. In 1915 he published his study on the Pagoda of Seoul. This was a more sub-stantial piece of work, but it proved to be his last essay in active historical re-search. Most of what he published after this was translation of Chinese texts.

He was intensely interested in the history of Korean printing type. The importance of early Korean achievement in this field had been noted by Griffis and others, especially Maurice Courant in his great *Bibliographie Coréenne*. Gale took the matter a stage further when he published in the *Seoul Press*, 11 October 1913, an article consisting of translations of early references to Korean movable metal printing types, drawn from the *Munhŏn pigo*, *Kukcho pogam* and *Tongmun-sŏn*. He added to these official documents the following informative passage from the jottings of Sŏng Hyŏn in the *Taedong yasŭng*:

They made the first type models of boxwood, and by means of them made an impression in a tray of mud gathered from the seashore where the reeds grow. When the boxwood model was thus pressed into the mud, the impression constituted the matrix. Then an upper tray, with holes in it, was fastened above. The copper was then melted and poured down through the openings of the upper tray, so that the metal went into the various matrices, each becoming a type. If any were badly formed, the corners of the irregularities were filed off. Bamboo slips were prepared to make all solid, that it should not shake. At first, not knowing how to prepare the plate, they had melted wax and poured it on; but the types were unsteady in the plate, and so bamboo slips were used to wedge it up instead of the wax. (*Yongjae ch'onghwa* VII)

The article dealt with the Korean metal movable type of 1403 as though it were the first ever made, and did not mention the movable metal type cast some time between 1232 and 1241 on Kanghwa Island. Details of this were not published until a posthumous paper by Bishop Trollope, written between 1925 and 1930, appeared in the Royal Asiatic Society's *Transactions* for 1935 (Vol XXV, pp 103–107). Gale, however, had mentioned the Kanghwa type in chapter xxiii of his *History of the Korean People,* written in 1925, and T. F. Carter, recording it in his *Invention of Printing in China and its Spread Westward* (New York 1925, p. 254) acknowledged Gale as the source of his information. Trollope's copy of Carter's book, now in Yonsei University Library, is annotated in the bishop's own hand giving the reference to Yi Kyubo's writings beside the acknowledgement to Gale.

Yi Kyubo is the sole source for the story of the Kanghwa type. Whether Gale or Trollope first lighted on it, he probably discovered it first in English, in the *Annual Report on Reforms and Progress in Chosen 1914–15,* page 17. The *Report* appeared shortly after the publication of the first modern reprint of Yi Kyubo's writings in 1913, and doubtless drew either Gale's or Trollope's attention to Yi Kyubo's mention of the matter. None of the Kanghwa type remains, nor any piece of printing done with it, but Gale possessed several pieces of early Korean type, which he believed to be from the fount cast in 1403. A facsimile impression of them was printed with a translation of his *Seoul Press* article in the Dresden magazine *Victoria* in 1914. He was mistaken about their date, for they were from a fount of either 1772 or 1777. After his death they were acquired by the Library of Congress, Washington DC.

Yi Kyubo, the Koryŏ statesman and poet, proved to be a discovery of major importance for Gale. He had included one piece of Yi Kyubo's prose in the 1904 *Readers,* but now he could see the whole of the man's work, and quickly recognized its unusual quality. With his friend Kim Tohŭi he began to translate the poems, and they made a pilgrimage to the poet's grave on Kanghwa Island. Gale told and re-told the story of that outing many times. One version is in chapter 19 of *The History of the Korean People.*

Some of his translations of Yi Kyubo were published in the *Korea Magazine,* of which he was chief editor for the whole of its life from January 1917 to April 1919. During his pre-breakfast study hours he wrote the greater part of all

53

twenty-eight issues. Indeed the magazine had to cease publication after April 1919 because Gale went on furlough in May that year. The articles signed with his name are mostly about the Korean language; many unsigned translations from Korean literature were later used in the *History of the Korean People;* a few articles are signed 'E.T.' for Esson Third, the pseudonym which he had used a dozen years earlier in the *North China Daily News.*

The unsigned articles betray his authorship by their style and subject-matter. The attribution is proved beyond doubt by the manuscripts preserved among his papers in Montreal. A signed article, 'Concerning the Occult', underlines one of his main interests, and he was also the author of a series of articles on 'Korea's Noted Women' by 'A Student of the Orient', for he was gallantly fascinated by the female sex, and made it one of the themes of his *History.* Many early mission-aries, especially spinsters, were misled by the social customs of Korea into think-ing that Korean women were downtrodden. Gale knew better, and presented Korean women as forceful and effective, usually beautiful, and always beguiling. His view was touched by romance, but it was fundamentally sound. In 1922 he wrote: 'The Korean woman has convictions of soul that hold fast through foul and sunny weather. Her influence on the present generation is the most hopeful possible. In study she is the equal of the man. Surely among the women of the world she will have a place of honour.' This is the other side of the coin he had written about twenty-five years earlier, in *Korean Sketches,* when he whimsically described petticoat government in the home, and rightly declared that it was the normal pattern of Korean life.

The same interest in women is seen in the translation of *Okchung hwa,* Yi Haejo's version of Korea's best-known folk romance, *Ch'unhyang chŏn,* published serially in the *Korea Magazine* under the title 'Choon Yang'. The style is un-mistakably Gale's, and his typescript has been preserved by his son, but the translator's name was not published in the magazine.

Gale's approach to pseudonymity and anonymity was curious. In the *Korea Magazine* he may well have been motivated by modesty, because he was writing so much of the journal's copy, but he had a puckish streak too. He happily quoted his own earlier writings, and did so several times in the *History* without admitting the fact. In one extreme instance, he quoted in the *History* a story from *Korea in Transition,* where the same story is attributed to Esson Third, 'himself an oriental writer'; but Esson Third was one of his own pen-names. 'Spectator' and 'A Student of the Orient' were simple enough noms-de-plume, but 'Yung Oon' is more puzzling. Probably it was an inversion of Unyŏng, the name of the heroine in a well-known Korean story he had translated with Kim Tohŭi in 1917. It means 'cloud bud', but when reversed to mean 'blossom cloud' it can can also be interpreted as 'British sojourner'. The articles in the *Korea Magazine* deal with such topics as tea, paper, dancing-girls, tobacco, chess, playing cards *(t'ujŏn),* the prohibition of alcohol, Korean religious ideas, and modern changes in Korean life. Gale thought Korean-language texts were meagre and uninterest-ing, so his articles are full of translations from Korean writings in Chinese. Fairy stories and lyrics predominate: he came to admire Korean philosophical writing, but did not translate much of it. At times he was schoolmasterly with his readers, upbraiding them for lack of background in Chinese literary culture; at other times he made careless slips himself and gave wrong attributions for the texts he translated.

The quality of the verse translations can be illustrated by comparing two of them with plain modern versions. He treated a poem by Ch'oe Ch'iwŏn as follows:

An Ancient Thought

> I am told the fox can change into a pretty girl,
> The wild-cat to a scholar-lord or chief.
> When creatures doff their forms so easily,
> Who then can tell what sort of beings
> Really walk around us? Again I think, well, yes,
> It is not hard to change the form or kind;
> What's hard is how to keep the soul and mind
> From changing. There's the rub. The true to false,
> The fair to foul, are changes to be feared.
> Keep bright the mirror of the soul, I pray.

The same poem more directly translated reads:

Determination

> A fox can turn into a lovely woman,
> A wild-cat change into a learned scholar.
> Who knows when he meets these wonders,
> These illusions under human form?
> But transformation is not really difficult;
> Controlling the mind is the greater problem.
> For the sake of telling the true from the false
> I will polish the mirror of my heart. (TMS IV 2)

Gale published his version as prose, but characteristically used far more words than were necessary to convey the meaning of the original. He took pains to unify the whole stanza by using the word 'change' in the latter part, whereas the Chinese demands that the reader perceive the link for himself. Gale ignored the structure of the stanza and made no attempt to convey the parallelism, but his rendering of the sense was correct, even cogent. He concerned himself first with meaning, and expressed it in diction that echoes Shakespeare and the Authorized Version.

The second example shows him working in a different way. The poem was written by Pyŏn Kyeryang. Gale gave it no title.   (Cf HKP chapter 24)

> So quiet sits this hamlet neath the hill,
> With softened shade and furrows freshly turned.
> I wander by the stream to seek for simples,

My books I spread out neath the drying sun.
Across the sky's blue vault the wild-goose wings,
Amid the moonlit bamboos calls the whip-poor-will.
I look toward Seoul, whence endless thoughts arise,
And jot a verse down for my friend of friends.

The plain translation is:

From the country to one Yi, a military graduate living in Seoul

The village still and quiet before the piled-up peaks,
Only a few mulberry-trees and two ploughed fields . . .
Searching for herbs, I often walk through the woods;
Airing my books, I fall asleep in the sun.
Clouds clear from the sky over the river
    where I see wild-geese returning,
Moonlight bathes the mountain bamboos
    when I hear the nightjar calling.
With feelings I cannot define, I turn towards where you are,
And write a new poem to send to you.

Here Gale paid all his attention to style, yet again he ignored the parallelism in the two middle couplets, which is an essential element in this type of poetry. He was intent on writing English blank verse, a medium for translation of Chinese seven-syllable verse that has been unjustly neglected by modern translators. He was given to mannerisms, and did not take the trouble to avoid repeating '*neath*', but made good use of alliteration. In each of the first six lines of the poem he sacrificed part of the sense for the sake of metre; yet he could have justified himself by claiming that he had retained the 'complete sense' of the poem.

Perhaps his most interesting work in the *Korea Magazine*, not excepting 'Choon Yang', was the series of excerpts from the diary kept by Kim Ch'angǒp while accompanying the Korean embassy to Peking in the winter of 1712–13. The series was interrupted by the cessation of the magazine, but it shows how Gale was translating prose at this time. The choice of book was characteristic. Kim's diary reflected Korean attitudes to foreign culture, and Gale selected passages that show Kim Ch'angǒp at his chattiest. Occasionally Gale baulked at a difficult passage and omitted it. Frequently he made mistakes that appear to be due to following his Korean pundit too closely. He confused official titles and was generally slipshod, as though trying to work too fast. He was prodigal of words, and his choice of expression very nearly succeeded in turning Kim into a mirror of James Gale. The extracts which were included in chapter 32 of the *History of the Korean People* were revised and improved.

Two concerns pervaded many of the *Korea Magazine* articles: the changes taking place in the Korean language, and the role of christianity in the modernization of Korea. Concern about religion shows most often in his translations of Korean writers. He translated a poem entitled 'Heaven' by the sixteenth-century scholar Song Ikp'il, boldly rendering the Chinese word for 'heaven' as 'God', and producing what might well be a christian text. He found also a letter written by Hong Yangho in the eighteenth century to the Chinese scholar Chi Yün in which Hong expressed his intellectual objections to what he had heard about christianity as it was being preached in Peking. The same letter shows that Hong knew of the muslim eunuch of the Ming court, Cheng Ho, who led several maritime expeditions across the Indian Ocean at the beginning of the fifteenth century, reaching Aden and Mogadishu, but not, as Hong Yangho imagined, the countries of Europe. Gale was also interested in contemporary Korean criticism of christianity, and at the end of 1918 gave a full account of some newspaper articles on the subject by Yi Kwangsu.

In lighter vein he contributed such pieces as this ode to tobacco by the seventeenth-century scholar Chang Yu. The style is reminiscent of those arch belles-lettres in the Canadian newspapers of Gale's youth.

> Thou loose-filled flower with oily seed
> And leaf that turns a brownish tan,
> Thou wert not born of Chinese breed
> But camest to us from east Japan.
> Across the sea in savage ships
> Thou mad'st thy way by lifted sail,
> O master of the heart and lips,
> Thou wonder weed, thou fairy tale!
>
> (*Kyegok chip* xxx 27)

There were also typical Korean yarns and anecdotes, sometimes didactic, sometimes good for little more than a chuckle, and often losing much when taken out of their original Chinese, like the following story from the fifteenth-century commonplace book of Sŏng Hyŏn:

There was in the days of Koryŏ an official named Yongdae, who dearly loved a practical joke. It seems a snake appeared on the shore of a dragon pool near his place, when the priests of the temple, thinking it a young dragon, caught it, kept it in a cage and fed it. Yongdae, hearing of this, had his naked body painted over carefully with scales in all the colours of the dragon. In this guise he came and called at the temple, saying, 'Have no fear, I pray your reverences. I am the dragon spirit from the pool. I have learned that you have kindly taken in hand my unworthy posterity to teach and bring up, and so I have come to express my thanks. On such and such a day I shall call again specially to see the teacher'. He said this and disappeared.

On the appointed day the priests, all dressed in their best, assembled to await him. He came, and calling for the teacher, took him on his back and straightway made off towards the pool. When he reached the edge he said, ' Now let go. Be careful not to hold on to me, but just shut your eyes and we shall be in the dragon palace in a moment.' The priest shut his eyes and released his hold. At once Yongdae swung round and flung him into the water with all his might, and then made off. The priest, almost drowned, floundered out at last, his clothes in a dreadful state and his body full of aches and pains. He made his way back to the temple and went to bed.

On the following morning Yongdae called again, but this time in ordinary guise, and asked, ' Are you ill? What's the matter?' The priest replied, 'The old dragon of the pool, knave that he is, has lost all his senses. He lied to me and got me into this plight.' (TDYS I 81)

It was now thirty years since Gale had arrived in Korea, and his reminiscences were part of what he had to offer, usually tinged with regret at the passing of so much that he had enjoyed:

When the writer came to this country, the first thing that completely bowled him over, speaking metaphorically, was the manner of dress. Men walked the streets in long tinted robes made of the finest silk, with a girdle across the chest of blue or green or scarlet. Nebuchadnezzar himself was surely never so adorned. The wide sleeves hung down on each side, deeper and more capacious than Aunt Miranda's pocket. Sometimes this robe was divided at the back, sometimes at the sides; sometimes it was a complete roundabout, or *turumagi*. On the gentleman's head was a headband, tied after long practice, tight enough to squeeze tears from the eyes. Above the band was a little cap, beautifully woven of horsehair. Above this sat the gauze hat, a cage for the topknot that you dimly glimpsed through the meshes. Over his eyes was a huge pair of spectacles, much like those Americans affect today, though more stunning in appearance. Back of his ears were gold buttons or jade; under his chin a lovely string of amber beads; in his right hand a waving fan; on his feet the daintiest pair of shoes mortal ever wore, wedded to a pair of socks white as Malachi's fuller never dreamed, the only really beautiful footgear in all the world. As he walked along with measured tread, the lengthy robe adding inches to his height, he was indeed one of the most startling surprises that the eye of the west ever rested upon.

From the time of the *Korea Magazine* articles onwards, Gale's written English style deteriorated noticeably. Harriet had helped him. Her own style was sweetly heavy, but her sentences were better shaped than his. He now lacked the assistance she had given him, and he lacked critics. He had only one more book published outside Korea, *The Cloud Dream of the Nine*, and that had been written before the *Korea Magazine* began. *Korean Folk Tales* was the best written of his books. After that he was at his best when writing most drily, as in his papers for the Royal Asiatic Society. Whenever he was passionately involved in his subject he became careless, till at the end of his life some of his essays seem like unconscious parodies of his own mannerisms.

The Cloud Dream of the Nine was a translation of *Kuun-mong*, the best of old Korean novels, written by Kim Manjung in 1687. Kim Tohŭi drew Gale's attention to it. Korean scholars differ as to whether the Chinese or the Korean text was the original. However, there are so many Korean versions, all of them faulty, that the best opinion now holds the Chinese text as the original. Gale did not say what text he had used, and it was for long assumed that he translated the only known Chinese version, a text printed in 1803; but since his translation contains matter not in that text, it was concluded that he must also have referred to a Korean version. This conclusion lent some colour to the theory that the novel was first written in Korean, and gave Gale's work a special place in the esteem of Korean scholars. Among his papers in Montreal, however, I found a note saying that he had worked from a Chinese text and had never seen a Korean version. He must have used a text unknown to Korean literary historians. Among my own books is a battered single volume from a two-volume Chinese edition of *Kuun-mong* which I found in an antique shop at Chŏnju in November 1970. It was printed at Naju in 1725, and contains the matter translated by Gale but missing from the 1803 text. Professor Chŏng Kyubok, an expert on *Kuun-mong* texts, obtained a similar volume in 1970 at Taegu, but, like mine, it was the second volume. If the first volume can be found, it will doubtless prove that this Naju edition is not only the text used by Gale, but the oldest printed version of the novel.

The Cloud Dream of the Nine was to have been published by The Open Court, of Chicago, but the world war intervened, and Dr Paul Carus, The Open Court editor, died—of a broken heart, if Gale is to be believed—so *The Cloud Dream* remained in typescript. In March 1919 Mrs Elspeth K. Robertson Scott, a resident in Japan, visited Korea for a holiday with her sister, Elizabeth Keith. Miss Keith's watercolours and etchings became well known, and Mrs Scott wrote the text for a collection of them published a quarter of a century later under the title *Old Korea* (London 1946). Much of the information in the book was obtained from Dr Gale, and she describes how she made his acquaintance while she was in Korea. Gale showed her the *Cloud Dream* typescript, which she took to the London publisher Daniel O'Connor. O'Connor published the book in 1922, with a rather silly introduction by Mrs Scott. Very shortly afterwards O'Connor went bankrupt, and the remaining unbound sheets of the book were acquired by the Christian Literature Society of Korea. The last copies were sold by Mr Yi Kyŏmno at his well-known bookshop, T'ongmun-gwan, in Seoul after the Korean War. (T'ongmun-gwan had previously been Paek Tuyong's famous Hannam Sŏrim, where Gale was a regular customer.)

The story is set in T'ang China, though the author was a seventeenth-century Korean. It tells of a young buddhist monk who sins against his vows and is condemned to transmigrate into the person of a poor country boy who eventually becomes the greatest soldier and statesman in the empire, marrying two princesses and six other women as wives and concubines. This paragon of confucian virtues lives to a ripe old age, when he is taken up in a cloud, only to discover that he is once again a young buddhist monk in his cell. The dream pattern for a novel was a commonplace; the best-known example is the Chinese *Hung lou meng*, 'The Dream of the Red Chamber'.

The real theme of the book is the tension between buddhism and confucianism in Korean thought, but the psychological interest centres in the female characters. All Gale's chief concerns are represented: religion, the mystic and occult, women and poetry. Opinions today are divided on the quality of the translation: the ornate diction is a faithful reflection of the original idiom, written just before his style began to lose its discipline. If one takes into consideration the inadequacies of the dictionaries available to Gale and the fact that in his day there were no annotated editions of Korean texts, it is remarkable that there are so few mistakes in the translation. For a third of a century it was the most significant work of Korean literature available to the English-speaking world.

Gale's marriage to Ada gave him a firm emotional base, but at the time of the first world war, trials and sorrows began to press upon him from outside. Not only was he constantly worried about money: his relations with other missionaries grew strained. Charles Allen Clark was increasingly critical of his activities and attitudes. After the June presbytery meeting of 1917 Gale recorded that Clark had offered a long prayer, and about this time Clark circulated a letter to all presbyterian missionaries complaining that Gale spent too much time on literary pursuits and neglected attendance at presbytery and other meetings. Clark was an uncompromising conservative with deep doubts about Gale's view of missionary life. The last jealousy between Gale and the Underwoods must have evaporated by 1918, when on Easter Sunday Gale baptized H.G. Underwood's first grandson, Horace. In the early part of the war period, however, there was a serious estrangement from his old friend Moffett. Moffett was the pioneer of the northern mission, than whom no single other missionary had a greater personal influence in moulding the Korean presbyterian church, and Gale had made him hero of *The Vanguard;* Gale owed his ordination to Moffett, and they expected to remain lifelong friends; but Gale's thinking had been moving away from Moffett's. Gale was less concerned about dogmatic theology, Moffett was deliberately unchanging in his views and policies. Dissension arose over the P'yŏngyang seminary. In May 1916 Gale sent a letter proposing his resignation from that institution. He disapproved of its methods, thought its standards too low, its teaching bad, its materials outdated, its student enrolment too numerous. He thought he discerned another way forward for Korean education, and he was possibly right. The issue between him and Moffett eventually expanded into complex alignments of theological liberals and conservatives; but that was after Gale's day, and Gale would have been shocked to think that he had in any way promoted the theological liberalism of the next generation. Both men were sincere, and both were deeply hurt. When Moffett wrote an eirenic letter in July 1917, Gale was relieved. He wept, and responded wholeheartedly to Moffett's advance.

It was well that he had this comfort in July, because at the beginning of August, when the family was staying with Father Drake at the anglican mission house in Chemulp'o, the baby Vivian went down with fever and acute diarrhoea. Four days later, on 7 August, he died, not quite fourteen months old. His father was heartbroken, and for months filled his prayer-diary with mourning for his 'angel laddie'. He even wrote the baby's biography. The funeral was at Yanghwajin on the 11th. There had been a long drought, and on the day of burial the rains came at last. Because they were so late that year Gale's trip to the Diamond

Mountains planned for mid-September had to be postponed for a few days.

In early years after moving from Wŏnsan to Seoul the Gales spent the hot summer weather at the temple of Tosŏn-sa, near the fortress of Pukhan, in the mountains north of Seoul. They continued to do so throughout Gale's missionary career, but in later years they occasionally took the children to the beach at Myŏngsa-simni near Wŏnsan, which was a regular summer resort for missionaries. There was a fine sandy beach near pinewoods on the Kalma peninsula. The name means 'ten leagues of shining sand' and is a poetic cliché for the east coast scenery, usually linked with the crimson sea-rose, the *rugosa* that grows wild there.

In the course of the trip to the Diamond Mountains from 21 September to 22 October 1917, Gale visited old haunts in the Wŏnsan area. (During the same year he also went back to Sorae, where another missionary vacation colony had been established.) The Diamond Mountains are renowned for the most beautiful scenery in Korea, rich in literary associations. Gale prefixed the diary of his trip with quotations from the diaries of Korean travellers, including these sentences from the fourteenth-century writer Kwŏn Kŭn: 'When I was young I learned how everybody wished to see the Diamond Mountains, and I sighed over my own failure to visit them. I heard too that many people hang pictures of them in their rooms and bow before them. Such is the burning desire that would peer into these mystic glades.' (*Yangch'on chip* XVII 9). Gale was accompanied by Yi Ch'angjik, Ada and six-year-old George. They went by rail on the Wŏnsan line to P'yŏngyang, then by pony through Hwach'ŏn to the mountains. It was autumn, when the reddening maple leaves gave the Diamond Mountains their greatest beauty. George was carried up and down the slopes in a jiggy, and delighted the nuns in the temples with his Korean speech. At the little temple of Changgyŏng-am they met an old nun of eighty-four named Myodŏkhaeng, 'mystic virtue', who spoke with a Hwanghae accent and was much taken with the little boy. Yi recognised her as the widow No whose only son, Ch'ilsŏng, 'seven stars', had been his childhood playmate. Yi's milk name too had been Ch'ilsŏng; his friend had died at the age of twelve, and soon afterwards the widow had disappeared. Yi told her who he was and there was a moving scene as she called him by his childhood name again. She put her amber rosary round George's neck and promised to meet him in paradise. Yi wrote a poem for her and pasted it up on the wall of her cell. The journal of the whole trip was published five years later by the Royal Asiatic Society, and still makes delightful reading; but it is wrong to say, as some Koreans have said, that Gale was a pioneer traveller in the Diamond Mountains. By 1917 he could record a postcard and souvenir stall for tourists by the Diamond Gate, and many foreigners had visited the area before that date.

Gale's increasing respect for buddhism led him to give more comfort than he knew to his old friend MacGillivray, who was now working with the Christian Literature Society in Shanghai, where a co-worker, the great English baptist Timothy Richard, had published in 1910 a book called *The New Testament of Higher Buddhism* that made a positive approach to buddhist thought. Two years later the aged bishop Moule had seen the book and written a scathing attack on

it. The ensuing rumpus might have caused an irreparable rift between MacGillivray and Richard, but in 1913 Gale wrote a letter giving a favourable opinion
of the book which helped to mould MacGillivray's thinking and to smooth over
the problems in Shanghai. Gale became more and more appreciative of the good
things in buddhism from this time onwards. In November 1915 he completed
an English translation of *P'alsang-nok,* a popular Korean life of Gautama
Buddha, but this was never printed.

Another trip was the guided one-day visit to Kaesŏng which Gale led in
June 1918 and soon afterwards briefly described in the *Korea Magazine*. Kaesŏng
was the capital of the Koryŏ dynasty from the tenth to the fourteenth century.
Gale had seen its sights first in 1891, on the way to Manchuria, and it was perhaps
on that journey that he visited the tomb of Wang Kŏn, the founder of Koryŏ:

> I found a little colony of latter-day Wangs nestled about its feet.
> One pretty lad with newly-fashioned topknot stood by the side of the
> way to watch. I asked him his name and he smiled and said, 'Wang.'
> The thirteenth generation removed, and yet as comely as a piece of
> *Koraiyaki* (Koryŏ celadon). I would have liked to have carried him
> home, preserved him, and kept him as a memento of the kingdom of
> the Wangs.

During the war years Gale suffered greatly from dryness of soul. He derived
much comfort from Bishop Trollope's friendship: Trollope's anglo-catholic
theology was so entirely different from any presbyterian style of thinking that
they were forced to meet on the basis of their common christianity, unhindered
by the differences that divided the American missionaries. They also had in common their loyalty to Britain and their interest in Korean literature. George
was a joy, and also an anxiety, because Gale shared the worry every Korean
feels as to how his son will turn out. He prayed earnestly that George should be
spared what he regarded as his own shortcomings, especially pusillanimity.

When on 4 August 1918 Ada gave birth to a daughter, Ada Alexandra,—
named after her mother and her great-uncle, the much-revered Alexander—he
felt that God was making up for the loss of Vivian. He doted on little Alex, and
she lighted the rest of his days. His Korean assistants pleased him by proposing
a Sino-Korean version of her name, transliterating Alexandra as Allaksŏn,
'peaceful happy fairy', which summed up what Gale wanted in a daughter. He
was not disappointed, but as a baby she was often ill, and he suffered agonies
of anxiety. Each time she recovered she gave him greater joy. A Chinese amah,
Ah Ming, was provided for her.

We have forgotten the exciting novelties of those days. At midsummer
1913 Gale wrote in his prayer-diary: 'I am to go for a motor-ride, I am told.
Go with us, dear Saviour, and make the ride one for thy praise and glory.' On
the other hand there was world-weariness. Gale in his forties felt the loss of
spirits common in his sex at that age. He worried about the prudence of Pastor
Kil Sŏnju's activities in the independence movement, and agonized for Yun
Ch'iho when he was imprisoned by the Japanese in 1914. Money was always a

worry. Behind all loomed the shadows of the Great War. Gale prayed for 'poor blinded Israel', and then for 'poor Belgium'. It was Belgium that caught the sympathy of the Seoul foreign community: there were rose teas at the Belgian Consulate, and benefit performances for the sake of Belgium, including a performance of *Ch'unhyang* at the Chosen Hotel. When the war ended there was a victory parade in Seoul with a procession of decorated motor-cars, and naturally Dr Gale was one of the orators of the occasion. The war, however, was a background to life rather than an immediate disruption. The biggest effect it had on Gale was to prevent him from making a visit he had planned to his stepdaughter in Shanghai in 1914, and from taking the furlough that he was granted for 1915.

The translation of the bible into Korean was completed in the month of Gale's second marriage. It was published in 1911, but its deficiencies were recognized immediately. Gale was one of the committee of fifteen appointed in 1912 for the revision of the Old Testament. Not all the other members had his feeling for Korean style. He relied increasingly on the opinion of Yi Wŏnmo, who was appointed in 1917 as one of the committee's four Korean members; but again and again the pleas these two made for smooth Korean diction were voted down by other members of the committee who favoured literal adherence to the grammatical structure, sometimes of the original tongues, but all too often of the English Authorized Version. Gale became the principal drafter of the revision, and in 1916 chairman of the revision committee, a post he held till he resigned from the committee in 1923.

He continued his work for the Christian Literature Society, reading tracts for them to publish, and also writing and translating. In 1911 he produced a curious mnemonic life of Christ in verse called *Yesu haengjŏk kinyŏm-si.* For several years he and Underwood collaborated in translating the Scofield Bible. The project suggested itself to both men independently before they decided to work together. Underwood was still working on it shortly before he died in America in October 1916, and the minutes of the presbyterian mission annual meeting in 1917 say that the New Testament part was in the press. There is no other trace of this project. Apparently the book was never published, but that it should have been undertaken is significant. Cyrus Ingerson Scofield (1843–1921) was a confederate soldier who became a lawyer and politician before he was converted at the age of 36, and three years afterwards, without formal theological training, became a congregational minister at Dallas, Texas. He later attached himself to the Southern Presbyterian church. His *Reference Bible,* which consists of the Authorized Version interlaced with his notes and explanations, gained the approval of the Moody Institute of Chicago and has been an important text in popular American protestant theology. It is characterized by an eclectic literalism in hermeneutics that results in three distinct but interrelated doctrines: dispensationalism (an arbitrary division of history into seven periods, each with its own mode of redemption); a form of chiliasm known as premillenarianism, teaching that the second coming of Christ will be followed by his reign on earth for a thousand years; and an ecclesiology denying that the Church is the new Israel. The eschatological concern that underlies this system is derived from the widespread interest in prophecy that produced such nineteenth-century movements as Mormonism, Adventism, Anglo-Israelism, the Russellites (or Jehovah's Witnesses), the Irvingites and the Plymouth brethren. The chief moulder of Plymouth brethren doctrines was John Nelson Darby (1800–1882), another lawyer turned freelance theologian, who was the paramount influence in the formation of Scofield's teachings.

Premillenarianism was the crux of the matter for the missionaries in Korea. It entered the Northern presbyterian mission in the eighteen-nineties. Mrs Swallen, a keen adherent of the doctrine, wrote in 1894 that the whole mission was premillenarian. Gale contributed to the spread of the idea when he translated Blackstone's *Jesus is Coming* in 1913, because that book, widely disseminated by the Moody Bible Institute, was important in promoting Darby's doctrine. Gale's *Bible Magazine* also contained articles on the Second Advent. The translation of Scofield's bible fits naturally into this picture. Possibly it was never published because it ran into trouble with the Japanese censors, who were always quick to resent any doctrine of universal rule that might jeopardize the reputation of the Japanese emperor; but if that were so, one would expect the story to be current among the tales of Japanese persecution. Scofieldism is not apparent in the Korean churches today, but it was important in the growth of Gale's own theological attitudes. Like Scofield and Darby, he was an untrained theologian; unlike them, he was not attracted by legalism. His approach to the subject was spiritual rather than intellectual: the part of him that was fascinated by the occult was drawn to eschatological speculation, and in later years was to find expression in Anglo-Israelism. Perhaps neither Gale nor Underwood realized what theological dynamite they were handling. Scofield's book had solid virtues which would appeal to them, and it was certainly convenient to have notes so close to the scripture text.

Gale worked on other helps to scripture study. He edited Korean Sunday-school lessons for several years. He was spending even more time on newspaper work. For the better part of twenty years he was one of the leading figures in Korean christian journalism. In December 1915 the chief Korean church paper again became a joint methodist and presbyterian organ, with the name *The Christian Messenger (Kidok sinbo)*. Gale was associate editor, or foreign editor, till he left for furlough in 1919. From February 1918 till his furlough, and again for several years later on, he also edited a Korean-language bi-monthly, *The Bible Magazine (Sŏnggyŏng chapchi)*, for preachers and other church workers, published by the Christian Literature Society. Its contents were mainly translations from the Chinese *Sheng-ching-pao*, edited in Shanghai by R. A. Jaffray, another Toronto man, and son of an editor of the *Globe*.

He maintained his interest in education. In 1912 an interdenominational Union Bible Institute for the training of unordained church workers was founded in Seoul, and in 1913 its name was changed to the Pierson Memorial Bible Institute. Arthur Tappan Pierson had been a great American presbyterian promoter of missions, for twenty years editor of the famous *Missionary Review of the World*. In 1910, when he was seventy-three, he visited Korea. A year later he died, and his family gave money for land and new buildings near the Great

West Gate, next to the Russian Orthodox Church. When the new school was opened on 20 May 1917, Gale was the administrator. From 1914 to 1919 he was the presbyterian delegate and teacher to the school, which was a joint methodist and presbyterian institution. He still spent a month and a half every spring in P'yŏngyang, teaching part of each day in the seminary and giving the other half to bible translation.

In 1911 he changed his listing from the New Albany presbytery to the presbytery of Washington DC, where he was the recognized missionary of the Sunday schools. He continued as pastor of the Yŏnmot-kol church, where the average Sunday congregations rose to 700 or 800, and there was a strong emphasis on Sunday school work. By 1918 his staff consisted of a co-pastor, Yi Myŏnghak, two helpers and three bible women. This team administered the largest protestant congregation in Seoul, and was also responsible for evangelistic work in the villages between the East Gate and the Han River. The Yŏnmot-kol congregation planned a surprise celebration in honour of the twenty-fifth anniversary of Gale's arrival in the country. The date was not quite right, but they decorated the church, and he was showered with prescnts and overwhelmed with congratulatory addresses.

He had intensified his studies of Korean literature and history, and now employed three Korean literary secretaries full time. He rose at five-thirty, and every morning spent the hours from six to eight in reading old books with these assistants. He was an object of reverence in the Seoul foreign community, famed for his brilliance, his urbanity and his knowledge of things Korean. He was frequently called on to deliver addresses before officials, and to help in drafting important Korean letters. His Korean speech is said to have been accurate and elegant, but slightly hesitant. Korean groups asked him to address them on Korean literary and historical subjects, and for some years he was overseer of his mission's language training programme.

To the surprise of almost everybody except the Korean organizers, popular demonstrations for Korean independence broke out in Seoul on 1 March 1919 and rapidly spread throughout the country. Japan's increasingly oppressive rule had at last provoked the Koreans, whom Gale had correctly described as dormant in his newspaper articles fifteen years earlier. Inspired by President Wilson's Peace Points, and agitated by the death of the retired King Kojong on 21 January 1919, the people organized non-violent demonstrations. A provisional government in exile was formed in Shanghai. The Japanese reacted with brutality, and quickly stamped out the movement within the peninsula, but they could not quell the new spirit. Ch'angjik's second daughter, Yi Hyegyŏng, was now a teacher at Chŏngsin School; she became vice-chairman of the Korean Women's Patriotic Society *(*Taehan Min'guk Aeguk Puin-hoe*),* which was founded in October 1919. As a result of this she was imprisoned with hard labour at Taegu for three years. One of her sisters also had to flee the country, and a brother died as a result of tortures inflicted on him in prison.

Gale reacted to these events by persuading Bishop Trollope to take a letter describing them to Lord Bryce in London. He had met Bryce in Seoul when Bryce visited Korea in 1916 on his way back to England after being British ambassador to the United States. The reply was sent to Gale by the bishop's hand, because they distrusted the security of the mails, even of diplomatic bags. Bryce noted that the United Kingdom, with its own problems in Ireland and elsewhere, was in no position to rebuke Japan for her conduct regarding Korea. He recommended fostering the Korean national spirit through education and literature, and using passive resistance. It was the sort of advice that appealed to Gale, because it coincided with his own ideas. Meanwhile he prayed:

> God, grant that this people may win out in their struggle for liberty. Thou seest the hard Hun rule of the Japanese, thou knowest how unjust it is, how false, how selfish, how unsympathetic. Hear the prayers that ascend from the torture-house of the prison. Hear all the prayers from the faithful wives and mothers who wait in deserted houses. Right is right, as God is God, and thou wilt see right through to the end. God bless Korea in these days of trial, and bring Japan to a place of true repentance and faith.

His friend Kil Sŏnju, who had baptized George, was one of the leaders of the demonstrations, on whom the wrath of the Japanese fell.

Gale's furlough had already been deferred twice, but on 26 May 1919 he left Seoul for his third full furlough in thirty years. It was less than a year since the armistice at the end of the Great War. Shipping was still not back to normal. After a month of waiting in Japan, the Gale family sailed from Moji on 17 July 1919 in the SS *Sado Maru*. Baby Alex's Chinese amah, Ah Ming, went with them. They sailed by Shanghai and Hong Kong to Singapore, crossed the Indian Ocean to the Suez Canal, narrowly escaped being delayed again by a dock-strike in Marseilles, but arrived eventually at Tilbury. In England they made their base at Grandfather Sale's house in Bournemouth while George was settling at Monkton Combe School, near Bath. Then the rest of them crossed the Atlantic for deputation work in the United States.

They spent the last part of this furlough in Canada. There was a great gathering of the Gale clan at Alma, and they celebrated baby Alex's birthday at Jenny's house in Kitchener. Dr Gale paid his first visit to Toronto in twenty-three years. The newspapers pressed him for his views on Japanese rule in Korea. He spoke of the brutalities of the police and military officials, but said he thought the Japanese elite had ideas diametrically opposed to those of the militarists. He blamed Kojong for his incapacity and for 'his attempts to win the favour of the Russians by allowing them to use the country for military purposes'. This was doubtless diplomatic talk on the part of one who hoped to return to work in Japanese-ruled Korea, but it was the opinion of Kojong sincerely held by the majority of westerners at that time. Gale added that during World War I some Koreans had hoped Germany would win, not so much because Japan was on the side of the Allies, as to put the world in a turmoil so that Koreans 'would have an opportunity to regain their lost independence. The Koreans are now intensely awake to the spread of socialist doctrines, and are waiting to see if Japan develops troubles of her own which might afford opportunity for the Koreans to take action.'

He was speaking with deep concern when he said: 'Whereas the Korean of thirty years ago was a scholar, the young Korean of today is in many respects an ignoramus. He has a smattering of western knowledge, and some little idea of his own tongue; but his knowledge of the ancient literature of his people is practically non-existent. Therein lies a great danger. That literature contains all the idealism of his race.'

Too few missionaries spoke in these terms; the quality of Gale's work during his remaining years as a missionary was inspired by this conviction.

vii Literature for Korea 1920 – 1927

The Japanese thought the whole affair of *Kimi undong,* the Korean independence movement of 1919, had been easily put down, though as a result of it they mitigated some of the harsher aspects of their rule. The demonstrations seemed to have been no more than a flash in the pan, and the provisional government in Shanghai meaningless. It is true that much Korean diplomacy during the next twenty years was ineffective, and that the immediate political effect of the movement was minimal, but 1919 proved to be a crucial year: the important results were spiritual. The Koreans were drawn together as they had never been before, and now that China's cultural domination had collapsed, one immediate effect of the 1919 movement was the blossoming of Korean culture. Modern literature is usually dated from the first western-influenced writing, published about 1906; but the proliferation of Korean writing did not happen till the twenties. By that time modern ideas were beginning to percolate beyond the small number of people educated in the early mission schools. Ironically, the Japanese themselves provided much of the education which reinvigorated Korea's national selfconsciousness. The famous literary magazines of the twenties, heavily indebted though they were to Japanese and European models, began to lay the foundation of what we now recognize as modern Korean culture.

The christian churches felt the effect of this new wave. They had traditionally emphasized the use of the Korean alphabet and pure Korean, as opposed to heavily sinicized, language. Their purpose had been single-mindedly evangelistic, but one of their effects had been to stimulate the development of the national culture. Christian churches, as well as buddhist and other religious groups, had played an important role in the 1919 movement. In the aftermath they were handicapped by their own success. The pace of christian growth slowed down; the fierce fervour of the politically uncertain years before the Japanese annexation of 1910 had cooled; the simple evangelical teaching of the first christian generations no longer satisfied the minds of young Koreans trained in Japanese and missionary schools. The problems of the Korean churches today are partly derived from the fact that many missionaries and Korean church leaders were tardy in recognizing this change of temper.

Gale was one of the few who recognized the emergence of the new mental climate. After his return from furlough on 11 October 1920 he published few christian books—a translation of H. E. Fosdick's *Manhood of the Master* in 1921, *Old Testament Types* and *The Gospel as Sung* in 1923, and a translation of Thomas a Kempis's *Imitatio Christi* in 1925 are all he did; he planned a life of Dwight L. Moody, partly done in 1924 but never finished. He spent most of his energies in translating non-religious books for the newly-enthusiastic reading public of young people. In 1924 and 1925 he published translations of *The Swiss Family Robinson*, Bruce's *Polar Exploration, Little Lord Fauntleroy, Robinson Crusoe,* Walter Scott's *Talisman, A Book of Strange Stories* (containing Washington Irving's 'Rip Van Winkle', Walter Scott's 'Tapestried Chamber' and stories from *The Century Magazine, Blackwood's Magazine* and *Chambers' Journal*), and a Korean and English translation of a confucian classic, the Great Learning. Charlotte Yonge's *Book of Golden Deeds in all Times and all Lands* was finished in 1924, but there is no evidence that it was ever published. This list of titles now looks dated, and was paternalistic at the time the books were produced, but it was meant for young people. The adventure tales were intended to hold interest, and all the books, even *Little Lord Fauntleroy,* whose very title raises smiles, were calculated to encourage sound morals and give a healthy introduction to western thought.

Recognizing the new literary climate of the twenties did not save Gale from the pains that changes in Korean culture were bound to bring him. *The Gospel as Sung* was a re-telling of the gospel story in rhythmic Korean phrases suitable for chanting in traditional story-telling style such as he had used with success in Wŏnsan thirty years before, 'an attempt to do something in Korean such as old Cædmon's poems did in English'. But by 1923 this style was already obsolete and a year later he publicly admitted that the book was published long after it would have been of any use.

Gale disliked the adoption by Koreans of the Sino-Japanese adjectival suffixes -*chŏk* and -*sang*. He wrote slightingly of modern books which used the newly-coined verb-ending -*yŏtta* and the fashionable vocabulary of students, whose 'principal stock-in-trade' was *insaeng, saenghwal, hŭimang,* and *hwalbal* —neologisms for humanity, life, hope and vitality. He did not acknowledge the epoch-making influence of the magazine *Ch'angjo* ('Creation') started by Korean students in Tokyo in February 1919. The newly-coined sentence-endings were created by this group: today they are standard Korean usage, and it is difficult to judge whether Gale was fighting the tide or whether he was essentially right. Many Koreans would like to purify the language of foreign vocabulary, though nobody now speaks of reviving the old literary grammar which Gale loved. In 1923 he wrote to the literary committee of the Christian Literature Society:

> The Korean language is fighting for its life as an intelligible medium of expression—can it survive against Japanese influence, western civilization, loss of classic Korean, introduction of illiterate writers? The worst enemy is the foreign missionary, putting out unidiomatic, ungrammatical, childish books. The bible is most defective, hymns are a literary disgrace, our books bad, Sunday-school lessons ditto.

He thought the Christian Literature Society should stand for good Korean. He opposed the introduction of western punctuation marks in Korean (in this he was misguided, though his principle is understandable), and he gave a rule for translation: 'Unless the translator can read through the paragraph in English and get it in mind so that he can close the book and reproduce it in Korean, he is not fit for his job.'

It may well have appeared to some that Dr Gale now typified a passing generation. His political views were conservative. Although he had come from stock politically liberal in the British tradition, he was a cavalier rather than a roundhead. He detested Bertrand Russell, the Huxleys and Ramsay Macdonald, whose stars were in the ascendant in England. He took the opposite stand to Bishop Trollope, who had worked as a priest in the London slums and held socialist views. Young Koreans were beginning to flirt with socialism, to Gale's distress. His affection for the older forms of the Korean language was consistent with this kind of conservatism. In 1923 he expressed his pessimistic view of Korean culture by printing two translations side by side. The first was from his old favourite, Yi Kyubo:

A Great Thunderstorm in November
The season's opening moon,
When winter airs break forth from out the deep!
The master of the thunder strikes his drum,
The splitting heavens rip wide from pole to pole;
Like glittering snakes of gold across the sky
Go thunderbolts, till all the frightened hairs
On every head stand up; the spouts of rain
From off the silver eaves shoot waterfalls,
And hail like eggstones falls with deadly aim.
The wind rips out by quivering root the trees
That guard the court; the whole house shakes its wings
As though to fly away. I was asleep
When this befell, the third watch of the night;
Wakened from dreams with all my wits at sea,
I could not rest, but tossed me to and fro.
At last I knelt and joined my hands in prayer:
'We are accustomed to thy might and power,
In spring the thunder, and in autumn frost,
But such a sight, with nature off its track
Makes mortals tremble, cold fear palpitate.
Our king's desire is how to govern well;
Why is it God should thunder thus, beats me.
In ancient days the tiger king of Chou,
And T'ang of Yin so acted that they changed
The threatening hand of heaven to one of blessing.
My humble prayer would have our gracious king
Bend earnest thought to make this stroke of thine

Turn out a blessing, and not grinding death,
But just a tickling on the skin
That leaves one feeling better.'
(TYSC XII 1)

With this Gale contrasted a poem published in 1921 by the 24-year-old O Sangsun in the second issue of the literary magazine *P'yehŏ* (Ruins).

Creation
Cackle! Cackle!
Does the sound mean pain?
Cackle! Cackle!
Or does it mean joy?
Cackle! Cackle!
My hand into the nest I reach,
I find an egg new-laid;
I take it out and go away.
There is life in the egg.
I think of its affinity with this life of mine.
I look and meditate upon its depth;
I stand like a road-post by the way.
The hen flies up on the roof.
With anxious look she gives a sideways glance at me—
Mother of the egg — creator.
She treats me with contempt, the young philosopher, me!
Cackle! Cackle!

'These two quotations will illustrate how far the centuries have pulled apart,'
wrote Gale.

P'yehŏ was started in 1920 by a group of young Koreans inspired by a
quotation from Friedrich von Schiller:

Das Alte stürzt, es ändert sich die Zeit,
Und neues Leben blüht aus den Ruinen.
(The old decays, the times are changing,
And new life blossoms from the ruins.)

The lines come from *William Tell,* Act IV, Scene 2, and are part of a speech
by the dying nobleman Werner von Attinghausen, who sides with the people for
liberation from the Austrian yoke, and appeals for unity among the Swiss people.
The implications of the quotation were both literary and political, because
independence from the Japanese was the burning desire of young Koreans in
1920. They felt the urgency of the changing times and looked for new life from
the ruins of their national culture. Their manifesto was irreproachably healthy-
minded, but by choosing 'Ruins' rather than 'New Life' for the title of their
journal they gave too much away. Orientals have always found romanticism the

most attractive element in western literature, and this group responded to romantic decadence in Europe. The only other western missionary who paid serious attention to Korean ephemera was W. C. Kerr; he and Gale deserve credit for recognizing the importance of the evanescent literary magazines of those years. This is the more remarkable in that Gale did not like them.

His choice of poem in this context was not a good illustration of his point of view. Had he not been distracted by the fact that O Sangsun wrote in Korean whereas Yi Kyubo wrote in Chinese, Gale might have noticed the affinity between the two poets. Yi Kyubo, when not in the exalted mood evoked by a unseasonable thunderstorm, wrote the same sort of self-deprecatory philosophizing verse as O; and though Gale's iambics fail to do justice to Yi Kyubo's Chinese verse, in his contempt for the young man's work he translated it in an unwarrantedly prosy fashion. Indeed it is hard not to suspect him of deliberately reducing its impact, which is felt in a more direct translation:

> 'Kgokgidak! Kgokgidak!'
> Do you complain about the pangs of birth?
> 'Kgokgidak! Kgokgidak!'
> Do you boast of the joy of bearing life?
> 'Kgokgidak! Kgokgidak!'
> I put my hand into
> the straw nest hanging from the roost
> and feel a beautiful warm egg.
> I take it out and hold it in my hand,
> and while I stand thinking about the affinity
> between man's life and the life hidden in the egg,
> staring at it in silence,
> still as a wooden devil-post,
> the mother of the egg, the creator,
> flaps up on the roof
> nervously cocking her head on one side
> to look down at me with a glassy eye,
> as though to mock the young philosopher,
> and cackles: 'Kgokgidak! Kgokgidak!
> Kgokgidak! Kgokgidak!'

There is much more of the old tradition in this than Gale allowed, as there is usually a much larger influence from the native tradition in modern Korean writing than western critics, quick to catch echoes of western influence, and distracted by accidents of diction, usually recognise. If Gale could have known O Sangsun in his later years when, still a bachelor, he was a tramp of the Seoul tearooms, eternally chain-smoking and talking of Nirvana, the Victorian Canadian would have felt justified in his pessimism. O's pen-name was Kongch'o, meaning 'Transcendental Void', but purposely punning on *kkongch'o,* 'cigarette-ends'. He died in a small room near Chogye-sa, the central buddhist temple, in 1963, and his friends made funeral offerings of packets of cigarettes. Yi

Kyubo also wrote magnificent poems on the Void, which are not spoiled by his dissipations.

Although Gale often said that the Korean alphabet was part of the divine *praeparatio evangelica,* he seems also to have believed that Chinese characters would never lose their pre-eminence in Korea. In 1918 he suggested printing all books in double columns of Chinese and Korean, but thought Koreans might settle down to use a mixture of Chinese and Korean script modelled on Japanese *kanamajiri.* He was wrong in thinking that literary Chinese would survive, right in believing that mixed script would become the norm—at least for the next half-century. Despite his lack of sympathy for contemporary fashions of script and style, however, young people responded to his efforts, and he was fifty years ahead of his time in his principles for the translation of the Korean bible.

He stayed on the Bible Society's revision committee as chairman till 1923, but grew increasingly dissatisfied with the processes that were used. His draft was criticized by missionary members of the general advisory committee of the Korean bible agency who had thought his translation, though approved by the revision committee, not literal enough. He said: 'My greatest ambition is to have the Book speak the thought, no more and no less, but to speak it in sweet easy-flowing Korean.' There was so much dissension that in September 1921 thirty-two pages of Genesis were printed in mixed script and circulated to all missionaries, who were asked to comment. A majority thought Gale had sacrificed meaning to style, because he had not kept closely to the English sentence structure. Some admitted that he had produced a smooth Korean version, but complained that he had 'shortened the original'. One crucial point was Gale's refusal to repeat nouns which Korean syntax did not require to be repeated, though the Hebrew did. This applied especially to some twenty omissions of the word for the godhead in the opening chapters of Genesis. One missionary asserted that Gale was leaving God out of the bible. Criticism was so strong that the London authorities of the British and Foreign Bible Society felt bound to apply their rule which said, 'Every version shall be as literal as the idiom of the language will permit.' Gale resigned from the revision board in March 1922, but was persuaded to return. The board was enlarged in the hope of effecting a compromise, but Gale was not disposed to let it tamper with his work. He considered most of the members inexperienced, and summed up his feelings as being much the same as Dr Avison's might be if his decisions in running Severance Hospital were submitted to the general public for final approval. In February 1923 an entirely new board was appointed to work on a final version, and Gale's work was to be printed tentatively. In March 1924 he was made an honorary member of the board. He understood that his draft, having been rejected by the Bible Society, was now his own, and he began making arrangements for its private publication. There was a new storm of protest, especially from some Southern Presbyterian missionaries, who did not want the work published under any circumstances, and claimed that though Gale had done it, the copyright belonged to the Bible Society.

For a time Gale despaired, believing that all his labour would be wasted, but the 'Gale Bible' was published on the last day of 1925. The event marked the end of four years of great unhappiness, and Gale was delighted to receive the first copy just inside the fourth centenary year of Tyndale's Bible. Yi Wŏnmo had been his chief assistant in preparing the text, but Yi Ch'angjik and Yi Kyosŭng, the other two members of his regular team, had also helped. He paid Yi Kyosŭng thirty yen a month, and tried to augment the sixty yen that Ch'angjik received from the Christian Literature Society. Yi Wŏnmo was paid ninety yen.

A curious feature of the bible was the indication on the contents page of the length of time required for reading each book of the bible, ranging from three minutes each for the second and third Epistles of St John to four hours forty minutes for the Psalms. This was intended to 'encourage the right use of spare time'. The text was printed in mixed Chinese and Korean script, that is, with the words of Chinese derivation printed in Chinese character, according to the usual style for secular books at that time. The Bible Society, aiming at wide readership, generally used the Korean alphabet alone, but Gale was concerned about educated readers. It pleased him, too, to think that the epigraphs to each testament (Psalm cxix 18 and 130) had been Ada's suggestion. The publisher was Kidok-kyo Ch'angmun-sa of Seoul, an enterprise of his old friend, Baron Yun Ch'iho, who is important enough to justify a digression about him.

Yun Ch'iho was born of a powerful clan in 1865. In 1883 when the first US Minister to Korea passed through Tokyo on his way to Seoul, he met Yun, who was studying in Japan. Yun accompanied him to Seoul as interpreter. In 1885 Yun's father was disgraced and the young man went to Shanghai, where he attended the Anglo-Chinese College and was baptized in 1887. He went on to study at methodist colleges in the USA till 1893, when he returned to China. After the Sino-Japanese War of 1895, he returned to Korea and joined the cabinet. Later he was a member of the Independence Club and edited its newspaper, the *Tongnip sinmun,* becoming a leader in the struggle for constitutional government. He was Korean delegate to various international christian conferences, and in 1906 founded the Anglo-Korean School at Kaesŏng. He has already been mentioned as one of the founders of the Seoul YMCA. In 1908 he was principal of the patriot An Ch'angho's Taesŏng School—where Gale gave Wednesday afternoon bible lectures. At first he suffered under the Japanese and was imprisoned as one of the 105 men convicted for their alleged involvement in a plan to assassinate Governor-general Terauchi Masatake in 1910. Later the Japanese succeeded in compromising him, and after the liberation of Korea he retired to his home in Kaesŏng, where he died of self-administered poison in 1946. He was one of the outstanding figures of his time. Gale had known him since he was governor at Wŏnsan in 1899, and his generosity made it possible for Gale to publish his Korean bible.

There was a strong feeling in the Korean church that there should be only one translation of the bible in the country. The Bible Society and its committees favoured this feeling, and disliked the idea of a 'rival translation'. Both Gale and the Society had tried to work in harmony, but he felt himself persecuted and many Koreans thought him badly treated. The Bible Society agent described him as 'a very delightful man, provided one could let him have his own way'; but today Gale's critics look more obstinate and less intellectually respectable than he does.

Gale's bible was never fairly judged, though it was compared to the Moffatt bible. He left Korea less than two years after it was published, it was never reprinted, and is now very difficult to obtain. Yet it was what he claimed, a smoothly-reading text, and when the Bible Society's revised translation was finally published in 1937 it bore a greater resemblance to Gale's bible than has ever been admitted. The revisers made such poor progress without Gale that they decided to base their work on his version after all, making only minimal changes. The resultant text was Korea's standard bible until 1967. No other single individual has made a contribution to Korean bible translation comparable to that made by James Gale. He also finished a Korean translation of the Apocrypha. The manuscript was given to the Anglican Church, which was the only group interested in publishing it, but unfortunately never had funds for printing it. The manuscript was lost during the Korean War.

The dictionary needed revision again. Gale completed the manuscript for a third edition, but it was destroyed in the great Yokohama earthquake of 1923. Some of his work-sheets were saved, and in 1924 he published a vocabulary of 3,000 modern words. The publication of the whole dictionary was delayed till 1931, four years after he left Korea. Its preparation was entrusted to Alexander Pieters, a senior presbyterian missionary. The number of entries was increased to 82,000, though the majority of the proper names in the 1911 edition were omitted. The Chinese character section was not re-issued. Gale's dictionary was partly superseded by Yu Hyŏnggi's *New Life Korean-English Dictionary* in 1947, and was out of print after the Second World War, but remained the most authoritative work of its kind until Samuel E. Martin's *New Korean-English Dictionary* appeared from Yale in 1967.

In 1923 the Gale family visited Annie and her husband, who were now stationed in Manchuria, at Changchun. This was the occasion of Dr Gale's last contribution, still under the pen-name Esson Third, to the *North China Daily News*. In it he described how he walked round Peking carrying Kim Ch'angŏp's eighteenth-century diary, which he had translated in the *Korea Magazine*. It was in Changchun that he received the news of the loss of the manuscript and proofs of his dictionary in the Japanese earthquake. He was shattered by the blow. The monsoon rains were at their height and the mud was tiresome. He was further depressed by the harsh treatment of White Russian labourers by the Chinese, who made the gangs work harder than Chinese had worked under Russians when Gale was last in Manchuria twenty years before. That same summer Dr Gale and Esson went to spend a week at Pogranichnaya (Suifenho) near the Russian border, and the family had a seaside holiday at Pehtaiho, where Jessie's husband taught little Alex to swim.

In spring of 1924 Han Sŏkchin invited Gale to visit Ŭiju with him on the anniversary of their first meeting there in 1891. Thirty-three years later to the day, they stood once again on the Soldier's Hill, and looked over to China together, in a sentimental pilgrimage which epitomized much of Gale's feeling for far eastern history and for his own mission.

During these last years in Korea, literary work was Gale's only official responsibility. He was no longer editing newspapers, apart from the *Bible Magazine*, and he had handed Yŏnmot-kol church over to a Korean pastor in 1919, but he continued to do some teaching at Kyŏngsin School. He preached as frequently as ever. The sermon notes were sparer, and he began to make use of mnemonics, which became more and more idiosyncratic. One address was summarized as *Shine my Dominus; take full power. What doest Thou?* which is an acronym of the real sermon outline: 'Sick, mad, dead; tree, fish, pigs; walk-on-water, disappear, to-heaven.' This must have been a sermon on the divine power shown in the gospel stories of Christ. Topical references to Lloyd George and Mussolini came in, but there was an increasing insistence on the heritage of Korean culture. Another favourite mnemonic, dating from 1922 and often used, was *Great things, pure, sweet, clear, come from China; China's prince, Prince T'ang,* an acronym for a list of things that originated in China; 'gunpowder, tea, porcelain, silk, compass, colour, flowers, chess, cards, paintings, paper, type.' A sermon on paradise had as its text Luke xxiii 43, our Lord's words to the penitent thief; it began with Adam and Eve, went through Dante, Thomas More and Milton to Hsi Wang-mu, and ended up in man's heart. This was a type of preaching almost as far removed from the hearty uplift of the Alma methodists as it was from Mr Duff's dry dogmatism.

Dr Gale was now even more of a revered pundit. One of his delights was to lead parties of guests round the historical sites of Seoul on Monday afternoons (traditionally the pastor's day off), when he enjoyed deciphering and translating stone inscriptions, some of which he incorporated into his *History of the Korean People*. 19 February 1923 was the emotional peak of his life in Korea, his sixtieth birthday by the solar calendar. For Koreans the sixtieth birthday is the apex of a lifetime, because it marks the completion of the sixtyfold cycle which is the basis of traditional Chinese chronology. It is called *hwan'gap,* 'return of the beginning', because the year again has the zodiacal sign of one's birth-year. Gale was born in a year of the Black Pig, and 1923 was a Black Pig year. A group of foreigners came to the Yŏn-dong house for a Korean supper, all wearing some sort of traditional Korean dress, from court robes to informal coats. Gale, in white clothes and horsehair hat with enormous brim, brandished a long tobacco-pipe. Korean friends, in larger numbers, gave a soberer party in the garden on 30 April, when the weather was milder.

George was not present at this family feast. He had remained in England at Monkton Combe School. In 1922 Jessie married a friend of Esson's named Charles Carroll, and they were now in Persia, where Charles had a government contract for work on ports and railways, and Jessie saw wilder adventures than she had ever seen in Korea.

Gale's diary for 1925 survives and gives vivid pictures of that year. On New Year's day he visited Saito, the Governor-general of Chosen, for the customary ceremonial greetings, and met the three Roman catholic bishops of the country, all of whom he counted as friends. He presented Saito with a copy of *The Cloud Dream of the Nine*, and received in return the Japanese edition of the *Tongguk t'onggam*. During January he was busy translating *Jesus, the Carpenter of Naza-*

reth, and had the anglican doctor, Anne Borrow of Yŏju, convalescing in his house—which meant constant streams of anglican visitors. His relations with anglicans were complex. Perhaps it was because their missionaries were British that they had always provided some of his best friends and his surest spiritual support. He frequently went over to the anglican church of the Advent in Chŏng-dong for evensong on Sunday afternoons. Yet when in 1926 Father Cecil Cooper presented a translation of A. H. McNeile's book *Self-training in Prayer* to the Christian Literature Society, Gale reported that it was

> 'a very advanced book, written as a cultured high-churchman would do it. Mr Cooper has made a brave attempt at a well-nigh impossible thing. It will be only for the leaders (for a few, perhaps, we may need such a book). I fear even the leaders, as they chew the cud of this kind of book, will lose both their simplicity of thought and their clearness of expression . . . I can scarce understand a high-churchman myself.'

Bishop Trollope was nothing if not a high churchman, yet when at the beginning of March 1925 he returned from six months in England, Gale was delighted to see him again, and after their first conversation confided to his diary that the bishop's mind and English training made him conscious of 'America's poor thin civilization'. On 28 March he and Trollope celebrated the latter's birthday with a two-hour walk beyond the Great East Gate of Seoul, returning to the Gale house for a tea-party with sixty-four candles on the cake.

During the early months of 1925 Gale was working on the *History of the Korean People,* sometimes writing two chapters a month, and always keeping more than a year ahead of the publication schedule. (It was finished in March of the following year.) In May work began on printing his Korean translation of the bible. During the same month he went to Andong for a week of special teaching. At the end of the month there was a visit from Oiesen, the Danish commissioner of customs who had been a friend in Wŏnsan thirty years before. In July the family went as usual for a holiday in the Underwoods' summer home by the Han river, where one of the rooms had been built round a pine-tree—a typical missionary whimsy. Gale took with him the proofs of the bible. Seven-year-old Alex took her private menagerie: Gamma the dog, Twit the turtle, Bunny rabbit and Nancy the canary. The holiday proved a nightmare. The monsoon brought devastating floods, and though the Underwood house was high enough to be safe, the Gales watched in agonized distress as weeping people clinging to wreckage were carried away down the swirling stream. Memories of the floods of that year *ŭlch'uk* ('the Year of the Blue Ox') and the toll they took of humanity still live in Korea.

Gale's reading during 1925 included Prescott's *Conquest of Mexico*, Defoe's *Journal of the Plague Year,* Froude's *Elizabeth*, Hawthorne's *Tanglewood Tales*, Motley's *Rise of the Dutch Republic*, Macaulay's *History of England*, and Gibbon's *Decline and Fall of the Roman Empire*. He did not care much more for contemporary writing in English than he did for the new Korean literature: Margaret Kennedy's *The Constant Nymph* had been published the year before and horrified him beyond words. In his spare time he was studying the Chinese classics. Since 1923 he had worked on the Confucian Analects and Mencius.

From 1923 to 1927 he was vice-President of the Korea branch of the Royal Asiatic Society, and after his 1920 furlough published two papers in the Society's *Transactions*. 'The Diamond Mountains'(1922), was an account of his trip there in 1917, together with a collection of Korean references on the subject, a brief topography, and translations from three famous Korean travelogues. Appended to it is a list of similarities between christianity and buddhism. In 1924 he published a translation of an account of a Korean shipwreck on Sakhalin in 1636. Only too typically, he gave no particulars of the original document, but it proves to be a work called *P'yohae-rok* or *P'yoju-rok*, contained in one of the Chosen Kosho Kanko-kai volumes. It tells how Yi Chihang of Tongnae, sailing up the east coast of Korea in the early summer of 1636, was blown by a storm to Sakhalin, later reached Hokkaido, and met some Ainu. After three months he was taken by Japanese traders to Tokyo and returned to Korea through Osaka and Tsushima, arriving in Pusan nearly eleven months after he set out.

Gale's final contribution to the *RAS Transactions* was 'A short list of Korean books' appended to Bishop Trollope's paper on 'Old Korean books and their authors' published in 1932 after the bishop was dead and Gale had left Korea. It is not without interest, but is a collection of notes and was clearly never organized into the form which its author intended.

He was not such an enthusiastic collector of old books as his friend the bishop, whose Landis Memorial Library now forms part of Yonsei University Library's collection of old Korean books, but in 1925 he negotiated for the American Library of Congress the purchase of 154 volumes from the library of his friend Kim Tohŭi, who had died the previous year. Kim, the man who had accompanied Gale to Yi Kyubo's grave, had taught classical Chinese at Kyŏngsin School. According to the report of the librarian of Congress for 1927, Dr Gale had 'for many years secured rare and valuable Korean works' for the library, and 'also analysed, indexed and otherwise helped.' In 1926 he had purchased the Kim Tohŭi collection for the library, and in 1927 he presented from his own collection 312 volumes, together with 33 rubbings of stone inscriptions and 150 christian books published in Korea between 1864 and 1899. So the library had doubled the size of the Korean collection it had held in 1924, entirely owing to Gale's efforts. The most significant feature of these accessions was the number of Korean works as distinct from the number of Korean editions of Chinese works. Two fine manuscripts especially delighted the librarian: a copy of *Nansŏrhŏn chip* with a preface by Chu Chih-fan, and Gale's treasured copy of *Chodu-rok*, an annotated list of confucian shrines and institutions compiled by order of King Chŏngjo. (The title is taken from the expression *tsu-tou*—Korean *chodu*—used in the Analects for ritual vessels.) The collection contained other important items, because Gale felt strongly that England and the USA were the only countries where the books would be properly looked after and made available to students.

The History of the Korean People was written for *The Korea Mission Field* magazine between 1924 and 1926, and was still being published in monthly

instalments when he left Korea. He was sixty-three years old when he finished
writing it. It summarizes his achievement, his virtues and his faults as a scholar.
No one was better informed on the subject, but he wrote for a middlebrow
audience that enjoyed the book's anecdotal style. This style, however, was derived
from the Korean historiographical tradition. There was a considerable Chinese
bias—though this has been over-emphasized by critics who have failed to observe
Gale's deep concern for native Korean culture and how far he was in advance
of others in his reading of Korean-language texts. The *History* also had a strong
missionary bias, and imputed to Koreans belief in a god not easily distinguish-
able from the God of the christians. Sometimes the style was jocular to a degree
that now seems fatuous, but the generous extracts from Korean writings gave
the work a quality not to be found elsewhere.

The book is limited chiefly in two ways, one arising from the nature of its
sources and the other from Gale's own temperament and training. In spite of
his interest in other religious systems, his sources were biased in favour of orthodox confucianism. He relied heavily on the *Samguk sagi* and the *Tongguk
t'onggam*. Both these were dogmatically confucian works, and his other chief
sources were only slightly less so. He has nothing to say of *sirhak*, the pragmatic
learning of the late eighteenth and early nineteenth centuries, which is now seen
to be a major current in the history of Korean thought, but which official confucianism disowned as heretical.

The limitations imposed by his own temperament and training are of a
different order. Several writers have complained that the work is not exhaustive,
and that it gives uneven attention to different periods, dwelling on some and skip-
ping over others. This is true, but the reader who expects a comprehensive history
of Korea is not looking for what Gale set out to write. The title is important.
His chief concern was to describe the sort of people the Koreans are, through a
medley of cultural and literary history, full of stories about individuals, rather
than to give a synthesized account of the forces that moulded the history of the peninsula. Gale was creative rather than scientific, not a trained historian, but a *littérateur* and an antiquary. These were natural avocations for a culturally-inclined
Canadian of his generation, and typical of the missionary community in which
he worked. Bishop Trollope wrote far less than Gale, and brought to the task an
education of far higher quality than Ontario could provide; his writing has
distinction and insight that are lacking in Gale's. It is not surprising that Gale
admired him. Yet Trollope, the best scholar in several generations of missionaries
to Korea, had essentially the same avocation: he was an antiquary rather than
an historian, who wrote less than Gale because he was not also a *littérateur*.

Gale left Korea for the last time without fuss in 1927. A party was given by
the International Friendly Association in the Chosen Hotel Concert Room
under the chairmanship of a Japanese named Niwa. Gale spoke, praising the
power and culture of Japan on the interesting grounds that Japan meant so much
to his wife. Then he turned to Korean culture:

> The east, i.e. Korea, saw, centuries before Abraham was born, that religion
> was of the heart, not of the nation, nor of the organization, nor of the period

of time, but that true religion was neither more nor less than the union of the heart with God . . . Confucianism, buddhism, taoism — the more I study them the more I honour the sincerity, the self-denial, the humility, the wisdom, the devotion that was back of the first founders, great priests of the soul. Their one desire was to overcome evil and step upward and upward, nearer to God. In this we are all alike, confucian, buddhist, christian—all brothers. Kind and sympathetic we should be to one another. Christ came to fulfil the ideals of each and every one of us. In Him, whatever our religion may be, we shall find the ideal of the soul. May He unite us all.

One could not wish for anything better at the end of his missionary career than this mature statement of the uniqueness of Christ and the respect one man should have for another's beliefs. In 1927 he wrote in an editorial report to the Christian Literature Society:

With what face can we talk to the oriental about anything we have, or anything we do, or have ever been? Let's cover our lips with sackcloth, never mention the west again, but rather enter into a life of silence and prayer, and see if we cannot render the east a better helping hand than heretofore.

After forty years of missionary effort, that statement expressed not despair, but humility.

The *Korea Mission Field* noted quietly, in the personal column of the July issue, that Dr Gale and his family had left on furlough.

viii Retirement in England 1928–1937

Though he left Korea on 22 June 1927, Dr Gale was not due to retire from the mission till 31 August 1928, and had a year of furlough before his contract finished. He arrived in Canada at Vancouver where he spent a week with an old varsity friend. From August to October he visited his native Ontario for the last time, and was fêted by the United Church of Canada, of which his own presbyterians had become part in 1925. He preached and lectured at Kitchener (where Alex's birthday was celebrated again at the home of his sister Jenny Cleghorn and Alex's cousin Corea), his brother's church at Bayfield, and other local churches.

In Canada on 22 September he copied into the book of farewell addresses given to him by his Korean friends a passage he had translated from Mencius:

When God intends to invest a man with high office, He first of all sends him disturbance of mind, weariness of body, hunger of appetite, emptiness of soul, and turns all he does into confusion. By so doing He works upon his heart and awakens him to a patient humble spirit, so that the man can then do things great and high that he never could have done before.

(Mencius VI 2 xv 2)

Beside it he copied a sentence from St Ignatius Loyola:

> If the Lord send you great tribulations, it is an evidence that He has great designs upon you, and that He wills that you become a saint.

The mere similarity of thought between the Chinese sage and the Spanish saint would have seemed noteworthy to Gale, but he was probably deeply moved by these passages. He had been wounded by the troubles over the bible translation, and it was far from easy to settle down in retirement. It had been hard to leave Korea, he was tired and had long been suffering from emptiness of soul. Even deciding where to live had been an agony. Just before leaving Korea he expressed this publicly in a report to the Christian Literature Society:

> In casting about for a place to retire to, the town of Victoria, Vancouver Island, offers special attractions, more even than London, England, or Washington DC. With an even climate, which is the principal consideration, it is Canada still, and in touch with the east . . .
>
> I confess that though the board lets me live in Canada, my church membership will be a question. I am afraid I shall have to leave it on the other side. Heart-union I believe in, as my life has ever proven . . . but organic union I would not lift my finger to bring about. I like differences; I like historic continuity. I like to think that there is a methodist church as well as a presbyterian.

Then, reminiscing on the part played in his boyhood by the presbyterian church at Elora and the methodist church at Alma, he continued:

> The dear methodist church! When home last, I preached there, and all the people listened with radiant faces. But I like the old presbyterian church too, for with all its chill and solemnity, it was there that I first caught sight of that heaven to come that has gone with me ever since. Would I vote for an organic union between these two? Never! Co-operation, then? Oh yes, yes, yes, all the time and everywhere. What shall I do then as to church membership if I go to Canada? Join the Union? I don't like the flavour of it, all mixed up, no taste, and a lot of confusions in its rear. What then? Join the old hard-shelled presbyterian group that has chucked my good friends out of Formosa? Never! I don't count that even christian . . .

Eventually he decided to live in England. He was offered a post as oriental specialist in the Library of Congress, but declined it for the sake of his wife. England was her native land, and George was living there. Annie and Jessie and Esson were disappointed, and felt that he could have lived more comfortably in America. In all probability he would have suffered from the economic depression of the times even more seriously had he been in the USA. Certainly his instincts were British.

He and Ada crossed the Atlantic on the RMS *Empress of Scotland* at the end of October. In the first week of December he was preaching at George's school. They took Alex to live in Bath, in a house obtained for them by the Sale sisters, so as to be close to Monkton Combe. The family were not united for long, however, because two years later the economic recession led to the decision for George to go to Canada, where he worked for the Bank of Montreal.

Bath still retains much of the aura of those days in the eighteenth century when the attractions of its ancient spa made it the most fashionable watering-place in England. The old-world elegance of the town suited Dr Gale's taste, and he lived, surrounded by his small but remarkable collection of Korean art and furniture, at 35 St James's Square. The house stands on the east side of the square built by John Palmer between 1790 and 1793. The poet Walter Savage Landor lived in it from 1838 to 1858. Gale claimed that Landor's best-known lines were addressed in 1849 to his landlady at 35 St James's Square after a quarrel with her:

> I strove with none; for none was worth my strife;
> Nature I loved, and, next to Nature, Art;
> I warmed both hands before the fire of life;
> It sinks, and I am ready to depart.

Landor's grandson, the explorer A. H. Savage-Landor, had visited Korea in 1890–91, and published a book about his visit, of which Gale kept a copy in his library in Bath. However, Gale relished more the fact that Landor the poet had entertained Charles Dickens in the house, and Dickens had conceived the idea of *The Old Curiosity Shop* while staying there. Moreover, the character of Boythorn in Gale's old favourite, *Dombey and Son*, was supposed to have been modelled on Landor. Gale was an enthusiastic admirer of Dickens, a member of the Bath Dickens Fellowship, to which in 1930 he read a paper on 'Charles Dickens and Oriental Writers'. A Canadian classmate who had visited Bath, addressing the Toronto Dickens Fellowship Club in January 1929, delighted them with a description of Dr Gale reading from *The Old Curiosity Shop* to ten-year-old Alex in an upstairs room of the house in St James's Square.

The guest book of the Bath house records a constant stream of visitors from Korea, especially the priests and doctors of the anglican mission. Father Cecil Chambers, who had worked in Seoul with Bishop Trollope from 1912 to 1918, came to Alex's birthday tea in 1928. His brother Basil had retired from his living as Rector of Ashchurch in Gloucestershire to live in Henrietta Street, Bath, and became a close personal friend of the Gales. (The same birthday was the pretext for the arrival of the last fox-terrier, Poong—so-called by a pun on the Korean *p'ung*, meaning wind, or Gale.) In September 1930 Bishop Trollope came to Bath and the two old friends went on an outing together to see the benedictine monks at nearby Downside Abbey. It was their last meeting: the bishop was on the eve of returning to Korea, after the Lambeth Conference of that year, and less than two months later he died on board ship in Kobe harbour.

Many interests filled Gale's eight and a half years of retirement. He had been made a life governor of the British and Foreign Bible Society, and was a well-known member of its Bath branch. He was active in the Bath branch of the Royal Empire Society, and the Bath Royal Literary and Scientific Institution. Bath is a famous centre for retired people, drawn by the curative effect of its waters on rheumatism, and such societies flourished. He was a president of the Bath branch of the Regions Beyond Missionary Union, a member of the Bath City Mission, and associated with the Somerset Diocesan Mission to the Deaf and Dumb.

For some years he was the much-loved president of the 135 members of the Bath branch of the British Israel World Federation, and only relinquished that position when his health failed. Although the British Israel theory had already been severely criticized by orthodox christians, it had not yet attracted the suspicions and distaste with which it later came to be viewed. The theory that the Celto-Saxon races are descendants of the 'Lost Ten Tribes' of Israel, who did not return from Babylon to Palestine in the sixth century BC, was held by some protestant groups in England during the seventeenth century. It was elaborated by a Scot, John Wilson, in some lectures published in Bath in 1843. Wilson was involved in the founding of the Anglo-Israel Association, which in 1919 became the British Israel World Federation. Most British-Israelites also accepted the theory first put forward in 1864 by Charles Piazzi Smyth, Astronomer-Royal for Scotland, according to which the Great Pyramid was built with the British inch as its unit of measurement, to demonstrate a time-scale showing the major events of Israelite and Celto-Saxon history. Gale had been fascinated by the pyramids since he had included a passage about them in the third volume of his *Korean Readers* in 1901. In 1920 he had made many pages of notes about them, and one summer during his last term in Korea he had given two or three lectures on the pyramids and prophecy to the holidaying missionaries at Myŏng-sa-simni. He is said also to have preached a series of sermons on the subject at Yŏnmot-kol. He was sincerely convinced by British-Israel theory, and it is not surprising that its ideas should have appealed to him. He had always been attracted by the out-of-the-way, he had been accustomed to thinking of mythical racial origins when studying Korean pre-history, and his political sentiments found echoes in Anglo-Israelism.

Rumours that he had become a Roman catholic floated back to Korea, and disturbed his old friends. C. A. Clark must have written to ask him the truth, because in June 1932 Gale wrote him a letter which was published the following September in *The Korea Mission Field*. Gale denied that he had anything to do with Roman catholicism. On arriving in Bath he had naturally begun to attend the presbyterian church, and had even preached at Holy Trinity, the presbyterian chapel in the Paragon. It was the original 'Chapel in the Vineyards' of Selina, Countess of Huntingdon, but had passed into presbyterian hands in 1922. This unusual history appealed to Gale, but he was soon disillusioned about the minister in charge. Robert Calder Gillie, who was only two years younger than Gale, and had arrived in Bath in the same year as Gale, was a modernist. He had written many books, but Gale was most deeply offended by *The Bible for Youth*, published in 1924. Dr Gale objected to Gillie's rationalization of miracles (such as that the walls of Jericho did not fall down, but the frightened inhabitants surrendered), to the textual criticism which denied the traditional authorship of the New Testament books, to the higher criticism of the Old Testament, and above all to the emasculation of prophecy. He wrote in the front of his copy that Gillie was 'a good, kind man' but 'the character of all these notes is such as to destroy SIMPLE FAITH'. He could not sit at the feet of such a preacher, so he went off to the Countess of Huntingdon's Connexion, the calvinistic methodist body founded by the Countess to introduce methodism to England's upper classes. Her Bath chapel had been opened in 1765, and though this had now passed to Mr. Gillie's congregation, another was functioning (and still is, in 1971, as one of the thirty-six that belong to the Connexion) in Trafalgar Road, in the village of Weston, a suburb of Bath. Gale became an elder there before he discovered that the pastor was another modernist, so he 'joined up with the Low Church, Evangelical (Church of England) at St Andrew's', a hundred yards from his front door. It is easy to understand how James Gale felt at home in St Andrew's, Walcot, where traditional evangelical orthodoxy was taught. The ceremonial, or lack of it, would have been strange to his high-church friends in the anglican mission in Korea. They would, however, have appreciated his pleasure in his pipe and the pint of beer with his supper which he could enjoy now he was no longer obliged to humour the puritanism of his missionary confrères.

He remained a member of the Presbyterian League of Faith, and wrote enthusiastically of the interdenominational City Mission prayer meeting held every Wednesday morning, 'an old-time revival prayer-meeting that does one's heart good'. He reiterated his belief in 'the infallibility of the bible . . . every jot and tittle of its prophecies will be fulfilled'. His orthodoxy did not allow of scepticism or rationalism, yet he did not lose his theological breadth: he was that rarest of christian types, the truly romantic protestant, and had little sympathy for the harsher kind of fundamentalism, though he was a man of principle, and the conservatism of his political views was mirrored in the strength of his orthodoxy. His appearance fitted his character, as he walked the streets of Bath in clerical subfusc with a high Roman collar and pince-nez spectacles, only his neat moustache betraying that he was a non-conformist minister.

He had disposed of most of his Korean and Chinese books when he left Korea, keeping only *Sambong chip* and the two treasured volumes of the Chosen Kosho Kanko-kai edition of *Tongguk Yi Sangguk chip*, the works of Yi Kyubo. It was nearly twenty years since he and Kim Tohŭi had visited Yi Kyubo's grave on Kanghwa Island and started to work together on translations of his poems. In retirement Dr Gale polished and repolished the translations. He sent them to Kegan Paul in 1933, but that publisher did not regard them as a paying venture and suggested Oxford University Press. Oxford also rejected the manuscript. It was a period of slump, but other factors weighed against the publication of Gale's work. Arthur Waley had long since revolutionized the English reader's idea of translations from Chinese poetry, and Gale's diction was now as outdated as the bustle and the brougham. The letters of rejection must have brought disappointment, but Yi Kyubo was an old friend, cheering Dr Gale with wry comments on old age, and comforting him with thoughts of God. Gale translated one such poem:

This long-drawn illness grows apace;
How many times this wavering pulse of mine
They feel! You say I'm not to die . . .
Still, why should God have special thoughts of me?
I'm seventy-three and more, and so my way
To heaven is open wide. When shall my time,
My day to go, come round? I'll ask of God;
And if he gives no answer to my call,
I'll look up his recorded notes and see
Where I've been out of reckoning.

(TYSC hujip VII 18)

The catalogue of his library was not finished until October 1933. He had kept one buddhist book, the popular life of Gautama Buddha called *P'alsang-nok*. He had a surprising number of Roman catholic devotional books, some books on astronomy, good collections on Scotland and Korea, some British Israelite works, and the beloved old Ontario Public School Books. He made an attempt to learn Sanskrit, but did not get very far: for Sanskrit to have been useful to him he should have studied it forty years earlier. His more absorbing and satisfying studies were on the bible, and in the last years of his life it was bible themes that filled his notebooks. There was little or no system about his studies now, but no sign that his passions were spent. When the socialist government of Britain was defeated in 1931, he declaimed *Nun danket alle Gott*.

He did a great deal of preaching and lecturing, in churches and schools and to various societies. The sermons tended now to re-live the earliest of his Korean memories, and almost always quoted his favourite Korean authors. In old-style English fashion he pronounced Seoul as 'Sowl' to rhyme with 'howl'; and gave imitations of Japanese officials to make his tales vivid. He sniffed again in imagination the smell of the lacquer on Korean gauze hats, which now seemed the most evocative of all his memories of Korea before she was modernized. Modernization had killed the Korea he loved. In a letter of 1933 he wrote:

Korea is dead and gone as a country. She was the most interesting of the Chinese group to the very last, for she had never been overrun, as China herself was overrun, by Tartars, Mongols, and Manchus, but had preserved in her thought, her habits and her writings the spirit of the T'angs and Mings. Now, however, Japan comes in like one of her own east coast tidal waves, and old Korea is no more.

In spite of this sadness, it was a retirement in grand style. On occasion he drank the amber waters of Aquae Sulis in the Pump Room. His health remained good: he was a little under six feet in height, and something over thirteen stone in weight, though he did not look portly, because he was broad-shouldered. He helped with church services until the latter part of 1934, when his health worsened. His biggest trial was the scantiness of his pension. Jessie used to send cheques from Iran asking for books on Persian history and including a handsome surplus, but he was sometimes so worried about money that the worry interfered with his ability to pray. In 1935 he had the joy of a visit from George, and his own brother Bob came over from Canada to see him. In 1936 news came of the death in Korea of Yi Ch'angjik. That summer the Gales had an August holiday, visiting Lyme Regis and Budleigh Salterton in the second-hand Standard car which Alex learned to drive at the earliest legal age. Later in the same year Dr Gale himself fell seriously ill. He recovered from the first stroke, which happened while he was doing business in a bank in Bath. Then one afternoon in November he sat by the fire laughing as he told an anecdote while his wife and daughter were getting ready to go out to tea with friends in the square. Suddenly he sneezed and looked pale; but made light of it. When Ada and Alex returned home the house was in darkness and he was sitting upstairs in the drawing-room unconscious and unable to move. He was taken by ambulance to a nursing home called Ormond Lodge. Consciousness returned, and he enjoyed being read to, but was weak and unable to sit up. At Ormond Lodge in the early hours of 31 January 1937, barely three weeks before his seventy-fourth birthday, he suddenly sat up, looked up, and said, 'How wonderful! How beautiful!' Then he fell back dead on his pillow. He was buried two days later at Lansdown Cemetery. The service was taken by Prebendary F. E. Murphy, assisted by Dr Rowland Grant, Rector of Walcot, and Basil Chambers. The least sectarian of presbyterians was laid to rest by anglicans. Ada died sixteen years later, at the age of seventy-seven, on 25 January 1953.

His adored Alex grew up as a confirmed member of the Church of England, and is now the wife of Alderman John Lloyd-Kirk of Bristol. Their three children are James Gale's only grandchildren.

ix   Scholar and missionary

The strain of high romance, that made James Scarth Gale both a pioneer missionary and an industrious translator, was evident in his selection of material whenever he wrote about Korean culture. It showed itself in his old-world feeling for women, his delight in strange tales and lyric poetry, his antiquarian pleasures, and his sense of the adventure of evangelism. He discovered in Korea a world of faery to which his Scottish blood responded—Scottish wraiths appear beside Korean ghosts in his *History of the Korean People*. The introduction to his *Book of Strange Stories* shows that he was aware of the dangers of this bent; but his millenarianism was its positive theological aspect. His dislike for Bernard Shaw and Bertrand Russell, and his hatred of theological modernism were not due to defensive fundamentalism: he could not conceive the world in materialist or behaviourist terms. He was anxious to teach science and practical skills to Koreans, but his passionate faith involved acceptance of miracle, and a love of prophecy sometimes so extravagant as to disturb some of his fellow-missionaries. His thinking was never subjected to the discipline of systematic theological education. Although this was part of the reason for the indiscipline of his writing, more formal training might have blunted his romanticism. Above all, he believed that the second advent of Christ was imminent, and this was probably why he worked so hard and completed so much.

His achievement as a missionary can no longer be measured in churches built or converts made. Even his Korean books survived for little more than one generation, and are not read today. The significance of his missionary work lay in its depth. In addition to pioneer work in Wŏnsan and a highly successful pastorate in Seoul, through the two presbyterian schools and the YMCA he influenced many Koreans who became christian or nationalist leaders. He was always alive to the needs of the moment: the need of early missionaries for dictionaries and grammars; the need of young Koreans for education in the first decade of the century, for a new kind of literature after 1920; and the need for a fresh approach to bible translation.

His romanticism had an effect on his techniques. He translated with panache, and never stayed closer than he needed to the sentence-structure of the original text. At the beginning of his career, when he was doing *Pilgrim's Progress,* the wide differences between seventeenth-century English and nineteenth-century Korean forced him to liberate himself from tyrannical literalness. The method suited his personality, and he produced important work. His *Cloud Dream of the Nine* is still read fifty years later, and his *Folk Tales* were reprinted a second time in 1971. Even though his essentially Victorian concept of poetry made him write usually in iambic metre and often with rhyme, his English versions of *sijo* were landmarks in literary history, and he unfailingly chose the best in Korean literature for presentation to the west. A comparison of his versions with the elegant paraphrases of them published by Joan Grigsby in *The Orchid Door* shows the honesty of his technique. As a translator of Korean writings in Chinese he suffered from a lack of adequate tools. It is quite understandable that he should mistake *lao-nu* for *kumis,* the milk wine of the steppes, when he had no modern Chinese dictionaries to explain that it is a specialised word for tea, and that he should sometimes trip up over obscure buddhist terminology. Such points can still hinder professional scholars.

He appreciated the virtues of scientific scholarship, and his monographs show that he was not bereft of them himself; but he was often so carried away by enthusiasm for his subject that he did not bother with the apparatus of scholarship. The fact that his readers were not interested in such detail was another reason for his failure to indicate his sources. There is a great difference between his Asiatic Society papers and his *Korea Magazine* articles: the former were more meticulously prepared.

The same duality shows in his romanizations of the Korean language. The preface to his dictionary presented a scientific system of romanization better than anything else proposed by his contemporaries. He never published an analysis of it, nor described rules for its use, but it closely resembles the McCune-Reischauer system of 1939, which has now become the norm. The differences are in the treatment of a few vowels. He wrote *ö* for McCune-Reischauer's *ŏ, eu* for its *ŭ, ai* for its *ae, oi* for its *oe,* and sometimes *öi* for its *e.* Otherwise there is no significant difference between the two systems. Gale's taste in the matter was remarkable. In writing for popular audiences, however, he bowed to the common, and deplorable, missionary custom of writing *u* for *ŏ*, and *oo* for *u*, omitted the apostrophe after aspirated consonants, and was inconsistent about medial consonants.

Even more than most missionaries, he recognised the remarkable qualities of the Korean alphabet and its importance for national development, but his appreciation of the Korean language was characteristically impressionistic rather than analytical. H. G. Underwood's *Introduction to the Korean Spoken Language* was a better-organized book, yet the fascinating collection of sentences and proverbs in Gale's *Grammatical Forms* had the wider vogue. His dictionaries show that he could handle large masses of material with competent attention to detail, but his articles on language show that he had less interest in its mechanics than he had feeling for its effect. This feeling extended, as that of few foreigners ever has, to details of style in Chinese poetry and prose written by Koreans.

His ability to interpret Korea to westerners, and his appeal to Koreans, were due to an affinity between his own personality and traditional Korean culture, with its mixture of moralizing and fairy lore. People described him as winsome, kindly, genial, sparkling. He could no more resist talking to a coolie or a sewing-woman than to a prince or a buddhist abbot. His old gift of mimicry, which made him so infuriating as a schoolboy, and so apt at learning Korean, betrayed him in later years. A friend commented that Dr Gale had adopted Korean gestures to the point that if he said, 'The fellow has no brains', he would tap not his head, but his chest, because the Koreans, like the Chinese and the Hebrews, think of the heart, not the head, as the seat of thought.

It is also said that he refused to attempt writing Chinese characters with a brush, because he believed it would be presumptuous for a westerner to attempt the art without the years of assiduous practice from early youth that go to make an oriental calligrapher. This was humility, and humility was a virtue which he came to love more as he grew older. An undated essay, written in his later years, sums up his romanticism and shows his deepest insights in praise of humility. It would have been surprising if a man so devoted to women had never written anything about the Mother of God. What he had to say about her was so untypical of presbyterianism that the version of the essay which he published in the Korean seminary journal in 1921 was much abbreviated and simplified. In the English text he compared the Blessed Virgin to Kuan-yin, 'goddess of mercy', but this was less original than what he said of the maternal element in the Godhead. He wrote of Mary's life as one of rejection and suffering, showing some protestant bias in working out the details of that essentially catholic idea; but he was completely in harmony with catholic tradition when he emphasized the centrality of Mary's *fiat* to the whole doctrine of the Incarnation. He did not wish to worship her or even pray to her, but he could not prevent himself apostrophising her in his peroration:

> Ave Maria! Thou lowly one, so gentle, so submissive, so truly one with God's great and wonderful purpose! A pattern thou for all ages and times to come. May we, like thee, gently, quietly, submissively, purged of self, lose our personality in the Father's will.

87

The lack of theological precision shows his lack of formal training and an absorption of buddhist ideas; but Mary had drawn from him his best mystical writing. It was something he could scarcely have imagined when he was dazzled by the candles in the church of St Sulpice.

The greatness of his achievement is enhanced if one knows his foibles and weaknesses. James Gale must have delighted in the parallel between the words St Paul wrote to the Corinthians about true strength being found in weakness and the words attributed to Confucius in the fourth book of the Analects: 'The faults of men are characteristic of the class to which they belong; by observing a man's faults it may be known that he is virtuous'.

THE HISTORY OF THE KOREAN PEOPLE

Editor's introduction

THERE is an appraisal of Gale's *History of the Korean people* at the appropriate place in his biography, and the principles by which I have edited it are described in the preface. Here are some notes on the place of the work in Korean historiography and on the poetry translations that form such a distinctive feature of it.

The oldest extant works on Korean history belong to the tradition of Chinese historiography established by Szŭ-ma Ch'ien in the first century BC. The form is annals accompanied by selected biographies and monographs on cultural and political subjects; the method is the collation of earlier sources, generously quoted. The aim was to be objective, but not impartial: right actions were to be praised and wrong actions blamed. It was a duty of the state for moral reasons to record the history of previous dynasties in this orthodox form, which assumed the validity of treating dynasties as historical periods.

As practised in Korea this type of historiography has given us the *Samguk sagi* and the *Koryŏ-sa,* essentially confucian (and hence to some extent distorted) interpretations of early and mediaeval history. During the Yi dynasty the same ideal produced the *Kukcho pogam,* whose purpose was to show the best examples of good government. In the fifteenth century the *Tongguk t'onggam* demonstrated a slightly changed approach. It consisted of annals alone, but was designed to be comprehensive rather than dynastic in scope; comments from moralizing writers were inserted, and the native legends of prehistoric Korea recorded in appendixes. Three centuries later, in the *Tongsa kangmok,* under the double influence of Chu Hsi's neo-confucianism and the Korean 'practical learning' *(sirhak)* school (which owed a great deal to the 'empirical research' *(k'ao-cheng)* school of Ch'ing scholarship), there was an attempt at further synthesis. This trend reached its zenith in the *Haedong yŏksa,* which, though its criticism of native legends had the flavour of orthodox confucianism, showed a rational scepticism that the modern student finds congenial. In the fourteenth century Kwŏn Kŭn had complained about the fantastic elements in Korea pseudo-history, and later writers had attempted to interpret prehistory so as to make it respectable for confucians, but the *Haedong yŏksa* went further and suggested that the truth about early Korean history was much as we now believe it to have been. This book showed a discriminating approach to sources which, while not wholly unbiased, opened the way for removing further biases.

The first western writers on Korean history were in no position to evaluate the qualities of Korean historians and tended to give them all equal credit. Only in their treatment of early myths did they express doubts—because of the inherent improbability of the material, not because they could distinguish the biases of the various chroniclers. The Japanese writers of the twentieth century, though using western disciplines, did little better. It is no reflection on the skill or devotion of the best of them to admit that they were concerned to establish the case for including Korea in the Japanese empire, and that paternalism was unavoidable for them even when they respected the Koreans and their achievements.

91

Since the second world war Korean historians have criticized Korean historical writings better than the Japanese were able to, and though they have sometimes over-reacted against misguided elements in the work of the Japanese, they have built on their native tradition and done the creative and imaginative work that was so sorely needed. The focus of study has switched from personalities and events to social, political and economic issues. To writers of this school, Gale's anecdotes seem not to be worthwhile history. However, the pendulum must swing, and the next stage in Korean historiography may well be the development of local history, for it is a reasonable proposition that the real stuff of history is to be found in that field.

Gale's work stands at the tail-end of the old Korean tradition and contains many elements from it, slightly modified by western nineteenth-century approaches and the protestant viewpoint. No protestant writer could fail to write with a moral tone, and Gale unwittingly took his cue from the *Tongguk t'onggam* when he filled his *History* with moral judgments. He wrote for western readers, but made little change in the Korean historian's technique when he did so.

His quotation of many poems has precedent in Korean tradition, but his reason for it was his conviction that the poems illustrated the Korean mind better than anything else did. He showed little interest in poetic structure, and although he was sensitive to style and feeling, his translations are cast in purely English literary forms. The proportion of old Korean literature not written in Chinese is small, and except for the few examples specifically described as having been written in the vernacular, what Gale calls 'Korean writings' were done in literary Chinese. Most of the poems consist of a single four- or eight-verse stanza, though some are longer. The verses have either five or seven syllable-characters each, and there is a regular rhyme-scheme. Where Gale uses rhyme it has no relation to the placing of rhymes in the original. I have pointed out in the biography that he did not concern himself with making clear in the English versions the parallelism that is an essential feature of Chinese verse. Where he translated the compositions called *pu* or *sa* (irregular or six-character verses, with some of the features of ornate prose), I have indicated the fact in a note, because there is nothing distinctive about his treatment of them. Yet in spite of these limitations, there still exists no other work on these poems which can be compared with Gale's.

FOUNDATIONS

1 Korean myths: Tan'gun and Ch'i Tzŭ

KOREA takes its beginnings in the misty ages of the past that elude all attempts at close investigation, ages that lie somewhere between that of man and those of angels and spirit beings, joining heaven on the one hand and earth on the other.

The first great father of Korea was a being called Tan'gun.[1] Be he myth or reality, he emerges from the shadowy prehistoric past and stands between Korea and Manchuria on the Ever-white Mountains. Here he gives the simple-hearted people their first lessons in right living, and in return, they call him *sinin*, which, translated, may mean divine man, angel, spirit, or god. His year date, marked with all the confidence of the Far East, is *wu-ch'en* of T'ang Yao, or 2333 BC.[2] A startling rumour comes down with him to say that he was the third person of a divine trinity. The *Kogŭm ki* reads, 'Hwanin is God *(ch'ŏn)*, Hwanung is the spirit *(sin)*, and Tan'gun is the god-man *(sinin)*; these three constitute a divine trinity *(samsin)*.'[3] What this means who can tell?

Tan'gun was the first great ruler of Korea, his capital, we are told, being at P'yŏngyang, which would make that town one of the oldest cities of the world, contemporary with Thebes and Shinar. Tan'gun did not know that on the other side of the world was Cheops of the Fourth Dynasty at Memphis, who had just built the Great Pyramid, or that Hammurabi was living in Babylon and working out his code of laws. An age of great masters it surely was, to be remembered for all time.[4]

Tan'gun's teaching was known as the Worship of God, and was observed by bowing before the Almighty and offering sacrifice. Quite different from Confucius, the buddha, and the Old Philosopher in his relation to the Great Unseen, he has been the guiding genius for Korean inspiration through all ages. Kim Saeng, born in AD 711, Korea's most famous calligrapher, prayed earnestly to God for his special gift of calligraphy, and in a vision he met an angel, who said to him, 'I am Tan'gun, and am come down to bless you according to the longings of your heart.'[5]

Solgŏ, the greatest of Korea's artists, prayed likewise that he might be divinely taught. This he did for many years. On a certain day an old man came to him and said, 'I am the god-man, Tan'gun. Moved by your earnest prayers, I have come to give you the divinely pointed brush.' Solgŏ was a master-hand ever after. He painted a pine tree on the temple gateway and the swallows beat their little breasts against the wall trying to alight in its branches. So thankful was he for the gift he received that he painted the aged Tan'gun more than a thousand times. Yi Kyubo, who lived about AD 1200, found one of his pictures and wrote a poem about it.[6]

These are witnesses to the fact that someone called Tan'gun sometime, somewhere, impressed the people of Korea with his power and personality. There stands in P'yŏngyang, Tan'gun's ancient capital, a temple erected to his honour in AD 1429. The wind and rain have beaten against its supporting pillars for five hundred years and still they stand. Inside the hall is a tablet before which worship is offered.

In the Kuwŏl Mountains of Hwanghae Province are shrines to his memory, but the most impressive witness of all is the huge altar on Mari Mountain at the south end of Kanghwa island, in sight of Chemulp'o harbour, where Tan'gun is said to have worshipped God so long ago. What inspiration moved an indifferent people to carry huge blocks of stone, like the foundations of Solomon's temple, fifteen hundred feet up the face of the cliff, I do not know; but some strange, impelling experience must have been behind the work, I am certain.

Songs innumerable have been written telling of Tan'gun. Here is one done when Shakespeare was alive:

> When did the heavens unfold?
> When did the earth take form?
> When did the sun and moon first rise?
> When did the trees take root?
> The sun and moon combined their spirits' power
> To greet the god-man neath the forest tree.
> Companion was he of the moon and stars,
> Great as the earth and sky; born clothed with power.
> Although he laboured not he wrought it all,
> And built the state of Chosŏn. And meanwhile
> One thousand years, yes, four have passed away.[7]

The name Chosŏn, given by Tan'gun, has outlived these long millennia. We date its beginning, according to oriental chronology, from 2333 BC, and follow it down till the beginning of the christian era. It was then dropped for one thousand four hundred years and restored in AD 1392. Today we still address our letters 'Chosen', quite as freely as we do 'Korea'. People ask whence comes the name Korea. Koryŏ, happened to be the name of the peninsula from AD 918 till 1392. Its ruling house was very intimate with China, the suzerain state, and so the Chinese learned that name and have continued ever since to call it Kao-li, or Korea.[8] We got the name, therefore, from them and have so called it, quite unconscious that the country's first, last, and real name is Chosŏn, the 'Land of Morning Freshness', the name given by Tan'gun.

Today, Koreans touched by a new spirit of investigation are asking each other who Tan'gun was and whence he came. A great mass of material pointing more or less directly to him has been gathered and yet the mystery remains. The echo of his mission on earth is like that of a Messiah who came to enlighten and save. Who he was, his place in that trinity, his identity, his character, remain to be more fully investigated.

THE PERIOD between Tan'gun and Ch'i Tzŭ is largely a blank. Only a few meagre droppings of chronology throw any light at all on Korea's world. Her people were called by the Chinese 'the Nine Barbarian Tribes' *(chiu-i),* the Chinese character for 'barbarian' *(i)* being made up of 'great' and 'bow'. It is thought by some that this may account for their name: famous handlers of the long bow. We read likewise that they were noted catchers of dragons. Whether by net or spear-hook is not said, but the date marked for it is BC 1879.[9] About this time the man of faith, Abraham, was leaving Babylonia, while Assyria was being freshly peopled by Nimrod and his race of hunters.

We are told that Korea now made her first ships, her first pieces of porcelain, her first calendar, her first swords of smelted metal. Oriental ceremony had already secured a hold; it was decreed at this time that the king on state occasions should sit facing the south while his ministers sat facing north.[10]

There appeared, too, in these days, so they say, a man known as a prophet who had learned the secret of rains, droughts, wind, frost and famine. Wang Kŭmsŏk was his name, and his mission to the people of Korea is said to have been greatly blessed.[11]

ALL THESE, however, pale before the coming of Ch'i Tzŭ.[12] A poem by one Kwŏn Kŭn (AD 1352–1409), a famous writer who was a contemporary of Chaucer, links Tan'gun with Ch'i Tzŭ.

'Tis said that when the earth was waste and void
Tan'gun came down and stood beneath the trees.
His world was in the region of the East;
His times were those of Yao and Shun.
How many tribes had come and gone I know not.
Thousands of years had passed; till in the end
Great Ch'i Tzŭ came, and called our state Chosŏn.[13]

In 1122 BC China fell on evil days. A monster, by name Chou Hsin, secured the throne and proceeded to carry out his evil purpose. Every law, human and divine, was cast aside, and the state given up to orgies indescribable. Devout men protested and were imprisoned. Among them was Ch'i Tzŭ (Viscount of Ch'i), a great and distinguished scholar. His protests were unavailing and he, too, was locked up in prison from which he escaped as by a miracle. On a stone erected in front of his temple at P'yŏngyang in AD 1613, is the following:

God's not permitting Ch'i Tzŭ to be killed was because He reserved him to preach religion to us, and to bring our people back to the ways of civilization. Even though Ch'i Tzŭ had desired death at that time he could not have found it, and though King Wu had determined not to send him to Korea he could not have helped it.[14]

This gives an interesting view of Korea's conception of the overruling providence of God. The wickedness of Chou Hsin is taken advantage of to bring Ch'i Tzŭ to Korea. The kings who came to power at this time, Wen and Wu, with Duke Tan of Chou, are the most famous of China's prophets and seers. They founded the line of Chou kings under whose rule came the great master Confucius. The *Chou-i* (Book of Changes), China's greatest classic, also dates from this time. The immanence of God was a vital issue in their lives, and their aim was to do those things that pleased Him. Thus the wicked king Chou Hsin departed and the virtuous king Wu ascended the throne, and yet Ch'i Tzŭ, one of his own trusted comrades, could not swear allegiance. Wicked though the former king was, and good though his successor was, still Wu was a usurper and Ch'i Tzŭ refused allegiance. King Wu, perplexed at this, suggested that he go to Korea and set up a kingdom of his own. In 1122 BC he came and thus restored the fading fortune of Tan'gun's people.

Ch'i Tzŭ was Korea's second great captain. Those accompanying him made him king and set up his capital at P'yŏngyang, calling his state once again Chosŏn. He brought with him the literature of China as well as its music and ceremonial forms. His stores of knowledge included medicine, magic, fortune-telling, all kinds of industry, the fine arts and the special output of five thousand skilled workmen. He could not talk to the people, and so had to approach them through an interpreter. P'yŏngyang's old ramparts and walls still keep the name of Ch'i Tzŭ. His tomb, though its authenticity has long been questioned, lies to the north of the city. Within the walls is a temple to his honour created in AD 1325, an extract from the memorial stone of which has already been given.

Many stories are told of Ch'i Tzŭ: one, that he promulgated the 'well-field law' *(chŏngjŏn pŏp),* under which one-ninth of all the produce of the state went to the king;[15] another, that he found the Koreans a fierce and ungovernable people, given to breaking each other's heads. To prevent this he had them don earthenware hats, wide as the moon, and fragile as eggshell porcelain. The extent to which the wide hat was preserved intact indicated a man's standing as a gentleman, while a broken hat marked him a thief and robber. The earthenware hat eventually changed to horse-hair and so it has come down till today. A very remarkable story!

Here is another: in order to work a change in the hearts of the people, he planted willows about P'yŏngyang. The sight of their soft and gentle leaves and lamb-like catkins was supposed to do it. Even today P'yŏngyang is called the Willow Capital (Yugyŏng).[16]

Thus Korea began her course in the world's history under the tutelage of two famous masters, one the mysterious Tan'gun and the other the sage Ch'i Tzŭ.

2 Chinese mythical emperors; taoism

ACCOMPANYING the dynastic line just recorded, the religious, moral, and philosophical lines keep pace in the mind of the Korean. Not only so, but they occupy a wider and more important place. Koreans have thought very little of their far-off race beginnings, but of the soul and its meanderings they have thought much. The inner man who thinks and dreams and meditates, who composes his poems and sings his songs, is much more truly the real Korean than the man who dons the white coat and wears the sagely solemn face. In heart he thinks not of Korea but of China; and not of modern China, but of ancient and mediaeval China, with a few scattered memories only for the present day. His views of creation agree somewhat with the 'waste and void' of Genesis: out of the shadows he sees P'an Ku come forth bearing in his hand the dual principle of nature, the *yin* and the *yang*. This ancient idea comes down from the legendary ages.

Great kings pass by as in a moving picture; the Heavenly Emperors, T'ien-huang Shih, upon the clouds; the Earth Emperors, Ti-huang Shih, on the land; and the Human Emperors, Jen Huang Shih, amid the congregated races of men. Following these comes Fu-hsi with his Eight Diagrams *(pa kua)*, on whose groups of three lines, divided and undivided, hang the mysteries of philosophy.[1] Then Shen-nung, the Spiritual Farmer, who has to do with agriculture and medicine. The native medicine shops of Seoul today still use his sign, *Sillong yuŏp* (The Calling of the Spiritual Farmer). He may have had in his pharmacopoeia 'eye of newt and toe of frog' and prescriptions to make the foreigner's hair stand on end, yet he had also many excellent remedies that have been tested and found not wanting through five thousand years. To complete the trio we add Huang-ti, the Yellow Emperor, or, as he is also called, Hsüan-yüan Shih, a great master of the mysteries of taoism. He lived among dragons and fairies, and his sphere of operation was not only the earth, but also the upper air and heaven, to which he finally rode on a dragon's back.

As TAOIST THOUGHTS occupy so great a place in the understanding and imagination of the Korean, a story of those far-off days will not be out of place.[2] Huang-ti had been nineteen years on the throne, and his heart was not at rest. He longed for a world of peace and plenty, but the power to bring it about was lacking. Hearing that a fairy, Kuang-ch'eng Tzŭ, who knew all the mysteries of life, was living in the K'ung-t'ung Hills, he went to see him. Said he, 'Understanding that you have attained to the highest place in religion, I have come to inquire concerning it. Could I but win the spirit you possess, so as to give abundant harvests to my people, I should be satisfied'. 'Away!' said the fairy, 'your thoughts are on material things. With such a mind no attainment is possible. Even the light of the sun and moon is full of evil to such as you.'

Huang-ti retired, ashamed; abdicated his throne, and built himself a little hut where he spread his mat upon the ground, and for three months gave himself up to prayer and fasting.

Again he went to see the fairy. Said he, 'They say you have entered deep into religion; tell me its meaning, please, and how I may attain unto it.'

The fairy said, 'How glad I am to hear your question now. Come close to me and sit down, till I teach you plainly. The meaning of religion is so deep that it recedes from view into the shadows and is hidden. It cannot be seen, even though we try to see it; it cannot be heard, even though we try to hear it. In the quiet of the soul it is sensed. Let your spirit be pure and take no anxious thought for the body. Let go the sight of the eyes, the hearing of the ears, and the understanding of the heart. Much knowledge destroys the soul. Put all your anxious care away, and bid a long farewell to every outward effort. By this means you will be guided on into the world of light and wonder.' He talked to him further, for

Huang-ti was now his true disciple, and became one of those who, we are told, never die, but are translated to the bliss of heaven as in Elijah's chariot. Now Huang-ti's date is marked 2697 BC, a thousand years before Tutankhamen, and yet the doctrine of the fairies, or taoism, was fully developed in his day.[3] We shall hear more of it, for it occupies a great place in the mind of the man of Chosŏn.

AS THE KOREAN runs his finger down his spiritual ancestry he comes to Yao and Shun mentioned in chapter 1, probably the two most famous names in East Asia. Yao was king of China and a contemporary of Tan'gun. Tan'gun was a Korean, and Yao a Chinese, and yet the Korean mentions Yao a hundred times to Tan'gun's once. There is a saying in Korea: *Ŏn p'il ch'ing Yo Sun* (When a man speaks, it is of Yao and Shun).[4] Yao's name appears in the first line of the Book of History, *Shu ching*, one volume of Korea's ancient bible, which reads, 'How great was Yao!' Shun, his son-in-law, who married Yao's two daughters, O-huang and Nü-ying, was also a model king and saint. With them begin the *wu-hsiang*, or Five Constant Virtues: benevolence, uprightness of mind, propriety in demeanour, knowledge, and good faith;[5] the *wu-lun* as well, the Five Right Relationships: between king and minister, father and son, elder brother and younger, husband and wife, friend and friend.[6] These are the Ten Great Commandments of East Asia, received on the misty mountain tops and handed down to future generations.

Associated with Shun, who is regarded as the first great filial son, were his two wives, models of woman's devotion. They were like Leah and Rachel, though their sisterly spirit was even sweeter and their lives of more perfect accord. Their husband went south to Tung-t'ing Lake and there died; his faithful wives followed, arriving too late. They wept such tears of sorrow that they marked the bamboo as by blood. Then they cast themselves into the Hsiao-hsiang River and died. To this today we have the *panjuk*, or spotted bamboo, that is said to bear witness to the old story of the faithful women.

With Yao and Shun begins Korea's calendar that measures the seasons of the year. It divides the circle of the sun into twenty-four divisions, each having a festival of its own. These twenty-four festivals hang on a fixed frame, as it were, whose four legs are the two equinoxes and the two solstices.[7] Attached to the same frame, but loosely hung, so that it can swing one twelfth of the circle backwards and forwards, is the lunar year. Its first day may be any time between 19 January and 20 February. An exceedingly interesting calendar it is, following in its course both the sun and moon, each festival, like a saint's day, marking off some item of interest that grew into the lives and fortunes of the people.

FOLLOWING Yao and Shun we have Yü, the king who drained off the waters of the Yellow River and saved China from a Noachic deluge, spending nine years of most arduous labour on behalf of his people. We are told that in this work he passed his home three times, and heard the crying of his little son, but did not even stop to inquire. His was the Hsia dynasty, that lasted, supposedly, from 2205 till 1766 BC, or from the Deluge to the death of Abraham. Yü is one of the great saints of Korea, great beyond words. The nine provinces of China, too, the first ordered geographic arrangement of the continent, were marked out by him.

This dynasty, that began so propitiously, failed in the end and went gradually down, till a horrible monster, called Chieh, appeared. Prince T'ang arose like Michael the archangel and, amid mighty portents and convulsions of nature, brought the tyrant down. T'ang is the fourth of Korea's great sages.

But how did T'ang attain to sainthood? Righteous though he was and backed by the will of heaven in his overturning of a dynasty, evil still followed in his train. A fearful famine lasting seven years came down upon the state. Seeing no hope but in human sacrifice, the king fasted, bathed, and then, arrayed in white robes, went to the mulberry grove hard by to make his final offering: he himself would die. This submissive will was accepted; T'ang's prayer was heard, abundant rains fell, and another name was added to the list of China's saints. His kingdom, called Shang, lasted from 1766 to 1122 BC, that is, from the time of Jacob till the days of the prophet Samuel.[8]

WE COME NOW to the real beginning of Korea's religious history.[9] As mentioned before, the Shang Kingdom fell into the hands of a second Chieh, a worse even: Chou Hsin. Every Korean who has made his entrance into the field of literature looks down with horror upon Chou Hsin—his wild forms of debauchery, his lake of wine, his abandoned women.

Then Wen, a wise and far-seeing statesman, arose, and was imprisoned for his attempts to set right the kingdom. While in prison he is supposed to have re-arranged the sixty-four combinations of the Book of Changes, *I ching,* that has come down for three thousand years as the greatest of the sacred books. He finally set his son on the throne, King Wu, the friend of Ch'i Tzŭ, and the Chou Kingdom began. With this great saint there came into being the Books of History *(Shu ching)* and Songs *(Shih ching),* the Pentateuch and Psalms of East Asia.[10] Every line of these was learned, recited; their texts were posted up as sacred writings, deeply to be revered; they were written as with a diamond point on the inner chambers of the heart. Here is one from the Book of History: 'The presence of God does not always abide with us; if we are sincere it abides; if not, it takes its departure.'[11]

Again in the Book of Songs I read, 'One must be correct in one's own deportment before one can expect to set right the four corners of the earth.'[12]

In the days of kings Wen and Wu there was a group of women of like mind with their masters, led by T'ai-jen and T'ai-szŭ.[13] Beautiful, and pure in soul and wholly devoted in their service, they form with O-huang and Nü-ying a special circle, the Hannahs, the Marthas, the Magdalens of the farthest East.

FROM THIS TIME down to the founding of the Han Kingdom, a thousand years, we have very meagre records of Korea's national history. Only a few scattered notes tell us that such a people lived and moved and had their being. Nevertheless, this period is the most important of all Korea's four thousand years of reckoned time.[14] During its span there lived the three great masters of the East: the Old Philosopher of *tao,* the Buddha, Confucius; besides, many great warriors and wise men whose names and memories are a part of Korea's inmost being.

Taoism, buddhism and confucianism are the three religions of the peninsula, and all three take their rise in the sixth century BC; how great they are, numbering their followers by millions and their length of service by thousands of years! Any history of the Korean people must take these three into account very carefully if it would weigh or measure aright Korean beliefs, character or attainments.

THE OLD PHILOSOPHER, Lao Tzŭ, (or Noja, as Koreans call him), was born in 604 BC and died in 522.[15] Late in life he met Confucius and asked this question,[16] 'Why trouble about ceremony while the greater question of religion remains unanswered? A rich merchant,' said he, 'looks as though he were poor, and makes no display of goods or wealth. Act the simple part if you would show forth true religion.' In his great book, the *Tao te ching,* he says, 'Religion is like water: it seeks the humblest place; it enriches and beautifies all it touches; it never boasts.'[17]

Joining up with taoism, though older by centuries than Lao Tzŭ, is the world of the fairy, the floating gardens of Eden that hang just over the mountains of Tibet. Here dwells a mysterious princess called the Western Queen Mother, Hsi Wang-mu. She and her fairy folk have a sphere of their own filled with the fruits of paradise, and to those who call there they hand the peaches of the immortals. She has at hand sky-blue pigeons who fly off at her bidding with messages to kings and princes, a radio service indeed, intended to hearten the poor dwellers of the earth.

What infinite comfort Koreans have gathered from the beliefs and delights of taoism. Here is a poem written by a famous Korean scholar named Chin Hwa, a contemporary of Francis of Assisi, Richard I of England, and Chinggis Khan. He probably realized more clearly than any of these the lost delights of Paradise.[18]

> The tangled grass with thorny tips points me
> Off to the east amid the smoky blue,
> Where fairy flowers encircle all the world.
> This is the place where refuge found its hold
> Against the rough compulsion of Ch'in-shih.
> The fairies' choicest garden is its name,
> Fresh limpid streams enclose it round and round.
> Its land is rich, its waters sweet and clear;
> Red fluffy dogs wake to its day
> And bark when clouds go by.
> The blooming flowers, kissed by the passing breeze,
> Drop, one by one, upon the grassy sward.
> We planted peaches out beyond the road
> To throw men off and keep the world away.
> We talk of things that happened ere the state
> Was burned and all its sacred books;
> We watch the grass and trees to tell
> How time goes by—the seasons of the year;
> We laugh as with our children we forget

The past and think of days to come.
Sometimes a fisher wanders in
And sees our joy, and goes to call his kind,
But later finds the way confused
And, hopeless, never sees our world again.

With taoism in his soul the Korean tells the most delightful stories of these dwellers in the higher sphere—how he meets them on occasion, the part they play in his world of imagination. A mayor of Seoul born in AD 1640, Im Pang, refers frequently to the fairy in his book of stories. Says he:

> Her world seemed filled with golden palaces and surrounded with a halo of light. Peopled it was with happy souls, some riding on cranes, some on the phoenix, some on the unicorn. Some were sitting on the clouds, some sailing by on the wind, some walking on air, some gliding gently up the stream, some descending from above, some moving west, some east, some gathering in groups. Flutes and harps sounded sweetly. So many and so startling were the things seen there that I could never tell the tale of them.[19]

THE great book of taoism is, as I have just mentioned, the *Tao te ching,* whose opening words run (I give the translation of Professor Giles of Cambridge, England):[20]

> The way that can be walked upon is not the eternal way;
>   the name that can be named is not the eternal name.
> All the world knows that the goodness of doing good is not (real) goodness.
> Therefore the sage follows a doctrine that does not find expression in words.
> When merit has been achieved do not take it to yourself; for if you do not take it to yourself, it shall shall never be taken from you.[21]

This will give a hint of the religion that underlies taoism, a religion that retires from the world into the mystic regions of silence and meditation. Taoism has played a great part in the thinking processes of the people of Korea, more perhaps than the average Korean is in any way aware of.

3 Gautama Buddha

THE second great master of Korea's fortunes was the marvellous man of India whom these people call Sŏkkamoni (558–479 BC).[1] It would seem as though the earth's soul in his day was charged with mighty men: Aeschylus the poet, Pythagoras the philosopher, Themistocles the writer, Herodotus the historian, all living and moving when the buddha was fighting his spiritual battles on the banks of the Ganges. Greek heroes, however, count but little before the might and majesty of this great Indian priest. Koreans have pondered over his life, and meditated on his mystic ways until he has become a part of their very being, seen by the eye of faith, gazed on through his portrayed countenance, talked of with the lips. The story of his birth as told in the *P'alsang-nok*² runs thus:

> On the eighth day of the fourth moon, Queen Maya came into the Lumbini Gardens with five hundred of her maids to see the *mandarava* flowers. As she looked about, pains suddenly came upon her and a sense of fear and mystery enveloped the world; flowers sprang forth at her feet and the light of glory filled the place. Overborne by the weight of it she sought refuge under the *asoka* ('no care') tree,³ where she threw herself down to rest. Suddenly a beautiful boy sprang forth from her side and took his seat in the calyx of a lotus flower. A moment later he arose and stepped hither and thither toward the four points of the compass, seven paces in each direction. Then he stood with his left hand raised, and his right turned toward the earth and said with a loud voice, 'In heaven above and earth beneath I alone am to be exalted.' When he had said this, he lay down, and, like any other child, cried himself to sleep.⁴

When he was twelve years of age he obtained permission of his father to go beyond the palace gates and see the world. He paid four visits in all, of great importance in their bearing on his own life and the future of Asia. On the first visit, boy-like and full of glee, he saw only things interesting or beautiful, until suddenly there crossed his path an old man with white hair and bent back, who could barely make his tottering way. He carried a staff and breathed with difficulty.

The Prince asked his attendant who this was that wore such a distressful mien. The reply was, 'He is an old man.' Again he asked, 'What do you mean by an old man?' The answer was, 'When a man is young his strength is firm; but when his years are many his hair turns white and his flesh and blood dry away; his back becomes bowed and his legs weak, so that he walks with difficulty. He needs must carry a staff as he goes forth on his feeble way. This kind of person we call an old man.'

The Prince again asked, 'Is this man alone thus, or do others grow old as well?' The reply was, 'In growing old, high and low, rich and poor are all alike.' The prince listened, then sighed and said, 'Though I have all the riches of the palace at my bidding, still I too must grow old, my back be bent, and my years, like others', fade and die.'

He came home from his outing, but joy had departed from his face. The king asked what the trouble was, and in his turn was rendered anxious.

The day following he had an equally unpleasant experience in meeting a sick man 'worn down to skin and bone', who breathed with difficulty and gasped forth his fears and dread.

On the next journey, worse than ever, he came on a dead body, 'wrapped and made ready for burial'. On inquiry he was told that the man was dead.

'Alas,' said he, 'life is a sad and woeful tale.'

On his fourth visit there came to him a new and wonderful experience. A man of religion crossed his path

dressed in green silk robes and a gold-embroidered vestment; he seemed unlike any dweller on the earth. The prince called to him, 'Who are you, so different from all I have ever seen before?' The stranger joined his hands and said, 'I am a *bhikku* (priest).' 'Why a priest?' His reply was, 'The world has nothing that it can give to satisfy the soul, and so I have broken away from it—parents, brothers, and relatives—cut my hair and become a religionist. The hills are my home, where I have fought my battle and passed over the troubled sea of mortal existence to the farther shore. On which attainment there came to me complete cessation from the miseries of birth, growth, decay, death, with all the pains of the endless *kalpas* (ages). Hence I am called a priest.'

When he had so spoken he shook his body and ascended into the upper air, riding on the tinted clouds, and went sailing off toward the western sky. As he went he sang:

'How vain this troubled earth,
    Its pain, its want, its woe!
Set free from life, from death, from birth,
    Upward I go.'

Thus he sang as he disappeared from view among the softly moving clouds. The Prince looked long and eagerly after him. Sorrow filled his heart, and till the day was over he remained in meditation, returning home by moonlight. The king waited anxiously, and when he came, took him by the hand and said, 'How has the day gone, my lad?' The Prince replied, 'I have journeyed forth by all the gates of the city, have seen every phase of human life and have just awakened to the fact that all things are vain.' The king made answer, 'Even though you have awakened to this sad fact, will that in any way help you to live a better life or be of greater benefit to others?' The prince replied: 'If your majesty will but consent to my departure, I am sure I can find a way to escape from earth's sorrow. I would cross to yonder shore where there is no birth and no death.' The king laughed and said, 'Though it would be a blessed experience to reach such a place, how could you think for a moment of leaving a king's throne with its endless delights?'

The prince answered, 'What delight, pray, has a throne for me?' The king's answer was: 'The begemmed palace, the pearly halls, the golden throne, your subject princes with their gifts of tribute, a thousand pretty faces to accompany the harps and pipes that play, fresh wine poured to the full, power and rank and high reward. When life has reached its limit you pass it on to your children to enjoy likewise through the ages to come, while you as a spirit, drink the offered blood and inhale the incense of the sacrifice. Thus may you enjoy life with all created things, and thus may your people look up to you with fear and

103

wonder, ascribing blessings to your name. What can equal such joy as this? Your leaving home for the sake of religion may be praiseworthy, but how can you think of leaving the shrine of your ancestors for such a visionary hope? My desire is that you give your heart to the service of your people and to filial devotion, and remember that all my accumulated hopes are centred in you.'

The prince bowed his thanks and returned to his room where, under the light of the lamp, he meditated on the song the priest had sung. How could he think otherwise? But the wishes of his father disturbed his heart and he passed an anxious night.[5]

This is a somewhat lengthy quotation from the opening pages of the story that has caught the imagination of the peoples of the East. Sŏkkamoni, or as he is usually called, Sakyamuni, left his home, his wife, his child, his father, his kingdom, his all, and thus became the first object of worship to the countless millions of Asia. Korea bends over this so-called gospel, from which we have quoted, with unwearying gaze.

Like the Scots, her people are of a sombre turn of mind, and, unless awakened to a livelier sense by the influence of wine, mainly see the dark side of life. One large hall in each of the buddhist centres is called the Hall of Hades, *Myŏngbu-jŏn*. On its walls hang the most dreadful representations of hell imaginable. For example: the Nail Hell, where sinners are battened down; the Grinding Hell, where they are put between the upper and nether millstones; the Hell of Wolves and Wild Beasts, where they are torn to pieces; the Knife Hell, where they are stricken through and through. As the gentle law of taoism woos men away to the bliss of Paradise, the buddha warns men by his hells to cease from sin. Koreans, however, have preferred the buddha to even the world of the Old Philosopher.

One illustration of the teaching instilled by terror, I shall give from this same *Life of the buddha*.[6] His brother Nanda[7] was a religious scoffer, which greatly disturbed the Highest. As he anxiously thought upon this,

Maudgalyayana[8], his faithful disciple, came and said, 'Though I claim no special skill to move the hearts of men, yet I feel sure I can bring your brother to repentance.' The buddha gave him full power to act as he thought best, and at once he called Nanda saying, 'You have come here, I know, from mere curiosity and not to learn religion. Come with me, I pray.' Nanda, full of the spirit of adventure, readily acceded. Maudgalyayana, endued with special power, picked him lightly up and went through mid-air till they reached a place that had great iron walls, high as heaven. Inside were keeps and fortresses filled with devils, who scurried about, peering through the gates. Nanda gazed with terror, for such a place he had never seen before. He turned to Maudgalyayana and asked, 'Where are we?' Maudgalyayana replied, 'This is the prison house of Hell.' Then again, crossing other heights and barricades, they came to a horrible place where a great assembly of priests and priestesses, laymen and laywomen, were gathered as prisoners. Here fires blazed up around metal pillar-prongs smeared with oil which stood in the flames. The victims were tossed into the glowing mass and commanded to make their escape up the pillars. If they went slowly they were beaten with iron whips. As the pillars were slippery they fell back again and again into the fires and were burned. Their screams resounded through the tumult. A respite was given at times, when they were spitted through with rods and hung up in the open. Snakes and hawks hurried forth to feed on their flesh. Blood flowed everywhere, a sight horrible to see.

When Nanda beheld this, he said, 'What sins have these people committed that they suffer so?' The guards replied, 'These men, while in mortal life, were disloyal to the king and unfaithful to parents. The women, too, were untrue to their husbands, and at enmity with their neighbours. They spoke against the buddha and when they saw anyone at prayer treated him with contempt. They drank wine, ate flesh, and did much evil. Here they meet their first punishment; afterwards they are sent to the greater hell which is of boundless width and immeasurable bottom.'

When Nanda saw this, his heart sank within him and he signified to Maudgalyayana that he wished to go. Maudgalyayana then took him to another place, where there was a great cauldron of boiling oil shot through with iron rods. Instruments of torture were placed in readiness, but no victims were to be seen. The demon soldiers stood at attention, their sleeves rolled up for action. Nanda asked the guard the reason of this special preparation and the guard said in reply, 'This is a place prepared for the boiling of Nanda, a brother of the Highest. We hear that he is already taken by King Yama (lord of the underworld),[9] but that he has been permitted for a moment to stop at the Spirit-Hill Assembly.[10] When that is over he will be arrested and we shall boil him here.' On hearing this Nanda turned ashy pale and asked, 'Why, what sin hath he committed?' The guards answered, 'He speaks against the law of the buddha, and refuses to listen to the teaching of the Highest, so the angels and archangels of heaven have sent word to the king giving his name, Nanda. You see we have it posted up on the walls,' to which they pointed.

When Nanda heard this, dreadful fears overcame him and without daring to look further he beckoned to Maudgalyayana, saying, 'Let's go.'

Maudgalyayana then picked him up and passed out over the gates. He threw his almsdish into the air and with Nanda beneath his arm, sat in it and went up to the abodes of bliss, where were innumerable beauties of bud and blossom. Angel children gathered to give them welcome, flowers bloomed everywhere, while phoenixes and peacocks adorned the scene. It was indeed a world of light and joy.

When Nanda saw it, he felt greatly refreshed. Said he, 'What sort of people inhabit this world?' Maudgalyayana replied, 'This place is

reserved for those who while in life worshipped the buddha, led their
parents and brethren away from sin, and with faithful, kindly soul did
what was right.' When Nanda heard this, his heart was greatly moved
and he turned to look elsewhere. 'Go,' said Maudgalyayana, 'and see
for yourself.' He went beholding this and that and saying, 'Wonderful!
Wonderful!' He reached a place where a beautifully-decorated pavilion
had just been built. A gilded throne stood in the midst of it with many
costly pieces of furniture round about, but there was no master to be
seen. Nanda asked, 'Is there no master here?' They replied, 'This home
was intended for the younger brother of the buddha, whose name is
Nanda, but now we hear that he has become an enemy of the faith;
has joined the Evil One, and that he will be sent to hell instead.' On
hearing this, Nanda hurried back to Maudgalyayana, took him by the
sleeve and prayed him to cease from further sightseeing and to take him
back at once to the presence of the Highest.

Maudgalyayana, grateful that his heart had changed, took him
under his arm and brought him back to the Spirit Hill where the buddha
was engaged in teaching the Law, and where, for the time being, he
paid no attention to the return of Nanda.

When occasion offered, Nanda, humbly entering the presence of
the Highest, shed bitter tears and said, 'I am a dark and ignorant soul,
an enemy of the Faith. I indeed deserve endless punishment, but today
my heart longs to repent. May the merciful and loving buddha save the
soul of Nanda!' When he had said this his hair dropped off and he was
found robed as a monk.

Such are a few quotations from the *Life of the buddha* that will give the reader
a hint of the kind of influence that has borne upon the people of Korea from that
quarter for fifteen hundred years.[11]

4 Confucius

THE third great master of this sixth century BC is Confucius. How different he is
from the others. He is neither up in the clouds with the disciples of Lao Tzŭ, nor
down in the deeps in the underworld of the buddha, but walks the earth as a
great and good Chinese.

The Chou Kingdom that had come into existence in 1122 BC lived and flourished for some four hundred years and then gradually began to disintegrate.
By the time of Confucius[1] it had fallen into many feeble states and the great
teacher went here and there trying to patch up the broken fragments and bring
back once again the happy days of Wen and Wu. In this effort he travelled the
empire from end to end, vainly endeavouring to call kings and courtiers back to
first principles. Here are some of his sayings:[2]

> Those who do right God rewards with blessing; those who do
> wrong God punishes.

He who obeys God, lives; he who disobeys Him, comes to grief.

If we sin against God, there is no place for prayer.

Life and death are ordered for us; riches and poverty are in the hands of God.

While your parents live, go not far afield; but if you have occasion to leave them, let them know where you go.

What all men speak well of, look nonetheless carefully into; what all men condemn, examine first before you finally decide.

Though bright and intelligent, be as modest as though you were ignorant; though noted the world over, keep out of the public eye; though brave as a lion, act as though you were possessed of fear; though greatly rich, be as humble as the poorest.

Fair speeches and an engaging manner are seldom based on character.

A government that stands on right principles is like the North Star that abides ever in its place, with all the other constellations circling round it.

Take note of a man's action, look well into his motives, see where his interests lie: no-one can hide this.

A man must be good indeed to know how to love and how to hate.

Riches and honour are envied by all men, but if they come by other than right means they are in no sense a blessing; poverty and low degree both are men's sore dislike, yet if they come to us by other than wrongful ways, they are not to be rejected.

If a man but meet true religion in the morning, he may meet death at night with no regrets.

When you see what is good, strive to emulate it; when you see what is evil, take note lest you do the same.

These sayings of Confucius are like Korea's coin of the realm passed from hand to hand. By the side of the picturesque Old Philosopher and the super-mystic priest Sakyamuni, Confucius seems a very ordinary person indeed, yet no one has touched the heart of Asia quite as deeply as he, or made so lasting an impression upon the sunburnt races of the Farthest East. He himself wrote almost nothing. The Spring and Autumn Classic *(Ch'un ch'iu),* specially attributed to him, bears little on his teaching, while the Great Learning *(Ta hsüeh),* Doctrine of the Mean *(Chung yung),* and the Analects *(Lun yü),* which are the most satisfactory works of exposition, were written and edited by others.[3]

As we read them we find the great subjects that he discussed, including God, whether under the name of T'ien or Shang-ti. Some scholars have thought that T'ien refers solely to the blue sky and never to the Supreme Being, possessor of heaven and earth, and fountainhead of thought and personality. We can best answer this by a quotation from Kim Ch'angŏp, a Korean scholar who was born in 1658. Speaking of this name he says, 'Now T'ien is not the blue heavens, but God who resides in the heart, and is the one to be feared.'[4]

Confucius also talked much of predestination, of sainthood, of the heart, of true religion, and especially of filial devotion. His grave is in Shantung, not in Korea, and yet I feel safe in saying that the people of Korea, man for man, know Confucius better than the ordinary Shantungese. Even Korea's coolie, who carries his rack on his back and bows before his poor little paper tablet, is a true disciple of the Master and a gentleman of the old school.

Without enlarging further here, I would repeat that these three masters more than any others have guided the destinies and fortunes of the people of Korea. They come forth from the 6th century BC, and so project an unbroken span of influence across two thousand five hundred years.

OUT OF THE CHOU Kingdom of China have come as well many of the habits and customs that specially mark the Korean people today. The division of society into four classes, expressed by the word *sanonggongsang* (scholar, farmer, manufacturer, merchant), belongs to Chou.[5] Low down in the list, number three, comes the worker. Consequently Korea dislikes what is regarded as industrial or manual labour. She counts farming and fishing less degrading, as they occupy the second place. In the immaculate garb of a gentleman she will look down with contempt on the Chinese merchant, uncombed, unwashed, untutored, as he gathers all her floating gear, ties it up in his greasy bag, and sends it back to the celestial abode of his grandfathers. She will not soil her soft tapering fingers: which accounts much for her unfortunate position today. The phrase *scholar, farmer, manufacturer, merchant,* has not only killed manufacturers of all kinds, but has put the merchant in a class little better than a pariah. Though rolling in wealth, he may not lift up his eyes to the lettered sage, who, deeply steeped in classic lore, knows not where tomorrow's meal will come from.

FROM THIS SAME kingdom of Chou comes that weird variety of the human species known as the eunuch. Twenty years ago there appeared in a Shanghai journal the following:[6]

> One of the influences that has borne upon Korea for woe rather than weal during its history is the eunuch. Smoothfaced and sallow, high-keyed in voice, and with the shadow of an old woman looking out over his cheek-bones, his tall gaunt figure has been seen for ages scuttling in and out of the palace. Mankind may be divided into three classes, male, female and neuter; and into the last class falls the eunuch. He is a monstrosity, of course, a contradiction of the eternal law, the product of a deformity, which shows itself in his face and renders him unpleasant to look upon, if not repulsive.
>
> When grown up, eunuchs are taller than other men. Nature, switched off one course, projects itself along another. Then, as to the voice, how shall I describe it? It is a girl's voice lacking the element of softness and charm that makes it a girl's voice. It is the ghost of a voice, like the clack of a cheap talking-machine; yet an excellent voice to whisper by.
>
> In disposition they approach more nearly to women, so Koreans say. There is a common expression, 'Bad-tempered as a eunuch'.[7] Their

rage, when once aroused, is said to reach beyond bounds; they are liberal and generous, are unforgiving if once wronged, are partial and one-sided in their views; all of which traits, according to the Korean, belong to women. I have some friends among the eunuchs and one I know particularly well — a jolly, free and easy, lively, girl-style of person, most refreshing to meet. He usually has some good story to tell or some droll experience.

In rank and position eunuchs stand high in society. This is accounted for by the fact that they wait specially upon the sovereign. They sweep his room, make his bed, draw the blinds, spread the quilt, put on his clothes, tie his topknot, fix his head-band and hat, bring in his table, light his pipe. They are all around and about him with their sallow, clammy existences. They move in and out of the kitchens and among the serving maids. There is not a corner of the palace, be it the emperor's or queen's apartments, that is not free to them. They take turns in waiting on His Imperial Highness and when off duty return to their private homes. (In order to be reckoned as men, and not as mere women, they have a wife and usually an adopted son.)

POLYGAMY, as well, came in from Chou and beyond. King Shun, the saint, had two wives, just as Jacob had, and from his day it grew to be the established custom, finally sanctioned by Confucius.[8] As the writer has viewed it in actual operation, he is inclined to think that the main thought behind polygamy is, 'A son I must have at all costs who will carry on the family line.' This habit has wrought much misery, especially within the palace. Dreadful tragedies, that we shall behold by and by, are often involved in the entanglements of the secondary wife. Confucius's own word was, 'One man and one woman.' Here are some notes on marriage, quoted from the Shanghai journal, that will give the reader a general idea of Korea's point of view:[9]

If there is any matter in which a Korean's spirit comes to a state of white heat, it is marriage. He is a born match-maker, a born marrier. He will have who married to whom, finished and done, before the sun goes down.

What money is to a son of the west, marriage is to the Korean; every man is after it. I have tried long and hard to see the full bearing of the marriage question upon the race, but I feel that as yet I know little of its mystery. The Korean's ideas are not ours. He never, never associates with marriage such a line as 'Kiss me softly and speak to me low.' Theoretically he says, 'Let me be married in the spring when the plum blossoms greet me, and when the peach flowers and apricots tint the hill-side;' but he never thinks of his bride as his peach- or plum-blossom. Spring is the mating season and he would mate. He wants to be married, not for selfish pleasure, nor because a little sugar-coated heart longs to rest in his love and be looked after. Not a bit of it: he wants a son, a son of his very own. He wants him wildly, unreasonably; anything for a son. Wife and love and poetry and domestic joy are unseen in this scramble for the *summum bonum* gift of the gods: a son.

In the choice of bride, the old elements are still consulted;[10] metal, wood, water, fire, earth. Everybody has his fixed element, according to the day, month, hour and year in which he was born. A girl marked 'metal' is crossed off when a 'wood' boy is in question. A 'fire' girl and a 'water' boy mated would mean fuss and steam and sizzle, while a 'wood' girl and a 'water' boy would fall within the encompassing sphere of good luck. Also an 'earth' girl and a 'metal' man might walk hand in hand and be partakers of conjugal bliss and never-ending posterity. A foreigner would go crazy under the restraining spell of it, while the Korean, delighted, has kept it up for three thousand years.

When the lots are cast and the elements are sufficiently juggled with, and the girl made fast, and the day settled, with its heaps of sewing and stitching done, the wedding takes place. The bride rides in a tiger-bedecked chair, and the bridegroom on the back of a prancing palfrey. They meet, (not easily, but in the stiff posturing manner of the East) drink, bow, are married. She swims in all the colours of the summer sunset, but never smiles, never. Her face is painted and pipeclayed, and her eyes are sealed shut. The groom is in the garb of a courtier of the king, but he looks scared and unmagnificent. They are married and live happily ever after. This is the only real marriage. Second, third, and fourth marriages are makeshifts, and but a shadow of the genuine thing.

The symbol of marriage that has come down from pre-Confucian days is the goose—a most proper bird: faithful, modest, wise, knowing the seasons. If a live goose cannot be obtained, a wooden goose will do. She suggests conjugal fidelity, which her image or likeness can do as well. I am accustomed to the live bird, however. The sage old goose will sit through a marriage ceremony today just as complacent as though she had been married a hundred times herself. All the onlookers know that in her heart of hearts she says: 'One husband only for me.'

The goose is the friend of all true lovers, of all forsaken wives. Thus they sing this very old song:[11]

> You clanging wildgoose of the night,
> Whither away? List for a moment, please!
> My master is in Seoul. Halt will you, pray,
> And say to him: 'Just as the moon goes down
> I feel your loss so great, my spirit dies.'
> 'I have a deal to see to,' says the goose,
> 'Am pressed for time. Whether I'll manage it or not. . .'

5 Customs of Chou and Ch'in

ANOTHER marked impress of Chou upon the people of Korea is their respect for the aged. As this is a most important tenet in their code of morals I mention it with some degree of care. Their way of expressing it can be most unusual. It cost a man something to be a filial son in the old days, as one who reads their history can readily see. In one group of devoted children mentioned in the *Yŏji Sŭngnam*[1] in connection with Seoul, I find that out of sixteen, five took a sharp knife and cut flesh from the lower limb with which to feed the revered father or mother who was doomed to die, with the result that the parent lived and flourished. Five cut off one joint of the third finger and used the drops of blood as an elixir of life, with marvellous results. Three made pictures of the deceased, hung them up on the walls and bowed daily for years before them, offering food and saying prayers. Two fasted and mourned through all the desolate years of sackcloth and ashes. Two built huts by the grave-side and cut themselves off from the world of the living to devote themselves entirely to the dead. One closed his lips to all passers and wept tears of blood, we are told.

While the influences and tendencies of the present day are directly against any special regard for parents or the aged, still deeply engraven on the Korean's soul is this religious tenet that has come down from Chou and the earlier ages of China. As comely as the precious ointment on Aaron's beard it is to see a family of thirty or forty stand at attention in the presence of father and mother, who are seated. Their one thought and object is respect and attention to the revered pair.

EXORCISM, a method said to be effective in devil expulsion, was practised by Chou and handed down to future generations. Korea inherited it, and has held to it faithfully through all these ages. Is a man possessed of an evil spirit? Let a séance of witches and sorcerers with tom-toms be called and have the demon expelled by a regularly ordered set of exercises and prayers. These so-called demons, allied to ghosts and spirits of the dead, have had a tremendous hold upon the people of Korea. They are said to be visible at times, their voices heard: shrill pipings, whistlings, wailings. There are haunted houses, demon-bestricken families, with individuals chased through years of miserable existence. These evils have doubtless been greatly enhanced by the fact that professionals were waiting near at hand to collect a fee and set the victim at liberty. Epidemics, like cholera and typhus, were so understood, and the witch and sorcerer were called in rather than the doctor. The weird world of witchcraft comes down like so many other habits and beliefs from the hoary days of Confucius.

Here is an illustrative case that will be accounted a mere ghost story by the westerner but true in every particular by the oriental.[2]

Yi Hangbok (AD 1556–1618) was for a time prime minister of Korea and is known as one of her great national leaders. In ability and uprightness of character he ranks with the highest. When young he had many friends among the gentry, one of whom had been ill for a long time. The friend's father was greatly distressed, as there seemed no hope of his recovery. The best physicians and fortune-tellers alike were helpless in his case. One day hearing of a blind sorcerer who had come by, a man specially skilled in casting lots and foretelling the future, the father had him called.

'Cast your lot now,' said he, 'and tell me about my son. Will he live, or will he die?'

The sorcerer shook his box, repeating a prayer meanwhile, and then finally threw and said, 'Alas, bad luck! He will die this year, in such a moon, on such a day, at such an hour.'

The father, in tears, exclaimed, 'Can't you do something for him? Save him, I beg of you.'

The sorcerer then shrugged his shoulders and said, 'There is only one way. I could tell you, but it would cost a life.'

'Help me, please!' cried the father.

'Help?' exclaimed the sorcerer, 'You would have others die, would you?'

'No! No!'

Just then out of the kitchen bounded a buxom young woman with knife in hand. 'I am the sick man's wife,' said she; 'had you not told us, we should never have known, but now that you admit that there is a way to save him, I am determined to have it. I demand that you tell us fully, otherwise I shall drive this knife into you and then run it through my own neck.'

The sorcerer, alarmed, thought for a moment and said, 'What the ancients remarked concerning unguarded speech is true. Swifter than galloping horses does it overtake you.' He then added, 'There is a man in the city named Yi Hangbok; have him come at once and remain with your son till such and such a time. If you do this he will live; but I myself shall be called upon to die. Please look after my wife and family when I am gone.'

He then took his departure and Yi Hangbok was called. The father told his story and Yi consented to remain.

On the night mentioned by the sorcerer he was sleeping at the side of the sick man, when suddenly, about the third watch, there came an eerie cry and a wild burst of wind. Yi suddenly awoke and lo, a spirit stood with drawn sword just before the door. He called, 'Yi Hangbok! Give that sick man over to me.'

'Why, pray?' asked Yi.

The spirit answered, 'He and I were enemies in a former existence, and now the time has come for me to square accounts. Hand him over at once.'

'Never,' said Yi. 'The master of this house has put his son in my charge and I shall die rather than give him up.'

'Then die,' said the spirit as he rushed on Yi with uplifted sword; but thrice he bounded back. Then he threw down his sword and bowing humbly said, 'Please, Your Excellency, take pity on my case and hand me over this young man.'

Hangbok asked, 'Why do you not kill me instead?'

The spirit answered, 'I dare not; you are an upright man whose name will be recorded in history. You will live as a pillar of the state.' The spirit then gave a bitter cry, 'Alas, I shall never again have a chance to take vengeance. You were warned by a certain sorcerer who lives in such and such a village. I shall certainly settle accounts with him!'

He then picked up his sword and was gone. The sick man at once passed out of his swoon. They gave him warm water to drink and in a little he awoke to consciousness.

On the following day word came that the blind sorcerer had died that night and so the father at once took his family under his care.

This is a sample of a kind of story attached to the ghostly world of demons and hobgoblins, not common in the west, but very common indeed in Korea.

FROM THE CHOU Kingdom also came the old custom of burial with the dead. Nine centuries before the Christian era it was practised in China. In the third section of the Book of Songs we read:[3]

The orioles call us from the darkened grove.
King Mu is dead, who dares to follow him?
Prince Tzŭ-chü, summoned thus to die, responds,
The greatest of us all.
Into the hollow grot he takes his way,
Fear on his face, and trembling in his soul.
Oh, thou great God, why hast thou ta'en our best,
To win back whom we'd give a hundred common men?

Today by special permit we are admitted to these chambers of the dead, decorated with symbolic paintings, a marvel to see.[4] Little comfort, however, would the paintings give to the imprisoned hearts who sat down by the coffin to await their own grim dissolution.

The custom of burying the living with the dead was begun in Ch'in, a subordinate state that occupied the west of China, where Szechwan now is. Korea picked up the evil practice as a rite sanctioned by imperial usage, and continued it till AD 502. We are told that the usual order was to have five young couples given up to join the dead in the darkened chamber. At the time when the Delphic Oracle was set up and young women were being sacrificed at the foot of Mount Parnassus to meet the requirements of the superstition of the day, ancient Korea was putting her fairest underground to please the spirits of the dead.

The *Arabian Nights*, in the Fourth Voyage of Sindbad, makes the burial of the living the theme of its story. Before Sindbad knew that he himself was to fall a victim to its frenzy, he remonstrated with the king saying, 'O King, I cannot express my astonishment at the strange custom which exists in your domains of interring the living with the dead.' Rumors of China and Korea, where this custom had existed for over a thousand years, had evidently made their way across the continent to far distant Arabia, and were now being told as something to make the hair stand on end.

THE CHOU kingdom fell into decay and disappeared, and the Ch'in kingdom, which had originally been a subject state modestly confined to the four corners of Szechwan, now arose in might and occupied all China. The only thing that Ch'in had been noted for heretofore was the burial of the living; now she was master of the 'whole world', and although her dynasty continued for only about thirty years she was to be remembered for all time. The great founder was Shih Huang-ti, Emperor Number One. It was the first time that the name Emperor, *huang-ti,* had ever been used in the Far East. He made his capital in Hsien-yang, the modern Sian (to which the Empress Dowager fled in 1901, a city that lies about a hundred miles west of the elbow of the Yellow River) and reigned from 246 to 210 BC. Here he built his famous palace, the A-fang-kung, 'five hundred paces by the front and fifty paces to the rear, with upper-story audience-hall that would seat ten thousand people'.[5] All the rich of the earth gathered about him and his glory seemed unbounded.

On the other side of the earth Greece was closing her long history when Shih Huang-ti awoke to fame and fortune. His great fear was the Hsiung-nu or Huns, toward the north. Not only were they a fear to China and the people of Korea, but they became a fear to the Far West as well, so that seven hundred years afterwards the Hun Attila, 'the scourge of God', was to ravage France and spread terror across the whole of Europe.[6] Shih Huang-ti, not liking the looks of this people, decided to build the Great Wall. It was the year 215 BC when he sent an army of three hundred thousand men to beat back the Hun, while Meng T'ien, his special aide, undertook the building of the wall. He asked the Koreans to lend a hand, which, out of fear, they did. So they had a part in this colossal under-taking. To stand on the hills behind Shanhaikuan and see the mass of masonry winding down into the Yellow Sea is impressive enough; but when you remember that 1,500 miles of it lie behind you over mountain and plain alike, you feel that it is more than the mind can grasp.

About the same time, in Europe (or was it three years earlier?)[7] Hannibal the Carthaginian was determined to get into Italy and so faced the greater wall of the Alps—not twenty feet high, but seven thousand feet at the pass of St Bernard, which he crossed. He brought an army of 26,000 men safely over: horses, elephants, and uncountable impedimenta. Shih Huang-ti, or as Koreans call him, Chin Sihwang, did not know that just round the shoulder of the north-ern hemisphere was a mighty warrior, mightier than he, before whose achieve-ments he would have stood aghast, a warrior who would have kicked his wall aside as a wisp of tangle and shaken his empire from end to end: they were con-temporaries, the first emperor of China and Hannibal the Carthaginian.

6 The Han dynasty and its Korean colonies

THE emperor who built the Great Wall was determined on one thing, and that was to be absolute. He would brook no opposition from any quarter, and when the literati rose to question his abolition of feudalism and other sweeping changes, he turned on them in blazing fury and issued an immediate order for their destruction. Not only so, but seeing the sacred books of China were the vademecum of the scholar, he determined to burn them all as well. Throughout the length and breadth of the land this order was carried out, but it availed as little to destroy them as did the burning of Tyndale's bible by Henry VIII. In the stampede to escape the labours of the Great Wall and the fate of the scholar class, numbers of Chinese made their way to Korea and set up what was called the state of Chinhan, the foundation of later Silla. This was China's second contribution to the racial stock of the peninsula.[1]

Though only the Great Wall remains today as a monument to the memory of Emperor Number One, or Shih Huang-ti, we know that he was a lover of architecture, for his palace and the wonders of it are a story-book for the ages. He also planted great blocks of granite by the highways, here and there, on the face of each of which was written an account of his famous deeds and high renown. This custom Korea has faithfully followed, so that today we have biographies dotting the land from north to south, books always open, that defy the rough hand of wind and weather for a thousand years.

Shih Huang-ti turned his attention to useful lines as well: paper, the brushpen, and other things. Like Napoleon he did much for his age and his people, and yet today his name is anathema. He was not a pure Chinese to begin with, but had a strain of savage blood in his make-up, and this Korea never can tolerate. His violent hand, too, on the scholars, the wise men of the East, she has never forgiven. Unwept, unmourned, his state fell in a few years, and crowds still go by today contemptuous of all his greatness, wagging their heads. He is called, by way of *plaisanterie,* ch'ŏnha hosi (World-wide Tiger).[2]

Every little Korean lad learns off by heart the history of this far-away period. On one occasion on a walk to a temple seven miles east of Seoul, I had with me Mr Kim, an accomplished scholar,[3] and proposed that he tell me what befell the Far East between the fall of Ch'in in 206 BC and the setting up of Han in 202. He was delighted to unroll before my awakened imagination the famous story of these four years BC that he had drunk in with his boyhood breath and knew far better than any event in his own national history.[4]

THE GREAT Shih Huang-ti had included in his sway all China from Peking to Canton, from the east coast as far west as the old kingdom of Shu, Chengtu. On his fall there succeeded these four years of anarchy with no emperor at the head, but many mighty chieftains fighting for the crown. It is known as the War between Ch'u and Han. It is interesting to note that on the Korean chessboard, but not on the Chinese, one king is marked Han and one king Ch'u.[5] Every game of Korean chess, therefore, calls back the memory of two thousand years ago. On the side of Ch'u was Hsiang Yü; on that of Han, Liu Pang. They hailed from the border-line between the provinces of Shantung and Kiangsu, near the old city of Suchow. Each made a dash for Hsien-yang, determined to be the first to win the capital. Liu Pang won. Hsiang Yü, a great and mighty warrior, showed matchless skill. In one encounter he captured Liu Pang's father and wife, but, instead of treating them as enemies, showed them all kindness. Like the knights of the Middle Ages he was a gallant soldier, who could treat his enemy with distinguished courtesy; or, on the other hand, could slaughter till the hills ran blood. No such general as Hsiang Yü has ever since appeared. He was defeated by cunning rather than by the spirit of the warrior. The final upshot of the struggle was that his forces were shattered, and, fearing lest he fall into the hands of his rival, he took his own life when crossing the Yangtze some thirty miles south of Nanking. As he was dying he told his general to have his head cut off and carried to Liu Pang: 'He will reward you well.'

How often little Korean boys have swelled out their chests and deepened their voice-notes in order to be like Hsiang Yü. Even the maiden all-forlorn sings of him and China's other heroes thus:[6]

> Outside the window wends the tinker-man,
> Who fixes pots and pans. But can he fix a broken heart?
> The tinker answers, 'Even Hsiang Yü of the Han,
> Who lifted hills and tossed them o'er the land,
> Could not do that; and Chu-ko Liang himself,
> For wisdom famed, who read both earth and sky,
> Not even he could mend a broken heart.
> How much the less a creature such as I.
> Don't ask me, please.

Liu Pang then ascended the throne as Kao Tsu, Founder of Han,[7] and made the old city of Hsien-yang, where Shih Huang-ti had ruled, his capital. He changed its name to Ch'ang-an, 'eternal peace'. Remarkable to relate, Koreans till this day call their own capital 'Changan' after this ancient Chinese city. Such expressions as, 'All the people of Changan are up in arms,' simply mean Seoul is in an uproar. Every footstep of China's pathway during this period is marked on the milestones of Korea's memory.

Just as Han came into being, Rome began universal sway; and just as Kao Tsu mounted the throne, the last remnants of Alexander's kingdom disappeared; Carthage, too, was wiped from the map. Rome became dimly known to the Far East, and was called Great Ch'in, the same character *ch'in* as was used by the builder of the wall.[8] Evidently the Chinese had been impressed with the wide extent of the Roman Empire to accord it such a name.

Kao Tsu was no sooner seated in his rule and had re-established the old feudal order, than the ancient enemy of Shih Huang-ti, the Huns, scaling the Barrier, appeared on the north border and threatened China's existence. Their leader's name was Mao Tun, who is said to have had in his train a million bowmen. Han Kao Tsu moved out with lofty indignation to meet the invader, confident that his trained cohorts would soon scatter these wild creatures from Lake Baikal and beyond. Matters turned out quite differently from his expectations, however, for he was outgeneralled and besieged in the city of P'ing-ch'eng for a whole week. Only through bribes, and by taking advantage of a dense fog, did he make good his escape.[9] Never again did he get into military entanglements with the Hun.

Kao Tsu had a dreadful woman for wife, called Lü Hou (the Empress Lü), who set the pace for all the savage dowagers and fierce queens of later ages. Her treatment of Lady Ch'i, one of her husband's concubines, was much like that of the Old Buddha of Boxer days, who, when the soft and gentle princess took to whimpering, had her promptly chucked into the well. This Lü Hou made Kao Tsu famous among Koreans and today they shiver at the sound of her name. She is the terror of all womankind, while poor Lady Ch'i who, with hands cut off and eyes put out, was cast upon the dunghill, is the acme of all that is pitiful.[10]

ABOUT this time (194 BC) a north Chinese by the name of Wei Man, who had run counter to the mind of Kao Tsu and had to make good his escape, came with a large following to Korea and settled in P'yŏngyang. He first offered his soldiers as a bodyguard, and then, by an act of treachery, turned and took possession of the throne.[11]

The king, who was called Mugang, made his escape, went south to Iksan and set up a kingdom called Mahan. Deserters from the Great Wall set up Chinhan on the east; fugitives from P'yŏngyang set up Mahan on the west, while Pyŏnhan, which came into being at about the same time, occupied the extreme south. These were the Three Hans, or 'Samhan', a name which came to mean 'Korea'.[12]

A remarkable accompaniment of the arrival of Wei Man was the topknot.[13] Koreans, therefore, have worn this peculiar form of head-dress faithfully for over two thousand years and still wear it in spite of all the twentieth century's newer and more attractive notions. It was originally the mark of the young man's coming of age, and the first making up of it constituted one of the four domestic ceremonies, the others being marriage, mourning, and ancestral sacrifice. A band was tied round the head to keep the hair in place, the strings that laced it being fastened to the root of the topknot. Behind the headband were two ring-shaped buttons, one on each side, that served for the lace strings to pass through. These buttons, made of horn, tortoise-shell, gold or jade, indicated the standing of the person who wore them.

One of my valued friends is a christian gentleman of high rank, a scholar of the old school whom the reader would be delighted to know. His father, a cousin of a former king, was informed in 1894 that an order had been issued to abolish the topknot. As a lad this young prince had been taught to count every hair of his head as precious, a link that bound him to his father and mother, and here was the topknot, a symbol of the past, a proof that he still held to the ways of the ancients, being ordered off at one fell swoop. Never would he do it: so he turned him home, set his house in order, called his children, bade them a dignified farewell and then quietly, by a sharp steel knife, departed this life. The topknot brought by Wei Man in 194 BC meant that much to him.[14]

AMONG the famous emperors of the Han Dynasty was Wu-ti who reigned from 140 BC. He greatly extended the borders of his empire and reached across till his long arm embraced Korea as well. He was a great scholar, a great soldier, a man of wondrous imagination. One of the dreams of his life was to become

117

immortal and never die. He drank of the dew of the fairies and gave himself up to the teachings of taoism. It is seriously told that the Western Queen Mother (spoken of in chapter 3), who was visited by King Wu of Chou in 1000 BC, hearing of this great king and his earnest search for immortality, sent her pigeons with a message to say that she was coming, and later dropped down from the clouds with all her fairy retinue and visited him in his capital, Ch'ang-an.

ALTHOUGH women are supposed to hold a very subordinate place in the Far East, they really occupy a very large space in its world. The Hsiung-nu were a constant menace during all this dynasty. It seems as though the Great Wall simply whetted their appetite for conquest and pointed them to unlimited plunder beneath its southern shadow. Over the wall they came again and again till the Han emperors were driven almost to distraction. Once, about the time Caesar was guiding his craft toward the shores of England, a great army of these barbarians swooped down on Ch'ang-an, and when the emperor, unprepared to fight it out, asked for terms, the Hun said, 'Give me the most beautiful of all your palace maids.' As it turned out, the Princess Wang Chao-chün was sacrificed to save the state. She is pictured riding a camel out through the gates of her fair city and disappearing into the mists and shadows of the Gobi Desert. She was guided by her tawny Tatar master, not into a desert of oblivion, but into world-renowned immortality. Some say she plunged in as she crossed the Amur River and so ended her misery; others, that she lived long and shed many tears, exiled in the home of her captor. Sir John Davis, Governor of Hongkong, in 1844 translated the story of Chao-chün from a Chinese drama called 'The Sorrows of Han'. Dead two thousand years, but still alive today in Korean song and story, she is the representative of all beautiful women who are born to tears and sacrifice.[15]

IN the year 108 BC Han took note that Korea had paid no tribute for eighty-six years, and so sent an envoy, She Ho, to P'yŏngyang to make inquiry. The king, a descendant of Wei Man, instead of treating him with the respect due, turned upon him and had him killed. Han then sent an army which so overawed the ministers of Korea that they murdered their king and surrendered unconditionally. Thus north Korea became a part of the great kingdom of Han, and was divided into four provinces: Lo-lang, Chen-fan, Lin-t'un, and Hsüan-t'u.[16]

In the year 1913 the Government-General, under the direction of Dr Sekino,[17] discovered the site of the ancient capital of Lo-lang, just across the Taedong River immediately south of P'yŏngyang City. Here were found many tombs, lofty chambers and high brick walls. The interstices between the bricks were, in many cases, filled with ancient tiles and pottery that point to the kingdoms of Han and Wei, while from the tombs there came forth many articles of a long-forgotten age: swords, mirrors, finger-rings, jars, pots, braziers. Studying these old remains we can guess what kind of people the Koreans were in those days of a hundred years before Christ. Judging from one tomb, fourteen feet high in the middle, with an anteroom of nine feet by six and an inner room of nine by ten, built of brick so substantially and well that it has outlasted two thousand years, they were assuredly great lords and kings in those days as compared with us ancient Britons who lived in the spheres of nakedness and painted noses.[18] A great splendid chamber was this tomb. In it, too, were many evidences of a high civilization. Those broken bits of tile tell of lofty halls and high palaces. The spears and swords mark the owners as warriors; the money, as traders. A decorated cross-bow found on one side, and many ornaments of gold give proof of an advanced culture.

Finally, amid these wonders that come forth to speak to us of the past, there is a mirror nine inches in diameter that has on the circle of its back two inscriptions. One reads, 'Something eternal for my posterity'. Who made it, I wonder? Little did he think that it would outlive all his children's children and last through millenniums to come. 'Something eternal for my posterity' is an inscription mentioned in the *Chung-ting kuang-chih*, (a book that gathers up the sayings of China found on pottery, household utensils, and such like), where it is noted as pertaining to the kingdom of Han.[19] A second inscription on the back in the outer circle reads, 'May your life be eternal as the hills, beautiful and good'. What fair lady trimmed her glossy locks by its shining face we can never know, but the wish of the maker for his mirror has indeed come true. This mirror of Lo-lang may be seen in the Industrial School, Tokyo, a model of beautiful workmanship for all time.[20]

This old site of Lo-lang's capital, that flourished in the days when King Jugurtha was being led in triumph through the streets of Rome, is one of the landmarks of East Asia.

THE THREE KINGDOMS

7 Foundation myths: Koguryŏ and Silla

WE come now to the setting up of the three kingdoms that occupied the peninsula of Korea for six hundred years. They begin in the world of myth and then gradually emerge into that of fact. Thus have they come stepping down to us from historian to historian and from one story-teller to another.

The oriental knows that the place of the myth in human experience is by no means to be ignored. It is often more powerful even than fact itself, for myth belongs to the region of the imagination, which has always been the power-house behind the brain. Probably the lower animals are without imagination and so have no fairy tales to accompany them; while man, blessed beyond measure, has at hand worlds they have never dreamed of. Out of these comes forth the myth, which, though nothing in itself, leaves its footprints on time and rock alike, to be wondered over by future generations.

For example, the imagination sees the maiden Helle holding on for dear life to the ram with the golden fleece as it speeds on its way through mid-air from Greece to Colchis. We behold her, as the Dardanelles yawn beneath, turn pale, grow dizzy, and then swoon off its back and go hurtling down into the grim swirling deep which is ever after called by her name Helle's Sea, Hellespont.

Likewise we behold Io, daughter of Inachus, changed into a little cow. The greatest gadfly of history comes to bite her and she kicks and runs for life. The fly, however, not discouraged, tightens his grip, while her wild escape takes her right over the site of Constantinople and with a sky-leap lands her in Asia. The strait is ever after called Little Bossy's Crossing, the Bosporus. Hard facts lie all about us dead, while myths live on and flourish.[1]

THE THREE KINGDOMS were called Koguryŏ, Silla and Paekche, and our knowledge of them begins with Kim Pusik who wrote the *History of the Three Kingdoms* in AD 1145.[2] He was a contemporary of St Bernard and the First Crusade, and was himself a religious man and a very great warrior. He saw also famous days in China, the Sung dynasty, where lived such scholars as Su Tung-p'o and the hazy political leader, Wang An-shih, who well-nigh brought the state to ruin. Kim was a man seven feet high, we are told, and when girt with the accoutrements of a great general must have been an imposing figure. He so won the confidence of his king that he received this commission: 'I make you', said his Majesty, 'dictator of all things outside the palace gates. Reward the good, punish the evil, and safely guard my people.'[3]

Kim wrote much. He wrote the king's prayers to the buddha, he wrote many poems, and among other things a little essay on 'The Cock that Failed to Crow' in which, with a touch of humour, he speaks his appreciation of 'every man to his duty'.[4]

The closing year speeds on:
Long nights and shorter days, they weary me.
'Tis not a lack of candle-light forbids me read,
But that I'm ill, my soul distressed.
I toss about for sleep that fails to come;
A hundred thoughts whirl tangled through my brain.
The cock-bird sits all silent on his perch.
Soon he will surely flap his wings and crow.
I toss the quilts aside and sit me up
And through the window chink come rays of light.
Wide out I swing the door and look abroad.
And there off to the west, the night stars shine.
I call my boy, 'Wake up! What ails that cock
That does not crow? Is he alive or dead?
Has someone thrawed his neck,
Or has a weasel-bandit done him ill?
Why are his eyes tight shut and head held low
With not a sound forthcoming from his bill?
In the 'Kuo-feng' book she thinks upon her lord
And says they crow though winds and rain cease not;[5]
This is the cockcrow hour and yet he sleeps.
Is he not breaking God's most primal law?
The dog who fails to see the thief and bark,
The cat who lets the rat go by, deserve
The direst punishment. Yes, death itself
Would not be too severe. Still, good men have
A word to say; love speaks, I dare not kill.
I'm moved to let you live. Beware, however,
And show repentance.

ACCORDING to Kim's account in his *Three kingdoms*[6] we read that a little state called Puyǒ lying north of the Yalu and the Ever-white Mountains had for king a man called Haeburu. No son had been born to him and this had been the burden of his woe. He went here and there offering sacrifice to hill and stream in a vain search for posterity. One day on this mission he passed a standing stone that looked appealingly at him while tears streamed down its gnarled face. Calling some of his retinue he had them overturn it. Lo, from beneath came forth a little boy, yellow as gold and plump as a rounded tadpole. The king, delighted, said, 'How happy! God has given me a little son'; and he called him Kŭmwa, 'Golden Froggie'. As the lad grew up he became the king's heir, and sunshine beamed on life.

About this time a minister named Aranbul received a divine message ordering the state at once, king and commoner, to move further east. Heaven had other plans for their future home. The king, persuaded, moved east and found a people already established who said that their ruler was of the gods, a divine being called

Haemosu, but that he had recently disappeared. Here Haeburu pitched his camp.

A little later when he died he made Kŭmwa his successor. Kŭmwa, out once on a tour of inspection, found a desolate woman wandering on the south slopes of the Ever-white Mountain. On his inquiry she gave her name as Yuhwa. 'I am a daughter of the river-god,' said she. 'Once when my sisters and I were off on an outing enjoying the freedom of the hills, a man suddenly appeared who announced himself as Haemosu, son of Heaven. He caught and carried me off to the Ungsim Mountains by the Yalu River where he compelled me to be his wife. He then disappeared and has never since been seen. My parents, shocked at my taking a husband without the proper forms, sent me off here into exile where I now am.'

Kŭmwa, hearing this, was greatly astonished, and taking her home locked her up in an inner room. The sun shot through the plated walls of her chamber like an X-ray and when she shrank from it the rays followed till they struck her squarely. She conceived and bore, not a son, but an egg as large as a market measure. The king, regarding it as uncanny, threw it out to the pigs but they refused to touch it; the dogs likewise. He left it on the highway to be trampled into the dust but both horse and bullock stepped over it with the greatest care. He left it in the fields and the birds came down and softly covered it with their wings. All creatures had apparently joined hands in its protection. The king himself tried to open it by force with hammer and chisel, but failed. He then gave it back to the mother, who covered it and kept it warm till finally a little boy stepped forth to greet her. This little boy was to be the proud founder of Koguryŏ, a kingdom that would last six hundred years, whose footprints we measure today.

From seven years of age he was a wonderful archer, so they called him Chumong, much as we should say 'Robin Hood'. His elder brothers, less gifted, were jealous and did their best to work him ill. Finally their wrath was so overheated that they decided to kill him. His mother, hearing of it, ordered him to fly. With a few followers he rode south-west along a line running from Khabarovsk to Port Arthur, his brothers in hot pursuit. The time of testing his inner mettle had surely come. A river lay ahead, his well-mounted foes were behind, and nothing was left him but to lift his hands and pray. This he did, and we are told that the river god, hearing, called all his turtle tribes and fishes together in a great concourse that formed a bridge right along his way. He passed safely over, he and his followers, and the magic bridge melted away, leaving the enemy baffled and thunderstruck on the other shore.

It is difficult to pick up the route followed by Chumong so long ago, but the old site of his capital city, which Kim Pusik could not locate in 1145, has been searched out and confirmed today by the clever eye of the archaeologist. It lies just across the Yalu and a little below the mouth of the Kanggye River—the old site of Kungnae-sŏng. It was Koguryŏ's chief capital from 37 BC till AD 427, nearly five hundred years.[7]

Today as we walk along the shore approaching the region of the walled city from the north, we pass on our right a magnificent tomb, evidently built by hands such as fashioned the pyramids. It is a vast pile of huge granite blocks one hundred feet square and forty feet high, one layer above another in seven terraces, capped by a kind of concrete that surpasses all modern attempts to imitate it. Down through this valley, just as we find in Egypt across the Nile from Thebes, are grouped many tombs of kings. We know they were of the same kind as Tutankhamen's, for we find inscribed on the bricks that served in the building such expressions as this: 'May this tomb of the great king be unmolested and last as long as the eternal hills.' The inner walls have on them pictures of warriors riding in coats of mail, lance in hand. Symbolic figures, too, look down upon us: the dragon, the phoenix, the lotus flower, and wheels of fiery flame.

From these tombs to the actual site of the old city is about five miles, the road leading south-west parallel to the course of the river. About a quarter of the distance along the way there, we meet the most interesting monument that remains of ancient Korea, some twenty feet high and six feet across the face, erected in AD 414. We shall read its inscription later.[8]

Before reaching the site of the old city we meet a group of eleven tombs, only one of which we need notice. It is the Tomb of the Three Chambers, these being separated from each other and yet united by subterranean passages. This tomb is evidently one of the halls of the buried-alive, a grim chamber of the dead. Was Chumong buried here, I wonder—five couples with bright cheeks and high hopes pushed alive into this cavern to keep the dead king company, the door sealed fast with a flat rock and marked with a signet ring, ten thousand tons of granite roofing to close out the blue sky forever? Alas, it is a sad picture. Imagine the sensation of these gay young birds clipped of hope and wing, dying in the dark and shut away from the world for two thousand years. But this was the custom of the day.

Such is the old capital of Chumong that lies silent, no longer a part of Korea but belonging to China just over the river, about half way down from its source in the province of Fengtien.

Koguryǒ grew from this modest beginning to a very extensive state stretching from Vladivostok all the way to Port Arthur, and from the south of Kangwǒn Province nearly as far north as Changchun, Manchuria. It took in Mukden, Liaoyang and the intervening cities, and made Newchwang its western gateway. It had three capitals in its history: first, the one we have mentioned, Kungnae-sǒng; second, one that lay about forty miles SSW called Hwando; and finally the city of P'yǒngyang which it occupied continuously for about two hundred years before its fall in AD 668.[9]

SILLA was the smallest of the three, geographically, but the most important. She also came into being on the bat-like wings of a myth. A man by the name of Sǒbǒl, out on a journey, suddenly heard the wild neighing of a horse, and, turning aside, discovered not a horse but a great egg lying on the roadway. He broke it open and a child stepped forth, a child that grew up to be the first king and founder of Silla. His name was Pak Hyǒkkǒse, *pak* meaning gourd or egg.[10]

In regard to these myths Kwǒn Kǔn, a contemporary of Chaucer, says:

> When Confucius edited the Books of History and Songs he cut out all the mythical parts that lay before the days of Yao and Shun, because in

those elementary times the earth was untutored and every sort of wild story gained credence. From Yao and Shun down, however, these extravagances disappeared and a reasonable world came into being. Our history, beginning so recently, with the Han Kingdom of China, should have known better, but it too has similar absurdities to relate. Not only in regard to the founder of the state does it speak thus, but it has all sorts of queer things to say in regard to the Kim, the Ko, and the Pak clans. It was assuredly an age of ignorance, and any man gifted with a little more than ordinary sense was accounted a wonder. Hence came these absurd stories.[11]

We feel that Kwŏn's words are wisely and well spoken, and yet if we strip these early records of all myth and fable we shall leave them as uninteresting as a magpie bird after the 7th night of the 7th moon.[12]

Under the date 53 BC in the *History of the East Kingdom*[13] I find that a dragon came forth from the Aryŏng Well of Kyŏngju. As to what a Korean means by a dragon, that we can easily know. Pictures of the creature abound in the East as do signs for Mellin's Food and other products over all the fair landscapes of the West. He may be of the order of the fish or of the snake, but, in either case, he is a terrible monster with awful eyes, and fangs and claws indescribable.[14] And yet in the mind of the Korean he is the author of much good luck, a semi-spiritual creature that stands for right royal kingship. Out of the side of this dragon of the Aryŏng Well flew a little child. An old woman picked her up and cared for her, and she grew up to be good and beautiful, and was finally chosen as queen by the founder of Silla. She and her husband, the king, were called by the people the Two Holy Ones. So are they marked in history and so have their names come down till today.

In the year 50 BC the Japanese came in ships to make an attack, but learning that the king was a holy man and that true religion prevailed in his state they quietly withdrew.[15]

In the year 28 BC a band of raiders from Lo-lang made an incursion from the north but finding the gates of the city open and unguarded, supplies untouched, and all things in peace and order, they withdrew ashamed and said, 'These people do not steal. They are indeed the sons of true religion, while we are a band of thieves in comparison'. So they turned home.[16] Okcho, a semi-barbarous state that lay off toward Vladivostok, hearing that Silla was ruled by a holy man, sent a gift of horses to show its high esteem.[17]

We are told that the king went about the country with his queen, encouraging agriculture and sericulture. One can hardly picture a more perfect state than that described by the outline sketches of Silla that come down to us in Kim Pusik's book, and the *History of the East Kingdom* (*Tongguk t'onggam*). Two daughters were born to the palace, beautiful of face and expert in the weaving of linen. So famed were they that the capital, which at this time was called Kŭmsŏng, 'the Golden City', became their special field of labour. Each had a ward, one to the east and one to the west, where they taught the daughters of the people how to weave. From the middle of September to the middle of October this course of study went on. Then there was a comparing of their work and prizes were awarded to the victors at a great feast with songs and dancing which took place about 15 October, called Kabae-jŏl (*Kawi*), whose happy memory still lives today.[18] Silla was indeed the woman's kingdom, famous from the very first when the daughter of the dragon set so fair a pace. Kwŏn Kŭn, the gentleman who was born in AD 1352, remarking on the queen's accompanying the king on his journeys said: 'Very bad; much better for a woman to stay at home and mind the house'. She and her daughters, however, have left a name that even the matter-of-fact and rather crabbed Kwŏn Kŭn can in no way discredit.[19]

On the death of King Pak, founder of Silla, Lo-lang once more made an attack. The young king, Namhae, said to his ministers, 'The Holy Ones have departed this life and I have no strength with which to rule. An enemy is at our doors; what shall we do?' The ministers said, 'The enemy think to take advantage of our loss, but God will never bless them in this campaign.' Shortly after, the Lolangites turned and went away.

These proofs of religion are indeed very wonderful, seeing that as yet there was no buddhism in the land and very little knowledge of Confucius.[20] It would seem to have been a case where the inner conscience recognized God as the ruler of the world, and man, His creature, as one to worship and honour Him. I may add another note of the chronicler which says, 'In the year *kapjin* (19 BC) when the king was urged to invade Mahan and add it to his territory, he replied, "Not on your life. No such act is blessed of God!"'[21]

Very propitious were these opening days of Silla, which was to last as a kingdom from 58 BC to AD 918, nearly a thousand years. Few kingdoms without a break in the royal line ever lasted so long or marked their days by ten centuries of recorded time.[22]

8 Foundation myths: Paekche; early Koguryŏ, and Silla

AS Koguryŏ was the son of Puyŏ, so Paekche was born of Koguryŏ. When Chumong left Puyŏ in his hot escape from his brothers he had to part from his wife who, as time passed, bore a son called Yuri. True to the spirit of being against the man that is down, the East taunted the lad with having no father and so plagued his boyish footsteps that his soul within him was worn thin to desperation. Being a skilled archer like his father, he carried his bow, partly for pleasure and partly for self-defence. As he went by, a woman with a water-jar on her head treated him to a flick of her ill-guarded tongue, and in return he shot through the earthenware jar and sent the contents flying, neck and crop. She cursed him as only an angry woman can curse. In his state of woe he came to his mother for consolation.

'Why have I no father?' asked he.

'But you have,' was her reply.

'Where is he then?'

'A great king,' said she, 'to the south, where he rules a kingdom.'

'But,' said Yuri, 'may I not go and find him? Everyone here hates me.'

'I fear,' said his mother, 'that will not be possible, for your father left a solemn charge with me to say that his son must answer this riddle before he could see his face: *Beneath the pine that stands upon the cornered rock is hidden the proof by which I'll know my son.'*

Yuri heard this with intense interest and immediately began his search. He looked in vain through hill and valley for an answer, till finally he thought of looking under a pillar that stood on its stone base just in front of his room. There indeed was a broken blade that awaited his hand, which was to be his token in the kingdom of Cholbon-Puyŏ.[1] (This is not unlike the old Greek story of Theseus, the son of Aegeus, as told by Plutarch. Aegeus leaves Aethra with word that if a son is born he must find his father's shoes and sword hidden beneath the stone and bring them to Athens as proof that he is his very own.)

Yuri arrived at Kungnae City and was welcomed by his father. He was his firstborn and to him the throne should pass. In the meantime Chumong had married and had two other sons, Piryu and Onjo. Their hopes for a kingdom were thus dashed in pieces in a single day and they resolved on flight. New worlds must be found to conquer. As people wait nowadays for a real leader to appear, so the world waited for them. Chumong had found his waiting people, and Onjo and Piryu must find theirs. They crossed the Yalu and came south. The next we hear of them is that in the summer of 18 BC they stood on the top of Paegun-dae (Pukhan), and looked with longing eyes toward the south. Let all who climb this highest peak of the capital remember that as it looked in the year 18 BC, so it looks today. The rocks are perhaps worn a little smoother by the many feet that have made their fearful way up its polished face, but they are the same. How many a slip of step has sent its victim hurtling over the brow of the cliff a thousand feet to a shattering death below we know not, but doubtless Paegun-dae stands today just as it stood when Onjo and Piryu each sought a kingdom.

They descended from the peak and Piryu went toward Chemulp'o where he built his city wall, dimly outlined today. Onjo crossed the river and pitched his capital on the top of Namhan. Piryu was unsuccessful and soon died of a broken heart. Onjo, however, of finer metal, held on and called his state Paekche, which means 'a hundred cross over'.[2] Like the name Hebrew, that is supposed to have underlying it the root *'eber*, 'from beyond' (across the Euphrates), so these Paekche-ites were known as a race who had come from beyond — crossed the river.[3] Their first capital was at Namhan, and here they remained till the year 6 BC, when, having repeatedly been annoyed by the Malgal (a Tungusic race related to Pohai, Khitan, and other tribes of the north), they moved the capital to Pukhan.[4] It is interesting to note that in 4 BC, the year in which Christ is supposed to have been born, Pukhan had its first wall built and its palace erected.[5] The names Pukhan and Namhan seemingly take their rise from the times of Onjo.

Onjo finally possessed himself of the old kingdom of Mahan[6] that fell before him in the year AD 9. Mahan is marked in the ancient chronicles as beginning in the year 194 BC with its capital at Iksan and including about fifty counties of Chŏlla, Ch'ungch'ŏng and Kyŏngsang. Its first king was Kijun, who made his escape from P'yŏngyang when chased by the semi-barbarian Wei Man. Coming south by boat, he set up his capital at Iksan, on the hills about three miles north of the present prefectural town. There today we find fallen stones that faithful hands carried for Kijun two thousand years ago.[7]

We are told in Chinese records of Korea[8] that the people of Mahan cared little for silks or satins, but that they loved gems and precious stones; that they did up their hair on the top of the head and wore straw and leather shoes; that the huts they lived in were built partly underground with mud walls and thatch roof. As yet Korea had not learned to use the *ondol,* or fire beneath the floor.[9]

Accompanying this Oriental kingdom in its fall were, as usual, comets, meteors, fires in the sky, earthquakes, famines, thunderbolts. Thus Mahan meets her end and goes down under the iron heel of destiny. It is interesting to note that in this very year AD 9 Rome got her first shock and warning of the end to come, when Quintilius Varus and his three invincible legions were annihilated in the Teutoburg Forest by the German Arminius. Creasy[10] mentions that, accompanying the catastrophe, Rome saw the summits of the Alps fall, fires on the mountain tops, lightning strike the temple of the God of War, flame flashes glaring in the night, comets blazing forth, sharp spears crossing the sky and shooting their points toward the Roman camp. As the Mahanite read his doom in the heavens, so imperial Rome at that very same time read her own dread destiny.

For the first two hundred years, little or nothing but misery is recorded in the annals of Paekche. In contrast to Silla, she was the unblessed state. Nothing is seen in the way of intelligent religion, nothing in the way of spiritual comfort. In 18 BC she builds a shrine to Onjo's father, King Chumong the first king of Koguryŏ, and there she offers sacrifice;[11] but apart from this no religion is evident. In these two hundred years are recorded six earthquakes, the first in AD 13 and the last in 199.[12] There were as well six great droughts, famines and pestilences. In the years AD 15 and 108 people killed and ate each other, a terrible story to be read in outline on the pages of Kim Pusik.[13]

KOGURYŎ, meanwhile, moves on her way. Yuri, who, like Theseus of Athens, had found his father, came to the throne in 19 BC. He married a daughter of the Marquis of Tamul,[14] who was chieftain of the Piryu tribes before Chumong came. She died the next year and Yuri unwisely took two wives, one a Korean from the Falcon River,[15] and the other a Chinese lady from the superior kingdom of Han. They quarrelled over the question of the king's love, these two; and his Majesty, to keep peace in the family, built them separate palaces, one to the east and the other to the west. The king, as was his wont, went on a hunting tour and remained seven days. The two queens in the meantime crossed the intervening space between the east and the west and had it out. She from the Falcon River, physically stronger than her associate, berated her soundly, calling her a foreigner, with the added words that she possessed an impudence beyond compare. Ashamed and humiliated, the proud daughter of Han left at once. When the king returned he found that she had gone. He followed hard after and overtook her, but she refused all explanation, all persuasion, all protestations of love, and bade her fond lover a last farewell. Yuri, desolate, returned on his way, and as he sat resting beneath a tree he saw a pair of orioles delighting in each other's company. This awakened in his soul a little song, dated 17 BC, the oldest piece of Korean composition extant:

Oh lilting, joyous yellow bird!
    You mate to live, and love each other;
While I, alas, unloved, unheard,
    Have lost my everything, sweet brother.

The great warrior and historian, Kim Pusik, has taken the trouble to tell of this domestic infelicity.[16] The West has many ideas regarding the sex questions of the East, imagining that we and they are worlds apart. Outward manifestations would seem to confirm this idea, but deep down in the heart feelings and emotions run about the same.

While Paekche shows a conspicuous lack of religious life, Koguryŏ strikes one as being religious but peculiar. At the point where we cross from BC to AD, that very year, the king was offering a sacrifice to Heaven—a pig. The animal, stricken with fear, made its escape and two officers, T'angni and Sabi, were sent in hot haste to recover it. They finally overtook it at Changok Lake, and, in order that it might not repeat the offence, had it hamstrung. When the king saw the wounded animal brought back, he was very angry and said, 'How dare you mutilate a sacrifice to be offered to God?' With that he commanded these two offenders to be destroyed—buried alive. Shortly afterwards, the king fell ill and a witch-woman was summoned to his side. 'What is the reason of my illness?' he asked. Her reply was; 'The spirits of the dead T'angni and Sabi are after you for your life.' He confessed to these dead souls that he had done very badly, and was at once forgiven and restored.[17]

Kwŏn Kŭn in the *History of the East Kingdom* remarks rather sarcastically:

> In the first place the Emperor of China alone could rightly offer sacrifice to God. A mere king of Koguryŏ had no business whatever to attempt such a thing. A humble mind and an honest effort in behalf of his people were the true kind of service he was called upon to render. Also, to kill two men for one pig shows how unenlightened and ill-guided he was.[18]

Other odd notes follow in the old chronicle. In AD 5 the king was out on a hunting expedition and met a man with a pair of wings growing from his armpits. He was known as Wing (U-ssi) and the king, interested in him, took him home and made him his son-in-law.[19] Another note, dated AD 8, says that Yuri had a son named Haemyŏng who was a great sportsman, a fine shot and as bold as a lion. A chieftain of the Yellow Dragon tribes, hearing of him, sent him a specially beautiful bow as a present. When the messenger brought it, Haemyŏng fitted the string and with one pull back to his ear drew the bow to splinters. His father was very angry at this act of disrespect and at once sent word to the Yellow Dragon Chieftain offering to hand his son over for execution. A messenger came requesting that he come. When one of his own officers warned him against the risk he ran, his answer was: 'Unless God means my death no Yellow Dragon tribesman can harm me.' He went and we are told that the Yellow Dragon chief was so overawed by his presence that he entirely changed his purpose and treated him with all courtesy.[20] Such notes may seem to have little historical value, yet they throw a measure of light upon the inner life of this ancient people.

During these first two hundred years of the christian era Koguryŏ greatly extended her borders. She completely conquered Lo-lang and added territory from Puyŏ on the north, thus gathering strength for her appointed destiny of six hundred years.

SILLA, launched on her way, moves much as the others.[21] Anxiety besets her from many quarters. Grasshoppers come, millions of them, and eat up all the crops. It is recorded that they appeared in the year AD 109 and the king, P'asa, who had been on the throne thirty years, went to the highest hilltop and made his prayer to God. We are told that the grasshoppers disappeared and plenty crowned the year.[22]

The year AD 28 records a unique happening. It reads:

> In the 11th moon the ruler of Silla while making a tour through his kingdom saw an old woman starving and freezing, ready to die. Said he, 'I am the basest of human kind, for I sit on a throne and at the same time allow my people young and old to come to such a dreadful pass as this.' He gave her food and clothing and, moved by her want, had his treasure-houses opened wide for the widow, the orphan, the sick, the suffering. Outside peoples, hearing of this, came in great numbers and settled in Silla. This was a year of special joy, for songs were first sung at public gatherings, and music and dancing accompanied the day.[23]

During the first four centuries of the nation's life the ruling family changed its name three times.[24] First it was Pak, then it became Sŏk, and finally Kim. Pak, as we have already noted, came forth from an egg or gourd, hence his name. As regards Sŏk T'arhae who ascended the throne in AD 57, we have the following story recorded by Kim Pusik. When T'arhae became king he was sixty-two years of age. His surname was Sŏk and he originally belonged to the land of Tap'ara that lies 300 miles north-east of Japan. His mother was a native of the Women's Kingdom. After seven years of married life, bird-like, she laid an egg. The king was displeased at this, regarding it as most uncanny. He ordered it to be thrown away, but the queen refused. Instead she wrapped it in silk, placed it in a box, and set it afloat on the deep blue sea.

It landed first off Kimhae, south Korea, but the people were afraid and pushed it back. It next appeared near Ajinp'o, where an old woman fished it out with hook and line, opened the box and found it contained a little child. She brought him up as her own son and he grew to be a giant, nine feet high, handsome and wise beyond his peers. A friend remarked at the time, 'We do not know the name of the child,' but when he landed the magpies flew about after him in great delight and made a wondrous uproar. 'Let's take the character for magpie,' said he, 'and strip it of the radical for *bird,* which will leave us the character *sŏk.* This will be his name. As he came out of a box, we'll call him *t'arhae*, 'drawn out', (or Moses).[25]

T'arhae became a fisherman and by this means cared for his mother. He was most diligent in all he undertook. His mother remarked, 'You are no ordinary person. Face and form mark you off from every other man. Make a name for yourself, I pray.' He gave his whole heart to the study of Chinese characters and to the mysteries of geomancy. In this connection he called attention to the site of Minister Hogong's house, which he said was replete with great good fortune. With this in mind he bought it, and in time made it the happy town of Wŏlsŏng.

King Namhae, in the fifth year of his reign, hearing of his great gifts gave T'arhae his daughter in marriage. In the seventh year he made him chief minister and entrusted him with full power of state. The throne was bequeathed him as well and he finally became king.

ANOTHER myth which marks not only a change of family name but that of the kingdom as well, pertains to Silla. It was in the year AD 65 that the king heard the crowing of a cock in the neighbouring forest. Cockcrowing is one of the characteristic sounds of this gentle nation. Practised through a long series of years, the Korean rooster is a perfect marvel as to crowing. Brass lungs with steam attachment can hardly express it. To have him break forth at 2 a.m. from the rafter point just over your cottage window, injects into your peaceful sleep a splitting sense of uproar beyond words. The king heard just such a sound as this, sat up to see, and then sent his minister Hogong to find out. A golden box was found hanging on a tree, while just beneath it a white rooster was announcing the fact to the whole world. The box was carried to the king, who opened it and found a beautiful cherub boy inside. 'The gift of Heaven,' said his grateful majesty. As he came out of a golden box, the boy's name became Kim ('gold'); and seeing that the rooster crowed beneath the tree, the state received the name of Kyerim or 'cock forest'.[26]

Kwŏn Kŭn (Chaucer's contemporary) adds this impatient note:

> The appointments of Heaven go forward in an orderly manner: things to grow, grow; things to die, die. How could a child ever find its birthplace in a golden box, and a rooster announce it to the world? Such nonsense! Bad men have made it all up in order to deceive the poor ignorant people and force them to associate marvels and miracles with kingship. It is one way, indeed, to rob a state and steal the throne.[27]

Very bad it is thus to tell a lie as some ancient Korean must have done, and yet how mild and gentle these little cherub boys and roosters seem when compared with the West and its doings on the other side of the world at this time. Nero, now on the throne of the great Roman Empire, must have excitement, you know, and must needs fill his days with well-rounded pleasure. To this end he poisoned his half-brother Britannicus, had his mother Agrippina quietly put to death, drove off his gentle wife Octavia (whom he later had beheaded), and then set on foot the first persecution of the christians. We of the Far West in those distant days wholly lacked the gentle spirit that ruled in the Kingdom of Silla.

9 Third-century Koguryŏ; the Chinese wars of the Three Kingdoms

THE gentle reader will now glance for a little through the mazes of the third century AD and see what part Korea took in the doings of the same. First of all I see scattered across its face about twenty Roman emperors dogged by murder, suicide, death in battle, deposition, assassination, and slavery. Koguryŏ, Silla and Paekche had each of them five kings during the same time and while a measure of human frailty and its attendant ills accompanied them, on the whole they enjoyed a large measure of quiet and lived out their little day better than did the Romans.

KOGURYŎ had grown to be a large kingdom with its centre on the Yalu, its doings being specially marked in the old chronicles. A king named Mountain-top,[1] who came to the throne in AD 197, had a variety of experiences that in the end reduced his name to great dishonour. His elder brother, called Kogukch'ŏn, had come to the throne in AD 179, having for partner a very masterful woman named U-ssi.[2] King Kogukch'ŏn had three brothers: Palgi, Yŏnu, and Kyesu.[3] One night in 197 the king died suddenly and U-ssi hurried to the home of Palgi. Startled at this unusual visit, Palgi exclaimed, 'What brings you here at this hour of the night?' Said she, 'The king, having no heir, is anxious about the succession. Come to the palace, I pray you, and let us consider it.' She did not tell him that the king was dead. He refused point-blank and told her to go, as he would have no hand in so grave a matter.

Indignant, she hurried away and went to see the second brother, Yŏnu. Said she, 'The king is dead and there is no one to take the throne. Palgi has insulted me. Come quickly to the palace and you shall be king.' Yŏnu responded and next morning the word rang out: 'The king is dead, long live the king!'

Palgi, surprised and startled, gathered a few soldiers and went to the palace. He called on his brother to come forth, but there was no answer. Finally, seeing his following melt away, he escaped to Liao-tung in South Manchuria, and there told his woes. Would they help him? The king of Liao, sympathetic, gave him troops, and so he marched on Kungnae-sŏng. Kyesu, the fourth brother, came out to meet him, and they had a battle in which the men of Liao were defeated. Palgi shouted in anger, 'You ought to be ashamed, thus to oppose your elder brother! What an evil heart you have!' Kyesu answered, 'Brother, I regret it all very much. Yŏnu should never have taken the throne from you, but you also have done badly in that you have brought an army of outsiders to destroy the inheritance of your fathers. What can equal that for downright evil?'

Palgi, hearing this stern rebuke from his little brother, was so overcome with shame that he hurried away to Paech'ŏn[4] where he cut his throat and died. Kyesu found the body, wept over it, and gave it honourable burial. Yŏnu, now King San-sang('Mountain-top'), called Kyesu and said, 'You let the wicked Palgi off without punishment and now you weep for him as though he were a saint, all of which proves that you condemn me.' When an Asiatic is thus spoken to by the king, be he brother or stranger, he gathers his robes about his knees and prepares to die. Kyesu, realizing this, said, 'One word, please, and then I surrender my life. Even though you took the throne by order of the queen, you can never be justified. You had an elder brother and should have kept the ancient faith of your fathers and stepped aside for him. To set matters right as nearly as possible, I had his dead remains brought here and in your name gave them honourable burial. Instead of being gratified, however, you are angry. I have nothing more to say, let me die.' The king, hearing this, arose at once and came to his brother. He knelt down and said, 'I have failed to do the good man's part and fear that I have lost your confidence for all time. Hearing what you have said, I realize how badly I have done. Do not blame me over-much.'

King Yŏnu made his widowed sister-in-law his wife, a very wicked act from an oriental point of view. Kwŏn Kŭn remarking on it said:

> This woman U-ssi was the wife of the late king. When he died she showed no sorrow, did not even let the fact be known, but with an evil mind went by night to Palgi's house and tried to inveigle him into her net. Palgi, not knowing that his brother was dead, sent her off with a refusal. If she had been at all human in heart she would have repented at this point, but she had no shame and went next to Yŏnu, and with him into the palace. Yŏnu, thinking only of his own gain, lost all sense of right and made her his wife. Such behaviour may be becoming in swine, but not in men. All the laws of heaven and earth were broken and morality cast to the winds. Such a man for king means, without doubt, destruction to the state.[5]

The year 203 had come, and yet no son was born to the king. Anyone acquainted with the place Korea gives to the son and heir can well realize how deep a distress this was to King Mountain-top in those far-off-days. Kim Pusik says:[6]

> The king went early in the 3rd moon and offered prayer by the hills and streams. On the 15th day God appeared to him in a dream and said, 'Be not anxious, a son will be born to you by a secondary queen.' On awakening, the king told his ministers and asked what he should do. Ŭlp'aso, a very wise and good man, said 'God's decrees are hard to fathom. Do nothing; simply wait.'
>
> In the 8th moon the great Ŭlp'aso died and all the state mourned his loss.
>
> In the year 208, in the 11th moon, the king was about to sacrifice a pig to Heaven, when the creature, terror-stricken, ran away. He chased it to the village of Chut'ong where, just as it was speeding by, a young woman of twenty years of age stepped out and, gently approaching, caught it by the leg. Thus it was taken. The king, beholding her beauty, wondered greatly. He went by night to the girl's home and took her to himself. Said she, 'I dare not refuse, seeing you are the king, but if a child be born I trust you will not cast me aside.' To this the

king readily gave consent.

The writer of the *History of the East Kingdom* adds:

> Yŏnu's taking his sister-in-law for wife lowered him to the level of the beasts. Now he goes by night to compass the dishonour of a village girl. A love of sensual pleasure was the motive behind all his acts. He carried on his relations with the foul U-ssi as well, and yet was not ashamed. How clearly it shows that Yŏnu had no religion.[7]

U-ssi, hearing of this village girl, sent soldiers at once to kill her. The girl, being warned, dressed as a boy and made her escape, but a soldier overtook her and was about to strike her down when she turned and said, 'Did the king order my death? I am with child; if you kill me it means the death of the king's son.' The soldier drew back alarmed at this, turned and quietly went his way. The king, hearing of it, again went to her home. She said to him, 'I have ever lived in strictest seclusion with my sisters, wholly apart from the world of men. My child to be born is one in flesh and blood with your Majesty.' The king, delighted, took her and made her secondary queen, and U-ssi dared not lift a hand. Finally the child, a son, was born and the king said, 'God has given me a son and it comes by reason of the sacrifice of the pig. His name shall therefore be Kyoch'e, 'Sacrificial Pig.'[8]

We read further that in the 9th moon of 234 U-ssi died, eight years after Yŏnu. As she was bidding farewell to the world she said, 'I have been a wicked woman, have lost my virtue and am now about to die. With what face can I meet King Kogukch'ŏn in the halls of Hades? If you do not cast my body to the dogs as I richly deserve, please bury me by the side of Yŏnu.' Thus was she buried. After the funeral a witch possessed by the spirit of Kogukch'ŏn said, 'When I saw U-ssi take to herself my younger brother I was very, very angry, furious in fact. I fought her and yet was ashamed that others should see me. Please set a screen before my grave that I may hide my face from all who pass.' Seven rows of pines were planted before the grave of Kogukch'ŏn.[9]

THE CHANGES and chances of the Orient that swing as on a roulette wheel brought Sacrificial Pig to the throne of Koguryŏ as King Tongch'ŏn in 227. He ruled for twenty years in comparative peace, but during that time great changes were taking place in China. Han, the mighty empire that had kept step with Rome for four centuries, went down in AD 220. It had occupied the two capitals of Ch'ang-an to the west and Lo-yang to the east and so made a broad base on the Yellow River.

The Yellow River is as much a source of song and story to Korea as if it flowed in her bosom. This famous stream is one of the mysteries of the Far East. Like a vast inland sea it comes rolling down from the mountains of Tibet, carrying all the world with it. Sometimes it reaches the sea by the Huai mouth south of Shantung, and sometimes by the Chih-li mouth three hundred miles further north. In Confucius's day it ran by the south route; in the days of the

Three Kingdoms it flowed north. In 1200 it broke its way through south again, carrying death and destruction with it; and in 1853 it swung back northward over villages and highly cultivated lands, winning its dreadful name 'China's Sorrow'.

Yi Chehyŏn, writing of it about 1319, says:[10]

> Down comes the rolling Huang-ho from the west,
> Its sources in the fabled Kuen-lun peaks.
> The envoy of great Han built him a raft
> To seek its fountainhead. From out the hills
> It thunders forth ten thousand measures
> Downward to the sea; he found it was
> The Milky Way, that drops here earthward
> And comes swinging forth; by nine great wheels
> It gathers in the circles of the sky.
> A battle fierce it seems 'tween Han and Ch'u,
> Crash of ten thousand horsemen on the plain,
> When slantwise it comes rolling, ever ceaseless,
> Mounting and overflowing fields and meadows:
> The people's hearts forsake them for pale fear.
> Through opening gates in mountainsides it cleaves
> Its mighty way: the fierce strokes of its blade
> Cut out a thundering pathway to the sea.

The Han empire will ever be remembered for the exploits of its famous emperor Wu-ti, who lived part time on earth and part time among the fairies of the upper sphere. It will also be remembered for the introduction of buddhism from the west and the setting up of this cult in the Middle Kingdom. The emperor Ming-ti (AD 58–76) had a dream in which he saw a giant riding from the west, some say with bow and arrows in his hand. The character *fu* for 'buddha' is written with elements meaning 'man, bow, arrows'. This, however, may be merely an attempt to explain the character, for on the authority of the K'ang-hsi dictionary it seems a much older character than buddhism itself. The dictionary says that the buddha came to China about the time the Great Wall was built, by the agency of a priest whom the Chinese shut up in prison. A 'golden man' came by night and set him free. Already the great buddha in his gilded armour was moving in the imaginations of men and was just beginning his long day of two thousand years.[11]

Now the end had come to the Han empire, and the three fighting states of Wei, Wu, and Shu had taken its place. Wei occupied all north China down almost to the Yangtze, Wu extended to the south and as far west as the border line of Szechwan, while Shu lay beyond. How Koreans have revelled in the story-books of these Three Kingdoms![12] They still hold a prominent place among the best-selling books in Seoul. Right across the middle of the third century their dashing warriors are seen to move, one moment doing gallant deeds to a fallen foe, and the next dealing death and indiscriminate slaughter.

I need mention only two great characters who step forth from the war of the Three Kingdoms: Kuan Yü and Chu-ko Liang. Kuan Yü was a native of Shensi, north central China, a pedlar of bean-curd by trade, till he met two strangers, Liu Pei and Chang Fei. After conferring on the fortunes of the day, they took the famous 'oath of the peach orchard' to live and die together. The book *San-kuo-chi* will tell the reader all about it.[13] As he reads on through its endless pages, his admiration for Kuan is kindled. More reading helps to quicken it into fire and flame till in the end he says, 'I never dreamed that long before chivalry was known to Europe, or the Knights of St John or the Templars had come into being, China had her soldiers of fortune, brave, generous and highly gifted.' Kuan's experiences were of the most varied sort: experiences to try his patience, his honour, his mettle. Never once in long years did he break the oath of the peach orchard. Once, captured by the enemy Ts'ao Ts'ao, he was locked up at night with Liu Pei's two wives, the Ladies Kan and Mi, whom Ts'ao Ts'ao had already taken. The enemy's thought was to create suspicion and so drive a wedge between Kuan and Liu. He failed, however, for Kuan mounted guard that night with a lantern in hand, pacing before the door the long hours through, and the ladies were doubly safe under his watchful care.[14] Later he squared things up, as the following song sung by Koreans today tells us:[15]

> A fierce sea-fight on Yangtze's main
> Lights up the sky with fire and flame.
> Great loss is Ts'ao Ts'ao's on this day,
> He flees, as rats run wild away,
> Before a chief whose righteous ire
> Flashes from eyes ablaze with fire;
> Whose threefold beard blows bristling high,
> Whose red horse leaps from sky to sky;
> Whose eighty-pound blue-dragon blade
> Is swung aloft, unmatched, unstayed.
> Ts'ao Ts'ao in flight, in feint, in fears,
> Begs for his life with humble tears.

Kuan's name and fame grew through a thousand years until he finally became Kuan-ti, the God of War. When Hideyoshi's army invaded Seoul in 1592, Kuan appeared in the upper air and gave notice of his presence as by aeroplane. In 1598, when the city had settled back to ways of peace, Kuan was remembered, and temples were built to his honour, one outside the South Gate and one outside the East Gate. The one outside the South Gate was burnt some years ago but the one outside the East Gate still stands as it did in 1599, the year in which Shakespeare wrote his *Julius Caesar*. Those interested in Korean thought and history should visit the East Gate Temple of the God of War and see the pictures of the Three Kingdoms that line the corridors; and then view the swarthy features of Kuan, the mighty warrior who counted his word greater than life itself.[16]

The second great character from the War of the Three Kingdoms who lives

immortal in the mind of Korea is Chu-ko Liang. He was sought out in 207 by
Liu Pei, who found him living in a grass hut. With the greatest difficulty he
was persuaded to leave his humble surroundings and give good counsel to these
mighty chiefs of war.[17] Kuan looked askance at him for a time, thinking him a
poor makeshift, in view of the grim realities that lay before them. Later, when
he saw Chu-ko Liang's wisdom he bowed deep down and did him reverence.
Among his many feats of war was his transport of supplies across the mountainous districts of Szechwan by means of 'wooden oxen and mechanical horses',
whatever these may mean.[18] His counsel won great victories. For wisdom and
sagacity without a flaw, Chu-ko Liang stands first in Korea, first in East Asia.
Much more than any war in their own peninsula this struggle of the Three Kingdoms of China is deeply engraved on every Korean heart.

LITTLE further need he said of Sacrificial Pig except that he came to be at
loggerheads with the rulers of Wei, descendants of Ts'ao Ts'ao, and in 246 had
to fly for his life, leaving his capital Hwando to be burned by the Chinese general
Wu-ch'iu Chien. He remained for a time hidden in the mountains of Hamgyŏng
Province.[19] In the end he shook off his foes and established his capital, not to the
west of the Yalu as heretofore, but in P'yŏngyang.[20] A hundred years later the
capital was moved for the last time back again beyond the Yalu, until the river
finally became the boundary.[21]

This is but a hasty glance across Koguryŏ during the opening years of the
third century, a time when Rome was filled with the persecution of christians
and ringing shouts of applause went up from the bloody contests of the Colos-
seum.

10 The fourth century; the coming of buddhism

AS THE THIRD century draws to a close I am reminded of Gibbon's stately account
of Zenobia, a queen descended from the Macedonian kings of Egypt, a distant
daughter of Cleopatra, trained in Latin, Greek and Syriac. How gracefully he
makes her ride her horse; how vividly he calls up her bronzed features rich with
beauty: her flashing eyes, her pearly teeth that glittered beneath the tinted skin.
And yet she had to see her faithful husband die, her fair city of Palmyra trampled
in the dust, and had to bow her own proud soul before the iron-heeled emperor
Aurelius.

While tears were flowing for Zenobia a somewhat similar scene was being
enacted in far-off Koguryŏ. In the year 248 Sacrificial Pig[1] died in P'yŏngyang
and the state was plunged into grief. The highest officers came forward clamo-
rously asking that they might be buried alive with his great and glorious Majesty;
but the son, now king, refused to allow it, saying that there were better ways of
expressing loyalty than that. Forbidden this final act, like General Nogi of Japan,
they took their own lives and passed on into the eternal shades with their beloved
chieftain.[2] His tomb, according to An Chŏngbok (1722–1791),[3] lies thirty *li* east of
P'yŏngyang, a high, conspicuous mound that recalls an ardour of devotion rarely
seen today. In these selfish days a world-wide pilgrimage to the tomb of King

Tongch'ŏn might well be in order, as a remembrance of him who by his life of devotion rose from pig to saint.

PRINCESS ZENOBIA is but one example of how fair women have suffered at the hands of men. Not so great by any means as she, not great at all, not noble, but just a common woman was Queen Kwanna. She was very beautiful, however, for her hair was nine feet long, and the king thought to make her his secondary wife. The first queen, Yŏn-ssi, whose hair was short and inclined to grey, feared that this might mean the complete loss of the king's love. 'I have heard', said she, 'that the state of Wei is on the lookout for women with long hair. A thousand pieces of gold, I imagine, would be gladly given for such a woman as Kwanna. Your father, the late king, failed in his tribute and had to flee before the Chinese army, nearly losing his life over it. Now if your Majesty will but send an envoy with this long-haired woman, Wei will accept it as a generous gift and all your fears for the future will be allayed.' The king said not a word, but Kwanna, hearing of it, was greatly alarmed. In return she informed against the queen, who had often reprimanded her saying, 'Out upon you, bold-face! How ever came you here into the palace? Away with you at once! If you do not take yourself off you will have occasion to regret it, I assure you.' Kwanna felt her danger. A little later she took occasion to meet the king on his return from a hunting expedition. Carrying a long leathern bag in her hand, she wept as she said, 'The queen has planned to put me into this bag and drown me in the sea. Please, your Majesty, save me from her and let me return to my home.' The king, imagining that this was a made-up story, flew into a rage and said, 'You really want to taste the bottom of the sea, do you? Taste it then.' He ordered her to be bottled up in the bag and thrown into the briny depths. Alas for poor Queen Kwanna! Even all her fine length of hair could not save her.[4]

Korea has had many examples not only of how kings and queens fall out and fight, but of how royal kinsmen quarrel as well. We read[5] that in the year 286 the king of Koguryŏ had two brothers, Iru and Sobal, with whom he was at odds. Once they went off to the hot-springs on a pretence of illness. Many friends accompanied them and they had a royal time with music and feasting. Unguarded words about the king were dropped and they came to his ears. He suddenly summoned his two brothers, pretending that he was about to appoint them to high office, and then ordered them to immediate death.

Kwŏn Kŭn, Korea's companion sage of the days of Chaucer, says;[6]

> Brotherly love is based on the fact that though the two are different in body yet they are one in spirit. There may be differences of opinion but there must never be a break in the bond that binds them. Good brothers never harbour hatred. Their only part is to love. This is one of God's first laws and one of the requisites of every clime. The king's two brothers pretended that they were ill and went to the hot-springs. They probably did so because they knew the king did not wish them near him. Their overfeasting and unguarded words were very wrong but a brother's part was to forgive. Instead of this, a spirit of murder possessed him. There

is no evidence of any rebellion on their part and the king's treacherous call was therefore wholly without excuse. By this one act he loses all his accumulated merit and stands before us condemned.

As we move along through the pages of Korea's history we are constantly reminded of the presence of the spirit world and the acts of an overruling Providence. Here is one dated AD 296 that comes in connection with the intended robbery of a royal grave. Korea's graves have always been her storehouses of treasure: paintings, porcelain, pottery, gold and silver. Wild Chinese, not the pure stock but the northern breed, allied to Mongol, Manchu and Khitan Tatar, came across the Yalu with intent to steal. They began digging into the grave of King West River, Sŏch'ŏn, grandson of Sacrificial Pig. Suddenly, as though electrocuted, the diggers fell dead. At the same time sounds of music came forth from the grave. The remaining wild men, terrified at this, fled, and Korea's graves remained unmolested.[7]

The century closes with this note, also having to do with the supernatural. A man of Silla named In'gwan went to market to sell unspun silk which one Sŏjo agreed to buy, but gave him grain instead of money. A day or two later a hawk came sailing past, picked up the silk, and, after carrying it round and round in mid-air, dropped it at In'gwan's home. In'gwan at once took it to the market and said to Sŏjo, 'A hawk brought your silk to my house. I hereby return it.' Sŏjo replied, 'The hawk's taking the silk and giving it to you is God's doing, not mine. I cannot take it.' In'gwan said, 'If you do not take the silk, then I shall send back your grain.' Sŏjo replied, 'Already two days have passed since I gave you the grain. It is yours, I cannot take it.' They both declined thus and left their goods in the market, the grain and silk. The master in charge of the market reported the matter to the king, who was greatly impressed and appointed them both to office.[8]

As WE TURN the corner of the century and pass into the year 300, in the western world we encounter Constantine and his newly-constructed city on the old site of Byzantium. He himself, though a professed christian, was a man of a miserable family, little better than that of Herod the Great—his sons and sons-in-law alike dying under the knife. In England we find Alban, the first martyr of Britain, laying down his life for the faith. He is one of the great army of heroes who demonstrate the fact that an idea in the soul may be more precious to a man than the earth and all its added treasure. Korea has had many examples of these in her history, not only men but brave women as well.

As we move on down through the years we find in Italy St Ambrose and St Augustine busy with the propagation of the gospel; and like them two priests in Korea, Shun-tao and A-tao who come bringing buddhism. We are not told much about what sort of men they were and what methods they employed that made their mission so successful. In an old buddhist record[9] I find that Shun-tao was sent by Fu-chien, king of Eastern Chin, in 372. He is said to have been a man of great virtue, handsome in appearace, full of love and patience, whose constant habit was the giving of alms. As a boy he had taken an oath to become a preacher of the buddha, and as such he had travelled far. Behold him now at the gates of Korea with letters for the king. Images too he brings, and sacred books. From this time on Koreans learn to say,' Namu Amit'abul, Namu Amit'abul' (I put my trust in Amida Buddha, I put my trust in Amida Buddha). This is the 'cross before the eyes' to guide the buddhist through all his wandering way. Is it cold, fit to freeze you? Namu Amit'abul! Is it hot? Namu Amit'abul! Are you hungry? Namu Amit'abul! Are you in dire straits and about to die? Namu Amit'abul! Wherever, whatever, time and place and circumstance count nothing if only you can say Namu Amit'abul!

The king of Koguryŏ went out to meet this first great priest, and 372 became one of Korea's most memorable years. As the religion of the gentle sage came forth, it suggested three words: 'humble, harmless, undefiled.' How self-renounced have been its priests who walked the humble way. As in our christian orders, there have been those who sought their own ends and lost everything, but the real thought of the buddha has ever been humility just as St Francis loved it. So harmless, too: no life was ever taken; even the noxious insect and the poisonous snake were allowed to go their way while the priest who saw them merely said, Namu Amit'abul! As for purity of life, this was indeed the buddhists' aim. False priests there have been, as in the west, but the ideal way to be trodden by the faithful was the way undefiled.

In the wake of Shun-tao came A-tao, the Augustine who followed Ambrose. He differed from his master in that he was part Korean. Years before, his father had come as envoy from the state of Wei and while here had married a woman of Korea and had this son whom he called A-tao. His mother had learned her lessons of the buddha and early in life had filled his little mind with the glory of the buddha's religion. A memorial stone erected in 544 in Kyŏngju, capital of Silla, still talks of A-tao;[10]

> It was in the second year of the reign of Mich'u (263) that he came. He had audience with the king and urged on him the acceptance of the buddha. The fact that this religion had never been heard of before made A-tao an object of suspicion and there were many who desired to do away with him. He fled to the home of a man called Morok. Three years later the Princess Sŏngguk fell ill and her case had become so hopeless that witches, fortune-tellers, and wise men were at their wits' end to know what to do. The king sent out messengers in search of someone who could come and save her. A-tao in response arrived at the palace and at once worked a cure. The king, greatly delighted, asked what he desired in return. 'Nothing,' said he, 'but a monastery on Ch'ŏn'gyŏng mountain.'

This the king gave a glad assent to and it was built, the first temple where the buddha was preached in Silla. Suddenly, however, the king died and A-tao's fortunes changed. He was looked upon as an alien, an object of suspicion, and had to retire. It is said that he closed the door of his hermit cell, made it fast and was never seen again. All this is recorded on the stone tablet that today stands as a witness in Kyŏngju. This stone, however, like many other buddhist records is quite wrong as to its date. Buddhists are often wrong as regards time. In this respect they differ from the confucians who have a definite imperial year on which to place their hand and are consequently right in their records. Thus have they recorded their doings with precision all the way from 1100 BC to AD 1900: no dates are more securely fixed than those of the scholar of the Far East. The buddhist, however, being unattached to worldly kingdoms, and unacquainted with annals and king-makers, has never been quite sure of just where he was. Thus he makes A-tao visit Silla in 263, a hundred years before the buddha was known in Korea.[11] As to other dates, he places Sakyamuni's birth at 994 BC, whereas it was really 558 BC.[12]

Korea has dated her national records, her biographies, her memorial stones, her halls, her palaces, and everything else, according to the Chinese name of the reign. For example, I discover a stone dated the 3rd year of Kuang-hua. I look up Kuang-hua and find it one of the names taken by the Emperor Chao Tsung of T'ang for a reign-period which began in 898. The 3rd year therefore is 900, the last year but one of good King Alfred.

JUST at this time there lived in China a great man whom Koreans have all but deified, Wang Hsi-chih. He was born in 321, died in 379, and had seven sons, all noted men, but his chief glory was his calligraphy. To this day Koreans taking note of specially fine calligraphy say, 'Wang Hsi-chih come back again.' Kim Saeng, who lived four centuries later, was called Korea's Wang Hsi-chih. Anyone who has through long years watched the Korean scholar's practised hand will readily appreciate his regard for China's great chieftain of the writing-brush.

The strokes used in writing Chinese characters number only eight, all of which appear in the ideograph for 'eternal', and yet it takes twenty years to learn to write them with skill.[13] Few attain perfection even in that time. Ferdinand Verbeist, a Belgian jesuit, who arrived in China in 1658 and finally became companion and preceptor of the great K'ang-hsi Emperor, is said to be the only foreigner who ever attained a perfect hand. He was an artist to begin with, which accounts for his delicate wrist muscles and fine sense of soul. The spirit set in motion by Wang Hsi-chih 1,500 years ago expired in Korea with the close of the nineteenth century. Nothing again so wonderfully picturesque or so delightfully exclusive will ever be seen as this freemasonry of the brush.

As WE CLOSE this rather scattered chapter it is interesting to note that when Kumarajiva, a priest from far-distant Kucha[14] in Sinkiang, Turkestan, was busy in Nanking, capital of East Chin, translating into Chinese the Diamond Sutra, the Lotus Sutra and other books of the buddha, the christian priest St Jerome, from far-off Dalmatia on the Adriatic, was in Bethlehem translating the Scriptures into Latin, which translation later became known as the Vulgate. The buddhist books done by Kumarajiva are still read in Korea today.

A very remarkable passage appears in the Chinese of the Diamond Sutra that would almost bring Kumarajiva and Jerome within speaking distance. It runs somewhat thus:

The buddha said to Subhuti; 'All that we see of the material universe is vanity, so we must view it as nothing if we would see the Coming One.' Subhuti said to the buddha: 'Thou Highest, if mortals hear such a word as this, can we ever expect them to come to the faith?' The buddha answered; 'Subhuti, do not say such things. Five hundred years after my death there will come One who will bring the Law with glory and blessing, and, understanding what these words mean, know their truth. This One will not only plant a virtuous seed through one, three, four or five existences of the buddha, but planting it through eternal ages, including all the buddhas, will know my words, and with a single and undefiled heart accept them. Subhuti! I know it all, have seen it all. All mortals likewise will receive endless blessing.'[15]

The buddha was born in 558 BC and died in 479. Some scholars regard this as a prophecy referring to Christ. Those books of the buddha that came to Korea shortly after their translation have occupied a very important place in the life of the nation.

MEANWILE the little kingdom of Paekche lived much by itself, till finally it found a friend in Japan. It had, like its companion states, come to a knowledge of Confucius, and, in the year 285 sent Wang In with copies of the Analects, the Thousand Characters, the Great Learning and other books to the island empire.[16] This, I understand, was Japan's first introduction to these, as the east calls them, the Sacred Books. What were her feelings, ever keenly alive to the latest and most up-to-date forms of teaching, when she read for the first time:

Confucius says:
'To go over again and again what we have learned is
    surely a delightful occupation.
A friend from faraway is indeed a guest to be enjoyed.
To be undisturbed because one's worth is unrecognized
    is an unfailing mark of greatness.
A man whose heart is dutiful to parents and faithful
    to his kin is not one to run counter to those in
    authority or stir up trouble in the state.'

All of which sayings are as wise today as they were then.[17]

Confucianism has never taken the same hold on the Japanese nation that it has on Korea, and yet the Japanese have always appreciated the merits and attainments of the scholar. In many cases that I have read of and some I have known, the Japanese people have almost killed the visiting Korean scholar by their requests for samples of his literary skill, and by their abundant feasting and over-generous treatment of him. Their admiration for Korean scholarship continues today in unabated measure.

AT THE CLOSE of the fourth century there lived the greatest Chinese scholar and poet before the kingdom of T'ang. He was a glorious dilettante, who hated all manner of official care. His pen was perfect and Koreans have well-nigh deified him through these long centuries. I asked a group of scholar friends if they could give me a sample verse or two from T'ao Yüan-ming, and they all replied at once with no end of special favourites. I selected the one that best reflects the mind of the poet himself and give herewith a very plain translation:[18]

> Behind my wattle gate, a harp to tune, a book to read;
> I touch the strings and joy descends, true joy indeed.
> A world of stored delights there are behind this favoured nook:
> At dawn a sprinkled cabbage patch, at eve a book!

11 Fifth-century culture and ideals

WHAT was the state of Korea's civilization at the opening of the fifth century and how does it compare with that of Europe? As we mention the fifth century, we are reminded that Alaric marched into Rome in 410 and brought the Mistress of the World down to the dust. Tens of thousands of Goths were let loose to work their will on the great city. Forty thousand slaves, too, were out to settle accounts for every ignominious lash they had suffered. The gay women of Rome, the soft and gentle maidens, fled for their lives only to fall into the foul grip of the savage. It was indeed Europe's midnight tragedy, when culture, refinement, grace, charm and beauty all went down in one vast cataclysm under the waves of Hun, Goth and Vandal. The Dark Ages settled over western civilization and did not lift for nearly a thousand years. Had it not been for the monasteries where men like Augustine, Cædmon, and Bernard of Clairvaux got their inspiration, we had gone back to be savages once again.

Meanwhile in this little country there were signs of great advances in religion, in government, in literature, in art, that leave us of the West far behind.[1] With the coming of the buddha, the easy-going master Confucius received a shock and decided to take a fresh hold of his task. Fearing that this new spiritual agency might greatly upset the even tenour of his way, he established schools and set about a renaissance. It is a remarkable fact that these two cults, buddhism and confucianism, have walked together through the history of Korea for fifteen hundred years and yet have never fallen out nor had a real religious war. They have manifested a strong dislike at times and shown black looks, but they have never come to persecuting or killing each other. We christians may well read Kingsley's *Hypatia* with shamed faces when we think that in 415, the very period we are writing of, this fair heroine was falsely charged with a horrible crime, dragged into one of the churches, stripped and cruelly murdered by a wild Christian mob headed by Peter the Reader. Korea knows of no such revolting scenes in her religious life.

ACROSS the Yalu, on the old site of Kungnae-sŏng (told of in chapter 7) there stands a tall monument—a rough block of stone, 20 feet high, 6 feet across the face, erected in 144 while Hypatia was still lecturing in Alexandria.

The long centuries that this monument has seen would alone make its inscription interesting to a student of the east. It first gives an account of the founder of Koguryŏ, Chumong, whom we already know. It tells how he crossed opposing streams on the backs of fishes and turtles, and how he rode the yellow dragon all the way up to heaven. Then it takes up the story of King Kwanggaet'o, whose stone it is. 'Peace-loving, great king,' it calls him. He became ruler at sixteen and was known as 'the master of eternal joy'. 'His power and might filled the world. His reign was marked by peace, while abundant harvests confirmed his righteous rule.' 'But God was sparing of His blessings,' the record says, 'for at thirty-nine years of age he was called to depart this life.' On the 29th day of the 9th moon of the year *kabin* (414) his remains were laid in this tomb, and this stone erected on which his virtues and good deeds were recorded in order that they might be known to future generations.[2]

This stone, that the Japanese have brought to light and given such careful details of in their *Pictures of Ancient Remains*[3] is a record of their greatest antagonist. In the year 399 Silla sent asking King Kwanggaet'o to help her against the Japanese, who were pouring into her cities. Kwanggaet'o despatched 50,000 men and from that time on his reign was a succession of hard fights against Japan, in which he was decidedly victor.[4] The Japanese, with their admiration for a stern fighting foe, have made King Kwanggaet'o's monumental remains immortal. Their investigations, the photographs they have taken, the great rubbings that hang in the Kŭnjŏng-jŏn,[5] all done by Japanese hands, tell what a strong fearless people the Koreans were in those distant days.

THERE are other proofs, as well, of Korea's high attainment. Recent investigations of ancient tombs have revealed a practised hand and a power of imagination hitherto undreamed-of. Twenty miles or so to the west of P'yŏng-yang, at a place called Uhyŏn-ni, are three great mounds, 30 feet high and 500 feet round the base. Their masonry is of granite cut in large blocks and built in the most substantial way, the skill shown by the masons being of a very high order. In the inner chamber are two tables of stone evidently intended as stands for coffins. The official record regarding this tomb says, 'The walls and ceilings are of granite, decorated with coloured pictures, strong in concept, beautiful for grace, and exquisitely fine as to execution.'

The four mural paintings[6] call for special attention, drawn as they are according to the symbolic law of Chinese philosophy. To the east is the Blue Dragon, blue being the colour that pertains to that compass point; to the west the Tiger; to the north the Turtle; and to the south the Red Bird. These figures are magnificently done with a power and wealth of detail that leaves one wondering whence they came. The Blue Dragon, with lifted paw and long spotted tongue curling upwards, is a very dreadful monster as he rides by amongst the clouds. His long scaly back has a curve of perfect grace, while his motion, attended by flames of fire, looks alive. The White Tiger is also a wonderful creation: the loose-flung tail; the strong rear foot, expressive of the driving force that sends the beast hurtling through the air; the fierce claws; the flashes of flame; the fanged jaws; the hotly glaring eye.

On the south wall is the Red Bird, another wondrous fabrication. It seems to have a double body with only one leg to each, beautiful scimitar-like wings and a sweep of uplifted tail. Its crowned head has a tip of red above the eye and a live coal in the beak. While the Blue Dragon has charge of wood in the east and the White Tiger charge of metal in the west, the Red Bird has fire as its element in the south. On the north wall is the strangest creature of all, an unimaginable turtle, lithe-limbed and long, with a snake, its mate, wound in folds about it. These two, both creatures of the shade, are supposed to represent the new year that comes forth out of darkness. They are symbols of the early beginnings of life. Such, as we see it pictured on these walls, was that distant day's understanding of Chinese philosophy. Who was the unknown artist? Even after one thousand years these pictures still hold their own. Some great king was buried here and given these symbolic emblems as companions. They were to be his guardians to ensure his safety through the ages to come.[7] Around and about the pictures are other representations. One of fire, matchlessly painted, was once thrown on the screen before a Boston audience and 'brought down the house'.

Not far from these three tombs, and about fifteen minutes walk from the Shinchido Station[8] on the Chinnamp'o line, is another wonderful palace of the dead that belongs to the century of which we write. It is called the Twin Pillar tomb. A few years ago it was but a dishevelled mound, no one knowing what it contained; today, with the imprint of the archaeologist's hand upon it, it has become one of the rare survivals of a long-forgotten age. Through the kindness of the government you are given a permit to enter. The low gate is unlocked to let you in, and you step down into a passage about 12 feet long, 5 feet wide, and 7 feet high. On the walls are pictures, pictures evidently of times then present: men, women, horses, oxen. On the east wall is a canopied cart drawn by a bullock. Under its outer covering, tent-roofed in shape, and hung about with lanterns, is a yellow-topped palanquin. That bull, fully accoutred, is harnessed into the shafts with the driver on his back. A woman in a full-pleated English skirt walks behind. A warrior, with pike in hand and dressed in armour, rides a horse equally clad in mail, showing only his head, his tail, and the tips of his hoofs. Here we have a comprehensive picture of these ancient days of Koguryǒ, of which so little is told in history, days when our wild Saxon forefathers were landing in Britannia. On the same wall are three stately ladies with caps of white bands, closely-fitting dresses, jackets and knife-pleated full skirts. A touch of rouge still adorns each long-forgotten cheek. True to life even today, behold here is a soft-looking individual of the male sex who droops his eyes before these fair ladies. On the west wall is a gallant horseman, his quiver on his back and two feathers in his cap, riding forth with his reins in one hand and a banner in the other. The equestrian gear of those days would seem to say that the Koguryǒans were a well-mounted people.

Between the long entrance passage to this tomb and the first chamber, there is a small gateway of about 3 feet by 4, with demon guards painted on the walls on each side. In the dim underworld you can see their rolling eyeballs flash lightning from their sockets as you go by.

When you enter the first, or outer chamber, you are in view of the octagonal pillars that give the tomb its name — Twin Pillar Tomb. They stand between the two chambers, the outer and the inner, and are about 15 inches in diameter and 7 feet high. They each have an artistically cut capital and base, are red in colour, and are coiled about by a yellow scaly dragon.

Passing between the pillars, we come now to the inner chamber which is 9½ feet long, 9 feet wide, and about the same in height. At the corners are painted imitation pillars which would doubtless have greatly upset Mr Ruskin. The Red Bird appears on the south wall above the door, walking, like Daniel's companions, unhurt amid the flames. Other decorations appear: the Seven Stars that are supposed to circle round the celestial throne; the *t'aegŭk*, a picture of the *yang* and *yin*. There are besides on the ceiling the three-legged crow that sits in the sun, and the squatty toad that occupies the moon. On the east wall of the inner chamber moves a procession of women, some in pleated skirts, and some in spotted dresses, jacket and skirt, red and black, and black and red. In the midst of these walks a buddhist priest very elaborately arrayed in what seem to be cassock and stole. He carries something in his hand, while before him goes a woman with a flaming candle on her head. Thus amid China's symbols, that touch every nook and corner of the chamber, walks the buddha all serene. It is indeed a picture of the moderation that obtained in the religious world of those ancient days. The west wall of the inner chamber is so marred and blurred that it is impossible of interpretation; but the north wall is clear to the eye and most interesting. Here sit his Majesty the King and her Highness the Queen in a special pavilion under a wide and highly-decorated canopy. Tongues of fire flash up over the pavilion behind the royal seat. The king has a horsehair cap on his head and wears a red robe. His queen is likewise in red and they sit in state while the world walks by in fear or bows at their feet. To the left of the pavilion appears a pair of dragons; but whether they are holding a friendly conversation, or joined in mortal combat, who can tell? A yellow matted walk leads up to the king's seat, while his discarded boots have a prominent place on each side. His face is kindly and courteous, and, like the buddha, his ears are large so as to hear the voices of his people.

Who was this king? Was it Changsu, who came to the throne in 413 and reigned for seventy-nine years? Perhaps! No inscription remains to tell us. A visit to this tomb is like a walk through Korea's fifth century. How beautifully dressed her people were! How keen their sense of graceful line and colour! What dainty hands they had for tracery! What a highly gifted state they were, that could ride forth so gallantly accoutred for war and so artistically decorated for peace.

So much for Korea's objective world of that day. How about her inner man? Was he brave, unselfish, truthful? Of all the heroic men of the fifth century that I have been able to find the world over, Korea's hero, Pak Chesang, surely stands among the first — a man who had within his heart ideals greater far than life itself. He seems to have had no son but only daughters, three or four of them. Doubtless he was their great chieftain and they his attendant fairies. In the year 418 the king of Silla gave a call for volunteers, someone to rescue his brothers and bring them safe home to him. His father Silsŏng ('truly holy') had fallen on evil days and had come under the hammer both to east and west. His second son Pokho was a hostage in Koguryŏ, and his third, Misahŭn, a hostage in Japan. The old king had died without seeing his children again and Nulchi, his eldest son, was now on the throne. His desire was to have his brothers with him but no way seemed open for their return. Someone suggested Pak Chesang as the man he needed, true-hearted and brave. Call him. Pak was called. Would he be willing to give thought to the deliverance of the king's brothers? 'It is difficult and dangerous,' said the king. Pak's answer was: 'I have always heard that the loyal courtier never thinks of danger or difficulty and that he does not fear to die. If we talk of danger or difficulty we shall lose sight of the spirit of devotion. I am quite unworthy of so great an honour; yet I shall do my best to see your Majesty's commands carried through.'

Thus he went. He met the king of Koguryŏ and said, 'I have heard that a great king's hold on the hearts of men is by confidence and good-will only. To keep a friendly prince as hostage wholly denies the spirit of confidence. Your prisoner Pokho is the beloved brother of our king of Silla. Ten years have passed since he was taken, throughout which time the king has longed for his return. I count on the great heart of your Majesty to give consent to his being set free. By this you will rise to the place of king indeed, and your esteem will be enhanced in all the hearts of Silla.' The king of Koguryŏ, Changsu, moved by this appeal, at once gave consent, and home came Prince Pokho. Changsu may have been the king through whose splendid tomb we have just made our way. How rejoiced Silla was at this valiant service.

Then came the greater and more difficult task of Japan. 'Only by strategy, not by appeal,' said Pak. 'Advertise me as a rebel making my escape, and lock up my wife and daughters. This will give me a good start.' Without farewell or any word to bid him *bon voyage* he left, and landed desolate and alone in Japan. 'Flying for your life, eh?' 'Behold me and see for yourselves,' was Pak's answer. 'What about rumours that Silla and Koguryŏ meditate an attack on Japan? Will you lend a hand to thwart it?' 'Certainly!' So Pak was engaged for the defence of the west coast and came daily into touch with the exiled prince. On one auspicious night, when a mist lay over the water, Pak had him shipped off by rowboat while he himself remained behind to hold back suspicion as long as possible. Prince Misahŭn got safely home, but Pak was arrested and brought before the Japanese king. 'You promised allegiance to Japan; have you now acted the part of traitor?' was the question. 'I did it for my king,' said Pak. 'But you are a minister of Japan and at her service.' 'A dog of Kyerim (Silla) I may be, but never a minister of Japan.' According to ancient custom he was put through various forms of torture, but not a word could they wring from him. Finally he was burned alive but his last shout was: 'Long live Kyerim!' After 1,500 years his memory is still fragrant. It was Prince Ito who had the different histories printed in which these valiant deeds are recorded. So fine a piece of *bushido* appealed to him and he feared lest the old records should be lost forever.[9]

Pak Chesang's wife, we are told, followed hard after her husband till she reached the Ch'isul-lyŏng (Eagle Pass). There she learned that he had already gone, and there she died. An ancient song that commemorates her spirit runs thus:[10]

Who first built ships to force this sad farewell?
Would that the wind and storms might block his way.
Who made the sea to bar all safe return?
Had I but power, I'd sweep the sea away.
Who gave the savage leave to kill my lord?
Would that the deeps might whelm his island o'er.
I'd cross mid-air had I but wings to fly,
An eagle bird that scorns the miles of space.
A spirit I'll return to guard this pass for ever.

Today a little shrine ornaments the hill-top. A note added to the old record says that Prince Misahŭn married Pak's second daughter.

Such is a glimpse of Korea's far-off fifth century. We see her people, we seem to hear their voices, we behold their dresses. We see their *esprit de corps* and kindly treatment of each other. We behold their devotion that leads to death itself.

12 Sixth-century Silla: Ondal

IN her long history Korea has had to deal with barbarian races that she has greatly disliked. One of the most powerful of these was the Wei,[1] a Tatar tribe that emerged, like the Mongols later, from the arid region of the Gobi Desert. These Tatars possessed themselves of all north China and pushed south till they reached a line midway between the Yellow and the Yangtze Rivers, having the old capitals of Lo-yang and Ch'ang-an firm in their grip. Not being confucian, but barbarian, they turned to the buddha for religion and said endless prayers to him for a hundred and fifty years: *Om mani padme hum* (Oh, the jewel in the lotus, amen!)[2] We find these Wei still in the saddle at the opening of the sixth century. During the past hundred years envoys had been sent to them from Korea many times. Safety demanded it, even though the feelings of the envoy were greatly outraged as he bowed before the unspeakable barbarian. Thus a close relationship had sprung up between this very select state of Confucius and the greasy, unkempt Tatar with his unlettered buddha.

Other states of China, more or less orthodox, composed of the men of Han, appeared and disappeared: Ch'i, Chou, Liang and Ch'en. Last of all came Sui. The Korean knows all about these fleeting national entities and gives you his estimate and feelings regarding them. King Yang of Sui who appeared in 605 was, says he, 'the wickedest monarch that ever lived.' His picture, so to speak, hangs still on the walls of Korea, as it has hung for a thousand years, a warning to all rulers. 'He poisoned his father, took possession of his father's concubines, kept dancing-girls like honking seagulls all about him, built an immense palace at Lo-yang with two million labourers under the lash. He stocked his capital with rare fruits and flowers, with beasts and birds gathered from all the world; and then to make his days flow soft and sweet, he dug the Grand Canal which extends from Chinkiang on the Yangtze, to Tientsin beyond the Yellow River, six hundred miles and more. Up and down this he sailed with endless delight. His restless spirit was not satisfied even with this, and so he fitted out an expedition to punish Korea for not paying tribute. Chinese records say he marshalled 350,000 men; Korean records, one million. At any rate his army was defeated by General Ŭlchi Mundŏk on the Ch'ŏngch'ŏn River, in north Korea, and this was the first step in his downfall. He was finally murdered by conspirators; and so China of the sixth century passes from us on its inglorious way.[3]

While these things were going on in Asia, Clovis (a name changed later to Louis) set up his capital in Paris, and founded the Frankish monarchy. France, how great to be, was emerging from the confused conditions of Europe, just as the T'ang Kingdom at the same time emerged from the broken fragments of China.

At this time, too, we begin to hear echoes of the Turk. He came in 551 like a midnight prowler, and looked over the Yalu, as he later looked over the walls of Europe. The Koreans, not liking his appearance, drove him off, sending ten thousand men after him. Had Korea fallen a victim at that time, the Far East might have wholly engaged the attention of the Turk, and Europe been spared all the miseries of Constantinople; but it was not to be. Korea was a fighting nation in those days and the Turks were out only for easy plunder. They turned their backs and moved off toward the Caspian Sea.[4]

This central region is the fountain-head of all the barbarian tribes of Asia, unlettered, untutored; whereas Korea has neither part nor lot with them, seeing she has drunk of classic lore from her earliest childhood. The writer's first recollection of Korea began with hearing the little children in the thatch-roofed school shouting in unison: *'Hanŭl ch'ŏn, tta chi, kamŭl hyŏn, nuru hwang, . . .'* All over the land went this sing-song: as you passed through the most distant villages you could still could hear it, under the very ears of his Majesty the King it sounded out. How many little faces, unwashed perhaps, were aglow with the steam and pressure of *'Hanŭl ch'ŏn, tta chi, . . .'* it would be hard to tell. What were they saying and what did it mean? They were all reciting the Thousand-character Classic,[5] the first book of the would-be Chinese scholar. It happens that this book was written in the period we are studying. It is called also the *Paeksu-mun*, 'the white-haired composition'. The writer was Chou Hsing-szŭ, a famous scholar of the Liang Kingdom of China (502–557). The common story, though unconfirmed by authority, is that Chou was imprisoned under sentence of death, when the king tossed him a thousand characters in the calligraphy of Wang Hsi-chih with a command that he make a composition before the next morning, to include them all and repeat none. Only thus would his life be spared. Chou accepted the challenge and by morning light, we are told, the task was done. His hair, however, had turned white in the effort. Hence it is called the White-haired Composition. This little book has become one of the landmarks of Korea, full of life and vigour still, though it has already seen 1,400 years pass by. It is older by far than our oldest English books, Beowulf or Cædmon.

In those distant days Silla had pushed her borders north and occupied the present site of Seoul and the magnificent hills that sit behind it. About the year 555 the king made a tour of inspection and placed on one of these peaks of

Pukhan a boundary stone that originally had on its face 199 characters.[6] Today only 128 can be made out, and these with difficulty. They seem to say that several chiefs met here and offered sacrifice, that victory was won by the king of Silla without soldiers or arms, that by way of high attainment he gathered to him the hearts of his people, that he visited all his state and rewarded those noted for sincerity of heart and true piety. As he climbed these hills he met a religious man who lived in a cave, and here he set up the stone. This stone can be seen today, standing on its lonely peak as it has stood since Ida ruled our rude forefathers as first king of Northumbria. Near the stone is the famous old temple of Sŭngga-sa where the holy man lived in that distant day. The writer has many times visited the sacred spot and peered into the cave.

Moving about at the same time, and touching this and that with his stick of charcoal, was Korea's most famous artist, Solgŏ. The old record reads: 'He was son of a farmer, and from earliest youth loved picture-making. When out cutting wood he used to make pictures on the rocks, and while he ploughed he would sketch in the sand with his ploughshare'.[7] Solgŏ is mentioned in chapter 1 along with Tan'gun and the swallows. His shadowy figure that bears the artist's touch moves dimly across the sixth century.

About the beginning of the sixth century Silla took a fresh start as a nation and revised her laws and customs.[8] In 503 she finally decided on the name Silla. Up to that time she had been called Sara, Saro, or Kyerim; but now Silla was fixed on as her one and only name.[9] In 502 she put an end to the custom of burial alive. She began also the custom of giving the dead king a posthumous name of special honour. The name was not given till the king was dead, so that today when we say 'King Sejong', we use a name that Sejong himself never heard. In England it was 'Queen Elizabeth', living or dead. In Korea while the king lived he had a special name, a *chonho* which appeared on his seal. King Sejong had four of them;[10] but only after he died was he Sejong. This custom dates from AD 514.[11]

WHILE buddhism had won right of way in the north, there had been many a tussle over its place in the southern kingdom, and only now, in 528, was it finally adopted as the state religion. The *History of the Three Kingdoms* gives this account of how buddhism became established in Silla:[12]

> The king had long desired to promote buddhism to a place of honour, but his ministers were opposed to it. While his Majesty was in these straits a courtier named Ich'adon came forward to say, 'I have a plan by which buddhism may succeed. Behead me, please, and you will dispose of the matter for ever.' The king said in reply: 'To begin a religion by beheading an innocent man would be a most contradictory act.' 'But', said Ich'adon, 'if you wish a right way for the buddha, my death is necessary.' The king then consented so far as to call his ministers. They said, 'As we see these buddhists, they are a most peculiar folk: their heads are smooth like children's heads, their speech is most obscure and difficult to follow. Assuredly if your Majesty makes this the state religion, you will repent of it later. We shall never consent, no matter

what you say.' Ich'adon then made his own reply: 'You ministers are quite mistaken. Only in the wake of a wonderful man does a wonderful religion appear. This religion is deep beyond words, one that we are compelled to follow.' The king, seeing it was impossible to move his ministers, said, 'You are the only one who speaks thus. I cannot follow you both, so we will have your head off and see.' Just before the knife struck, Ich'adon said, 'I die for religion's sake. If the buddha has spiritual powers he will manifest them now.' Then they took off his head and the blood that spouted forth was white as milk. The onlookers wondered at this and regarded it as a miracle. No further opposition was made to the buddha.

From this time on, the buddha increased and grew in Silla. His commands were written large for all to see: 'Do not kill. Do not steal. Do not commit adultery. Do not lie. Do not drink. Do not seek renown. Do not overdress. Delight not in what the eye sees or the ear hears'. So markedly was the buddha in favour those days that King Sammaek in 576 cut off his hair, dressed as a priest, and had his queen become a nun.[13] Famous women donned the coarse dress, took the alms-bowl and rattle in hand and went about saying, *Kwanseŭm posal, Kwanseŭm posal* (Saviour Kuan-yin, Saviour Kuan-yin). The casting of a great image, too, was begun—one that occupied a place in the Yellow Dragon Monastery swallowed up 30,000 pounds of brass and 11,000 *pun* of gold.[14] Think of it! Though the buddha was born 3,000 miles away on the distant banks of the Ganges, yet, after a lapse of a whole millennium, he was here the mightiest influence moving in the hearts of men in this distant corner of East Asia.

Shall we glance for a moment at the life of one of the great priests of that day? His family name was Sŏl and his priestly name Wŏn'gwang. At thirteen years of age he became a teacher of the buddha. His mind was broad and clear, and his wisdom far beyond his day. He loved to study and among his best friends were confucianists and taoists. His desire was to ascend far into the heights away beyond the noisy, jarring world.

When thirty years of age, he went to live in solitude in the hills that sit behind Seoul, Samgak, 'the Three Horns'. There came a priest there, a stranger, who built a temple and practised the faith. Sitting one night reading his books and telling his beads, Wŏn'gwang suddenly beheld an angel who came forward and, calling him, said, 'Good! There are many who walk the way, but none more faithfully than you. Yonder priest has not as yet entered the outer portals. Because he fails of attainment, a jealous spirit possesses him. Go and tell him to move away, for if he remains here danger threatens you both. Go to him early in the morning and say, "Move away at once. Escape for your life." ' On hearing this Wŏn'gwang said, 'Why be anxious about the words of a disembodied spirit? I refuse to go.' About midnight of the day following there was a great noise, like thunder. When Wŏng'wang hurried out to see he found that a tremendous landslide had occurred that buried priest and temple alike.

Shortly after, the angel came again and ordered him to China. 'Go', said he, 'and learn; and later you will come back to save your people from destruction.'

151

'But', said Wŏn'gwang, 'the sea is wide and blocks my way. Please guide me.'
He finally reached China and, travelling here and there, learned many of the
deeper teachings of the buddha. As Moses saw a burning bush, so on one occasion
a pagoda just in front of Wŏn'gwang took fire and, flaming up, blazed high. The
general of Sui, thinking Wŏn'gwang an incendiary, had him arrested and bound
hand and foot. Suddenly the flames died down and the pagoda was untouched
by even the smell of smoke. On this the general let him go, regarding him as a
prophet.

In the 22nd year of King Chinp'yŏng, 605, he returned in the train of the
envoy, and while on the tempestuous sea was met once more by the angel who
said, 'When you are safely home, build me a temple in order that many may be
blessed.' As the years passed, he became known as the good father of his people
and all the world rejoiced in him. The king himself showed him great favour and
looked up to him as he would to the buddha. Thus did buddhism become firmly
fixed in the land of Silla.[15]

YOUNG people, in all lands and at all times, have had their special place.
Forty years ago in Korea they were the most respectful and reverent of all youth.
In the presence of their seniors they stood with hands crossed and most attentive
mien; their behaviour to father, mother, king, and courtier was perfect; good
wishes at night and greetings in the morning were made with all reverence and
a deep bow that touched the ground. Korea has shown many excellent qualities
in the handling of her youth. One of her earliest attempts to specialize in
this matter was when the king of Silla gathered carefully-selected lads and
had them sit under masters duly qualified to teach them every department of
learning. These boys were called the *hwarang, 'flowery lads.'* They were taught
duty, service, loyalty; their grace and beauty filled the land.

Before this a similar group for girls existed. Among these daughters of the
East two were specially noted, Nammo and Chunjŏng. Delightful was their
world till jealousy, with its root of bitterness, sprang up between them. Chunjŏng
('Honesty'), forgetting her beautiful name, invited little Nammo to her home
in a garden by the river. There she made her drink much wine — forced her, in
fact, to drink till she was dead drunk; then dragged her out and dropped her
into a yawning pool that waited beneath the cliff. A great to-do was made, and
the end of it was that one of the first ladies' colleges of the world was suddenly
closed and its four hundred pupils dispersed. Shortly after this, in the mid-sixth
century, the boys' *hwarang* group was started.[16]

IN SPITE of this failure the young Korean woman has won great renown
during her long journey. A marked faithfulness and devotion of soul has lifted
her from the shadowy inner chamber to the highest places of honour. Under the
year 577 I find in Koguryŏ a famous minister called Ondal.[17] He was a beggar in
his early years, with a twisted countenance and dishevelled hair, so widely known
that even in the palace Ondal the beggar was a name passed from lip to lip. The
king's little daughter, it seems, was given overmuch to crying, which caused the
king great annoyance. 'You wretched child,' said he, 'I've decided to marry you

off to Ondal the beggar.' Then when she was sixteen, he made arrangements for her marriage, not to Ondal, but to the son of a noble chief of state named Ko. She objected, saying, 'I am already plighted to Ondal by your royal command and cannot break troth to marry another.' The king, disgusted, said, 'Then marry whom you please.' In the night she gathered together ten highly-bejewelled daggers that were among the possessions of the palace, and made her lonely exit. She sought the home of Ondal, where she bowed reverently before his mother. Ondal, at that moment, had just returned with a load of *nŭt'i* (zelkowa) bark on his back. She told them why she had come, and the two were married. The princess then brought forth her daggers and by exchange bought fields, house and slaves. She then had Ondal buy up the cast-off horses that were dropped from the king's list. These were specially fed and cared for and were soon equal to the best.

It was the custom of Koguryŏ to have a great state hunt on the borders of Lo-lang (Manchuria) on the 3rd day of the 3rd moon. All game taken on that occasion was sacrificed to Heaven and Mother Earth. The king went forth to share in the sports and the ministers followed him with officers of the army. Ondal, too, brought up the rear. His horses were the best in the field and outrode all others, his bag of game was the heaviest. The king called him and asked, 'Who are you?' The answer was 'I am Ondal,' which greatly astonished his Majesty.

Just at this time North Chou, which lay to the west of China, invaded Chi, whose centre was about Peking. Her armies conquered all before them and marched on to Liaotung, threatening Korea. As the king went forth to stop this tidal wave, Ondal was the officer who led the van, and from the first he gained a signal victory. When rewards were distributed, Ondal stood highest. The king sighed and said, 'He is indeed a worthy son-in-law. Let's call up the belated forms of royal marriage and have him and the princess crowned with honour.' He was made minister-in-chief and is indeed one of Korea's great men, still spoken of today; a man made out of nothing by his determined, resourceful princess.

As WE CAST our eye across the century once again, we find it included the first Korean history ever written, now gone, alas, beyond recovery.[18] This was also Korea's opening age of music. As we listen today to the unusual strains that accompany the sacrifices to Confucius, or hear the weird bag-pipe whistle that keeps pace with the modern theatre, we naturally ask whence come these far-away notes blown on pipe or struck from harp-string. We are informed by the *Tongsa Kangmok*[19] that a music teacher named Urŭk came to Silla from Kaya, a little state near modern Masan, bringing with him a harp. The king, hearing him, was delighted, made him his music master and asked him to prepare new tunes for him and his people. Urŭk made a special kind of harp with twelve strings, one answering to each month of the year. It was called a *kayagŭm,* or 'harp of Kaya', which name it still retains today. A contemporary it was, though no man knew it, of the 'harp that once through Tara's halls the soul of music shed'. The king appointed for Urŭk three specially gifted disciples: Kyego, Pŏpchi, and Mandŏk. Kyego was taught the harp, Pŏpchi song and Mandŏk the dance. The king listened and said, 'Happy, but not loose in soul; sad, but not to tears. This is true music.'[20]

What did they sing in those far distant days? Let me suggest a sample as I seek through the old records:[21]

> O rapid stream that flows through mountain gorges,
> Pray don't be glad swift-winged to fly away;
> When once you fall into the deep blue sea,
> There's no return. Let's wait before we go.

Here is an expression of filial piety:

> That ponderous weighted iron bar,
> I'll spin out thin in threads so far,
> To reach the sun and fasten on
> And tie him in before he's gone,
> That parents who are growing gray
> May not get old another day.

Here is a love token:

> That rock heaped up on yonder shore,
> I'll chisel out and cut and score,
> And mark the hair and make the horns,
> And put on feet and all the turns,
> Required for a cow;
> And then, my love, if you go 'way,
> I'll saddle up my bovine gray,
> And follow you somehow.

UNITED SILLA

13 Seventh-century unification of Korea

WITH the seventh century we arrive at one of the most important periods in the history of Korea, where we behold her no longer three kingdoms but one. Out of a great struggle she comes forth a united people. As we pass the years in review, in spite of war and confusion, we are more and more impressed with her superior civilization and her high attainment: but let us note first how Korea rises to be a military power. As mentioned in the last chapter, King Yang of Sui sent his finest troops and greatest generals to deal Koguryŏ a death-blow. His forces reached the Yalu in 612. The sedate old historian goes on to say that there each Chinese soldier was given a hundred days' rations, in weight equal to two bags of grain. A note appended to the order read: 'Any man found shirking his load will have his head struck off.' In true Chinese fashion the soldiers set themselves to thwart the orders of their chief. They dug holes under their tents and buried the obnoxious weights, while at the same time they stuffed their load full of soft and easy-going hay. Soon supplies gave out and they were in dire straits.[1]

A minister of Koguryŏ, a man of great resource, trained as scholar and soldier alike, Ŭlchi Mundŏk, was ordered to the front with soldiers to make a mock surrender. General Yu Chung-wen of China received Koguryŏ's message and at once arrested Ŭlchi; but his commanding presence and distinguished manner so moved the conclave of generals that they let him go. Across the Yalu he retired, while China, regretting her magnanimity, made after him in hot haste. Ŭlchi eluded her best endeavours and allowed himself to be defeated seven times in all, till he had drawn the enemy well on towards P'yŏngyang. Here he sent a very submissive letter to the commander-in-chief with a poem attached:[2]

> Your strategy is like the gods,
> Your calculations high as heaven;
> You've hit me hard time and again;
> With such a record hie you home, I pray.

The Chinese answer was; 'Not on your life. First and foremost: unconditional, immediate surrender.' Ŭlchi answered, 'Of course, of course! If you will please to retire a little, I'll follow and yield you all.' The Chinese moved back foolishly, with dire result: a fearful fight on the Clear River (Ch'ŏngch'ŏn) at Anju, where the army of Sui was trapped, drowned, trampled upon and cut to pieces. 2,700 men were all that were left of nearly half a million. Korea says little of General Ŭlchi because his memory lies buried forever beneath the fallen fragments of Koguryŏ, but surely if great achievement marks merit he might well be named the equal of China's highest hero, Han Hsin.[3]

These were fighting days, and women too came bravely to the front. There lived in Yulli, Silla, a man named Sŏl who had a very beautiful daughter. No son was born to his house and so the father, though advanced in years, was called to take the field. Sŏl-ssi, only a girl, was grieved to think that she could not stand in her father's place. Tears were of no avail, and she was obliged to see him prepare to go. At this moment there called at their home a gallant knight named Kasil. 'My greetings to your ladyship,' said he. 'I have sworn to give my life to any great cause I meet and especially to the service of others. Here is my chance; let me go, I pray you, in place of your revered father.'

Sŏl-ssi hurried forth with this delightful message. The father expressed his thanks, and at once offered his daughter in payment as the partner of the good knight's fortune. Kasil bowed and asked that a date be set.

Sŏl-ssi answered, 'Marriage is too important a matter to decide lightly. I am yours by heart and promise, let that suffice. Meanwhile I shall await your return.'

In answer he took his metal hand-mirror from his pocket, broke it in two, and gave her half. When he departed, he presented her with his beautiful horse. 'Feed it well,' said he, 'You may need it later.'

The country's troubles kept him long away, and six years passed with no message of return. Sŏl-ssi's father said, 'We agreed to three years, but that is long gone by. You had better marry someone else.'

'But', said she, 'Kasil has gone in your place and has suffered much for you; if I broke faith with him how dreadful that would be.'

Her father tried to force her and, in fact, concluded an agreement with a village neighbour. Seeing this, Sŏl-ssi drew her belt tightly and made her horse ready to flee. Just then Kasil returned, but so worn, thin and poor that she did not know him. His clothes, too, hung in tatters. Only when he brought forth the broken mirror did she recognize her knight returned. According to their plighted faith they were married and lived together in all happiness. Such are Korea's women dotting the pages of her history. They give their word and it proves as safe as the soundest merchant's bond.[4]

THESE are among the mightiest days of East Asia, for they mark the rise of the T'ang kingdom, which was to last 300 years and give the world great poets, great statesmen, and great warriors. The founder, T'ai Tsung, was a Li, descendant of the Old Philosopher and a great-great-great. . .grandfather of Li Hung-chang.[5] He was steeped in religious lore. A couplet ascribed to him runs thus:[6]

> Enlightened souls see ere the form appears,
> And sainted spirits hear when sounds are absent.

So often is the name T'ang T'ai Tsung on the lips of the Korean that I must endeavour to make some mark here that will impress him upon the memory of the reader. Perhaps I cannot do better than call to mind the halfstone of Wŏnju now in the Kyŏngbok Palace Museum in Seoul. Let all readers examine it carefully as they pass it. I quote a note written by Hong Yangho,[7] who was highpriest of Korea in 1776, and head of the Confucian College. He wrote as follows:[8]

> The half-stone that is on the Yongbong Hills of Wŏnju has on it an inscription prepared by the founder of Koryŏ (A D 940). He gave orders to his literary master, Ch'oe Kwangyun, to collect examples of the written characters of T'ang T'ai Tsung and so compose the inscription. As the Japan War of 1592 was in progress the enemy placed the stone on a cart and started off with it toward the east coast, but when they reached the Bamboo Pass (Chungnyŏng) the stone fell and was broken in two. Half of it they took away with them. When the war was over the governor of Kangwŏn province brought back the remaining half to Wŏnju, placed it on its base and called it the Half Broken Stone.

This gives the reader some idea of the rough hand of time and chance that the stone has seen. It remained in Wŏnju and at the site of the monastery of Hungbŏp-sa till 1913 when it was removed to the museum where it now is. The remarkable feature of this stone is the wonderful calligraphy of T'ang T'ai Tsung that adorns its face. Hong describes it thus:

> I got a rubbing from it, and the lines of the characters are strong beyond compare—the very brush-strokes of the man of God. I had learned that T'ai Tsung liked best of all the style of Wang Hsi-chih, and now that I see these characters I realize that he had indeed acquired the mastery for himself. They are of the most splendid form, like Heaven's horses galloping across the sky, something that no other hand can ever hope to rival. Even though untaught and untrained, the enemy could not but fall in love with such a trophy. Thus it was they stole it away. They were not daunted by a thousand pounds of weight or ten thousand *li* of distance. Fortunately, by the overruling of providence, half remains with us. This stone might be called a great world wonder. Hereafter if any great scholar should ever come from China inquiring for priceless treasure, please show him this.

And yet to our untrained western vision how dull it seems, though to every quickened Korean eye this stone stands for the greatness and glory of T'ai Tsung, founder of T'ang. At this very time, when T'ang was rising, Muhammad was making his mark on the glaring sands of Arabia. He appears not, however, like the silken-coated monarch of the Far East, but as a wild Beduin of the desert, armed and cloaked to defy the sun's rays and every mortal man that might cross his path. He, too, sang hymns and spoke praises, but in less gentle tones than China. Here is a poem of his from the Koran, compiled in those very days:[9]

> By the Sun and his noonday brightness!
> By the Moon when she followeth him!

By the Day when it revealeth his glory!
By the Night when it enshroudeth him!
By the Heaven and Him who built it!
By the Earth and Him who spread it forth!
By a Soul and Him who balanced it,
And breathed into it its wickedness and its piety!
Blessed now is he who hath kept it pure,
And undone is he who hath corrupted it!

WHILE MUHAMMAD was on his long search after God, and the T'ang king-dom was awakening, a Korean named Kim Yusin, greatly distressed by the con-flicts and enmities of his native land, was in the mountains behind Kyŏngju, pray-ing. Kim is one of Korea's greatest characters, as his tomb, that stands on the hills behind Silla's old capital, indicates today. We are told that in early years he was specially taught by his mother. Once, inveigled away by evil companions, he spent a night in the haunt of a dancing-girl called Ch'ŏn'gwan, 'Heaven's Queen'. His mother met him with tearful face; 'I had hoped', she said, 'that you might have become one of Korea's great, good men, but my dreams are done and all my plans have fallen.' Kim bowed before his mother penitently and swore a solemn oath that never again would he fail of her highest hopes. We are told that he never afterwards failed. Once his horse inadvertently turned aside into the gateway of the temptress, where Heaven's Queen was awaiting him. Kim dismounted, drew his sword and struck the horse's head off. Thus he refused all her advances. Tradi-tion says she died of a broken heart and that a monastery was built in Kyŏngju to her memory, named Ch'ŏn'gwan-sa, Heaven's Queen's Temple.[10]

We next behold Kim, as recorded in the *Samguk Sagi*,[11] greatly distressed by invasions of the armies of Koguryŏ, Paekche and Malgal; he left his friends and his life of pleasure and retired to a cave on Chungak Mountain, where, having performed the necessary acts of purification for body and soul, he prayed, saying, 'Enemies that have no religion invade our land like wolves and take by force the fields apportioned us. Peace has departed from the earth. I, a mere servant of the state, helpless to right these wrongs, make my humble prayer to God. Be pleased to condescend and lend thy powerful aid.'

After he had thus passed four days in prayer an old man in rough reed garb appeared and said, 'There are many venomous serpents and dangerous beasts in these hills; why should a handsome lad like you abide here alone?' Yusin replied, 'Whence comes your Excellency and what is your name?' The genius answered, 'I have no fixed abode, but visit where destiny calls me; nor could I ever explain to you fully the meaning of my name.' Yusin, hearing this, came forward, bowed twice and said, 'I am a man of Silla whose heart is sore over these inroads of the enemy. My coming here is in the hope that I may meet someone who will lend me help.'

The genius was silent for a time while Yusin's tears flowed as he earnestly besought pity. At last, breaking the silence, the stranger said, 'You are still young and yet your thoughts go out to unite these kingdoms into one—a great purpose indeed.' He then taught him the 'hidden law' by which all things are done, and said, 'Be moderate in your ways and speak only with discretion. If you misuse the gift I give you it will be your destruction.' Thus he finished speaking and went on his way, and though Yusin attempted to follow, he was gone and out of sight. Only a cloud of light rested on the mountain-top.

THE YEARS that followed were full of fateful consequences. In the great clash of arms Kim is ever constantly to the fore, while a host of China, 200,000 men under the command of Su Ting-fang, moves on Paekche, which goes down in the 2nd moon of 663, followed by Koguryŏ in 668. A sad day it was for Korea, surely, and yet in the end it doubtless worked weal, for it made her a single people, undivided.

The old capital of Paekche was Puyŏ. Immediately north of the ancient site is a mountain fortress about 400 feet high enclosed by an earthen wall, the north-west angle jutting out into the river. This rock that overlooks the watery depth has a name: the Rock of Falling Flowers. The story is that when General Su Ting-fang entered the city with his army, the maids and dancing-girls of the palace, unwilling to yield to the enemy, went up to the fortress rock and threw themselves into the river. Hence its name, Nakhwa-am, 'Rock of Falling Flowers'.[12]

In the centre of the city limits stands one of Korea's great wonders—a pagoda built by the same great T'ang in the days of the beginning of their glory.[13] They were marvels at the pen, the chisel, the plummet-line, the trowel, and have left their impress on the east as no other kingdom has. Here in Puyŏ is one of their masterpieces, this old pagoda that has stood one thousand three hundred years lifting its graceful form against all wind and weather. It is called the 'Pagoda of T'ang Peace to Paekche', though peace meant the silent grave, utter extinction. On it is written the story of T'ang's greatness; how she was destined to rule the whole world, Paekche and all other states; how her generals carried everything before them; how her virtue, her goodness, her glory were to be extolled. Anyone desiring to read this in the original will find it in the *Haedong yŏksa* volume xlvi. This is the oldest pagoda in Korea, not Korean at all, but planted here by one of the greatest of Korea's teachers, the T'ang. It has looked out toward the silent south during the same long period that the Mount of Olives has been gazed at by the Dome of the Rock, the Mosque of Omar.

General Su took back with him the captive king, the crown prince and three other sons, eighty-eight ministers and generals, and 12,807 of Paekche's best people.[14] We can behold in imagination this long procession wending its way out of Puyŏ much as the Jews did out of Jerusalem under the lash of Nebuchadnezzar. A dreamland region is this old site enclosed in the elbow of the White Horse River, Paengma-gang.

FROM NOW ON for three hundred years Korea wore just one name, Silla. Before this, there occurred an event of great importance in the history of Korean womanhood. King Chinp'yŏng died in 632 without a son. Boldly he passed the throne on to his daughter and she became 'king', her given name being Sŏndŏk, 'Sweet Virtue'. She was the first queen that I know of in East Asia to come to the throne by ordinary succession. There have been many dowagers who have usurped power, but Sŏndŏk was a queen in her own right and ruled Silla from 632 to 647.

A story is told by the sage chronicler which in his mind marks her wisdom: when she was a little girl there came, among other gifts from T'ang, the seed of the peony and several beautiful paintings of this famous flower. How greatly they were admired. 'But', said little Sŏndŏk, 'they have no fragrance. What a pity!' 'How come you to think that?' asked her father. 'If it had fragrance,' said she, 'there would be bees and butterflies about it.' They planted the seed and in due time flowers bloomed, but fragrance they had none. 'My wise little daughter!' said the king, 'She shall reign when I am gone.'[15]

Anyone visiting Kyŏngju will be deeply interested in the old observatory that stands as firm on its base as ever, built by Queen Sŏndŏk in the year 647 for the purpose of reading the stars. It is said that she sat in this high tower to watch the constellations go by.[16]

I look across the world of those times to the advancing hosts of Arabs and while I find great palaces and beautiful ornaments and carpets eighty feet long, no woman who can compare with Queen Sŏndŏk of Silla appears either in the Arab world, or east or west the wide world over.

As THE SEVENTH century drew to a close the one great and wise man of the peninsula was Sŏl Ch'ong, son of the noted priest, Wŏnhyo. In 692 King Hyoso had just come to the throne, and, having his counsellors about him, called on Sŏl Ch'ong. 'Today,' said the king, 'the long rains have ceased and the soft breezes blow. Tell us a good story, please. Recall something specially interesting from what you have seen and heard.'[17]

Sŏl Ch'ong replied, 'Your humble servant once heard that when the king of flowers first came to dwell among us he was planted in a garden with beautiful palings about it. Spring came and he opened up his wonderful world of colour. How proud he felt and with what contempt he treated all others. The common flowers and buds that bloomed jostled each other in order to do him honour. Among them was the sweetest of all, the *changmi,* the rose, with her soft tinted cheeks, ivory teeth, pretty dress and graceful mien. She came stepping forward to say, "Your humble servant has heard of the virtues of Your Majesty and so desires to give herself to you and share your pillow. Will you accept me?"

'Just as she said this, a gentleman stepped forward called the anemone, dressed in sackcloth, with leathern belt on his waist, a white cap on his head and a staff in his hand. He seemed awkward as he came forward bowing low and saying, "I your humble servant am from the country, where I dwell, a very common mortal, by the public highway. As I thought to myself I said, We need not only solid food but occasionally dainties, too, and medicines as well. We can have silks and satins without looking askance at ruder fabrics. Has Your Majesty thought it well through?"

'The king replied, "Your words are good words, indeed, and yet so rare is perfect beauty that one knows not what to do."

'The stranger then answered: "The ruler who makes wise men his counsellors lives and flourishes, but he who gives himself up to pretty girls goes the downward way. It is easy to lose one's heart to a pretty face, but very difficult to lend companionship to the good and wise. Mei Hsi brought destruction on the state of Hsia, and Hsi Shih on Wu, while Mencius looked in vain for a wise king to guide and counsel."

'The king asked pardon, saying, "I have done very badly." He added: "Your story is full of wise counsel. Write it out, please, and let it stand as a warning."'

Thus was Sŏl Ch'ong called and appointed to high office.

The peony girl, the tinted rose, the smiling-faced chrysanthemum were always a danger against which oriental kings were warned. Yi Kyubo wrote 400 years later:[18]

> Have you not heard that the glance of her eye
> Is a sharpened blade?
> That her eyebrows are a double-faced headsman's axe?
> That her red cheeks are a deadly potion,
> Her soft flesh a hidden demon that demands the soul?
> With her axe she strikes, with her blade she thrusts,
> With her hidden wiles she seeks my life,
> With her deadly draught she brings me down
> To guilt and shame. Is she not a danger?
> Among all my deadly foes, who can equal her?
> Therefore is she called a thief, a robber,
> One who means my death.
> How dare I make friends with her?
> So I say, put her far away!
> To the eye she is a delightful invitation,
> But in reality she is a fearful evil.

14 Eighth-century T'ang and Silla culture

WITH the dawn of the eighth century we are introduced to some of the most noted characters of the Far East, perhaps the most noted of all being Yang Kuei-fei, queen of T'ang. Twenty years ago Yi Yongik,[1] the sturdy finance minister of Korea, who had more than once faced tigers in the north, almost lost his life by likening Queen Ŏm to the famous, or rather, the infamous, Yang Kuei-fei. In the *China Journal of Science and Arts,* September 1923,[2] we find a long account of her, the most beautiful woman in the world and also the most abandoned. She forced her way into the palace and became her father-in-law's concubine, holding him as by a leash, her subject and her slave. In her train came intrigue, rebellion and war, the end of which was her own tragedy, her strangled body hanging by the roadside. Tears and songs and stories are the memorials of her wilful way. Here is one:[3]

> At her sweet smile fades every other beauty,
> On her soft charm kings marched ten thousand *li,*
> Now her fair soul, hung from the crags of Ma-wei,
>> Pipes through the night.

All Koreans know Yang Kuei-fei as the most beautiful, the most accomplished, the most wicked, the most wonderful of womankind. She lived in the days of Bede and Charlemagne and yet she had already reached the acme of woman's fame and fortune. How crude the dames of Merovingia or Byzantium would have looked beside her. When she danced and sang, Europe would have felt as the writer did in early days when, in rough tweed suit and woollen footgear, he stood in the presence of Korea's nobility, who were cloaked and clad in silk and shining gold, jade and amber.

EQUALLY famed with Yang Kuei-fei was her great contemporary Li Po, most gifted of China's poets. He is the joy and delight too of the children's world. How has the air of Korea resounded with

Tara, tara, palgŭn tara! Yi T'aebaegi noldŏn tara!'

(O moon, o moon, o shining moon, the master Yi T'aebaegi's moon.)[4] Wine and women have not occupied the poet's attention in the Far East as much as wine and the moon have. The wind, the flowers, the pine, all have their part, but none can equal the moon. Here is a song written by Yi Kyubo, born in 1169, showing how Li Po's moon had not waned in five hundred years:[5]

> Viewing the moon has ever been a pleasure.
> In ancient days, so now: the sages left
> Their moon with us. If we should fail to view it,
> How bad the moon would feel.
> Once her resentful anger rose, she'd shine no more.
> My fear is that the whole creation,
> Thus grown dark, would lose its eyes, go blind.
> Let's take a cup and go tonight to see the moon!
> We went. Delighted was the moon:
> She swept the clouds aside and shone for us.
> A million pupils of the eye, all centred
> In her disk, shot up their spears of light
> To make her brighter still.
> If eyes should fail to see, how soon the moon
> Would lose its ray! List now, my friend,
> Until I sing you of the moon.
> Let's have a cup, and still another cup,
> And watch the night through till the morning breaks.

As the newer generation of Koreans comes forward, fewer and fewer will know how to appreciate this master spirit of China; in fact few will even be able to understand the thought that underlies his writings. Li Po, like the customs, ideals and ceremonies of his native world, will go down into a long Van Winkle sleep and wake—who knows when?

IN THE FIRST chapter of this history I mentioned Kim Saeng, Korea's most famous calligrapher, and how, after earnest prayer, he met the old man Tan'gun.[6]

Kim was born in 711 and so belongs to the period of which we write. Though 1,200 years have trodden thin and rolled out and rarefied his memory, it still survives clear and matchless as ever. To show how great his spirit was, the delightfully innocent historian tells how he wrote the name of the temple Anyang-sa in large characters and hung them up. Shortly afterwards, it was noticed that the temple had begun to lean over on the side of the name. Kim was hastily called to write a corrresponding balance for the other side, which he did, and at once the great structure swung back into place and sat square.[7]

Yi Kyubo sees in Kim Saeng's writing wonders such as these:[8]

> The morning dew alights, the evening mist is there,
> The angry dragon lifts his claw, the phoenix flies;
> 'Twas God who made you what you are:
> Wonderful! No words can tell.

As Wang Hsi-chih 400 years before had become a name to thrill all China, so now Kim becomes the Tintoretto, the Angelo, the da Vinci of his people; his brush-strokes, pictures that can never die.

THESE were propitious days, as one learns from ancient remains, conspicuous among which is the great bell of Kyŏngju cast in 771.[9] It was made in honour of the king's grandfather, Sŏngdŏk, who had reigned from 702 to 737. No wars marred his rule; peace, pardon, and plenty were the footmarks of his way; the needy were fed, the old and sick cared for; the king himself was a true Sir Lancelot who went out to do deeds good and great. The bell was cast in bronze, its diameter being $7\frac{1}{2}$ feet, its height 12 feet and its weight 80 tons. It is sounded by beating with a swinging ram of hardwood, and its vibration can be felt thirty miles away. The greatest scholar of the land wrote the inscription on its face, which the wise may read today. Thus it runs:[10]

> True religion lies beyond the realm of visible things; its source is nowhere seen. As a sound heard through the air without giving any clue to its whereabouts, so is religion. Thus we hang up this great bell that it may awaken the call of the buddha. So ponderous is it that it can never be moved: a fitting place on which to inscribe virtues of the king. Great Sŏngdŏk was his name, his deeds eternal as the hills and streams, his glory as the sun and moon. He called the true and noble to aid him in his rule. Fitting ceremonies and music accompanied all his ways. He encouraged the farmer to joy in his work and the merchant to the exercise of honesty. Gold and jewels were counted nothing in his sight, while useful knowledge and skill of hand were treasures above compare. His great aim was the right-ordered life. For this reason people came from afar to seek his counsel and all revered him for his worth.

As proof of the high place held by the kingdom of Silla at this time we read that T'ang China closed her palace gates for two days when King Hyoso died;

and, also, that she sent a special envoy to be present at the funeral.[11] Silla, desirous of showing her deep appreciation, sent as gifts some of her finest horses, rolls of her most beautifully woven silk, lovely sealskin garments and, to cap all, two of her most beautiful princesses. Hsüan Tsung of T'ang, who was by no means a saint and loved the light and easy way well enough, was so moved to pity by these beautiful women exiled from their native land, that he sent them back under safe escort, with word that no such gifts could be accepted, seeing they were of royal blood of the honourable house of Silla.[12]

Buddhism, as represented by the monster bell at Kyŏngju, was in great vogue in those days. Its echoes rang over the land in the sweetest, softest notes ever heard. The twentieth century stops with attentive ear today to listen to its vibrations. Wonder-struck it says; 'What matchless tones!' How this bell world surprises and delights one. Among the mountains of Kangwŏn, at Sangwŏn-sa, seemingly far away from human habitation, you may hear its softest ringing— a five-foot bell hung in P'yŏngch'ang when the Venerable Bede was fifty-three years of age. It tolled the knell of Osric, King of Northumbria, as it has tolled the knell of all kings and counsellors since. Such are the footprints of the buddha: on the earth, great temples; on the rocks, vast images like the Manjusri of the Diamond Mountains; in the air, the ever-recurring echoes of the temple bells.

In a monastery of Kyŏngju, named Kamsan-sa, was an image of Maitreya made in 719.[13] Prince Kim Chisŏng had it made in memory of his father and mother. This prince, as shown by his composition, must have been a master of all three religions. In the confucian style of script he is unsurpassed; in the depth of his buddhist peace and quiet, kings and courtiers are as nothing. As for taoism, he knew all the old philosopher by heart. Scholarship in those days had attained to its highest mark, and yet we have no collected writings remaining to us till 200 years afterwards. Somewhere, sometime, in some way, all the famous books went down to the eternal shades and left us nothing but what is carved in stone or moulded on the shining face of a temple bell.

Under the date 778, I find mentioned a very remarkable character named Kim Am. Early in life he went to T'ang where he found service at the court and learned of the latest developments in science and philosophy. Among other things, he attained to the exercise of *tun'gap*, by means of which he could make himself invisible. With such manifestations of power he greatly overawed his king and people. In this year he was sent as envoy to Japan and she, taking note of his remarkable gifts, had a mind to ask him to stay and cast in his lot with her. Just then, however, there came an envoy from T'ang who, delighted to meet Kim, showed him every honour. When the Japanese saw the respect with which the T'ang envoy treated him they concluded that he was too great a man to be moved by reward or gain and so they withdrew their intention.[14]

What was this law of *tun'gap*? We used to hear of it constantly in the old days. It was often spoken of as the *tun'gap changsin*, the 'law that hides the body'. Curious Chinese books are sold even today in the streets of Seoul with this as the central thought. One of these, *Chi-men tun-chia,* is believed to have been written by the wise Chu-ko Liang, who the maid in chapter 6 said could not mend a broken heart.[15]

THESE WERE DAYS of mighty builders. Fifteen miles behind Kyŏngju is Pulguk-sa, a temple set up in 751. The entrance way, the pagodas, the halls, still demonstrate the master hand of Silla. So beautiful a structure, built by such simple people, seems a contradiction in itself. The story of its building is this: there lived in the valley of Moryang a poor widow, mother of an only son named Kim Taesŏng. He was indeed her joy, till suddenly one day he died and left her desolate. On the night of his death, a voice was heard calling from mid-air over the home of minister Kim Mullyang, 'A child is to be born to you named Taesŏng. A son of the widow of Moryang he was, but now he comes to you.' For seven days his baby hand remained tight shut. At last when it opened two characters were seen written in the palm, *taesŏng,* 'great city.' Thus was he named and it was he who in 751 built the beautiful temple of Pulguk-sa.[16] On the one hand we smile at the absurdity of the story; on the other we behold the beautiful Tabo Pagoda and ask who built it.[17] This story alone gives an answer. What could be more graceful than this landmark of Silla's soul? Loosely flung together as though it could be toppled over with a hearty push of the hand, it has yet outlasted the earthquakes, wars and tempests of 1,200 years. As we pass the Tabo Pagoda of Pulguk-sa it is fitting that we doff the hat in memory of Kim Taesŏng, the little lad twice born, with the two characters hidden away in his crumpled baby hand.

As you walk about the hills and tombs and temples of the old capital of Silla you meet with mystery on every hand. What do these great mounds at the entrance mean?[18] The great bell with the voice of a dragon? This observatory tower of Queen Sŏndŏk? This Pulguk Temple with its pagoda? They strike the visitor as marvellous footprints of ages gone by. The most striking, however, is still to come. Over the hills behind Pulguk-sa, along a giddy way that looks out on the sea of Japan, is a cave-temple of the buddha, called Sŏkkuram. With flashlight in hand you step into its shadows. Of eleven figures ranged as bas-reliefs along the wall we would call attention to Kuan-yin who stands on his lotus leaf, capped with a crown of golden faces, a halo about his head and a vase of the flowers of Paradise in his hand. At his side stands a queenly lady with uplifted chalice, clad in soft robes that cross her graceful form. Her face, her poise, her manner might easily make her Semiramis, or Dido, or Cleopatra, or Zenobia, from the other end of Asia. Was she copied from a picture or from a living model? Nearby stands another bas-relief, a modest, meditative man, who might easily be Saul of Tarsus. Whence came he? On either side are guards with drawn swords, who, like St George of England, or Michael the Archangel, trample evil under foot. The Japanese art world has been so greatly struck by these bas-reliefs that Count Terauchi had them cast in plaster and the casts placed in the Seoul Museum. Let all passers take note of these and remember that they represent Korea of the eighth century. What have we of that period that can equal them or spell so clearly a high refinement of state and nation?[19]

THESE WERE indeed anxious days for Europe, full of fear and weird foreboding. The Saracens had swept across north Africa, which they held still, under the name of Moors. Tariq ibn Zayid, one of their generals, had captured the straits of Spain and threatened western Europe. The rock where he landed was called Jebel Tariq (Mountain of Tariq), hence named Gibraltar. They had landed, these Moors, Arabs and Saracens, and getting Spain into their grip were across the Pyrenees into France. Before this hurricane of mounted sabres, it was touch and go as to whether European civilization would become muslim, or be annihilated. Charles Martel, the Frenchman, answered the call. He was the master-spirit of the hour. Rising in his might he met the muslim at Tours and fought, as Creasy says, one of the fifteen decisive battles of the world.[20] It was a great victory and we were saved by it in 732. I look through the annals of East Asia to see what was going on but find nothing recorded of that year except that Silla took stock of its city walls and saw to their strengthening.

These were the days of the Nestorians in China and the setting up of their famous monument at Ch'ang-an, nine feet high, three feet across, and one foot thick. The excellent composition and beautiful characters on its face tell of the superior world to which it belonged. It was erected in 781 and then lay buried in the ground for nearly a thousand years, till 1625. It describes the creation of the world and gives an outline of christian doctrine: good and evil, God, the incarnation (specially mentioning the cross), baptism and the scriptures. All Koreans of any scholarship know of the Kyŏnggyo-bi, the Nestorian Tablet. An English lady, the late Mrs E. A. Gordon, has placed a copy of it at the entrance to Changan-sa, in the Diamond Mountains.[21]

As mentioned before, Korea remembers nothing of the great scholars who adorned her state at this period. That there were such we know full well, for who wrote the inscription on the monster bell at Kyŏngju if not a great and noted scholar? Who indited the story of the merciful buddha in 720 and wrote it on the stone that still remains?[22] Who was it in 784 that inscribed the memorial to the great priest Sŏdang? Thus it still clearly reads:[23]

> The religion of the buddha goes not, comes not, loves not, hates not. Like a shadow it follows in silence. Its influence lies in the mind only. How great its power! Such was the master Sŏdang: a man who cast the world aside that he might give his whole soul to the onward march of the buddha.

THESE WERE indeed great men, but Korea knows them not. None of her own great literati of the eighth century remain. Two Chinese on the other hand, born in 772 and 768 respectively, have come to more than take their place, and live as household words: Po Chü-i and Han Yü. Po Chü-i was a great poet whose smiles and tears poured out upon his paper. The dancing girl of Seoul still sings his songs as a sort of psalm of life. One in memory of Yang Kuei-fei runs thus:[24]

> One turn of head, one softly moving smile
>   Shot other beauties dead;
> The maids, in all the glimmering palace halls,
>   Turned ashy pale and fled.

Such songs of Po Chü-i are sung still today, and his name lives green while Silla's music is forgotten. Han Yü too, the contemporary of Po Chü-i, wrote much that Korea reads still. Here is one sentence of his that begins an essay:[25] 'Widely-extended kindness is called love; acts that move in line with truth are called righteousness; a life lived in accord with these is true religion.'

As we think regretfully of Korea's forgotten dead, we are reminded of a somewhat similar phenomenon in our own race. We know much of the Jewish women Mary and Martha, but little of their contemporary Boudicca, the British warrior queen. As Judea was the fountain-head of our religious inspiration, so was China to Korea. Consequently China's heroes, China's warriors, China's saints, and China's scholars have become Korea's master spirits.

DURING this century the influence of the buddha was felt more and more, so much so that orders were sent out forbidding all slaughter of animals. There should be no taking of life. This doctrine went so far as to protect even insects, vermin, and reptiles. All were as lost souls to be saved by the mercy of the buddha. Let me close this chapter with a quotation from the *Life of Sakyamuni:*[26]

> In a past existence Ananda and Kasyapa were farmers living in the country ploughing their fields. On the side of the road a great snake had been wounded by a boy who was passing with an ox. Ananda saw it and ran away in fear but Kasyapa left his plough and, seeing the creature dying, scolded the boy, took up the snake and put it where the ants might get it, saying, 'Make haste to rid youself of your ill-fated body and so attain to some better form.' Because of this prayer the snake became a rich man of the world, and all the people of his town were the ants who had befriended him. The farmer who looked at it with disgust and ran away was Ananda, and the one who took pity on it and placed it by the ant-hill was Kasyapa. Because of his dislike, the one was punished; and because of his pity, the other was richly rewarded.

15 Ninth-century Silla culture

A great century of the buddha opens before us, its years marked by the footprints of many famous priests. Mountains, pagodas, stone pillars and temples, remind us of how great they were. Some were called *kuksa,* royal teachers; some *taesa,* rulers in the world of the buddha; some *sŏnsa,* masters of meditation. Two of supreme importance span the century: one called Nanghye, 'Peerless Wisdom', and one Nanggong, 'Nothing of the World'.

Nanghye's biography, written by Ch'oe Ch'iwŏn,[1] the father of Korean literature, is carved on a stone that stands today among the weeds under Sŏngju Mountain, Poryŏng County, half way across the province of South Ch'ungch'ŏng hard by the Yellow Sea. The other, that of Nanggong, is in the museum of the

Kyŏngbok Palace.

The old stone of Nanghye was set up when Alfred the Great was thirty-one years of age. Before telling what is on the stone, we glance for a moment at the writer, Ch'oe Ch'iwŏn. Like modern students he went abroad for study. He reached China when about thirteen years of age, and remained there for seventeen years. His name was enrolled among China's noted scholars, for he was made secretary to the commander-in-chief of the army and so must have won great renown. He wrote much, though only a few spare remnants from his gifted pen survive. This is what he says[2] about

The Swallow

She goes with the fading summer
   And comes with returning spring;
   Faithful and true is she,
Regular as the gentle winds
   Or chilly rains of autumn.
   We are old friends, she and I.
You know, ungrateful bird, that I have always
Consented to your occupying a place
In my spacious home, but more than once you soiled
The painted rafters. Are you not ashamed?
You leave hawks and uncanny birds far off
In islands of the sea, and come to join
Your heron friends in streams and sunny shallows.
Your rank is equal to that of the goldfinch,
I should think; but when it comes, finch-like,
To bringing home finger-rings in your bill
As gifts to your master, you fail me!

The Seagull

So free you are to ride the running whitecaps,
Rising and falling with the rolling waters!
You lightly shake your feathery skirts and mount
Aloft, indeed the fairy of the deep.
You soar and sweep, serenely free; no taint
Have you of man or of the dusty world;
Your practised flight must have been learned
In the abodes of genii. Enticements
Of rice and millet fields have no power
To woo you, but the spirit of the winds and moon
Is what delights your soul. I think of Chuang-tzŭ,
Who dreamed of the fairy butterfly; surely
I too dream as I behold thee.

The Tide

Like a rising storm of snow or sleet you come,
A thousand rollers from the deep, dark tide;
Over tracks so deeply worn, again you come
And go. As I see how you never fail
To keep the appointed time, I am ashamed
To think how wasteful all my days have been,
And how I spend in idle dissipation
The precious hours. Your impact on the shore
Is like reverberating thunder, or
As if the cloud-topped hills were falling.
When I behold your speed, I think
Of Tsung Ch'üeh and his wish to ride the wind;
But when I see your all-prevailing might,
I think of sleeping dragons that awake.

HEREWITH a line or two from the old stone to show how a great confucian scholar in those days a millennium ago estimated a priest of the buddha. There were no religious persecutions then, and no feeling that 'I' was right and every other man wrong. Over 5,000 characters cover the face of the stone to tell of the good priest's being and doings:[3]

> Teacher of two kings of Silla, master of meditation. It was as though the people of the kingdom had lost their eyesight when his light went out. His Majesty said, 'His late Excellency was indeed the reincarnation of the buddha. My father as well as King Mun, my uncle, made him teacher and learned the grace of his guiding hand. I was desirous to make him my chief counsellor but God has taken him away. Alas, how destitute I am! All I can do now is to honour him who was so truly honourable. Hence I enroll his name, Tae Nanghye, Greatly Enlightened One, and call his pagoda Paegwŏl-pagwang, "The Pagoda that outshines the Moon".'

The record goes on to say:

> His mother once in dreamland saw a hand reach down from heaven and pass her a lotus flower. On accepting it she was found to be with child.

His desire as he grew up was to see China and study there. With this in view he joined the envoy's company, but was wrecked in the Yellow Sea. For a fortnight and more he and his companions were driven about on wreckage. Finally cast ashore, they were saved. On returning, his influence grew so great that people came from far and near to learn of him and to become his disciples. The old stone says:

> He was like the bell that waits but the hammer-stroke to give the sound, or the mirror that needs but to be looked into to tell what manner of man you are.

YOUNGER by thirty-two years was Nanggong, whose stone was found in North Kyŏngsang. Even after a thousand years it too speaks unstinted praise. The inscription was written by Ch'oe Inyŏn, a cousin of Ch'oe Ch'iwŏn, and set up in 954.[4] It begins:

> I have heard that the true boundary is indistinct and the dark ferry is dim and far away; but I know that it yet is pure as the boundless sea and unalloyed as the immensities of space. Even the boat of wisdom fails to reach its distant bounds; the chariot of knowledge, too, would fail to carry us over. How divinely deep it is, closed away from common mortals. If one does not overcome the monkey in one's soul and drive the horses of thought straight across the sky, one is sure to land where there is no truth, sure to be shipwrecked amid the vain allurements of the day. The man of enlightened soul, however, who bids farewell to earth, and with truth for his guide dips deep into religion, can realize the mysteries of the kalpas and enter the beautiful gates of the buddha. Such an one indeed was the Great Master who knew deep in heart the jewelled ornament for the head, the true stamp to put upon the soul.
>
> His religious name was Haengjŏk, 'Walking in Silence', while his lay name was Ch'oe. His forefathers were distant descendants of the great Chiang T'ai-kung[5](1100 BC) of the kingdom of Chou. His later forefathers became kings of Chi and finally, when that state disappeared, became dukes of Ting. Such was his family line. In the days of his happy boyhood he played at buddhism; his custom was to gather sand and build pagodas, and to find spices and compound sweet incense. When he attained to youth he used to take great subjects and write essays thereon. While at his studies he fasted and lived with the closest strictness till his spirit was wearied and his flesh worn down. So vehement was he in his labours that his pent-up soul would boil the sea. In his service he passed through all manner of hardships and lived for others with all lowliness of soul.

He visited China and was given audience on the birthday of the emperor in 870. The emperor asked, 'What is your desire in coming thus across the great sea?' 'My desire,' said he, 'is to follow the spiritual footsteps of the masters and attain to the pearls that lie in the red waters of the brain. Thus would I bring greater light to my people and leave a mark for the buddha on the hearts of my fellow-countrymen.'

The emperor, delighted at what he said, loved him greatly and showered favours upon him. He returned home and made the Odae Mountains his residence. There, on the high peaks, he used to converse with a divine being 'whose hair was white as snow'.

At this time (AD 912) King Sindŏk ascended the throne of Silla and summoned the master to the palace. In the spring of 915, at command of the king, he called his priests together to the capital and had them assemble in the Silche Temple. This became the master's residence, and frequently the king went there to receive 'the favour of his countenance'. 'Here his longing hopes were fulfilled, for he heard the words of supreme wisdom.' As the master returned once from the royal presence he met a lady, a special admirer, whose name was Myŏngyo, 'Bright Jewel'. One of the fairy group, she was of the royal descendants who dwelt in the dove-forest of Kyerim. Her one desire was to follow the master and so to attain to the spiritual heights of the buddha. Among gifts that she gave him was the Sŏngnam-san temple to be held as a perpetual memorial.[6]

In regard to his death Ch'oe writes: 'His departure from earth was like the fairy's ascent to the abodes of bliss. In life, in death, his influence never failed to show forth the graces of religion. There was no limit to his wisdom and his spiritual understanding was perfect.'

A THOUSAND YEARS is a long stretch of time and yet today whether to a listening world, to the silent hills, or to the echo of the pheasant booming by, these stones speak out with accents unimpaired the high praises of the great masters of Silla. Religion was indeed one of the heart treasures of the state. Literature, ceremony, poetry, and music likewise. When Alfred was spelling out his first lessons before his mother Osburga and leaving his unlettered brothers far behind, Silla was writing with master-hand essays that today are the wonder and admiration of Oxford and Cambridge and other great schools of the west. Could they but have seen her literati construe a piece of complex confucian Chinese so as to bring the thought out clearly, they would have bared their heads in reverence most profound. But Oxford and Cambridge were not dreamed of for 400 years still to come.

As Silla paid her tribute to T'ang—beautiful furs, rolls of grass cloth, silken fabrics, inlaid boxes, mats in dragon pattern—nothing pleased the Chinese more than Korean paper. Here are some notes that I gather from the *Haedong yŏksa:*[7]

> 'Korean paper is of superior quality, very white, tough and smooth. The Chinese paper has been but poorly developed, and so we have had to depend on other countries, especially Korea, for our supply. In the poems of the T'ang dynasty we find many references to Korean paper. Even then (AD 618–905) it was reckoned the best of all.'

A thousand years before the first patent was taken out for its manufacture in England in 1665, it was known to Korea, and such high skill developed in its manufacture that it won the admiration of the great kingdom of T'ang. We are informed that in the imperial archives the finest models of calligraphy, precious writings of kings and princes, masterpieces of Han, the Three Kingdoms (AD 220), the Six States (AD 439), Sui (AD 600) and T'ang were all preserved on Korean paper.

The Chinese, always an inquisitive individual, in his astonishment over this paper's excellent quality, undertook to make a minute examination and see what it was made of. His wisdom decided that it was made from the cocoon, like silk, and he called it *chien-chih,* 'cocoon paper', which name it still bears, though the idea behind the name has long since been exploded. It is interesting to think that Korea was able to fool the Chinese for 500 years in something that his hands could handle and his eyes could see. We are doubtless safe in saying that no other people in the world have ever done it before or since.

The great K'ang-hsi emperor, who seems to have discovered the mistake, says:[8]

> In days gone by we were told that Korean paper was made of the silk of the cocoon but now we find that we were mistaken and that it is made of the bark of the paper mulberry. The skill with which it is manufactured surely surpasses everything. I tested a piece of it with fire and discovered that it was the bark of a tree and not silk thread. When I enquired of the Korean envoy how they made it, he told me that it is made of the bark of the *tak* tree (*Broussonettia kazinoki*), the white part of the bark alone being used. Tough, smooth and soft, it glistens as though made of the finest windings of the silk-worm.

As paper is the special accompaniment of the scholar I have taken this occasion to tell how long Korea has had its gentle service at her disposal. When the mulberry failed, Koreans found a good substitute in old mats and oat straw. They have had paper from the earliest times.

In return for the beautiful paper, T'ang sent the seeds of the tea plant. Korea had talked of tea and used it since the days of Queen Sŏndŏk (632–647) but had never grown it herself. Now in this year 828 she began to cultivate it in the Chiri Mountains. The question is frequently asked: 'Why does Korea drink no tea today when Japan and China are so devoted to its culture and to the rites and ceremonies that attend it?' There is no answer that I know of. She drank it for 500 years and then gave it up. She had tried it and refused it 300 years before we knew that tea existed. One feels quite a shock of surprise to think that Queen Elizabeth, with all her graces of soul, never enjoyed afternoon tea. Tea came to England too late for her day, but just in time to brace up the nerves of Oliver Cromwell for his rough task. From 800 to 1400 Korea rejoiced in its sweet fragrance. Hsü Ching, a Chinese, envoy of Sung, who came in 1124 and wrote a book called *Kao-li t'u-ching*, 'Korean Pictures', says:[9]

> The tea of Korea has a slightly bitter and astringent taste, disagreeable to a Chinese. Of late, however, she has become addicted to tea drinking and makes many varieties of beautiful teapots. Her teacups are decorated with gold and flowers. There are black teacups, too, and small pots of green-coloured ware. On occasions of entertainment they provide tea and as they bring it into the room they walk very slowly and say, 'Tea, please.'

Ch'oe Ch'iwŏn, who wrote about the swallow, wrote also about tea.[10]

> Today a gift of tea comes to me from the general of the forces by the hand of one of his trusty aides. How deep my appreciation! Tea was first grown in Shu and brought to great excellence of culture. It was one

of the rareties in the gardens of the Sui Kingdom (AD 589–618). The practice of picking the leaves began then, and its clear and grateful flavours from that time were known. Its specially fine qualities are manifest when its leaves are steeped in a golden kettle. The fragrance of its brew ascends from the white goblets into which it is poured. If it were not to the quiet abode of the genii that I am invited to make my respectful obeisance, or to those high angels whose wings have grown, how could such a gift of the gods ever come to a common man like me? I need not now a sight of the plum forest to quench my thirst nor any day-lilies to drive away my care.

KOREA, with her great priesthood, her devotion to China, her high literary excellence, dots all her pages of history with stories that turn on religion, especially piety. Under the date 835 I find the following:[11]

Son Sun was a man of Moryang, sincere and upright by nature. When his father died, he and his wife went out as servants and so fed and clothed his widowed mother. Sun had a son of evil nature who made a habit of stealing his grandmother's dinner. Greatly disturbed by this, Sun said, 'We can easily get another son but not another mother; I propose that we do away with him.' So he took the boy on his back and went to the hills. There he dug the ground to bury his evil offspring out of sight; but in the digging he came on a wonderful stone bell. His wife exclaimed, 'This marvellous thing that you have found just in the nick of time will save my child. He shall not die.' Thus they returned home. The bell was hung up and struck. Its wide encircling vibrations took in the whole city. The king, hearing the sound, inquired and the story was told. Said he, 'In ancient days Kuo Chü intended burying his son, and God gave him a golden bowl that he dug up. Here too, Son Sun would bury his son and a stone bell appears. These are similar marvellous happenings.' So he gave him a house and fifty bags of rice each year.

Here is a word that shows how the 'New Woman' existed at that distant date as well as now. Ch'oe Ch'iwŏn writes:[12]

This was written for Hsü Ching on the occasion of his wife Liu-shih's desire to take the field and offer her faithful services as a soldier. I was greatly impressed by it and have failed to find words for all I desired to say by way of appreciation. In the *History of Later Wei* we read of a General Yang who was given the name of Ta-yen, 'Great Eyes'. His military talents were of the first order. He was a master of the confusions of the battlefield. He had a wife called P'an-shih who was a practised rider and a great shot with the bow. When her husband was called upon to attack, advance, retreat, or pitch camp, she too was on hand, dressed in uniform, keeping pace with his rough life and hard riding. She also sat with him in his tent, a companion of his aides and officers, and laughed and talked with the greatest freedom. Great Eyes used to say concerning his wife: 'She is General P'an sure enough.' I had known of Liu-shih for a long time but had never before been so impressed with the excellence of her behaviour as I am now. This lady who today marches with us I shall call General Liu.

KORYŎ

16 Tenth century: foundation of Koryŏ

THE year 900, which marked in Europe the rise and progress of the Saxon people, saw in Korea a period of disturbance. Three men come to the fore: one very bad, one very good and one a nondescript, contemptible creature. Let me deal with the bad man first. His name was Kungye, 'Son of the Bow'. The bow has had much to do with the imagination of the east. It occurs in the ideograph of the buddha with its two arrows; and a spirit, a ghost, has a string of bows hung by the girdle in its ideograph.[1]

Kungye,[2] only one degree better born than Jephthah, was the son of a concubine, his father being King Hŏnan who reigned from 857 to 861. A rainbow announced his birth, and he was born with strong teeth fully-developed. The state astrologer said, 'This boy brings signs of evil fortune, put him out of the way.' Like Paris of Troy, like Oedipus of Thebes, he was flung aside, but rescued by his nurse, who in her hot haste to save him poked out one of his eyes. He grew up, therefore, as a priest with only one eye and with no mind for religion, his thoughts being entirely on earthly things. A passing crow once let fall an ivory book-mark that struck him on the head. Carved on it was the character 'king'. 'My lot is kingship' said he, and the times favoured his wish, for they were sadly out of joint, and the end of Silla's days had come.

Son of the Bow, he gathered about him like minds with himself, every man with his quiver full of hates and resentments. These he set to work to thrash north Korea into line with his wishes, his headquarters being at Ch'ŏrwŏn on the way to Wŏnsan. Here it was that he first met a young man named Wang Kŏn whom he induced to join his forces. Wang Kŏn is the second of the famous three. Already Kungye had welded together a large part of Korea under the strokes of his hammer and had set going a system of terror in order to win it all. He called his state Taebong, his own title being Mirŭkpul, 'the messiah of the buddhas'. He wore a golden crown and a purple robe and as he went from place to place he rode a large white horse whose mane and tail were plaited with coloured tinsel; boys and girls carried umbrellas, banners and flags before him; two hundred priests brought up the rear singing psalms. He wrote many books—'all proud, senseless stuff' remarks the later historian. Sometimes he would sit and preach by the hour, showing an immense amount of windy conceit. One of the priests, of a bolder turn of mind than the others, said, 'From a religious point of view, sir, your talk is all meaningless bosh.' Kungye turned on him like a tiger and knocked his brains out with a club. Wang stood by and took note.

Kungye then inaugurated a reign of terror. Every suspect was at once taken and handed over to a violent death. The old record reads, 'A hundred and more innocent people were killed every day', so that the region about Ch'ŏrwŏn was paralysed with fear. Said Kungye, 'I am the buddha and can read every man's innermost thoughts. I know even the evil intentions of my wife.'

He had an iron baton three feet long that he used with terrific effect. When a palace-woman offended he had this heated red hot and driven into her body. His wife remonstrated at this and Kungye made a counter-charge against her, impugning her morals. She defied him and the red-hot bludgeon with its nameless torture was resorted to. 'The smoke came out of her mouth and nose', says the record. Having killed his wife, like Herod the Great, he killed his two sons.

His range of suspicion now enlarged and took in Wang Kŏn. He called him up and inquired, 'What were you and your henchmen plotting last night?' Wang Kŏn coolly replied; 'Plotting? What should I plot, pray?' Kungye roared, 'Don't dare answer me thus! I have power to read your heart—your very inmost soul. I shall retire for a moment and read you through and through.'

So, with his hands behind his back and his eyes shut tight and turned up toward heaven, he meditated. At this moment a recorder, Ch'oe Ŭng, who was waiting on the king, purposely let fall his pen in front of Wang Kŏn. As he stooped to pick it up, he whispered, 'There is danger in standing by your innocence.' Wang Kŏn caught the hint and replied submissively, 'I am indeed a rebel and deserve death.' Kungye gave a great laugh and said, 'There you are a straight and honest man at last.' He then gave him a gold-mounted saddle and said, 'Now don't deceive me again.'

As the heart of Kungye grew more and more hardened, people turned with longing toward General Wang Kŏn. In the 3rd moon of 918 a Chinese merchant from T'ang came to Korea with a wonderful mirror. Turned one way to the light it revealed in its depths the inscription: *Behind the three waters and beneath the four nets, Heaven will give to Chin and Ma a son, who will first catch the chicken, then the duck*. It also read: *Two dragons there are, one in the pines and one in the shadow of the black rock*. The merchant, regarding it as a very wonderful mirror, made a gift of it to King Kungye. Kungye handed it over to three of his wise men who at a private sitting worked out its mystery. 'The three waters,' said they, 'are the three seas about Korea; the Chinese characters for 'four' and 'nets' together make the character for Silla; Chin and Ma are Chinhan and Mahan: green wood or pine refers to Songdo where the son of the dragon will become king.' Wang Kŏn, it seems, had scales under his arms and so was accounted a dragon in his descent. The chicken was the cock of Kyerim and the duck the *ya* character in the name of the Yalu River. All from the far north to the far south were to come under his sway. To speak this openly, however, would have meant instant death at the hands of Kungye, and so the wise men cleverly arranged a second interpretation which gave all to the Son of the Bow. This greatly pleased His Highness.

Meanwhile secret meetings were held in the quiet hours of the night. Retainers gathered round Wang Kŏn and said, 'This man means the death of us all. He has already killed his wife and children and will have the rest of us with no long delay.' But Wang Kŏn made answer: 'I can't interfere. I have sworn an oath of good faith which I mean to keep, no matter what he does. Who strikes him down strikes me.'

'But', said his retainers, 'it is now or never. You are our man; not only are all eyes on you but the mirror from China flashes its light as well. You must lead us forth or we shall all die.'

Yu-ssi, Wang Kŏn's wife, came in at this point, but Wang Kŏn, wishing her away, asked her to go to the garden and get some melons. Yu-ssi pretended to go, but instead she slipped into a corner of the near room and listened. Overhearing the proposition she rushed into the room and said, 'Do the right. It is your duty to rid the earth of this bloody-handed monster. My heart leaps at the chance. Will you, a warrior, be less valiant than a woman? It is God's will; accept it.'

With her own hands she got out his coat of mail and put it on him, and made his helmet fast round his chin while his generals stood wondering by. When day dawned a throne was improvised — a heap of rice bags — and from the top of this he received their oaths of allegiance. A shout was raised, 'Long live the King.'

When Kungye heard it and saw the rush to the standard he said, 'Wang Kŏn has won. This is the end of me.' He hurriedly donned a suit of hempen cloth and fled for his life. For days he hid in a cave in the Sambang Pass, (to which my attention has frequently been drawn), and subsisted on roots and tufts of grain. The country people hunted him as they would a wild beast. At last they found him, surrounded his cave, and beat the life out of him with savage glee. For twenty-eight years he had been the scourge of this unhappy people.

On the word of a woman, Yu-ssi, 'daughter of the willow', hung the fate of the kingdom. It was her decision and her deft fingers buckling the helmet strap round the faltering Wang Kŏn's chin that decided the fortunes of the day. Let Yu-ssi be held in highest honour. Wang Kŏn was great, but not greater than she.

AT THIS same time there arose in South Korea a robber chief named Kyŏn Hwŏn.[3] His original name was Yi which he changed to Kyŏn, 'the potter'. When he was a child, it is said, his mother left him once under an oak tree while she ran with a noon-day luncheon to his father working in the fields. When she came back, what was her surprise and fear to find a tiger suckling her little son, as Romulus was mothered by the wolf 1,500 years before.

Kyŏn grew and prospered, nearing seven feet in height. He gathered five or six thousand like-minded followers and set up a kingdom with Chŏnju as capital, calling his state 'Later Paekche'. In a campaign of plunder he marched on Kyŏngju, stormed and took the Golden City, murdered the king, violated the queen, and left Silla in ruins. A wild Muhammad of east Asia he was, with many wives and many sons, but of all his varied brood the fourth child was the offspring of his choice, 'Diamond', Kŭmgang. He made him Crown Prince, which greatly angered his firstborn, Sin'gŏm. Full of fierce resentment, Sin'gŏm made war against his father and, carrying all before him, took both him and Diamond prisoner. Diamond he killed, while he ocked his father up in Kŭmsan Temple. From this place, however, Kyŏn Hwŏn made his escape and went with a pitiful story to Wang Kŏn at Songdo. King Wang, kindly of soul, listened. His feelings rose against the unnatural son, and he marched south with 5,000 men. A great battle was fought near Kongju, where Sin'gŏm was defeated. He surrendered and Wang Kŏn forgave him. Kyŏn Hwŏn, on the other hand, had no mind for this and called for vengeance, but Wang Kŏn would have no more killing. Furious at the thought of the rascal getting off, Kyŏn Hwŏn worked himself up into madness and died of an abscess of the brain or, as we should say, of a broken heart.

WANG KŎN in conference with his scholar attendants decided on a name for his country, a name that has had a remarkable history. They called it Koryŏ, 'high hills and sparkling waters'. Silla means 'new silk', and Chosŏn means 'morning freshness'. Both these names had passed away and now it was called Koryŏ. China learned the new name so well that even today (1925) she says Kao-li, not Ch'ao-hsien. Westerners, as mentioned in chapter 1, learned the name of the country from her and so now, though this name has been discarded by the Korean people for 500 years, we still use it and call the land Korea.⁴

The old bases of pillars and high foundation stones that still stand show Songdo was a great and prosperous city; but it had many fears to encounter and many battles to fight. The barbarian of the north has always been a nightmare to Korea and especially one terrible variety that appeared at this time known as the Khitan Tatar.⁵ His original home lay east of the Khingan Mountains and north of the Sungari River, where he had been subject to Turks, to Chinese, and to the Khakan tribes each in turn. In the year of grace 936 these Tatars suddenly overflowed their borders and swarmed forth like the grasshoppers that multiply by the million in one season and fade away in the next. They swept down on the Yalu, over-ran north China and finally took possession of everything to the banks of the Yellow River, making Peking their capital. Nine kings ruled during their dynasty,⁶ and the terror of their name was felt through the whole Far East. Their eyes were on Korea, too, and when Wang set up his capital at Songdo they sent gifts of camels, their real intention being a sudden and swift invasion. Wang Kŏn banished the emissaries to an island and starved the camels to death.⁷

Among Wang's kind acts was a visit paid to the last possessor of the house of Silla. He remained with him twenty days and they had a right royal time. Thus was it that Wang Kŏn won over the whole peninsula without force of arms or recourse to the assassin's knife.⁸

As in 1777 a Scottish widow of Ayr saw her son, Jock Hempy, lying dead on the battlefield 3,000 miles across the sea, and caught visions of his wraith again and again, so certain people in Korea 900 years before had seen in advance the fall of Silla. Among these was an odd creature named Ch'ŏyong whose appearance was strange and his dress peculiar. He came and sang and danced before the king, and so fascinated his Majesty that he made him a *kŭpkan* or state minstrel. On moonlight nights his custom was to go out and dance in the market place, where he would utter strange cryptic sounds like the oracle at Delphi. Even today, after a thousand years, Koreans talk of Ch'ŏyong and dance his dance. One night in the wake of his weird goings-on came four men, 'dress peculiar and faces terrible'. They danced before the king and in raucous tones sang: *Chiri tado top'a top'a,* which translated ran: 'Chiri (Silla) broken, all will fly; fallen her city, fallen her city.' Ch'ŏyong by his mysterious doings became the father of maskers, the lowest of Korea's social scale. From now on, on special occasions, they would appear with horrible faces: lions, dragons, devils, to the amusement of the children and the disgust of the ancient confucian scholar. Maskers and actors became in Korea the pariahs of the world, lower than the scavenger. They were ordered to keep away from sacrificial ceremonies, as the spirits of the dead would never deign to descend on seeing them near.[9]

In the dignified behaviour of Confucius where every step is taken according to a fixed and inflexible law, the wild jumping of a set of clowns was the limit of indecency, at which the scholar would not even look. Accordingly the masker went down to oblivion, taking with him the theatre, the stage and all their accompaniments.

AT THIS PARTICULAR PERIOD, in view of kingdoms rising and falling, Korea resorted to a very strange expedient to hold the state steady. Here and there throughout the land she erected geomantic masts that were supposed to be safety pillars to which the ship of state could moor. The custom began about 900 and continued till 1100 or so. Two huge pillars of stone were erected first as holders, then the mast clad in bronze was placed between the holders, bolted firm and bound about. It might reach sixty or seventy feet high and speak its prayer for good luck to all the world.[10]

Such a pair of ancient holders, fifteen feet high I should think, still stands a mile or so to the north of P'yŏngyang city. What an immense mast must have been required to fit closely between them — gone now under the 'whips and scorns' of a thousand years. Another pair at Chiksan, the mining centre, still speaks its long-forgotten message.[11] In Ch'ŏngju there is a bronze mast still standing, with an inscription upon it that may interest the reader. It was erected in 962.[12] The writer, a *hallim* doctor named Kim Wŏn, says:

> I have heard that such a mast as this, set up before the gates of the buddha, serves as a spiritual guard to the palace of the Master. It suggests the blue crane flying up to heaven, or the dragon winging his way towards the illimitable expanse. Those who set it up did so as an act of faith and from a pure heart. It is an iron staff for the suppression of the devil, a divine arrow from the sky to daunt all rebels. Sixty feet upward it rises to touch the clouds and prop up the sun. It pierces the fogs and rides clear beyond the mists. Master Lu of China failed to make a ladder to the sky, or an umbrella for the gods, but we have done better, we have made a rope of silk to make fast the ship of state, a pillar to which to tie for safety. The mind that reared it is a mind deeply imbued with religion. A glad assurance rests on its being set up. By means of this mast all fears are dispelled and a place of safety is made sure.

These masts, while associated with the buddha, have in them as well a taoist element, where *feng-shui* plays a part. As to whether they come from China or are of purely Korean origin I am unable to say.[13]

About this same period pagodas began to be erected, some of stone, some of brick, in every variety of form.[14] How solidly they were built to have outlived the thousand years. In meaning they differ from the mast, for they are supposed to cover the relics of some faithful priest and are intended as an inspiration to generations to come. Many carved images of the Merciful Buddha, Mirŭk (Maitreya), came into being at the time, the greatest of them being at Ŭnjin.[15] What a busy world it was. We are informed that the number of houses in Kyŏngju was 180,000. Five to a house would mean a population of nearly a million. A note reads, 'The great houses of Kyŏngju were called *kŭmipt'aek* — "wealth abounding". There were thirty-five such. Houses and halls of amusement, too, were built for the four seasons, beautifully decorated, with the accents of sweet music always about them.' But the end had come, with handwriting on the wall: Silla, silken-coated, soft-fingered, highly bejewelled, went down; while Songdo, rough-riding, hard-handed, kindly-souled, came into being.[16]

SONGDO was much colder in winter than Kyŏngju. How did they heat the houses then? As now, by this *k'ang* floor *(ondol)*. Here is what was written around 1200 about these floors:[17]

> Beneath the winter's moon the biting cold
> Sharp-toothed sets fingers on my quivering skin.
> At last — good luck — a fire blows 'neath the floor
> With heat awakening from its faggot brand.
> The welcome warmth is like the breath of spring,
> And friendly grows the blanket at its spell.
> I speak my satisfaction: all may hear;
> Once more I feel myself in hand and live.
> Not that I greatly care for comfort's cheer,
> But how to meet the cold's the question.
> The really great feel neither cold nor heat,
> But I am no such breed, blue shivering I.

17 Eleventh-century Koryŏ culture

THE foundations of the wide-flung walls of Songdo, or Kaesŏng as it was also called,[1] can still be seen. The old South Gate, that lies nearly two miles eastward from the present railway station, was the needle's eye that cut through the mighty fortifications winding over hill and valley, today given up to the silence of the dead. The narrowest limits of the city were four miles across, crowded, when full, with 200,000 houses, or a million and a half people. This is what General Wang Kŏn had been called upon to rule over like King David. The names of the city wards still speak for the manner of man he was: Sunset Ward, Twin Cascade Ward, White Cloud Ward, Early-to-rise Ward.[2] Thus the great city spread its wings for its flight of 500 years. It was a fresh start with new life in every nerve and blood in every vein. A great poet who appeared later in Songdo, Yi Inno, gives his idea of a fresh start in a short poem entitled:[3]

Combing the Hair

The jade-like flame that lights my room burns low;
Across the boundless deep the dawn shafts rise.
I sit in silence and close down my wakeful breath,
While with my hands I hold its will in leash.
The locks beneath my ears grow gray;
With moon-shaped comb I smooth and brush them out.
White flakes drop round me like the falling snow.
As gold by passing through the fire, not once,
But many times, is rendered pure,
So does a combing-out make new the man,
And help his soul to live and flourish fair.
'Tis like the cock refreshing in his dust-bath,
Or when the horses roll and roll again
Upon the sand: Such is a good head-comb.
The master, Tung-p'o, too, hath said the same.

Korea had had a thorough combing out. The scurf and dandruff had gone with Kungye and Kyŏn Hwŏn and a new day had dawned.

COMPANIONS with her were the sons of China, famous for literature, philosophy and art. There came to Korea in 957 a famous Chinese named Shuang Chi of the rank of *han-lin*.[4] It was he who suggested and outlined and put into action the government examinations called *kwagŏ* that for a thousand years constituted the centre of Korea's civilization. On their outcome hung preferment to office, a place in the sun and a name never to be forgotten. The *kwagŏ* were indeed a field of battle. From tiniest boyhood to youth and full-grown manhood, beginning with the Thousand-character Classic (mentioned in chapter 12), study continued on its endless course. Day after day, morning, noon and night, the ceaseless hum of the schoolroom accompanied the ordinary round of life. All one's days were required from five years of age to twenty-five filled out to fullest measure, with only fifteen days of New Year's rest in the whole circle of the sun, if one would be a successful candidate for the honour of the *kwagŏ*. Many died under the weight of it, few reached a place of special mention. Those who did, shone as the stars in the sky. Their course of study was threefold: reading, writing, and composition. There were those who rose from nothing to be great men under its exacting spell. Korea's land rang with the echoes of the scholar; the pen, not the sword, was the fairy wand.

Many of Korea's great men came from the lower classes and gave rise to tales that brought hope to the humblest village lad. Here is one about Ch'oe Ip.[5] His family was nothing to the world. In his village fifteen of the literati met once in a contest of skill. Ch'oe, seeing this, asked if he might join. The answer was: 'No! You have a slight measure of ability, it is true, but no style. We could not think of it.' This was said, not because Ch'oe was ignorant, but because he was unknown to rank, a mere middle-class man. He petitioned again, however, very gently, very persistently, and finally won. They divided into two parties, eight on each side, and made a piece of prose composition their test. When each had done his part and sealed his name, the papers were submitted for decision to No Susin who lived in the village and had formerly been prime minister. He read them, marked them Good, Fair, or Medium; and then sent them back. Ch'oe's paper alone had no marks upon it, and only his name had been unsealed. His seven companions gathered around and berated him: 'Didn't we tell you not to butt in? With your blundering ignorance, you have lost us the game!' The members on the other side were highly delighted and sang, 'Hurrah! The day is ours!'

A moment later the call of outrunners was heard, and messengers hurried in to say, 'The minister is coming!' All were wonder-struck and asked what this could mean. Ch'oe was ordered to betake himself to a place of hiding in the kitchen. The fifteen then went out to meet his Excellency and make their bow. When the greetings were over and the minister had taken his seat he said, 'I have come to congratulate you young men on what you have written. Very good indeed! You will all make your mark in days to come, I have no doubt. May I see Ch'oe Ip? Who is he?' One student answered, 'He is of the lower classes, sir, gifted somewhat, yet with little idea of true literary form.' 'Indeed!' said the minister, 'I'd like to see him.' Ch'oe was called. He came modestly in and stood in the humblest corner of the room. 'Come here,' said the minister. When the boy was close up he took him by the hand, made him kneel down, and said to him: 'For five hundred years we have waited for you. Who would have guessed that you were the lad gifted to succeed? Your genius means not only honour to this little room and its company, but unbounded felicitations for the state. In days to come you will write despatches to the emperor and win undying fame. Go forward in your studies with all diligence.' The fifteen looked on with faces ashy pale.

This is a characteristic story showing how Korea's great and good men came out of the struggle for literary fame. The master Ch'oe Ip fulfilled all that Minister No had predicted of him. A year or more ago the writer despatched a set of his collected works to the Library of Congress, Washington DC.

THE examination arena awakened in the Korean his sense of verse and song. It was the usual thing, when scholars met, for them to write poems which passing years and keen competition whetted into compositions of wondrous skill. To translate them gives only the merest suggestion of their meaning without any of their literary beauty, but even a translation may be of interest. Here is one that shows the young candidate ambitious and highly-keyed for action. He entitles it:[6]

This World
I set out in my cart to thump upon
The gates of heaven and ask that God let down
The Milky Way to wash this wicked world.
Its insane calculations blear my eye.
How many fish can hope to swim in hoof-tracks?

So 'tis with men in this brief round. I play
My harp with practised hand: none comes to hear;
I bare my arms and show a tiger's strength,
But never meet my man. Life's disappointing,
Sad my song. My sword, shut in its sheath
With nought to do, cries as dragons cry.

IN THE YEAR 991 the Sajik-tan, the most sacred spot in the land, was set up in Songdo.[7] Already seventy years had passed without its presence in the city, an ominous lack indeed. This double platform of earth, 50 feet square and $3\frac{1}{2}$ feet high, surrounded by cut stone and approached from the four sides by stairs of three steps, was an altar to the god of the soil and to the spirit of the harvests that grow therefrom. Uncooked flesh of animals, grain and wine were offered three times a year: in spring, in autumn, and at the winter solstice. Its origin is to be found in China, where it represents one of the oldest forms of oriental worship. The prayer offered ran something like this: 'How good thou art that bearest on thy back all things that live and move, and how good the grain thou givest that we may live.'

According to the Dual Principle that rules the philosophy of the East, heaven and earth, the divine pair, unite in their activities for the good of man. Earth is the ever-present mother and prayers to her are made at the Sajik, while at the Altar of Heaven that stands in the imperial city of Peking prayers are offered to the father. Much as many christians today feel that the approach to Mary is gentle and sweet while the direct approach to the Father is beset with fear, so Korea would gather her skirts about her and kneel to offer a petition to Mother Earth while only the emperor of China, the Son of Heaven, might venture to approach direct to God. The Sajik-tan is therefore a very sacred spot and a common saying among the people is, 'If you lose the Sajik you lose the nation.'

The old Sajik-tan of Seoul stands under Inwang Mountain on the west side of the city, a link with the unseen that accompanies the Korean down through the centuries.

ATTEMPTS were made at this time to cast copper coins such as were used in the great Middle Kingdom. They failed, however, and it was not till 1101 that coins actually came into being, with a hole in the centre so that they could be strung on a string.[8] Four characters were engraved on them that read, 'Korea's Circulating Treasure'. These strings of money were called 'cash' by the foreigner. Their weight and bulk were enormous: to purchase a house meant a long procession of ponies, ten or fifteen, like Joseph's brethren going down to Egypt, their backs heavily laden with what might seem to be bundles of rope, but which, on close inspection, turned out to be cash. Once on a journey to Ŭiju, thirty-five years ago, the writer and his companion had to walk every foot of the way, 350 miles, the horses being wholly engaged in the task of carrying these heavily charged strings of cash. One of the largest and most ornamental pieces of furniture that helped to decorate a Korean home was the *pandaji* (half-closer), a box to hold these ropes of copper cash. Today we gather the

183

remaining pieces as treasured reminders, mementos of a finished past that will return no more.

THE OPENING of the eleventh century held dark and troubled days for Korea. Evil deeds had been done in the palace, and according to ancient Korean thought, evil deeds call down judgment. Hwangbo-ssi, mother of King Hyŏnjong, was a secondary wife and now widow of King Kyŏngjong, who died in 982. She fell into evil ways and was found to be having illicit relations with all sorts of men. It was discovered that she was with child, and the disgrace of it was so terrifying to her that her pains started as she made her escape by the back entrance. In her distress she caught at a willow tree to support herself and beneath its shade King Hyŏnjong was born.⁹ Years later Hyŏnjong's confederate, Kang Cho, had King Mokchong killed and Hyŏnjong placed on the throne.¹⁰ We are told that the people were greatly incensed and regarded these doings as presaging a day of doom. They had not long to wait, for in less than two years' time disaster came.

An ominous cloud had been gathering for years beyond the Yalu River. Forces of the Khitan Tatars were there in countless numbers, cohorts waiting for the word to march. The king sent his trusty friend Kang Cho, who still, like Macbeth, had the blood of Duncan on his hands, to drive these Tatars back. A battle was fought and Kang Cho was taken and beheaded. The king in Songdo, hearing of this, fled for his life while the enemy swarmed into the city. Seldom has Korea been subject to such a scarification as she went through in 1011 when Songdo's palaces, tablet-houses, pavilions, halls, hearths, and homes went up in clouds of smoke, while hundreds of thousands of the inhabitants fled. The king reached the far south, Naju, before he stopped in his flight, and the people thus left helpless waited for the end to come.¹¹

For the salvation of Korea at this time, there appeared from the mists and confusion an old soldier seventy-one years of age, Kang Kamch'an, who had been forgotten. Like Joffre he came forth to save the day. The king appointed him to the chief command. One of his first acts was to dam a stream in the north that overlooked the broad way along which the enemy was to come. The sluice-gate was timed to swing just as the host came broadside on. Great numbers of Tatars were overwhelmed in the rush of water while the whole army was put to confusion. Battle after battle followed in which Kang's strategy drove the enemy to the wall every time. The year 1019 saw Korea cleared of the pest and the king went forth to meet the conquering hero.¹² He gave Kang thanks and placed a wreath of golden flowers on his head. It speaks volumes for the bravery and wisdom of a man like Kang Kamch'an that he drove from Korea an army that possessed itself of half China down to the Yellow River and made Peking its capital. The Khitan continued as a nation for a century longer, departing from history in 1110, but never again did they try odds with Korea. The Tatar king would send envoys with the compliments of the season and gifts from his rough-riders, but never again did he cross the Yalu in the guise of a wild Hunghutsu.

DURING this period the greatest literary light was Ch'oe Ch'ung, a man of commanding presence and uprightness of heart. From his earliest years he loved study and in 1005 he was first in the examination list. He was a great official and real ruler of the land. Some of the Jürched barbarians, from the neighbourhood of modern Vladivostok, had encroached on the territory of Korea and had been taken prisoner. The question was what to do with them. Ch'oe Ch'ung said, 'They are barbarians. They have faces like men's faces but their hearts are beasts' hearts. They cannot be corrected by punishment, nor can they be taught by the Cardinal Virtues. We have had them on our hands for a long time now and they are no better. They only fret and pine for their native lairs. Let us give them freedom and let them go.' The king agreed and it was done.[13]

Because the land had been disturbed for many years by war, education had fallen by the wayside. Now under the leadership of Ch'oe Ch'ung nine orders of schools were established and a regular revised course of study adhered to. Students in those days measured their time by candlelight and so read and studied. Rewards were given to successful candidates, and rejoicing accompanied the winners of the day. Ch'oe Ch'ung in command sat supreme above all and was called the Confucius of Korea.[14]

Fifty miles south of Seoul, on the Pusan railway line at Sŏnghwan, there is a plain that a thousand years ago was infested with robbers, a danger to all passers-by. As it was one of the great highways of the nation, the king, (the lad born beneath the willow tree), had a sort of hospice of St Bernard built there in honour of the buddha and in memory of his mother. His desire was to aid travellers through the dark and dismal way. Ch'oe Ch'ung wrote an account of it for the stone that still stands in its memory:[15]

> The Master Hyŏnggŭng was the overseer and he never ceased from the task till the work was done. So blessed was it that not a sound of complaint or resentment was heard through all the time of its building. No one was called away from seed-sowing to help, nor was anyone discommoded or pressed into service. The result was that multitudes came, those who made tiles and those who could handle axe and saw to work in wood. Others again, though having no special skill, came to lend a hand.

Thus it was all completed in the year *sinyu* (1021). The inscription reads:

> A warm and cosy place was prepared for the winter passer and an open and refreshing one for him of the summer season. There were supplies on hand sufficient for all, and forage stored away for the cattle and horses. Aid was given to all in need. Not only were they who wore the robe provided for, but lay folk as well were given refuge at night and refreshment by day. Here they heard the truths of religion with no fear of robbers to distract their thoughts. His Majesty the King commanded your humble servant to write this memorial and I have not dared to refuse, even though my thoughts resemble dry leaves and my learning a toothless soul. Still, what I have written I offer with a sincere heart.

185

Thus Ch'oe Ch'ung, the great confucian scholar, joined with the buddha in blessing this house of alms that stood not far from the present Sŏnghwan station. He was a great writer, legislator, poet, and teacher. Here is a poem of his that is famous in its original form as a song to be sung with harp and drum.[16]

> *By Night*
> The light I saw when I awoke,
> Was from the torch that has no smoke;
> The hill whose shade came through the wall
> Has paid an unexpected call.
> The music of the pine-tree's wings
> Comes from the harp that has no strings.
> I see and hear the sight, the song;
> Would I could pass its joys along!

As King Hyŏnjong had built his temple and smiled with favour on the poet, so King Cnut in England on the other side of the world had done likewise.[17] 'He had a singular affection,' we are told, 'for the fen country (like Sŏnghwan) and for their church which even then was a magnificent structure. He several times took occasion to keep the festival of the Purification of the Virgin Mary with great solemnity and a boundless hospitality at Ely Abbey.' Ely Abbey was not unlike the great buddhist temple built at Sŏnghwan, while the Virgin Mary and the gentle Kuan-yin might easily have been siblings.

18 Twelfth-century Koryŏ and Sung: the rise of the Mongols

As we approach the year 1100 there pass across our line of vision many famous persons whose names are remembered even today. There was Su Tung-p'o, a Chinese, referred to in the song 'Combing the Hair' in chapter 17. He was a great scholar and a wonderful calligrapher. Today his characters limned in folded albums hold the Korean spell-bound with ecstatic admiration. His picture adorns the palace scroll where he and the shining moon illumine all the guests that enter. To the men of Chosŏn, Tung-p'o has always been the greatest master of the famous Sung dynasty. Opposed to the socialist Wang An-shih, he was a firm champion of imperial rule. Korea, however, has a grudge against him, for on one occasion, we are told, he treated her envoy with marked contempt and suggested that the 'uncouth outlander gather up his traps and betake himself home.' This may only be hearsay, for it has made no appreciable difference to the standing of Su Tung-p'o in Korea.[1]

There were at this time no great writers in England. After the Conquest, the Anglo-Saxon Chronicle which had begun to take shape was buried beneath the weight of Latin, the literary language of Europe. Even Anselm himself, the archbishop of Canterbury, was not an Englishman but an Italian born in Piedmont. St Bernard of Clairvaux, a Frenchman, was the great light of the christian Church. In his lone retreat near Lake Geneva, where with fasting and prayer he meditated on the smiting, the mockery, the nails, and the tears of our Lord, he met the worldly but intellectual Abelard, whom he warned against a day that most tragically came. There was Peter the Hermit, too, preaching a wild drive to Jerusalem to rescue the Holy Sepulchre.

Kim Pusik, spoken of in chapters 7 and 9, lived at this time but was all unaware of Abelard and Heloise or the Holy Sepulchre. Kim was a great scholar as well as a great soldier and his book, the *Samguk sagi* ('History of the Three Kingdoms'), is still read today. In a collection of his poems I find this one first of all—a lay sermon that preaches to the world in general:[2]

> The terrace heap on which King Yao took stand
> Was only three feet high, and yet his name
> Resounds through all the ages since his day;
> Ch'in built the wall that guards ten thousand *li,*
> Yet the next generation saw his fall.
> Throughout the vivid annals of the past
> Models are set before us for reflection:
> Think deep of Sui who perished in luxury,
> And spent his people's blood in wild display.

These were days of mighty changes on earth. The Normans were in England, never to leave; the Turks in Palestine. Feudalism was raising its head, while the Crusades, with clash of steel, were attempting to turn the Saracen and Turk into humble christian believers.

THESE WERE the days, also, of recreation, leisure, pleasure. We surely got our chess and backgammon from their relaxations. It pleases one to think that the east and west sat down somewhere, at some time, and played these kindly games together; perhaps a little before the Crusades, perhaps during that time. In a Korean book called *Ahŭi wŏllam* (Children's Primer), written by Chang Hon in 1803, we read that chess was invented by King Wu of China (1122 BC). Some again say its author was Prince Hsin-ling of the Divided States (244 BC). In any case it is older than the Great Wall and so outdates our game by 800 years at least. Still it is easy to see that they are the same, and that our game was evidently modelled from the Korean or Chinese board. There are thirty-two pieces on each, though we have changed the general into a king, which was most natural, since the western ruler combined kingship with leadership. Instead of aides, which are common in the east, we have a queen. Women had already come into their own to some degree in Europe when chess was decided upon, hence the queen has a place, though in Korea she never thus appeared in public. Instead of a cart or chariot we have a castle: how true to the age of chivalry! It seems absurd, however, for a castle to go moving about with all freedom toward the four points of the compass, until we remember that the castle borrowed its moves from the Chinese chariot without troubling about the inconsistency of the thing. Our knight is like the eastern horse and moves in the same irregular way: the prominent place won by knighthood in those days would easily account for its being on the board. We in Europe had no idea of elephants and so, of course, the elephant had to go. What more natural than to fill the place with a bishop? As the elephant had to do with splendour and imperial movings in the east, so had the bishop in the west. A glance at the Oriental board will show that our bishop got his powers from the Chinese elephant, for he too crosses the squares diagonally and as many as he pleases at a time. Our gunpowder is supposed to date from the fourteenth century, and as the beginning of chess is much earlier, we did not know what to do with pieces of Chinese artillery that used gunpowder, so we did away with the two guns and blended them with the rank and file of the soldiers or pawns. The age of chivalry, antedating gunpowder, evidently modelled our chess after the Chinese. How our forefathers got it at the time we are writing of, and by what route it came are questions whose answers are lost to us.

Backgammon, a game known in Korea since 1300[3] and probably much earlier, is exactly the same game as was played by Queen Elizabeth in 1600, with the same number of pieces similarly placed. Some think Plato refers to it in his *Republic* in the expression 'on a throw of the dice', but this is very doubtful. Chaucer makes one supposed allusion to it. However this may be, we have the two games today exactly alike, but do not know the circumstances by which they are linked together.

IT WOULD SEEM as though the spirit that dominated the age was likewise common to both sides of the globe. As St Bernard and Peter the Hermit, each in his own way, called the world back to religion, so the east made the buddha its all-in-all. Kings gave their own sons to be priests. The fourth son of king Munjong (1047–1083) was a master of the sacred mysteries, and his memorial stone, beautifully inscribed, was set up in 1101.[4] Today it may still be seen in the Kyŏngbok Palace museum. Sukchong's sixth son, Master Wŏnmyŏng, was a disciple as well, and the stone that marks his memory is of such delicate and beautiful workmanship that the Japanese have taken it to Tokyo to adorn their museum there.[5] Westerners can never sympathetically enter into the beauty of the Chinese ideographs that give such delight to the man of the east. Magnificent photographs of these memorial stones appear in Volume VII of the Government's *Album of Ancient Remains.*[6]

A great monastery called Hŭngwang-sa was built at this time at Songdo of 28,000 *kan* or 168,000 square feet, one and a half times the floor space of Winchester Cathedral. Here a golden buddha was set up, and a feast of five days prepared for 1,000 of the chief priests of the realm. Such pomp and display and high-hung lantern festivity had never before been seen.[7]

It must not be thought, however, that Confucius was forgotten in the glory of these buddhist days. Books, especially the classics, began to be printed from wooden plates most skilfully made. Lands were given as rewards to successful candidates at the government examination, and much was done to encourage learning and beautiful calligraphy. Scholars of today gaze with wonder at the inscriptions of this time, which show the degree of perfection to which the practised hand could come.

AMONG domestic affairs I mention one of special note. It is this: if a man had no posterity he was permitted to adopt an orphan and make him his legal heir, while a man with children might not. Between ordinary generation and family readjusting and out-and-out adoption, there is such confusion in Korean households that the foreigner never really knows where he is, who are brothers, or cousins, or sons, or daughters. These very definite relationships with us sail about here on the misty wing of custom and supposition, till there is no saying what brother means, or son, or uncle, or grandfather. However, we find in the year 1068 a definite law that reads: 'If you have no son you may adopt an orphan and make him your heir.'[8]

A good son, found in this way, was indeed a windfall — which reminds the writer of something other than a windfall. About this time (1057) a meteor dropped from heaven into the county of Hwangju and caused considerable consternation. Someone said that the end of the world had come. The Master of Ceremonies, however, drew attention to similar phenomena in the ancient kingdoms of China and asked that the man be punished who said it meant the end of the world. We can, in mind, see the guilty offender, all his superior knowledge gone by the board, sitting with a *cangue* about his chafed and begrimed neck, realizing that as far as he was concerned the end had already come.[9]

IN THE YEAR 1126 there came to Korea as envoy a distinguished Chinese, named Hsü Ching, mentioned in chapter 15. He was a famous scholar and wrote among other things a book called *Korean Pictures* in which his observations were jotted down:[10]

> When Koreans drink, they drink in the night, and when they feast, they feast in the night. Country gatherings spread their mats in the open and by the help of high-hung lanterns make their joys known . . . Some of the candles I have seen are several feet long and as large round as a weaver's beam. On such occasions young men of the best families carry these silken-crowned lantern masts.
>
> As for the grains grown, rice is chief, wheat being very scarce. It seems strange to me (a Chinese) that wheat should be so rare.
>
> As for attendants and servants, a minister of state may have four secretaries, thirty servants, and sixty hangers-on. When he goes out, these carry a great umbrella twenty paces before him. Two men lead his horse, each holding a bridle rein.
>
> Ordinary people who ride may not have a servant to direct the way. They must handle their own reins and carry their own whip.
>
> When women go out it is on horseback, servants following in the rear. They go veiled in black gauze down to the feet. A hat is worn outside the gauze mantle. The queen, while she wears the same kind of veil, has it broidered with red. There are no chairs or carts even for queens to ride in.
>
> The people of Korea are very clean in their habits. They laugh at us Chinese and think us dirty. Every morning at first call is the bath. In summer, when the weather is warm, they bathe twice a day. Men and

women seem quite free to bathe together in the open stream, their clothes lying along the bank. Washing and weaving are the two chief callings of the women: they keep at it night and day with no complaint.

Though there are pigs and sheep in abundance, only the king and high officers of state may slaughter them. The people must depend on fish for their fare; eels, crabs, shrimps, clams, oysters, turtles, and the like. Hence their world has a disagreeable fishy odour.

There are no distinct wood cutters among the Koreans. Anyone may take part in gathering fuel. People in the city, however, think it means bad luck to cut down a tree. It breaks the law of *yang* and *yin*. Thus trees have been left to grow as they please, some of them attaining to enormous size, two arm-spans round. While in Korea I noticed that people who brought wood into my compound carried it not on the shoulders but on the back.

The Koreans do not know how to slaughter animals as we do. When our envoy arrives, pigs and sheep are not knifed as with us but are taken whole and thrown into a blazing fire. Only when life is extinct and the hair all burned off are they taken out to be dressed. A disagreeable burnt odour accompanies all their subsequent use.

These are a few extracts from Hsü's book. One can read through them the influence of the buddha as seen in the abundant use of water and the dislike of taking life. And yet along with this great buddhist reverence at the same time runs Korea's powerful confucian strain, a strain that lifts her far above the barbarian tribes in which the Far East abounds.

PROBABLY the most mysterious region on the face of the earth is that which lies east of Lake Baikal and far south into the Gobi Desert. It is a wild and barren waste, and yet out of its mysterious depth have come myriads of human-kind that have shaken the world to its foundations: the Hun, the Turk, the Khitan, the Jürched, the Mongol, the Manchu. Today as we cross Siberia and see the Kalmuk, the Kirghiz, and the Samoyed, we look with wonder to think that this is all that is left of those famous rough-riders of the world, Chinggis and Khubilai. There had been for many years a strange, undeveloped race moving about the regions of Vladivostok and beyond. Many times its bands had joined up with Korea and become loyal subjects, and again with the restless soul born in them they had revolted and broken away. In 1104 there was a raid of these tribes in which Korea's troops were badly beaten. This gave kings Sukchong and Yejong much cause for concern. Formerly Koreans had regarded the Jürched much as passengers on the Limited Express in America look out on the Cheyenne and Cherokee riding by in long feathers and red blankets; but what was their amazement now to behold these barbarians, reinforced by countless numbers on horseback, drive straight into the heart of the Khitan Empire. T'ien-tso, the Khitan ruler, went out to meet them with an army of 700,000 men, but was overwhelmed in a signal defeat and the Khitan Tatar was no more. The Jürched flood poured straight on into China, taking the name Chin (Korean

Kim). They made a dash for Kaifeng, the capital, and took it, obtaining hostages and an immense indemnity, then moved directly on to the Yangtze.

KAIFENG continued as their capital for 118 years till a similar tidal wave of Mongols swept the Chin from the earth, as the Chin had destroyed the Khitan. How Korea was saved from this conquering host right on her border I do not know. Yun Kwan is said to have saved them. That great scholar, a *hallim haksa* (doctor of letters), was said to have stemmed this mad rush of barbarians and won the day.[11] He died in 1128 with honours heaped upon him. I have not been able to find any of his writings, but I specially appreciate two of his friends, Kwak Yŏ and Yi Chahyŏn. I substitute their writings for his. They were fellow-students in youthful days, equally gifted in their contests before the king, but in the course of years their lives drifted apart. Kwak Yŏ became governor of Kang-wŏn Province, while Yi Chahyŏn was a dreamy hermit hidden away somewhere among its hills. We are told that Yi retired to the mountain fastness of Chŏng-p'yŏng, to the monastery of Munsu. His life was rapt in endless meditation. In the deepest gorge of the hills he built a little egg-shaped hut that he could barely creep into. Here he would pass the days in utter silence, sometimes for months at a stretch. The governor, Kwak Yŏ, hearing of this, went to pay a visit to his old companion. As they met Kwak wrote a poem which runs:[12]

> Far to the east, off here among the hills
> We meet again who never thought to meet.
> Full thirty years ago before the King
> We wrote our best for fame and fortune's sake;
> But lengthening suns have drawn us far apart,
> And clouds in spotless white have led you on,
> The moon too, silver shield across the water.
> We meet, we look, but have no words to say
> Our spirits hold their silent intercourse.

The hermit Yi Chahyŏn answered with his brush[13]

> This grateful visit turns the seasons round
> And brings me orders from my lord the king.
> Shu Ch'i and Po I rose and left the world
> To save their souls, while Chi and Hsieh marched on
> To please high heaven; your honoured self likewise
> With stamp and seal. When will you doff your hat
> And shake your soul from out this dusty world?
> Is it not here that you and I may hide
> And bend our steps to where immortals dwell?

Speaking of the Hermit Yi 400 years later (1550), Yi Hwang, the greatest master of his day, said as he passed the Ch'ŏngp'yŏng Hills:[14]

He was a son of highest fortune and sailed right into office. Everything of riches and honour was at his hand, but he cast it all aside and betook himself to these hills where he bowed in prayer for thirty-seven years. He would listen to no word from the King. People questioned why he did so, but assuredly his soul was in it, otherwise he would never have done it. I have seen many notes and comments that sought to do him wrong, but he rises superior to them all. For him to toss aside the world's best offers and spend his years thus is proof that he was the rarest of human kind. Some say he did it for a name, but I say No, for had he chosen to take it, a name ever awaited him amid all the splendours of the state. He did it because his soul was great and had joys that the outer world never dreams of. How I revere his matchless worth!

Yi Hwang ends his comments with this verse:

> These hills crowd up, while off the river swings.
> My ladder leads me o'er the giddy way
> Where tinkling streams abound.
> Men tell us still of these same Yŏsan Hills,
> For here the master ploughed his simple field.
> Just as the moon fills all the waiting sky
> So his great soul is with us.
> Mere gossamer web that leaves no trace behind
> Such was the glory of the world to him.
> Who writes his story now?
> Doth not his simple life film dim your eyes?

19 Yi Kyubo

As we cross the dividing line into the thirteenth century we behold a wonderful procession of greathearts and heroes leading the way. We see King Richard of England in the van, helmeted and girt about with rings of steel; and at his side, high-horsed and curved-sabred, with bright colours round his head, the Mongol, Chinggis Khan. Richard is the elder by five years, but Chinggis outlives him by twenty-eight. What a commanding pair! Chivalry and knighthood in company with the master of all rough-riders, the great Asiatic chieftain.

Behind them, thin of garb and spare of face, riding a little donkey, I see a man with eyes that look you through, eyes that soften the evil heart within you and turn it into tenderness: sweetest Francis of Assisi! Beside him rides an old Korean priest named Chŏnggak, 'Wide-awake'.[1] The biographer says of him: 'He made men over to righteousness as the potter moulds the clay.' He was older by forty-three years than St Francis, and yet they crossed the century line together. I can hear how gently Francis talks to him and see with what high regard he looks upon his dreamy, wrinkled face: both were priests of God, both sincere, both calling men back to what is right and true and pure.

Following them comes another pair, one in Lincoln green with long bow and short sword, a smile on his face and the light of eternal youth in his eye. Who is he? Robin Hood. 'Such archers as he and his men will England never see again.' At his side rides a lithe, swarthy cavalier whose face, whose form, whose wondrous magnetic eye hold the imagination and crown him master of the day: the noted Saladin.

Behind these again rides another strange pair, one an Englishman and one a Chinese. 'Who are you?' I ask. 'I am Robert Fitzwalter, a baron of England, who carried through the Magna Carta.' I ask of the Chinese, 'Who are you?' and he says, 'I am Chu Hsi, professor of classics, interpreter of the Great Master.[2] My age is seventy.' So the procession passes on its way. Could such a sight be promised today, a London Lord Mayor's show would be nothing to it. How men would cross continents to see such a triumphal progress! Excursion ships would be weighted down to the load-waterline; points of vantage from which to watch would engage the pocket of the millionaire, so great are these names as they pass from the twelfth century to the thirteenth. They were all on earth together, looked for the same moon to rise each night and saw the same changing sky, without in the least dreaming that they would one day keep step in the minds of men and hold companionship through the ages.

Of this procession, the one that most filled Korea with awe was the Mongol chief, Chinggis. He set in motion the warriors who were to take possession of all Asia — China, India, Persia, clear from Korea to the streets of Baghdad and Jerusalem — the leader in one of the mightiest adventures of the human race. The next great man was Chu Hsi, who has ever remained the only authoritative interpreter of the Chinese classics to the Korean scholar.

ON the eve of this march-past, Korea had had one very bad king called Ŭijong, who ruled from 1147 to 1170. He was a lover of strong drink and loose women, and spent his days in a way that scandalized the better-thinking population. One of his delights was to play hockey,[3] or shinny as it is sometimes called, a game for schoolboys but not for kings. This served for his round of the day, while the night was taken up with music and dancing. The state fathers bowed their heads and uttered earnest protest, but the king treated their remonstrance as a joke. Feasting, sightseeing, gaming were the measure of his soul, and no good counsel could make him amend. Only once was he called up with a sharp shock. He had fallen foul of his step-mother and by way of retort addressed her in insulting and contemptuous terms. Woman-like, she heard him out, then bounded into the palace court and gave full vent to her bottled-up indignation. She called down heaven's curse on this unfilial son. We are told that in answer to her imprecations a sudden thunderstorm came on, with lighting that struck the palace hall before their eyes and sent splinters flying in all directions. The king, frightened out of his wits, rushed to his step-mother and hid his face in her voluminous skirts till the terror had passed by.[4]

The law of the curse has continued to be one of Korea's weapons for the weak. Our old saying, 'Curses, like chickens, come home to roost', is not true in the East. The curse of Asia goes straight after the man cursed. Like the evil eye of ancient Rome which, as Vergil says, 'could spread terror among men and shrink up cattle and horses into skin and bone,'[5] the curse of a withered old Korean woman or toothless hag could scare both king and courtier. At this time the king learned that a woman in Kamŭm county, abetted by an official secretary, had cursed him and all his entourage. At once he had her and her associate arrested and both thrown into the river. He then shook off his fears and went to see a game of ball.[6]

When Balak, the king of Moab, sent to hire Balaam to curse Israel he was no doubt acting in accord with the recognized custom of the day. Recently a sojourner in China told the writer that professional cursers abounded among the celestials, and had no scruple whatever as to heaven above or earth beneath, but were ready, for money, to curse whom you pleased. The curser, it seems, may stand in the middle of the street, or on the door-step of the one to be cursed, and, according to the amount of money paid by his employer, will open the sluice-gates of his invective and pour out death and destruction on the head of the victim.

This king of Korea had been well cursed and he knew it. Neither the buddha nor the Old Philosopher could absolve him. When the year 1173 drew to a close, instead of being ruler of the world, as he foolishly thought, his majesty found himself tethered, a prisoner in Kyŏngju, and his uncle, whom he hated, sitting on the throne. The king remained in prison some time in uncertainty till at last one night a band of assassins, the servants of the curse, led by Yi Ŭimin, 'a giant eight feet high', strangled him, ran him through and then, stuffing his body into a rough kettle, dropped him into the deep water of the lake. So ended the wretched, cursed existence of Ŭijong, king of Korea.[7]

A FEW years before this, in 1169, was born a famous master of the pen: Yi Kyubo. His life, like that of Boswell's Johnson, is recorded year by year, carefully marking the ups and downs of each round of the sun. Ease and plenty by no means attended his way. The freedom of his written speech made him many enemies: he was too straightforward for his generation and this stood in the way of his upward course, but finally he came into his own and was recognized as the greatest scholar and statesman that Korea had yet seen. The book *Koryŏ myŏng-sin chŏn* ('Famous Courtiers of Koryŏ')[8] says:

> Recalled from exile after a year, he was appointed to the office of Royal Secretary. At that time the Mongols began their incursions into Korea; frequent messages and threatening demands came from them to His Majesty, and Yi Kyubo was entrusted with the writing of replies. He made Korea's case abundantly clear. Influenced by these communications, the emperor of the Mongols recalled his troops and the land was left in peace.
>
> Yi Kyubo had an alert, active mind, a kindly liberal soul, a clear and gifted understanding. He paid no attention to the trivial affairs of domestic life, but yielded himself up to the joys of the scholar — music and poetry. His writings, both in verse and prose, were unlike anything that had ever gone before. In literature he went his own way, as the

waves of the sea do theirs. All the famous writings of the time came from his hand. He was Prime Minister and three times Chief of the Board of Official Examiners.

I herewith append a quite literal translation of a few of his short poems.

The old home

The morning's late and yet I lie abed,
While swallows on the eaves make sport of me.
The servant lads, bound for the field,
Haul by their cart: 'Come, come,' they shout, 'It's late!'
Up quick I get, unwashed, my head uncombed;
Whistling my thoughts, out through the pinewood gate,
(Beneath the shade, unfingered by the sun,
The glittering grass hangs wet with morning dew),
Slowly I wend down to the sparkling brook,
Across whose stones skid spouting streams of rain.
The women, dressed in creeper coats, weed o'er the field,
While men outdecked in hempen blue, work by and sing;
The hand-hoes move like waving clouds.
The season of the iris and the apricot,
The time to plough, the time of seed is here.[9]

This seems a familiar picture of Korean life today though painted 700 years ago.

Here is a poem marked *Beasts and Insects,* through which we trace some of the thoughts and habits of the day:[10]

The toad

You warty lumpy beast, a sight to see,
With fingered feet you grip the crumpled ground.
Yet other creatures must not view you ill,
For you have climbed aloft into the moon.

As the Korean sun has a crow in it, so the moon has a toad in its bosom. An old lady, Heng-o, wife of the famous archer, Hou I, who lived about 2400 BC, had stolen from her husband the elixir of life, a gift he had received from the Western Queen Mother (mentioned in chapter 2). Heng-o stole and drank it and, in order to escape his wrath, flew into the moon where she became a toad. She amuses herself today by weaving and unravelling the twisted fortunes of young lovers who dwell down on the misty earth. There she sits, all toad-like, just as Yi refers to her.

The frog

No angry words or fierce looks cross your eyes,
And yet at times your stomach swells with fire.
Proud of the music of your band you sing,
And yet, uncharmed, we turn our ears away.

The rat
Your eyes, like lentil-beans,
Lead you to scamper wildly through the night;
You pierce my walls and do your wilful way,
A thief you are indeed, a thief of thieves.

The snail
A man appears; at once in go your horns,
And into home, your shelter, there you hide.
Such horns were never made for battle-fields
Whose rivers run with blood.

The ant
Out from the winding of the way you come;
You rush about the circling millstone, wild.
Who'd ever guess that 'neath this quiet tree
A whole state organized doth live and dwell?

The spider
Athwart the eaves you hang your silky web,
Or on the wall weave soft an entrance hole.
You land upon the needle finger of the maid
And speak good luck for her.

The fly
You buzz as all the rooster tribe that crow,
And spot my jade with marks of foulest gray.
Though driven off you come again, you pest!
I'll get the king to turn his thoughts on you.

The silkworm
You vomit up long threads of twisted silk,
A spun cocoon that finds the boiling pot.
So highly gifted, yet so great a fool,
I'm truly sorry for your luck, I am.

He writes this on seeing a picture:[11]

Picture of a tiger
Not a real tiger, only make-believe,
And yet I shrink before those awful eyes.
The sparrow looks with terror on the hawk
That's dead: I, too, as I see thee.

His reflection in the water[12]

Along the edge I walk and gaze into the water;
My windy image dances to my eyes,
My form vibrates in a hundred odd contortions.
I think of Su Tung-p'o and how he saw
Deep in the Ying-shui Pool, a hundred beards,
Two hundred eyebrows quivering clear.

Here is another, somewhat similar:[13]

Looking into the well

For long I have not looked into a glass,
And what I'm like, I'm scarcely free to say.
But now by chance I gaze into this well
And seem to catch a face I've seen before.

He clearly saw the need of social reform in his day:[14]

Moved in heart

I have a tongue and yet I dare not speak;
Eyes too, that cannot weep. Who'd ever guess
The sorrows of my soul? The long day through
Distressed am I. Is it the cold that bites,
Or that my clothes are threadbare, thin and poor?
Comes it from lack of food and eating weeds,
This my distress, beyond what words can say?
My trouble lies down deeper far than that.
I set my feet and gaze toward the sky,
Yet heaven itself makes thoughts grow sadder still:
I long to grasp the heavenly Dipper's ends
And vault me up into the stellar lights.
Some men go by, seals dangling from their belts,
And others wear high hornèd caps of state;
The little birds find nought to wet their beaks,
Nor can the prisoned phoenix hope to fly;
The deadfall traps have failed to do their work,
Tigers and leopards rampant rage around.
Though Chia Yi saw there were two things for tears,
And Cheng Hsüan spoke of ten ways states could fall,
Who now will rise with such a mind as they?
A brave outspoken word no echo bears;
What I might say, man greets with scornful ear.

Here is another poem.[15] Korean scholars regard the Chinese of it with marked admiration. Any attempt by the writer to render it into English is very poor, yet even its gist is worth consideration:

> *A pinetree picture screen*
> Who was it built his house beside the pines
> And saw their tufted tops against the sky
> With all his powers of vision squarely set?
> Through days and months and years, his soul was lost,
> The world of pines became his second sight
> That overflowed; then quivering needle tips
> And waving breaths he vomited in bloom
> Upon the six folds of this painted screen.
> Elsewise how could an inch of weasel-tail
> Have wrought so vast a scene of deathless wonder?
> How dark the background hills, deep the far shore!
> Black in the darkness, shining serpent forms
> Wriggle seawards. The tide has swung away
> And left behind great monsters of the deep:
> Whales, stripped of their flesh, stand in bony forms,
> Lean against cliffs and hang the valleys o'er;
> Their pillowed heads are close against the sky.
> In openings of the scene I catch a view
> Of eyes and mouths, odd faces, peering through.
> On misty days when winds awake,
> I doubt not dragon wails and calls will come
> From out this shadow screen. Throughout the day
> I sit with chin in hand and gaze my fill:
> To think that ink could work so great a wonder,
> Or human hand be found the brush to swing.

This is what Yi Kyubo thought of his little daughter 700 years ago. She was not with him and he longed to see her.[16]

> *My daughter*
> I have a dainty little daughter
> Who smiles and calls me Papa,
> Holds my coat and plays upon my knee;
> Mirror in hand, she does her hair like Mama's.
> It's months since we have met,
> And yet she seems to nestle at my side.
> I am a wastrel, careless, wayward man,
> With restless soul that never finds me peace;
> Drunk days at times, I then am sick for months.
> I face the city of my father's pride,
> But hills and streams lie limitless between
> Alone, I think of her by early morn
> Till tear-drops wet my robe. Boy! Get my horse
> Well groomed and fed; I'm off for home today!

A love-song will close these selections from the famous poet Yi Kyubo:[17]

The little ducks
Soft water like a silken sheen's their world,
All day they sport without an hour apart.
He cannot think to let her from his sight,
Nor she to see him for a moment go.

Like a pilgrim to the sacred shrine of Canterbury, the writer once paid a visit to the grave of Yi Kyubo. It was a spring morning, 18 May 1914, before the world had tasted of the bitter war and its attending woe. The little donkey I rode seemed happy of heart as he tripped merrily along at an even pace. A Korean scholar friend was with me. The call of the pheasant greeted us right and left. Across the paddy fields, here and there, were patches of softest green where seedlings grew. Early morning farmers were out making their way with plough on the back, and the ox, by a halter, following behind. Men were already knee-deep in the fields ploughing, levelling, trimming, combing their world of rice that lies under water. Others were swinging huge ladles, hung on tripods, to spoon the passing rivulets up into the paddy fields. After a ride of two hours across the interesting island of Kanghwa we turned east from the roadway and entered a grove of pines where we found the great master's grave. In front, an inscription on the stone, dated 1733, reads: 'Minister Yi of Koryŏ, Duke Munsun, Earl Haŭm, Kyubo's grave.'

Prince Ito decided in 1909 to publish the best Korean writings, one volume each month.[18] This was continued for nearly eight years, making in all nearly eighty volumes — an excellent library of pure Korean literature. Two volumes contained the works of Yi Kyubo, whose name adorns this nineteenth chapter.

UNDER THE YEAR 1155 in the *Tongguk T'onggam* I find this story:[19] The king summoned to his presence Minister Ch'oe Chayŏng, Vice-minister Yang Wŏnjun and State Secretary Ch'oe Nubaek and took counsel with them regarding affairs of state. Now Ch'oe Nubaek was a man of Suwŏn, the son of a common yamen secretary. When he was fifteen years of age, his father went out one day on a hunting expedition and was killed by a tiger. Nubaek took the matter so to heart that he made up his mind either to die or to wreak vengeance on the horrible beast; but his mother forbade him.

He answered, 'But, Mother, shall I not take revenge on the enemy of my father?' With that he shouldered his axe and was gone. The tiger, meanwhile, overgorged, had retired to a cave to sleep off its surfeit. Nubaek, following its tracks, reached the cave, and going boldly in, shouted, 'You have devoured my father, you monster. Take note, I am here to settle accounts and to eat you.'

The tiger whipped an angry tail and glared at him, but before it could rise to spring, Nubaek had dealt it a fatal blow. Ripping it up he took out his father's remains and packed the tiger's flesh and bones in a crock, which he buried under running water at the side of the stream. The father was given burial on the hillside, where Nubaek built a thatched hut and gave up his time to fasting and prayer. When the period of mourning was ended he unearthed the crock with the tiger's remains in it which, the chronicler goes on to say, 'he ate to the last mite.'

This may seem a trivial story to the foreigner, but to the east it is not so, for I find it recorded in four great histories of Korea, the *T'onggam*, the *Yasŭng*, the *Kangmok* and the *Sŭngnam*, to the eternal honour of the man who avenged his father's ghost.[20] It was the doctrine of the sages in those days and, according to the light she had, Korea lived out the fourth commandment of the scriptures. So she kept her nation intact for 1,300 years.

20 Thirteenth-century Mongol domination

For a troubled period in East Asia, nothing can surpass the early years of the thirteenth Century. The Golden Horde[1] had gone down before the house of Chinggis, and China had entered on a new era. China — a most strange country indeed — accepts defeat at the hands of this one and that, and then sits quietly down and proceeds to absorb its enemy, body, soul and spirit, much as the cobra does the ass that threatens to trample his head into the dust. Thus has it been with the Khitan, the Mongol, the Manchu: each and all in turn have defeated and taken possession of China and settled down to rule her, and in the end each has melted away like a vanishing picture, leaving China to stand out more clearly defined than ever.

Just now (1220) China herself steps aside and watches while Khitan, Jürched and Mongol devour each other. The Khitan had their day from 907 till 1119, and the Jürched till 1233, when Khubilai's father, Tuli, brought them to their knees. The result was that fugitives from all parts of China made their terror-stricken way to Korea and kept the country in a state of constant fear.

While the Mongols did not assume the Dragon Throne till 1260, already in 1215 they were pressing Korea hard all along the north from their great cavalry camps in Manchuria. At the same time a remnant of the Khitan was bearing down on Songdo, and it looked as though Korea's end had come. The Mongol emperor, however, sent help that arrived in the nick of time. In response to this aid Yi Kyubo was commanded to write Korea's thanks. He said:[2]

> Our little country had been long under the hard heel of the enemy when Your Divine Majesty came to our aid and your angel soldiers scattered the foe. This most grateful help saved us at the very point of death. Reverently would we state that the land first given to Ch'i Tzŭ, and ever since possessed by us, is a joint neighbour of the Khitan. They and we had lived heretofore very happily together, and why they thus ruthlessly invaded our bounds we know not. Like a swarm of angry bees they came killing our people with great slaughter, and, though we resisted them with our best soldiers, we could do nothing, till your Majesty, out of pity for your little neighbour, came with timely help and brought these tormentors to swift account. The Khitan leader died by his own hand: the remainder of his forces came and bowed submission. Our whole nation lives again and sings its songs of joy.

Your servant prays that your Serene Highness may be long spared to rule, and that he himself may be permitted to repay at least one part in a thousand of your gracious favours. I offer herewith my most faithful service to your high Majesty.

DURING THE TIME when Korea needed the help of great and good men she had battening on to her, like a giant vampire, the terrible Ch'oe family of Ubong in Hwanghae province. To recite all their crimes and evils would fill a volume. There were two brothers and a son, all equally bad. In 1196 Ch'oe Ch'unghŏn, the arch-criminal, won favour with the king by capturing a rebel named Yi Ŭimin. He sought permission of the king, and when it was given, slaughtered Yi and all his relatives far and near. The extermination of the clan is a Chinese custom. The reason is that filial piety requires the son, even though he never saw his father, to requite the enemy and appease the wandering ghost of his lamented sire. To guard against this, the whole family of an executed criminal must be exterminated, and Ch'oe Ch'unghŏn was a greatly gifted expert in this method of operation.[3]

Ch'unghŏn and his brother Ch'ungsu later had their family differences. They fought as to who should possess the king, and when their mother interfered Ch'ungsu knocked her down. Ch'unghŏn then gave his little brother the *coup-de-grace* which rid the world of him forever.[4]

Ch'unghŏn built himself a palace and, as the historian relates, in order to give his halls good luck, had children dressed in gaudy colours, boys and girls, and buried alive at the four corners of the main hall. So terrible was the fear of him that people guarded their offspring as though a man-eating Polyphemus was abroad.[5] About this time a courtier called at the palace with a special message to Ch'unghŏn as he waited on the king. The message was not unlike that of Ehud to Eglon, king of Moab. The courtier's name was Wang Chunmyŏng and he had a sword girded at his side. Ch'unghŏn suspected him and on his first attack called to the king for help, but his Majesty darted into a side room and bolted the door. Ch'oe finally overcame his antagonist and then, in anger, sent the king into exile and appointed a successor. All the Wangs, high and low, old and young, were immediately put to death.[6]

Ch'oe next learnt that his son-in-law, Pak Chinjae, was party to a plot to do him evil. So he had him destroyed and found a fresh applicant for the hand of his daughter. An *ajŏn*, or yamen secretary, now tried his hand and plotted to kill Ch'unghŏn but he too failed and he and all his tribe entered the wailful regions of the dead.[7]

When Ch'oe Ch'unghŏn finally died he left a son, Ch'oe U, as bad as himself, to take his place. Wealth and power and idleness had wrought so great a change in Korea: from being the land of the 'superior man' of Confucius she had become a den of thieves. For fear of Mongol and Jürched the capital was moved in 1232 to Kanghwa. In 1260, however, at the urgent request of the Mongol emperor, it was restored to Songdo.[8]

Little by little the Mongols increased their power in the direction of all south Asia, Korea included. They tried friendship, but Korea stood aloof. They then began a campaign of fishing for Koreans, catching them unawares. In the year 1254 they captured no less than 200,000 and made prisoners or slaves of them. To the terror of all the people they would appear here and there, rising as it were out of the ground on their swift-moving horses. At times, too, they came down to the very landing stage on the straits near Kanghwa to peer across at his Korean Majesty on the other side.[9]

In 1260 Khubilai came to the throne and a change took place. He withdrew all troops from Korea, and sent home all captured Koreans.[10]

We learn that during 1269 Mongolia made herself an alphabet of forty-one letters, renouncing the wilderness of the barbarian for the enlightened sphere of the 'superior man'. This may have been the example that gave King Sejong of Chosŏn the first thought of the Korean alphabet 200 years later.[11]

At this time we find Korea apologizing for tardiness in sending samples of the best brass to China, 20,000 lbs in one lot; also the best falcons.[12]

Khubilai, who was always most friendly, invited the king of Korea to visit him, which he did in 1264, leaving in the 8th moon and returning home in the 12th. The kind treatment accorded Korea by Emperor Khubilai changed the whole spirit of the east. Kings and princes went with confidence now to Shang-tu, or to Peking, knowing that generous treatment awaited them.[13]

Seeing that Korea had become the firm vassal of Peking the advisers of Khubilai urged an attack on Japan, the Koreans being asked to show the way. This they did as far as Kŏje. There, however, the wild wind and fierce sea, lying between the Mongols and the object of their desire, gave them pause and they retired. Again an attempt was made that finally reached Tsushima, where they took two Japanese prisoners.[14] The final attempt was made in 1281 when, as Li Ung-bing says,[15]

> An armada of 4,500 ships manned by Mongols, Chinese and Koreans sailed in the direction of Hakata. The resistance offered by the Japanese was such that for two months every attempt at landing was frustrated. While cruising fruitlessly in the vicinity of Hichiku the fleet encountered a severe storm which sent the majority of the ships to the bottom, leaving but few survivors to return home and tell the sad tale. Further attempts at revenge were given up because of the unpopularity of the venture.

So contrary was this campaign to the general mind of Khubilai, that one feels that he was led into it against, rather than in accord with, his better will.

Now began a relationship with China, very pleasant and agreeable, but which had most serious consequences to the ruling house of Korea. Shang-tu, like Mecca, was the object of a lifetime's visit. Interesting Mongol women were there, women much freer than Chinese to meet and catch the smile of the Hermit man, who for a thousand years held his own fair sex locked behind bars, or hidden under a double-twisted silken veil. He was amused and interested to see these red-checked, round-faced, bright-eyed Amazons come and go at will, or ride wild horses that would have taxed the powers of a Buffalo Bill. In 1271 the Korean Crown Prince married a Mongol princess, daughter of Khubilai, and in 1274 she came to sit on Korea's throne beside her goodman King Ch'ungnyŏl. Later they had a son whom they called Wŏn, grandson of the great Khubilai, half Mongol, half Korean.[16]

Soon afterwards a school for the study of the Mongol language was set up in Songdo[17] and the refined attachments that had held Korea so long to the great houses of Han, T'ang and Sung began to break from their fastenings. How changed too the women's life, almost as much as today, for lo, the queen rode out in the open, side by side with her husband; rode better and carried a bow and arrows with which she could shoot like a daughter of William Tell, or handled a falcon with a skill that would have done honour to Simon Latham.[18]

A law was passed at this time making Mongol dress the rule, with an added injunction that the hair be shaved just over the brow.[19]

In 1282 the queen fell ill and she and her husband made a hasty journey to Peking to inquire of a doctor, also to consult a witch. All's well that ends well, and we find her back a few months later, in full enjoyment of a hunting expedition in Ch'ungch'ŏng province.[20]

While the king and queen of Korea were in Peking at the feet of her father Khubilai, a strange, weird creature from the outer world of the barbarian was seen to come and go through the streets of Shang-tu. It was Marco Polo, the famous Venetian, who remained in China from 1275 to 1282. His description of Khubilai's palace (found in chapter lxi of his *Travels)* is most interesting. Built partly of permanent materials, marble and the like, yet having a roof suspended on tent lines, it makes a unique picture. This may account for the style of architecture seen in Korea today, and yet the best authorities maintain that the tent-roof line has come down from far distant days a thousand years before the Mongol. Marco Polo says further: 'Emperor Khubilai had a stud of 10,000 horses, his mares as white as snow.' The milk of these mares was scattered to the winds on the 28th day of the 8th moon in order to bring all spirits into loving accord with the great Chinese empire.[21]

On special occasions such as New Year, 100,000 horses marched in procession and 5,000 elephants.[22] Surely the father-in-law of Korea in those days was a man of unusual parts. It came about, however, in the process of time that Korea felt the loss of her exchange of the refined type of queen of ancient days, gifted with the excellence of Han and T'ang and Sung, for the wild Mongol. Notwithstanding the height to which Khubilai had, for the time being, risen above his low estate, he was still barbarian and all his women with him. These greasy, cheesy-smelling Mongols were wholly unfit to command the respect of Korea's court, unfit to take charge of her children, or prepare them for the gentle life ordered by the nation's standards. Thus the line of kingship began to fail.

KHUBILAI did not die till 1294, so practically saw Korea through the thirteenth century. Just as the 'flu', an undiscoverable microbe, attacks and decimates the human species today, so in 1246 a terrible creature appeared in the east called *sigin-ch'ung* (man-eating bug). It was less treacherous than the influenza for it was apparent to the eye. It fell, as the rain falls, over the whole land. The history says, 'These insects had around their bodies a fine netting like silk. When they

203

touched anyone it was like the sting of a sharp knife. If their hair got into the food or under the skin it caused instant death. Various remedies were tried but onion juice was the only thing that could withstand them.' Nothing more is said and there is no further word of explanation. The echo dies away and apparently the obnoxious creature has not appeared again in all these 800 years.[23]

These were the days when Dante was deep down in Hell where he saw inscribed over the door, *Lasciate ogni speranza, voi ch'entrate* (Abandon hope, all ye who enter here).[24] Dante's contemporaries in Korea sang in a more hopeful tone:

> I spent some years in pleasure trips down south,
> Mid hills and streams too wonderful to tell.
> Bright grows the grass down to the ferry's edge,
> And green the willows on the standing shore.
> The breeze tiptoes it o'er the shining stream
> And round the wall hang wreaths of ivy hue.
> The rain sweeps by and joyous workers sing;
> Dim in the distance comes the woodman's raft.
>
> (U T'ak 1262-1342)[25]

> The dew has washed
> The Milky Way and polished bright the moon;
> Brimming, the wine-cup flouts the winter's cold.
> My friend, who sings, shines like the polished jade,
> Outmatching candles as the night sweeps on.
>
> (Kwŏn Pu 1262–1346)

> The yellow flower, the coloured leaves, the autumn moon!
> Golden the wine-cups, bright the shining fire!
> My children come to wish me weal, how dear!
> Old bones like mine wake as on fairy-wing.
>
> (Kwŏn Pu 1262–1346)[26]

The fairy that appears in all Korea's writings came originally from China and yet the Korean has put upon it his own impressions and interpretations. The Chinese character *hsin* (fairy) is made up of 'man' and 'mountain,' because the fairies are supposed to inhabit inaccessible hills.[27] In story-books they are usually like angels. When they meet humankind and converse they usually begin by saying that they have been exiled from heaven for some fault, but that the time of their return home is near at hand. Frequently they speak of their beautiful Nirvana, where the Western Queen Mother lives, as being among the mountains of Tibet. The fairy, however, may also be an old man, very old and very wise. In Japan his tall head sometimes rises a foot above his ears, but in Korea it is the long beard rather that the long head that marks him out.

WE HAVE a picture of this period of which we write, given us by a great doctor of the *hallim,* Ch'oe Hae.[28] So closely does it resemble the features and characteristics of the present day that we give it in full as of special interest.

> Men of today look down on those who are gone,
> And children disrespect their parents.
> The former scholar class is dead,
> Now none left know the simple joys of yore.
> Contempt for others is the order of the day,
> Each thinks himself a model and so plans to do
> His wayward will. A century more and none will know
> Which is the male and which the female of the crow.
> I am distressed that I am born so late:
> I love the past and would reform the world,
> Would speak my inner soul to men. We are divided,
> They and I, even more than Yüeh and Ch'u.
> I'm out of gear with all with whom I have to do,
> And weep my eyes out through the hapless day.
> Why should I fare as those who plot and scheme?
> My heart is set on what is right.
> In place of halls and palaces
> My soul sits happy in its wattle hut.
> Last fall I turned me home toward the south;
> I rode far off, and in my dreams
> Outdistanced e'en the wild-goose flight;
> I saw the hills and all their wondrous store.
> Pent up, my feelings found a swift relief
> And waited for a time to rest
> And let the world wag on its dismal way.
> I had set out upon a round of pleasure,
> But hastened back once more.
> Religion rests in the heart,
> While being in and out of the world.
> Within the sacred books all may be found:
> I am not anxious now, though left alone.

Ch'oe Hae was master of the Confucian College. He gave another interesting picture of the times, their trials, their hopes, their satisfactions, in a short essay on rain:[29]

> Last year the sun and rain turned out awry,
> And all the farmers failed to plant their seed,
> The world dropped down low to starvation point
> And faces looked through lines of anxious care.
> This year again the spring broke endless dry
> And hands were folded in the scorching sun;
> The green moss in the well was shrivelled up,

And red blood marked the morning sky.
Along the highways were the starved, the dead,
And all the fields lay wasted, bare as bone.
I in my little hut lay long asleep,
When suddenly I hear the sound of rain.
I hear it patter on the famished court,
And fall in gems from off the hanging eaves.
I start, I wake, I rise in wonder wild,
I fling the window wide and mad delight
Looks out upon the scene: across the hill
The willow-treetops shine and laughing flowers
Awake along the lea; all things take on
Divinest shades, and fragrance fills the air.
I know now that the mind of God
Thinks of the needs we mortals bear.
Out go the ploughs, the harrows, hoes and spades,
A presage of abundant crops to come.
We thank God for a leaky thatch;
I shall forget my mouth and stomach now.

SUCH was Korea in those distant days. What was England doing? She was fighting against two indomitable Scotsmen whose names we still sing:[30]

Scots, wha hae wi' Wallace bled,
Scots, wham Bruce has aften led;
Welcome to your gory bed
Or to victorie.

These were the days of Wallace and Bruce, who were champions of fair play, and who, perhaps as much as any two that ever lived, have given the world its measure of liberty. Khubilai never met Wallace and never met Bruce. Had they met and could they have talked, what fire would have danced from their animated souls as they told of mighty deeds seen and done. Khubilai could have said, 'Gentlemen, you have had hard luck; I have never been beaten myself.' Khubilai had been dead four years when Wallace went down at Falkirk; but Wallace's name will live as long as Khubilai's.

21 Fourteenth-century Mongol domination

IN the summer of 1797 Samuel Taylor Coleridge, suffering from an attack of pain, had occasion to take an anodyne — how strong a dose we are not told — but after it he slept and had a dream. The dream picked up the last sentences that he had been reading in *Purchas' Pilgrimage:* 'Here the Khan Kubla commanded a palace to be built,' and thus, in a sleep of some three hours, a wonderful poem came to him, moving on in stately measure, 300 lines and more. So vivid was the impression that on awaking he caught up his pen and wrote:

> In Xanadu did Kubla Khan
> A stately pleasure dome decree
> Where Alph, the sacred river, ran
> Through caverns measureless to man
> Down to a sunless sea.

Just at this moment the wind off the Bristol Channel blew in some straying caller from Porlock, who broke the spell and summoned the poet away at the end of his fifty-fourth line. Coleridge came back to the task but Khubilai and his palace had vanished from his imagination for ever. What the other 246 lines might have said about Xanadu we can only guess. In the hands of a great master like Coleridge they could doubtless have spoken something wonderfully well.

At the very time to which Coleridge refers, the Korean government had set up a special line of communications by post-horse with Xanadu one thousand miles distant.[1] In the year 1300 the king and queen of Korea paid a visit to this great capital, called not Xanadu, but Shang-tu. Here the emperor invited them to a special banquet and among the many subject kings who sat at the table Korea was number four. So highly did the king appreciate this honour that the next day he made his Imperial Majesty a gift of 200 sheep, 200 bottles of wine and a beautifully-written prayer for long life and blessing. Catching a suitable occasion, he sang a song, 'The Two Swallows', and danced before their Majesties while, with rattle in hand, he kept the measured time. Mongol royalty was greatly charmed by this expression of good will — all of which happened within the stately halls that Coleridge saw in his misty dream 500 years later.[2]

While dealing with royalty we may say that the dancing of King Ch'ungnyŏl before the son of Khubilai by no means expressed the real heart of Korea's ruling family. They were very unhappy in their home life. A Mongol princess had come to Korea as daughter-in-law, who was of an exceedingly jealous disposition and hard to get along with. Her presence so disturbed the royal household that the king asked his brother-in-law, the emperor, to have her divorced; but no such light and easy law as exists today was known in the world of Chinggis. It could not be done and the Crown Prince was asked to endure his misery in quietness.[3]

King Ch'ungnyŏl, who reigned for thirty-four years, spent most of his life in Shang-tu, and let Korea go her own untutored way. In 1308 he died, and the Crown Prince[4] who came to the throne was a dissolute young man, half Mongol himself, who quarrelled incessantly with his Mongol wife. So outraged were the better classes of Korea by his unseemly conduct, and his illicit commerce with loose women in general, that U T'ak, the famous scholar from whom we quoted in the last chapter, made his way to the palace with an axe in his hand and a rough mat under his arm. What he meant by this accoutrement the west would hardly guess. He knelt on the rough mat and said, 'I have come to offer a humble man's protest against the evil ways of your Majesty. Be pleased to accept my warning; or else I pray you strike off my head with this axe that I bring.' The axe was not intended to brain the wicked king, as one might think: no renowned confucian scholar would ever dream of such a thing. The axe was for the king to use against U T'ak himself, in case his counsel was not received.[5]

KING Ch'ungsŏn had an altogether demented career. He ostensibly reigned for the four years 1309–1313, though for nearly all this time he remained at the Mongol court at Shang-tu. In the end, he resigned his throne when he was forty-five to his son Ch'ungsuk, then twenty years of age. So obnoxious had his presence become to the imperial government that they exiled him to Tibet where he remained for four years.[6] It took him seven months to make the journey and seven months back. This year and more may be subtracted from the actual time of his exile. He was an ill-starred monarch, yet he had an appreciation of letters, for he took with him on his long journey, (or on part of it at least), Yi Chehyŏn, one of the greatest writers and statesmen that Korea has ever known. It was he who wrote the poem on 'China's Sorrow' quoted in chapter 9. In his collected works we find light thrown on that long journey into exile, for here is a snow-storm they encountered:[7]

China's Snow

The wild north wind rolls up the trembling earth,
And flings its shadows over hill and river.
In the bosom of the clouds is heaped up snow
That gives the traveller anxious thought. All heaven
And earth are blotted out in whirlwinds of confusion;
The ground is robed in glistening white,
A new and fresh creation. First I thought
It was the Milky Way had broken loose
And fallen earthward, or that the hilltops,
Struck by the storm, were down upon us.
The angels of the sky, robed in rainbow garb,
Fluttered around like phoenix birds,
Fairies of the deep flashed forth dragon scales.
My horse's hoofs slip as he steps in fear;
He moves not though I let him feel the whip.
My robe takes on a hundred pounds of weight,
While I, inside it, think of Meng Hsiang-yang,[8]
Of how he rode a donkey through the snow
And thought out verses to relieve his hunger.
How very kind the master of the inn,
Who dips a cup of wine to cheer me!
I take my seat beside the cat
That sleeps upon the softly heated floor.
Have you seen Chu-saeng's picture of the snow,[9]
How on one sheet he piles its vast creation?
The willows by the river-bank are weighted down
Where crow-birds used to light. The little inn
Has closed its doors, no breath of life appears.

A guest is starting off upon his cart
Into the wilderness; official duties
Make him pull his bridle-rein and twist
His horse's nose. How happy is his lot
Who draws his quilt around his ears
And floats off into common country dreams,
To let the world of heat and cold
Drive forward as it pleases.
I too behold the scene that Chu-saeng pictured,
And ne'er forget the meaning of his pen.
If some day we should meet, Chu-saeng and I,
I'll clasp his hand and talk with him
About the landscapes of the snow.

So much for Chinese snows as told by Yi Chehyŏn in the year 1319. About the same time William Tell shot the apple off his son's head in the snow-capped canton of Uri. Men now say there never was a William Tell, that doughty hero of the storybook whose inspiration has lasted six hundred years; while Yi Chehyŏn, a master, not of the bow but of the pen, who really lived, they have never heard of. Let me show how he fought his battle for liberty as compared with the Altdorf archer. The palace of Songdo was deserted by its king, who was far away in China. His country was left to the tender mercies of those who happened to be in power. It was argued in Shang-tu that Korea was Mongol as to royalty, and Mongol as to rule, so why not make it a Mongol province? Thus it was decided in 1323 to make Korea a part of the great Mongol Empire.

Yi Chehyŏn then came forward to plead for his country's life. His practised pen and skilful hand represented longer years of study and hard labour than even Tell's unerring bow. How powerfully he marshals his Chinese paragraphs, how deftly his phrases run, with what persuasive effect he presents his case we can gather from the fact that the Mongol emperor was moved by them to say to the government, 'Hands off!'

A paragraph or two from his paper will give the reader some idea as to how he won his case;[10]

The Doctrine of the Mean says that true government gives its heart to mend the broken line of royalty, to restore the state that has fallen, to bring order out of chaos, to steady those of feeble step, to give liberally but to receive sparingly. This is true rule, that will win the hearts of all men. I learn that the Imperial House meditates making Korea a province of the Empire. Will not such an action run counter to the commands of the great Emperor Shih Tsu (Khubilai) and to the spirit of those emperors who have have helped us so greatly heretofore? Our little country measures only about a thousand *li* at best, and of these, seven-tenths are waste land. Though you should receive all the taxes therefrom, the amount gathered would not equal the cost of transportation, and though you levied a polltax it would not pay the salaries of those required for its collection. Though all our humble state were added to the Empire, it would appear scarcely more than a grain of sand on the face of T'ai-shan Mountain. No profits would accrue therefrom. It is miles away in distance and its people are a very ignorant folk who speak a language entirely different from that of the Empire. Its customs, too, are odd and its ideas wholly unsophisticated. If a rumour of this should get abroad fear and suspicion would take possession of my people. How could one ever hope to go from house to house to clear up so great a misunderstanding? Japan also watches us with wakeful eye: if she should hear of it, she would advance to lay a claim.

I pray that your Majesty will think carefully, and, remembering the Doctrine of the Mean, leave us as we are, a separate nation, a contented people. In doing so you will awaken thankfulness in all hearts and grateful tears from the spirits of the kingly dead. Graciously pardon my presumption in thus writing, but this is my petition. This I humbly beg and pray.

On reading this the emperor at once vetoed the project and never again did the question arise.

Before we leave Yi Chehyŏn, let us give a common-place picture or two as they dropped from his pen.[11]

Domestic animals

The cat

Two ears you have, and two green eyes,
And claws and teeth;
And yet how rats abound and gnaw and scrape!
Why sleep? Wake up, I say!

The dog

You wag your tail, so glad to greet my eye;
You lick me with your tongue most dear!
Now, never fight, and don't o'er friendly be,
But watch the holes that poke beneath the fence.

The cock

See, when you crow, that 'tis the proper time;
And when trespassers come, stand up and fight.
You pick your living from the refuse heap
To make a sacrificial meal for me and mine.

THERE APPEARED at this time in Korea a wonderful Indian priest called Chigong, whose name means 'up yonder'.[12] He was dark of face but most attractive of soul. Some ten miles east of Seoul, under the Ch'ŏnbo mountains of Yangju, stands a stone that commemorates this great Indian master with nearly 4,000 characters. The composition is by Mogŭn, Yi Saek, Korea's noted man of letters.[13] He had seen Chigong, for he had companied with him thirty-five years on earth and his knowledge was therefore first-hand. This biography, so favourable to the buddhist teacher, cost Yi Saek his place of honour in the Temple of Confucius. In the council of great masters the vote went against him because he had spoken so highly of the dark-faced Indian stranger. He tells how he came of a royal line of kings, of how he first awakened to a knowledge of religion, of his startling methods of conquering evil. For example, he found the priests of his day noisy and quarrelsome, so he quietly withdrew and, taking careful thought, gave their confusion a death-blow by himself not speaking for ten long years. The power of silence on his part drove unseemly discord from the presence of the buddha. Yi Saek tells of his long journeys past this kingdom and that; how his life was beset by every form of evil; how lions and serpents beset his way. In many places kings and ministers were so impressed that they made an image of him and bowed before it night and morning. In other places fierce rage and jealousy possessed their hearts. As he preached against murder, lying, robbery, and adultery, one evil king sent a dancing-girl into his bath to tempt him, but as the writer puts it, Chigong, though on other occasions greatly alive, was, to her, a dead man. Others set upon him with clubs, beat him and broke his teeth, but these things in no way changed the gentle tones of his voice, or the kindly purpose of his mission. The emperor of China made him for a time his counsellor, the king of Korea looked upon him with wonder. Queens and princesses listened as he discoursed. Among his disciples was a famous character known as Naong ('Lazy old man'), born in 1320, who died in 1376. It was he, lazy though he called himself, who hammered out the Manjusri or Great Buddha of the Diamond Mountains and the small images that mark the rock face in front of P'yohun Temple.[14]

THESE were days of exceptional religious fervour, when the first catholic missionaries arrived in China. John of Montecorvino, a Franciscan, was the leader. He arrived in Cambaluc (Peking) about 1300, and so won his way with the rulers and the people that he became bishop of Peking and died at eighty years of age, honoured by all. In his short term of service he gathered into the Church more than 30,000 believers. But how lonely he was. Once he wrote, 'It is now twelve years since I have heard any news from the western world and I am become old and gray-headed.' He translated the whole of the New Testament and the Psalms of David into the Mongol language. In 1336, the Emperor Shun-ti, whose wife was a Korean, sent a certain Andrew the Frank as a special envoy to the Pope.[15]

These were the days, too, that saw the beginning of the Hundred Years War (1338–1453), when Crécy and Poitiers were fought and Edward III of England spoke his *Honi soit qui mal y pense*. When Crécy was fought, Chaucer was a little boy of six learning his lesson at his mother's knee. In Korea another little boy of six, called Yi Chono, was taking his first arduous lessons in writing. When they grew up what did they write about? Chono, a Korean scholar, would scorn to write about girls — no gentleman ever did. As I make this note I can see from my window Samgak-san, the Three Horned Peaks that stand nearly

3,000 feet high behind Seoul. These hills have seen Korea's world march by for as many years as they have measured feet. Wonderful hills! Yi, 600 years ago, falls in love with them and writes:[16]

> Behold these shafts three-sparred against the sky,
> Their lights and shades like clouds piled mountain-deep.
> I gaze straight up where stand the armèd peaks,
> I look across at lotus flowers between.
> For long I studied in a temple there,
> But two years stayed beside the River Han.
> Who tells me mountains do not have a soul?
> Today we meet, and tears are in our eyes.

Chaucer, on the other hand, just the same age as Yi Chono, breathing the same air and seeing the same moon, writes in quite a different strain. It is not the hills that attract him, but the sweet prioress of whom he says,

> Ful wel she song the service divyne,
> Entuned in hir nose ful semely;
> And Frensh she spak ful faire and fetisly,
> After the scole of Stratford atte Bowe,
> For Frensh of Paris was to hir unknowe.[17]

I can imagine Chono and Chaucer meeting and the former saying from the depths of his confucian heart, 'Don't you feel a little demeaned in taking note of a mere woman, a nun, too, and writing thus?' I hear a great laugh on the part of Chaucer and a thoroughly English answer. How different they must have been; Chono much more the finished gentleman; Chaucer rude, but with the youth and vigour of the west lighting up his eyes.

IN THESE DAYS a young Korean woman who had won her way into the palace at Shang-tu suddenly rose to the place of empress. Yi Kok, the father of Mogŭn, whom we quoted in this chapter, writes of her saying:[18]

> When the emperor of the Mongols had been on the throne some seven years, the palace lady-in-waiting Ki-ssi became empress. She was a Korean and her promotion was due to the fact that she had given birth to a son. 'I am blessed', said she to the eunuchs, 'with this high office and in return I desire to pray to God for eternal blessings on the emperor. Without the help of the buddha, however, these cannot be obtained.' She sought far and wide for blessings and at last hearing that the Changan Temple of the Diamond Mountains was a place of special prayer she gave of her own private means in order to beautify it and make it a place of abiding worship.

At the fall of the Mongol dynasty before the Ming, the Empress Ki-ssi made her escape and, it is said, carried the imperial seal with her. Some years ago the newspapers of Seoul reported a lawsuit in which the Ki family sued a magistrate for the imperial seal of Khubilai's house. Ki-ssi had brought it to Korea, they said, and the county magistrate hearing of it had come and taken forcible possession. They now demanded it back as a priceless treasure.

As A RELIC of this period let the reader take note of the bell in the South Gate of Songdo. It was cast in the year 1346 about the time that the battle of Crécy was being fought and when Chaucer and Chono were both six years old.[19]

22 The end of Koryŏ

WE come now to the close of a great chapter in Korea's history. Koryŏ, the state from which we derive our familiar name, Korea, had been stricken with a mortal sickness and was going down. The end had come, and no balms of Gilead could suffice to restore her. Kings came and went, while the fortunes of the day fell lower and lower.

King Kongmin, who ascended the throne in 1352, was a dainty, delicate, soft-fingered individual whose hand loved best of all the artist's brush. Even today, in the royal museum of Seoul, we have a specimen of his highly finished work.[1] Tradition says his most famous picture was that of the A-fang Palace of Emperor Ch'in-shih, who built the Great Wall of China told of in chapter 5. King Kongmin was a man of timid soul, easily alarmed and influenced by dreams. One night when he was in the grip of a dreadful dream-spell he dreamt that a man attacked him with a drawn sword. The king cried out for help, when suddenly a priest appeared and struck down the assassin. Next day, when a minister named Kim Wŏnmyŏng came into audience, he brought with him a strange priest who had never been in the palace before. The king gave a sudden start, looked closely, and recognized him as the priest of the dream who had saved his life.[2]

From this day on Sin Ton, for that was the monk's name, became the evil genius of the palace. He was a man of no learning, but quick of eye and glib of tongue. The king was interested, yes, charmed by all he said and did. Wise ministers shook their heads in warning. One, an old man, Yi Sŭnggyŏng, said, 'Mark my words, that fellow with the shaven head will give us trouble.'[3] Several of the higher officials planned to do away with him, but the king got wind of it, and whisked him safely out of sight. Later, when the great Yi was dead, Sin Ton returned, with long hair that had grown in the meantime, and made his way into the palace. Immediately all power was put into his hands: Prime Minister he was and father confessor to the king, to the ministers, and to their wives and daughters as well, with whom he carried on illicit commerce that lasted for years. One of the last words recorded of Yi Chehyŏn, was this warning: 'The expression of his face betrays him.' But the king refused to hear.

The foolish Kongmin had no son born of the queen. Word came to him that a very beautiful serving-woman in Sin Ton's house, with whom he had had to do, had a child, his child they said. He accepted this as true and had the child

213

brought up as his adopted son — though he was really of the line of Sin Ton, not of the king. Amid Korea's cataclysmic fortunes this same youth ruled from 1374 to 1388.

Sin Ton, well aware of the fact that he had many enemies, remarked, 'I have heard it said that your Majesty lends a ready ear to tale-bearers. If so, you will hear much ill of me.' On hearing this the king with his own hand wrote out an oath that ran: 'May the teacher be my saviour, as I the teacher's. Let us live and die together. Let us pay no heed to those who speak against us or defame us. May the buddha and God bear witness.' Sin Ton set to work to have all those who opposed his will sent into exile, and each vacancy filled with one of his own henchmen. Thus he stepped into the place of absolute power. His actions were announced to the world as purity itself: 'Guarding the right, doing the good, living with God, ruling as just, holding the world'; while his titles ran: Three-Times-Great Lord of Samhan, Prime Minister, Chief-Justice, Prince Ch'wisŏng etc., etc.[4]

The great literary master of the period was Yi Talch'ung (1328–1385). The king, appreciating his high attainments, appointed him to office. Once, on Sin Ton's entering the council, Talch'ung was heard to remark, 'I hear Your Excellency is much given to wine and women. Ha, ha!' Sin Ton resented this and shortly after had Yi Talch'ung dismissed.[5]

Herewith I add a short extract from the writings of Yi to show the manner of man he was. He calls it *Whom to Speak Well Of*.[6]

> Once a man, not much of a man, called on a certain old man and spake thus: 'There's a company not far from here that meets daily to talk over mankind in general. They also speak of you. Some among them say you are a man, and others say you are not a man. How comes it, my Lord, that you are a man to some, and not a man to others?' The master listened and then made reply: 'Though there are those who say I am a man, I am not pleased at that; and though there are others who say I am not a man, I am not distressed. When a real man says I'm a man, or one who's not a man says I'm not a man, I'm interested. What kind of man is the man who says I'm a man? And what sort of man is the man who says I'm not a man? When a real man says I'm a man, I'm pleased; and when one who is not a man says I am not a man, I like that too. If a real man says I'm not a man, then I am anxious; and when he who is not a man says I'm a man, I am anxious also. My one desire is to know whether the man who says I'm a man is really a man; and whether the one who says I'm not a man is really not a man. The saying is, *The good man alone can truly estimate others*.[7] Is the man who calls me a man a good man? Also is the man who says I am no man, no man? This alone I care to know'. The questioner then laughed and went away.

Such were the scales in which this great scholar weighed men, who said to Sin Ton, 'I hear Your Excellency is exceedingly fond of wine and women. Ha! ha!'

Yi Chono also wrote of Sin Ton: 'A devil has got control of our race and nation. We must get rid of him at all costs.' He and another high officer, Chŏng Ch'u, wrote a petition, the closing paragraph of which reads with a truly oriental flavour.[8]

> Since your Majesty has entrusted all power to this Sin Ton, the seasons have quite fallen out of gear: we have had thunder in the winter time, yellow mists overlying the land for days, spots appearing on the sun's face, glaring red clouds riding across the midnight sky, meteors dropping earthward with deadly aim, trees broken down with ice and snow, wild beasts from the hills appearing in the streets of the capital in open day. Does it look as though your Majesty's promotion of Sin Ton was in accord with the will of God and man?

The king, greatly enraged at this, threw it into the fire and had Chaucer's contemporary put to torture. Chono was only twenty-five years of age at the time (1365), but he stood the torments as only the brave can stand them. He never really recovered, for he died at the age of thirty-one. One of his last words was, 'My regret in dying is that I do not see this monster, Sin Ton, dead before me.' History says: 'In the long course of 500 years the greatest, the truest, the bravest censor that lived was Chono.' Rest to his ashes![9]

So brazen was the audacious impostor Sin Ton in his life and ways that a horror grew up over the whole land regarding him. The Queen Dowager, for one, felt that he must be destroyed. Ex-ministers consulted together as to what to do. But how difficult it was to oust him! A veritable reign of terror set in. Every man who dared raise a protest was killed; even Yi Wŏnmyŏng, who had introduced Sin Ton to the king, was beaten to death because he dared peep a remonstrance. But the net began to close upon its victim. Little by little rumours of his evil deeds, his murders, his foul life, came to the king's ears, till the credulous, foolish monarch was astounded. 'I thought him a saint of God,' said he, 'but behold he is as black as Pluto.' Sin Ton was questioned but failed to clear his name. On seeing his danger he determined to strike for his life, decided even on the death of the king himself. The plot was discovered, and he was taken prisoner and sent in irons to Suwŏn in 1371. There he was followed by an executioner, Im Pak, who had a written statement from the king saying: 'You swore to me that you lived a religious life to the full, and never had illicit commerce with women, but now I hear that your progeny is everywhere and that you have seven houses of your own in the city.' Thus were his sins read off. He was then beheaded, his body divided into fragments and sent abroad throughout the land, while his head was hung up on the East Gate of Songdo.[10] This man's career, perhaps more than anything else, hastened the fall of Songdo and the setting up of the Yi dynasty with its capital at Seoul in 1392.

KING KONGMIN survived the death of his favourite only three years, when he was murdered by a disgruntled eunuch and an over-pampered minister. His

215

10–year-old son, Sin U, whom the serving woman Panya was said to have borne to him in the home of Sin Ton, succeeded him. Before Sin U came to the throne, however, he had been adopted and made the son of Queen Han. This Queen Han ruled the palace. Suddenly the forgotten serving-woman appeared and laid claim to Sin U as her child, which he really was. A great disturbance followed. Panya was arrested and imprisoned and finally dropped into the Imjin River, which put a quietus on the unhappy question.[11]

The Mongols, from being friends, suzerains and guardians, had become the enemies of Korea, and, as their day in China drew to a close, they vented their evil feelings on their poor eastern neighbour. Japan too, was abroad in pirate ships everywhere, attacking the peninsula from right and left. Two generals appear at this time, Ch'oe Yŏng and Yi Sŏnggye, on whom King Sin U depended for the defence of the realm. These brave soldiers held back the Mongols until they finally disappeared into the Gobi Desert; then they fell at loggerheads with one another over the king. Sŏnggye, who afterwards became T'aejo, founder of the Yi Dynasty, was sent off with troops to attack the newly-risen power, the Ming, who had driven out the Mongols and gained control of China. Sŏnggye offered many reasons against attacking this new dynasty, but Ch'oe Yŏng and King Sin U urged him on. Finally, blocked by rains and innumerable obstacles, he wheeled about and came back against the king with all his force. The king, who was in P'yŏngyang, fled to Songdo and Sŏnggye followed. A skirmish took place in which the royal forces were outgeneralled. Ch'oe Yŏng was taken prisoner, but Sŏnggye treated him considerately and sent him into exile.

One of Sŏnggye's best friends was a man named Cho Chun who afterwards built the walls of Seoul. Sŏnggye made him Grand Counsellor, so that the trembling king took from him whatever was given in the way of orders. One night, in desperation, the king and eighty of his eunuchs donned coats of mail and crept stealthily to the homes of Yi Sŏnggye and Cho Chun, determined to settle the matter once and for all; but they were doomed to failure, for both these generals were away with the army and the king and his aides had to go back disappointed to the palace. Ch'oe Yŏng's daughter was queen and naturally worked in the interests of her father, who was in exile. Yi Sŏnggye noticed this and asked King Sin U to send her away, but he refused. On this Yi Sŏnggye had him and his queen and concubines bundled out of Songdo and sent off to Kang-hwa, the island home of royalty. There Sin U died the next year, aged twenty-five.[12]

GREAT NAMES appear at this time associated with the palace: Yi Saek, Mogŭn, Korea's mighty master of the pen; Chŏng Mongju, whose blood marks are seen still on the Bamboo Bridge of Songdo; Kwŏn Kŭn, whose comments appear in this history; Chŏng Tojŏn, the friend of Yi Sŏnggye, who later died under the knife.

When the first envoy for the Ming was called for in 1389, Yi Saek was sent. His chief officer was Yi Sungin (1349–1392), also a literatus of great renown, though twenty-one years younger; and his secretary was T'aejo's second son, who afterwards became King T'aejong.

Great fears for the state possessed everyone, for there was a general impression abroad that the end of the world had come. We see it in this essay by Yi Sungin, the second envoy:[13]

How sad this autumn night!
The witch-wind and the rain drive through the dark.
I long to sleep my griefs away
And free my soul. My spirit takes its flight
And upward wings its ready way;
Into the depths of space I whirl, all landmarks gone,
Until I light upon the windy height
That leads to heaven. In a flash I feel myself
Before its gates, where God sits throned on high.
Wide out they swing and then a voice calls, 'Come!'
Who would turn back from such a call as this?
So in I go, and kneeling down speak out.
God looks at me with kindly face
While I make bold to speak:
'I live a humble dweller in the lower earth,
With heart and soul distressed.
A day or two ago I was a child
In swaddling clothes. By slow degrees I waked
And longed to live as did the saints of old—
Just as Confucius taught. His words:
Deny yourself and live a life of love.[14]
He also said: *Let not the thoughtful scholar*
Ever forget he is a child of sorrow.[15]
The Master Mencius loved to speak these words,
And yet he failed and had to die. I too
Have buckled on these precepts, strong to act,
To do my best and be a faithful minister,
A loyal subject of the state.
But evil habits of the day make all depraved;
Flattery and falsehood are round about the king.
I am a fish drawn from the sea,
Destined to be sliced and cooked.
Already do they lift their eyes and clean
Their teeth for action; yet though I should die
A thousand deaths, my mind dare never change.
I come up here to have a wide extended view.
If Thou hearest not, whither shall I go?
Thy justice is exceeding great: save me,
I pray thee, from my lost and foundered state.
My tear-drops fall like rain,
My heart so pent-up wild, I gasp for breath.'
God looked with pity on my low estate

217

And said, 'Come near and hear what I shall say.
You must adapt yourself to times and needs,
For e'en the sun, when once it tops the height,
Goes down; and the moon whose full face fades away.
Even religious views will vary with the times.
Why should you wonder at men's changing ways?
The world hates most a sharply-cornered soul.
Why not round off your roughened edges
And think of others? The world loves white:
Why should you stand by black and win ill-will?
I pity your hard lot; and yet the fault
Is all your own. If you would shake free
From such distress and come to peace with men,
Then you must change your ways.'
Now as I think it o'er, God's grace is boundless,
And yet for me there is no way of change;
I can but hasten on unto the end.
A thousand years ago men lived and died,
A thousand years to come they will live still,
But change I cannot. This dark world knows me not.
Hence I have spoken.

BY MANY SIGNS and omens the end of Koryŏ was seen approaching. For 500 years she had carried on as a distinct part of the great Chinese system, distinguished in literature, in fine arts, in religion; her footsteps are seen in heaps of gathered volumes in the great libraries of the world, in choice porcelains that decorate the palace halls of the west, in stones that stand by her own wayside and sing her eternal praises. With much tender sympathy we watch her go down and see from her ashes rise another kingdom that will also ride the rough waves of time for 500 years, but will not touch the heights, nor yet the depths, that marked this ancient kingdom's joys and griefs. Let me close with a plaint by Yi Sungin.[16]

Feelings

But yesterday I felt the blazing heat,
And now today I'm chilled clear to the bone.
The frost nips hard the leaves of every flower,
The sun swings, wheel-like, past my window chink.
Frail man, that's born of time and earthly clods,
Labours his day and generations through.
His body, lacking iron-will and stone,
Fails long before its hundred years are up.
From this grim fact the ancients used to say,
'Guard well your time; 'tis short.'
I've heard of Wang Tzŭ-chin and how he fared
Among the fairies in the Kou-shan Hills:[17]

The pipe he played was heard in many lands,
His white cranes flew like steeds across the sky.
All worldly trammels far he cast aside,
And, stripped of every cark and grinding care,
He looked far down upon these fields of strife,
Where life is but the fever of a day.
If, after all, I'm but a hand-cuffed slave,
Let's rid me of my stocks and get me free.
Whom shall I tell this inner mind of mine?
Come tune my harp and sing a roundelay:
The constellations ride across the sky,
The autumn comes with sad and shrivelling breath,
The west wind blows on rattling wing as well,
And whistles through the leafless boughs at night.
My master long has dwelt an exile drear;
He left me with no message of return.
I live alone in this deserted room
And think and think the weary daylight through,
But thoughts have failed to bring him back again.
My sadness and my grief alone remain.

THE YI DYNASTY

23 The founding of the Yi dynasty: T'aejo

To BE SUDDENLY transferred from the life of a commoner to the majesty of a throne might well turn the head of any man. Theoretically, what a wonderful thing kingship is — to be the ruler of a nation, as free as Halley's Comet to swing among the suns, appear and disappear at pleasure, and do all one's own sweet will: in fact, be a king. Actually however, Korean kingship was no such soft sinecure, but, rather, a round of most exacting service, bitted and bridled at every turn, and beset with a thousand petty annoyances. T'aejo[1] till 1392, fifty-seven long years, had been a free man to go his own way; from this date on we behold him king, with all the cares and miseries that kingship entails. Probably there has never lived anywhere a man more utterly miserable than T'aejo.

He was large-hearted to begin with, and kind, for instead of wiping out the ancient house of Songdo, as one might have expected from an oriental usurper, he let King Kongyang go off into easy exile, first to Wŏnju in Kangwŏn province, where he retained the title *kun* or 'prince'; and two years later to a place called Samch'ŏk, on the south border line of the same province, where he died, not wholly without suspicion of foul play. His departure is somewhat like that of Richard II of England, who disappeared behind the plated doors of Pontefract Castle in 1399 and was never heard of again.

T'aejo had swung most of his world into line, but there were some souls he could neither move nor shake. One was Chŏng Mongju, a great scholar and statesman, who had been sent as envoy to Japan, and also to China. Among his writings we find reference to the great Ming court, and see the awe with which he looked upon its favours. He writes:[2]

> 'I, Chŏng Mongju, in the year *pyŏngin* (1386) was in Nanking in the fourth moon, with my commission from my king. On the 23rd day the emperor, while seated in the Gate of Divine Worship, sent a palace maid to say that it was his imperial will that I should come. I went and he talked with me face to face. What he said was most gracious. He ordered our yearly tribute of gold, silver, horses, cotton goods, etc., to be entirely remitted.

'Blessings on his name!' says Chŏng as he closes his memorandum.

On state business, also, he was sent to Japan, and, while there, among other things wrote:[3]

> A thousand years have stood these islands of the deep;
> By raft I come, and long I linger here.
> Priests from the hills bow, asking for a song;

My host, too, sends me drink to cheer the day.
I'm glad we can be friends, kind to each other;
Let's not be mean in mind because of race.
Who'll say one is not happy on a foreign shore?
Daily we go by chair to see the plums in blossom.

Chŏng was a great friend and admirer of T'aejo, and wrote of him thus:[4]

His presence is the mighty warrior, firm
He stands, an eagle on a mountain top;
In wisdom and resource none can compare,
The dragon of Namyang is he.[5]
In judgment on the civil bench,
Or counsel from the warrior's tent, he rules:
He halts the waves that roll in from the sea,
And holds the sun back from its heavenly course.

When it came, however, to Chŏng's swearing allegiance to him as king, he refused. One of the old tenets of the east is to stand by your king through weal or woe. Chŏng's mind was as immovable as the grey rocks that guard the entrance to Pusan. He would not swear, never! As he returned from an ill-fated conference held in Yi Sŏnggye's house by the old East Gate of Songdo, he was crossing the Sŏnjuk Bridge when an assassin suddenly darted out and struck him from his horse with an iron bludgeon. There he died 533 years ago, and there today we stop to behold with wonder the blood marks that sank into the stone. T'aejo had eight sons and five daughters. The fifth son, Yi Pangwŏn, later known as T'aejong, was a masterful, overbearing man who seems to have been the moving spirit behind the whole plan of changing the dynasty. He was twenty-five years old when Koryŏ came under his hammer and it was he who set the assassins to await the return of Chŏng.

Notwithstanding the evils that necessarily attend such a line of action, T'aejo, being a soldier of resource and quick of action like Napoleon, struck with all his might and settled in a few hours what had proved a lingering sickness to the state for years. His ascent to the throne was, through the diplomatic skill of his son, Pangwŏn, confirmed by the Ming emperor, and so he set about the organization of the state. He chose as his new capital a place called Hanyang, fifty miles south of Songdo, where he set up the Sajik and the ancestral shrine of his fathers, the name ever after being Seoul, a common noun meaning simply 'capital'. It occupies a favoured site, between the Three Horn and Mongmyŏk[6] Peaks. Tosŏn, the famous priest of Wang Kŏn, had spoken of it as the future capital, and now Muhak, another great master of the buddha, pointed out its way. In the year 1394 T'aejo moved all his paraphernalia and established new laws and customs, calling the state not Koryŏ but once more the old name of Chosŏn, 'Morning Freshness', the name Ch'i Tzŭ had given it in 1122 BC.[7] The walls of the capital were built in 1396, the whole work being done by 200,000 labourers in about six months.

THE CHIEF INTEREST centres on the household of T'aejo. He had two wives and, as already mentioned, thirteen children. One wife, Queen Han, who had been the companion of his earlier years, was the mother of six sons and two daughters; while Queen Kang, the aristocratic wife of his choice, had two sons and one daughter. Queen Han died in 1392, the great year of change, leaving Queen Kang in sole possession of power behind the screen. Naturally she felt all a woman's ambition for her own sons and desired one of these to be appointed Crown Prince, though Korea's usual custom was to appoint the eldest son in the family line. The case, however, was unusual in that Lady Han had never really been queen. She was only a plain country-woman, who died before the honours of queenship could be put upon her. Queen Kang, on the other hand, was the royal companion, sharing the throne. At her urgent request T'aejo made her second son, Prince Pangsŏk, his heir. This was done in 1393. Inextricable tangles of intrigue were at once set in motion which Pangwŏn, the masterful fifth son, watched with ever-wakeful eye. He saw that Chŏng Tojŏn, the great literary master and one of the chief architects of the newly-erected city of Seoul, was set straight against him. Chŏng had been his father's chief-of-staff in all the changes wrought and was now naturally behind Queen Kang's party. He suspected Pangwŏn and regarded him as a dangerous man.

In 1396 Queen Kang died and the king sincerely mourned her loss. She was buried where the British Consulate now stands[8] and the evening call of her temple bells awakened his Majesty's most tearful, tender memories. After her departure the king, now aged sixty-one, turned his whole attention to the children she had left him, two sons, Pangbŏn and Pangsŏk, and a little girl named Kyŏng-sun ('submission'). Pangwŏn saw the net slowly closing around him, the most powerful agents of the state in league with these lads of sixteen and seventeen, bent on his destruction. All unexpectedly he struck. Pangbŏn and Pangsŏk rose against him, and a battle was fought in Seoul of two engagements from which two wards of the city are still called (though the Chinese characters do not indicate it) First Fight and Great Battle.[9] The beloved sons of Queen Kang were killed, and Chŏng Tojŏn, the scholar who had abetted them, was taken and beaten to death without trial. On this the old king, enraged beyond words, cut off his daughter's glossy hair, shook the dust of the accursed city from his feet and made his way back to Hamhŭng.[10] For ten long years he remained in exile, a grinning spectre, his empty title being *Taesangwang*, 'Great Superior King'. His eldest son nominally occupied the throne wearing the title *Sangwang*, 'Superior King', while the fiery fifth son of the family, Pangwŏn, actually ruled and was called king. More than once he sent messengers to ask the old father's forgiveness, but these failed. One messenger, Pak Sun, thinking he had been successful, turned to take his way home and was struck in the back by an arrow; his body was dismembered as though he had been a criminal of the deepest dye. Others went and came, always at the risk of life. Finally, after many invitations and requests, the old king came back to a point ten miles beyond the east wall of Seoul, where Ŭijŏngbu railway station now stands.[11] Here he was met by Pangwŏn, who came to ask forgiveness. The answer of the great chief was a shaft that went flying with deadly aim from his bow. Pangwŏn just in time dodged behind a tree which caught the deadly arrow deep in its heart. On this the old man threw him the state seal and said, 'Take it, you rascal, since that's what you want.' The next year he died in Seoul in one of the buildings of the present Royal Gardens.[12]

Following this, in order to clear away all memory of his ill-fated half-brothers and step-mother, T'aejong (as Pangwŏn is now called) had Queen Kang's body removed from the confines of the present British Consulate hill and buried hastily outside the Little East Gate. For nearly two hundred years, till 1581, the site was lost and no sacrifices were offered. Finally, through the writings of Pyŏn Kyeryang it was rediscovered and she was restored to honour. Today the reader may visit Chŏng-nŭng, 'the Pure Tomb', in a half-hour's walk from the north-east of the city.[13]

Shakespeare says, 'The course of true love never did run smooth.'[14] History surely has proved, both in east and west, that the way of kingship is likewise beset with briars and thorns. Henry IV of England who, like T'aejo, ousted the real king from the throne and took forcible possession, was beset by an equal distress of soul. While T'aejo, self-exiled in Hamhŭng, was growling over his wrongs, King Henry was tossing the night through and mumbling, as Shakespeare puts it:[15]

> O sleep, O gentle sleep,
> Nature's soft nurse, how I have frighted thee,
> That thou no more wilt weigh my eyelids down
> And steep my senses in forgetfulness?
> Canst thou, O partial sleep! give thy repose
> To the wet sea-boy in an hour so rude;
> And in the calmest and most stillest night,
> With all appliances and means to boot,
> Deny it to a king? Then, happy low, lie down!
> Uneasy lies the head that wears a crown.

Could King T'aejo and Henry IV have met together and talked over king-ship, how much they would have found in common, and how many serious looks and noddings of the head would have confirmed what they had to say.

HOWEVER, in spite of domestic infelicity, progress was made. One of the greatest events in the history of East Asia was the invention of movable type, *chuja,* 'cast type', as it was called. The idea of it went back as far as 1390 and farther. In that year we find Chŏng Tojŏn, the unfortunate victim of Queen Kang's intrigue, writing thus:[16]

> Our scholar class, though imbued with a love of literature, has few
> books to draw upon, and so, however learned it may be, its range of
> reading is very narrow. I have felt this lack of books all my life. For
> this reason I propose that we set up a publishing house supplied with
> movable type in order that the Sacred Books, the histories, the masters,

the poets of all ages, as well as books on medicine, military tactics, etc., may be printed, and no more sighs be uttered over lost opportunities. May you all feel a personal interest in this matter and help make it go.

'Cast type' was known to Korea as early as 1232, for in that year, when the capital was moved to Kanghwa, Yi Kyubo had, of his own accord, twenty-eight sets of a book of ceremonies printed by movable type, as his record clearly tells today in Volume xi of *Yi Sangguk hujip*.[17] Leaving this first and earliest reference out of account, however, there is no doubt that the general use of movable type began in the year 1403. For two hundred years movable type had been used in Korea privately, but now in this third year of T'aejong a government printing office was set up. A record from the *Kukcho pogam* reads:[18]

His Majesty, regretting the fact that there was so little opportunity for the extension of literature, gave command that there be established an Office of Type for type to be made of brass. From these, books were to be printed.

As THIS FIRST CENTURY of Seoul opens, three names occur to the writer, with which he tries to match something from the east: Joan of Arc, Dick Whittington, and Thomas à Kempis. There is no other Joan of Arc, she stands alone — a simple country-girl who saw visions of God and came forth, the spotless maid of France. Korea has had no-one so great, and yet among her good daughters there was one Kim-ssi of this same time, whose name is well worth remembering. Her story is told in the *Yŏji sŭngnam*.[19] Her husband, (for she was married), was of the Yu clan, a soldier called to active service on the frontier. Said he, 'As my life of roughing it is to begin, I propose to start tonight and sleep in the open.' His wife said, 'Then I'll go with you.' She went; and in the night a tiger came prowling by and, before she knew it, had her husband in his fierce grip and was off. As on wing, with bow in hand, she followed. There was no time to string the arrow, but with limber arm she struck the beast again and again across the eyes till he let go his hold and sat back blinking at them. Kim-ssi said, 'You would kill my husband, would you, and devour me as well? Horrible beast!' The tiger, hearing this, turned tail and went away. Meanwhile, since her husband was unconscious, Kim-ssi took him on her back and carried him home. When the day dawned he returned to life. The next night the tiger came again and roared out his fury time after time. Kim-ssi took a stick in her hand, opened the door and went out. 'Tiger,' said she, 'you have that modicum of sense that knows what is right and what is wrong. Why act thus?' The tiger in reply turned and bit furiously at the pear tree under which he sat and then departed. 'At once', says the historian, 'the pear tree sickened and died.'

I can find no story corresponding to Dick Whittington's. As the bells of Bow Church were ringing for Dick's return to London, T'aejo was hearing the call to kingship. Happy was Whittington's lot, however, as compared with that of T'aejo, first king of Korea's Yi dynasty; and blessed was his cat above many.

One Korean cat story carefully recorded in history falls about eighty years later, telling of a cat that brought good luck, as did Dick's. This I quote from the *Inmul chi* or 'Record of Famous Men'.[20] Chang Sunsŏn was a man of south Korea, an excellent scholar, who passed his examinations brilliantly. Unfortunately he had a face as homely as a savage, and a head like a pig's. For this reason he was called Chedu, 'Pig-head'. Among the *kisaeng* or dancing-girls of Sŏngju we are told there was one whom he regarded as a special favourite. Later this *kisaeng* was removed to the capital to wait on the king, the infamous Yŏnsangun.[21] It happened one day when the food intended for sacrifice before the royal tablets was brought in for inspection, that there was a pig's head among the dishes. The *kisaeng* saw it and laughed. The king noticed and inquired, 'Why do you laugh?' 'This pig's head here reminds me of the head of Chang Sunsŏn of Sŏngju; that's why I laughed.' He turned on her and roared, 'It looks as though you had had more to do with him than you ought.' At once in a jealous fit of rage he ordered an officer to Sŏngju to have Chang Sunsŏn's head off. Chang was eating breakfast when this pressing order came. The officer, however, instead of carrying out the order at once, bound him and ordered him to start for Seoul. They reached the lake of Konggŏm-ji that lies at the south side of the mountain pass. Here the road divides, one fork bending slightly east and one west. They did not know which to take. Suddenly a cat appeared, passed in front of them and dashed along the east road. Chang said to the officer, 'Years ago when I was on my way to examination the road was crossed by a cat just as now. She brought me good luck and I won first place. Today the cat passes me again. I feel that her way leads to great good fortune.' 'Then let's go her way,' said the officer. They went, and crossing the hill met a messenger in hot haste who came armed with a pardon. The evil Yŏnsan had been driven from the palace and his gifted brother Chungjong reigned in his stead. Chang lived. 'My luck', said he, 'is with the cat.' He rose to be chief of a department and later, Prime Minister of Korea. He was fifty years behind Whittington, but his cat was almost, if not quite, the equal of Whittington's in its beneficent spell.

Two great priests of religion lived at this time, one in the West and one in the East. The western priest was Thomas à Kempis, who spent his life in devotional writing and silent meditation,[22] the eastern priest was Muhak, 'Ignorance', whose life was given up to silent prayer and deeds of self-renunciation. His memorial stone stands at the foot of Ch'ŏnbo-san, 'Divine Treasure Mountain', in front of Hoeam Temple, ten miles beyond the East Gate of Seoul. From the time of his conversion he refused sleep and gave himself up wholly to prayer. At times, too, he would live all unconscious of food. Once his companion, Naong,[23] the great priest of the Diamond Mountains, asked, 'Are you dead? Why not eat?' Muhak merely laughed, and made no reply. One of his remarks was, 'True religion is like the elephant's tusk: no matter how much he may seek to hide it it persists in appearing.' He also said, 'Great responsibility is not to be compared with a life of retirement.' Yet he was called on by King T'aejo to be his mentor. How he loathed it; but he did his duty. It was Muhak who saw the old king safely on his way. One of his well-known sayings was: 'Among all the actions of life, those of a tiny baby are best.'24

If Korea had no one quite to measure up to Joan of Arc, nor any cat to equal Whittington's, she had this great priest, who might well walk the companion saint of Thomas à Kempis. Pyŏn Kyeryang, the confucian scholar, writes of him:25

> The religion of the Master
> Is beyond ken such as mine.
> He was a peerless son of meditation,
> A teacher of the Fathers.
> While he lived on earth
> He was a little child.
> When he met with one enlightened
> It was like a charge of armies flung together.
> An almoner's cap and one spare dress his all,
> How lowly did he seem;
> And yet in majesty and greatness none his peer.
> As one born to highest honour
> He cared not for sounding praises.
> His prophet-vision was unlimited;
> God gave him lengthened life,
> Seventy and nine long years.
> Whence came he at his birth?
> The sun's rays shot him forth.
> Whither now depart his steps
> Up beyond the lotus flower?
> In all places his disciples
> Leave his marks and memories.
> The strongest things 'tween earth and heaven
> Are rocks and stones:
> So write we deep in stone
> That he may long endure.

24 The fifteenth century I: T'aejong

OLD T'AEJO, who really never ruled the kingdom, was dead, and his son T'aejong, without any hand to hinder, now sat squarely on the throne. It was the year 1408 and he was forty-one years of age. His coming to the place of power had been through many tears and much blood, for he was a man of ruthless will who put down all opposition with an iron hand. Since he had overridden father, brothers and ministers, the east regarded him as out-and-out a king.

We are told that at times he had serious doubts as to his own virtues. In the winter of 1410 he was on his way with soldiers to Haeju for military manoeuvres, when a great storm of rain and hail with thunder and lightning overtook him.1 Suddenly two of his horses were struck down at his side. At once he stopped the procession, fasted, and called off the programme of the day. Said he, 'I am a sinful man, unfit to rule a kingdom; let me resign my throne in favour of my son.'

Yi Sukpŏn, his minister, hearing this, said in reply, 'Parents reprimand their children when occasion requires; likewise God, who loves your Majesty, has sent this lightning stroke to remind you of your duty. Throwing up your office will make no amends, but a humble heart and a renewed determination to do the right will be pleasing to God.' T'aejong, subdued in spirit, resumed his duties.

ALL THE STATE now underwent a renovation as regards dress, from that of the commoner to the robes of the king. In chapter 11 we told something of the dress of Koguryŏ; since that time many changes had come to pass. Koreans, on the one hand conservative, are yet on the other very ready to adopt the customs and habits of their big neighbours. They had become more and more Mongol. This awakened the contempt of the Mongol emperor himself, who said, 'why do you people change so readily and set aside your own customs?'[2]

In the year 1357 a state astrologer wrote a memorial which read:[3]

> Our country takes its rise in the Ever-white Mountains to the north and extends to the Chiri Hills in the far south. We have therefore *water,* which pertains to the north, as our distinctive element, as well as *wood* to the east, their corresponding colours being black and green. If we follow nature's law, therefore, we should have black for our head-dress and green for the cloak we wear.

Through the long lapse of years Korea still stands by her gauze-like black hat and associates her origin with the deep shades of the Ever-white Mountains.

'The Korean's headband', says the *Munhŏn pigo,*[4] 'was unknown till the early days of Ming (1380), when a Chinese taoist priest brought it, with the request that we make it a part of our national costume. This we did, and have continued to wear it ever since.' This headband causes the young man who first dons it almost as much pain as the bound foot does the Chinese princess, but he has manfully stuck to it till the present day.

In ancient time Korea used hempen fabrics and silk for dress goods. Only at the close of the Koryŏ period was the wonderful plant known as cotton first introduced (1369). Mun Ikchŏm brought it from China, as he brought also the spinning-jenny and the cotton-gin. The Korean people took to this new discovery with great avidity; before a hundred years had passed the whole land was growing cotton, and white-coated people walked on all the highways. The question is raised as to what kind of white dress-goods Koreans wore in the days of Ch'i Tzŭ, 1122 BC, a question not yet satisfactorily answered. Even in the times of Confucius cotton was known and had won a large place in China. That Korea should have let this pass her notice for 2,000 years seems very improbable.[5]

IN GLANCING across the face of the peninsula we find a people highly favoured and blessed, and cared for by a most watchful king. Among T'aejong's first acts was an order against alcoholic drinks.[6] Said he,

My desire is to see my people happy, but drink makes them miserable. Let us use the past as a mirror into which to look and learn from our forebears. Let their experience be known and read of all men, for it proves conclusively that drink spells wretchedness. If we see the ruin it has wrought and yet take no warning, what miserable sinners we must be. Though you do not think of the state, think, nevertheless, of your own heart and your own life. If the wise are unconscious of the evil, what can you expect from the common run of men or from ignorant fools? Crime and lawsuits are the natural results of drink.

I write this with an eye to the past and a desire for the future, and ask, therefore, that all officials, out of regard to my wishes, make themselves examples for good and so avoid excess of this kind.

At this time a great stream of remarkable books came from the Ming. With the return of each envoy samples of China's best literature were brought, books on religion, on philosophy, on history, on morals. In one embassy I find 128 different sets, many volumes in each set, all gifts to Korea from the benign suzerain state. China was and had been from time immemorial the fountainhead of the lights and liberties of the east.

Along with the many books came the water-clock, a huge machine having four casks for water, the largest being called Night-Heaven-Tank, and measuring twelve feet round.[7] Arranged on a kind of stairway, this intrument told off the hours drop by drop.

T'aejong, as a great scholar, did his best to have the people redeem the time. A huge memorial stone set up by him in 1409, that gave the reader some inkling of his ideals, once stood under the ginkgo trees inside the entrance to the Confucian Temple. Said he:[8]

As I ponder on the religion of the Master, I am profoundly impressed. It is beyond our powers meetly to extol his virtues; an attempt at praise is like venturing to picture the sun and moon, the heavens and all the stars thereof. Our Master, born toward the close of the Chou Kingdom (551 BC), gathered together the best writings of all time and chose therefrom precepts and examples that have served a hundred kings for their illustrious models. This may be regarded as the first real establishment of religion.

One can gather from such quotations the serious purpose of King T'aejong's mind.

In order to impress the state with good morals he had pictures of the saints and masters of the past painted on the inner walls of the palace. Here appeared King Wen (1100 BC) saying good morning to his revered father; the founder of Han (200 BC) passing the wine-cup with all good wishes; the queen of Hsüan Wang of Chou (800 BC) with gentle touch calling her husband to consciousness of the new day: 'Wake up, my lord, wake up.'[9] With such pictures King T'aejong adorned his palace halls while William of Wykeham was saying to the boys in

Winchester, 'Maners makyth man!' It would seem that T'aejong was as anxious to make a great and intelligent people of his subjects as the founder of New College, Oxford, was to brace up and renew the flagging spirits of the men of England.

THERE WERE religious confusions attending these days in Korea just as there were in Europe. In the *Lighted Bramble Records* I read:[10]

> In the first year of T'aejong buddhist priests were forbidden the palace, and all worship of the buddha ceased within the city.
>
> In the second year the Astronomer Royal wrote, 'In the first year of Koryŏ (918), there was a man who said, "The land that bears the hills on its back and holds in its hand the waters that go by, needs the buddha and his temples to make it live and flourish." The king then gave command to his officials to build a temple; he gave fields and slaves to its priests, and the temple was called "the House of Blessing". Later the king and his people accepted buddhism and made it the state religion. So from that date on for 500 years temples arose in great numbers. When prosperity overtook buddhism, it split into two sects, the *sŏn* (meditative) and *kyo* (dogmatic) that disputed as to who owned the fields and slaves.[11] Priests cast aside their poverty, dressed in silk and rode beautiful horses. Many of them fell victims to wine and women. All sorts of vicious habits were their portion. Though there was said to be happiness in these practices it was not true, for happiness is not found in actions such as these. My suggestion now is that seventy temples alone be spared and that the rest be given up to the service of the army.'
>
> T'aejong gave his assent to this and it was so ordered.

For one hundred years, from the departure of Muhak in 1405 till the coming of Sŏsan in 1560, no great priest appears. The frown of T'aejong had withered this spirit away. Buddhism survived, however, not so much in great men of state as in such characters as this that I gather from the *Lighted Brambles:*[12]

> There was once a buddhist very badly dressed but very honest and kindly of heart. If clothes were given him he would pass them on to the first beggar he met shivering in the street. He was most gentle of soul, and never found occasion to quarrel with anyone. It was his practice to call every man by his first name, regardless of rank or station. He himself was known as Chabi Sujwa (the compassionate priest). Wherever there happened to be an offender to be beaten, at temple or government hall, he would call and offer himself as a substitute, accepting all the pain. The great were only simple people in his eyes while the humble folk were very dear. Once, when he was staying at the Wŏn'gak Temple, a great feast was held. Princes and ministers of state came in all their glory. Chabi looked on, and, forgetting himself for a moment, sat with knees locked in his arms, a manner not permitted in the presence of

royalty. Just at this time Prince Insan, a man of iron will who made all the world to tremble, appeared.[13] Chabi said, 'You are a great man, aren't you?' The prince, astonished at such a rude remark, asked, 'You impudent creature, who are you?' and gave him a resounding blow on the ear, repeating it. The priest dodged and said, 'Don't beat me, Insan, please. It hurts, it hurts!'

Again he met Yi Sŏkhyŏng, known as Prince Yŏnsŏng, who was the great chief of the Confucian College.[14] Chabi winked at him and said, 'Your face I know but your name I've forgotten.' A moment later he added, 'Why of course, I know it now, your name is Yi Sŏkhyŏng.' The other priests hurried forward and begged pardon for this ill-mannered address.

Such was the Compassionate Priest, a messenger of unconscious good to many people who have gratefully recorded his name; such were the footsteps of the buddha across this unfavourable century.

ABOUT THIS SAME time there may be noticed a marked recurrence of reports of the reappearance of the dead. In the mind of Korea, as truly as in that of the London Society for Psychical Research, appearances of the dead are possible, and these appearances have been definitely recorded. One I take at random from Yi Yuk (1438–1498) who lived somewhat later than T'aejong, about the same time as Chabi Sujwa, in the reign of Sejo. The story runs:[15]

Prince Hasŏng, who was son-in-law of the king, had in his entourage a serving-woman of Yangju County who was accounted rich. She had a very pretty daughter whose name I have forgotten but whom I shall call *Mo*.[16] A scholar, An Yun, fell in love with her and took her by a marriage contract as his secondary wife. Prince Hasŏng, hearing of this, was furiously angry and demanded a separation. 'How did you dare', said he to the serving-woman, 'send your daughter to the home of a scholar without permission?' He at once had the girl arrested and locked up, intending to marry her off to one of his slaves. Mo learned of this, and, in desperation, climbed the wall and made her way to An Yun. She wept, saying, 'I shall die, no one can help me.' Yun, equally distressed, could do nothing. A day or two later she was again arrested and made secure. This was the final act of her poor little play: with her girdle string she made her quietus and was found next day hanging dead. Some time later An Yun, returning in the evening twilight from the Confucian College, reached the little hill behind the Kyŏngmo Palace. It was early autumn. The moon, too, was softly rising over Camel Mountain to the east and everything was perfectly still. Alone he walked on, thinking sad thoughts of Mo and recalling tenderest memories. Suddenly he heard a soft tread and turning to look, there she was. But she was dead; that he knew. It could only be her spirit. Nevertheless he so longed for her that he turned at once and took her by the hand saying, 'Is it you, Mo?' when suddenly she vanished. An Yun wept and from that day on a sickness of heart overcame him so that he died a year later.

Kim Ch'amp'an's son,[17] a friend of mine and a cousin of An Yun, told me the story, (says the writer). Yu Hyojang, a brother-in-law of An Yun, also told me the same tale with tears in his eyes. Said he, 'It is very rare that we see even a daughter of the gentry give her life for her convictions, how much more wonderful on the part of one who was only a slave. She knew nothing of the great teachings of the sages and yet she possessed them all: courage, conviction, and devotion. Her faithful heart was her most priceless possession. "I shall die rather than yield up my husband." Thus she died to save her soul from shame. Was there ever a more wondrous example of the virtuous woman?'

So asks Yu Hyojang nearly 500 years ago. We may well ask the same as we read through this sad little story of the fifteenth century.

KING T'AEJONG had twelve sons and seventeen daughters. The great question was which should succeed him in the royal line. His first son was inclined to religion, to be a buddhist priest; his second was a worthless character; but the third was a student, a scholar gifted with all the graces of the ancient sage. Him he would make his successor. The tablet that stands guard before the third son's tomb reads, 'While still a little boy in his mother's room, he was most diligent, never laying aside his book. His father, seeing him look pale, at times ordered the books away.' Student and master-mind, his merits have won much glory for the house of Yi.

T'aejong abdicated in 1418 and placed this son, now known as Sejong, on the throne. It was evident, even in this act, that T'aejong sought only the welfare of his people. He indeed beheld the attainment of his wishes, beyond his highest hope, in this gifted son who was only twenty-two when he took the reins of state in hand.

After having resigned the throne, T'aejong built himself a palace where Chosen Christian College now stands,[18] and called it Yŏnhŭi-gung. There he lived quite privately and often walked far out over the hills and by the river, greatly to his soul's delight. He said to his ministers, 'I have a good son to take my place; surely never was a man so free from care as I.' This was indeed a great recommendation from so grim a father.[19]

Sejong's care for his mother, too, was another proof of his goodness. He watched by her bed, walked by her chair, and tenderly closed her eyes when she passed away. The Ming emperors were charmed with reports of him, and every year sent books and gifts innumerable.

Sejong lived in the days of the large family, and had eighteen sons and four daughters. A line on his ancient memorial stone runs thus; 'His sons came night and morning to wish him peace and make obeisance. They were like a string of jewels, a flock of wild geese, as numerous as the grasshopper, and as propitious as the gentle steps of the unicorn.'

His elder brothers, as Reuben and Simeon gathered unto Joseph, came up to Seoul to live with him. He and they were a united clan, linked most happily together. He had a gentle but compelling manner that kept eunuchs and palace maids in their place. His father, like King David, had been a man of war, but he himself, like Solomon, was a man of peace. His relation with the suzerain state, the Ming, was perfect. Great ministers went as envoys and China's leading scholars made return. In sending the annual tribute Sejong made it a point to go over the list himself to see that all things were in order. He and his father worked out the problems of movable type, made their own waterclock, prepared an almanac for each year, and drew up rules of propriety such as would do credit to the most orderly christian assembly.

T'aejong died in 1422, and Sejong, his son, went into mourning for three years. No music, no meat to eat, no colours to wear, no joy in life, was accepted willingly for three years as a proof of his grief at his father's death. The old king was buried at the foot of Great Mother Mountain fifteen miles from Seoul across the Han to the south-east.[20]

ONE of Sejong's special favourites was the scholar Pyŏn Kyeryang, who for twenty years was chief of the Confucian College, a man of unexampled learning and deep religious piety; but, like mortals in general, he had his personal idiosyncrasies and defects. His chief fault was a rat-like stinginess that coloured all his doings, and gave the wags and wits of the time no end of stories to tell. The old record *Lighted Bramble* says:[21] 'Even in the case of the pumpkins that he had cut up, he counted every slice lest any thing should be missing. He took note of the glasses of wine as well, and had the bottles recorded with exacting care. Guests seeing his stingy manner would often get up and leave indignantly.'

While Pyŏn was preparing the *Kukcho pogam* or 'National History' in the Hŭngdŏk Temple, his Majesty frequently sent dainties and sweetmeats. Officials also added their contributions. The old scholar would regale himself liberally and then, most un-Korean-like, lock up the remainder and keep firm hold of the key. Not a crumb did he give to the servants. Finally, when the accumulated mass went foul he would have it thrown out to the pigs.[22] Still he was the great Pyŏn Kyeryang, and so will live long after his little foibles and failings are forgotten.

He writes thus about movable type:[23]

> The purpose of the invention was to supply the state with books and a better means of gaining knowledge. This would mean endless blessing. Our first cast of type was defective and the printers grumbled much over the time spent in adjusting and putting it into shape. In the 11th moon of the year *kyŏngja* of Yung-lo (1420), his Majesty took note of this and put the matter into the hands of a Board Secretary, Yi Ch'ŏn, who had a new fount cast. In seven months the work was done, a great improvement over former efforts. The printers were highly pleased and were able to set up more than twenty pages a day. This work, begun by his late Majesty, was thus successfully carried on. We are prepared now to print any book there is and all men will have the means of study.

Literature will increase and grow, and religion flourish in the earth. The
kings of T'ang and Han spent their strength in the training and equip-
ment of armies; how much better this work of our good king. As high
as heaven overtops the earth so does this deed outshine theirs. Endless
blessing for Korea.

Pyŏn wrote many poems; in fact all great scholars counted themselves poets.
Here is one:[24]

> So quiet sits this hamlet 'neath the hill,
> With softened shade and furrrows freshly turned.
> I wander by the stream to seek for simples,
> My books I spread out 'neath the drying sun.
> Across the sky's blue vault the wild-goose wings,
> Amid the moonlit bamboos calls the whippoorwill.
> I look toward Seoul, whence endless thoughts arise,
> And jot a verse down for my friend of friends.

25 The fifteenth century II: Sejong

THE reign of King Sejong marks the most illustrious period in the history of the
Yi Dynasty. The greatest and best king ruled, the most distinguished minister
helped to direct the affairs of state, the finest achievements in 500 years were
now brought about.

Sejong, as has already been told, was chosen by his father to succeed him,
and the wisdom of the choice was demonstrated through a long reign of thirty-two
years. Many kindly stories are told of this democratic king. He was gentle and
considerate, and had a bright eye to see true worth wherever it might be. His
benevolent soul appears on all occasions. One of the old laws of Korea commanded flogging, not on the buttocks, but across the back. King Sejong ordered
this to be changed. Said he, 'It endangers a man's life to beat him after this
fashion; we shall have no more of it.'[1]

His elder brother, Prince Yangyŏng, was given to drink and debauchery,
and a petition was presented from Kwangju, where the brother lived, asking that
he be punished. But the king said, 'It is the duty of brothers to cover each others'
faults and put the best face forward. How unbecoming it would be for me to arrest
my elder brother and announce his failures before the world. I could never do it.
Bear with him as best you can.'[2]

With his trained army he beat off the inroads of barbarians across the Tumen
on the northern border and so gave a settled peace to the province of Hamgyŏng
with strong garrisons at Chongsŏng and Puryŏng which remained for many a
day. In 1438 the king improved the clepsydra, and made an instrument like the
cuckoo clock that came forth and struck the hours. He was all for diligence, that
not a moment be lost.[3] *Feng-shui*, regarded as of so great a consequence to east
Asia, he set aside as meaningless. 'The prosperity of the state,' said he, 'depends
on the character of the government and not on the vagaries of wind and
weather.'[4]

THE KING'S KEEN EYE for worth is seen in his selection of the scholar Yu, who was of humble origin and whose name was far down on the list.[5] Little could Yu hope even to glimpse the great monarch, much less be admitted to his presence. Many laboured efforts of his had ended in failure. It was evident that he was not born to fame or fortune and that he had better betake himself to the quiet of the far south and forget the world. Still, Yu was a very great scholar; few were his equals. Before starting out he applied to a friend who held a minor position at the palace gate, asking that he might be admitted to the outer enclosure so as to gain some idea of the fairyland where the king lived. The friend replied that he would meet him the next night and that he should come straight in just at curfew time. Yu went, his heart beating excitedly. When he entered, he found that his friend had not been there that day; something had detained him. But the gates were closed and he could not get out. He was assigned a lowly corner in the gatehouse where he might huddle up till morning, when the gates would open again.

On this night the moon shone full as day. Just in front of his window was a piece of wall broken by a recent rain. Could he but climb that, he might be able to look in. Not a sound was to be heard. He would try. Over the wall he went and into a wondrous park of trimmed walks and stately trees. Suddenly a gentleman appeared, who asked, 'Who are you?' 'Oh, I beg your pardon, sir,' said Yu, and went on to explain. The stranger listened. 'You say you have studied the Book of Changes?' 'Just a very little, your Excellency.' 'Come with me,' said he, and Yu went, wondering who he was. They reached a pavilion and at the call of a servant a beautiful copy of the Book of Changes was brought. The stranger asked the meaning of one passage, and another, and another, to all of which Yu answered with wonderful skill. The stranger, speaking as to himself, said, 'Ha! ha! With such knowledge, to think that this man has never been used. Alas for my country when such as he are set aside.' Yu was most kindly treated and sent off. Next day his name appeared on the roll of those given office. Other officials, surprised, questioned this appointment. Who was Yu? The king settled the matter by a banquet to which the wondering Yu himself was invited. On arrival he discovered that the master of the occasion was the king, in whom his astonished gaze recognized the kindly gentleman of his midnight adventure. King Sejong, for it was he, took occasion to show Yu's superior knowledge to all the assembled guests and thus it came about that he was appointed to office, which he held throughout his Majesty's reign.

KING SEJONG's first and great counsellor and prime minister was a man thirty-four years his senior called Hwang Hŭi. It was due, no doubt, to this man's wise counsel that Sejong ruled so well. Many stories are told of Hwang Hŭi which show the kind of man he was.

A woman servant once came to him and made complaint against another, recounting her evil deeds. 'You are quite right,' said Hwang Hŭi; 'quite right!' Later the other woman came and presented her case. Hwang Hŭi, patiently hearing her, said likewise, 'Exactly so, quite right!' His wife taking note of this said, 'If one is right, the other is wrong, and yet you say to each, "Quite right!

Quite right!" How absurd!' He looked up for a moment and said, 'Why yes, wife, I expect you are right,' and then went on reading his book.[6]

Again, one day he saw a man ploughing with a red cow and a black, and he called, 'Which of your cows is the better, the red or the black?' but the man made no answer. Finally, when he turned the end of the furrow he came over to Hwang Hŭi and whispered in his ear, 'The red is the better.' 'But why whisper?' asked Hwang Hŭi. 'Whisper?' the man replied, 'Why don't you know, sir, that even beasts feel hurt if they hear another referred to as better than themselves?' Hwang Hŭi learned a lesson from this and never afterwards criticized people before others.[7]

ONE OF THE GREAT achievements of Sejong's reign was the invention of the alphabet.[8] Gibbon says, in chapter ix of his great work, where he deals with the northern barbarians: 'The Germans in the age of Tacitus were unacquainted with the use of letters, and the use of letters is the principal circumstance that distinguishes a civilized people from a herd of savages incapable of knowledge or reflection.' Korea had had what was equivalent to letters, the wonderful Chinese character, an exquisite instrument for recording thought, but the middle and lower classes were civilized and ennobled only by the reflected light of the scholar, for they themselves had no power whatever to dip into the wells of past history or experience till Sejong came and made his alphabet. It was the king's desire to let the rank and file of his people into the joys of literature that prompted its making. Many officers of state opposed the project, saying it would degrade literature and bring it down to the level of the dust, but Sejong, undaunted, went straight forward to the accomplishment of his magnanimous purpose.

In the making of the alphabet the king used the musical scale *(kung, shang, chüeh, chih, yü)* as the basis of the operation, so the account of the alphabet in the *Encyclopaedia* appears under the subdivision 'Music'. The letters are hung on the old Chinese philosophic wheel which revolves to the tones of Confucius. To the east is the letter *k*, to the south *t*, to the west *s*, to the north *m*. It is a very simple set of twenty-eight letters made from variations and combinations of the circle and the line.[9] A verse that is sung as a market ditty gives some idea of the shapes of these letters,[10]

With an *iŭng* (ring) in my ox's nose,
And my *kiŏk* (sickle) in my tightened belt,
I amble forth to behold the *siŏt* (Chinese character for 'man'),
Whose only thought is of their *miŭm* (Chinese character for 'mouth'),
I tell them take care about their *riŭl* (Chinese character for 'self')
Or I'll put a dot upon their *tigŭt* (the Chinese character for 'damned').

I said there were twenty-eight letters. Three of these originals, however, have been discarded and the remaining twenty-five fill all the needs of today.[11] Never before had Korea been able to record the spoken language. The Chinese written script, no better suited to the Korean native tongue than Egyptian hieroglyphs are to English, could never record the simple speech of the people; but now by means of this happy invention the songs, sayings, and speeches of 500 years were accurately noted down. Especially is this true of market catches, folk-lore, folk-songs and the like, which express the emotions and feelings of the race. Love songs are among the most commonly recorded. Here are two or three samples literally translated. These songs, be it remembered, are the call of the secondary wife, the concubine, or perhaps the dancing-girl, for the one who has deserted her. The prosaic first wife, who merely serves to propagate the family line, has usually no part in such expressions.[12]

I   Buy me love! Buy me love! I say,
     But who sells love?
     Buy my parting! buy my parting!
     Who will buy my tearful parting?
     No one sells and no one buys,
     My lover's gone; my spirit dies.

II   My dreams last night, how fair!
     A letter from my love, so rare!
     A hundred times I read and read:
     It slept with me, it shared my bed.
     So light its weight, so fleet its part
     And yet it almost broke my heart.

III You cuckoo bird, why cry?
     What use however much you cry?
     But if you cry, then cry alone, and don't wake me;
     Your cries at midnight break my anxious sleep.

IV   On the wide lifting sea, ye waterfowl,
     Curlews and gulls and divers of the deep,
     Could you but know how far the water lies beneath,
     As on its face you softly rise and fall,
     Then you might know my lord, how deep his soul;
     I know it not.

V   O moon, o shining moon,
     My master's shining silver moon!
     Tell me he sleeps alone.
     Or has some partner won her way?
     You know and see. Tell me, o moon,
     My life hangs on it.

VI   The third watch of the night, with roaring rains
     That slash the *odong* trees! I turn and turn
     As endless thoughts race madly through the brain,
     No sleep, no sleep!

> The cricket in the inner room cheeps out:
> The wildgoose calls across the blinding sky
> The endless longings of my soul.
> Know, crying wildgoose, in your flight,
> My heart is broken! Dreadful is the night!

Here is a glimpse of a hermit's abode, something very dear to old Korea. This mountain retreat appears again and again in the songs.

> VII   My home is in the White Cloud Hills
>   Who knows to call on me?
> My only guest a clear soft breeze;
>   My ever-constant friend, the moon.
> The crane-bird passes back and forth;
>   He stands my guard.

We find Korean ideas regarding drink recorded by these same wonderful letters:

> VIII Deep drunk with wine, I sit here like a lord,
>   A thousand cares all gone, clean swept away.
>   Boy, fill the glass! Let's make an end
>   Of anxious thought.

Here again is a whimsical snatch such as Koreans love to indulge in:

> IX   Hello!
>   Who dyed thus black the crow!
>   Explain!
>   Or bleached so white the crane?
>   Who pieced the legs of the heron tall
>   And gave the duck no legs at all?
>   I wonder!
>   Still, black or white, low-set, long-reached,
>   Pieced out, or clipped, black-dyed, or bleached,
>   Who cares? What matters it?

IN THESE DAYS Korea had the Sacred Books done into native speech.[13] It was an event like the opening of the treasure-houses of Greece to Europe about the same time. From now on even the untutored could read in their own language the sayings of the Great Master:[14]

> The godly man's life is the simple life; the man without religion hates
>   simplicity.
> The simple life is the highest possible attainment. How long it seems
>   since any man has attained thereto.
> The good man accepts his place and acts accordingly. He desires

nothing better. If he is rich and great he acts his part; if he is poor and mean, he takes his place as such; if he is a barbarian he does his duty as a barbarian; if he meets misfortune he finds his service there. There is no place in life where the good man cannot fulfil his part: though he sit on high he looks not down upon the low; though he be low he counts not upon the great. He does his part honestly, asks no favours and makes no complaints, blaming neither God who dwells above nor his fellow-man who sits below. The good man, therefore, accepts his place and waits on the will of Heaven.

As has already been suggested, this was a day of days when not only were the treasure-houses of Chinese literature thrown open to the average Korean but also the wonderful writings of Greece began to be known to the western barbarian. In 1453, three years after the death of Sejong, the Turks battered down the defences of Constantinople and took the famous city of the first christian Roman emperor. So great a disaster to Europe, yet it had a blessing in it. The learning that fled from the wild inrush of the Turks came into the possession of the western world and the Renaissance made its beginning. Just as Korea read her famous messages from the ancient masters, so Europe began to read her books in Greek.

'There is no wealth save the soul's wealth alone,' says one of these, Lucian of Samosata, 'All other brings us more of grief than joy.'[15]

Older far than Lucian was Pythagoras, a contemporary of Confucius. Now, after a space of two thousand years, he began to speak to Europe and said much as Confucius might have said:[16]

Better that you should throw a stone at random than let fall an idle word.
We ought so to behave to one another as to avoid making enemies of
    our friends and at the same time to make friends of our enemies.
No man can be free who is a slave to or ruled by his passions.
While harbouring anger, we should refrain from both speech and action.
Show rather in your actions what should be done than in your speech
    what should be thought.
Choose rather to be strong of soul than strong of body.
Do not talk a little on many subjects, but much on a few.
Those who do not punish the wicked are willing that the good should
    be injured.
Do what you believe to be right, though it be at the sacrifice of your
    reputation; for the mob is a bad judge of noble conduct.
Do great deeds without making great promises.
Nor e'er let sleep fall gently on thine eyes,
    Till thou hast made a three-fold inventory
    Of the day's doings: where thou hast transgressed,
    What rightly done, where fallen short of duty.

How much, then, these two great masters were alike, one a Greek and one a Chinese. At one and the same time they each walked this earth's widest measure, telling to all they met the true philosophy, honest words of duty. Each knew what it was to escape for his life, each felt the shame of a scanty hearing, each held his message in hand for 2,000 years to give it at last to a waiting world of aliens. Surely a similar spirit must have enwrapped the earth, east and west, to have brought forth these two great men of the same time—the spirit of genius, the spirit of mastery, the spirit of religion.

A VERY DIFFERENT SUBJECT now presents itself. There was an attempt about this time to introduce into state ceremonial a 'jazz' dance, that is commented upon by Nam Hyo'on, a man of great learning and integrity. In order to appreciate more clearly the force of Nam's remarks we will give the following definition of the modern jazz from E. C. Brewer's *Dictionary of Phrase and Fable*:[17]

> The jazz is a voluptuous dance of negro origin accompanied by a wild irregular kind of music. Originating in New Orleans, it has aggravated the feet and fingers of America into a shimmying, tickle-toeing, snapping delirium, and is now (1919) upsetting the swaying equilibrium of the European dance.

Before America was discovered, for Nam Hyo'on died in that very year 1492, he says:[18]

> We Koreans have learned the dances of the barbarian in which we bob our heads and roll our eyes, hump our backs and work our bodies, legs, arms and finger-tips. We shut them up and shoot them out, bound after bound, like a twanging bow. Then, bouncing forth like dogs, we run. Bearlike, we stand upright, and then, like birds with outstretched wing, we swoop.
>
> From highest lords of state down to the lowest music-girl all have learned these dances and take delight therein. They are called *homu*, the Wild Man's Dances, and are accompanied by instruments of music. At first I rather favoured them myself, though my dead friend, An Chajŏng, was much opposed. Said he, 'Man's attempt thus to show himself off is unworthy of a human being. Such actions lower him to the level of the beast. Why should I take my body and put it through the motions of an animal?' I thought this remark somewhat extreme until I read, in the *Han-shu*, Ho Tz'ŭ-kung's comment on seeing Lord Tan Ch'ang perform the dance called 'Monkey's Bath'.

Korea had undoubtedly as much concern to keep her customs, habits and ceremonies pure in those days as we have today.

AT THIS TIME Gutenberg, out of much tribulation, lawsuits and financial loss, brings forth the first Latin Bible printed with movable type. It was a triumph over which Europe, and especially Germany, has exulted for nearly 500 years.

Why should she not? Could there be given to mankind a more beneficent invention? Still the book-maker's palm of victory, the Nobel prize of those days, goes not to Gutenberg but to T'aejong and Sejong, kings of Korea, who on the other side of the world saw their invention of movable type completed fifty-two years before Gutenberg's came to pass.

WE CLOSE this chapter by expressing our regret that good kings have to die. As the beneficent rule of the Antonines of Rome gave place to a terrible creature called Commodus, so, as Sejong passes, we see the eyes of a human tiger glare out upon us in the person of his second son Sejo. But of him we shall hear later. A paragraph in the *Taedong kinyŏn* under the year 1450 runs thus:[19]

> Sejong was by nature very quiet, a man of few words, very gentle. He loved peace and harmony. Bright he was and wise, too, a sage indeed beyond his fellows. He was most considerate of his people, greatly inclined to forgiveness, while at the same time underneath he was strong and forceful. One with the eternal spirits, he enjoyed their aid in literature and art. His daily round was like this: by the fourth watch of the morning he was up and dressed ready for audience; not a lazy moment was there in his life; every department of government he took a share in, and all he touched was blessed. When his mother died he mourned her loss as did the ancients, and cried aloud for several days, eating nothing. It was the hottest season of the year but he discarded his softer *yo* (mattress) and used only a rough mat to lie on. Those about him placed oil-paper beneath lest the dampness should harm him, but he refused it and had it taken away.

So lived one of the best kings Asia, yes, the world, has ever seen: the great and good Sejong.

26 The fifteenth century III: Munjong, Tanjong, Sejo, Sŏngjong

WHEN Sejong died his eldest son, Munjong, aged thirty-six, came to the throne. Immediately on his accession there broke out in Hwanghae Province a terrible epidemic of typhus that swept away great numbers of the people. The king, groping uncertainly after the cause of the scourge, arrived at no better conclusions than London did 214 years later on the coming of the Great Plague. Comets appearing at that time foretold destruction, so London said. Defoe himself writes, 'I saw and looked upon them as forerunners of the judgments of God.'[1] King Munjong, in a statement that he has left us, remarks,

> The present epidemic is not due to malignant spirits, as some think, or to the fortunes of the *yang* and the *yin*, but to the faults and sins of men. For this reason I erect an altar, offer sacrifice and make a prayer. Let good works follow on good works; let all cease from distressing, evil ways; and may the law of life reign once more.[2]

We are told that after this sacrifice was offered, the epidemic gradually declined. Munjong seems to have been a very gentle soul with but a frail hold on life, for in the year following he committed his son, eleven years of age, to the tender care of his chief ministers, and softly passed away. The little king, Tanjong, though but a youth when he himself died, is known far and wide throughout Korea. His name stands for innocence and gentleness against a black background of great wrongs done.

Sejo, uncle of Tanjong, now thirty-six years of age, set his determination on obtaining the throne. To do so he must strangle his nephew, the helpless little king, the unfortunate lad who had been entrusted to his care; he must knock on the head with an iron bludgeon Kim Chongsŏ, Prime Minister, a man of great wisdom and integrity; he must poison his own brother Anp'yŏng, the picturesque prince and scholar who was the centre of the poetry and music of his age; he must employ all the official thugs and assassins possible to carry out his schemes: Kwŏn Nam, Han Myŏnghoe, and the like. It is sad indeed to find Chŏng Inji, the author of the *Koryŏ-sa*, a famous literary work, acting as one of his henchmen. It was at his request, in fact, that Prince Anp'yŏng was foully done to death. How Sejo went out at night beyond the West Gate to Kim Chongsŏ's house, summoned him and, while engaging his attention in unsuspecting conversation, had the murderer approach from behind and deal him a death blow, is unfit to be recorded after the virtues of his father Sejong.[3]

Finding this evil group led by the son of a saint surely provides a sad comment on human nature. Could the race, by some method of rivets and bolts, be keyed up or braked at the highest points of attainment so as never to slip back, leaving the children free to take a fresh hold and move on, we might gradually hope for a perfect age to come; but, with every new generation up against the same old problem of depravity we make no real headway, and are sometimes up and sometimes down. This seems abundantly to be the case with Sejo, a much worse apostate from his father's faith than was Julian of Roman fame.

King Tanjong was carried away a prisoner to Yŏngwŏl, one hundred and thirty miles distant. No kind Hubert was at hand to melt in heart and soothe his sorrows; like Arthur, son of the Norman Geoffrey, Tanjong tasted bitter death under his murderous uncle's hand. The old record reads,[4] 'In the tenth moon of the year *chŏngch'uk* (1457) the hemlock was sent to the boy king.' It seems that the ministers, under the leadership of Chŏng Inji, made an urgent request that he be put out of the way, so as to remove temptation from the people. The official historian declares that Chŏng Inji gathered the ministers together for this sole purpose and thus made himself, to the end of time, a traitor of the blackest dye.[5] Closely associated with him in the crime was Sin Sukchu, also a great scholar, to whom good King Sejong had once said, 'You'll stand by my little grandson, won't you?'[6]

The warden of the Kŭmbu Prison,[7] we are informed, carried the deadly draught down to Yŏngwŏl; but a sense of fear possessed him and he did not readily enter the *kaeksa*, or detached palace, where the young king was. The ruder servants who accompanied him, fearing the loss of a liberal reward, urged him on; but the warden, entering the court, simply bowed. King Tanjong came forth to meet him, wearing a royal robe and a crown. He kindly asked the warden why he had come, but the latter's feelings so choked him that he made no reply. An *ajŏn*, or secretary, who attended Tanjong, seeing how matters stood and fearing lest the eyes of the king should melt the heart of the warden, flung round the king's neck a long bow-string that he had ready, drew it tight and strangled him before the entrance door. Thus died king Tanjong at the age of sixteen. The women of the household and female servants with one accord made a rush to the deep Han River and perished together in a fatal plunge.[8]

ON THE SAME NIGHT in which Tanjong died the ghost of his mother, Queen Kwŏn, who had been dead for sixteen years, suddenly appeared in the palace of Seoul, stood boldly before King Sejo and cursed him to his face. Immediately on her uttering the dreadful sentence, Tŏkchong, the Crown Prince, nineteen years of age, fell dead at his feet.[9]

Sejo, though now seated squarely on the throne, realized, nonetheless, that a terrible black-skirted Nemesis whisked in and out and was ever round about him. He sought refuge for his guilty soul from her ghostly attacks. Not only was he an apostate from the virtuous ways of his father, but like Julian again, he was an apostate from his father's religion, for he gave up Confucius and took to the buddha. In his zeal he has left in Seoul two monuments of his reign: one, the Great Bell that hangs in the pavilion in the centre of the city, cast in 1468; and the other, the pagoda in the park that marks the site of his famous monastery of Wŏn'gak-sa.[10] Sejo later paid a visit to the Diamond Mountains, where he attempted to wash away the curse of Queen Kwŏn and the hateful memories of Tanjong. On approaching this region one encounters a high ridge called the Hair-cut Pass. Rumour says that Sejo on reaching this point cut off his topknot and assumed the smooth shining head of a disciple of the Indian priest, but this is questioned.[11] He became a buddhist, however, as far as outward profession could make him, and his tomb today stands under the shadow of the Pongsŏn Temple, twenty miles north-east of Seoul.

Koreans may support an unworthy cause from a sense of fear or advantage, but in their hearts they are sound as to true honour, and their historical judgment is eminently fair. No amount of scholarship can save Sin Sukchu from the shame of having deserted Tanjong in his hour of need; and no disgrace that Sejo could put upon Sŏng Sammun and his associates—not even the dismembering of their bodies—could in the slightest degree dim the glory of their fame. Sŏng Sammun, who had been an associate of Chŏng Inji and Sin Sukchu in the making of the alphabet, was now led out to death under their orders; but he was really the victor, not they; and the true heart of Korea was his, not theirs. A great scholar, he was accustomed to jot down his thoughts and feelings in poetic form. Thus he wrote as the death-cart trundled him out of the city on his way to doom:[12]

> They beat their drums to hasten life away;
> I turn my head toward the setting sun.
> There are no inns within the Yellow Shades:
> Where shall I sleep tonight?

SEJO'S ELDEST SON, Tŏkchong, stricken by the curse of Queen Kwŏn, died and left his brother Yejong as heir. He came to the throne in 1469 and reigned only one year. Tŏkchong's son Sŏngjong was only thirteen when he was summoned to take the state in hand. He was, however, a good king with a large measure of literary and artistic taste. King Sejo had commanded Ch'oe Hang to undertake the preparation of a history of Korea, to be called the *Tongguk t'onggam*, 'Mirror of the East Kingdom'.[13] It was completed later by Sŏ Kŏjŏng, under the direction of Sŏngjong, and is still regarded as a standard work. It begins:

> Korea had originally no king till a god-man came down and stood beneath the sandalwood trees. The people hailed him as their ruler and called him Tan'gun; and the name of their state they called Chosŏn. All this happened in the times of Yao of T'ang (2333 BC).

And it ends:

> King T'aejo was a great and highly gifted man, who saved the world and gave peace to the troubled tribes thereof. God therefore gave him the throne of Korea and all the people gathered to his feet. (This was in AD 1392.)

MANY GREAT and gifted scholars lived at this time who were specially famous as men of religion. One of these, Chŏng Yŏch'ang, has his tablet placed number fifty on the west side of Confucius in the great temple.[14] He was born in 1450 and died in 1504. He studied the *Hsiao hsüeh* for thirty years, saying, 'When I live up to what I have learned in it, I shall pass on to something else.' He had no hard and fast rule about drink, and so, on occasion, imbibed freely. Once he over-drank, and his mother in deep grief cried over him. Seeing this, he swore a solemn oath and never drank again. King Sŏngjong later passed him the cup, and he said, 'Many thanks, but once I grieved my dear mother by drinking and swore an oath never again to touch it. Please excuse me.' The king looked at him and his eyes were filmed with tears. When his mother died Chŏng spent three years by the side of her grave in the hills, all alone, meditating on the teaching of the sages and thinking over her faithful ways.

When he was a little lad a Chinese envoy called at his home and, seeing how bright he was, gave him the name Yŏch'ang, meaning 'You'll shine'; and shine he did.[15] The world thought him a lonely silent soul who cared for nobody, but it was not so, for Master Chŏmp'il-chae (Kim Chongjik), also a great and good man, was his bosom friend. As Chŏng Yŏch'ang was master of his soul, so also was he master of his body, which he brought under control so that even the hottest weather could not move him from his ordered way. He went to the Chiri Hills, we are told, and built a little hut there where he said his prayers, and grew rush-reeds and bamboos for company. Here he wrote:[16]

> The rush-rods flutter in the flying wind,
> So light, so lithe, so free;

'Tis May and yet the barley's rolling ripe
As autumn fields should be.
I view the hills of Chiri, height on height,
Then turn my boat and lose me in the night.

He was appointed magistrate of Anŭi and was indeed a prefect of prefects. He taught the children of the district to read, appointed them lessons and carefully drilled them in how to treat the aged. When his mother died the district officials proposed to bear the expenses of the funeral, but he said, 'No. Those taxed might feel unkindly toward my mother.' At night, when in company with others, he would pretend to be asleep, though his companions noticed that he was not sleeping but was really praying or meditating on the sayings of the Masters.[7] He wrote many books: notes on the Doctrine of the Mean, the Great Learning and others, but in the *muo* year of troubles, 1498, his wife burned them all for fear that they would involve them in the general disaster.

KIM KOENGP'IL, who died a martyr, also specially studied the *Hsiao hsüeh*, which begins:

It is God who makes things live, and grow, and round out, and come to fruition; it is man's part to show love, righteousness, courtesy, and wisdom.

Why was he killed? Because he was the disciple of Kim Chongjik, and Chong-jik's sin was that he wrote in his historical records an account of the evil deeds of the king's great-grandfather, Sejo. He did it in veiled form, which made it all the worse. Listen to what he says.[18]

In the 10th moon of 1457 (the month in which Tanjong was murdered) while on my way from Miryang to Sŏngju I slept the night at Tapkye post-station. There I had a dream in which an angel from heaven, shining in royal robes, came sweeping in before me. He said, 'I am a descendant of kings, was king of Ch'u (200 BC) in fact, but Hsiang Yü killed me and flung my body into the Pin River.' Thus he spoke and was gone. I awoke with a start. Now the king of Ch'u lived in the far south of China, ten thousand *li* from here, and removed from me by more than a thousand years. What could his sudden appearance mean? I read my history, but find no mention of his body being thrown into a river. I wonder if Hsiang Yü sent a secret agent to do the deed? One cannot say definitely. Let me, nonetheless, write out my feelings. When God first created the world he gave man an appreciation of truth. He did not give it more fully to the man of China than he did to the man of Korea, neither did he mean it for ancient days any more than he means it for today. Although I am but a poor barbarian and am born a thousand years behind the times, I give my sympathies to the King of Ch'u.

In days of old, Ch'in Shih-huang, like a great dragon with horns and teeth, wrought his works of evil. All the waters of the Four Seas were turned to blood by his deeds. Even the whales and sea monsters suffered; their only thought was to find a way of escape. The state fell and the descendants of royalty were left as beggars in the land, but I specially regret the fate of the king who fell into the hands of Hsiang Yü. Still, God so ordered it, his body was thrown into the river. In the darkness of the night he killed him. The waters flowed by and he returned no more. Earth and heaven remain as of yore, but when will his sorrows be wiped away? The soul, unrequited, flits though the night and now appears to me in dreams. When Chu-tzŭ wrote his history he made first mention of this foul murder. I follow Chu-tzŭ and offer my sorrowful soul's sympathy to the King of Ch'u. I pour my glass and trust that his bright spirit will come and drink.

Thus wrote Kim Chongjik making Ch'in Shih-huang the dragon-parent of Sejo. The murdered king of course is Tanjong, the great whale is Kim Chongsŏ. This passage, quoted by Kim Ilson in a history, was read with glaring eye by Sejo's great-grandson, King Yŏnsan, who at once had Kim the historian killed and all his associates. The body of Kim Chongjik, taken from the grave, was beheaded, and the faithful Kim Koengp'il, who was his disciple and whose tablet now sits number fifty on the east side of Confucius, was done to death. This passage, written under the guise of a perusal of Chinese history, was the cause of what is known in Korea as the *muo sahwa*, the destruction of the scholar class in the year 1498.[19] A minister by the name of Yu Chagwang, an illegitimate son of Yu Kyu, a man of powerful physique, who could climb trees and do all sorts of monkey tricks, was from his youngest days an exceedingly bad character. He gambled and stole and prowled about at night. None of the young women that crossed his path escaped outrage. Sejo picked on him as a trusted aide, and so he remained in the service of royalty till the ill-fated piece of writing by Kim Chongjik awakened his desire for revenge on all the scholar class, seeing that they looked with contempt on his low social position and his ill-conditioned soul. The brightest and best in the land, the real scholars, the religious teachers, the models for the generation to come, were stricken down in the dread *muo sahwa*.[20]

On the other side of the world a group of boys, all more or less in their teens, full of life and zeal, were busy at their lessons, never dreaming that their names would become famous and 500 years later stand side by side with far-off Korea's Chŏng Yŏch'ang and Kim Koengp'il: Copernicus, Sir Thomas More, Luther, Zwingli, William Tyndale, Michelangelo. It has always been a long and difficult journey toward sainthood in the old Church: even Joan of Arc did not attain to it till five hundred years had borne witness to her memory. So the Korean saints who sit on each side of Confucius in the great temple in Seoul have had not only centuries of time to back up their high claim, but the universal judgment of the enlightened classes to confirm their place of honour.

As the fifteenth century draws to a close, a new world has opened to the eyes of the west, but not the world they thought it. The Indies were not the Indies they supposed them to be, though they still wear their mistaken name. Columbus said, when he touched the Bahamas, 'Behold this is India, and all these people are Indians.' Likewise the Lachine Rapids ('China Rapids') on the St Lawrence River were so called, seriously or otherwise, because of their nearness to China. Such names mark the bold, blind gropings of the West in those days, unhappy for Korea, when the spirits of the great and good had departed and devils had come up in swarms to guide the fortunes of men.

BORN at this time was a noted literatus, Yi Chun'gyŏng, who later became prime minister. He leaves us, in his collected works, an interesting note on the ways of providence that shows something of the best mind of his times. Says he;[21]

> There is co-operation between the two spirits, God and man, seen in the meting out of blessing and misfortune. In form, God differs from man, yet, according to the law of the Dual Principle, which interweaves as warp and woof, God and man work together. God holds the eternal principles in his keeping, but man receives them; God possesses life, but he makes man a sharer in the same; so the principle that God works by, pertains also to man. Man's religion, too, finds its origin in God Himself.
>
> Man, however, being a material creature, with a tangible body, easily concentrates his thoughts upon himself and so misses the thought of God altogether. He foolishly leaves Him out of his reckonings saying, 'What can yon blue heaven have to do with me?' or, 'What concern can a crawling creature like man have with God?' So he gives free rein to self-will and yields himself up to loose and lascivious ways, in the end calling down disaster and making God, who ever lives, dispense calamity instead of blessing. Man shares a similar life with God; and the king, who is exalted above all, God's appointed head of the people, has a special interest in the life that pervades all nature. The prosperity of the world depends on the attitude and doings of the king. So the Book of Poetry says,[22] 'The Great God is the light that shineth forth on thee and maketh thee king. God Almighty will meet thee early and be thy play-companion.' So the good kings of the past beheld God everywhere and were most careful to fear and obey His commands.
>
> Now, however, this teaching has fallen by the way, and men no longer reverence or worship God, but daily seek their own will and pleasure. Pretty birds, strange beasts, fascinating flowers, blind the vision; while flattery captivates the ear, high flavours and rich foods lead away the taste, sweet perfumes turn the sense of smell. As the moth doth corrupt, so their hearts are eaten away by the songs of the dancing-girl. Thus do they lose all sense of what is right, and every desire to return to the straight and narrow way, their conscience being so defiled that an evil-doer seems to them a good man, and a good man an evil-doer. God looks down and beholds it all. Should we not fear and tremble in view of what He thinketh?

27 The sixteenth century I: Yŏnsan-gun, Chungjong; T'oegye

As we turn the page of a new century and note its date, AD 1500, we find ourselves in a greatly changed world. The Tudors are on the throne of England. A great Portuguese by the name of Magellan has made the first heroic voyage round the world. With his little ships he sailed boldly into the yawning maw of Tierra del Fuego, ever after to be known as the Straits of Magellan. These were the days, too, of the gallant Frenchman Bayard, a soldier who by his loyalty, benevolence, and integrity won the admiration of his age and the honourable degree *sans peur et sans reproche*. Korea also had her great hearts, of whom I shall mention one from the writings of Yulgok. He says:[1]

> Yi-ssi, wife of Sin Chinsa, was the daughter of a confucian scholar. She was gifted by Heaven with a very beautiful nature: sweet, retiring, reserved, given to few words, delighting in her work, doing everything with kindly care, and ever ready to lend a helping hand. She had been educated in the Chinese character but never indulged in poetry or essay-writing. Her husband, an official, was held fast to his post in Seoul while she, by special request, remained to care for her parents in Kangnŭng. Sin Chinsa, finally given a holiday, made haste to cross the peninsula, eager to see his wife and daughters. On the way, however, he fell ill and, by the time he reached his home, was down with fever, quite unconscious, evidently at the point of death. Yi-ssi, who had waited with inexpressible longing for his coming, was stricken dumb. Her mother had just died and here was her husband, also about to leave her. There was no one to whom her soul's distress could be spoken. In this strait she prayed earnestly day and night, not once closing her eyes. Then she bathed, trimmed her nails, and taking a short knife under her belt, went up to the mountain peak behind the family cemetery, where she burned incense and offered her prayer. 'O God,' said she, 'Thou givest blessing to the good and trouble to the wayward. Evils abound and yet my husband has ever been a man of honest heart whose acts and words are without guile. Why is it that Thou hast put so sore a trial upon him? We have each served our parents and, in order to do it well, have been separated for sixteen years. Only a few days ago I suffered the loss of my dear mother, and now my husband lies at the point of death. If he recover not, I shall be left in utter desolation. The same laws that pertain to man pertain to God, for nothing is hidden from Thy sight, great or small. Thou, Highest of All, look down in pity, I pray Thee.'
>
> Then she drew forth the knife from under her belt and struck off two joints of the big finger of her left hand. She beat her breast saying, 'Evidently my faith and devotion are a failure, and so I am brought to this place of deep distress. Great God, Highest of the high, behold my severed finger as proof of my sincerity and accept my prayer.' She ended and retired to where her husband was lying, peace written on her face.

That night an angel appeared, they say. However that may be, the day following the patient had safely passed the crisis and all the people of the village, filled with wonder, said, 'It is an answer to Yi-ssi's prayer.' This happened in the days of Chungjong, and His Majesty, hearing of it, had mention made thereof in the nation's archives and a shrine of honour erected to her memory.

We might almost say of her as was said of Bayard: *sans peur et sans reproche.* Her valiant soul is recorded in the forty-fourth volume of the *Yŏji Sŭngnam* under the heading of Kangnŭng.[2]

THERE WAS SEATED on the throne of Korea at the opening of the sixteenth century a very objectionable ruler by the name of Yŏnsan.[3] He was the eldest son of King Sŏngjong and had been in his younger days a dissipated, idle youth. His rule was one of exceptional evil, so much so that officers of state met in secret conclave and proposed to dethrone him and put someone else in his place. Sŏng Hŭian, who later became prime minister, had tried by hint and precept to set the unworthy king right, but failed. Once, on an outing by the river side, pen and paper were called for and the king asked each minister to write a verse. Sŏng's turn came and he wrote *Sŏngsim wŏn purae ch'ŏngnyu*, which meant, 'Your Majesty has a natural dislike for clean water,' or as the king read it, 'Your natural bent is for things unclean.' Instead of treating it as a piece of good advice, the king was furiously angry and ordered Sŏng to be dismissed from office. Had he taken the sharp reproof and profited thereby he would doubtless have lived and ruled in peace, but he was self-willed and went straight to his ruin.[4]

In the year 1506 Sŏng Hŭian, by careful and wise counsel, succeeded in bringing about the king's dethronement. He was aided by Prince Pak Wŏnjong, whose sister had been outraged by Yŏnsan and had died of shame and mortification. Driven from the palace, Yŏnsan was exiled to Kyodong, an island to the west of Kanghwa. Two months later he died. A natural death? Who knows? History tells how the palace women screamed out on the night of his expulsion till the noise of it was heard through the whole city.[5]

CHUNGJONG, a younger brother, became king. Now *chung* means 'middle', 'mediocre', and Koreans say that no king who wears the cognomen 'middle' can ever be great.[6] Chungjong was not great, and yet in his reign some greatly terrible things happened. One was another *sahwa* or slaughter of the literati. It happened that there was in the palace a certain Cho Kwangjo, twenty-five years of age at the accession of Chungjong, a very just man though rather given to over-assertive manners before his seniors. He interfered so much with military operations that had been undertaken against a rebellion in the north, that the officers in command were amazed at his untutored insolence. From this slight irritation grew serious trouble. Factions arose, pitted one against another, and a deadly feud began. Suspicions were awakened against Cho: he was the evil genius of the state. The very air whispered his name in condemnation. Leaves were brought in from the palace garden perforated thus: *Chuch'o wi wang*

(Chuch'o would be king). Now if the two characters *chu* and *ch'o* are united they make *cho*, the surname of Kwangjo. Someone, with evil intent, had written these words upon the leaves with honey as ink, and the 'mountain bug' had come and bitten them through in order to get at the sweetness, leaving the perforated leaves to say, 'Cho would be king'. Poor muddling Chungjong, seeing this, in his simplicity felt that the overruling fates had intervened, and that Cho should hang for it. He died and many others with him, showing the king to have been a very great fool. A later day honoured Cho by placing him among the saints and seating his tablet number fifty-one to the east of the Master.[7]

Koreans have always associated natural disturbances with errors in government. Gibbon indicates something of the same when he tells in his chapter xliii how comets, earthquakes and plagues beset the unhappy years of Justinian. In the same way the Korean tells of Seoul's dreadful earthquake in 1518, the year in which Cho and his associates were unjustly tried. In the month of June the whole peninsula began to tremble. The *Yŏllyŏ-sil kisul* says:[8]

> On the 15th day of the 6th moon an earthquake occurred. Rumblings were heard like the roll of thunder and then the ground began to bounce up beneath the feet of the people. The roofs of the palace went heaving up and down, like a boat at sea that rose and fell on the waves. Men and beasts were so frightened that they lay down in terror on the ground. Walls fell and houses toppled over. It did not pass in a moment, but came on again and again. People rushed out into the courtyards, afraid lest they should be crushed in the general destruction. Little by little it decreased and when a month had passed it finally ceased altogether. The whole eight provinces were equally shaken.

This was read as a warning sign from high heaven against the evils of the day. The scars of that great earthquake are still to be seen in the repaired portions of the city wall, one fifth of which is said to have gone down.

A son was born to King Chungjong and named the Prince of Kindness, Injong.[9] Joy filled the palace. One day, however, a dead rat was found hanging from a tree just behind the prince's sleeping-apartment. Accompanying it was a written curse. The great question was: who did the cursing and who was intended to be cursed? The rat, being a second-cousin of the pig,[10] in whose year Injong was born, was supposed to have his evil-eye on the prince, while the curse was traced to one of the king's secondary wives, the mother of Prince Poksŏng. Many people besides this mother and her son died because of the 'rat curse', and the terror of it lasted for seven years.[11] Four centuries earlier, as we saw in chapter 19, the mighty influence of cursing was known in Korea, and its influence had in no sense abated.

There were good and honest ministers during these opening years of the sixteenth century, but one *soin*, or flatterer, a man of insincere soul, Kim Allo, held high office and was for a time one of the three chief advisers of state. He has left many writings. I select the following as a sample of the spirit of this day:[12]

In the year *ŭrhae* (1515) I was an officer in the College of Literature and had to do with the entertainment of the Japanese envoy at Yongsan. I went with him as far as Ungch'ŏn. At that time we were undergoing state mourning that occupied the official world and so the other members of the party were not present, and I was left alone for the night in the Mangho Hall. It was beautiful moonlight with the sea and the hills as open as the day. The clear air seemed to enter my bones with a joy inexpressible. My heart went out in boundless delight and I thought of jotting it down, so I turned for my writing-brush. Drawing it out of the holder, I was surprised to find the weasel-tail point missing. I spread out my bedding, shook my clothes and looked everywhere but it was not to be seen. I wondered what sort of visitation this meant and was struck by it as the oddest thing I had ever known. Later, by morning light, my horse was saddled and I was about to set out when I again picked up my brush; and there it was in perfect order. The night before I had written a few notes and then inserted it into the holder myself. It could not have left me of its own accord, and there was no place for it to be lost. It was a very little room, floored with shining paper that was as smooth as glass. The walls too, had just been freshly done. There was no place in which to hide: even a single hair or the finest size of needle would be readily noticed. The doors that joined with the main house were all locked; the south side alone, before which I slept, was open. The brush and inkstone were just beside my pillow. How odd that this weasel-point should be missing. Where could it have gone? Its dropping out was a mysterious thing; its being nowhere in the room was a second mystery; but its coming back into place was the most mysterious thing of all. I could see no solution to it and told my chief so. He said he had heard that in ancient days anyone who wrote exceptionally well was the object of envy on the part of the spirit world, so much so that at times the spirits shed tears. It looks as though there might be something in this.

ON THE OTHER SIDE of the world, wholly unconscious of Korea's tears and sorrows, moved a stately procession of great men; great painters: da Vinci, Raphael, Holbein; great scholars: Erasmus, Sir Thomas More, Copernicus; great religious teachers: Xavier, Calvin, Luther; great statesmen: Loyola, Machiavelli, Wolsey; great rulers: Charles V, Francis I, Henry VIII. What a world of mighty men it was, and yet not only Korea but China herself had arrived at one of the low ebbs in her history. The Ming were on the throne and Wu Tsung was emperor. He was a scholar and could read the Chinese ideograph, as well as Sanskrit, Arabic, and Mongol; but the eunuch class, baleful as ever in their effect on royalty, were all about him, so he saw but few and evil days. The west was rising, but the east was already old and showed signs of going down.

Two great men of the period were accorded a place in the hall of Confucius, Korea's real Temple of Fame. One sits number fifty-one to the west and the other number fifty-two to the east. The one to the east was four years older than John

Knox and five years older than St Francis Xavier. His name was Yi Hwang and he was called Master T'oegye. Xavier landed in Japan in 1549 and was, therefore, a close neighbour of Master T'oegye, though they never met. Could Xavier, a man of unbounded zeal who spoke his mind fearlessly to high and low alike, have come into touch with so great a scholar and so sincere a soul as T'oegye, how delighted he would have been. I once heard a wise Korean say that if T'oegye had lived to see the coming of the missionaries he would have been a christian. Had he met Xavier he might readily have accepted the great missionary's message. Here is one of his expressions of good counsel to King Sŏnjo,[13]

> Let your Majesty with a sincere and honest heart realize just once what the love of God means. You have been on the nation's throne barely a year and yet we have had many signs of Heaven's disapproval. Nature is out of gear; cold and heat are badly distributed; wheat and barley crops have failed; over-abundant rains beset us on one hand and drought on the other; never were such plagues of wind, hail, worms and parasites seen before. This is proof that God by means of terrible signs would awaken you to repent. My one wish is that your Majesty would serve God with the same heart that you serve your parents, that fear and reverence might attend all your ways. Even though in your acts you may not be conscious of sin, look well to your heart lest self-will gain the mastery and little sins become a great delusion like a mountain in the soul. They must all be put away.

As T'oegye lived in Yean and gave good words of counsel to the king, so Xavier just across the straits in Yamaguchi was endeavouring to impress the truths of the christian religion on the Daimyo of Bungo. Xavier wrote poetry. One well-known hymn is usually ascribed to him. The last verse is:[14]

> Sed sicut Tu amasti me,
> sic amo et amabo Te,
> solum quia Rex meus es,
> et solum quia Deus es.

The translation from Stead's book of hymns:[15]

> So would I love thee, dearest Lord,
> And in thy praise will sing;
> Solely because thou art my God
> And my eternal king.

At this same time Master T'oegye wrote in quite a different strain:[16]

> I do forget so soon,
> And have to read again my scattered books;
> Now I gather and place them on the shelf.

The sun is late and swings off to the west,
The stream that ripples by reflects the shade.
I take my staff and step into the court;
I look out at the clouds that touch the hill.
The rising smoke proclaims the evening meal;
A clear cool breath floats freshly o'er the plain.
The reaping time is near and harvest joy,
And all the hands who beat the grain are glad.
At even the crow flies by on easy wing,
The crane stands out clear-cut against the shade.
I, I alone, am wrung with anxious thought
That fills my soul, alas, too deep for tears.
No place is there where I can tell my grief,
I take my harp and wake the silent night.

T'oegye had lost an elder brother in the troubles of the *sahwa* and all his days were darkened by the memory. He asked that no lengthy biography should mark his grave but that his simple stone should say:

The grave of Yi of Chinsŏng,
Who retired to Tosan, and later left the world.

As I close this chapter I am reminded of Yi Sun, an astronomer who, on receipt of books from China, made a wonderful telescope by which he could read the moon and stars.[17] In this very year, Copernicus, who was fifty-three years old, had grown almost blind with watching the stars and writing at night. Great souls, though separated by 10,000 miles, they were in sympathy, their searching minds were one.

28 The sixteenth century II: Injong, Myŏngjong; Yulgok

IN the year 1545, the year of the Council of Trent, King Chungjong died and his son Injong came to the throne.[1] His title, 'Kind King', was surely well merited, for though he reigned only a year his renown has never faded through these four long centuries. An indefatigable student, by his diligent ways he greatly raised the literary standards of his day. Young men who observed him with deep regard rose to be Korea's saints and scholars: Yulgok, Kim Inhu, Song Ikp'il and others. His influence for good during his short life of thirty years can hardly be measured. The envoy of the Ming was greatly impressed by him and called him 'the youthful Yao-Shun'. In the summer season the crops failed and the prince prayed for his people out in the open, exposed to wind and weather. During the hard stress of famine that followed he refused meat and drink till finally, worn down and weak, he could hardly walk. Exhausted at last and probably assisted in his demise by the cruelty of his step-mother, Princess Munjŏng, he died. Queen Elizabeth of England was a little girl of twelve at this time and her great father Henry VIII had four years still to run. How little each guessed the sorrows of the other side of the world. Sir Francis Drake was only five but he was already fortifying his young spirit for the task of seeing what lay on the underside of this restless revolving planet.

INJONG WAS SUCCEEDED by his half-brother Myŏngjong, a kindly disposed but weak and fear-driven king. His mother, Munjŏng, second wife of Chungjong, whose name has come down on batwing like that of Jezebel, was in complete command and drove the state at her bloody chariot-wheel. The palace, invested by a legion of harpies, hung upon her word. Meanwhile great men and saints like Kim Inhu looked on but were powerless to mend the day. It was the first time in the history of Korea that a demon-possessed woman had control of the state. She was forty-four years of age when she entered upon her career, and for twenty years held the land in a reign of terror. Even in 1532, before she came to full power, she had made use of omens and curses to work her will. Whether it was, as mentioned in the previous chapter, a dead rat that hung from a tree with a written curse dangling on its tail, or a letter dropped as though mysteriously from the clouds, or an inscription written on the wall that threatened the life of the king, she made use of any device to fasten guilt upon this one and that whom she hated and thus to compass their destruction.

To the gentle king all this was most abhorrent. His mother must have seemed in his eyes the reincarnation of Empress Lü of Han, for hers was indeed a repetition of that terrible story. He, however, never ventured to oppose or criticize her. On one occasion she is said to have struck him a blow in a fit of fury, but his only reply was, 'Dearest Mother, I am your son.'[2]

Envoys came regularly from the imperial court of the Ming, which had its capital at Peking. We find them bringing large gifts, and receiving in return beautiful things from Korea, her paper, her silks, her flower-patterned rush mats. How small her tiny world must have seemed to these ambassadors from the limitless bounds of the Celestial Empire.

IN THE YEAR 1543 the king gave directions for the setting up of a *sŏwŏn* or country school for the study of the Sacred Books, the first of its kind. It was to rest under the shadow of the Sobaek Mountains in Kyŏngsang province at Sunhŭng.[3] Two classes of scholars were present throughout the long history of Korea: the literary master, whose intellect was trained for the superior handling of the pen; and the religious master, the sage whose whole study was the right direction of the heart. In the centuries that followed there grew up scores of such study-halls, each dedicated to a great religious teacher whose spirit-tablet was a little plaque of wood with his name written on its face, before which, at appointed seasons, a sacrifice of raw food was offered. Here also the scholars of the district met to discuss the sacred books, to study, and to teach. It was the religious teacher rather than the intellectual who presided.

This first school was dedicated to An Yu (1287–1350), one of the great literary masters of the past dynasty, Koryŏ. He was a contemporary of U T'ak and Kwŏn Pu mentioned in chapter 20. One asks what An Yu did that made his name a perpetual remembrance to be sacrificed to for six hundred years. He was born of a humble family but by dint of great faithfulness and diligence won a name for integrity and profound scholarship. Early in his career he was made magistrate of Sangju, and while he was there, the country was startled by the passing of three witches, marvellous in the power they possessed. They could call voices from mid-air and bring down curses on whom they pleased. An Yu, hearing of this, had them arrested, and when he attempted to cross-question them they cursed him to his face. Undaunted by a terror which even today makes great China tremble, An Yu had them imprisoned on 'bread and water', and only after receiving a full confession of their fraud did he set them free. We are told that the women were found to be no longer possessed of demons, but were happy in a great deliverance.[4]

Another story told of An Yu is that on one occasion he asked one of the yamen secretaries to wash his feet. The secretary objected, and attempted to raise a strike on the part of all the serving corps, saying that no such indignity had ever been put upon him before. Then an old writer came forward and said, 'Men, you make a great mistake. If I read the master's face aright he is a sage whom we may well delight to honour.' Not only were his feet washed, but his name grew apace till in 1337 his tablet was placed on the east side of the Master Confucius in seat number forty-nine.[5]

Now again in this year 1543 his was the first name which was honoured by these country schools. A verse by him expresses his zeal for the confucian cause:[6]

> Incense and lamps here, there, and everywhere
> Help on the prayers to Buddha; high harps and pipes
> From house to house ring out his noisy praises;
> While all the time the sacred temple of the Master
> Rustles with grass and footsteps of the dead.

These country schools increased in number till abuses grew up about them and idle people made them their rendezvous. Seeing this, the old regent, the late king's father, had them abolished in 1864, leaving only one school to each revered sage.[7]

AT THIS TIME appears Korea's master-saint Yi I, commonly called Yulgok, 'Chestnut Valley' (1536–1584). It is impossible to pass this period without giving him special mention. He was greater than king or courtier, his name outshone all others. Four miles from Munsan Station on the P'yŏngyang railway line stands his school, or *sŏwŏn*, his quiet grave, and his memorial stone, the inscription on which was written by the famous scholar and envoy Yi Hangbok.[8]

Yulgok's mother was a most gifted woman, not only in Chinese but in art as well, whose pictures are admired today. About the time of her famous son's birth she dreamed that a dragon arose from the sea, came into her room, picked up a little child and placed it in her bosom. Such is the story that the old stone has told the passers-by for three centuries and a quarter. When he was five years of age his mother fell ill and the little lad went alone to the family tablet-house and prayed for her recovery, prayed that the gentle spirits of his ancestors would make his mother well. At twelve, when his father fell ill likewise, he went to the hills and offered his prayers. He was sixteen when his mother passed away. His love for her was so great that he built a hut by her graveside and remained there three years, never putting off his mourning garb. The record reads, 'The three years seemed to him as but a day.'

At eighteen years of age a great desire to know religion overcame him. He went to the buddhist monasteries in search of it, and finally took up his abode at Chŏngyang Temple in the Diamond Mountains, a house which looks out on all the wildering peaks. After a year of study he said, 'I have thought it through and through, but see no light,' gave up the buddha and came back to Confucius. The conservative school, however, the old hands who surrounded the king, more or less questioned his motives and sniffed at him. The smell of the buddha was still on him.

Yulgok found his master T'oegye, Yi Hwang (spoken of in chapters 27 and 28), and inquired of him about religious perfection. The master could only give him a very modest and indeterminate reply. Perfection was a high attainment; few could hope for it. Apart altogether from religion, Yulgok was a great scholar. In each of nine examinations, open to all, he passed first and so was nicknamed, partly in honour, partly by way of pleasantry, 'First in Nine', *Kudo changwŏn.*

Early in life he resigned from political affairs and with his brothers and other members of his family retired to Haeju. We are told that the day began with a prayer before the family shrine, after which the sacred books were read. How gentle he was, and how kindly disposed toward the needy and poor! Against his will, time and again, he was called to office, and at the age of forty-four was made high-priest of Korea, head of the Confucian College. In 1582 he was sent to meet the envoys from China, but those savants, seeing his plain attire, were highly offended. One of them, Huang by name, asked, 'Why does your king send us this country lout? Has Korea no scholars that she calls a farmer from the plough?' 'Far from it,' said the interpreter; 'this gentleman is the first scholar in the land, who has won highest honours at every examination and is now head of the Oktang, or Council of the Literati. His appearance is his own choice, a plain country farmer.' The envoy on hearing this made a deep obeisance and showed him from that time forward unbounded respect.

With prophetic vision Yulgok urged the training of 100,000 troops to meet a great and coming need, but his words were laughed at, as were Lord Roberts's in England in 1914, laughed at till the laughter was drowned in appalling thunder (the first roar of cannon Korea ever heard) and the great Japanese invasion was on.

In summing up his life Yi Hangbok says,

> He never laboured to find out anything, but seemed to know it by intuition. He seemed to ride on the wind, rise above all barriers that blocked his way, wave the gates open before him and see as God sees. Because of his loving heart he never feared to disagree with others. He

made straightforwardness his rule of life, and as his duties presented themselves did each and everything to the profit of all. The whole world sings his praises today.

A selection or two from his writings may be of interest as showing something of the spirit of his age. Here is part of an essay entitled 'God hath done it'.[9]

God's way is difficult to know and beyond our powers to explain. The sun and moon are in the heavens; the days and nights go by, some longer, some shorter. Who made them so, I wonder? Sometimes these lights are seen together, sometimes they part, occasionally each eclipsed and narrowed down. What causes this? Five of the stars pass us on the line of the celestial warp, while the rest swing by on the wings of the woof. Can you tell definitely why these things are so?

When do propitious stars appear, and when will such uncanny things as comets come again? Some say that the soul of creation has gone out and formed the stars. Is there any proof of this? When the winds spring up, whence come they? Sometimes, though they blow, the branches of the trees scarcely sing, while at other times forests are torn from the roots and houses hurled through the air. There is the gentle maiden wind, and there is the fierce typhoon. On what law do they depend? How do the clouds form and how do they dissipate into original space? Who has charge of the thunder and the sharp strokes of lightning, the blinding flashes that accompany them and the roarings that shake the earth? What does it mean? Sometimes they strike men dead and sometimes other creatures. What law holds this in hand? The frost kills the tender leaves while the dew makes all fresh and new again. Can you guess the law by which frosts and dews are given? Rain comes from the clouds but again some clouds bear no rain. What causes this? In the days of Shen-nung (2800 BC) rains came at the people's call, and ceased when their wishes were fulfilled. So it was in the Golden Age. Was it because God in His dealings was specially favourable to those people? When soldiers rise in defence of the right, rain comes. It comes too, when prisoners are set free. What do you suppose could cause this? Flowers and blossoms have five petals while the flakes of snow have six. Why should this be? Is there any law by which we could do away with eclipses altogether and have the stars keep their wonted courses, so that the thunder would not startle the world, nor frosts blight the hopes of summer; snows not afflict us, nor hailstones deal out death and famine; no wild typhoons rage, there be no floods; all nature run straight and smooth, and heaven and earth work in sweet accord for the blessing of mankind? When shall we find such a religion? All you great scholar chiefs, who are so deeply learned, I think some of you should know. Open your hearts now and I will listen.

Yulgok wrote many poems. Something of their flavour may be gathered from the following renderings:[10]

The windy world has whipped my whiskers gray;
How vain it seems as home by boat I come.
The hills before me beck with kindly mien,
'Twould seem that they alone have hearts to love.

No fleck bedots the boundless azure blue.
From misty hills the palaced moon peers up
Of which the world sees only wax and wane;
It never guessed the moon is always round.

While digging roots I've lost my mountain way,
Mid coloured leaves by countless peaks I come.
A priest returning from the spring, I meet;
He points to a curling cloud, announcing tea.

The world is tasteless, less than water-brew;
My life alas, has fallen quite away.
But those there are I dare not leave behind,
The little tots who play about my knee.

Across Asia gleam the teachings of Chuang-tzŭ — the search for the inner life. The buddha, Confucius, Mencius, the Old Philosopher were all seekers for the inner light. Yulgok sought earnestly; and in the end very humbly, very sincerely, became the patron saint of his nation.

On one occasion in Seoul the writer was asked to say a few words to the very exclusive Literary Association. In so doing he touched on many great names and assured the assembled company of his high regard for men so great, so truly gifted. The next day the president of the association called to express his thanks; 'I have only one comment to make,' he said; 'hereafter make perhaps a little less of some others, but even more of Yulgok.'

Looking through his writings I come upon what he calls the 'Diary of Sŏktam' (Stony Pool), in which he says,[11] 'In the year *pyŏngin* (1566) the scholar class of Songdo set fire to the joss-house that stood high up on the mountain behind the city.' The queen dowager, a lady of much force of character and fifty-two years of age, sent a strong protest and had the responsible parties arrested, but the fire had done its work and the guardian spirit of the mountain had disappeared in smoke. What to do with the offenders was the question. When they were brought to Seoul the head of the Confucian College attempted to exonerate them, declaring that the worship of spirits on a hill-top was the height of folly. The queen dowager, however, highly incensed, spoke her mind and maintained that the women-folk were greatly comforted by it, and that she would by no means give it up. How strange to think that in this very year, in this same month, probably on the same day, Queen Mary of Scotland in high dudgeon was having it out with John Knox on a like delicate point of doctrine, the victory going to Knox by a slim majority. So the master of the Confucian College barely succeeded in holding his own, and saving the necks of the scholars who had interfered with the gentle worship of the Korean women.

King Myŏngjong died in 1567 and his nephew Sŏnjo came to the throne. He was only fifteen when he assumed the high office of state. His aunt, now the dowager queen, thirty-five years of age, sat behind the screen and gave her queenly orders. About this time strange signs appeared in the sun, red and black circles. The queen seeing them said, 'An unpropitious omen! Surely it is due to the fact that a woman is ruling the state. I will resign at once and let my nephew take full control.'[12]

29 The sixteenth century III: Sŏnjo; the Hideyoshi invasions

AMONG the active forces now at work in the east was christianity. The arrival in Japan of Xavier and the missionaries who followed him caused a great stir. They were met by the forces of the buddha that objected to a religious invasion of his peaceful kingdom and were determined to oppose it. Nobunaga, the regent, however, received the missionaries kindly. The dignity, the piety, and no doubt the learning of the priests accounted for the standing they so readily won. We can imagine what Xavier's influence would be among this exclusive, hero-wor-shipping people. Some of the most powerful families in the land, led by him, were represented among the christian groups from the first. Later, when per-secution arose, many of them sealed their devotion with their blood. Women too, were baptized in those opening days of oriental missions.

Hirado, to the extreme west of Japan, the island where the foreign mission-aries foregathered, was one of the stepping-stones to Korea. Doubtless Xavier looked with longing eyes past Iki over Tsushima and on toward the dimly out-lined coast of the Hermit Kingdom, but Japan more than occupied all his thoughts during his short stay: his hope was that the emperor himself might yield to his persuasion and be baptized. On the long journeys he took from Hirado to Kyoto he visited temples, talked freely with the priests, rebuked evil when he saw it, and made himself the friend of all men. Mobbed, insulted, threatened, he never turned aside from his faithful way; at times walking wet-footed through the mud or fording icy waters waist-deep. One of his followers, Juan Fernandez, was preaching in Yamaguchi when he was approached by a Japanese who pre-tended to have something important to say. The man leaned forward as though to whisper in the preacher's ear, and spat upon his cheek. Fernandez showed no anger in return but, gently wiping away the insult, continued his speech.[1] Those who saw this were much impressed. One prominent Japanese who had been opposed to foreigners made the remark, 'A religion that enables its dis-ciples to act thus must surely be true.' Following this, in less than two months, more than 500 persons had become christians. Xavier, after two years and three months, left Japan in 1551, but so mighty had his influence grown that his name and fame were found in the highest places.

Year pass by and we reach 1569, when one day a contest was going on between Brother Laurence and a champion of the buddhist faith named Nichijo in the presence of the regent, Nobunaga. In the process of argument Nichijo, feeling his position give way, grew very angry and drawing his sword rushed forward to strike Brother Laurence dead. He would have done so, without doubt, had he not been caught and held by a young samurai whose name was Hideyoshi. Thus one of the truly great men of East Asia first comes to our attention as shield and protector of the foreign missionary.[2] Later, when he became regent, his attitude changed: he feared that christianity might be a political power and ordered its complete suppression. Of the 205 martyrs who suffered under his hand at Nagasaki, nine were Koreans. They shared with their Japanese brethren the honour of beatification by Pope Pius IX on 7 July 1867.

WE must return somewhat on our tracks and take up the story that brings Hideyoshi into touch with Korea. It was a time when many great men lived. Shakespeare had a host of contemporaries in the Far East, any one of whom he would have been most interested to meet, but, alas, they were as far from his comprehensive ken as if they lived on another planet. The head of the Korean state was Sŏnjo, a weak and wavering monarch, wholly unfitted to meet the difficult times that were approaching. Already signs and omens were giving warning, and fearsome stories were passing from lip to lip. One of these, mentioned in in the *Taedong yasŭng* and quoted by Yulgok, says that in 1573 the water of the Naktong River failed for a whole day.[3] Such a happening, real or imaginary, at once set the people in dread of disaster. Shortly afterwards, in 1574, a snowstorm in which insects were seen to be mixed with the falling flakes occurred in Hamgyŏng province.[4]

As time went on, each year more scary than the other, everything was magnified into a portent of evil. In 1589 a miserable fox was found seated on the Dragon Throne of the royal palace.[5] In the Far East the fox won a place of most eerie eminence. He is one of the dreaded manifestations of the devil. In the form of man or woman, but usually woman, he comes forth from his sinister lair to work all manner of evil. Men live in fear of him. A temple stands in Mukden where worship is offered to the fox in order to propitiate him. The very thought of his sitting on the royal throne was enough to give the whole nation, as Dickens says, 'a turn'.

Following this, rumours got abroad that Japan was making great preparations for an attack on China and that her way of approach would be through the Hermit Kingdom. Envoys were sent from Korea to inquire: one Hwang Yun'gil, a west-man or, as we might say, a conservative; and one Kim Sŏngil, an east-man, a liberal. They found no ground on which to agree and when they returned their reports were diametrically opposed. Hwang said Japan was making preparations for a great attack on Korea, while Kim maintained that there was nothing in it. Just then a letter from Hideyoshi confirmed Hwang's conclusions, and caused profound consternation. In this letter Hideyoshi said,

> I am a mighty chief. Time and again rebels have thought to thwart me, but I have put them down with a heavy hand. When I was conceived my mother dreamed that the sun dropped from the heavens and entered her bosom. Astrologers who heard it said, 'The sun shines over all the earth; this child, born to fame and fortune, will rule the world.'

His letter, in substance, went on, 'Seeing how short life is I am not content to sit quietly at home in Japan but intend to reach out to wider worlds. Korea therefore must help clear my way to China. By so doing she will save her own soul and we shall be friends indeed'.[6]

On the return of the two envoys King Sŏnjo had asked, 'What sort of man is this Regent Hideyoshi?' Hwang answered, 'His eyes flash fire and he is brave and wise.'[7] How true Hwang's estimate was Korea learned later. The army he transported, given in Korean records as 250,000 men, was landed at Pusan almost as skilfully as we would land an army today.[8] It was the 4th moon and the 15th day. At once the general in command took possession of the fort held by the Korean officer, Chŏng Pal, who bravely faced the overwhelming numbers, did his best, and died. On the same day the whole Japanese force was set in motion toward Tongnae. Here the magistrate shut the gates and prepared to defend himself, but in less than three days the walls were battered down and Japan had made another step in her march toward Seoul. From here on the army went forward in three divisions by three different routes. Two of them met a week later at Sangju, where a battle was fought. The Koreans under General Yi Il were again defeated. The Japanese had already learned the manufacture and use of short firearms from Europeans, and, of course, were greatly at advantage. Word got abroad that every man of the enemy carried 'a dog's hindleg' over his shoulder. So firmly was this saying fixed in the minds of the people that even down to the close of the last century those who shot well and won their degree in military arts were called 'dog-leg graduates'.[9]

These two divisions of the Japanese army then crossed the Bird Pass[10] and reached Ch'ungju on the 28th, when another battle was fought. Sin Ip, the Korean general, was defeated and killed, and the armies moved on toward Seoul. One division, swinging to the right, made a half-circle through Yŏju and approached Seoul by the East Gate; the other crossed the river Han immediately and went through Chuksan; while the third came by way of the west. Their plans succeeded, and the three armies were united before the capital on the 3rd of the 5th moon.

The king, hearing of the defeat of generals Yi Il and Sin Ip, had taken fright and made his escape north on the 30th of the 4th moon. Yi Yangwŏn, the officer in charge of the defence of the capital, alarmed at the forces moving against him, made his escape likewise and followed hard after the king. Yi Kŭngik, who writes the story,[11] goes on to say that the Japanese remained in Seoul for a few days only, and then, leaving an army of occupation, started north in pursuit of the king. Generals Kato and Konishi met their first difficulty at the Imjin River, where they were delayed for eight or ten days. Here the Korean generals Yi Yangwŏn, Yi Il, and others, were waiting for them with an army of five thousand men. On the 17th a battle was fought in which many Korean officers were killed. The Japanese finally crossed on the 27th and moved past Songdo to P'yŏngsan, where one division led by Kato turned north-east toward Hamhŭng, while the other under Konishi pushed on toward P'yŏngyang. The latter reached the Taedong River on the 8th of the 6th moon while the king was still in P'yŏngyang.

At once a message was sent by a Korean prisoner, asking for an interview with the scholar Hanŭm, Yi Tŏkhyŏng, who had been in Japan the year before and had been kindly received. Yi offered to go and so took boat on the Taedong on the 9th. The Japanese sent a buddhist priest to meet him and they had a conference in mid-stream. 'Why have you come?' asked Tŏkhyŏng, 'Urge General Konishi to go back at once.' The Japanese replied, 'You mistake us. We are simply on our way to China; if you but grant the right to pass, all will be well.' Yi Tŏkhyŏng said this was quite impossible and that they must go back by the way they had come. The conference settled nothing and Yi returned to the city. Seeing the hopeless plight he was in, the king left P'yŏngyang on the 11th of the 6th moon and fled to Ŭiju, while on the 14th the Japanese army entered P'yŏngyang, where General Konishi took up his headquarters and remained.

On the 11th the king despatched word from Pakch'ŏn to the Ming emperor asking for help. At once general Tsu Ch'eng-hsün, in command of the Liaotung forces with an army of three thousand men, hastened across the Yalu. On the 19th of the 7th moon he fought the Japanese at P'yŏngyang, but was beaten and retired. Many Chinese officers and soldiers were killed in this engagement. From Ŭiju the king again sent a messenger to Peking with a still more urgent call. In response General Li Ju-sung was despatched with 40,000 men. On the 24th day of the last moon of the year he crossed the Yalu on the ice and arrived before P'yŏngyang on the 6th day of the 1st moon, having made the distance of 150 miles in twelve days. Konishi was waiting for him. Early on the morning of the 8th Li Ju-sung had his soldiers well fed and put in order before the north-west gates. The Japanese, with white and red flags flying, came forth to the attack. Li Ju-sung met them with a hundred or so horse. He had with him cannon which, when they were fired, could be heard for miles. The writer says, 'It was like the sound of thunder, and clouds of smoke arose.' Under this barrage the Chinese general made his way up on to the wall, but the defenders fired back with short guns and hurled stones so deftly that he was obliged to retire. Li Ju-sung, seeing his troops give way, had one man beheaded on the spot and his grim remains carried round the camp by way of encouragement. Following this, General Li himself led the van and shouted, '500 *liang* of silver to the first man over the wall!' Lo Shang-chih, a Chinese officer, won it and many troops followed in his wake. The men of Chekiang captured a number of Japanese flags and planted Chinese ones in their place. Already part of the city was on fire from the cannonade, and the Seven Star Gate (Ch'ilsŏng-mun) had been battered in. Here the Chinese army entered. They were now through the outer wall from three points and converging on the inner city. More than a thousand prisoners were taken and the Japanese, unable to withstand a further attack, withdrew behind the inner fortifications, where they built mounds with port-holes that looked like beehives. From these they shot bullets with great effect so that many Chinese were killed.[12]

Li Ju-sung withdrew, pitched his camp and sent a messenger with a despatch which ran: 'My army is quite sufficient to destroy yours, but I desire to spare the lives of your men. The way is open for you to go at once.' Konishi replied, 'I shall go as you request. Please see that my way is not blocked.' To this General Li agreed and sent messages to the Korean army to let the Japanese pass. Konishi accordingly departed in the night. The other divisions of the army joined him till on the 24th of the 1st moon they all arrived in Seoul. The chronicler says, 'They set fire to the city and killed many of the people.' On the whole, however, judging from the Korean records, the march through the country seems to have been a very orderly one, and Konishi a man of kindly spirit.[13]

During these engagements we are told that to Chinese eyes at least the God of War, Kuan-yü, was seen with his armies in the upper air fighting Korea's battles. He appeared in P'yŏngyang during the first attack, again in other places, and finally over Seoul in the year 1599. He was first descried outside the South Gate. He and his warriors crossed the city among the clouds and disappeared beyond the East Gate. Two temples were built commemorating this miraculous appearance, one to the south (destroyed by fire some years go), and one to the east of the capital (which still stands).[14] What a very strange idea, we say; and yet, in this very year Shakespeare in writing *Julius Caesar* ascribes these words to Caesar's wife Calphurnia:[15]

> Fierce fiery warriors fought upon the clouds,
> In ranks and squadrons and right form of war
> Which drizzled blood upon the Capitol.

Li Ju-sung remained in P'yŏngyang until the 8th moon, when he began a march toward Seoul. On hearing this Konishi turned back and the armies met at Pyŏkche-gwan in Koyang County. A battle was fought and Li Ju-sung was badly beaten. Konishi inveigled him and his whole force into a morass where his cavalry foundered. Li himself was knocked from his horse and almost killed. Many of the Chinese fought their last fight here. A retreat was ordered and the whole Chinese army crossed the Imjin River. The Koreans urged Li to make a second stand but he refused. But on the 19th of the 4th moon, just about a year after their first landing, the Japanese again crossed the Han River and made their way back toward Pusan, joined as they went along by the scattered guards that had been left here and there to hold the south.

WHEN THEY FIRST landed there was in the province of Chŏlla a man named Yi Sunsin, chief of the naval defences of the south coast.[16] He at once mustered all his sailors in the port of Yŏsu. Calls for help had come from the officer in command of the Kyŏngsang coast. He had been defeated by the Japanese and was in dire straits. Yi refused at first to respond to these, till one of his aides, Ŏ Yŏngdam, earnestly besought him. 'I should be glad to answer his request,' said Yi, 'but am uncertain of the way.' Ŏ answered, 'I know the way: I'll answer for it and will serve as guide.' Yi then called together his turtle fleet and set out on the 4th day of the 5th moon, with eighty war-boats in all. In his preparation for defence Yi had devised what the Koreans called a 'turtle-boat', a very cleverly-armed vessel. It was covered with planks thick and hard. On the top, running lengthwise, was a narrow footway and another ran across. All the rest of the surface was occupied by spikes, spears and blade points. Each boat had a dragon's head carved at the prow for good luck, the mouth fitted with a rude cannon such as the Chinese had long known and made use of. At the rear, underneath the tail, was another porthole for cannon shot. There were six openings on each side, one for a cannon muzzle and the others for the soldiers to shoot through. Sailors, too, had their places down below where they handled the oars. When moving into battle these boats were covered with light fluff or matting so as not to show their teeth. Any attempt to board them ended in hopeless confusion. Whenever they were surrounded the guns belched forth fire on all sides. Fearing nothing, they drove straight into the heart of the enemy fleet.

This invention was wholly from the mind of Yi Sunsin. Born in the same year as Sir Francis Drake (1545) he seems to have been gifted with a spirit similar to that of the great Englishman. He was great in high command, but surely greater in the inventive genius that fashioned his ships from models never seen before, models that existed in his imagination only. He met Wŏn Kyun, his fellow admiral from Kyŏngsang, in the straits of Noryang-jin, and they moved out into the open sea before Kwangyang. There they met five or six ships of the enemy, which withdrew at once. Yi gave chase and the Japanese, who were slower, made for the shore. Finally their boats were captured and destroyed, and the Korean fleet returned for the night.

On the day following Yi started for Kyŏnnae-ryang and on the way he met a great fleet of the enemy covering the sea. The officer in charge of the turtle squadron moved forward while Yi with the main fleet tacked back. The enemy, seeing this, set sail and followed hard after him. This continued till they reached the neighbourhood of Hansan Island, where Yi suddenly turned and, after a fight of several hours, sank the whole Japanese fleet.

At the same time Ŏ Yŏngdam fought another engagement off Chinhae against twenty-five of the enemy's ships, which were all sunk or destroyed. On the 7th the remainder of the enemy set out from Kŏje Island and made for Japan. Yi followed and overtook them in the sea off Kadŏk Island where he defeated and sank more than a hundred of their craft. Among them was one fine vessel that stood over twenty feet out of the water. It had a curtain of red silks about it, and beautifully gilded screens stood upon its decks. An inscription written and posted up told that it was the admiral's ship. Here a fan was picked up that had on it the writing of Hideyoshi, dated 8th day of the 6th moon. When the enemy had been destroyed, and all trace of his fleet had disappeared, Yi returned to his station.[17]

30 The seventeenth century I: Kwanghae-gun; Yi Kwal

THE slumbering war and unsatisfactory negotiations dragged on, soldiers of Japan going and coming till the year 1598, when Hideyoshi died. In that same year Yi Sunsin fought his last fight off Noryang and when victory was won, like Nelson he was struck by a stray bullet and killed. His success at sea upset all Hideyoshi's plans for a further advance on China. As the Scots, and English too, sing the praises of Bruce and Wallace, so valiant Japanese as well as Koreans will ever account Yi Sunsin a hero equal to Drake or Hawkins. The records of his exploits are so definite and so many that, no matter how much times and seasons may change, his memory will abide for ever.

In Korea's straightening out of her domestic affairs after the war, she found that she had lost the golden crown given her some two hundred years before by the founder of the Ming. She had this replaced.[1] The Confucian College, too, that stands near the wall of the north-east part of Seoul, had been burned down but was restored in 1602, the inscription being written by the Minister of the Left, Yi Chŏnggu, and deciphered for the writer (J.S.G) by his descendant of the eleventh generation. It speaks in high praise of Confucius, 'No sage like him, no master so great.' Why does Korea pay this ancient Chinese so deep a meed of gratitude? Because she owed him practically all she had: her civilization, her religion, her social structure, her ranks and offices. All these hung upon the teachings of Confucius. When they were given up in 1894, Korea lost her soul, and by degrees has arrived at the intellectual and social chaos of today. Out of the broken fragments of the present it will take generations to build up as substantial a civilization as that which came down from the Great Master through 3,000 years. The building of the temple in 1602, the year in which William Shakespeare wrote *All's Well that Ends Well*, reflected a similar sentiment: 'The war is over, all is well.'

Much had to be done in shaking off the grim remembrance of war. Many Koreans had been taken prisoner, and they had to be ransomed and brought home. I find this note in the *Taedong yasŭng*:[2]

Seventeen Korean women had been captured and were kept in the house of a Japanese officer named Omoiye. They each came with a petition to the Korean commissioner asking that they be delivered from exile and returned to their native land. Among these was a pathetic note from the daughter of a gentleman of Seoul. Her petition ran thus: 'I am So-and-so's daughter, from such-and -such a place. On the opening of the war, I made my escape with my parents, they holding me by the hand as we ran for our lives. In their distress they cried, "Our death is nothing, but what about our daughter?" We rested occasionally and gazed into each other's faces while tears streamed from our eyes. It was as though a sword had passed though my body and soul. I thought, "If I am not to live and serve my parents, better die and be done with it. As it is, I am only an anxiety to them." Just at that moment a troop of the enemy came rushing upon us, and, in our attempt to escape, we were separated and lost sight of each other. Then I was seized and taken prisoner by a fierce fellow and carried off. Oh, my God, my God, what sins have I committed that I should have been made to suffer such a painful, dreadful fate as this? If my parents be already dead there is no need for this appeal, but if perchance they live, when will their sorrows find an end? Why do such things as these happen with their tears and agony? Two years have passed. The fact that I am still alive and have not died by my own hand is due only to the hope that I may yet be returned home to see my father and my mother. But if perchance they be dead? Still, even the sight of the home where they lived would gladden my eyes. After that I could die in peace. So every morning as the

265

sun rises and each night as the moon goes down, I pray to God asking Him to grant me this one blessing, namely, to see my father and my mother. Where are they now, o God? As they love and think of me, so I love and think of them. Look, o God, on this thought of mine and be pleased to grant us a happy time of meeting.'

The reader will judge from the fact that this record is here that she was brought home and restored to her grief-stricken parents. It affords a pathetic picture of the sufferings of war three hundred years ago, and of the soul of a Korean girl in those distant days.

AS THE HUMBLE SUFFER, so the high in station. One of the most pathetic notes sounded in all Korea's history rings out at this time. King Sŏnjo's queen died in 1600. In 1602 he took a second queen and in 1606 a son was born to him who was called Prince Yŏngch'ang. But the little lad was destined never to be king. When his father died, his half-brother Kwanghae, a rough unkempt creature born of a concubine, pushed him aside and later, when he was eight years of age, got possession of him, imprisoned him in Kanghwa and burned him to death in an overheated room. Kwanghae-gun however, after a reign of eight years, was ejected from the throne by his nephew Injo, who was backed by an indignant people. Kwanghae was sent to exile on Quelpaert, where he lived in poverty for eighteen years, and so atoned, in part at least, for the murder of Prince Yŏngch'ang. Korean scholars are all poets, and the history of the country is dotted with odes and songs that record every possible feeling. Kwanghae was no mean scholar, but he had no writing-brush in his exile and no paper. He wrote on the wall of his prison with a stick of charcoal thus:[3]

> The north wind blows the rain across my way,
> And mists hang deep upon the city wall;
> The sea roars in upon the evening tide,
> And all the hills are wrapped in anxious gloom.
> My homesick heart hangs by each blade of grass,
> And in my dreams I wander by the shore.
> I know not how my state goes, up or down,
> And passing boats speak not nor give a sign.

In the meantime, broken-hearted Queen Inmok at thirty years of age saw her son dead. She also had nineteen years of long agony. In the valuable library of Korean books collected by Bishop Trollope is to be found an original letter of Queen Inmok, done in Korean script, and inscribed as with drops of blood. Her son, her only son, her dearest, the light of her eyes, born to a kingdom, was foully torn from her, what words could suffice? When could her agony fade? To quiet her soul and find rest, she copied off the Mit'a Scripture of the buddha,[4] a little saints' book, in characters of gold. The writer saw this 300-year-old treasure at the Yujŏm Temple in the Diamond Mountains in 1917. A note at the end says, 'May my parents and relatives and especially my son, Prince Yŏngch'ang, find eternal blessing in the world beyond by my having copied this out.'

I have only been able to find one little poem of hers, though her name is famed as a princess great in scholarship. It is this:[5]

> The weary ox, grown old through years of labour,
> With neck sore chafed and skin worn through in holes,
> Nods off to sleep. His ploughing now is done,
> And harrow days are over, spring rains fall:
> Why does his master still lay on the goad
> And cause him pain?

THE EVIL-DOING KING Kwanghae, whose name is today expunged from Korean state records, died in 1641. Before his exile he had already become addicted to tobacco and the loss of it was a torture to him. We are told that he improvised a pipe-stem from a twig of bamboo and a bowl from a piece of broken tile. Begging a leaf from a passer-by through the chink of his prison wall, he solaced himself with this extraordinary weed.

Tobacco first came to Korea from Japan about 1616. Japan, it seems, got it from foreign merchants who had imported it from Europe, name and all, *tambakko*. The following comment by Yi Ik, a Korean born in 1681, is of interest.[6]

> Tobacco became generally known in this country in the closing years of Kwanghae. The common story is that it came from a place in the far south called Tamp'a, hence the name. I asked of Teacher T'aeho, 'Do you think tobacco is good for the health?' He replied, 'It is good for those troubled with phlegm, and for those inclined to have spells of nausea. People, too, who suffer from indigestion and insomnia are benefited by it. It allays bitter flavours in the throat and is a protection against colds in the winter season.'
>
> 'But is it not hurtful as well?' I inquired. His reply was, 'There are dangers that go with it. It may be hurtful internally to the mind, or externally to the eyes and ears. On the continuous use of it, no doubt, the hair grows gray, the teeth fall out, the flesh dries up and age rushes on. The smell of it too, is dreadful and no man using it can ever expect to come into touch with the immortal gods . . .'

Tobacco took the people of Korea by storm. On its approach, tea, which had been in use 800 years, faded away never to return.

On the writer's taking train at Toronto, Canada, for Korea in 1888, strange to say, he met Mr W. W. Rockhill, afterwards American minister in Peking and ambassador in St Petersburg, who had already been in Korea as US chargé d'affaires.[7] He knew Seoul and the hermit people well, and kindly gave much interesting information regarding them. Among other things he said, 'They are the greatest smokers in the world.'[8] Judging from the length of pipe-stem and the long hours occupied in tending it, we might say so; but considering the effect of the more deadly short pipe or of endless cigarettes, we conclude that old Korea's was a gentle smoke compared with that of the occidental.

To CHANGE the subject: as the Earl of Mar in 1715 took umbrage at a slight given him by George I, and stirred up no end of Jacobite hornets to sting and terrify the state, so about a hundred years earlier, Yi Kwal, a Korean, indignant at being poorly rewarded by King Injo, did the same. He had ousted Kwanghae and set Injo on the throne; now in the distribution of rewards he was overlooked, an insult he could not brook. Added to this, the king, to get him out of sight, made him captain of that region in the farthest north where exiles go, and a man of far less experience was set over his head, Chang Man. This was the last straw that broke down his allegiance. With the soul of the Korean tiger glaring from his eyes, he trained his army of 12,000 men, joined by 130 skilled Japanese swordsmen, men taken prisoner in the Imjin War who were afterwards content to dwell in Korea and share its fortunes. Yŏngbyŏn, sixty-five miles or so north of P'yŏngyang, was the point from which his expedition moved. He pretended to be marching south to rescue the king from dangers that threatened him. In reality he was on a warpath of revenge, with anger intensified by the news that his son had been arrested and was in danger of his life.

There was great consternation in the capital. No plans were forthcoming; the various cities along the way seemed ready to submit. The king, at his wits' end, decided to take his family tablets and his household and escape to Kanghwa; later however, his destination was changed to Kongju.

Yi Kwal was opposed all along his way by Chŏng Ch'ungsin, a general of great courage and ability, who repeatedly attacked and weakened the rebel forces. Suspicion was felt everywhere; suspects were arrested and cross-examined, some families were entirely wiped out—during all of which time Yi Kwal was drawing nearer the capital. There was no time for proper trials, *habeas corpus* was thrown to the winds. The historian says, 'There was no time to consider whether men were beautiful porcelain or only earthenware; all were bundled together and smashed. Such pandemonium the state had never seen before.'9

Songdo fell before Yi Kwal, who left at once, crossed the Imjin River and on the 10th of the 2nd moon marched into the capital and pitched his camp in the grounds of the Kyŏngbok Palace. Chŏng Ch'ungsin followed hard after and came hurrying over the Peking Pass and down the side of Lone Tree Mountain.10 Here the armies met on the hills behind Yŏnhŭi College and fought it out. At the sound of a false alarm shouted by Nam Ihŭng, 'The enemy are beaten!' Yi Kwal's troops began to give way, breaking their ranks here and there till at last all was flight and confusion. Chŏng Ch'ungsin rode forward to capture Yi Kwal when Nam Ihŭng stopped him saying, 'By the grace of God victory is ours. In a day or two all heads will be in our hands. Why follow at unnecessary risk?'

Later the rebel chief fled by the Water Gate and made his escape to Ich'ŏn where he was assassinated by one of his own followers, Ki Ikhŏn, who brought his head to Chŏng Ch'ungsin and won the reward. So ended the rebellion of Yi Kwal, with many dead bodies dotting the sides of Lone Tree Mountain which the inhabitants of Seoul gazed upon with fear.

THE AIR SOON CLEARED and Korea settled down again to its quiet life of the pen, not the sword. It has always been the land of the literati, a scholars' world, noted for its distinguished writers. As an example I shall present one whose name I mentioned before, he who wrote the inscription for the Confucian College, Yi Chŏnggu. Born in the same year as Shakespeare (1564), he outlived him by nineteen years. He was not only a man of great literary attainments, but also a master of the state. He went north on the occasion of the old king's flight before the Japanese and in Yi Kwal's invasion he again accompanied his Majesty to a place of safety in Kongju. His collected works number twenty-two volumes printed from wooden plates and titled with his pen-name: Wŏlsa, 'Moonlit Sands'. A note of introduction says, 'On the day of his birth a tiger came and stood outside the gate.' A good omen, no doubt, but people were alarmed and afraid to come near. He began his studies at eight years of age, matriculated in 1585, and graduated in 1590. At eleven he lost his mother. He was once Minister of the Left[11] and nine times Minister of Home Affairs. Heaped high with honours, he was made head of the Confucian College and Chief of the Literati. His grave is in Kap'yŏng.

The so-called 'inner volumes' of his works number seventy-seven.[12] Eighteen of them are taken up with poems, and two with an explanation of the Great Learning, a Chinese book that Korean students know by heart. Then the list of contents continues: memorials written for the king of Korea to the Ming emperor; explanations of the sacred books for the help of his Majesty; inscriptions for memorial stones; biographies; prayers on sacrificial occasions; miscellaneous writings; and so on. From these I select a passage from an account of a trip he made to the Diamond Mountains in 1603. Among those hills is a peak where the fairies are said to come forth at times and play upon their pipes. As Yi and his party were seated before it on the great flat rocks of the gorge, he had his musician secretly sent round behind into the grove of pines, unknown to the rest of the party.

> Softly and sweetly, as though from the Ninth Heaven, sounds of music were wafted on the air. The assembled guests looked at each other in wonder, listened and said, 'Does your Excellency hear it?' I made as though I heard nothing and so they all kept perfectly still and said, 'Wonderful! The music of the upper spheres! Tradition says that the fairies used to live here, and now we actually hear them play!' The sound was especially sweet and clear, and it really did seem to come from the clouds. As the wind blew, it would cease and then be heard again. I knew what it was, and yet I, too, was inclined to think it was the fairies playing.[13]

Another story is told of Yi Chŏnggu that well illustrates the spirit of the age.[14] The king, hearing that Chu Chih-fan, a great Chinese calligrapher, was on his way to Korea as envoy, sent Yi Chŏnggu with a number of his associates to meet him. Arriving in P'yŏngyang, the Ming envoy stepped from his chair and greeting Yi, said, 'Delighted to meet your Excellencies, all gifted writers, I know. Please write me, will you, a poem of a hundred couplets about this famous city of P'yŏngyang before cockcrow of the morning. A hundred thousand thanks to you!' He then bowed and took his departure to rest for the night after his long journey. Yi called his friends together and said, 'Here we are with this high request on our hands, what shall we do?' 'I propose,' said one, 'that we each write a part and piece them together.' 'Never!' said Yi, 'Such a composition would be an offence to his high Excellency.' He then called on Ch'a Ch'ŏllo, a famous scholar, and said, 'Ch'a, you are the man to meet our need.' Ch'a thought for a moment and then replied, 'I'm a fool, I know, but let's try.' He called for a tall screen which he placed round him so that he was quite hidden from view, then for a fire-box, a bowl of drink, and a fan. Han Sŏkpong, a marvellous calligrapher, sat outside the screen with a roll of beautiful paper in hand and a well-watered ink-stone. Ch'a took a long drink from the bowl and then began with a deep mumbling hum to collect his thoughts, tuning up as it were. He beat time with measured fan on the rim of his brazier and then springing to his feet shouted, 'Ready!' Like a rippling stream from a fairy fountain, soft couplets came tripping forth in song. His spirit heightened as he gathered speed and his whole soul vibrated for joy. Off went coat and outer garb to clear his decks for action, while all the time the couplets raced upon each other's heels. The company could see his head bobbing up and down above the screen while Han, racing as if for life, was dashing the poem characters all down the roll of paper. In a trice it was done, rolled beautifully, sealed as a picture is sealed, and carried to the Chinese envoy who had just entered upon his first delightful sleep. 'Who is it?' inquired he, 'and why am I waked at this hour? 'The poem,' they said, 'the poem is here.' 'Already, so soon?" said Chu, 'Impossible!' But here it was. He unrolled it with his attendants about him and, taking up his fan, beat its rhythm on the rim of his brazier. How sweetly and beautifully it ran. Chu gathered inspiration as he went sailing along and sang out clearly so that all could hear. The delight of it banished his thoughts of sleep and carried his soul up into the ecstatic regions of saints and sages. We are told that he beat his fan to flinders before he reached the climax at the end. 'A wonderful poem!' said Chu, 'Korea is indeed the land of the Superior Man.'

Yi was later sent as envoy to China to show Korea's regard for the high honours done her. Let me close this chapter with a little poem of eight lines that he wrote on his long journey:[15]

> The little inn upon the river's brink
> Waves bright its willows o'er the passing stream;
> While soft the springtime breaks the morning blue,
> And evening drops behind the mountain wall.
> The sparkling water tells the time of year,
> Though weary miles mark lines across my face.
> The wandering thought finds nothing worth the while
> And lets its rhymes drop from a pointless pen.

31 The seventeenth century II: Injo; the Manchu invasions

KOREA'S contact with foreigners dates from the beginning of the seventeenth century. True, 400 years before this Marco Polo must have seen her white-coated people, passing and re-passing along the streets of Cambaluc city—but he makes no mention of it. The Korean, too, being by far the most exclusive of all Orientals, would not have deigned to look at Polo had he crossed his path. Western nations were bundled unceremoniously together by him under the name of 'yangin from yangguk', men of the sea, who knows whence. Korea had no idea whatever, even down to 1885, of the tremendous part played in the world's affairs by Europe. That Europe embraced many different races, many different languages, many different nations, she never dreamed. The first real announcement of the foreigner's presence was in 1627 when a Dutch ship, off its course and short of water, sent three sailors ashore into Chŏlla province. These lads were taken prisoner and never saw their good ship or Holland again. Two died fighting for their captors against the Manchu; and one, John Weltevree, remained at the call of the court for more than thirty years. He must have been a man of some education and some sense of dignity, to have held his post so long.[1]

On 15 August 1653 a Dutch ship, making its way to Nagasaki, was wrecked off Quelpaert, and thirty-six men were cast upon the rocks. With the exception of Hamel, their leader, they were all very ignorant, very common sailors. While Weltevree had won a place by his good bearing and tact, this party, including even a Scotsman, won nothing, but remained as the very dust of the betrodden street. No mention is made of them by the great lords who swept by daily and took careful note of all they saw and heard. Low-caste outlanders such as they were not for gentleman of high repute even to remember, and so, tossed here and there, they were kicked about the country, till 5 September 1666.

On that very day the Great Fire of London began. Pepys wrote: 'About two in the morning my wife calls me up, and tells me of new cries of fire, it being come to Barking Church, which is the bottom of our lane.' At this same time, too, eight Dutchmen, including Hamel, made their escape from Korea in a little boat that finally reached Nagasaki. After an exile of thirteen years and twenty-eight days they were among their countrymen again. The others were never heard of. No mention is made of them, favourable or unfavourable. It is as though they had never been. As Koreans looked on these degraded exiles day by day, their peculiar hair, their irregular features, and their ugliness in general, a definite impression of the inferiority of the European race must have formed, which determined Koreans more than ever to live an isolated life untainted by these creatures of the west. It took a great priest like Matteo Ricci, whose fame has outlived 300 years, to tell Korea what the West had done with its mighty men.[2]

BUT THE PRIDE of the nation was to get a sore shock as it approached the middle of the seventeenth century. Since time immemorial, Korea had learned to look upon China as the suzerain state, the great Middle Kingdom, the mother-hen with her ducklings gathered around her, all her very own except Japan. Like

England, aloof from the continent, Yamato never sent tribute to anyone, least of all to the capitals of Han. Korea, however, was not only a dependent state, but loved to be so, especially when China, true to her real self, was a Chou, a Han, a T'ang, a Sung or a Ming; when she changed into a Jürched, or a Khitan, or a Mongol, or a Manchu, Korea loathed her. These barbarian races were robbers, who for the time being had got possession of the mother-state, and so were more than ever to be despised. Not even great names like K'ang-hsi or Ch'ien-lung[3] could make Korea forget that the ruling house was a *ho*, a barbarian.

Gradually the Manchu, from being a mere tribe of the Jürched, had grown to be a great state under the wise rule of Nurhachi, and now had a flourishing capital at Mukden. In 1644 their forces were set in motion toward Peking, the real centre of the world. A Chinese army of 200,000 came out to meet them, but in a great battle this host was totally defeated, and the orthodox imperial line perished, leaving the Manchu as emperor of the Middle Kingdom. His rule lasted till 1912 when a republic was set up with Yüan Shih-k'ai as its president.

From the day the Manchu came into possession of Mukden, Korea set about putting her house in order for defence. In 1627 a real danger arose, for forces of the enemy crossed the Yalu,[4] took possession of Ŭiju, and quietly settled down for a number of years. This was a constant source of alarm, for the Manchu, unlike the permanently settled Korean, is a nomad who, with his horse, occupies everything within a hundred miles range of his camp. At what hour he pleased he was on the way, always ready, and always armed. Who could withstand him? Outriders spread terror everywhere, as far as Seoul and Kanghwa, extorting oaths and promises that were never kept. At last, however, the khan determined to bring matters to a head, and set his main army in motion in the 12th moon of 1636.[5] Everywhere the fields were frozen, and the whole world was a highway for him and his men. Before they started, a conference was called in which a high officer, Guyen baturu,[6] rose to say, 'Korea is a land of the gentleman and scholar; from a military point of view she is of no account whatever. Let us leave her alone. When once we settle matters with China, she will come to us of herself.'[7] The khan, a broad-thinking man, counted this reasonable and agreed; but two generals, said to be Korean renegades, Lunggultai and Mabutai, opposed it so vehemently that the march went forward.

On the 13th they were in P'yŏngyang.[8] The government in Seoul, hearing of this, decided that the family tablets, the king's wives, crown-princesses, daughters-in-law, grandchildren and others of the royal clan should be shipped to Kanghwa under special guard of the chief civil officials. Beacon fires on the hills hastened this move by announcing that the Manchu were on the way. Before the king himself decided what to do, already the enemy's army had debouched from the hills, and was covering all the lower lands behind the Peking Pass. The king also made an attempt to escape to Kanghwa, but he was intercepted and came flying back. On the advice of his wisest counsellors he started for Namhan. When the people saw his Majesty and the Crown Prince flying for their lives along what is now Kokane-machi that leads to the Water Gate, a general panic took place. History says, 'The cries of the trampling multitude went up to heaven.'[9] In the night of the 14th, after great fatigue, his Majesty finally reached the South Fortress,

Namhan, while Ch'oe Myŏnggil, one of the ministers of state and a very wise man, was holding the Manchu in leash by a never-ending consultation. Ch'oe promised a speedy reply from the king, but it did not come, till the Manchu finally threatened his life. In the nick of time, however, messages got through. The reader may well appreciate the difficult place in which Korea stood. Here was this all-powerful enemy, dressed in his quilted garb, fearing neither cold nor fatigue, his long sleeves dangling by his elbow, his pig-tail hanging from beneath a dog-skin cap, his overall breeches a wonder to behold, carrying a villainous bow and swinging a broadsword at his side, claiming imperial honour, though the Ming were still in Peking and presided over the Temple of Heaven. What could Korea do? She had once entangled herself with Khubilai's Mongol tribe to her lasting confusion; and here now was another barbarian, equally loathsome, threatening her. To yield was unthinkable; to fight probably meant death and destruction.

The king, attempting to make his escape from Namhan to Kanghwa, set out on the night of the 16th, but snow and rain and a biting frost had turned the mountain into a world of glass. Outside the South Gate of the fortress the feet of his horse gave way and he fell. He himself then tried to walk, but fell also. Finally, unable even to stand, he was made to seat himself on a mat while his servants, shod in straw shoes, dragged him back. Flight was now given up and a strong defence decided on.[10]

The whole Manchu army had moved out to the level ground before Namhan, while Ch'oe Myŏnggil went back and forth to confer. 'We are come,' said the Manchu, 'to settle matters definitely. You have broken faith twice now and we are here to see that you do not do it a third time.'

Already Namhan was completely surrounded, and all communication with the outside world cut off. Expected Korean reinforcements had not come. The Manchu called loudly for the Crown Prince, and many excuses and evasions were made, but all of no avail. The name also by which the Koreans should address the khan, 'Your Highness', or 'Your Majesty', or 'Imperial Majesty' was argued and fought over. Finally it was agreed to give him the best there was, namely, 'Your Imperial Majesty' *(Hwangje)*. This aroused great opposition on the part of some high Korean officials, but the Crown Prince thought it best and asked that he might go and present their case in person.[11]

Before this was carried out, however, as the morning of the 18th dawned bright and favourable, Wŏn Tup'yo, the guard of the North Gate, darted out and killed six of the enemy. So lively a feat set the garrison in high spirits. The king on the other hand was not at all uplifted: he fell into utter despair, wept and bemoaned his lot. To give up the Crown Prince was unthinkable, and yet Ch'oe Myŏnggil, his wisest counsellor, advised it. Many arose at this, threatening to kill Ch'oe.

On the 19th the king made a desolate round of the fortress and talked with his ministers. He conferred over a proposed sortie to capture the Iron Pass[12] that formed the gateway of the southern provinces.

For several days Manchus had been taken and killed, and now a messenger of theirs came with a rather submissive look and asked for a conference. They talked with him for a time over the walls, till the king stopped it and said, 'Have nothing more to do with him.'

At this point he called on Na Man'gap, an official who had charge of the commissary, and made inquiry as to supplies on hand. 'There are', said Na, '9,300 people now in the fortress, and probably there will be 12,000 by the time all get in.' 'How many bags of grain have you: rice, lentils, beans?' asked the king. '18,000 bags!' 'How long will it last?' 'Sixty or seventy days. We have also 220 jars of soy.'[13]

On the 24th the king, seeing the wild wintry weather, was in great distress and suggested that they offer a prayer to God. He went out into the court, where, with only rough straw-matting spread beneath him, he bowed four times and said, 'We have come to this place of desolation where our only hope is in Thee. Under such rain and snow we shall all die. For myself I am not concerned, but these my people, what evil have they done? Give, I pray Thee, fair weather and save us from death.' Drenched through, he knelt still and wept 'till the tears ran down his chin'. Finally his ministers raised him by force and helped him back into his room. On his way he saw the guards watching by the gate in the cold, and, flinging off his beautiful fur robe said, 'Here, cut this into pieces, and give each man a bit to wrap his ears with against the biting blast.'[14]

The Manchu, seeing the hills too steep to climb, and the fortress an ugly problem to tackle, built a pine branch wall round it and hung every part with clattering gongs, bells, or whatever would make a sound, so as to announce any attempt to creep out in the night. Inside this they erected a wooden stockade, and between the two — wall and stockade — kept soldiers on guard, four to every hundred paces.[15]

On the 27th the king sent out a feeler to the enemy, two cows and some bottles of wine; but the Manchu general said, 'Take this stuff back to your starving soldiers, I don't need it. My master owns all your eight provinces, cattle and wine as well.' There was in this Manchu's proud confidence something completely discouraging to the national spirit of the Korean.[16]

Very foolishly, on the 28th the king allowed a company of 300 men to set forth under the command of a stupid official named Kim Yu. Against the warnings of Ch'oe Myŏnggil and Na Man'gap, they passed through the North Gate, noble three hundred, but they came back no more. When the Manchu had lured them on, beyond the pinewood wall, to which the Koreans set fire, he turned on them with his horses and rode them down. The Koreans had guns and used gunpowder, while the Manchu had only bow and broadsword; but his horsemanship, his rough-rider methods, his wild outdoor life made him a perfect demon to the silk-coated Korean. From this time on the spirit of the Korean soldiers was completely broken.[17]

The governor of Ch'ungch'ŏng province, hearing of the plight of the king, raised 8,000 troops, and, passing the royal tombs a little to the west of the fortress,[18] was leisurely making his way toward the gate on the 29th. Suddenly the Manchu was upon him. Again it was a fight of untrained foot against horse, where the whole force was cut to pieces. Chŏng, the general, a brave man, fell, but was carried off by a soldier, who took him on his back and fled to the hills.[19]

On the next day, the 30th, the last of the year, the Manchu khan arrived. He had lagged behind his main fighting force. On the same day a magpie came and began building his nest before the room occupied by the king. Some thought it a sign of good-luck, but not his Majesty. He maintained that it would take more than one magpie to set things right. Urged on by the distress around him, his generous heart shared the last of his bedclothes with his men while he slept in his day-clothes only.[20]

During all this time the father of the first Manchu emperor to reign at Peking, now forty-four years of age, looked on at Korea's predicament and waited. Negotiations again began, most distasteful. What could Korea do? Die and be done with it? The great question was the Sajik and the tablets, the Sajik being the royal altar to God, and the tablets the seat of the royal ancestral souls. The negotiations were interrrupted, for the last great stroke came. On the morning of the 4th of the 1st moon of the year an army of 40,000 men, (so it was said), under command of Generals Hŏ Wan and Min Yŏng, on their way from the south, entered the Ssangogae Pass, near Kwangju, not far from Namhan. As they moved on, quite unaware of danger, they saw a line of suspicious-looking horsemen moving down the hill and veering towards them 'like fish upon a string'. One of the Koreans, a sharp-shooter, took aim, struck the leader and brought him down. This awakened a call to 200 horsemen in the rear who rose as out of the ground. At once they came thundering down and a dreadful mêlée resulted. The Koreans having shot away their little supply of gunpowder had nothing left with which to meet the deadly bow and arrow of the Manchu, his trampling horse, his death-dealing broadsword. First the left wing gave way, then the right until, as Hong Kyŏngmo the historian says, the whole 40,000 were utterly destroyed by 300 horsemen. Korea, like many another nation, had been caught napping, so that a single trained trooper of the Manchu type was a match for a hundred men. The theory of the soldier may be ever so well learned in the gentle school of the inner court but in the end it is the practised hand that tells.[21]

On the 5th Kim Ch'unyŏng, military governor of Chŏlla, repulsed a minor attack of the Manchu and held his own, but the day was already lost.[22]

On the 9th Kim Sanghŏn suggested that they offer worship to the spirit of King Onjo, who had reigned there in Namhan from 18 BC to AD 18, during the very days that Christ was on earth; and the king approved.[23]

Signs and omens were carefully watched, but all to no purpose. The Manchu set watch-fires about his camp and waited. On the 16th, when a messenger was sent to enquire something of him, he was told that 70,000 more men, reinforcements, were on the march with 28 pieces of cannon.[24]

For days the question remained undecided, and the Koreans bravely beat off the enemy from the walls. On the 24th, however, cannon were brought to bear that battered down the gates. Finally on the night of the 30th matters had reached an impossible pass and Korea surrendered.[25]

At once the Manchu turned his face homeward, taking with him as hostages two of the princes.[26] A stone, 11 feet high and 5 feet across, still stands on the banks of the Han River ten miles from Seoul, written on the face in Chinese, and on the back in Manchu, telling of all the valiant deeds of the famous horsemen. Its inscription, among other things, reads: *Ch'ŏn kang sang no, chae suk chae yuk:* 'God gives frost as well as dew; behold his severity as well as his loving-kindness.'[27] For 300 years Korea faithfully bowed her head and sent her tribute, always reserving to herself the private right, whensoever she pleases, to turn up her nose at that uncouth barbarian, the Manchu.

AMONG THOSE bottled up in Namhan who had protested against the miserable surrender was a young man of twenty-nine named Song Siyŏl. He is perhaps the most famous scholar of the seventeenth century. For the thirteen years that Injo still remained on the throne, Song would accept no office, because the shame of the Manchu defeat was always before his eyes. Only after Hyojong, son of Injo, succeeded to the throne, did he accept and finally become Minister of the Left. He was the head of what was called the Noron, or 'Older Party'. Korean parties in those days had no clearly-defined policies of government like ours in the west. Each, however, just as with us, claimed all the virtues of the state and made it loudly known that their opponents were a set of scoundrels. Thus it was in Korea when Song held office and power for so long a time. Consequently he was greatly loved and greatly hated. Numberless schools dedicated to his memory are scattered over the land, but in the end his downfall came at the hands of his enemies, the Namin ('south-men'), who prevailed upon the king to send him into exile, and later to give him, an old man of eighty-five, a glass of arsenic and croton oil mixed — the favourite hemlock dose by which mortals were sent on their eternal way. Song drank it with as steady a hand as did Socrates and died, in 1689. He was a brave old soldier and attained to highest honour in the end, for his tablet stands today as one of the attendants of the Great Master in the Temple of Confucius.

ANOTHER noted character of this reign was Kim Sangyong, a fierce old scholar, seventy-five years of age, who had followed the queen and the princess on the 14th of the 12th moon in their flight to Kanghwa, and helped to look after the royal tablets. These were brought along in small chairs like living people. Finally they were safely taken across the ferry at Kapkot-chin and deposited in the ancestral hall where they remained in comparative quiet till the 22nd of the 2nd moon. Suddenly on this day word came that the Manchu was just across the straits, in fact was pushing over. Great consternation followed. Many of the women, some of the highest in the land, threw themselves into the river to escape disgrace, and old Kim, feeling that the day of doom had come, called his servants, divided his goods and clothing, ceremonial coats, caps, and so forth, and asked that they be given to this one and that. Then he went up to the tower of the South Gate of Kanghwa town, where was a large chest of gunpowder on which he sat himself down and called for a tobacco light. This startled the servants for old Kim was known to be not only a non-smoker, but, like James I of England, a great opponent of the 'filthy weed'. Kim's call for a light for his pipe raised a smile even amid the grim surroundings of the day. No response came but a little later, who knows how, he got fire and as he sat on the chest dropped a spark through a chink in the lid. There was a tremendous explosion that blew the gate of Kanghwa to pieces. Along with Kim died two of his best friends, his servants, and a little grandson of thirteen years. So perished Kim Sangyong, a victim of his country's shame. He was a great scholar and like all the literati wrote many verses of poetry.

Here is one of eight lines marked 'An'guk Temple' ·— some buddhist retreat in the hills, no doubt:[28]

> The shining moon rides o'er the sky
> A large and rounded platter:
> The windy road that's pitched on high
> Chills all my dreaming matter.
> The flowers, o'ershadowed, fill the plain
> The hills look downward coldly;
> The stork that leads the fairy train
> Pipes through his whistle boldly.

When the Manchu departed, as we have already mentioned, he carried off sons of the king and three high officers of state: Hong Ikhan, Yun Chip and O Talche. Those three sturdy old knights of the pen refused to bow before the evil-smelling Manchu and were beheaded in Mukden. They died heroes: their ideals were greater than life itself or any pain that man could inflict. Only after seven long years were the princes allowed to return.

32 The seventeenth century III: Hyojong, Sukchong; Kim Ch'angŏp

THE conduct of Korea's women during these trying times might well arrest our attention, though the only women seen abroad were of the dancing-girl and coolie classes. I recently read this of the former:[1]

> One of the noticeable features of Korean life is the dancing-girl. You see her in the street dressed in all her fluff and feathers, coloured like a bird in green and pink and yellow. She appears thus in all the colours of the rainbow, tipped with ermine edges: a picture for the eye to see, not often pretty in feature from the western point of view, but striking. She rides about in the best of rickshas with up-to-date pneumatic tyres, and holds her head up like a queen. It might seem to a foreigner that a woman who not only sells her gift of song and her grace of foot but her body as well, ought to hide her head, and be seen only lurking about hidden corners, or dodging here and there in the twilight. Not so the ki-saeng; she is as blithe a bird as ever hopped, with never a shadow across her easy-sitting conscience; happy in the role she is called upon to play, and feeling that she is a very important part of what the east calls 'society'. If we reckon her cultural ancestry according to the books and documents on hand, she is a thousand years old; and as far as physical ancestry is concerned, she probably comes down from some of the best families of the day in which her fathers lived.

Many noble deeds are told of the dancing-girl. One, specially known, comes from Chinju in the far south. The Hideyoshi invasion had pushed forward till, at last, Chinju fell. Non'gae, a dancing-girl of the place, the best-known of her group, prepared as for her wedding day. She stood on a high cliff, just beneath Rock Point Pavilion, Ch'oksŏng-nu, and awaited the conquerors. One officer, struck by her beauty, wished to approach, but, seeing how near she stood to the place of danger, withdrew. Another, of more dauntless spirit, named Ketani, came forward. She smiled to greet him. As he put out his arms toward her, suddenly, like a mountain tiger, she sprang upon him, gripped him fast, and with one bound went over the cliff where they both perished together. The other girls, seeing this, flung themselves after her, and so passed the famous group of kisaeng of Chinju. The spot is still marked today *Ŭirang-am,* 'The Rock of Faithful Women'. Recorded beneath it is an inscription which runs:

> *Eternal as the ever-flowing river,*
> *May the memory of her faithfulness never fade.*

One of Korea's commonest stories in that of the dancing-girl, telling how by dint of faithfulness she rises from a place of obscurity, yes, of shame, to become one of the first ladies of the land. In accord with this same spirit we find gentle women, too, ending their lives in the wild tides off Kanghwa, or hung by the neck from the rafter rather than suffer shame at the hands of the Manchu. One of these was the wife of Yun Sŏn'gŏ,[2] who no sooner heard that the enemy had crossed to the island than she slipped on the noose and swung, a lifeless body, in her softly embroidered room. Likewise was it with the second daughter of Wŏlsa, told of in the last chapter but one. She too was found dead in the rafter-room, determined that her life should end rather than that her name should be fouled. Her mother-in-law, wife of the famous minister, died at the same time from distress of soul over the sights she saw. I find this written of her:[3]

There was a wedding ceremony in the home of one of the royal princesses. Her son was to be married. The king commanded the wives of the ministers to be present. The ladies, delighted, came dressed in their very best. It was a great occasion; for silks and costly gems the like had never been seen. Last of all there came in by the gateway a humble two-man chair, from which an elderly matron stepped out, leaning on a staff. She was dressed in plainest garb, and yet made as though she would mount the steps into the gorgeous assembly. The princess in charge, suddenly noticing this, pushed everything aside and hurried down to meet her. The guests looked with wonder at the plainish old woman, questioning who she could possibly be; but the princess led her up, seated her in the highest place of honour, and treated her with the most exacting forms of ceremony. They were more mystified than ever to see that when the feast tables were brought in, one for each guest, the table of honour was placed before her. 'Thanks very much,' said she, 'but I shall have to go as my old man and my two sons, who have been busy all day, will be home shortly and I must see to their meals'. Then the assembled company recognized her as Kwŏn-ssi, the famous wife of Wŏlsa.

THIS IS A PERIOD of which Macaulay writes in his *History of England*. Great men like Walsingham and Burleigh were dead and gone, while a degenerate race of successors held their place. There was talent, but very little uprightness of soul to be seen. On his employment of the Duke of Marlborough a friend protested to the Prince of Orange, saying something like this; 'Don't you know, sir, that he is the biggest rascal that ever walked?' 'I am quite aware of it,' was the answer. 'Then why use him?' 'If', said King William, 'I am to use only honest men, where in this fair land of England shall I find them?' Something of a similar flavour marked the closing days of the seventeenth century in Korea. King Hyojong, who as Prince Pongnim had been tried in the miseries of the Namhan siege and found worthy, went as a willing hostage to Mukden to save the kingdom and his father's 'face'. There he uncomplainingly bore seven years of exile. He was a good scholar and wrote the classic style well. He also had a deep sense of religion. One of his recorded mottoes was made of two phrases, one from Mencius and one from the Book of Songs. The first read *Tangsŏk-punŭm*, 'Redeem every moment of your time';[4] and the second, *Taewŏl-sangje*, 'Live ever as in the presence of God.'[5]

When Prince Pongnim and his elder brother had been about to leave Peking for home in 1645, the emperor asked them what they would like to take as a souvenir. The Crown Prince replied, 'That beautiful inkstone, sir, from which you write.' 'Good,' said the emperor, 'you may have it.' He then asked the second prince what he would like, and he modestly replied, 'The gift of all my people who have been taken prisoner.' They were released and sent home. The king of Korea, Injo, on finding out about the gifts, said to the Crown Prince, 'Did you have the face to ask for an inkstone in such a day as this?' With that he caught it up and flung it at his son's head. Had it struck, it would have ended his days forever; as it was, a few months later the Crown Prince died, probably of distress of soul, leaving the succession to his brother who came to the throne in 1649, and is now known as Hyojong.

HYOJONG died at forty years of age and his son Hyŏnjong, eighteen, succeeded. The most notable event of his reign was a sharp controversy on the part of the government over hats and dress colours. Koreans have always worn white, as has been said before, but frequently orders were sent out to get them back into blue, blue being the colour of the east point of the compass, on which yard-arm Korea hung, and white the property of the west, where the unwashed, tousle-headed Tibetan lives. Blue it must be, and for twenty years, in accord with the order, the officials and literati dressed in blue; but, by and by, it fell back to white again, where it has remained as it is today.[6] Hats too, came in for review. Since 1649 they had been getting narrower in the brim and lower in the crown, till at last in 1660 an emphatic order went forth: 'Hat crowns shall be 9 inches high, with a diameter of 6 inches to sit on the head. The brim shall be 9 inches all the way round', thus making the diameter of the whole hat 24 inches, or 2 feet.[7] Very little space remained over when a scholar with a 2-foot hat bowed his head to enter the door. Hats too, were never taken off during a call, but kept rigidly on as a necessary mark of respect. Four gentlemen seated at a game of padŭk or backgammon would thus occupy sixteen square feet of room space.

IN 1674 King Hyŏnjong died and his little son of thirteen, Sukchong, came to the throne. He was to reign for forty-six years and to leave a considerable impress on the memory of his people. One historical note dated 1701 deserves mention. It had been the custom to exile medical officers who waited on royalty and failed to effect a cure. Sukchong's queen, Inhyon, fell ill and died. Her lingering complaint had outlasted two years, and now that the end had come the physician, Ch'oe Sŏngim, was arrested. The High Chief Justice and his associates were for sending Ch'oe to the ends of the earth, adrift on the open sea, where she might die at her leisure; but the king remonstrated saying, 'The ancients held that life and death are wrapped up in mystery, and that the days of even common mortals are in the hands of God. How much more those who share in kingship? Why should we put the fault of death upon the physician? How foolish! You men are supposed to be scholars. How you could have come to such an absurd conclusion is more than I can comprehend.' From this time on the royal physician drew a longer and freer breath.[8]

THESE were the times of Peter the Great and the rise of the Russian Bear. Peter, slaving like a coolie in the shipyards of England and Holland, would, in the eyes of the Korean, be the last man in the world to set up a kingdom that would stretch from the rising of Asia's sun to the setting thereof, but he did, and gradually swept into his comprehensive net the miscellaneous tribes of the unknown; Buryat, Kirghiz, Kalmuk, Samoyed, until his long arms swung down and touched Korea, marking off all the Russias — a weird, mad empire that was to end 200 years later in an unparalleled tragedy.

Korea and Russia have always had a distant speaking acquaintance only. A Korean girl-baby, cast away in the snows about the year 1875, was picked up by a Cossack guard and given to the governor's wife, who trained her in all the knowledge of St Petersburg, so that when the storm with Japan broke in 1903 she was governess to the little daughter of the Grand Duke Constantine. How she fared in the Great War is unknown.

IN GLANCING over the literary records of this period near the close of the seventeenth century and the opening of the eighteenth, I stumble upon a family of famous brothers surnamed Kim,[10] who dated their ancestry eighteen generations back, all carefully recorded, to a certain Kim Sŏnp'yŏng who flourished in 918 and helped Wang Kŏn to the throne of Songdo. The family had always been distinguished, so that in 1706 the eldest brother, Ch'angjip, was prime minister, and later, in the winter of 1712, was sent as envoy to the imperial court of Peking. He took with him as companion his fourth brother, Ch'angŏp, who recorded with great care his impressions along the way.[11] They bore with them the yearly tribute and Kim Ch'angŏp gives among other long lists of goods these as specially to be presented to the emperor:[12]

200 rolls of white grass-cloth
100 rolls of red silk
100 rolls of green silk
1,000 rolls of white cotton cloth
2,800 rolls of unbleached cotton cloth
2 grass mats with five-claw dragon pattern
20 grass mats in flower designs
100 deer skins
400 sable skins
300 black squirrel skins
10 swords
2,000 rolls of large-size white paper
3,000 rolls of small-size white paper
70 bags of glutinous rice
30 bags of white rice

As we follow Kim Ch'angŏp along the dusty trail through Manchuria we hear him say,[13]

All the way from Ŭiju to Peking is a world of sand, and, from Liao-tung on, the carts and horses are without number. The dust they raise is a cloud in the sky, finer than the finest haze. On the slightest wind the whole air is blinded with it, and those coming cannot see those going; while beyond Shan-hai-kwan it is total obscurity. Even on days when there is no wind, the air is impregnated with fine sand by the mere passing of the wheels of the carts and hoofs of the horses, so that people's clothes, hats, faces and eyes are covered thick. Your whole appearance is changed so that you look like another order of being; people cannot recognize each other. Though you attempt to wash it off your face and whiskers, it does not yield readily. Instead, it gets into the mouth, so that you can hear a gritting sound between the teeth. A basket may be wrapped in ten folds of paper, or a bottle have a double case over it, and yet the sand finds its way in. It is a mystery that I cannot fathom. In markets and houses, where goods and chattels are displayed, people have whisks made of feathers and keep up a constant round of dusting. To fail to do so would soon leave an inch of stive covering everything. Men water the streets of Peking in order to keep it down.

Kim tells of the wonderful sights of the imperial capital, and of how the great K'ang-hsi emperor went forth escorted by banner-bearers, horses and elephants.[14] K'ang-hsi, it seems, took a special interest in the books the Koreans had brought along. He asked most particularly for everything they had, and one secretary when questioned was indiscreet enough to say that Kim, the brother of the envoy, had kept a diary. 'Just the thing,' said the emperor. When this word was brought, Kim was struck dumb, for all through his blessed diary he had referred to the Manchu as *ho*, 'barbarians.' This would never do for the emperor to see, so he set to work and wrote the night through, preparing a new barebones diary that only said: 'Reached such and such a town, did so many miles, saw so and so, and slept' — a very dry affair which evidently awakened no comment whatever.[15]

Kim's visit to Peking is full of interest. The fact that he could write so well and that the classics were so familiar to him gave him entrance everywhere. He was treated as a distinguished guest. Shortly after their return home the state fell on evil days, called the *sinim sahwa,* the troubles of 1721–22. Sukchong died and his son Kyŏngjong came to the throne at thirty-eight years of age. He was defective in his physique, and this raised the question of posterity and the succession.[16] It was proposed by one party that he abdicate in favour of his brother, or at least appoint him Crown Prince. So great a disturbance was created over this that Kim Ch'angjip, who had journeyed so successfully to Peking, and three of his companions had to drink the hemlock draught and die. His faithful brother Ch'angŏp also, who wrote the diary, seeing his beloved chieftain fall, wasted away and accompanied him, not to Peking now, but to the eternal shades.

I jot down one or two more notes of Kim the scholar to show you something of his mind:

Peking: 21st day. Weather fine. Light wind. Very warm. After breakfast Kang Uyang brought in a man who was skilled in removing wax from the ears, and I had him try mine. Truly he could go to the very depths, clear out everything, and never hurt you in the least. He had six or seven instruments all of which were fitted to the shape of the ear, with hooks and spoons at the end. He had also a kind of pincers for extracting the wax. The other instruments I cannot describe fully. One was like a tiny brush with a horn handle. This he used to clean the ear perfectly after the wax had been removed. He charged five cash each for every man's ears he cleared. He could barber well too, could clean the feet and finger- and toe-nails. All his various instruments he carried in a box that he strapped to his back. Thus he was ready for whatever he was called upon to do. He would put his box on the ground and have his patient sit upon it while he leaned forward and did the work. He did not seem in the least ashamed of his calling, though it was surely the most contemptible of all professions.[17]

Peking: 1st moon 4th day. Not cold. Cloudy toward evening. Today a friend sent me a pot of narcissus flowers, a dozen or more stalks, all out in the richest bloom. These flowers are as large in the face as a peach blossom, the soft white petals being most delicate and beautiful to behold. I had bought a number of them before, but they had failed me and never bloomed. Now I see them at their best and am delighted.[18]

Peking: 19th day. Fine weather. Fresh wind. The traffic on the main street was so congested with carts, horses, and passers-by that it was exceedingly difficult to push one's way along. One of our horse-attendants, who had his animal loaded with water buckets, was not paying strict attention as he walked, and his horse kicked over a hot-food vendor's stand. The Chinaman gathered up his dishes and wares, but said not a single word. I was so chagrined that I wanted to give the groom a blow with my stick, but the Chinese on each side stopped me, and would not let me do it.[19]

THESE WERE the days of the South Sea Bubble when the whole world of London went wild in the hope of getting rich out of nothing. In the end they were overwhelmed with loss inexpressible, poverty, misery, suicide. About the same time Alexander Selkirk, the original of Robinson Crusoe, equally wretched, found himself sitting alone on the deserted island of Juan Fernandez, listening by day 'to the bleating of the shoals of seals along the shore' and by night to the wild 'howlings and whistlings of the spirits in the air'. In spite of an occasional political set-to, which ended in a Socratic drink of hemlock, Korea seems to have been as peaceful and comfortable a part of the earth as any there was. America was fighting the Red Indians, France was all of a turmoil over the Spanish succession, Spain was down and out. Two doughty chieftains of the north, Peter the Great of Russia and Charles XII of Sweden, were at it hammer and tongs. What a mass of tumult, during all of which time a young Korean prince of the royal family, seeing the troubled world, looked on.[20] He was seventeen when the Kims died. Like St Benedict, he hastened away to escape the evil, and withdrew to a quiet retreat of the buddha. He finally became a great priest called Sŏlp'a whose memorial stone stands today in the south, not far from Chŏngŭp. In the quiet of the Yŏngwŏn Temple nearby he learned the sacred books by heart, saying a thousand times a day to the beads of his rosary, *Namu Amit'abul, Namu Amit'abul,* 'I put my trust in buddha, I put my trust in buddha'. Thus he passed on peacefully to the great beyond in the very year when Louis XVI, king of France, endeavouring to escape from his unhappy country, was captured at Varennes and brought back to die. Louis and Snowy Hill (Sŏlp'a) were both royal princes. How blessed the one, how miserable the other!

33 The eighteenth century I:
Yŏngjo; folk festivals; the 'Coffin King'

WE come now to the longest reign in Korean history, the reign of king Yŏngjo[1] from 1725 to 1776, exceeded in English history only by George III and Queen Victoria. Yŏngjo was thirty years old when his father died, so we see he lived to be an old man, very grim we are told, not unlike the Frenchman Clemenceau, much of the tiger in him. Could he have cast his eyes round the world he would have seen a goodly company of occidentals on the other side keeping step with him along his way: Captain Cook, Voltaire, Rousseau, Samuel Johnson, Benjamin Franklin, Frederick the Great, Tobias Smollett, George Whitefield, Handel. Few indeed were the opportunities for the east and west to meet in those days. Unknown seas lay between.

THROUGH this long reign the affairs of state moved with a regularity of custom thoroughly Korean, and left but little in the way of event or happening to take note of.

The seasons in their round, of course, make great occasion of the lunar New Year (*sŏllal*). It can fall any time between 21 January and 20 February but, early or late, it is a joy-ride for the whole nation. Sacrifices are offered to the ancestors; salutations are made to the district fathers; while its beauty of dress, fabric and colour, tell all the world how the women's kingdom rejoices.

The 14th, when the first moon of the year is at the full, is the great night (*taeborum*). Under the rounded moon, health, hope, and happiness are compounded by all the fortune-tellers of the land. Straw mannikins (*cheung*) tossed beside the way and carried off by beggars, take with them the evils, ills, and ailments of the family. The kite flown in the silver sky has written on its face the bad luck of the flyer. When it reaches its full length of string, it is cut and left to float away into the limitless blue carrying the worries with it.

One of the common salutations on the 15th is, 'I say, Jack!' 'Yes!' 'Buy my heat-stroke.' If Jack had not answered Yes, he might have escaped, but the word Yes pins him.[2] A call for good luck is everywhere in the air, from the crown of the head to the sole of the foot, and from the outer cuticle of the skin to the innermost weavements of the soul, good luck, great fortune. Stone-fighting, drum-beating, *yut*-throwing,[3] all mean sweetness and light for the coming round of the sun.

On the 6th day of the 2nd moon the Pleiades are looked at to see if they are before the moon or behind it (*chŏmsaengi pogi*). From the position they occupy, people judge as to the coming season's poverty or plenty. The moon is the rice-mother and the Pleiades are her children. If the children are hungry and are seen running in haste to catch the moon, it will be a year of want. If on the other hand they are satisfied and are jogging sweetly along with the moon behind them, it means a year of plenty.

On the 3rd of the 3rd moon, cakes (*hwajŏn*) are made with azalea flowers on them, first offered to the ancestral spirits, and then partaken of by the family.

The 8th of the 4th moon is the Feast of Lanterns, the birth of the buddha, the night of all belighted nights (*ch'op'ail*). Great poles are erected from which hang many shapes of lantern: drum-shape, bell-shape, gourd-shape, fish-shape. They are lighted, but the smoke of the kitchen fires and the dust of the multitudinous feet dims much of their glow. In every home the flame of the lantern is watched with eager eye: the brighter it shines the better the luck; the lower it burns, the less will be the joy.

The 5th day of the 5th moon (*tano*) is the day of swings. From every high-limbed tree ropes are hanging and, as joy gathers strength, up and down the brightly coloured swingers go. On this day also offerings of cherries are made at the family shrine.

In the 6th moon fall the dog days (*pogil*), when dog soup and red-bean porridge are eaten, not so much for food as for a medicine against the baleful heat. Every kind of flesh has its medicinal value in the east, from the flesh of the dog to that of the snake, the scorpion and the centipede. 3,000 years of experimenting has told the orient in unmistakable terms that these values are real. If we of the west are just beginning to find certain animal secretions of immense value, who am I with my meagre years to say Nay to the hoary east?

On the 7th night of the 7th moon (*ch'ilsŏk*) all China, all Japan, all Korea, gaze heavenward. This is the night when the fluttering magpies make a bridge over the Milky Way, across which the Herdboy hastens to meet his sweetheart, the Weaving Damsel. Only one night in all the year are they permitted to meet. Across the softly matted bow that spans the sky they step. How it comes let those explain who know, but the next day the neck feathers of the magpie are hopelessly awry, and for a whole month afterwards he looks as though he had been trampled upon ruthlessly by all the caravans of the night.

The 15th day of the 8th moon (*ch'usŏk*) is Harvest Home. It may fall on any date between 4 September and 4 October, according to the swing of the sun, but it is the great day of sacrifice to the ancestors and of rejoicing for the harvest. Tables are spread before the graves and the spirits are bowed to.

On the 9th day of the 9th moon (*chungyang*) again a sacrifice is offered, when chrysanthemum wine is mingled with the cakes and wafers. The 5th of the 10th moon too, is the Home Day (*hyangsan-je*) when an offering is made to the spirit of the house, with a request for added safety to the family line.

The winter solstice month (*tongjit-tal*) watches the sun drop to its lowest point, and then, as by a great effort, helps to lift it backward on its return journey. Red bean porridge is offered to the spirits, and some of it is tossed outside the gate as good luck against disease. Thus in Korea there are two New Years, one of the sun, and the other of the moon. As the moon has ever held in the minds of the people a tender place of deep regard far beyond the sun, so the New Year of the moon is the season of all seasons. Long before the christian era the east made the winter solstice its new year, but the great Han kingdom broke away from this dark forbidding season, to make the New Year accord more nearly with the smiling return of spring.[4]

These are a few among many days on which the ancestors are specially remembered, for to the Korean the main thought of any holiday is a visit to the ancestral graves and a spread of food for the revered shades of the fathers.

WE SEE how great a part religion played in the affairs of the Korean people. How evident this is, too, in any diary or book of travel notes. About this same time, in 1719, an embassy started on its way to Japan with compliments to the Shogun. It had reached Pusan, and there, before venturing out into the uncertainties of the deep, it proposed a religious service with prayers to God that He would grant a safe and prosperous journey. Those who had charge of the ceremony took a special oath, swearing as follows:[5]

> We, a company of six boats on our way across the sea, ask the blessing of the Great Spirit. For two days we have purified ourselves and for one day fasted and prayed; we have cut off wine, smoked no tobacco, have partaken of no strong food such as onions or garlic, have heard no music, have shared no feasts, have engaged in no foolish talk, have taken no part in services of the dead, have visited no sick, but have lived day and night in all reverence, and thus we approach the service.

If any one of our company swear falsely may his sins be exposed to the light of day.

Thus they prepared their hearts, and made their prayer to the Great Spirit who rules the sea.

The Korean scholar has always been a verse writer. Along his way he drops his softly limned couplets to express his heart or record the doings of the day. The Great Spirit had safely conveyed the fleet across the straits, and Sin Yuhan, who saw himself in Japan for the first time, wrote:

This night I could not sleep for some reason or other, so I wrote a verse or two to while away the time:

> With flags and banners o'er the deep blue sea,
> We sailed into the port at eventide.
> Beyond the clouds lie ancient Silla's state,
> While all around lift high Yamato's hills.
> Dear thoughts of home come crowding on apace,
> And valiant verse steps proudly through the soul.
> The waning moon hangs by the hawser's line;
> I laugh to drink Japan's most honoured health.

THUS THE KOREAN'S ROUND of the years took its course through the eighteenth century, unconscious of *The Heart of Midlothian, Redgauntlet,* or *Guy Mannering* whose dauntless deeds were being chronicled beyond the horizon's rim.

Yŏngjo, though he reigned long and peacefully, had his troubles. Apart from his two wives, he had a specially beloved concubine who, though very dear and faithful, brought him his heaviest weight of woe. At the entrance to the grounds of the Yŏnhŭi College stands her memorial stone, with an inscription on it composed by the king's own hand. It reads:[7]

On the 26th day of the 7th moon in the year *kapsin* (1764) she left me and took her long departure. For thirty-eight years we had journeyed together and now it is all a dream. Who knows what life means? Her nature was most gentle and loving, and she devoted her soul to me without reserve. In the troubles of *imo* (1762) it was really she who saved the state. This is not overpraise, for she truly deserves it, as I can fully testify. She lived three years more, saw the sacrifices to her son completed, and the next month passed away. Alas! For three days I remained by her failing form. In the evening, when she died, I had her remains carried to her own home in Chŏng-dong, and there performed the ceremony of wrapping her in her coffin. On the last day of the 8th moon I wrote this inscription and got some relief from my sorrow. On the 27th of the 9th moon we buried her here by the Yŏnhŭi Palace in a tomb that faces a little west of south.

This looks like a very loving tribute of the old king to his dearest companion. Her name was Yŏngbin, 'Bright Princess', and in 1734 she bore him a son, Prince Changhŏn. He was a great athlete, full of new and daring notions. One of these was to beat off China and make Korea independent. Another rumoured plan was to get rid of his old father and rule a new kingdom in a new way. The old king, who was no more inclined to let his will be thwarted than was King Saul of Israel, looked into the matter, spoke his condemnation, and issued orders for his son's death. A glass of poisonous hemlock seems to have been given, but — a most unusual thing — the son refused to drink. The order then went forth to nail him up in a coffin. Long spikes were driven in and his cries were heard for days from the inner regions of the horrible box. Grass was piled upon it to deaden the sound, while Bright Princess looked on at the tragedy of her only son. Her ten-year-old grandchild, his own little heir, later called King Chŏngjo, wept to hear the last cries of his father, who was ever after known as 'Coffin King', *Twiju Taewang*.[8]

The conscience of Korea fully justified the old king in what he had done: for a son to rise against his father is the blackest crime imaginable.

MANY noteworthy statesmen and scholars cross the eighteenth century. Two of these we select as fairly representative of the mind of the Korean people: An Chŏngbok (1712–1791) and Hong Yangho (1724–1802). An was twelve years older than Hong, but they were men of like mind, both scholars of the old school.[9] Hong rose to be what is called Taejehak, Secretary of State; he went also as special envoy to China and was in every respect a man of the world. He lived to be seventy-eight. An lived to be seventy-nine and was a religious man of great renown. He took no examinations and never sought office, but was called upon at times by the king out of regard for his great learning and sincere heart. These two speak the sentiments of their day very interestingly. They were gentlemen of true refinement, both of whom would have regarded Laurence Sterne and Tobias Smollett as very vulgar individuals, yes, and Henry Fielding too. They would be ashamed to face the world had they written some of the pages of *Tristram Shandy,* and they would no more have kept company with Peregrine Pickle, or Count Fathom, than they would with an unwashed, evil-smelling, Mongol cameldriver.

Each left volumes of his collected works. From Hong's I select two or three poems.[10]

Autumn

My horse treads fallen twigs along the way,
And step by step awakes the sounds of autumn.
Wind whips the leaves and whirls them o'er the hill,
And, roaring, calls the echoes from the clouds.

Our meeting

Athwart the bridge the shadow of a priest—
I ask him, 'Whither off among the hills?'

Slow the soft-stepping staff makes no reply,
But lifted, points me to the clouds.[11]

His eldest son had died and he visited the grave. We read through the following lines an oriental's deep sorrow:[12]

Since you are dead
Twice have the hills been brown and sere;
The bitter frosts have veiled your eyes,
And saddened winds have chilled my soul.
But what's my soul, for I am dead,
And strength has left me bare;
The days and months go fleeting by,
Earth and heaven stretch to infinity.

Your little lad has learned to speak,
But he knows only 'mother' and 'grandpapa';
So busy is he at his letters,
Yet I cannot teach him the word for 'father'.
When he grows up and asks me what it means,
What shall I tell him?
His little voice sounds more and more like yours;
This ought to be a comfort to me.

Your grave rests on the hillside
That overlooks the stream;
'Twas here you begged me, years ago, to build.
The house still stands, but you are absent.
Alone in my old age am I;
You doubtless have a place of rest.
But my thoughts of you are ever restless.

Now I am off on a thousand-mile journey
Where the blue sea murmurs.
Your brothers have come to say farewell
And all the neighbours;
Drink and refreshments abound,
But I have no heart to taste.
I long to go to your grave and weep,
But fear lest I make your soul feel sad.

I was so happy when you were young, and loved
To write the character and compose verses.
What I dictated you wrote
And marked my couplets for me;
But now that you are dead,

I have no heart for verse.
I compose this as a last farewell,
But who is there to write it down?

An Chŏngbok, who was, as I have said, a religious man, was greatly exercised over the arrival of christianity. Books had been brought from Peking, a great number of them:[13]

In the years *kimyo* (1603) and *kapchin* (1604) christianity became popular with a certain class of young men who contended for it, saying that God had come down to earth and had given commands through his angels. Alas, in a single day how greatly their hearts had been changed, and turned away from the writings of the Sages. It is like the boy who graduates from the classroom and then comes home to call his mother by her first name, a sad story indeed.

Let me give herewith my opinion as to what is written in these books. One called *Truths About God*[14] by Matteo Ricci says, 'In the 2nd year of the Emperor Yüan-shou (1 BC), on the third day after winter solstice, God made choice of a virgin, and by means of birth came and dwelt among men, his name being Jesus. Now the name Jesus means 'saviour'. He taught his disciples for thirty-three years on the western frontier of Asia, and then ascended up to heaven.'

But I would ask: has the worship of God not been known to us in the Far East from the earliest ages? It certainly has, for the Book of History says, 'God gave man his conscience which, if he preserve it clear and undefiled, will find him the way of peace'. The Book of Songs, too, says, 'King Wen safeguarded his heart and so served God acceptably.' Again it says, 'In fear of the majesty of God one can preserve one's faith under all circumstances'. . . . Mencius says, 'To set one's energies to the training of the heart, this is the service of God'.[15]

By these quotations An Chŏngbok would make it clear that the Far East has never been without the knowledge of God. He praises the western missionary for his abstemious life and surpassing knowledge, especially of astronomy and the use of gunpowder. Still he thinks that western countries are like the extremities of the great body of creation, while China, the Middle Kingdom, is the true heart and lungs from which the real saints should spring. He goes on to say that there had been other missionaries before these christians, who had taught much the same. For example there was Mo-tzŭ (450 BC), who wrote a book called *The Hidden Will of God* (*T'ien-pi-p'ien*), in which he says,[16] 'Those who follow the will of God, know only love for all mankind, and seek by love to benefit others . . . Doing so', says he, 'they will find their reward; but men who run counter to God's will hate each other, and in their friendship seek only selfish gain. Unquestionably they will be punished.'

An Chŏngbok labours to prove that nothing new comes to them from the missionary except his scientific knowledge. One feels great sympathy for the east fighting for the best she has, namely the teaching of the sages, a teaching that had held society safe and in comparative peace through a longer succession of ages t han any other part of the earth has ever known. No wonder An Chŏng-bok bristles a bit in view of the dogmatic west that too often speaks with gleaming steel and cannon roar. What he says is undoubtedly true: there were real saints in the east before the days of the christian missionary.

34 The eighteenth century II: Yŏngjo; memorial stones

IN these uneventful days of the Georges (1714–1830), Korea seems to have lived a very even life. Happy? Not entirely so, but as much, on the whole, as most countries. Her standing in comparison with other states, her attainments in the superior ways of civilization are more or less reflected in a composition by Hong Yangho of whom we spoke in the last chapter. True there were contests of political parties more or less vehement, and at times there were jealousies, bickerings, spites, and bloody revenges. In one of these Hong was banished to the far north. It was there that he wrote this essay in the form of a poetical composition:[1]

> *Letting go the wild geese*
> In the late autumn of the year *chŏngyu* (1777), a farmer from the Tumen River caught two wild geese, cut their wings and brought them to me. They were kept in the courtyard, where the steward looked after them. One day he came to me and said, 'These birds, sir, are better-flavoured than pheasant. I advise your Excellency to kill and eat them.' 'God forbid,' said I. 'Wonderful birds such as these were never intended for slaughter. Have not you noticed that when they fly they observe the strictest order (*ye*); when they mate, they are true to another, righteous (*ŭi*); in their migrations they follow the warmth of the sun, wise (*chi*); and though they go far afield you can always depend upon their sure return, trustworthy (*sin*); they never make war on other creatures with bill or claw, they love (*in*). Only mere birds with feathers, and yet they possess all the Five Virtues—*in, ŭi, ye, chi, sin*. They are mentioned in the classics; their note is accounted a song; the *Li chi*, Book of Rites, talks of them. They are present on wedding occasions, and are carried along as good luck for the happy bride and bridegroom. Kill them? Never!'
>
> I therefore fed them every day, gave them water to drink, fixed them a shelter to keep out the cold, shut them up at night from foxes and rats, and let a moon and more go by till their wings were grown. Then I took them to the peak near by and let them fly off with this message:

> Now don't go North
> Where larchwoods moan, and hairy beasts go by,
> Where roaring speeds the Amur on its way,
> Ice piled aloft stands high in horny heaps,
> And bearded men slink by with green-grey eyes,

Men who have claws and teeth like tiger's fangs.
The bow they twang; and the far-hurtling spear,
Swift from the hand, drives straight its barbet home.
If you go there you're dead, and that's the end.

Nor yet go South,
Where fiery dust breaks on the smothery air,
With boiling waters seething everywhere;
Where snakes with venom fill the empty void,
And spin tail-tipped with tongues like forks protruding;
Hills all asmoke and rocks red with the sun,
With rays that pierce and flames that blind the eye.
If you go there, your quills are burned away.

Nor go you East. Cross not the sea;
For wild waves mount and echoing roar their will,
Great whales appear that swallow down the ship,
And glancing sea-snakes spring upon you whole.
Black, too, the women's teeth, tattoed the men,
Equipped with cunning and a practised hand
That wields the gun, and waits the deadly aim:
A thunder-clap, a fiery flash, 'tis all.
Avoid it on your life, go nowhere there,
Where bones and joints are ground to powder small.

Avoid the West—the treacherous Yalu's stream,
For there the great unwashed barbarian hides,
With wild disordered speech and half-hung hair;
A dirk at belt and arrows on his arm,
He hunts for flesh to stuff his ravenous maw.
He loves the fishy smell and rancid hide,
Long pheasant tails he swings upon his spear,
And every feathery thing he takes with guile.
If you go there, a wandering ghost you'll be.

But here's the place for you, in this green land
Of ours where first the sun alights, safeguarded
By the stars and sheltered by the sky.
Here on our hills with all their circling streams,
So cool and yet not cold, with endless miles
Of fertile soil—rice too, and beans to spare.
The children of the sages, we: how wide
And far-extended is our favour. No chicks are killed,
Or egglings stolen away; abundance rules.
Go nowhere; find your place within this land.
Bring wife and weans and all your kindred dear,

> Dance 'neath the clouds and sing out to the moon,
> Dine off the reeds: but guard the passing spear,
> Take note and lend an eye: avoid the net.
> With springs that go and winters that return,
> Live out your life in peace.
>
> Again I say, spread wide your wings and ride
> Between the clouds, cross o'er the Mach'ŏn Pass,
> The long straight route to Iron Hill; still on
> Unto the peaks that guard the fair spot, Seoul.
> Dance your glad joy to his high grace the king
> And step your welcome home. Trim off
> Your morning quills within the palace park,
> Then light and play and dip upon the Han.
> Sing out clear notes to please his royal ear,
> Tell his Majesty how I am an exile
> Grown grizzly grey, but that my heart is true.
> True, yes, as ever.

Here we behold Hong's high estimate of his own country, an estimate made in the days when the wild goose might have sought long to find as peaceful a spot in England.

DURING these quiet years we behold the state erecting memorial stones to mark great events, great people, great ideals that His Majesty hoped would never be forgotten. I note first a stone set up before Anju, a city of the north, a stone intended to comfort and quiet the spirits of the restless dead.[2] Nearly half a million Chinese had died before Anju in AD 261, inveigled into a terrible net by the Korean general, Ŭlchi Mundŏk. The writer says how many the world over have died this violent death, filling the universe and all space with their unhappy wailings; spirits everywhere calling out their resentments, unappeased. Hence this service known as *suryukche,* or 'water and land sacrifice', was offered for their comfort.

The late Dr T. J. Hudson, of Washington DC, an authority on psychic matters, says[3], 'The resentful soul will remain nightly rehearsing its tragedy for days and months and years until someone with nerves strong enough demands to know the object of its quest. When this is done and the information given, the phantom will fade away forever.' So the king of Korea, having this very thought in mind, was anxious to give rest to these troubled shades that elude the common eye and yet are known and talked of by all men. The stone was set up in 1731, and still stands, reminding Korea that she has a duty to the dead as well as to the living.

ANOTHER stone, erected in 1728 at Haeju, recalls one of the famous stories of the east, almost as famous as that of the Magpie Bridge and the Via Lactea Damsel.[4] Po I and Shu Ch'i, two brothers in the far-off days of Samuel the prophet, each so humbled himself before the other that both have lived forever. The elder was Po I, the younger was Shu Ch'i. Both were princes, sons of the king, but the father loved his Jacob better than his Esau and gave him the throne; Jacob said, 'I shall never deprive my brother Esau.' Esau replied, 'I shall never accept a throne contrary to my father's wishes.' Here the matter hung, each fully determined. No yielding possible, they finally both gave way, locked arms and retired into the Shou-yang Mountains of Shensi where the world lost sight of them forever. Near Haeju, Korea, are hills also called Suyang (i.e. Shou-yang) and the names of Po I and Shu Ch'i have been associated with them as well. If you raise a question as to Po I and Shu Ch'i ever having been here in Korea in 1100 BC, the ordinary citizen of Haeju will bristle up and treat you to a volume of proofs that will silence you forever.

These two famous ones belong to the same class as Hsü Yu, who lived two thousand and more years before Christ. So good he was that the king, the great Yao, offered to resign the throne in his favour. Hsü shuddered at the thought and the remembrance of it so worked upon him that he washed his ears to clear his soul of the hateful sound. Korea lived on these stories for ages, counting them pure gold: 'Seek not, give up everything, resign sense and soul, count all as nothing, and nothing as all.' Hence the raising of this stone to the memory of Po I and Shu Ch'i nearly three thousand years after they had left the world. 'Forget them not', was the old king's exhortation and the stone still stands in this year 1927 for all who can read it.

ANOTHER stone, erected at Taegu in 1737, tells of the building of the walls of that southern city.[5] These walls were late in being built, and they soon vanished from the scene, for they are entirely gone today. On Tuesday 31 December 1889, however, they were standing, for the writer on that day visited the place. The gates were closed against him till a special permit came from the governor permitting him to enter. Crowds gathered in the streets to see the stranger go by, and only with difficulty could he extricate himself from the multitudinous mêlée that pressed upon him in the public square. Gradually they grew quieter and finally withdrew. Next morning with his Korean companion he made a round of the walls as one views Peking from the height of the Ch'ien-men. They looked down into many a busy courtyard and were in places dangerously near peering into the women's quarters; but these walls are gone today like a dream, for where they stood is now a wide road along which motor-cars speed by with honk and dust and evil odour.

IN 1740 King Yŏngjo erected a stone in Songdo to the memory of Confucius's father.[6] 'That we have not dropped to the level of the beasts; said he, 'is indeed his merit — Confucius, or rather, Confucius's father.' So this stone was set up in the year when Frederick the Great came to the throne and when Europe entered upon one of its most devastating wars. How quiet in comparison were the halls of Songdo in which the teacher discoursed on the merits of the Great Master. Linking Confucius with his father helped also to keep alive that vital relationship on which Korean civilization hung: filial devotion. Confucius himself, and all his great disciples, Yen Hui, Tseng Ts'an and others, have receded into the shadows; Yŏngjo, seeing how vital their teaching was to the existence of the state, had the stone set up to remind the people whence their felicity came.

IN AN OBSCURE corner of the far south called Tasan-ni, accompanied by a memorial stone that was set up in 1766,[7] is a shrine called Samgang-myo, the 'Shrine of the Three Virtues': state loyalty, filial piety, wifely devotion. They pertained to the home of a noble gentleman named Yi Hŭiryong, whose memory King Yŏngjo specially lauded as a model for all his people. Yi himself was a good horseman and fought in the war of 1592. Hearing that the king had made his escape to Ŭiju, he set out at once to offer his services but fell in with the enemy at Ch'ungju and died for king and country in the defeat that Korea suffered there. Thus was the virtue of loyalty demonstrated, remembered and carved on stone by King Yŏngjo nearly two hundred years later.

When the son heard that his father was dead he set out to recover his body and give him honourable burial, but in the search he met the enemy and in the fight he also was killed. This was the filial piety that King Yŏngjo wished his people to take note of and emulate.

The young wife, learning that her husband was dead, set out likewise in search of his dear remains. These were days when honourable young women did not show themselves abroad without a loss of name and place, but what was place or name to her when her dear one was lying dead? Love was stronger than death. She sought for three months, and failing, came home, called her servants and said, 'My father died for the king, my husband died for his father, I shall die for my husband. When I am dead let a suit of his clothing be my winding sheet and so bury me.' With this quiet leave-taking she disappeared and was found later hanging from the rafter beam. 'Take note of her,' said the king, 'and let all good wives so honour their husbands. I write on stone this story of devotion that future generations may never forget its meaning.' So the shrine is called the House of the Three Virtues.

THESE WERE the days of George Washington, who was now thirty-four years of age, deeply engrossed over resolutions against the Stamp Act, and meditating with his friend Patrick Henry certain actions to be taken in opposition to George III. George III's was a long reign of fifty-nine years, filled with wars with France; fightings with the red man, Pontiac; bickerings with colonists; Bunker Hills and Benningtons. Much happier were Yŏngjo's years of rule, and quite as enlightened. We think of the oriental as under the iron heel of despotism, whereas the truth is he was usually very content and in most cases left happily alone. Our ideal of government is a noisy democracy; his, a wise and good ruler. If one but take the trouble to read and compare history carefully, the conclusion will undoubtedly be that on the whole his is much the better choice. Tyrants sometimes he has had, but single ones; we have had tyrants, swarms of them. Aristotle knew well what he was talking about when he said, 'democracy is the acme of tyranny.'[8]

King Yŏngjo died in the famous year 1776 at the age of eighty-one and was buried in a beautiful spot on the wooded hills ten miles east of Seoul.[9] The whistle of birds, the ripple of water, the murmur of the wind through the pines, the endless colour of the flowery pageant that moves before his grave make it a charming spot. Unbroken quiet with the soft suggestion of life still about, so gentle, so perfect, so unmarred by man's brutalities—a world indeed where the fairies dwell! Here sleeps Yŏngjo after his long years of joy and sorrow.

What religion did the king have to comfort his soul? Let me quote in answer from Hong Manjong, who wrote:[10]

> There are three religions in the world: confucianism, taoism, and buddhism. Now confucianism makes love and righteousness its basis. By a life of virtue it aids others to virtue, and by keeping the Five Commands makes peace the universal law, so that even birds, beasts and insects are blessed thereby. When one's appointed days are numbered one is called to another world, submissive always to the will of God. This is confucianism.
>
> Taoism has to do with purity and by means of water and fire lifts its subject to a place of refinement where the spirit sloughs off its outer shell and guards only the essence; so that one may journey freely outside the body, drinking the dew of the morning and the glow of the evening sky; absorbing the light of the sun and the soft radiance of the moon; looking on the world as but a passing phase of the day, and all the ages gone by as but the breaking of the morning; living in the world, and yet not of the world. This is taoism.
>
> Buddhism dwells in the regions of silence where wisdom is reckoned mother, gentleness father, joy one's wife, love and tenderness one's son and daughter. With all sensations of the mind and body cast aside as worthless, and zero as the object of attainment, it moves by meditation through the immensities of space with nothing to trammel the soul, leaving its transmigrations far behind, hell and terror forgotten forever. It grows brighter and clearer in mind as the body decays, and increases in strength and vigour as the eternal ages go by. This is buddhism.

King Yŏngjo knew all these, but just what his inner thoughts regarding them were, we may never know.

35 The eighteenth–nineteenth centuries: Chŏngjo, Sunjo; Roman catholicism; Hong Kyŏngnae

CHŎNGJO,[1] grandson of the old king, came to the throne in 1776 when he was twenty-four years of age. Doubtless his day of state honour was saddened by the memory of his father's death and the inexorable box that held him in its gruesome grip. Still Chŏngjo showed no signs of weakness and came on in a stately manner to his own — a true gentleman and scholar. In fact his erudition was renowned the whole oriental world over. More than a hundred volumes remain from his own pen: poems, biographies, prayers, words of warning, letters, answers to petitions, recorded judgments, essays, inscriptions, congratulations, commentaries on the classics, notes on buddhism, dictionaries of classical terms, stories of the great and good, compilations of state laws, and more.[2]

But to return to his year of coronation; Napoleon and Wellington were little boys of seven then, and while Chŏngjo as a boy amused himself with book, inkstone and writing-brush, Napoleon found his delight in a little brass cannon that he planted on the sea-shore among the rocks of Corsica. Wellington, a little lad of seven, was on his way to England to the home of his fathers, happy with a shilling in his pocket that a friend had given him. Too widely sundered were they for King Chŏngjo ever to know anything of them and yet in this chapter, for the first time, we see some points of contact open where each looked distantly at the other with a doubtful and questioning eye.

King Chŏngjo was the companion of his mother, who was of the same clan as Hong Yangho the poet and statesman. She was only eighteen when her distinguished son was born. How happy! Chŏngjo's one great desire was to please his mother. Among other things, in 1794 he planned a great celebration in her honour and wrote,[3]

> Next year, *ŭlmyo* (1795), will mark my mother's years as sixty, the twentieth of my reign. How can I express my gratitude for the blessings of Heaven that are mine? What God has given me would take more than one year of time to tell, for all my life has been filled with proofs of His kindly favour. I therefore command a celebration this year and next. Let the assembled officers of state go to my mother's palace on the 1st day of the 1st moon and sing their congratulations. In order also that the whole country may share in the joy, I order every official of seventy years and more to be present, and all people over eighty, and all such old couples as have spent their lives together. I shall have those over a hundred ennobled with the title *sungjŏng taebu,* 'Excellency'; all married couples of seventy and over given rice and materials for wear; officers of whatever degree advanced in rank; and old men of eighty honoured by the king.

Were so many aged feet ever seen on the highway before in any land? 75,145 all happy as the miles were long! The king added:[4]

> I wonder if the old people of the Chou kingdom when assembled made such a concourse as this? A happy year indeed! If our house had not been one of good deeds and beneficent action how could I have come to such a day as this?

As mentioned in the state records, there were present on this occasion fifty-eight persons over 100 years of age. Two, the oldest, were 108. People of the west sometimes lose count of their age and are not sure of their year and day of birth, but it is not so in the east. The exact year, month, day, and hour of birth are the four pillars on which hang life's good fortune, and are known to the poorest in the land, so that age records are not open to doubt or question.

What a delight it must have been to the Dowager Queen to look from her apartments upon these happy hearts and faces. Was such an assembly of music and dancing ever seen or known outside fabled Arcadia? While the slow graceful swing of the dancer was the delight of all hearts, higher still and more keenly appreciated were the contests with the writing brush: the rhyme character, the measured foot, the balanced phrase, the soft running rhythm, the pictures called up to the mind which really constituted Korea's most thrilling exercise. As the king was a master-hand himself, I can imagine his lively soul suggesting this subject and that to be done in four lines of seven characters each. Here is one of the king's own. No translation can bring out the finished features of the Chinese, or its expression. The thought, the order, the feeling alone are barely possible:[5]

The sun
The sun's round face a-blazing bright
Spans all the world with kingly rule;
No one can fly his searching light,
So fair, so wondrous wide, so cruel.

Another by King Chŏngjo:[6]

The Great Bell
Here sits the Time Tower high aloft
That guards a monster in his pride,
A bell wrought of ten thousand tons,
That rings at dawn and eventide.
Ye toilers of the dusty day,
You rest and rise as rings the bell,
For while at e'en it says: 'Asleep',
With waking morn it booms: 'All well!'

WE TURN AWAY from this happy picture to a scene of great sadness, a scene overshadowed by misunderstanding and suspicion. These were the days when Korea first came in touch with the foreigner. In 1776 Yi Sŭnghun, a gentleman of P'yŏngt'aek, met Jesuit priests in Peking and brought home with him news of christianity. One of the first to embrace its teachings was a famous scholar Chŏng Yagyong (1762–1836), author of many books, whose brother Yakchong (Augustine) died a martyr in 1801. As yet no foreign priest had reached Seoul and for thirty years still the converts were left alone to meet the brunt of all the powers of persecution.

Recovered from state documents piled up for more than a century was a letter of a certain Alexander Hwang Sayŏng, done on silk, beautifully written, about 24 inches long and 16 wide, having on its face 13,000 characters. It was a letter to the Bishop of Peking asking for help for the Church of Korea, not financial help, but spiritual oversight and counsel. This letter begins:[7]

We sinners, Thomas and others (Thomas was the messenger), in tears

address you, our venerable Bishop. Our sins so heavy on the one hand
that we have drawn down upon us the anger of the Lord; and our
wisdom on the other so poor that we have lost the sympathy of men!
A great persecution has broken out, a calamity that has taken in as well
our spiritual father. (This was the Chinese, Father James Chou, executed
31 May 1801.) With what face can we who have not known how to
meet danger and give our lives, as he, for the Lord, dip our brush and
forward to you these complaints?

This famous document never reached Peking but was intercepted and Thomas,
the messenger, as well as Alexander Hwang, the writer, were both beheaded,
faithful martyrs to the last. It seems very fitting that this letter, so feared by
those opposed to christianity, should be preserved through all the years of
persecution and a century and a quarter afterwards be safely lodged amid the
music of St. Peter's with the great head of the Catholic Church in Rome.

The first missionary to enter Korea was Father Maubant, a Frenchman from
the town of Vassy, Calvados, born 20 September 1803. He arrived in January
1836. A note regarding this reads:[8]

At last on the fifteenth day we beheld, in the middle of a valley crossed
by the River Han with its many windings and surrounding hills, wooded
and grassy or bald of peak, a long line of walls lifting their battlements
against the blue of the sky and pierced with gates, the larger of which
were surmounted by a pavilion in the Chinese style. In this vast enclosure
were grouped low houses with tiles, which, here and there, were overlooked by imperial palaces, official halls, homes of the gentry, and buddhist pagodas. This was Seoul.

Father Maubant's entry wound its way, not by the main thoroughfare but
by narrow and tortuous streets.

A Christian led the way on horseback, followed by two on foot. Others
kept at a distance lest they might draw attention by too numerous a
company. Thus led, Père Maubant at length reached his destination,
where he found the Chinese priest, Liu, and twenty or more christians
assembled. All together they hailed the stranger with deep respect and
knelt to receive his blessing.[9]

He was followed later by Father Chastan and Bishop Imbert. For three
faithful years they continued their work till finally on 21 September 1839 they
suffered death. No more touching story of christian martyrdom was ever written
than that which tells of Korea's great persecution of 1839 and the passing of
these lonely missionaries.

As to the character of their converts one story will suffice, that of Protase
Chŏng.[10] A christian at thirty years of age, he became one of the leaders till,
informed against in April 1839, he was arrested. The judge called on him to recant,

but Chŏng refused. He was then put to torture but remained firm. Finally, in a moment of weakness, won over evidently more by the gentleness of the magistrate than by the fear of pain, he apostatized and was at once released. Scarcely, however, had he reached home before a terrible sense of his shameful act overcame him. He could not eat, he could not sleep; tears were his only portion. At last, encouraged by his friends, he went back to face the judge.

'Hello!' asked the guards, 'What are you here for?' 'To set right the sin of yesterday,' said Chŏng. 'I apostatized and I repent of it and want to see the magistrate.' In saying this he attempted to enter the courtroom. 'Nonsense,' said the guard, 'your case is finished. Home you go!' He went, but three days later was back again. Not being allowed entrance to the court, he finally met the judge on the road and said, 'I have sinned, your Honour, my mouth has spoken what my heart denies. I repent. I am a christian still.' 'I don't believe it,' said the magistrate and went on his way, but Chŏng followed crying, 'I am a christian. I want to die a christian.' 'What a race of impossibles these creatures are,' said the magistrate. 'There is no getting at them at all,' and he ordered his arrest. Chŏng stretched out his hands, grateful to be tied, and was led back to prison. Later, sentenced to twenty-five blows of the big paddle, he was carried insensible to his room and died a few hours afterwards, aged forty-one. Faithful christian! Worthily was he beatified in 1925 along with the French martyrs.

I mention this with some degree of detail as it marks Korea's first real touch with the western world. The shipwrecked Hollanders, 200 years previously, did not count; but these Frenchmen did.

ALREADY in 1816 two British men-of-war had touched Hwanghae at the line of 38 degrees north latitude. On 1 September they sighted land and proceeded to a group of islands where they anchored. Crowds of people came down to meet them. Some of these, says Captain Basil Hall,[11]

> who appeared to be superior to the rest were distinguished by a hat the brim of which was nearly 3 feet in diameter and the crown about 9 inches high, shaped like a sugar !oaf with the small end cut off. The texture of this strange hat was of fine open-work, in appearance not unlike a dragonfly's wings, evidently horse-hair, varnished over. It fastened under the chin by a band strung with large beads, for the most part black and white, but occasionally red or yellow. Some of the old men wore stiff gauze caps over their hair which was formed into a high conical knot on the top of the head. The dress of these islanders consisted of loose wide trousers with a sort of frock reaching nearly to the knees made of coarse open grass-cloth. On their feet they wore neat straw sandals. They were of middle size, remarkably well-made and robust-looking. At first they expressed some surprise on examining our clothes, but afterwards took very little interest in anything belonging to us. Their chief anxiety was to get rid of us as soon as possible.

Captain Hall had some drawings made of the varied groups he met and these he carefully took with him on his return. On 11 August 1817 he called at St Helena where Napoleon was in exile. The morning following, a message came to him: 'General Buonaparte desires to see Captain Hall at 2 o'clock.' 'I carried with me,' says Captain Hall,[12]

> some drawings of the scenery and customs of Loochoo and Korea, which I found of use in describing the inhabitants. When we were speaking of Korea he (Buonaparte) took one of the drawings from me and, running his eye over the different parts, repeated to himself, 'An old man with a very large hat and long white beard — hat — a long pipe in his hand — a Chinese mat — a Chinese dress — a man near him writing — all very good and distinctly drawn.'

This is the nearest perhaps that the great Napoleon ever came to speaking terms with Korea.

Korea had heard many unhappy stories of the approach of the foreigner, stories wafted from China, from Japan, and from other points beyond the sea, till she had become exceedingly suspicious, desiring nothing less than to come into contact with these rude gun-carrying tribes. So the French missionaries and also the native christians suffered for the sins of others, for the accumulated misgivings of a hundred years and more. The government was not willing to look at christianity. It was the slogan of the foreigner and must be fought to a finish. The truth of the matter is, that King Sunjo's mind and Bishop Imbert's were very much in accord, could they have seen and known each other better. King Sunjo, who reigned from 1801 till 1835, wrote a book called *Kundo-p'yŏn* ('Handbook of the king').[13] There were eight headings: Worship God; Love the people; Offer your prayers with sincerity; Honour your parents; Be frugal and careful; Make friends of the good; Take rebukes kindly; Be sparing in meting out punishment.

> The ancients said, 'God's warnings to kings are like the warnings of a parent to children, prompted by love.' King Yŏngjo ruled for fifty years and all that time he made these two characters his rule: *Kyŏng Ch'ŏn* (Honour God). When therefore the wind blew or rain fell or when the elements seemed out of season he used to rise in the night, dress fully, kneel and say to those about him, 'I wonder if I have done something wrong that these warnings come?' and so he would pray that he might be enlightened. Sometimes too, when he was ill, he would have his ministers called into his bedroom to talk to them of God.

Could, therefore, Bishop Imbert and King Sunjo have known each other's thoughts we can imagine their being good friends at once. The world's greatest griefs have grown out of misunderstandings.

IN 1811 the quiet of Korea was upset by a rebellion in the north. A person named Hong Kyŏngnae, claiming to have magic powers, so bewitched the people that by the end of the year he had in his train thousands of followers ready to die any death in behalf of his vagaries. From youth he had been followed by strange stories that prepared the way for his wild venture. Here is one:[14]

A great gymnast named Mun lived in the south, known far and wide as a Herculean champion who could lift a mountain off its hinges. He was out fishing one day alone by a quiet brookside, when a boy came by carrying a box on his back. He dropped it near Mun, bowed and said, 'May I ask a favour, please? I am obliged for a moment to run to the village beyond the hill but will be back instantly. Will you kindly look after this box while I am gone? Guard it well, I pray you.' 'All right,' said Mun, 'I'll see to it, don't be anxious.' The boy left and Mun wondered what the box contained that could so deeply concern the lad. He took hold of it to lift it, but it was heavy and would not budge. He bent his back till the very tendons of his being cracked, but the box was glued to the ground like primaeval rock. Sitting down, ashamed, Mun wondered. Then the boy reappeared and, thanking Mun kindly for his care, whipped the box on to his back and was gone. Mun called after him, 'Who are you?' 'I?' asked the boy in apparent surprise. 'Why, I am Hong Kyŏngnae from Yonggang.'

Such were the stories that prepared the way for Hong's rebellion. With his followers keyed up to fighting pitch against the state, its greed, its injustice, its tyranny, he marched into Kasan and killed the governor, his father and his retinue; thus the rebellion was begun. The court, getting wind of it, sent forces at once to put it down. The king remarked, 'A rabble of ragamuffins, what can they do?' They did more than he bargained for. To hearten the people, the government dispensed much rice and gave liberally to the poor. In the battle that followed gunpowder was used on both sides. Finally Hong was trapped in Chŏngju, North P'yŏngan province. Here the troops blew up the walls and in the mêlée that followed Hong was killed and his head severed from his body. So the rebellion ended after about six months of great distress for the northern people. From this time on Hong's mystic box of magic gradually faded away. China, hearing of the trouble, sent troops to defend the king against his own people, but the storm was already over before they reached the Yalu. Grateful for this well-intended aid, the king sent his thanks and large supplies of beef and grain to feast the troops.

All that is left of the redoubtable Hong today is a story that Korean children read as English boys read Robin Hood. It begins:[15]

In North P'yŏngan in the county of Yonggang lived a man whose family name was Hong and whose given name was Kyŏngnae. Tall of body, eight feet high, with a tiger's head, a wolf's back, a swallow's chin, a monkey's arm and a voice like resounding thunder, he had gifts and wisdom beyond bound. Such a shot was he with the bow that spirits and devils looked on with amazement.

But it all passed off in powder smoke, this famous rebellion of Hong Kyŏng-nae: like Jack Cade he calls today for no more than passing notice.

36 The nineteenth century I: Hŏnjong, Chŏlchong, Hŭngsŏn Taewŏn'gun

KING Sunjo died in 1834, but his son and heir, though later canonized as Ik-chong, had already passed away. A little grandson, Hŏnjong, seven years of age, was the only representative of the royal line. He came to the throne, and his grandmother, the Dowager Queen Kim, now forty-four years of age, ruled for him from behind the screen. He died in 1849 at the age of twenty-two, and so, although he saw the two great christian persecutions of 1839 and 1846, he had really no part in them. They were directed wholly by the powerful Kim clan.

Various political parties had lived and flourished for more than two centuries, but now their power began to wane. One ruling family, the Andong Kim, more and more elbowed itself to the front, until under the leadership of Kim Mun'gŭn, it became what was called *sedo*.[1] As the Shogun of Japan had for centuries been a shield to protect the sacred person of the Mikado from the rude thrusts of the untutored world, so this ruling family set itself up as the protectors of royalty in Hŏnjong's day,

Their residence courtyard became the pivotal point of all the world's doings. They, not the king, were in command. One writer says;

> Before their great gate were wheeled carts and horses no end, servants and followers galore. Some sat gazing dreamily into space, some sound asleep, some were fighting in a death grip. It was a greater confusion than any market-place ever saw. Within was worse still, the inner court all a hubbub: a theatre could not equal it. Every schemer in the land was there: a stream flowed in from morning till night without interruption. Some sat and waited the day through, some came twice in the same morning. People cast aside the duties of their distant country home and came up to spend years in this outer court of the capital.

This *sedo* system continued, more or less, till the year 1905, when General Min Yŏnghwan took his own life and carried away with his memory the last of the ruling clans.[2]

GREAT changes were taking place in the Far East. Odd ships with unimagined sails were seen to pass and dip below the horizon; sudden awakenings would announce a whole fleet in the harbour. China, determined to have nothing to do with the western barbarian, shut her doors, tightly barred and locked them. But it was all unavailing to keep him out; it was just the invitation the bluff English dog liked. He went at his work, resolved to surmount all obstacles and come to close grips. Finally in 1842 a treaty was signed on board Her Majesty's Ship *Cornwallis*, and from that day to this, relations have continued, sometimes serene, sometimes highly ruffled.[3]

It was a new world in the west as well. The electric telegraph had been invented or discovered in 1844; ships were driving through every sea by steam; newspapers were pouring forth from steam presses, thousands of copies an hour; flint and steel had been buried forever and the smelly, evil-breathed sulphur match was here in their place; sewing-machines were heard to hum ten thousand stitches to the old-fashioned finger's one. The mighty Bank of England had been set up; and the power of finance began to tell; the Jewish people had been released from bondage, and Baron Rothschild took his seat as a member of England's parliament.

Korea, being off the main line, did not feel these throbbing forces, and kept her house walled up for nearly forty years longer. Travellers and foreign government agents in Peking looked with wonder upon these strangely-coated people, so proud, so thoroughly uninterested in strangers, so exclusive, so content to go their own way.

APART from the christian persecutions the years of Hŏnjong are barren of great events. Only one child was born to him, a little daughter who died early. In the hot season of the year 1849 he himself also passed away, leaving his throne vacant. As hearts trembled in England when no heir was forthcoming, so likewise in Korea it was a visitation of terror for a king to die without posterity, an evil portent, over which the nation whispered, 'An end has come to the house of Yi.' However, it could be patched up by adoption from some outlying branch of the family, though the chances of trouble accompanying this were abundant. Chŏng Wŏnyong, prime minister and sixty-six years of age, knowing the danger, went quietly to the inner palace and consulted Dowager Queen Kim through the screen. She was fifty-nine, and had had long experience in affairs of state. Her opinion was that the third son of Prince Chŏn'gye should be chosen, the eldest being dead and the second a cripple. Prince Chŏngye was the grandson of the Coffin King, and nephew of Chŏngjo, the monarch who organized the old folk's feast to please his mother. Since he was of no account, the son of a concubine, he had fallen into poverty, and at last his dilapidated fortunes had exiled him to Kanghwa island. Now he was suddenly called to kingship.[4] Minister Chŏng, afraid to let the decision of Queen Kim be known, started off for Kanghwa wholly unannounced, carrying her order in his coat-sleeve. When he arrived he informed the governor of his errand and Kanghwa awakened as from a dream. The king was dead, long live the king—Prince Chŏn'gye's third son. The governor was astonished at this announcement, as was the prince's whole household. Consternation seized them. Did it mean their doom, or their fame and fortune? Minister Chŏng looked for the lad, the third son, but failed to see him, for he was out in the fields ploughing. When called, he turned out to be a strapping boy of nineteen, his hair in a queue down his back and his face tanned by the sun.

On the way to Seoul, a distance of about thirty miles, Chŏng sent word in advance saying, 'I am accompanying the king to the capital, send a guard of honour as far as the river, pray.' He added to those who were with him, 'If the guard is there we live; if it is not, we shall all die.' However, the guard was there,

GENEALOGY OF THE LAST SIX YI KINGS

Dotted lines show adoptions. Numbers show order of reigning kings of the dynasty. Surnames of wives do not necessarily indicate maternity of the kings' sons.

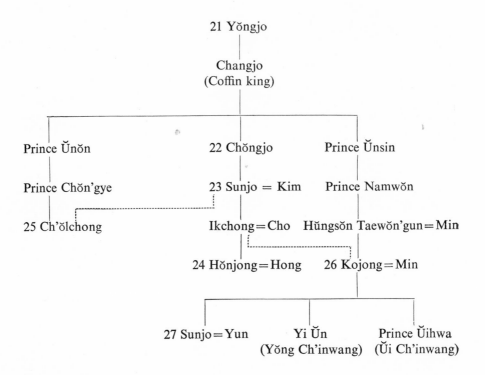

EXTRACT FROM THE GENEALOGY OF MIN showing relationships with the royal family in the nineteenth century

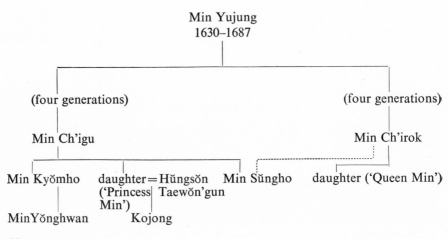

and so Ch'ŏlchong passed triumphantly into Seoul to take his seat on the throne. Then his hair had to be done up, and he himself married to the fairest lady in the land, who happened to be a daughter of Kim Mun'gŭn, the *de facto* master of the capital. Ch'ŏlchong was regarded as a son of Queen Kim, consort of Sunjo, passing over the intervening royalties, Ikchong (who never reigned) and Hŏnjong. Thus the stage was set for all sorts of palace intrigues. There were three dowagers: Queens Kim, Cho, and Hong, aged respectively sixty, forty-two, and nineteen. Naturally forty-two and nineteen had to give way to sixty, and Ch'ŏlchong became Queen Kim's son, with whom she might play as a college girl does with her tennis ball. This irregular line of sonship brought with it many evils: contests between queens, clan fights, palace intrigues, all of which lent themselves to Korea's speedy downfall. The noble line of kings had departed, and the whim of the moment served in its stead. Ch'ŏlchong had been summoned not for any qualities he possessed or any special preparation he had for kingship, but simply because he would be a ready instrument in the hands of those who sought to use him. Taken from poverty and obscurity, and introduced to the extravagances of the palace, he naturally fell a victim to excess and died at the early age of thirty-two. He had five sons and six daughters, all of whom passed away in infancy except the fourth daughter, who became the wife of Marquis Pak Yŏnghyo.[5]

As THE power and personality of the kings declined, so clan rivalry increased: Kim against Nam, Cho against Yi, Yi against Kim. We see a great man like Nam Pyŏngch'ŏl tossed about from pillar to post, a victim of this frenzy.[6]

There was one prince of the royal house, named Hŭngsŏn-gun, who was regarded with more or less question.[7] He was given to light and easy ways—so much so that the mighty lords among the Kim looked askance upon him. Among his accomplishments, however, was a ready hand with the artist's brush. He could draw orchids beautifully, and made them his special delight. Being poor and without influence, he was anxious to win over the head of the great Kim clan. For this purpose he made a beautiful screen, and, after inquiry, had it presented to the powerful Kim Pyŏnggi;[8] but Kim merely gave it a glance and put it aside. Again, Hŭngsŏn-gun took special pains to invite Kim and Nam to his home on his birthday. Both these lords, feeling themselves superior to an impoverished prince, gave half consent but failed to put in an appearance on the day. Prince Hŭngsŏn inquired later as to the reason, and Kim said, 'Remember you stand close to the succession. It would not look well for me to be seen going to your house as though I were backing your end of the family line.'

King Ch'ŏlchong died in the 12th moon of 1863 (16 January 1864 by the solar calendar) and at once the great ministers met to decide on his successor. They discussed long but came to no conclusion. The second son of Prince Hŭngsŏn had been mentioned, a bright and gifted lad who seemed to have in him the makings of a king. He was two generations further removed from Prince Chang-hŏn, the Coffin King, than Ch'ŏlchong and so was a great-great-grandson. It was a time of intense anxiety. Kim Pyŏnggi and Kim Pyongguk[9] were in tears over the loss of the late ruler, and here was the problem of his successor bearing down upon them that brooked no delay. A council was called to decide.

It has often been thought that Korean women have no part in state affairs, that they are mere nonentities who sit by with folded hands. Never was there a greater mistake. In many a crisis of the east they have glided in and decided the fortunes of the day. There were, as already mentioned, now three dowagers in the palace: Queen Cho, wife of Ikchong who never ruled, but mother of King Hŏnjong, who ruled from 1834 to 1849; Queen Hong, wife of Hŏnjong; and Queen Kim, wife of the deceased Ch'ŏlchong. To which of these should the adopted new king belong? For seeing the direct line had failed, whoever ruled must do so in the line of adoption. While the councillors and great lords were engaged in the discussion of this vexed question, Queen Cho was in the palace—having a secret conference with Prince Hŭngsŏn. At this moment the youngest Queen Dowager, Kim-ssi, knowing that she had the backing of her father's clan, summoned the former minister, Chŏng Wŏnyong, to her presence. It was he who had safely brought Ch'ŏlchong from Kanghwa and she now ordered him to bring the second son of Prince Hŭngsŏn to her at once. The 80-year-old minister wended his way to the Unhyŏn-gung, the 'Cloud Hill Palace',[10] but the lad was not there. Finally he found him in a neighbouring garden flying a kite. The prince was eleven years old and he wondered what all this pother meant — minister Chŏng's coming and what not. To his surprise, high lords came and bowed to him. What was up? Here was a royal chair with runners ahead who beat off the people high-handedly. The lad was tender-hearted; he had the chair stopped, and asked where they were taking him and what this beating meant. 'We are to make you king,' was the reply. 'Then don't beat the people.' Hearing his young and kindly voice, the world was greatly delighted.

When he entered the palace the Dowager Cho, tossing all forms aside and overriding ministers and younger queens, came right out from the women's quarters into the open and took the lad by the hand saying, 'My son!' The chiefs, overawed by this, merely bowed low, though the aged Chŏng did say, 'No, no! Go back, please, into the inner quarters.' She obeyed, but did not let go the lad's hand, who followed as she led the way. She had a throne set up in her inner room with a screen hanging before it, and at once issued orders for the ministers to assemble and receive her commands. 'I have made the new king,' said she, 'the son of Ikchong. Be it known to you I that have hung up the screen and now take command of the government.'[11] The ministers were paralysed to find their conference thus abruptly broken up and the all-important matter of kingship so arbitrarily decided, but it was a *fait accompli*. There was no help for it, and they bowed their heads. That was how the late emperor, Kojong, who was summoned to become the successor of Ch'ŏlchong, turned out to be the son of Ikchong, who had died twenty-two years before his birth.

A day was chosen for the doing-up of the king's hair, which would make a man of him. Formerly he had been but a boy. Partly in weeping, and partly in shouting *manse* (Long live the king!),[12] the occasion passed. Since he was a generation younger than his late majesty, the new king was required to wear mourning and weep and bow before the royal bier. Queen Cho became ennobled with the title, *Taewang-daebi*, 'Supreme Great Queen Dowager'; Queen Kim was merely given the title *Taebi*, 'Great Queen'; while Queen Hong was called *Wang-*

daebi, 'Royal Great Queen'.

IT WAS a question, indeed, what to do with Prince Hŭngsŏn, father of the king.[13] What forms of ceremony should be accorded him? What dress? What place in the government? He could not bow as other officials did because that would mean bowing to his son. He could wear a horn belt and use black for the colour of his dress. Let a stone be erected before his gate commanding all to dismount, but let him have no part in state affairs. Through the influence of Queen Cho, however, he became regent and ruler absolute with the title *Taewŏn'-gun*, 'Prince of the Great House.' For nine years his heavy hand was felt. Several definite lines of action clearly bore the stamp of his will: he was against foreigners, he opposed the great clans that had formerly looked down upon him, and he was set on his own greatness. A double fan-banner was carried before him when he rode, whereas a minister had only a single one. The eunuchs met him at the palace entrance and supported him on each side as he moved in, his seat of honour was loftier than that of any prime minister, medicines were dealt out to him from the royal dispensary, fields and paddy flats were his — a gift of the nation.

His first great enterprise was the restoration of the Kyŏngbok palace,[14] which had lain in disorder for 273 years since the war of 1592. Taxes were levied, collections were made, goods were appraised and properties valued, and yet there were not funds enough. A great cry went up from the people claiming that they were being mulcted on false pretences, but the Taewŏn'gun was not a man to be daunted by an outcry. Dealing out punishment here and there, he went straight forward to the end contemplated: the great halls and palaces of the Kyŏngbok enclosure. How well he did his work we can still see by the Kŭnjŏng Hall, and the Kyŏnghoe-ru or lotus pavilion. The breadth of his mind and the mastery of his hand are evident.

MANY stories are told of his squaring accounts with his old enemies. Once he had overheard the two great Kims, Chwagŭn and Hunggŭn,[15] propose that he be set aside and given no part in state affairs. This he never forgot. Some time later the young king went on a progress to Suwŏn to visit the tomb of his adoptive great-grandfather Chŏngjo.[16] The journey was long, and it was thought that on his return the king would arrive late at the crossing of the River Han. Custom required the great ministers to be there at his landing, ready for audience. The Kims sent a message of inquiry: 'Doubtless it will be late', said they, 'when His Majesty returns; shall we trouble to take ceremonial robes or not? There will hardly be an audience at such an hour.'

The regent answered, 'Never mind about your robes.' At the same time he sent a message to old minister Chŏng, 'The king crosses the river at such and such an hour, have your robes ready without fail.' In the meantime he instructed his son thus, 'When you arrive at Nodŭl[17] be sure to call for the two Kims and Minister Chŏng.' All came about as planned, and the three were summoned. Chŏng, robed as the state rites required, bowed low and said, 'Peace to your high Majesty.' But where were the Kims? Consternation fall upon them, no robes, great loss of face, blundering excuses—and the procession moved on. Next morning they wrote humbly, 'Your Majesty, pardon, pray: we have sinned.' The king sent word, 'What is past and done is over with. Be at peace!' The Taewŏn'gun, the old tiger, sat back and grinned.

AGAIN, Chwagŭn, according to ancient custom, kept a favourite concubine. Her name was Yang. She came from Naju and ruled the ex-prime minister with a high hand. She sold offices at will to the benefit of her own private affairs. She was a bold engaging wench, and when her master did not please her she slapped his cheek. Her nickname was Nahap, 'Minister of Naju'. She smiled at this complimentary cognomen, till one day a summons came from the palace commanding her to the presence of Queen Cho. The grim old queen said, 'You are a servant of Minister Kim, and yet you deserve instant death on three counts: you have presumed to sell office and take bribes; you are disrespectful to your superiors and have been known to slap the minister in the face; and you have won a detestable name, Nahap, that you pride yourself on. I would have you beheaded at once were it not that the old minister would grieve over it, because he cannot exist without you. My sentence is that you take yourself off out of the city and never let me see you again.'

Minister Kim, distressed at this decision, took his young concubine away to Son'ga-jŏng, a quiet spot at the foot of Pukhan.[18] There he remained in hiding till some days later a caller was announced. The Taewŏn'gun came in, all smiles. 'Why are you here, your Excellency?' 'My young wife is ordered from the city and I have come too, as I cannot live without her.' 'You care for her, do you?' 'She is all I have.' 'But does she care for you?' At this, bubbling sobs were heard from behind the screen. The minister called her in, and she came and made a deep bow before the Taewŏn'gun, and again a deep bow. 'Please forgive me,' said she, 'I have done very badly.' 'I cannot do that', said the regent; 'it is a state matter and has been decided.' She put her head down and wept bitterly. The old minister too was deeply moved and pleaded for her. 'I'll tell you,' said the regent, 'I promise to speak for you.' 'So many thanks,' said Yang-ssi.

'In case I am successful and you are forgiven, what acknowledgment, pray?' At once she said, 'Sim-man yang,[19] a hundred thousand *yang*, I'll give to the palace building.' 'Good,' said the Taewŏn'gun, 'I'll speak for you.' She added, 'And a hundred thousand more for the king's wedding.' The next morning a letter came from Queen Cho: 'You are forgiven, my dear; see now that you walk circumspectly in all your ways.'

37 The nineteenth century II: Kojong

WHEN the young king had completed his three years of mourning, his marriage question came to the fore.[1] In this, as in all other state matters, clan intrigue was at work. The late Min Ch'irok had left a daughter three years older than the king,[2] and Princess Min, wife of the regent and mother of the king, had fixed upon her as the queen-to-be. She was a Min, and would keep the Min influence well grounded. The regent said there were difficulties that made it impossible. In the first place, Min Ch'irok had adopted as his son Min Sŭngho, a uterine brother of Princess Min, mother of the king. If the king now married Min Ch'i-rok's daughter he would be marrying his uncle's sister, which would be equivalent to marrying his aunt. Furthermore, as Min Sŭngho was a brother of Princess Min, he was brother-in-law of the regent; and if the king married the daughter of Ch'irok, whose adopted son was Min Sŭngho, the king would become a brother-in-law of Sŭngho. That is, the father (the regent) and the son (the king) would both be brother-in-law of the same person, Min Sŭngho. It was one of those inextricable tangles of relationship that only Asia possesses and for this reason the regent objected. Said he to his wife, 'This will not do. You are a sister of Sŭngho and he is therefore my brother-in-law. By his adoption into Ch'irok's family he has become the brother of the proposed queen and so, in case of marriage, would be my brother-in-law and my son's brother-in-law as well. Ridiculous! Never do in the world! Also, such a marriage would mean my son's marrying his uncle's sister, practically marrying his aunt.'

But Princess Min, being a woman of much force of character, was not to be daunted by any such mathematical calculation. She bore down all opposition and finally won her way. When Min-ssi was brought to the home of the Taewŏn'gun to spend the preliminary days in preparation for her marriage, the grim old father-in-law-to-be took note of her and remarked that she was a woman of great determination and much poise of manner. He was somewhat disturbed at this. Later, when he saw a letter that she had written, he said, 'She evidently aspires to be a doctor of letters; look out for her.' Thus there grew up between them a rift that never closed, but Min-ssi never failed in all the required forms of deportment.

1866! IT WAS the happy year of the king's marriage, yet it was a terrible year for Korea. Russians, French, British, Americans, Germans were all waiting just outside the barrier, intent on forcing an entrance. This roused the ire of the Taewŏn'gun against the whole western world. He would have none of them, and set to work making buff-armour, casting cannon, buying guns from the Japanese, building forts, experimenting with gunpowder, anything to make his hermit home secure. He was alarmed at the increase of christianity and the many rumours he heard of its advance. When heated to blazing point he unleashed the full force of his fury upon the heads of the French missionaries, who were the only foreigners within his reach. In February orders were issued for the arrest of Bishop Berneux. The bishop made no resistance but came submissively as ordered. A native record says of him: 'Height, eight feet; eyes, deep; nose, prominent; flesh, white; beard, long; accent, strange.'[3] Fifty-two years of age, he had been in Korea ten years, and now the end had come. Still, thousands of Koreans were his devoted disciples and really did lay down their lives for him, as well as with him. No servant of the state perhaps ever had as many true followers as Bishop Berneux, but they were powerless against the regent. Among those who exercised influence on his behalf was Princess Min, the regent's wife. Hearing that he was arrested, she sent her eldest son, the king's elder brother, to obtain his release. He failed, however, and not even her tears and petitions could avail. The case went forward and on 8 March Bishop Berneux and three of his younger associates were beheaded on the banks of the Han at Saenamt'ŏ, the old execution ground. Later in the year five others followed. During all this time foreign men-o'-war went round the coast, helpless to rescue these who with the thousands of native christians passed on to martyrdom. The modest records that remain speak in a spirit of gentleness and quiet simplicity. Young, as well as old, were not only glad to preach the Good News but were ready also to die for the name of the Lord Jesus. Let us protestant missionaries humbly remember this, and place a wreath of honour on the graves of these gallant Frenchmen and faithful Koreans who have shown such remarkable examples of the soul's supreme devotion.

AMERICAN ships, among others, had come and gone. A schooner called the *Surprise* was wrecked off the coast of Hwanghae, where the kindly people rescued the survivors, fed them and finally saw them off safely by way of Ŭiju. A month later, in July, the *General Sherman* left Tientsin for the coast of Korea, where, unfortunately, groping its way up the Taedong River to P'yŏngyang, it grounded on the mud and met with dire disaster. As this was one of the first introductions of America to Korea, it merits attention. The writer once encountered a sturdy old-time hermit, Chŏng Hŭijo of P'yŏngyang, who had seen it as a boy and told it as only a beholder can tell.[4] 'As the American ship', said he, 'came up the river, news of its approach was sent by courier post.' The governor at the time was a great scholar and highly-honoured gentleman, Pak Kyusu, whom Yüan Shih-kai once called *sich'e saram*, 'man of the times'. Chŏng went on to say;

> Little by little the boat came further up, the water being exceedingly high at that season. When the news of it got abroad the people of the city fled for their lives out of the gates and, when the gates were ordered shut, over the walls. Many like myself, however, were moved by curiosity and desired to see who Ch'oe Nanhŏn was, for this, we were told, was the name of the foreigner in command of the fearful expedition. Governor Pak summoned Colonel Chŏng Ch'ihyŏn, who was in command of the troops, and sent him to make inquiry. He went, but for some reason was detained on board and not allowed to return. Seeing this, crowds of people armed with stones, sticks, and bows and arrows went out on the river to get within throwing distance. Suddenly a cannon shot was fired from the ship and wrought great havoc among those who had ventured near. Some lost an arm, some a leg, some were blown up and killed altogether. The colonel made every effort to get away, but the foreigners held him fast and finally took his seal from him.
>
> By means of the written character he conversed with a Chinese, Chao Ling-feng, who happened to be on board. In this conversation Chao wrote, 'Is there a stone pagoda anywhere near?' The colonel replied Yes and asked what he meant by such a question. Chao made answer, 'Before coming on this trip I met a fortune-teller who read my chances for the journey and wrote: *Ch'ien-nien-ku-ch'eng shih-t'a ko-wei* ('A thousand-year-old city, stone pagoda, very terrible') which

means that a stone pagoda standing before a certain thousand-year-old city is greatly to be feared.' Strange as it may seem, a stone pagoda did stand just over Ch'i Tzŭ's dyke in the willow-grove opposite to where the ship hung fast. The same pagoda stands in front of P'yŏngyang railway station today.

The governor then summoned the guard, several hundred men, and a group of fifty or more tiger hunters, and ordered them to fire on the ship. But the cannon shots that came in reply spread terror everywhere and ploughed the land where potato patches now are. This continued for several days, during which time news was being constantly sent to Seoul. Finally word came back from the old regent: 'Destroy them utterly.'

Among those who ventured to try a hand against the foreigner was a man who had a boat protected by bull's hide. A cannon shot sunk him and blew him up, his bag of gunpowder and all. He was killed and my father took pity on his son and brought him into our home where he lived for many years.

While the ship was still fast aground a bold sculler went close up and called on Colonel Chŏng to jump. The colonel, being free at the moment, did so, and also one of his attendants; but another, Yubogi, missed his footing, fell into the water and was drowned.

Though the attacking party was balked for several days, at last, by loading a scow with brushwood sprinkled with sulphur, they got the ship afire and the crew smoked out. They dashed into the water and Ch'oe landed with Chao the Chinese. Both offered submission, bowing deeply, but this was refused. They were pinioned at once with the rest, among whom were two black men, negroes, and led over Ch'i Tzŭ's wall to the willow-grove where the fated pagoda stood. There they were beaten to death. The man who first struck the American Ch'oe[5] was a brother of the colonel's attendant who was drowned. There were about twenty in all and they met their fate on the 22nd day of the 7th moon in the year *pyŏngin* (2 September 1866).

This was Chŏng's story. I photographed him while a man with a bullock and a plough of the era of Abraham were busy at my side tilling the soil.

IN OCTOBER French men-of-war came asking the reason for the murders, and pounded the forts of Kanghwa; an American squadron did likewise but the old regent, undaunted, refused all negotiation and ordered them about their business. One cannot but admire the persistence with which he held to the way of his fathers. Only after his hand was removed from the helm were the doors finally opened. Even the treaty with the Japanese,[6] which came in 1876, was not signed till after the Taewŏn'gun had retired from active participation in state affairs. The rift, too, between him and his daughter-in-law had widened ominously. While watching her he was alert to the changing age into which the fates had thrust him.

The king, now twenty-eight years of age (1880), and governed more and more by the advice of the queen, sought to rule apart from his father. France came again in 1880 with Russia, seeking trade relations, but they were once more told, 'No!' Commodore Shufeldt called at Pusan in the USS *Ticonderoga*, but could arrive at no understanding. In 1881 Li Hung-chang wrote Korea a note advocating limited treaty relationships with the foreigner. The American minister, with the help of Shufeldt, kept the matter on the *tapis* in Peking. These were the levers that finally got behind the tightly barred door and swung it back on its hinges. In the meantime British ships had surveyed much of the coastline, so that when 1882 dawned, and treaties were signed, the seas were open and ready.[7]

THE EIGHTIES constituted a decade of disturbance, as all transition periods do. First, there was a conspiracy against the state, in which the king's half-brother, Yi Chaesŏn, was involved. Condemnation quickly followed, and so, under the knife and by hemlock, he and his associates were sent forth on their eerie way.[8]

Committees sailed abroad at this time on tours of investigation: one to Tientsin,[9] the home of the great Li Hung-chang, and one to Japan, where western ways were known and studied.[10] A Japanese officer named Horimoto Reicho was engaged to teach the troops modern methods of military tactics.[11] This new order of soldiers aroused fierce indignation among the old tiger-hunting companies who had been the nation's standby in the past. It was rumoured that the latter were to be summarily dismissed with months of pay still in arrears. A little rice was given to pacify them but chaff and sand were mixed with it that gritted their angry teeth. Whether this was true or merely a rumour I cannot say, but these old-timers were so enraged over the monstrous changes of the day that they broke into the palace and killed two high officers, Min Kyŏmho and Kim Pohyŏn, before the very eyes of the king. Min Kyŏmho was the father of Min Yŏnghwan, who later figured so prominently, and Kim Pohyŏn was the famous Min Yŏngik's father-in-law.[12] The wild soldiery burned the homes of these great lords, let out the prisoners from the prison, and, as they could not find Queen Min, whom they were after (by direction of the Taewŏn'gun), they burned the monasteries round about Seoul that she was supposed to have under her wing. Was the Taewŏn'gun really behind this foul attempt on the life of her Majesty? Some think he was. Later events would seem to say that it was probably true. She, clever woman, always alert, had disappeared. Carried off on the back of her faithful servant, Hong Chaehŭi, she was found two months later seventy miles away in Ch'ungju,[13] in the home of Min Ŭngsik. On her return the nations' weeds of mourning were cast aside,[14] and the group of henchmen of the old Taewŏn'gun who had set this outrageous sackcloth going were all given their cup of arsenic and sent in haste to the fated shades.

The soldiers, not satisfied with taking revenge on those who had withheld their pay, went raging through the barrack grounds and wreaked their vengeance on Captain Horimoto, who was in no sense to blame, since he was merely employed as a military instructor. The tiger-hunters, however, were determined to wipe this new order of military off the face of the earth, and so they killed him and as many of his men as they could find. Finally they were overcome, their leader beheaded and quartered, and the old Taewŏn'gun, who was acknowledged to be behind the anti-queen disturbance, was shipped under guard to Tientsin and kept in durance by his august excellency Li Hung-chang.

The first foreigner to be engaged by the government of Korea was a German, Paul Georg von Möllendorff, thirty-four years of age, a student who had already published his *Manual of Chinese Bibliography*,[15] and therefore was acquainted with the east. One of the first recollections the writer has of the Orient is the wonder-struck expression on the faces of Japanese and others who saw the tall von Möllendorff dressed as a Korean, in black hat and long white robe, walking through the streets of Tokyo. He organized the very efficient customs service that continued to operate till the days of the protectorate of 1905, and started an English school that continued for many years under the efficient direction of Mr T. E. Hallifax.[16]

During the year 1883 a Korean embassy, headed by Min Yŏngik, the adopted son of Min Sŭngho, and therefore nephew of the queen, made its way to Washington DC. On its return in the USS *Trenton* it was accompanied by Mr Percival Lowell, who wrote a book called *Chosön,* and was the first, if I mistake not, to name the country 'the Land of Morning Calm'.[17]

In October a British treaty was signed by Sir Harry Parkes, who twenty-three years before was a prisoner in Peking and had been tortured, the brand marks being still upon him. Business companies came as well and modern Korea settled down with its Jardine, Matheson & Co; J. H. Morse, Townsend & Co; and Meyer & Co. The various consuls arrived, even the Russian Waeber. Mints were started, glass factories, model farms, powder mills, mining outfits, electric light plants — all to be given up later and cast on the dump heap like discarded playthings. Korea was not yet ready for such a flood of change, not yet in touch with such a degree of modern life. This the innovators did not seem to know or understand.[18]

IN SEPTEMBER 1884 Dr H. N. Allen[19] arrived, but scarcely had he set foot on Korean soil and learned his first lessons before the great *émeute* of Kim Okkyun broke out. Kim Okkyun was of the same family as the famous Chwagŭn spoken of in a previous chapter. He had been in Japan, had seen the advantages of modern government over the antiquated methods of his fathers, and now set himself to carrying them out, but he was unwilling to bide his time and go slowly. As with all inexperienced politicians, everything was haste; he must do it at once, do it today. A great feast was called for the 17th day of the 10th moon (4 December 1884) by Hong Yŏngsik, who was in charge of the new Post Office.[20] The foreign consuls were invited and the chief ministers of state. In the midst of the dinner a fire broke out the other side of the wall and the guests fled in dismay. Men suddenly appeared with swords, and Min Yŏngik was cut down near the entrance of the hall but not killed. Dr Allen's good care staunched the blood and saved his life. Several of the leaders of the plot hurried into the palace and informed his Majesty that Chinese troops were up in arms and the whole city afire. 'Escape,' said they, 'and we will have the Japanese troops protect you.' The king was not inclined to move. At last he was carried off by force and for some hours made prisoner. The next morning, however, changed the fortunes of the day, for a 25-year-old Chinese officer named Yüan Shih-k'ai made his appearance with troops to rescue the king. At first his Majesty was nowhere to be found, but already a provisional government, backed by Japanese soldiers and supposedly called by the king, had taken action, appointing ministers, and so on. Needless to say, the city of Seoul was worked up to an indescribable pitch of excitement.

One Korean record says, 'The Chinese general sent a message to the Japanese consul, "Why do you not call off your troops who are interfering with the liberty of the King?" but no answer came.'[21] When hostilities opened the Japanese, having not only the Korean guard against them, but also the Chinese army of occupation, beat a retreat to save their lives. Hong, the master of the feast, and Pak Yŏnggyo, brother of Marquis Pak Yŏnghyo,[22] were taken and killed by the mob. Yüan set up his camp near the king's quarters in the East Palace, and matters quietened down. The people, regarding the Japanese as abetting the enemy, burned their legation outside the West Gate, 'and the conspirators', says the Korean record, 'were smuggled aboard ship in boxes and so made their escape.'[23] The Taewŏn'gun, a prisoner in China, knew nothing of what was going on. 2,500 Japanese troops and 3,000 Chinese landed, the former at Chemulp'o, the latter at Asan, and for a time it looked like war, but finally matters were adjusted satisfactorily and they returned to their homelands. To end it all the old Taewŏn'gun was brought back and Yüan Shih-k'ai was appointed representative of Imperial China in Seoul.

38 The nineteenth century III: the end of the Korean kingdom

FOR ten years one of the most fascinating parade groups seen whisking through the streets of Seoul was that of Yüan Shih-kai.[1] He was the representative of the great mother state, and took precedence of all other nationals. When he entered the palace, it was through the great central gates reserved for royalty. He himself was a young man of pleasant manner, genial expression and agreeable tone of voice, a fitting agent of the great Li Hung-chang.[2] Korea was the stage on which he made his début and Seoul the decorated scene of the first part of his play. From then until 6 October 1913, when he was elected President of the Chinese Republic, he kept steadily on his upward way. Then, like a rocket that explodes and is gone, he and his imperial robes and all his high-falutin paraphernalia were suddenly snuffed out, and China was left to the confusion of darkness in which we behold her today.

KIM OKKYUN had fled to Japan after his political fiasco, and lived there for ten years until the matter was forgotten; then a friend of days gone by, named Hong Chongu, paid him a visit. Hong gave him much interesting news. How charmed Kim was to have this call. Later on, urgent business summoned Hong to

Shanghai and he invited Kim to accompany him — no danger whatever: Korean police were not there. Kim, never a very wise man, went. On a gusty March day in 1894, as he was having a quiet siesta, friend Hong stealthily drew a gun from his pocket and quick as lightning blew Kim's brains out. Had it happened in Japan Hong would have swung from a rope-end, but knowing this, he had inveigled his unwary victim to China, where men may do what is right in their own eyes. China took note, commended the act as a very proper squaring of accounts with a rebel, and sent Hong and the body home to Chemulp'o in a man-of-war. On 14 April the gruesome remains were divided into portions and hung up to public view.[3] This revolting custom of old Korea is akin to what existed with us a hundred years ago; it need call for no surprise, nor any special comment. Human nature feels more keenly the horrible things done by others than those done by itself. Cromwell's grinning head set on a pike-point on Westminster Hall continued for twenty-three years to scare the kiddies of St Martin's Lane. The mistaken notion that this would warn the world and dissipate the spirit of rebellion seems to have been common to all humankind.

KOREA was nervous over the sudden influx of foreigners who, like uncanny birds, swept in on all hands uninvited. Following in their wake were rumours of every sort; one, peculiar to 1888, was that Korean children were missing here, there and everywhere, seen today and gone tomorrow. Most weird stories were told the writer, which ended in the general conclusion that foreigners had a bent for the flesh of little children. It seems to have been a view common to all East Asia and doubtless took its rise from the Chinese text of St John's Gospel: 'Except ye eat the flesh of the Son of Man', which a person ignorant of the proper interpretation could easily render: 'Except you eat the flesh of a man's child and drink his blood.' The passing of time gradually dissipated this monstrous misconception and wafted its remains away.[4]

DURING these years a very peculiar person rose to fame and fortune out of a witch's den hidden in a deep recess behind the Confucian College. I find a record written in scholarly Chinese that reads,[5]

> She was like a fox full of evil and called herself a daughter of Kuan-ti, the God of War. She took princes and prime ministers by storm with deceptive words, and had herself named Chillyŏng-gun, 'Princess of the Immaculate Spirit'. To this one she said, 'Brother'; to that one, 'son'; and all the world was at her feet. So mightily did her power prevail that even provincial governors were sent out at her bidding.

She once called on the writer with her numerous retinue, explaining that she was in touch with spirit beings and asking that he pray to his God for her, so that all power might be committed to her keeping. She presented him with a gilded dragon seal two and a half inches square on which is carved, 'The seal of Marquis Han-shou' (*Han-shou ting-hou;* i.e. Kuan-ti, the God of War). She was a woman of very gentle manner and refined speech. I marvelled that one so softly and engagingly equipped could be the driving-force that she was said to be. She was the first woman commoner ever denominated 'Princess' by a Korean king. At her bidding, all the joss-houses of the land swung open, and Kuan-ti's side temples were engaged for prayer.

One Korean writer says, 'The purpose of prayer is blessing, but here we were cursed instead.' Finances ran low, while in and out of the palace went characters not unlike Sin Ton 500 years before. Every weird creature who had even a ghost to tell of was assured of a hearing.

UNDER THE YEAR 1893, the 30th year of His Majesty's reign, I find this record:[6]

> In the last years of Ch'ŏlchong there was a man of Kyŏngju named Ch'oe Poksul who, in the name of religion, gathered about him a sect called the Tonghak. Orders went out for his arrest, so that finally he was taken, tried at Taegu and beheaded.

Among his disciples was a certain Ch'oe Cheu, who came up to Seoul with a great concourse of followers, and bowed before the palace gates. Many called for his execution but the government hesitated. He was said to be in touch with invisible spirits and Princess Chillyŏng counselled care. His Majesty issued a proclamation that read in part:[7]

> 500 years have passed and the world has fallen into exceeding great evils, so that every man does what is right in his own eyes — very bad! The law of the curse has upset the whole human race and totally blinded my people. What you call *hak* or 'learning', said to be to the honour of God, is in reality an attempt to deceive God. For what purpose do you act thus? Your building of walls, your flying of flags, your scattering of leaflets merely stir up the people. Such practices will bring a sea of troubles on Korea and end in war.

But the Tonghaks kept on,[8] and a succession of failures on the part of government troops aroused his Majesty's fears for the state. He sent a letter calling on Li Hung-chang for help. At once, as a kind suzerain should do, China sent a force to Asan. Before the landing, one of the Chinese transports, the *Kowshing (Kaosheng)* encountered a Japanese man-of-war and after a short sharp parley was sunk with all on board. War was declared by Japan soon afterwards and China was defeated in several engagements. The order, discipline, and excellent methods of the Japanese drove all before them and changed the face of the Far East in a few months. Korea's fortunes were reversed. Her revered suzerain, her mother state, her 'guide, philosopher and friend' from time immemorial, was reduced to nothing, and Japan, as yet hardly recognized, had risen to be a world power. New understandings had to be arrived at, new treaties, new declarations, new adjustments. From henceforth China was left out and Japan was the masterhand that held the balance of power in East Asia.

OPPOSING parties immediately sprang into being in Korea: the pro-Japanese party, in which the leading character was the old regent, and the conservative party, backed by Queen Min. Many things were happening, many changes were coming about, but the enmity of the king's father toward his strong-minded daughter-in-law did not change. It continued till one sombre morning, 8 October 1895, the echoing of gun-fire was heard from the direction of the palace. What did it mean? Later in the day it was announced that the queen had been assassinated and that Japanese *soshi* (agents) has been used to do the deed. So ended the life of the kindly, brilliant, strong-minded, too-superstitious woman, who allowed her great influence to be used in a way that enfeebled and impoverished the state. The so-called Reform Party controlled the palace till February 1896, when the king and crown prince made their escape, hidden in sedan chairs, and arrived at the Russian legation, where they resided for a year. This struck the spark for a new and more terrible explosion.

Russia's hold on the king was in direct defiance of Japan, and this the latter saw and took note of. Little by little, under favour of his Majesty, the Russians were given Yongam-p'o,[9] promised Masan-p'o[10] and blessed with this and that, so that the day could not be far distant when Japan would have to settle accounts or for ever knuckle under. With the most exacting care, and counselled by the wisest military experts, she again made her preparations for land and sea attacks and bided her time. This continued until 1904 when one day, 9 February, the booming of heavy guns in Chemulp'o shook the entire city of Seoul. It was the opening announcement of the Russo-Japanese War. The result of this first engagement was that there lay in Chemulp'o harbour, like dead corpses, three Russian ships: the *Varyak,* the *Koryeets* and the *Sungari*.[11] Half-drowned and wounded Russians were everywhere, but not a Japanese was to be seen. The fight was over and they were off for fresh fields.

The rest of the war was little noticed in Korea but had a tremendous influence on her future. The great sea victory off the Yalu, the battle of Mukden and the final expulsion of the Russians from Port Arthur settled all questions of dominion as far as the east was concerned. Russia had been great: in stature, in empire, in name (the Chinese characters for 'white' and 'tsar' together make 'emperor'),[12] but she was gone, never to return, and her fall in the Far East had much to do with the great European War and the final fate of the Russian Empire. An old Korean scholar,[13] careless in dress and droll of speech, but sound of understanding, once said to the writer, 'We Koreans started the World War — and so we really are a world-wide people after all.' 'How do you make that out?' I asked. 'Follow me now', said he, 'and you will be convinced. We called forth the Tonghaks, didn't we? The Tonghaks made it so uncomfortable for his Majesty and the home government that they had to call in China. China came; which at once roused Japan to take a hand. There was war and Japan beat China, to the astonishment of the world and especially of Russia, who said to herself, "I must checkmate this Island Empire or I am in for difficulties." For this purpose she won over the king of Korea and lodged him in her legation. Japan meanwhile tightened her belt and got ready. When the time appointed by the fates came, they went at it hammer and tongs and — who would have thought it? — Russia was beaten, and up went

Japan. Germany seeing Russia knocked out said, "Now's the time for me to deal with her too; something that has to be done sooner or later," and so she turned her empire into a mighty training camp that lasted for ten years. Then the Great War broke on the world. Assuredly our little Tonghaks set a-going the mightiest conflagration that world history records.' I listened to this, and said, 'Why, yes, it looks as though there were something in what you say.'

FOLLOWING the Russian defeat Ito Hirobumi came to Korea as Minister Plenipotentiary, determined that never again should a foreign power gain such a foothold in Korea to the damage of his country as Russia had gained in Yongam-p'o. He forcibly hurried the government through a form acknowledging the suzerainty of Japan, and from that day to this Korea's fortunes have been one with those of the Island Empire. Ito's death[14] speeded up the annexation, which took place in 1910. With regret we see the little kingdom go down after having played its part so valiantly through two millennia. All things—fate, fortune, and the times she had fallen on—combined against her. Her king was unwise, his advisers untutored, so the days that should have been spent in useful preparation were frittered away in useless talk, to the sacrifice of those essential activities on which a country's foundation must rest.

Many changes have come to pass in the habits and lives of the people. The dark streets of Seoul have been lit; cholera epidemics have given way to a 'pest of bicycles' as Dr Allen well denominates them in his *Chronology;*[15] the Taewŏn'gun and Queen Min have both passed on their way to the spirit world; women are out in the open, veiled habits flung aside; tram-cars now vigorously sound their gongs, and railway trains go screaming through the night. The old hat and headband are off and the Barber's Guild is running a lively business at every street corner; western cut of garb, western hats, western boots are everywhere. The sedan-chair, relegated to the East Palace Museum, has been replaced by the ricksha, and the ricksha has been jostled off the highway by the motor-car. Schools have been opened everywhere, and farmers' sons are labouring alongside princes and peers to grope their way through problems of geometry and cube-root.

Many famous men of the west have come and gone in recent years, and have seen the declining fortunes of this ancient, cultured people with saddened eyes. Among them was Prince Henry of Prussia.[16] He found in Korea what princes seldom know, the joy of a walk, unnoticed and unmolested: he and his dachshund, free as the humblest, no man caring anything about him. Curzon came, peeped in and spoke of the problem of the east.[17] William Jennings Bryan, in a genial speech of an afternoon, told a congregation of young men where Korea's only hope lay.[18] Jack London browsed about till he had picked up materials for his terrible story *The Jacket.*[19] Lord Kitchener landed and looked for a moment with his cold, unresponsive eye.[20] Lord Bryce was tremendously interested in this people whose lives were impregnated with the spirit of literature, poetry, colour, ceremony, music and all the other things that combine to make a high culture. He wrote of them and thought of them to the last.[21] A long line of passers-by has come and seen and taken note that, though Korea was part of the Far East, she differed from China on the one hand and Japan on the other. China had mixed with many barbarian races, and Japan was a buddhist people thrilled by a sense of enterprise and a boundless future; Korea, overburdened by the weight of confucian dignity, treated all innovations with contempt.

THE END of the nineteenth century marks the end of Korea. Since then western so-called civilization has come in with overwhelming volume that nothing could withstand. Before this juggernaut the Chinese classics have gone down, together with the old course of classical study that prepared men for public office. Old religions, that comforted the soul and held society together for centuries, have been forgotten. All the ancient forms of the east have been flung to the winds in exchange for the inextricable confusion that we see today. China, to be sure, is in a similar plight: with the downfall of the old empire and the inrolling tidal wave of western notions, she too is drifting, none can tell whither. We weep over old Korea, a victim, not so much of political agencies, as of the social and intellectual revolution that has come from the west.

We have unwittingly brought about the destruction of East Asia, in which Korea is involved. To her the west evidently does as it pleases, why should she not? The west does not bother about father and mother, why should she? The west has no barriers between the sexes, why should she have? In everything that she has seen of the west, religion counts as nothing: why should she bother about it? Labour-unionism, communism, socialism, bolshevism, and anarchism express the real mind of western nations; why should she not take them up and be the same? Why should she sing in falsetto when the west sings with the whole throat open and full steam ahead? Why use the brush pen? Why not paint in oils as the west paints? Why not play on trombone and violin? Why not go whirling off for joy-rides, boys and girls? Why not be divorced at pleasure? Why not be up-to-date as the west is up-to-date? This wild dream, outdoing anything Jack London ever envisioned, well expresses the mind of the advanced youth of the city of Seoul in these days of confusion.

Let us glance once more at the Korea that is gone, 'the land of the superior man', as China long ago called her;[22] land of the scholar, land of the book and writing-brush, land of the beautiful vase and polished mirror; land of rarest, choicest fabrics; land of poems and painted pictures; land of the filial son, the devoted wife, the loyal courtier; land of the hermit, the deeply religious seer whose final goal was God.

HERE I repeat the earliest recorded verse I can find, written in 17 BC by King Yuri of Koguryŏ and quoted in chapter 8.[23] King Yuri's wife had left him and he, seeing a pair of orioles so happy together, says to the male bird:

> Oh lilting, joyous, yellow bird!
> You mate to live and love each other;
> While I, alas, unloved, unheard,
> Have lost my everything, sweet brother.

Finally let Viscount Kim Yunsik, who died on 21 January 1922, speak. Head of the Confucian College, a true Korean chief and patriot, how much he suffered for his country. Long years in exile, disgraced by the old government, imprisoned, degraded, condemned; yet always a gentleman, kindly of speech, temperate in habit, beautiful of face. One of the treasures the writer carries away from Korea is a copy of Kim Yunsik's works in eight volumes, given with his photograph and an autograph letter. One of the first poems I find is this:[24]

The departing swallow
You guard your fledgling's budding beak,
And twittering teach him how to speak;
Your thousand labours eve and morn
Declare him dearest ever born.

Upon our coloured eaves you light
And build a nest in Madame's sight;
She loves you, dear, both she and I,
And yet you think to leave us, why?

With endless twittering spring has fled
And here is autumn, rustling, dead.
'Mid waxing cold you sit so still,
And show no life or wingèd skill.

When you arrived 'twas two, no more;
But now, on going, you are four.
You said, as wide you circled free,
'Our coats are black, great lords are we.'

You skimmed the flower and tipped the stream
But now you're gone, a dream, a dream . . .
The cricket, whiles, a witless wight,
Keeps up his cheeping all the night.

NOTES AND BIBLIOGRAPHIES

TO

THE HISTORY OF THE KOREAN PEOPLE

Abbreviations used in the notes and bibliographies

CKK Chosen Kosho Kanko-kai (p. 356)
CKS   Chosen kinseki soran (p. 372)
CLS   Christian Literature Society of Korea
HDYS   Haedong yŏksa (p. 359)
HKP   History of the Korean people
KB   Korea Bookman (p. 377)
KCPG   Kukcho pogam (p. 360)
KM   The Korea Magazine (p. 376)
KMF   The Korea Mission Field (p. 377)
KR   The Korean Repository (p. 376)
KS   Koryŏ-sa (p. 360)
KSK   Korean sketches (p. 374)
MHPG   Munhŏn pigo (p. 359)
NHC   Chungjŏng Namhan chi (p. 363)
NTK   Namhun t'aep'yŏng ka (p. 365)
PCUSA   Presbyterian Church in USA
SGYS   Samguk yusa (p. 368)
SGSG   Samguk sagi (p. 360)
TC   T'oegye chip (p. 367)
TDKN   Taedong kinyŏn (p. 362)
TDYS   Taedong yasŭng (p. 361)
TGTG   Tongguk t'onggam (p. 361)
TKBRAS   Transactions of the Royal Asiatic Society, Korea branch
TMS   Tongmun-sŏn (p. 364)
TSCS   Tongsi chŏngsŏn (p. 365)
TSKM   Tongsa kangmok (p. 361)
TSYP   Tongsa yŏnp'yo (p. 362)
TYSC   Tongguk Yi Sangguk chip (p. 367)
YC   Yulgok chŏnsŏ (p. 367)
YJSN   Chŭngbo Tongguk yŏji sŭngnam (p. 359)
YLSK   Yŏllyŏ-sil kisul (p. 361)

NOTES

Chapter 1

1 A palaeolithic culture of hunters and foodgatherers seems to have existed in Korea by 25,000 BC. Neolithic cultures, which have left various kinds of pottery, existed from 3000 BC onwards. Bronze culture, associated with the dolmens that dot the country, entered around the 6th century BC; and ironwork, domesticated horses, and the heated floor now called *ondol* were known from the 4th or 3rd century BC, in the civilization now called Ancient Chosŏn. The name Chosŏn is probably cognate with Su-shen, the name of another non-Chinese people of the Korean-Manchurian region. Its meaning is not clear, but is unlikely to have any connexion with the meaning ('morning freshness') of the Chinese characters now used to write it.

Han'guk or Taehan, the modern names for the Republic of Korea since 1948, mean 'Land of Han' or 'Great Han.' They were also used from 1897 to 1910 (during which time the monarch was styled 'emperor') and are derived from the name of the Han tribes described in chapter 6 below.

The earliest form of the Tan'gun story in writing is in the thirteenth century *Samguk yusa*, written at a time when the myth was used to foster Korean national identity during the struggles with the Mongols; but the essentials of the legend are illustrated in Han dynasty reliefs carved a millenium earlier at the shrine of the Wu clan at Chia-hsiang in Shantung, an area which in prehistoric times belonged to the same cultural region as Korea. The myth therefore probably dates from the period of Ancient Chosŏn. The date 2333 BC for Tan'gun's appearance is taken from the *Tongguk t'onggam*, which differs slightly from the *Samguk yusa* on this point; both make Tan'gun contemporary with Yao, the sage-king of Chinese legend, much venerated by Confucius. It is possible that Tan'gun commemorates a culture-hero of neolithic times, but the date is more likely a simple matter of emulation.

The meaning of Tan'gun's name can only be guessed. As now written in Chinese character it means either 'sandalwood king' or 'altar king', but the first syllable may be a translation of a non-Chinese word meaning 'nation'. Some have suggested that *tan'gun* is transliteration of an Altaic word meaning a shaman-king. In early forms of the story Tan'gun is not the progenitor of the race, but a divinely appointed ruler and lawgiver. The traces of a bear cult in the story suggest either a bear totem or reverence for the bear as an earth god (because it hibernates), and link prehistoric Korea with other peoples of north-east Asia.

The Ever-white Mountains (Changbaek-san) are on the Manchurian border of north Korea. Their highest peak is Paektu-san.

2 The legendary emperor Yao lived at T'ang. See chapter 2 below.

3 Cf Ŏ Yunjŏk *Tongsa yŏnp'yo* p (1). *Kogŭm ki* is otherwise unknown.

4 Hammurabi lived in the 18th century BC.

5 TYSC *hujip* XI 3. Cf *Korea magazine* I ix 404–414, where Gale quotes *Tongsa yugo* (Various studies of Korean matters). *Tongsa yugo* has not been traced. Yang Chudong believes that it must have been a modern compilation (cf *Han'gugŭi in'gan sang* V 19, Seoul 1965).

6 These stories are both from *Tongsa yugo*, but cf the biography of Solgŏ in SGSG XLVIII. For Yi Kyubo see below chapter 19. The poem mentioned is not in TYSC.

7 According to Gale's article in *Korea magazine* I 404 and 413, this poem is 'Taebaek tan'ga', written by Sim Kwangse (1577–1624) and included in his *Haedong akpu*, but the text has not been found.

8 The literal meaning of the Chinese characters *kao-li* (Korean *koryŏ*) is 'high and beautiful', but the name is a contraction of Koguryŏ, possibly a transliteration of a native Korean word resembling the modern *koŭl*, 'settlement'. The English word Korea is derived through the Portuguese Corea from the Japanese pronunciation *Korai*, and dates from the sixteenth cen-

大
great
弓
bow

chapter 1 *i*: barbarian

イ
man
弓
bow

佛

chapter 9 *pul:* buddha

昔
sŏk
鳥
bird

鵲

chapter 10 *yŏng:* eternal

1 slant
2 bridle
3 strive
4 spring
5 whip
6 skim
7 peck
8 tear

chapter 8 *ch'ak* : magpie

イ
man
山
mountain

仙

chapter 20 *sŏn:* immortal

弓
bow

霘

chapter 16 *yŏng:* spirit

白
white
王
king

皇

chapter 38 *hwang* : tsar

走
chu
肖
ch'o

趙

chapter 27: *Cho* a surname

井
a well

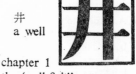

chapter 1
the 'well-field' pattern

tury. Gale used the Japanese form *Chosen* for Chosŏn because when he was writing, Japanese was the official language of Korea.

9 Ŏ Yunjŏk *op cit* p (46). All the history in this section is fictitious, except for the name of the *chiu-i* or *tung-i*. See Chinese characters, p 324.

10 Ibid pp (55), (57), (74). The directions at court were those in use until the end of the Korean kingdom in 1910.

11 Ibid p (97). This entry was deleted from the second edition of *Tongsa yŏnp'yo* in 1929. Wang Kŭmsŏk is otherwise unknown.

12 The story of Ch'i Tzŭ (in Korean Kija) migrating to Korea is not believed by most historians. It occurs first in the *Shih chi* of Szŭ-ma Ch'ien (1st century BC). The establishment of the P'yŏngyang shrine mentioned by Gale dates from the early twelfth century AD, and the whole cult of Ch'i Tzŭ in Korea seems to belong the China-worshipping mentality which grew up from that time onwards. It has been suggested that a religious cult of Ch'i Tzŭ may have been brought to Korea by emigrants from China to Ancient Chosŏn, and Chinese historians later invented the legend of his settlement in Korea to explain the presence of this cultus in the peninsula. There is no evidence for Chinese cultural influence in Korea as early as the traditional date of the Kija legend.

13 *Yangch'on munjip* I 4

14 CKS II 828 *Sungin-jŏn pi*

15 Ŏ Yunjŏk *op cit* p(122). The square fields were divided into nine smaller squares of equal area. Eight families tilled one field, giving the produce of the central square to the ruler. This system was said by later writers to have existed in Chou times. The four lines crossing the field in two pairs at right angles make the Chinese character for 'well'. Cf Mencius III a 3 xviii-xix. See Chinese characters, p 324.

16 Cf Ŏ Yunjŏk *ibid*

Chapter 2

1 The *pa kua* (Korean *p'al kwae*) are, strictly speaking, trigrams showing the eight combinations and permutations of broken and unbroken lines in groups of three. Their origin is unknown, but they form the basis of the *I ching*. They have been of cardinal importance in divination and four of them appear in the flag of the Republic of Korea.

2 Cf *Chuang-tzŭ* XI Tsai-yu

3 Taoism is a name for a varied conglomeration of Chinese myths and philosophical ideas, now used to cover the sophisticated thought of the *Tao te ching* and the fairy stories mentioned by Gale in this chapter. Chuang-tzŭ represents sophisticated taoism. The dating of Huang-ti belongs to legend.

4 Mencius III a I ii: '(Mencius) always spoke in praise of Yao and Shun.'

5 *Jen, i, li, chi, hsin* (Korean *in, ŭi, ye, chi, sin)*; Gale's reference is to Mayers's *Chinese reader's manual* 311.

6 Mencius *T'eng Wen Kung* III a 4 viii, where the *wu-lun* are attributed to Shun.

7 The 24 divisions of the year were not kept as holidays, but were, and still are, important in the popular calendar. Their origin is not known. The list is as follows (the precise date of each varies from year to year):

3– 5	February	*Beginning of spring*	7– 8	August	*Beginning of autumn*
18–20	February	Rainy and wet	22–23	August	End of heat
5– 6	March	Excited insects	7– 8	September	White dew
20–22	March	*SPRING EQUINOX*	22–24	September	*AUTUMN EQUINOX*
4– 5	April	Clear and bright	7– 8	October	Cold dew
20–21	April	Grain rain	23–24	October	Hoar frost
5– 6	May	*Beginning of summer*	7– 8	November	*Beginning of winter*
20–21	May	Swelling grain	22–23	November	Little snow
5– 6	June	Grain in ear	6– 7	December	Great snow
21–23	June	*SUMMER SOLSTICE*	21–23	December	*WINTER SOLSTICE*
6– 8	July	Little heat	5– 7	January	Little cold
22–23	July	Great heat	20–21	January	Great cold

8 The Shang era is well attested by archaeological remains, but the Hsia period is legendary, as are the stories of Shang personalities. The traditional Korean style for Yu of Hsia is *Ha U-ssi.*

9 I.e. the Chou period, during which Confucius lived. It is the beginning of Korean religious history only in the sense that Korea held to Confucius's doctrines, which arrived in the peninsula at a much later date.

10 For an account of these sacred books see the bibliography, pp 369–371.

11 *Shu ching* (Ku-wen text) xv 2 Hsien-yu-i-te

12 *Shih ching* III iii 2 I-i-wei-i

13 T'ai-jen was king Wen's mother. T'ai-szŭ was his wife, and mother of Wu, the founder of Chou.

14 Koreans speak of their national history as going back 4,000 (or even 5,000) years, but their recorded history goes back only 2,000 years and is in this respect comparable with the history of western Europe.

15 Various traditional dates are given for Lao Tzŭ, who is said to have been a contemporary of Confucius, but sober opinion discounts the legends and believes that *Lao-tzŭ* was the original name of the *Tao te ching,* treating that work as anonymous. See p 371.

16 The story of the meeting with Confucius is in the biography of Lao Tzŭ in the *Shih chi* (early 1st century BC).

17 *Tao te ching* viii

18 TMS VI 7 *Towŏn ka* (Song of the peach-blossom spring), an old-style seven-syllable poem, of which rather more than half is translated here. It is based on the famous fragment *T'ao-hua-yüan-chi* by the 4th century poet T'ao Ch'ien (see below chapter 10), which tells of a secret valley where lived refugees from the violent reign of the tyrant Shih Huang-ti, known in Korea as Ch'in-Shih (221–209 BC. See below chapter 6).

19 Gale *Korean Folk Tales* p 119

20 Herbert A Giles *The remains of Lao Tzu* Hongkong 1886 p 6 ff

21 The references to *Tao te ching* are I 1, II 4, II 6, and II 7a.

Chapter 3

1 Sakyamuni ('the sage of the Sakya clan'), also known as Gautama, from the sacerdotal name of his family. His personal name was Siddhartha (Korean *Siltalta*). His life cannot be precisely dated; Gale gives a traditional date which is probably not far wrong.

2 *P'alsang-nok* is a popular life of Sakyamuni written in Korean. The version used by Gale has not been traced. He completed his translation by 1915. See bibliography p 368.

3 In Korean the tree is called *musu*, which is a common element in Korean place-names.

4 *P'alsang-nok* II Suha t'ansaeng

5 Ibid III Sa mun yu-gwan sang

6 Ibid VII Nogwŏn chŏnbŏp sang

7 This Nanda (Korean *Nant'a*) is distinguished from others of the name as Sundarananda. He was king of Kapila-vastu and half-brother of Sakyamuni.

8 Maudgalyayana (Korean *Mongnyŏn*) was one of Sakyamuni's ten disciples and a great thaumaturge.

9 Yama-raja (Korean *Yŏmna wang*) is an ancient Indian figure who became ruler and judge in purgatory according to later buddhist mythology. He is very popular in Korea.

10 The Spirit-Hill Assembly (Korean *Yŏngsan-hoe*) was the imaginary meeting on the Vulture Peak, Grdhrakuta, where Sakyamuni expounded the Lotus Sutra.

11 Gale's account of buddhism in this chapter is perfunctory, and even misleading. He proves elsewhere that he had a deeper appreciation of it.

Chapter 4

1 The traditional dates for his life are 551-479 BC.

2 The first of these aphorisms is attributed to Confucius in the *Myŏngsim pogam*, where it is the first entry. The idea goes back to the *I ching*, commentary on the second hexagram, *K'un wen-yen.* See pp 365, 369.

The references for the remaining aphorisms are: Mencius IV 1 vii 1; Analects III 13 ii; XII 5 iii; IV 19; XV 27; VIII 5; I 3; II 1; II 10; IV 3; IV 5 i; IV 8; IV 17.

3 For all these books see bibliography, pp 370f.

4 The original of this quotation has not been identified.

5 The phrase is found in the *Kuo yü*, a book that purports to date from Chou times.

6 *North China Herald* 19 May 1905 pp 375–6. The author was Gale himself.

7 Cf *Naegwanŭi saekkina kkojipkido chal handa* and *Naesich'ŏrŏm kol nanda*.

8 Confucius is here used by synecdoche for confucianism. 'One man, one woman' was first recorded in *Yen t'ieh lun* ('Discourses on salt and iron'), a treatise on economic problems compiled in the first century BC, which affirms that this was the ancient ideal of marriage.

9 The passage was printed in the *Korea Magazine* I viii 360–361. No publication in Shanghai has been traced. It was written by Gale before June 1912.

10 The earliest literary reference to the five elements is in the *Shu ching*, where the concept is attributed to Ch'i Tzŭ in the *Hung fan*. The theory was later elaborated in connexion with the doctrine of *yang* and *yin*, especially by Tsou Yen in the fourth century BC. The accompanying table shows some of the ramifications as commonly understood in Yi dynasty Korea.

	lesser yang	YANG	neutral	lesser yin	YIN
elements	wood	fire	earth	metal	water
colours	blue/green	red	yellow	white	black
seasons	spring	summer	——	autumn	winter
cardinal points	east	south	centre	west	north
denary signs	*kap, ŭl*	*pyŏng, chŏng*	*mu, ki*	*kyŏng, sin*	*im, kye*
musical notes	mi	fah	doh	re	soh
quadrants	dragon	phoenix	——	tiger	tortoise
planets	Jupiter	Mars	Saturn	Venus	Mercury
weather	rain	heat	wind	fine	cold
natures	mild	inflammable	moist	cool	frigid
fortunes	infestation	war	abundance	mourning	floods
metals	tin	copper	gold	silver	iron
grains	barley	millet	rice	hemp	pulse
animals	scaled	feathered	naked(man)	furry	shelled
organs	muscles	blood	flesh	skin/hair	bones
viscera	liver	heart	stomach	lungs	kidneys
tastes	sour	bitter	sweet	peppery	salt
smells	musky	scorched	fragrant	rancid	mouldy
senses	sight	taste	touch	smell	hearing
feelings	anger	joy	thought	sorrow	fear
virtues	benevolence	ceremony	sincerity	justice	wisdom
consonants	palatal	lingual	guttural	dental	labial

11 The song is a *sijo*, a form of short lyric in the Korean vernacular which became very popular during the Yi dynasty. This is a *sasŏl sijo* (a longer form of the genre) written probably in the eighteenth century. Gale's text was NTK 11b (125).

Chapter 5

1 YJSN III 44–45

2 A note among Gale's MSS says the story comes from *Kimun ch'onghwa*, but I have not been able to trace it.

3 *Shih ching* I xi 6. This is the first stanza of three describing the three noblemen who were buried alive with Prince Mu of Ch'in at his funeral in 621 BC.

4 See below chapter 7.

5 The description is from the *Shih chi*.

6 The Hsiung-nu were nomads of the northern steppes. Their identity with the Huns is conjectural, though it is generally accepted that the Huns who later appeared in the west were

elements of the same Turkish-speaking peoples.

7 The second Punic War began in 218 BC.

Chapter 6

1 See below note 12.

2 Literally: 'world-wide tiger's glare'.

3 Probably Kim Tohŭi.

4 The traditional Chinese history textbook used in Korea was the *Shih-lüeh* (Korean *Saryak*). The stories told in this chapter are succinctly recounted in it. See bibliography p 372.

5 For other differences between the Chinese and Korean games, see Stewart Culin *Korean games* (Pennsylvania 1895, reprinted as *Games of the Orient* Tokyo 1958) pp 82–91. The Chinese sides are called black and white.

6 The song is another eighteenth century *sasŏl sijo* in the Korean vernacular. The broken heart in the poem is caused by a separation. For Chu-ko Liang see below chapter 9. This version of the song is at NTK 8 a (84).

7 Kao Tsu, a posthumous title meaning 'high progenitor'.

8 Ta-ch'in probably meant the eastern provinces of the Roman empire.

9 *Shih-lüeh* II has the story but credits Mao Tun with only 40,000 cavalrymen.

10 The story of Lü Hou is in *Shih-lüeh* II. Gale's vulgarism 'chucked' is a pun on the Korean pronunciation of the name of Lady Ch'i: *Chŏk,* which he spelled 'Chuk'. The 'old Buddha' was the dowager empress of China, Tz'ŭ-hsi. She had her nephew appointed emperor (Kuang-hsü 1875–1908); in 1901 she had his favourite concubine ('the Pearl Concubine') wrapped in a mat and thrown into a well.

11 The story of Wei Man (Korean *Wi Man*) is given by the *Shih chi*. Wei Man was a lieutenant of Lu Kuan, ruler of Yen, who rebelled against the Han and failed. Lu took refuge among the Hsiung-nu, and Wei fled to Korea, where he was made a border commander rather than a bodyguard. His superiority over the previous residents in Korea may have been due to his knowledge of iron weapons. Some historians think he assumed leadership of Chinese elements already in Korea, but some Korean historians believe he may have been from non-Chinese stock, nearly akin to the Koreans. Cf TSKM I i (*musin* year 28) p 111.

12 The Han of the Chinese dynasty and the Han of Korean states are written with different Chinese characterrs. For the material in the paragraph see TSKM I i pp 111–12 and TGTG *oegi*. Modern Korean historians discount the possibility of Chinese blood in the Han communities and regard them as confederations of Korean groups. Cf chapter I note 1 for Han as a modern name for Korea.

13 TSKM I i (*pyŏngo* year 26) p 111. The headband (Korean *manggŏn*) has been traced in China as far back as T'ang, but it became widespread only in Ming times and is now presumed to have come into use in Korea in early Yi. Gale's treatment of his sources here is uncritical.

14 There is a similar story in Isabella Bird Bishop *Korea and her neighbours* London 1898 (II 180). There were several such suicides.

15 The story of Wang Ch'iang or Wang Chao-chün is one of the most popular in the Far East. The oldest and probably truest version tells that she was a court lady married in 33 BC to a Hun chief whose son succeeded on the death of his father and married her, according to Hun custom, along with his father's other wives. Late versions of the tale say she took poison rather than follow the incestuous barbarian custom. An even later version tells how she refused to bribe the court painter Ma Yen-shou and he deliberately painted her ugly, so she was selected to marry the Hun ruler. The confusions are shown by the reference to the Amur as a boundary of the Gobi. Gale omits the story of her 'Verdant Tomb', which is said to remain green in the midst of the desert. In the thirteenth-century play *Ch'u-chai Chao-chün,* translated by Davis as 'The sorrows of Han', she drowns herself rather than marry the Hun.

16 TGTG *oegi* and TSKM I i (*kyeyu* year) pp 115–17. The Han army was sent to subjugate Wei Man's kingdom, either because it was hindering trade with the tribes in southern Korea, or simply because its existence was a threat to the security of the empire. Korean historians tend to believe that the four Han provinces or commanderies were situated mainly in present-day Manchuria, and only partly in northern Korea.

17 Sekino Tadashi (1867–1935), was a Japanese architect and lover of Korean antiquities who visited Korea first in 1902. Then and later he conducted official surveys of ancient remains in the peninsula. His chief publications apart from his share in editing *Chosen koseki zufu* and *Koseki chosa tokubetsu hokoku,* were *Rakuro-gun jidae no iseki* (Remains of the Lolang period) 1927, *Chosen bijutsu-shi* (History of Korean art) 1932, and *Chosen no kenchiku to geijutsu* (Korean architecture and art) 1941.

18 Gale accepted the still common error which underrates the Britons and overrates the Koreans.

19 *Chung-ting kuang-chih* was edited by Hsüeh Shang-kung of the Sung dynasty. The Chinese inscription reads *Hou-jen-ying-pao* (Korean *Hu-in-yŏng-bo*).

20 *Chosen koseki zufu* I 10. The mirror then kept in the Tokyo Koka Daigaku was inscribed *Shou ju chin-shih chia ch'ieh hao hsi* (Korean *Su yŏ kŭmsŏk ka ch'a ho hye*). Gale drew this material from his article in the *Korea magazine* II viii 354–6.

Chapter 7

1 Helle and Phrixus were the children of Athamas, king of Thebes, by his first wife, Nephele. Ino, his second wife, hated them so much that they fled on the golden ram. Helle was lost but Phrixus arrived safely in Colchis, where the ram was sacrificed to Zeus and its fleece hung up till it was recovered by the Argonauts.

Io was beloved by Zeus, who changed her into a heifer to hide her from Hera's jealousy. Hera had the heifer persecuted by a gadfly that chased her to Egypt, where she was later worshipped as Isis. *Bosporos* means 'ox-ford', but 'bossy' is a colloquial word for 'calf', derived from the bosses on its head rather than from the Greek *bous,* 'ox'.

2 I.e. *Samguk sagi.* See bibliography, p 361.

3 The foot by which Kim was measured was smaller than the English foot. The king was Injong of Koryŏ and the date of the commission 1135. If refers to Kim being made commander-in-chief for the quelling of Myoch'ŏng's rebellion. KS XCVIII 4 yŏlchŏn 11, and TGTG XXIII Injong 13.

4 TMS I 10 *Agye-bu.* Not an essay, but a long poem in six-character lines, called *pu* (Chinese *fu*). The lines are arranged in paratactic couplets, there is a rhyme scheme, and the subject is usually moral or descriptive, rather than lyrical. Chinese and Koreans, like westerners, suffer from the delusion that there is some peculiar connexion between dawn and the crowing of cocks.In fact, they crow at all hours of day and night.

5 This couplet was omitted by Gale. I have restored it by reference to his first draft, in which he marked it for excision, presumably because he never checked the reference to *Shih-ching* I (Kuo-feng) vii 16, where a woman waiting for her husband says that storms do not stop the cocks crowing.

6 SGSG XIII 1; TGTG Silla sijo year 21 *kapsin*

7 The foundation myths of the early Korean states are extant in forms dating from the twelfth century or later. They have much in common with other myths of heroes, but usually suggest an immigrant leader from an advanced culture moving in to marry a woman of the local less culturally advanced group. The hero is born from an egg, gourd, or sea-borne box, which may stem from a myth about a 'cosmic egg', or merely indicate miraculous birth, or hint at a bird totem (in the egg stories) or a folk memory of choosing leaders by casting votes (or lots) in a receptacle. The Koguryŏ foundation myth may have been borrowed from the Fuyu people of Manchuria. The state of Koguryŏ probably emerged in the last century BC; it was established by the second century AD. The dates given by Gale belong to legend. The capital described by Gale, Kungnae-sŏng, is on the Manchurian side of the Yalu at T'ung-kou.

8 See chapter 11 below.

9 By many historians Hwando is now equated with Kungnae-sŏng.

10 SGSG I 1; TGTG I 1

11 TGTG I. This is a summarized quotation.

12 The story of the Magpie Bridge is an ancient Chinese legend which is extremely popular in Korea. See below chapter 23.

13 I.e. *Tongguk t'onggam.* TGTG I Silla sijo year 5 *mujin*

14 The legend of dragons may have taken shape in China from the sight of salmon leaping up-

river during the spring rains.

15 TGTG Silla sijo year 8 *sinmi*
16 TGTG Silla sijo year 30 *kyesa*
17 TGTG Silla sijo year 53 *pyŏngjin*
18 TGTG I Silla Yuri year 9 *imjin*. *Kabae* is a Chinese transliteration of the Korean *kawi*, the mid-autumn moon festival, which seems to have been introduced into Korea through Silla. It is kept on the 15th—i.e. the full moon—of the 8th lunar month and is essentially a harvest celebration. The modern name of the festival is Ch'usŏk. See chapter 33 below.
19 TGTG I Silla sijo year 17
20 Confucianism probably did not arrive in Koguryŏ and Paekche until the third century or later, and in Silla about the seventh century.
21 TGTG I Silla sijo year 39 *imin*
22 It is not certainly true that there was no break in the royal line of Silla.

Chapter 8

1 SGSG XIII Yuri. The token was that the broken blade fitted the piece that his father had retained.
2 HDYS IX 1. The etymology is a back-reading from the Chinese transliteration of Paekche.
3 'Eber (Gen x 21, etc) may have been the eponymous ancestor of the Hebrews, but the meaning of his name is not known. If the word 'Hebrew' has any connexion with *'eber*, it probably means that the Hebrews were wanderers. The whole question is a matter of conjecture. The river crossed by Paekche was either the Yalu or the Taedong. For the full story see SGSG XXIII sijo.
4 SGSG XXIII sijo year 14
5 SGSG XXIII sijo year 11. Paekche evolved out of Koguryŏ, in the Han River basin. It was well established as a state by the middle of the third century.
6 SGSG XXIII sijo year 27
7 HDYS III and TSKM Ia Han Hui-ti year 2
8 I.e. the *Wei chih*. See TSKM Ia Han Hui-ti year 2, and TGTG *oegi*.
9 But see chapter 1, note 1.
10 Sir Edward Creasy *Fifteen decisive battles of the world* 1851. See below chapter 14 note 20.
11 SGSG XXIII sijo year 1
12 Ibid year 31; Sogo-wang year 24
13 SGSG sijo year 33; Kiru year 32
14 SGSG XIII Yuri year 2. Tamul may have been modern Sŏngch'ŏn, South P'yŏngan province.
15 Kolch'ŏn. Gale mistranslated 'Magpie River' (Chakch'ŏn). The place is not identified.
16 SGSG XIII Yuri year 3. The poem is called *Hwangjo ka*, and may be either an extract from a longer poem or a snatch of folk song which has had a legend attached to it. It is preserved in the Chinese language, and the claim that it is the oldest piece of Korean literature in existence can therefore not be taken very seriously. The other lyric for which Gale made the same claim in *Korea Magazine I ii* 59 (*Konghu-in*, ascribed to Yŏ Ok) is probably a Chinese song which has been attributed to Korea owing to a confusion of place-names (See HDYS XLVII 1).
17 SGSG XIII Yuri year 19
18 TGTG I Koguryŏ Yuri year 19
19 SGSG XIII Yuri year 24
20 SGSG XIII Yuri year 27
21 Silla, originally called Saro, was effectively organized as a kingdom in the mid-fourth century, and grew out of a confederation of Chinhan communities.
22 SGSG I P'asa year 30
23 SGSG I Yuri year 5
24 Or, more probably, the kingship rotated among these three families. Another theory holds that the rulers were Kim, their consorts Pak. The Sŏk may be legendary.
25 SGSG I T'arhae. There may be further signs of a bird totem in this story. Ajinp'o is the pre-

sent Yŏngil. Tap'ara may mean Cheju, formerly known as T'amna. '300 miles' is a translation of '1000 *li*', a vague expression. 'The Women's Kingdom' may hint at an earlier matriarchal system. See Chinese characters, p 324.

26 There is some confusion between this myth and that of Pak Hyŏkkŏse in the preceding chapter. It doubtless marks the settling of the royal line in the Kim dynasty. 'Kim' means 'gold'. See SGSG I T'arhae year 9, and TGTG II T'arhae year 9.

27 TGTG II T'arhae year 9 note.

Chapter 9

1 King Sansang, personal name Yŏnu.

2 SGSG XVI Kogukch'ŏn year 2

3 The following story is in SGSG XVI Sansang year 1

4 Unidentified.

5 TGTG III Koguryŏ Sansang year 1

6 SGSG XVI Sansang years 7 and 11

7 TGTG III Koguryŏ Sansang year 11

8 SGSG XVI Sansang year 13

9 SGSG XVII Tongch'ŏn year 8; TGTG III

10 *Ikchae chip* I 3. The translation given here amounts to rather less than half the full poem. For Yi Chehyŏn, see below chapter 21.

11 The Chinese character *fu* (Korean *pul*) was appropriated to the buddha because of its sound. These stories of the introduction of buddhism to China are apocryphal. The reference to K'ang-hsi's dictionary is to a quotation given under this character from *Cheng-tzŭ-t'ung*, compiled by the Ming polymath, Chang Tzŭ-lieh. For the dictionary see bibliography, p 372.

12 *San-kuo-chih yen-i*. See bibliography, p 372.

13 *San-kuo-chih yen-i* 1

14 *San-kuo-chih yen-i* 25

15 The song is a Yi dynasty *kagok*, based on the *Chŏkpyŏk ka*. The text is in Yi Ch'angbae *Chŭngbo kayo chipsŏng* Seoul 1966, p 83, and Yi Hyegu *Kugak tae chŏnjip* Seoul 1968, p 205. It refers to an incident after the famous battle of the Red Cliff (Ch'ih-pi, Korean 'Chŏkpyŏk') (*San-kuo-chih yen-i* 50). The red horse was the famous charger Ch'ih-t'u, 'Red Hare', and the sword was called Ch'ing-lung, 'Blue Dragon'. Gale translated the last line incorrectly as 'Gives up his name to after years', owing to a forgivable misunderstanding of *myŏng*.

16 The Tongmyo outside the East Gate still stands in 1972. The Nammyo, outside the South Gate, was burnt in 1898 and again in 1950. In the latter part of the Yi dynasty the cult of Kuan Yü became very popular and a number of private temples to him were built in Seoul. See below, chapter 38 note 5.

17 *San-kuo-chih yen-i* 37, 38.

18 *San-kuo-chih yen-i* 102

19 SGSG XVII Tongch'ŏn year 20

20 SGSG XVII Tongch'ŏn year 21

21 SGSG XVIII Kogugwŏn year 12

Chapter 10

1 I.e. Tongch'ŏn.

2 SGSG XVII Tongch'ŏn year 22

3 TSKM IIa Chungch'ŏn year 1

4 SGSG XVII Chungch'ŏn year 4

5 SGSG XVII Sŏch'ŏn year 17

6 TGTG III Sŏch'ŏn year 17

7 SGSG XVII Pongsang year 5

8 TGTG III Silla Yurye year 15

9 SGSG XVIII Sosurim year 2; SGYS III. Cf *Chosŏn pulgyo t'ongsa* I 1, and III 70ff.

10 CKS I 25 Ado hwasang pi; SGYS III Ado ponbi: cf *Chosŏn pulgyo t'ongsa* I 7–10. The stone had disappeared before Gale's time.

11 Koguryŏ officially recognized buddhism in 372; Paekche had missions from Koguryŏ in 384; Silla officially established buddhism in 527 or 528.

12 See chapter 3 note 1.

13 The origin of the *yung-tzŭ pa fa* ('eight principles of the character *yung*') cannot be traced. They have been attributed, but with little reason, to Ts'ai Yung (133-92). Because *yung* was the first character in Wang Hsi-chih's fabulous *Lan-t'ing hsü* (Orchid Pavilion Essay)—the most famous piece of Chinese calligraphy ever written—and there is a story that he spent fifteen years perfecting his writing of that character alone, the eight principles have also been attributed to Wang Hsi-chih. His seventh-generation descendant, the calligrapher-monk Chih-yung, developed the theory in the late sixth century, and the names now given to the eight elements were explained by the thirteenth-century writer Ch'en Szŭ.

The eight elements are not the strokes of the character (*yung* is written with six strokes, not eight) but a system for teaching the requisite force of each stroke. Each element is denoted by a verb describing the force it represents: slant, bridle, strive, spring, whip, skim, peck, and tear. At least 32 different shapes of stroke are used in Chinese calligraphy, but these eight elements epitomize the dynamic technique required to draw them all. Correct shapes without dynamic force would produce inferior calligraphy. See Chinese characters, p 324.

14 Kucha was one of the buddhist Indo-european oasis kingdoms of the Tarim basin, culturally heir to Alexander the Great as well as to Gautama. It declined after 650. Kumarajiva was an Indian monk captured by Chinese about 382. He translated 98 scriptures, of which 52 are now extant. The Lotus Sutra is the Saddharma-pundarika-sutra, 'The lotus of the wonderful law' (Korean *Myŏbŏp yŏnhwa kyŏng* or *Pŏphwa-gyŏng*) and the Diamond Sutra is the Vajra-prajna-paramita-sutra, (Korean *Kŭmgang-gyŏng*). The 'diamond' or thunderbolt *(vajra)* symbolizes indestructible truth. See bibliography, below p 369.

The translation is wrong and the prophecy cannot refer to Christ. For 'the Coming One' read 'buddhahood'; for 'Five hundred years' read 'During the five-hundred-year periods'; for 'One who will bring' read 'those who will keep'; and for 'This One' read 'They'.

15 Vajra-sutra v and vi. Previously published *Korea Magazine* II ii 52.

16 The story and name of Wang In (Japanese: Onin) are in the *Nihon shoki.*

17 Analects I i 1, 2, and 3; I ii 1

18 *To Chŏngjŏl chip* I 9 Ta P'ang Ts'an-chun. See bibliography p 372.

Chapter 11

1 This was a common nineteenth-century misassessment of early mediaeval history. The European 'Dark Ages' compare favourably with contemporary oriental civilization.

2 CKS I 3 Koguryŏ Kwanggaet'o Wangnŭng pi. The reign of Kwanggaet'o (391-413) was the beginning of the golden age of Koguryŏ. He first used a Chinese-style reign title, Yŏngnak (Gale's 'Eternal Joy').

3 *Chosen koseki zufu* I plates 89-95

4 Cf SGSG III Soji years 19 and 22; CKS I 5

5 The main court of the Kyŏngbok Palace, Seoul.

6 In the Great Tomb (Taemyo, late sixth or seventh century).

7 In fact the tomb was painted as a microcosm. Cf table on p 327. It was believed that all tortoises were female and that snakes performed the male role for them.

8 Shinchido is Japanese for Chinji-dong. The Twin Pillar Tomb is called Ssangyŏng-ch'ong. It probably dates from the early sixth century, too late for Changsu.

9 SGSG XLV, SGYS I, TSKM IIb Nulchi year 2 summer

10 The original text has not been identified.

Chapter 12

1 Also known as Toba, they played a major role in introducing buddhist art to China.

2 A Sanskrit lamaistic formula, said to be a prayer to Padmapani (Kuan-yin holding a lotus flower) and used as a potent charm. Korea was not yet, in fact, a Confucian state.

3 SGSG XLIV; and XX Yŏngyang year 23. Gale has confused the chronology of his account by telling here the story of seventh-century Yang, which he repeats in the following chapter.

Sui replaced the Wei and other kingdoms towards the end of the sixth century.
4 SGSG XIX Yangwŏn year 7
5 The *Ch'ien-tzŭ wen* was the standard primer for all Korean boys to learn their first thousand characters from. The phrase quoted is the famous opening phrase, 'Heaven and earth, the dark and the dun', in the form in which it was memorized by Korean children.
6 CKS I 10 Silla Chinhŭng wang sunsu pi. The stone is now thought to have been erected about 569 to commemorate the king's visit of 555, soon after the annexation of the Han basin by Silla. Two similar stones stand in South Hamgyŏng and one in South Kyŏngnam.
7 This story is from *Tongsa yugo*. See chapter 1 note 5.
8 In fact Silla deliberately Sinified herself, the last of the three Korean kingdoms to do so.
9 Sara, Saro, and Silla are the same name in different Chinese transliterations.
10 The naming of Korean royalty is a complex subject, and Gale has here only touched on one aspect. Using his example, King Sejong of the Yi dynasty, the matter can be further illuminated as follows:

(1) Sejong: temple name (*myoho*) given after death, and the usual way of referring to a former king. The temple name is not given to deposed kings, who revert to their princely title after death. Sejong means 'regenerating ancestor'.

(2) To: personal name (*myŏng* or, more properly, *hwi*) given early in life and, in the case of kings, thereafter treated as tabu till the end of the dynasty. When the character was needed in writing, an approved substitute had to be used. *To* means 'a sleeve-cuff' or 'blissful'; the approved substitute was *hyul*, meaning a sleeve, and associated with *to* as a compound word. Both are very rare characters and are entered only in the largest dictionaries.

(3) Wŏnjŏng: *cha*, a name for familiar use, commonly given at marriage. Wŏnjŏng means 'fundamentally upright'.

(4) Some kings used also a literary name or style (*pyŏrho, tangho, aho,* or *ho*) but none is recorded for Sejong. A man might have several *ho*, chosen by himself or given by friends or teachers.

(5) Ch'ungnyŏng: his princely title. Such a name, prefixed to *kun* or *taegun*, according to rank, was given to all royal male offspring. The title is usually a real or imaginary geographical name. Sejong was originally Ch'ungnyŏng-gun, then promoted to Ch'ungnyŏng-taegun before he was made Crown Prince.

(6) Yŏngmun-yemu-insŏng-myŏngho, meaning 'florescent scholar, sagacious warrior, benevolent sage, resplendently filial son', was his honorific name (*chonho*), referred to by Gale as four names because it has four elements. Such names were created by a government department specially set up when they were needed—usually after a king had died or honourably abdicated. They could be changed and added to, if need be, centuries after the king's death. Some seals with *chonho* survive, but Sejong's personal seals have disappeared.

(7) Changhŏn; the posthumous honorific *(siho)* bestowed by the Ming court. It means 'good and respected ruler'.

A former king's full name consists of his temple name followed by his posthumous honorific and his other honorific names. Thus Sejong is formally recorded as Sejong-changhŏn-yŏngmun-yemu-insŏng-myŏngho taewang. The longest of such names is that of Yŏngjo, which has 58 syllables.

During their lifetime members of the royal family were referred to by titles rather than names. *Wang* is strictly a subsidiary king, and Yi dynasty Korea used *taewang* ('great king') with occasional variations such as *sang'wang* for retired monarchs. The crown prince (the selected heir to the throne) was known as *wangseja* or *seja*, with or without titular name prefixed; the king's sons by the queen consort were *taegun* (great prince); the king's sons by concubines, the eldest son and grandson of any *taegun*, and all the sons and grandsons of the crown prince, as well as certain meritorious subjects, were called *kun*. The royal son-in-law was called *puma*, an abbreviation of *puma-towi*.

After 1897 the monarch was called emperor (*hwangje*) and the princes of the blood were called *ch'inwang*.

The names and titles of royal women corresponded in the main to names and titles used for royal males, except that women normally had no personal names.

11 SGSG IV Chijŭng year 15
12 SGSG IV Pŏphŭng year 15
13 SGSG IV Pŏphŭng year 37
14 SGSG IV Pŏphŭng year 35
15 SGYS IV; cf SGSG IV Chinp'yŏng year 22
16 SGSG IV Chinhŭng year 37. The myth of the founding of the *hwarang* suggests the change-over from a matrilineal to a patrilineal society. The exact dating is not to be taken seriously: the story is added in at the end of Chinhŭng's reign, and so appears to belong to his last year. The institution for youths lasted a long time, and has probably left its final relics in the male shamans of Korea. Another version of the story occurs in SGYS III. Gale had the material garbled, as though the *hwarang* were founded before the girls' band. I have amended his text. In modern Korea the *hwarang* have been widely misinterpreted as a military organization; in Gale's day they were little talked of, because they were not strictly confucian.
17 SGSG XLV
18 SGSG IV Chinhŭng year 6. Kŏch'ilbu and others were ordered by the king to compile *sagi* (annals, a title copied from the *Shih chi*). SGSG XXIV Kŭnch'ogo year 30 mentions without conviction a similar attempt in Paekche in 375.
19 TSKM IIIa Chinhŭng year 12. Kaya was a league of small states between Silla and Paekche, which was absorbed by them by the last third of the seventh century. It had close relations with Japan, and a distinctive culture.
20 SGSG IV and XXXII
21 All three songs are sijo, written in the Yi dynasty, probably in the eighteenth century, although the first one is attributed to Hwang Chin (fifteenth century). They were all written a thousand years after the days of Urŭk. The second and third as here translated were published in the *Korean Repository* April 1895 in the first selection of *sijo* poetry ever published in English translation. The texts are NTK 4a (38), 5a (49), and 5a (48). Gale did not know of the existence of *hyangga*, which are lyrics dating from Silla times.

Chapter 13

1 SGSG XX Yŏngyang year 23
2 TMS XIX 1; HDYS XLVII quoting *Sui shu*.
3 Han Hsin won great victories for the emerging Han dynasty in the second century AD.
4 SGSG XLVIII
5 See chapter 37
6 The correct translation of this couplet is:
> Keen ears hear where there is no sound,
> Keen eyes see where there is no shape.

It occurs first in *Shih chi* CVIII in a speech by Wu Pei, minister of Huai-nan, reprimanding his king for plotting a revolt. The passage occurs again in *Han shu* XLV. Gale's attribution to T'ang T'ai Tsung is either an error or a reference to a quotation which has not been identified. The two parts of the sentence have been reversed and the words referring to hearing and sight have been misunderstood.
7 See chapter 33
8 The stone is known formally as *Hŭngbŏp-sa Chin'gong taesa t'ap pi*. The text is in CKS I 144. Hong's text is in *Igye chip* XVI 44.
9 Qu'ran, sura 91
10 YJSN XXI 29
11 SGSG XLI
12 YJSN XVIII 23
13 It is now known that the traditional account of this pagoda, give here by Gale, is wrong. It is a Paekche pagoda, originally belonging to the temple Chŏngnim-sa. Su Ting-fang had the story of his 'pacification' of Paekche inscribed on it. The remains of Mirŭk-sa pagoda, near Iksan, are in fact older (c 600).

14 SGSG XXVIII Ŭija year 20
15 SGSG V Sŏndŏk wang
16 YJSN XXII 24. It is not known how the observatory was used.
17 SGSG XLVI
18 TYSC XX 8, extract from 'Saegyu'

Chapter 14

1 Yi Yongik (1854-1907) was a conservative politician and doughty fighter against Japan, who favoured pro-Russian policies. He was finance minister at the time of the modernization of the currency. Lady Ŏm was not officially queen, but *kwibi (kuei-fei)*.
2 The article is in the issues for September and November 1923, and January 1924, written by Wu Shih-huan.
3 A *sijo*. NTK 8b (88)
4 These are the opening lines of a favourite old Korean nursery song.
5 TYSC II 17
6 See above chapter 1 note 5
7 TYSC *hujip* XI 3
8 TYSC *hujip* XI 5
9 The Pongdŏk-sa bell in the Kyŏngju museum.
10 CKS I 38 Silla Sŏngdŏk wang sinjong myŏng
11 SGSG VIII Sŏngdŏk year 1
12 SGSG VIII Sŏngdŏk year 22
13 CKS I 34 Kamsan-sa Mirŭk posal chosang ki. Removed to the Government-general Museum in 1915.
14 TGTG X Hyegong year 15; SGSG XLIII yŏlchŏn 3
15 *Chi-men tun-chia* is a book of magical calculations.
16 SGYS V
17 The Tabo-t'ap (Prabhuta-ratna stupa) or 'Many-jewels' pagoda, was probably built at the same time as the temple. Prabhuta-ratna was an ancient buddha, long in nirvana, who appeared in his stupa to hear Sakyamuni preach the lotus doctrine. Cf Lotus sutra XI.
18 The mounds are tombs.
19 The lovely relief of Kuan-yin shows him with eleven heads as Ekadasamukha, looking for suffering in all directions. Gale made the widespread error of thinking Kuan-yin is female. The 'queenly lady' with the chalice is the boddhisatva Samantabhadra, the 'all-gracious', special patron of the Lotus Sutra school. The other figures are Manjusri, Brahma, Indra, and ten arhats or disciples. The 'modest man' is one of the disciples. The guards trampling on devils are the four Deva kings. All the figures are male.
   The famous golden crown of Silla had been discovered in 1921, but Gale had obviously not seen it.
20 *Fifteen decisive battles of the world,* 1851. The battles were: Marathon, Syracuse, Arbela, the Metaurus, the defeat of Varus, Châlons, Tours, Hastings, Joan of Arc's victory at Orleans, the Spanish Armada, Blenheim, Poltava, Saratoga, Valmy, and Waterloo.
21 Mrs Gordon set up this facsimile of the Nestorian tablet in the Diamond Mountains in 1916. She wrote a number of books on buddhism. Some idea of her mind and methods can be gleaned from her paper, 'Some recent discoveries in Korean temples and their relationship to early christianity' TKBRAS V i 1914. She was more enthusiastic than scholarly.
22 CKS I 35 Kamsan-sa Amida yŏrae chosang ki. The inscription is on the back of a stone buddha. Cf Kim Chewŏn and Kim Wŏnyong *Treasures of Korean Art* London and New York 1966 pp 149-50.
23 CKS I 41. A conflated and free translation. The stone is in the Kyŏngbok Palace museum. Much of the inscription is obscure.
24 *Ch'ang-hen ko.* The fourth couplet from a poem of some 70 couplets. It is included in the eighteenth-century anthology *T'ang-shih san-pai-shou* (300 poems of T'ang) and was available in Korea in *Komun chinbo* I. Koreans usually refer to Po Chü-i as Paek Nakch'ŏn (Po Lo-t'ien).

25 *Yüan tao*. Koreans knew this essay through *Komun chinbo* II. They usually referred to Han Yü as Han T'oeji (Han T'ui-chih).
26 *P'alsang-nok* vii Nogwŏn chonbŏp sang: Aran sugin. Young Ananda and aged Kasyapa are Sakyamuni's typical disciples.

Chapter 15

1 Ch'oe Ch'iwŏn was born in 857 and died about the end of the century. He is regarded as the first Korean writer, though he wrote in Chinese after the style of later T'ang, and it was a long while before anyone else followed his example in Korea. He was fundamentally buddhist, though the confucians claim him. His chief remaining work, *Kyewŏn p'ilgyŏng*, was composed entirely while he was in China.
2 The original texts of these three poems are in *Kyewŏn p'ilgyŏng*: XX 8 Kwiyŏn-ŭm hŏn t'aewi; XX 9 Haegu; and XX 9 Chorang. All these poems were later criticized for their mannered richness. The reference to Chuang-tzŭ's dream that he was a butterfly, and his failure, on waking up, to know whether he was not a butterfly dreaming it was Chuang-tzŭ, is very common in Korean writing. It comes from the end of the first book of the *Chuang-tzŭ*. Tsung Ch'üeh of Southern Sung was asked by his father what his ambition was and replied that he wanted to 'ride the long wind'.
3 Nanghye is the posthumous honorific name of Muyŏm (801–888). He became a monk in Sorak-san in his early teens, and went to China for studies from 822 to 845. He was a propagator of *ch'an* (i.e. zen) buddhism. The memorial inscription is in CKS I 72ff Sŏngju-sa Nanghye hwasang Paegwŏl-pogwang-t'ap pi.
4 Nanggong is the posthumous honorific name of Haengjŏk (832–916). He was trained at Haein-sa, went to China in 870 and visited many famous shrines, travelling as far as Chengtu. He returned to Korea in 885 and died at the age of 85. CKS I 181ff T'aeja-sa Nanggong taesa Paegwŏl-sŏun-t'ap pi.
5 Chiang T'ai-kung, also known as Lü Shang, was the fabulous old counsellor whom king Wen of Chou found fishing in the River Wei. He was so wise that he could catch fish with straight hooks.
6 Cf CKS I 184–85
7 HDYS XXVII
8 HDYS XXVII Munbang-nyu
9 *Kao-li t'u-ching* CKK edition Bk 32 p 528. Cf HDYS XXVI. (See bibliography p 372.)
10 *Kyewŏn p'ilgyŏng* XVIII 14 Sa sin t'a chang; TMS XLVII 17
11 TGTG XI Hŭngdŏk year 10. Kuo Chü is one of the Chinese paragons of filial piety, said to have lived in the second century AD.
12 *Kyewŏn p'ilgyŏng* XII 1 Chŏju Hŏ Kyŏng wigok. This Hsü Ching is not the Hsü Ching of note 9 above.

Chapter 16

1 See Chinese characters, p 324. This is an ancient form of the character *ling* (Korean *yŏng*) for 'ghost' or 'spirit'.
2 The story of Kungye as given here is based on SGSG L, with some details from TGTG XX.
3 For sources of the Kyŏn Hwŏn story see note 2 above. Gale's account obscures Kyŏn Hwŏn's qualities. This 'robber chief' maintained a kingdom for thirty-five years, with diplomatic skill during turbulent times.
4 For notes on the meanings of these names see chapter 1 note 1 and note 8; also chapter 11 note 9.
5 The Chinese for Khitan is *Ch'itan*, the Turkish and Arabic is *Khitai*. *Khitai* became the Turkish and Russian word for China, and is the origin of Marco Polo's 'Cathay'.
6 The dynasty was known as Liao.
7 TGTG XIII T'aejo year 14
8 SGSG XX
9 SGYS II Ch'ŏyong-nang. The dance appears originally to have been an exorcism, and was

developed during Koryŏ days. The other mask dances referred to by Gale have independent origins in religious folk drama.

10 The mast is called in Korea *tang-gan* or *chimdae,* the pillars *tanggan chiju.*

11 Ch'ŏnhŭng-sa tanggan chiju

12 Yongdu-sa ch'ŏl-tanggan still stands in a square in Ch'ŏngju. Its date was 962, but Gale failed to calculate correctly from the Japanese imperial era Koki, and wrote 1182. The text of the inscription is in CKS I 194f.

13 They were originally flagpoles at buddhist temples, but geomantic meanings were given to them later. They were erected also in China.

14 In fact pagodas had been built as early as the sixth and seventh centuries. See page 334.

15 The Kwanch'ŏk-sa Mirŭk near Ŭnjin dates from the late tenth century. Many other *mirŭk* figures are several centuries older.

16 SGYS I Chinhan; Sajŏl yut'aek.

17 TYSC *hujip* VII 19 Nandol

Chapter 17

1 Songdo is the popular name of the city. It was originally created out of the two districts of Songak and Kaesŏng in 919 and called Kaeju. In 959 the name was changed to Kaegyŏng and in 995 to Kaesŏng. It is commonly but wrongly said that the name was changed to Kaesŏng for the Yi dynasty.

2 The Korean names of the wards are Chaha-dong, Ssangp'ok-dong, Paegun-dong and Chogi-dong.

3 Yi Inno (1152–1220) wrote the *P'ahan-nok* and is the typical poet-dilettante of middle Koryŏ times. This poem ('Chogi sodu hyo Tongp'a'——Rising early and combing my hair: in imitation of Su Tung-p'o) is in TMS IV 5. Tung-p'o is Su Shih or Su Tung-p'o, the calligrapher-poet of Sung; see below chapter 18 note 1.

4 KS LXXIII sŏn'gŏ-ji; and II Kwangjong year 9

5 Ch'oe Ip (1539–1612) and No Susin (1515–1590) doubtless knew one another. Gale's draft of this story has an MS note saying that it comes from *Hadam-nok* i.e. Kim Siyang *Hadam p'ajŏk nok.* The story does not occur in the version of *Hadam-nok* printed in the CKK *Taedong yasŭng,* nor in the fuller manuscripts I have been able to examine. It is suspect because by the time No Susin retired as premier Ch'oe Ip was a 49-year-old local governor.

6 The poem is 'Sok haengno nan' by Yi Inno. TMS VI 1. Also *Taedong sisŏn* I 30

7 KS III Sŏngjo year 10 moon leap 2

8 Cf KS LXXIX Sukchong; TGTG XVIII Sukchong year 7 moon 12. The inscription mentioned by Gale was *Haedong t'ongbo,* though other inscriptions have been found on coins of this period. Gale relied on Ichihara 'Coinage of old Korea' in TKBRAS IV ii 48f. The earliest coinage found in Korea is the copper 'knife money' (*ming-tao-chien*) of Chinese style discovered in P'yŏngan and in south Chŏlla. It is believed to belong to the Wei Man period and to have been brought from China. Quantities of Chinese Han period coins have been found in Lolang tombs, and there are legends of coins being produced in the south Korean Han tribes, but sober history believes that Korean wealth and trade depended on grain and linen as bartering staples until the middle of the Koryŏ period. Even in the Yi period these commodities were still so used. At times Chinese coins seem to have had limited circulation. There was a relatively unsuccessful minting of iron coins in 996, and silver ingots in the form of small bottles were used from 1101 to 1331. Yüan paper money, which so impressed Marco Polo, was used in Kaesŏng at least for trade with China, and Korea used mulberry-bark paper money during the fifteenth century. Copper coins were minted from time to time, but the first successful copper coinage was instituted in the late seventeenth century. During the nineteenth century the instability of the economy played havoc with the coinage and produced the inflation described by Gale in this paragraph. At that time foreigners were using either Japanese currency or Chinese sycee ('silver shoes'), and sometimes even quinine, to make their payments.

The *pandaji* is a traditional form of Korean chest. The top half of the front is hinged at the lower edge so that it will open outwards and downwards. *Pandaji* were usually chests

for clothing.
9 TGTG XIV Sŏngjong year 11 moon 7
10 TGTG XV
11 TGTG XV Hyŏnjong years 1 and 2
12 KS VIII Hyŏnjong year 10 and XCIV Kang Kamch'an chŏn
13 KS XCV 1 yŏlchŏn 8 Ch'oe Ch'ung
14 KS XCV 6
15 CKS I 260ff and TMS LXIV 18 Pongsŏn Honggyŏng-sa kal. The stone stands on the east side of the road in a grove to the north of Sŏnghwan.
16 TMS XIX 14. The original is a brief quatrain. The smokeless torch is the moon.
17 This extract has not been indentified. The Ely story is from the *Liber Eliensis* and is connected with the famous song of the monks. Canute went there on 2 February because on that day the abbot of Ely entered on his annual four months as chancellor of the realm of England. The king went by sled across the frozen fens from Soham, and on one occasion was preceded by a skater, the heaviest man who could be found, as tester of the thickness of the ice. The man's name was Budde ('Pudding').

Chapter 18

1 Su Shih (1037–1101) the greatest of the Sung poets. His most popular poem in Korea was the *Ch'ih-pi fu* (Song of the Red Cliff) included in *Komun chinbo*. The Red Cliff in this case is not to be confused with the one mentioned in chapter 9 note 15, nor are the two poems of the same name indentical. The incident referred to is documented in HDYS LVI *Su Shih ch'i-ling Kao-li-seng ts'ung Ch'üan-chou kuei-kuo chuang*. While Su was an official in Hangchow he wrote several memorials about Korean trade embassies, which he considered more nuisance than benefit to the Sung government. In 1089 he suspected the intentions of the Korean monk Sugae, who was in China for study, and asked for his extradition.
2 TMS IV 2 Kyŏlgi-gung ('The Chieh-chi Palace' of Chang hi-hua, concubine of the last ruler of Ch'en before his ruin in 589). The third couplet is missing from Gale's text and I have restored it.
3 The reference is to a poem by Yi Kyubo, TYSC VI 24 b 4
4 CKS I 293 Hŭngwang-sa Taegak kuksa myoji
5 CKS I 393 Hŭngwang-sa Wŏnmyŏng kuksa myoji
6 *Chosen koseki zufu* VII 958–9 and 961
7 TGTG XVII Munjong year 21
8 TGTG XVII Munjong year 22
9 TGTG XVII Munjong year 11
10 *Kao-li t'u-ching* CCK edition 489, 490, 491, 492, 493, and 494.
11 TGTG XIX Yejong year 2
12 TMS XII 14; YJSN XLVI 12 (slightly different text)
13 YJSN XLVI 12. For Shu Ch'i and Po I see below chapter 34. Chi and Hsieh were ministers of the emperor Shun (see chapter 2). Chi became deified as the god of agriculture, the *jik* of the *sajik* (see above chapter 17 note 7).
14 *T'oegye sŏnsaeng munjip* I 12 ff

Chapter 19

1 TYSC XXXV 1. Chŏnggak was a posthumous honorific title. His secular name was Chŏn Hakton and his religious name Chigyŏm (1145–1229).
2 Chu Hsi, known in Korea as Chu-ja, 'Master Chu', (1130–1200) the neo-confucianist thinker whose doctrines became standard in Korean orthodoxy of the later Yi dynasty.
3 The game had two forms: one was like field hockey and the other a kind of polo, played on horseback. TGTG XXIV Ŭijong year 6
4 TGTG XXIV Ŭijong year 11
5 *Georgicon* III 103
6 TGTG XXIV Ŭijong year 18 moon 5. Kamŭm is now Anŭi, South Kyŏngsang.

7   TSKM IXa Myŏngjong year 3 moon 10; TGTG XXVI ditto
8   *Koryŏ myŏngsin chŏn* (written by Nam Kongch'ŏl 1822) V 2. Yi's biography is in TYSC.
9   TYSC II 7; TMS IV 12 'Yu kagun pyŏrŏp sŏgyo ch'odang' (On a visit to my father's thatched house outside the west of the capital)
10 TYSC III 11–12
11 TYSC III 22
12 TYSC VIII 1 'Kye-sang u chak' ('Written by a brook')
13 TYSC XVIII 13
14 TYSC VIII 17 Kamhŭng. This translation differs from that in the original text of HKP. It has been amended according to a later version by Gale.
15 TYSC VII 3–4 'Ch'an sujwa pangjang soch'uk hwa nosong pyŏngp'ung sa-yo fu chi'('Written at the request of abbot Ch'an about his screen painted with old pinetrees').
16 TYSC VI 15. Verses 7 to 9 are missing in the original HKP. I have supplied them from Gale's MS draft.
17 TYSC XII 18. The original title is 'Mandarin ducks — a diversion'. Mandarin ducks pair for life and are a traditional symbol of conjugal fidelity.
18 I.e. the Chosen Kosho Kanko-kai editions. Gale had several details wrong in this paragraph. I have emended the text. See bibliography pp. 357, 358.
19 TGTG XXIV Ŭijong year 9
20 TDYS XIX Haedong chamnok 1 Ch'oe Nubaek (CCK ed vol IV p 427), and XXIII Haedong chamnok 5 Ch'oe Nubaek (CCK ed vol V p 148); TSKM IX a Uijong year 9; YJSN IX 8.

Chapter   20

1   Gale was misled into thinking that 'the Golden Horde' was a name for the Jürched because they called themselves Chin ('gold' or 'metal') in Chinese. The Golden Horde was not the Jürched, but the western Kipchak tatars of Khazan, who in the thirteenth century established an empire in south-east Russia under Batu, grandson of Chinggis. The name came either from their splendid court or from the association of the element metal with the west. Their empire disappeared in 1481.
2   Cf TGTG XXX Kojong year 3; TYSC XXVIII 3
3   TGTG XXVI Myŏngjong year 26. The Ch'oe founded an hereditary 'shogunate', which was really a militarist bureaucracy.
4   AD 1197. Cf TGTG XXVI Myŏngjong year 27
5   TGTG XXIX Hŭijong year 6
6   AD 1211. Cf TGTG XXIX Hŭijong year 7; but there Wang is said to have been exiled.
7   AD 1207. Cf TGTG XXIX Hŭijong year 3 moon 5
8   For the move to Kanghwa see TGTG XXXI Kojong year 19; for the return to Songdo TGTG XXXV Wŏnjong year 11 moon 5
9   KS XXIV Kojong XLI moon 12
10 TGTG XXXIV Wŏnjong year 1; TSKM XIa Wŏnjong year 1 moon 3
11 A young Tibetan lama named 'Phagspa was made *kuo-shih* ('national preceptor') and commissioned to create a new alphabet for use in writing all the languages of the Mongol empire. He created 42 letters based on Tibetan script, but they were ill-designed and never supplanted the modified Uighur script which continued to be used for Mongolian. It is certain that Sejong and his scholars referred to this 'Phagspa script when they were devising the Korean alphabet. Gale got his information on this subject from Ŏ Yunjŏk *Tongsa yŏnp'yo* p 360 (AD 1261). I have corrected the errors he copied from this source.
12 TGTG XXIV Wŏnjong year 3; KS XXV 25. The Mongols held Korean falcons in high esteem.
13 TGTG XXIV Wŏnjong year 5. Peking was then called Ta-tu or Khanbaligh (Chaucer's and Marco Polo's Cambaluc).
14 AD 1274. Cf TSKM XI Wŏnjong year 15
15 Li Ung-bing (Li Wen-pin) *Outlines of Chinese history* (Shanghai 1914) page 219. Khubilai was more civilized than his predecessors but Gale's gentle view of him is not supported by

other historians. Li Ung-bing lived in Soochow.

16 For the marriage see TGTG XXXVI Wŏnjong year 15 month 5, for the birth of Wŏn (later King Ch'ungsŏn) TGTG XXXVII Ch'ungnyŏl year 1. The element *ch'ung* in Korean kings' posthumous names during the Mongol domination means 'loyal' and was purposely chosen to emphasize their dependent status.

17 TGTG XXXVII Ch'ungnyŏl year 2 moon 5. This was the T'ongmun-gwan.

18 TGTG XXXVII Ch'ungnyŏl year 2 moons 1, leap, 9, etc. Simon Latham (fl. 1618) was the chief English authority on falconry.

19 TGTG XXXVI Wŏnjong year 13 moon 2. The crown prince (later Ch'ungnyŏl) introduced these customs in 1272. The wearing of white was forbidden in 1275, cf TGTG XXXVII Ch'ungnyŏl year 1 moon 6

20 TGTG XXXVIII Ch'ungnyŏl year 8 moon 8

21 Marco Polo *Travels* I lxi

22 Ibid II xvi

23 TGTG XXXII Kojong year 33

24 *Inferno* III 9

25 TMS XV 2 Yŏngho-ru, 'The pavilion of shining waters' at Andong. Cf YJSN XXIV 9.

26 Both these poems are from TMS XX 25. The first is entitled: 'Verses on rhymes proposed at a night banquet' and the second 'Grandchildren celebrating an eightieth birthday'.

27 See Chinese characters, p 324.

28 TMS IV 13. An old-style five-character poem entitled 'Written in reply to a poem by Chŏng Chahu and using the same rhymes'. Ch'oe Hae (1287-1340)

29 TMS IV 15 'Rain on the 23rd of the 3rd moon'. Not an essay, but a five-character old-style poem.

30 Robert Burns 'Scots wha hae'.

Chapter 21

1 TGTG XXXVIII Ch'ungnyŏl year 5 moon 6

2 TGTG XL Ch'ungnyŏl year 26 moon 6. The song was called 'Ssangyŏn'gok'.

3 TGTG XLI Ch'ungnyŏl year 28 (1302)

4 Wŏn became King Chungsŏn.

5 YJSN XIV 24

6 TGTG XLII Ch'ungsuk year 7 moon 12

7 TMS VII 4 (also *Ikchae chip* II 1). Yi Chehyŏn lived 1281-1367.

8 I.e. the T'ang poet, Meng Hao-jan.

9 Chu-saeng means merely 'the scholar Chu'. The text says *Wu-chung Chu-sheng,* and appears to refer to the T'ang dynasty landscape artist, Chu Shen, who came from the district of Wu.

10 This text is printed in many places. Cf TMS LXII 13-15; TGTG XLII Ch'ungsuk year 10 moon 11; *Ikchae chip* VI 1-3, 'Chae Taedo sang chungso-todang so'. The translation given here is incomplete.

11 *Ikchae chip* IXb 28

12 Chigong means 'pointed to the void'. His original name was Dhyanabhadra. He was a prince of Magadha who went to Yüan China and visited Korea in 1328 for some years. He died in Peking in 1363 and some of his relics were brought to Yangju in 1368.

13 TMS CXIX 6-14

14 This attribution seems to be traditional.

15 See below note 18 for the Korean empress. Andrew the Frank went to Rome with a group of Alan chiefs. The christian Alans had been conscripted by the Mongols for the conquest of China. The object of this embassy was to obtain a bishop to replace John of Montecorvino, who died in 1328, and to persuade the pope to send envoys and presents to the khan. The envoys and presents were sent, but, apparently, no bishop.

16 TMS XVI 1, also YJSN III 4 'Hwanjo nosang mang Samgak-san' (Seeing Samgak-san on the way back to court). The third couplet is missing from Gale's printing of HKP, and I have supplied it.

17 *Canterbury Tales* Prologue 122-26.

18 YJSN XLVII 10. The empress Ki is known in Korea as Ki Hwanghu. Shun-ti became enamoured of her in his teens. Although she was a powerful and conspiratorial influence in Chinese politics for thirty years, she was officially created empress only one year before the fall of the dynasty. She seems to have fled to Manchuria.

19 CKS I 490 Yŏnbok-sa chong myong

Chapter 22

1 The painting is known as 'Ch'ŏn-san taeryŏp to' (Picture of the great hunt in T'ien-shan). Three damaged fragments remain, one each in the Toksu Palace Museum, the National Museum of Korea, and Seoul National University Library. Yi dynasty historians accused Kongmin of homosexuality, but some modern writers regard the charge as unfounded.

2 KS CXXXII yŏlchŏn 45, biography of Sin Ton. Gale gives the traditional Korean account of Sin Ton. It has been credibly suggested that the king tried to use Sin to achieve much-needed reforms, and that Sin was falsely impeached by those with vested intersts in the *status quo*. The truth of the surviving records is in doubt.

4 TGTG XLVIII Kongmin year 14 month 12

5 KS CXX yŏlchŏn 25.22

6 TMS XLIX 12 'Aeo cham pyŏng sŏ' (Epigram on praise and blame, with preface). Gale has translated the preface only and omitted the epigram.

7 Analects IV 3

8 KS CXX yŏlchŏn 25. 19–20

9 KS loc. cit; TGTG XLIX Kongmin year 20 moon 5

10 KS CXXXII 19

11 TGTG L Sin U 2.3

12 TGTG L Sin U 14.7 During this period Yi Sŏnggye and Cho Chun were preparing the land reform which was an essential element in Yi's policy.

13 TMS I 7; *Toŭn chip* I 'Ae chusŏk'. Written in 1375. Not an essay, but a *tz'ŭ* (Korean *sa*). The Korean *sa* resembles the *pu* (see chapter 7 note 4), but its subject-matter is usually lyrical. Gale may have used the term 'essay' because he had not polished these translations into regular blank verse, and printed his drafts as prose.

14 Analects XV 8

15 Mencius IIIb Iii,

16 TMS V 10; *Toŭn chip* I 2 'Kamhŭng'

17 Wang Tzŭ-chin, also known as Chiao, was a prince of Chou in Ling Wang's day, who became an immortal on Kou-shih-shan.

Chapter 23

1 T'aejo (Chinese T'ai Tsu) means the Prime Ancestor, and was the posthumous title customarily given to the founding monarch of a dynasty. Cf above, chapter 12 note 10 and the passage there referred to. The suffixes -*jo* (or –*cho*) and -*chong* (or -*jong*) have no significant difference in literal meaning, but since Han times *cho* has been regarded as the more honorific. The *Han shu* (*Ching-ti chi*) says that *cho* is given to kings who achieved great things, and *chong* is given to kings of virtue. In practice rulers who took the throne by other means than peaceful succession, or who lived through great wars, tended to be named *cho*. Some kings were first termed *chong* and later changed to *cho* (see below chapter 33 note 1) when it was politic to refurbish their reputations. Kings not deemed worthy of either continued to be called by their princely title of *kun*. (See above chapter 12 note 10).

2 *P'oŭn chip* I 9

3 *P'oŭn chip* I 24

4 *P'oŭn chip* III 1 'Songhŏn Yi sijung hwasang ch'an' (Encomium of a portrait of Songhŏn, Yi Sŏnggye)

5 I.e. the beneficent dragon from the southern ocean.

6 The south mountain of Seoul, Nam-san.

7 See chapter 1 note 1. T'aejo first called his kingdom Koryŏ but later asked the Ming emperor if he could use either Chosŏn or Hwaryŏng ('Peace'– a name for his own birthplace in Ham-

gyŏng). The emperor chose Chosŏn, which was officially used from the 15th of the 2nd moon, 1393.

8 Now the British Embassy. The exact site of the grave is doubtful.

9 The two districts in question are Ch'ojŏn-gol, now Ch'o-dong and Ch'ungmu-ro 3-ka; and Taejŏn-gol, now Sup'yo-dong and Ulchi-ro 2-ka. The derivation of both names is contested.

10 YLSK I

11 Ŭijŏngbu, 'government office', takes its name from this story. The colloquial expression *Hamhŭng ch'asa* ('Hamhŭng messenger'), meaning a messenger who returns late or not at all, takes its rise from this story.

12 YLSK I. 'The Royal Gardens' means the Ch'angdŏk Palace.

13 YLSK I Chŏngnŭng p'yebok

14 *A midsummer night's dream* I i 121

15 *Henry IV Pt 2* III i 5–8 and 26–31

16 *Sambong chip* I 18a Ch'i sŏjŏk-p'o si pyŏng sŏ. Gale translates from the preface.

17 TYSC *hujip* xi 7. See also the discussion of this story in the biography of Gale, above, p 53.

18 KCPG III T'aejong year 3 *kyemi.*

19 YJSN XXIV 20

20 *Kukcho inmul chi* I 234

21 See below chapter 27

22 Thomas à Kempis cl380–1471.

23 See above chapter 21

24 TMS CXXI 8–10

25 TMS CXXI 10b Myoam chonja t'ap myŏng

Chapter 24

1 KCPG IV T'aejong year 10 winter

2 KS XXV 19 Wŏnjong sega year 1 moon 8 *imja*

3 KS LXXII chi xxxi 11-12. 'Green' includes shades of blue as well as green. The argument is not clear.

4 MHPG LXXX 9, quoting Yi Sugwang (16th century) *Chibong-yusŏl* xix 14

5 HDYS XXVI; TDYS VI Ch'ŏngp'a kŭktam p 56. Cotton is native to India, where hand-spinning is believed to have begun about the fifth century. It was introduced into China about the eighth century. The word later used for cotton is used as a proper name and as an adjective in the Book of Songs, the Erh-ya and other confucian writings, and Gale is wrong in supposing the the cotton plant was known in China in Confucius's day. The early textiles of China and Korea were hemp and silk. Hempen clothes of light cream colour would be regarded as white by the ancients, but hemp can also be white.

6 KCPG III T'aejong year 1; also KCPG VI Sejong year 15 *kyech'uk,* reprinted in *Yumong Sokp'yŏn,* where Gale gave the Chinese text. See page 380.

7 MHPG III Sangwi-go 3 additional note: Nuguk

8 CKS II 850 Munmyo pi

9 YLSK II

10 YLSK pyŏlchip 13. 'Lighted Bramble' is one translation of the literary name of the author of *Yŏllyŏsil kisul* (Literally 'Records of the Lighted Brambles Study').

11 *Sŏn* is *ch'an* in Chinese, and *zen* in Japanese (Sanskrit *dhyana*).

12 TDYS VI Ch'ŏngp'a kŭktam 2. See also Gale *Korean folk tales* 198. Not from the *Lighted Brambles.*

13 The title which Gale here translates as 'prince' is *puwŏn'gun*. It was given to the king's father-in-law and meritorious subjects of the highest rank, prefixed by the man's place of origin. Insan Puwŏn'gun was Hong Yungsŏng (1425–1475) a supporter of Sejo.

14 Yŏnsŏng Puwŏn'gun, Yi Sŏkhyŏng was another favourite of Sejo (1415–1477).

15 TDYS VI Ch'ŏngp'a kŭktam: Puma Hasŏng Puwŏn'gun. See Gale *Korean folk tales* 30.

16 *Mo* means 'a certain person', or 'so-and-so'.

17 Ch'amp'an means a royal counsellor.

18 Subsequently called Yŏnhŭi University, from the name of the palace. In 1957 it amalga-

ated with Severance Medical College to become Yonsei University.

19 YLSK III
20 The tomb is called Hŏn-nŭng, and the mountain Taemo-san. The location is Taewang-myŏn, Kwangju-gun. The mourning lasted actually little more than twelve months.
21 YLSK II Munhyŏng
22 YLSK loc. cit.. For *Kukcho pogam* see bibliography p 361.
23 TMS CIII 18
24 TMS XVII 11. This translation is discussed in the biography of Gale, above page 55.

Chapter 25

1 TDKN I 14
2 Ibid, loc. cit.
3 TDKN I 18
4 TDKN I 19. The Korean *feng-shui* is *p'ungsu*, a traditional geomantic system for estimating the influence of sites on human activities.
5 This story probably refers to Yu Pangsŏn (1388–1443), a scholar whose writings were printed as *Taejae chip*. The story was originally published by Gale in *Korean folk tales* 133–40, as a translation from a manuscript of anecdotes by Im Pang.
6 TDYS LVI Songwa chapsŏl
7 Ibid
8 Gale's account of the invention of the Korean alphabet is based on his own article, 'The Korean alphabet' in TKBRAS IV i 13–16. The alphabet was created by 1443, but not promulgated until 1446. It was known in Gale's day as *ŏnmun*, 'vulgar script', but is now known as *han'gŭl*, 'Korean script'.

   Gibbon's work is, of course, *The decline and fall of the Roman empire.*
9 The rationale of the Korean alphabet was scientific phonetics, but the forms of the new letters were designed in accordance with neo-confucian ideas of cosmogony developed by twelfth-century Chinese thinkers. According to this doctrine there are correspondences (described above, chapter 4 note 10) between the five elements, the five directions of the compass (the centre is added to the four cardinal points to make five), the five colours (black, white, red, blue/green, yellow), the five viscera, the five notes of the scale, the five types of sound, the five tastes, and so forth. These correspondences can be diagrammatized in a circular table which is what Gale means by 'the old Chinese philosophic wheel'. 'The tones of Confucius' ought to be 'the tones of neo-confucianism', because the system involved was worked out by Sung dynasty synthesizers, and does not appear in the writings of Confucius himself.

   The five notes of the musical scale are *kung, shang, chüeh, chih,* and *yü* (Korean *kung, sang, kak, ch'i, u*) and correspond to the western doh, re, mi, so, lah. They belong to vocal rather than to instrumental music. Chinese and Korean vocal music, like that of most early cultures, is pentatonic. This scale was derived from the twelve-tone scale of instrumental music, and was already known in the time of Mencius. It is therefore at least as old as the fourth century BC. The reference is MHPG CVIII Akko 19
10 Gale's 'market ditty' is a conflation of two popular parodies, both Chinese five-syllable quatrains, which use the name of a Korean letter for the last two syllables of each line. The first two lines as given by Gale are an inversion of part of a quatrain attributed to the vagabond poet Kim Sakkat (1807–63):

> You with the sickle in your belt
> And a ring in your ox's nose!
> Go home and wash yourself,
> Or you will be disgraced.

It is said to have been addressed to a cheeky oxboy. The Korean letter *kiŏk* is shaped like a sickle, *iŭng* is a circle, *riŭl* is the same as the Chinese character *ki* ('self') and a dot on the letter *tigŭt* makes the Chinese character *mang* ('to be disgraced').

   The remaining four lines form a quatrain recorded by the great scholar-poet, Yi Sŏgu (1754–1825):

> I see the men of this world
> Depend on the lips for praise or blame:
> If I do not take care of myself,
> I am bound to be disgraced.

The Korean letter *siŏt* is the Chinese character *in* ('man'), and *miŭm* is the Chinese *ku* ('mouth'). Gale may have used a variant of the second line of this quatrain, because his translation does not fit the text given by Yi Sŏgu. (Cf Yi Ŭngsu *Tae chŭngsu p'an: Kim Ip sijip* Seoul 1944, page 177.)

11   The number of letters has now been reduced to twenty-four. One of the original twenty-eight was dropped in Sejong's day. It was written as a circle with a horizontal line over it and re-presented a Chinese initial sound not used in speaking Korean; it was artificial in the first place. The next two letters disappeared in the sixteenth century: a triangle pronounced as *z*; and a circle with a dot on the top, which was used for *ng* and was redundant because the plain circle could serve both for that letter and the soft breathing sign. The fourth letter was the dot, a vowel now usually called *arae-a*. It represented an indistinct vowel sound that had effectively disapeared by the eighteenth century, though the letter continued to be written until well into the twentieth.

12   These nine songs are all sijo written long after Sejong's time and are all anonymous, though the third is sometimes attributed to Yi Yu of the eighteenth century and the seventh to Yun Sun of the same period. Gale translated them from the *Namhun t'aep'yŏng ka,* and the translations show the peculiarities of the texts in that anthology. Numbers ii, v, vi, and ix are not found in other old anthologies. The references are NTK 5b (55), 6b (64), 7b (76), 3b (36), 11a (118), 14a (153), 15a (160) 15a (161), 18a (192).

  In iii the cuckoo bird is the same as the whippoorwill in the poem at the end of chapter 24, and probably means the nightjar, though it is usually translated as 'cuckoo'. The text of iv is particularly corrupt and difficult. The *odong* tree in vi is now called the *pyŏg-odong,* the the 'Chinese parasol tree' or 'sultan's parasol' (*Firmiana platanifolia,* the Chinese *wu-t'ung*). It is a member of the chocolate family whose bark keeps green throughout its life, grown for the elegant appearance of its foliage and bark, but traditionally esteemed because the divine phoenix will perch in no other tree. Since the phoenix is a symbol of conjugal affection, the tree figures frequently in love poems.

13   Some buddhist works were published in *han'gŭl* in Sejong's time, but confucian works were not printed in *han'gŭl* until the latter part of the sixteenth century.

14   These three passages are quoted from the *Chung-yung* II i, III, and XIV 1–4

15   Lucian of Samosata (AD c125–c190). The quotation is taken from Harbottle's *Dictionary of quotations (classical)* 2nd ed London 1902, page 481. It comes from the *Epigrammata (Luciani Samosatensis opera* Leipzig 1887, III 462).

16   No authentic wiritings of Pythagoras have survived. Gale's quotations are all spurious, taken from late anthologies; the *Anthologion* of Joannes Stobaios, compiled probably in the 5th century AD; the writings of Diogenes Laertius, dating probably from the 3rd century AD; the *Aurea carmina* commented upon by Hierocles in the 5th century AD; and a manuscript of John Damascene's *Parallela sacra* copied in the 12th or 13th century and kept in the Laurentian Library at Florence. Gale's source for all the quotations was Harbottle's *Dictionary of quotations.* Harbottle used the 1759 Leipzig edition of Diogenes Laertius, and Thomas Gaisford's editions of Stobaios, the *Florilegium* (Anthologion) (Oxford 1822) and the *Ecloga* (Oxford 1850). The latter contains the extracts from the *Aurea carmina* and the Laurentian MS of St John Damascene.

  The references for Gale's quotations from Harbottle, with Harbottle's indications of sources, are as follows:

  (1) 315, Flor xxxiv 11; (2) 320, Diog viii 1, 19, 23; (3) 367, Flor xviii 23; (4) 370, Diog viii 1, 19, 23; (5) 373, MS Laurent I 7,35 (Gaisford 700); (6) 396, Flor I 22; (7) 415, Flor xxxv 8; (8) 435, Flor xlvi 112; (9) 481, Flor xlvi 42; (10) 487, Flor I 24; (11) 419, Aur carm 40 (Gaisford 114).

17   Brewer *Dictionary of phrase and fable* New edition (London, 1923) p 607

18   MHPG CIV 6 Akko 15 (*Han-shu: Ho K'uan-jao ch'uan*). Translation emended.

19 TDKN I 20

Chapter 26

1 Defoe's *A journal of the plague year* is an historical fiction, published in 1722. Gale's quotation is not verbally exact.
2 TDKN I 21
3 TDKN I 22
4 YLSK IV
5 TDKN I 31
6 TDYS XXII Haedong chamnok 4; Sin Sukchu
7 The Kŭmbu was responsible for the punishment of high-ranking criminals.
8 YLSK IV
9 Tŏkchong was the name given to the prince posthumously by his son, King Sŏngjong, who in so doing raised his father to kingly rank, although in fact he never reigned. His title as prince was Towŏn-gun. The story of his death is widely known.
10 For Wŏn'gak-sa and its pagoda see Gale's article in TKBRAS VI ii ((1915) 1–22. Gale is wrong in saying Sejong did not honour Buddha.
11 The story of Tanbal-lyŏng, the Haircut Pass, is told in *Chibong yusŏl* and YLSK, where its veracity is questioned.
12 YLSK IV
13 See bibliography, p 362.
14 The tablets in the confucian temple in Seoul, the Sŏnggyun-gwan, were: (a) that of the sage Confucius himself; (b) those of this four closest associates, the 'four sages' or 'four assessors', Yen Hui, Tseng Ts'an, Tzŭ-szŭ, and Mencius; (c) the 'ten disciples' who earned special praise from Confucius; (d) the six sages of Sung who were together the framers and developers of the neo-confucian doctrine which was the only orthodox doctrine in Yi dynasty Korea: Chou Tun-i (1012–73), Ch'eng Hao (1031–85), Ch'eng I (1032–1107), Shao Yung (1011–77), Chang Tsai (1020–77), and Chu Hsi (1130–1200); (e) ninety-five Chinese scholars; and (f) eighteen Korean scholars. The Koreans on the east side were Sŏl Ch'ong (c 700), An Yu (1243–1306), Kim Koengp'il (1454–1504), Cho Kwangjo (1482–1519), Yi Hwang (1501–70), Yi I (1536–84), Kim Changsaeng (1548–1631), Kim Chip (1574–1656), and Song Chun'gil (1606–72); and on the west side, Ch'oe Ch'iwŏn (859–c910), Chŏng Mongju (1337–92), Chŏng Yŏch'ang (1450–1504), Yi Ŏnjŏk (1491–1553), Kim Inhu (1510–60), Sŏng Hon (1535–98), Cho Hŏn (1544–92), Song Siyŏl (1607–89), and Pak Sech'ae (1631–95). The list was last added to in 1883. In 1949 all the tablets to Chinese personages were removed except Confucius, the four assessors, Chu Hsi and Ch'eng Hao. The Koreans were moved into the central sanctuary.
15 YJSN XXXI 33
16 Stories and poem from TDYS VIII Haedong yaŏn, and III Pyŏngjin chŏngsa-rok
17 TDYS XXIII Haedong chamnok 6 (CCK ed vol V pp 189—193)
18 YLSK VI. For *Hsiao hsüeh* see bibliography, p 371. Chu-tzŭ is Chu Hsi.
19 TDKN I 53; cf YLSK VI
20 YLSK VI Yŏnsan-jo kosa ponmal
21 *Tonggo yugo* II 9 Pyŏngin pongsa
22 *Shih ching* III 2 x 8

Chapter 27

1 YC XIV 27 chapki 1; Yi-ssi kamch'ŏn'gi
2 YJSN XLIV 22
3 Yŏnsan was pathologically deranged, and there are various explanations, all connected with his feelings for his mother. His troubles were exacerbated by the factionalism of his court. The traditional account, written by his enemies, contains deliberate vilification.
4 YLSK VI. Sŏng's verse is better translated: Your Majesty does not care for the Clear Stream.
5 YLSK VI
6 Chungjong was not as dull as Gale suggests. He was at pains to restore the confucian state

largely destroyed during Yŏnsan's reign. The name *chung* was given posthumously, and denotes a key concept in the confucian doctrine of the mean.

7 TDKN I 71. Cho was a government censor, and the real crux of this struggle was the control of the censors' powers. For the message on the leaf cf Chinese characters, page 324.

8 YLSK XV Chaesang: Chungjong 13

9 Injong was a posthumous name, never used during his lifetime.

10 The twelve zodiacal animals used to denote the years are the mouse, ox, tiger, rabbit, dragon, snake, horse, sheep, monkey, cock, dog, pig. Each sixty-year cycle contains the whole series of animals five times, and it is conventional in English translation to distinguish the five occurrences by prefixing the animal name with the colour appropriate to each pair of the 'ten heavenly stems' that are combined with the twelve 'earthly branches' to produce the sixtyfold cycle. Thus Injong was born in the 'year of the red pig', which was followed at twelve-year intervals by the 'blue pig', 'yellow pig', 'white pig' and 'black pig'. These terms play a leading role in Korean horoscopy. See table of the five elements, p 327.

11 YLSK IX Pak Kyŏngbin Poksŏng-gun chi ok

12 TDYS XIII Yongch'ŏn tamsuk ki

13 TC *naejip* VI 53ff Mujin yukcho so (summarized). T'oegye is Korea's greatest philosopher.

14 It is now known that this hymn is not the work of St Francis Xavier, but is a Latin version of a seventeenth-century Spanish sonnet.

15 W.T. Stead *Hymns that have helped* London 1896, page 66. Stead was the English journalist who edited the unofficial journal of the second peace conference at The Hague in 1907, and through it gave great help to the Korean envoys. The translation of 'Xavier's hymn' is the work of the English Roman catholic priest, Edward Caswall, originally published in *Lyra catholica*, London 1849. Stead's book contained christian and non-christian hymns.

16 TC *munjip* I 22

17 TDKN I 73

Chapter 28

1 Gale's account of Injong, while it reflects the attitude of the *Kukcho pogam*, and is based on that work and YLSK, is confused. According to YLSK, it was the Korean scholars, not a Ming envoy, who compared the prince to the mythical Yao and Shun (see above, chapter 2), and the king's health was damaged more by his mourning for his father than by his prayers in the drought. The role of the royal wives in promoting factional strife complicates the story of Injong's reign.

2 YLSK X Taebi suryŏm

3 YLSK pyŏlchip IV Sŏwŏn. The school was founded in 1542/3, but the inscription was dated 1549/50 (TDKN 1550). It was founded by the local magistrate Chu Sebung, then honoured by the king with a calligraphic nameboard, tax exemptions and grants of books, lands and slaves. By 1600 there were a hundred such schools throughout the country.

4 KS CV yŏlchŏn 18.28; YJSN XXVIII 14

5 KS CV yŏlchŏn 18. 28

6 TSCS I 26a Yugam; YLSK pyŏlchip 7 Sŏnggyun-gwan

7 47 buildings were left as shrines to noted sages.

8 YC XXXVI 34ff. The following account is based on this text.

9 YC XIV 54 Ch'ŏndoch'aek (Heaven's Design)

10 These four quatrains are found as follows: (1) TCSC I 30 (cf YC II 7b 11) Kwi P'asan ki Song Unjang; (2) YC I 23 Sanjung sa yŏng 4; Wŏl (cf TSCS I 30a Yŏng wŏl): (3) YC I 20 San chung (cf TSCS I 23); (4) YC II 24 Uŭm (cf TSCS I 23)

11 YC XXVIII 6 (Kyŏngyŏn ilgi 1) TDYS III 368. 'Kyŏngyŏn ilgi' is another name for 'Sŏktam ilgi'.

12 YC XXVIII 26; TDYS II 392

Chapter 29

1 Cf H J Coleridge SJ *Life and letters of St Francis Xavier* 4th ed London 1912 II 306, Oct-Nov 1550. Brother Laurence, a blind Japanese and the first Japanese lay-brother of the Society

of Jesus, was converted on this occasion.

2 I have been unable to confirm this story, though Hideyoshi was present on this occasion,which is well documented, except for the role Gale claims for Hideyoshi. Cf Jesuit *Cartas* II f 177v.

3 TDYS III 440; YC XXIX 10

4 MHPG XII 6

5 MHPG XII 20

6 TDKN II 24–5; YLSK XV. The comparison of Korean factions to western political parties is not intended to mean more than that they opposed each other, though at times the 'westmen' took a conservative line. The party titles derive from the sectors of Seoul in which the leaders lived.

7 Ibid, loc. cit.

8 TDKN II 26. This was in 1592, the year *imjin* of the sixty-fold cycle. Hence the war that followed is called the Imjin War.

9 Korean: *kaedari ch'ulsin*. The expression is old-fashioned slang.

10 Sae-jae, otherwise known as Cho-ryŏng, in Mun'gyŏng-gun, North Kyŏngsang province.

11 If Yi Kŭngik is indeed the author of *Yŏllyŏ-sil kisul*. See bibliography, p 362.

12 TDKN II 48

13 YLSK XVI

14 See above chapter 9 and note 16 there.

15 *Julius Caesar* II ii 19–21

16 This account of Yi Sunsin is based on YLSK XV

17 Yi Sunsin's seamanship was the deciding factor in the defeat of the Japanese. He was also a a man of unusual nobility of character, who patiently suffered perverse impeachment.

Chapter 30

1 In 1370 and 1403 and on several other occasions the Ming emperors sent royal and court insignia to Korea, granting the Korean king the crown of a prince. The shape was that of a jewelled turban, not a circlet such as is typically used for a crown in the west. During the Imjin War, court dress went out of use. It was restored in 1600. (YLSK XIII Kwanbok).

2 TDYS XXXVIII Chaejo pŏnbang chi 4 (p 639)

3 *Taedong sisŏn* III 165. Quelpaert is Cheju.

4 *Sukhavati-vyuha-sutra*, popularly known in Korea as *Mit'a-gyŏng*. What remains of Bishop Trollope's collection, called 'The Landis Library' after Eli Barr Landis (1865–1898) the scholarly doctor and first American anglican missionary to Korea, is now in Yonsei University Library. Queen Inmok's letter has been lost.

5 I have been unable to discover the source of this poem, which was frequently quoted by Gale and others in this translation.

6 *Sŏngho saesŏl* Manmul-mun 9 (II 9). T'aeho was the style of Hong Wŏnsŏp; but the reference may be to Yi Wŏnjin.

7 William Woodville Rockhill (1854–1914), US minister in Peking and Seoul 1884–7. In 1888 and 1891 he led Smithsonian expeditions to Tibet and Mongolia. He was US minister in Peking 1905–09, and died in Hawaii in 1914 while on his way to advise Yüan Shih-k'ai in Mongolia. He wrote much, and presented many Chinese books to the Library of Congress in Washington, DC.

8 Cf J S Gale *Korea in transition* page 9. The incident is alluded to twice in the biography of Gale. See above pp 12 and 54.

9 YLSK XXIV

10 Kilma-jae, otherwise Anhyŏn or Muak.

11 *Chwaŭijong,* i.e. first deputy prime minister.

12 'The inner volumes' are the *naejip*, the original or basic collection.

13 *Wŏlsa chip* XXXVIII 6

14 This story is contained in *Taedong kimun* II 32. I have not traced an earlier source for it. Bishop Trollope in TKBRAS XXI 5, where he copies out Gale's version, slightly rewritten, gives the date as 1606. This is wrong, because Sŏkpong died in 1605.

15 *Wŏlsa chip* II 20

Chapter 31

1 Jan Janse Weltevree (c1595–1670?) was actually sailing on a pirated Chinese junk when he arrived in Korea, more likely on the south coast of Kyŏngsang than of Chŏlla. He was employed by the Korean government as a cannon-founder. See Gari Ledyard *The Dutch come to Korea* (Seoul 1971) pp 25–37.

Hendrik Hamel (c1630–92) was a ship's writer of the *Sperwer* (Sparrowhawk). He was 23 when the ship was wrecked on Quelpaert (Cheju) in 1653. He became leader and recorder of the group, probably because he was the best educated. One of them was a boy of twelve and two were fifteen-year-olds. They were kept in Cheju till June 1654, when they were transferred to Seoul and put into service as royal guards. The following spring two of them contacted the Manchu envoy in an attempt to escape, so they were all sent to south Chŏlla, where they lived more or less poorly until eight of them escaped by boat to Japan in September 1666. Their escape led to a diplomatic problem between Japan and Korea, as a result of which the seven Dutchmen surviving in Korea were released in the summer of 1668, and all returned to Holland. (The evidence for this return was not available to Gale, who relied on *T'ongmun-gwan chi* Hyŏnjong 7 and the translation of Hamel's account in TKBRAS IX [1918] pp 91–148.)

Gale was mistaken in thinking that upper-class Koreans took no notice of the Hollanders. The exhaustive treatment of the whole story given by Gari Ledyard in *The Dutch come to Korea* details the Korean documentation. Ledyard doubts whether one of the castaways was a Scot, but the idea would naturally have appealed to Gale, and there is some evidence to suggest that he was correct.

2 Ricci's effect on Korea was slight, and entirely through his writings; he never visited the country.

3 K'ang-hsi (1661–1722) and Ch'ien-lung (1736–95) were the reign titles of the two emperors who gave the greatest splendour to the Ch'ing dynasty in China. Both were Manchu. Many Koreans continued until the end of the nineteenth century to date documents according to the Ming era.

4 This invasion is now known in Korea as the *chŏngmyo horan*. The Manchus occupied Seoul.

5 This invasion is known as the *pyŏngja horan*.

6 Guyen baturu *(Kuei-yung-chieh)* was the title of Nurhachi's second son, Daisan.

7 YLSK XXV. The 'khan' was Abahai. Lunggultai and Mabutai are tentative romanizations.

8 NHC IX 255. 8 January 1637.

9 TDKN III 34b. Kokane-machi was Kuri-gae, now Ŭlchi-ro.

10 NHC IX 258

11 NHC IX 260

12 Ihyŏn.

13 NHC IX 264

14 NHC IX 266

15 Ibid, loc. cit.

16 NHC IX 267

17 Ibid, loc. cit.

18 The tomb was Hŏn-nŭng.

19 NHC IX 268

20 NHC IX 269. 25 January 1637.

21 NHC IX 271–2. Abahai, Nurhachi's eighth son, was father of the Shun-ch'ih emperor.

22 Ibid, loc. cit.

23 NHC IX 273

24 NHC IX 274

25 NHC IX 277. 24 February 1637.

26 The crown prince Sehyŏn and his brother Prince Pongnim.

27 CKS II 874ff. The stone is known as *Taech'ŏng hwangje kongdŏk pi* (Stele praising the Ch'ing emperor) or *Samjŏn-do habi* (Shameful stele of Samjŏn ferry). One side is inscribed in Chinese and the other in Mongol and Manchu. All three texts are given in CKS. The site is Samjŏn-do,

Songp'a-ri, Chungdae-myŏn, Kwangju-gun. During the administration of Syngman Rhee, the president ordered the stone to be destroyed. The Cultural Affairs Office demurred, and a compromise was made by burying the stone. After Rhee was expelled by the student revolution of 1960, the tablet was resurrected. It now stands a kilometre south of the river near the village of Songp'a-ri.

28 *Sŏnwŏn yugo* Ia 13a; *Taedong sisŏn* IV 3, The site of one An'guk-sa is in Sŏsan county.

Chapter 32

1 The passage was written by Gale himself and printed in KM II v 198. His story of Non'gae comes from Chang Chiyŏn *Ilsa yusa* Seoul 1922 p 32.
2 Yun Sŏn'gŏ (1610–69) was a famous scholar. His works are collected in *Nosŏ yugo*.
3 *Kimun ch'onghwa* II 3
4 *Tsin-shu: T'ao K'an chuan*, not Mencius. This and the following motto are recorded in KCPG XXXVII Hyojong year 2 month 8.
5 *Shih ching* IV i 1
6 YLSK pyŏl XIII Kwanbok
7 Ibid. *Padŭk* is the Chinese *wei-ch'i* (Japanese *go*); the pebble game.
8 KCPG LI Sukchong year 27 moon 8. Palace women were attended by medical kisaeng.
9 Gale learned of Anna Ivanovna from her adoptive brother, Captain Crown of the *Argun* (see above, p 41). Cf *Korea Mission Field* May 1927 page 103.
10 The father of this remarkable family was Kim Suhang (Mun'gok), a member of the pro-Ming Noron faction and friend of Song Siyŏl. He was prime minister in 1680. In 1689 he was ordered to drink hemlock.
   The sons were (1) Ch'angjip (1648–1722), prime minister in 1717, and one of the ablest statesmen of his day, but executed during political intrigues in 1722; (2) Ch'anghyŏp (Nong-am 1651–1708) a distinguished calligrapher and scholar, who retired from politics in disgust; (3) Ch'anghŭp (Samyŏn 1653–1722), the least brilliant, but a competent poet; (4) Ch'angŏp (Noga-jae 1658–1721), painter and writer, whose diary is discussed here by Gale, spent his life on his country estate; (5) Ch'angjŭp (P'oŭm 1662–1713) passed his whole time in scholarship; (6) Ch'angnip (T'aekchae 1666–83) died at 17 but was considered a remarkable poet.
11 Parts of the translations given here are reworkings of the translation previously published by Gale in the *Korea Magazine*.
12 *Noga-jae Yŏnhaeng-nok* CKK edition 9. The audience was on New Year's morning.
13 Op cit 17
14 Op cit 137 (1st moon 1st day)
15 Op cit 214–5
16 Kyŏngjong was accused of sexual impotence.
17 *Yŏnhaeng-nok* 175. All three dates belong to the 1st moon of 1713.
18 Op cit 147
19 Op cit 167
20 The 'prince' was Yi Sangŏn (1707–1791). He was not a king's son, but a descendant of Hyo-ryŏng-taegun, second son of T'aejong. Gale is incorrect in calling him a prince, and was mistaken in identifying Yŏngwŏn-sa as a Diamond Mountain monastery. I have corrected the latter error. See *Chosŏn pulgyo t'ongsa* I 568. The memorial stone is at Sŏrun-sa, Sangin-ni, Asan-myŏn, Koch'ang-gun, North Chŏlla, about 35 kilometres from Chŏngŭp.

Chapter 33

1 Yŏngjo was called Yŏngjong by Gale. I have changed the text to accord with the change of title in 1899, when this king was raised from -*jong* to -*jo*. Cf above chapter 23 note 1. Yŏngjo's administration was enlightened, and although Gale's picture of pastoral peace is overdrawn, its insertion at this point has a certain appropriateness.
2 This game is still popular with boys. If a sleepy boy answers a call on this morning of the year he is supposed to have bought the caller's sufferings from the following summer's heat. If he does not answer he is safe.
3 *Yut* is a game played with four wooden sticks, bevelled on one side and flat on the other, which

are thrown instead of dice. It is still one of Korea's most popular games.

4 Chinese histories, following the *Shih chi*, attribute the fixing of the lunar new year to the emperor Wu-ti of Han when he came to the throne in 140 BC, changed the calendar and took the first reign-title in Chinese history, Chien-yüan, meaning 'the fixing of the beginning (of the year and the reign)'.

5 *Haeyu-rok* (Han'guk chinsŏ edition) page 8

6 Op cit page 14

7 The tomb of Yi Yŏngbin was moved from the Yŏnsei campus to Sŏo-rŭng on 8 September 1970.

8 The 'coffin king' was later honoured by his repentant father with the title Prince Sado. In 1899 he was canonized as a king and called Changjo. He was accused of many misdemeanours. Some historians believe he was a victim of political factionalism. The facts of the case are far from clear. The spikes in the box, which was a rice-chest, not a coffin, were the nails that fastened it, not spikes driven into the dying man.

9 They were of the 'old school' so far as Gale's day was concerned; in their own day they were up-to-date, since both of them, but especially Hong, were influenced by the *k'ao-cheng* (empirical research) methods of the Ch'ing scholars. They belong to the history of *sirhak* (practical learning) in Korea. It was typical of *sirhak* scholars to be interested in the ideas newly heard-of from the west.

10 *Igye chip* II 4

11 *Igye chip* II 2; cf a *sijo* of the same meaning by Chŏng Ch'ŏl, (*Songgang kasa* no. 71) and the traditional song *Paekku ka* ('Song of the white gull'. NTK 23b).

12 *Igye chip* VIII 10

13 *Sunam chip* XVII 1 and 8, Chapchŏ: Ch'ŏnhak-ko and Ch'ŏnhak mundap. An Chŏngbok also compiled the *Tongsa kangmok* (see bibliography, p 362).

14 *T'ien-chu shih-i (De Deo vera doctrina)* Peking 1601.

15 The references to the classics are: *Shu ching* Shang-shu T'ang-kou; *Li chi* XXXIII 10 (not *Shih ching*); *Shih ching* VII 1 vii; Mencius VII a 1. Before the quotation from Mencius, An Chŏngbok inserts: 'Few think of heaven' (Analects XVI 8) and 'What heaven ordains is called nature' (*Chung yung* I 1). Gale omits these two less cogent quotations.

16 *Sunam chip* XVII 10a, referring to Mo Tzŭ XXVIII 3.

Chapter 34

1 *Igye chip* I 1

2 CKS II 1121 Suryuk-che sajŏk pi

3 Thomson Jay Hudson 1834–1903, journalist and lecturer, who popularized the expressions 'subjective mind' and 'suggestion' as psychological terms. His religious attitudes spoiled his reputation among scientists. The passage quoted by Gale is not an accurate quotation but a conflated summary of *The Law of psychic phenomena* (London and Chicago 1893) page 296.

4 CKS II 1118 Paekse ch'ŏngp'ung pi. For the Magpie Bridge story see chapter 33 above; the story of the Chinese loyalists refers to the time when Chou took over from Shang. Confucius praised their virtue.

5 CKS II 1135 Yŏngyŏng ch'aeksŏng pi. The Ch'ien-men mentioned later in this paragraph is the Cheng-yang-men, the great south gate of the city of Peking. See also above p 15.

6 CKS II 1145 Kyesŏng-sa pi

7 CKS II 1202 Samgang-myo pi. (Kyŏngbuk, Kyŏngju-gun, Kangdong-myŏn, Tasan-ni)

8 Not a quotation, but the general sense of the *Politics* III 9.

9 The tomb is Wŏn-nŭng, one of the East Nine tombs.

10 *Suno chi* II (Kungmun chaeryo che 3 chip, Seoul 1959, page 70). Hong Manjong, however, was dead before Yŏngjo reigned. For the 'five commandments' of confucianism (*wu-lun*) see chapter 2 note 5. Gale seems not to have known that Hong Manjong and other confucian writers also edited collections of scatological and pornographic anecdotes.

Chapter 35

1 Gale writes Chŏngjong throughout, but this king was raised from *-jong* to *-jo* in 1899. Cf

above chapter 33 note 1.
2 The collection is called *Hongjae chŏnsŏ* and consists of 184 books in 100 fascicules.
3 *Ŏjŏng insŏ rok sŏ* I 2
4 KCPG LXXIV Chŏngjo year 18 moon 9
5 *Yŏlsŏng ŏje: Chŏngmyo ŏje* XXXVIII 1
6 Op cit XXXVIII 31
7 *Lettre d'Alexandre Hoang à Mgr de Gouvea, Evêque de Pékin, 1801.* Traduction française, Hong-kong 1925. Gale handled the original, which was obtained by his friend, Archbishop Mutel, and sent to Rome in 1925. See KMF XXIII iv April 1927 page 70.
8 Launay *Martyrs français et coréens 1838–1846* (Paris 1925) page 17
9 Launay op cit page 18. The Chinese priest was Liu Fang-chi, otherwise Pacificus Liu.
10 Launay op cit page 44. Protase's Korean name was Chŏng Kukpo.
11 Basil Hall *Account of a voyage of discovery to the west coast of Korea* London 1818 pp2–3
12 Hall *Narrative of a voyage to Java, China, and the Great Loo-choo Island* London 1840, page 80
13 *Yŏlsŏng ŏje* (1924 edition page 515)
14 Source unidentified. Gale is wrong in suggesting that Hong's revolt was singular. At this period peasant unrest was widespread and there were several such insurrections.
15 This is the beginning of a popular novel called *Sinmirok* or *Hong Kyŏngnae silgi*. As with most such novels, there are a number of editions.

Chapter 36

1 *Sedo* is the sound of two different Chinese expressions which have come to be confused. It is commonly now understood in the way in which Gale uses it, and practically synonymous with the Andong Kim clan during the time of its power in the nineteenth century. It has also been used of the Ch'oe family during Koryŏ times (see above chapter 20). At the end of the nineteenth century the *sedo* passed to the Min family. Gale's quotation is from Pae Chŏn, quoted by Yi Nŭnghwa in *Chosŏn Kiddokyo kŭp oegyo* II 2. The Andong Kim were descendants of two of the five Kim brothers mentioned in chapter 32 note 10.
2 See below chapter 37.
3 The treaty of Nanking was signed by China and Britain, as a result of the opium wars, on 29 August 1842. It regularized the trade of Britain on the China coast, opened the first treaty ports, attempted to control the opium traffic, and granted Hongkong to Britain.
4 Chŏn'gye, who was already dead, was not to be called king, but regent for his son. When the succession was manipulated in this fashion for political reasons, by a fictitious adoption of the chosen boy as son of a former king, the boy's father might be enfeoffed as *taewŏn'gun*, 'prince of the great palace'. Cf *puwŏn'gun* ('prince of the palace') above chapter 24 note 13. Cf genealogical table p 304.
5 Pak Yŏnghyo (1861–1939) was a pro-Japanese statesman, son-in-law of Ch'ŏlchong, who after a stormy career in Korean politics was given a marquisate by the Japanese government. Gale met him while Pak was exiled in Japan during 1895–96.
6 Nam Pyŏngch'ŏl (1817–1863) was a scholar related by marriage to Kim Mun'gŭn. He was an unusually skilled geographer, astronomer, and calligrapher, who received the highest administrative appointments but was deposed during factional struggles.
7 His name was Haŭng; Hŭngsŏn was his princely title. He was a great-grandson of the 'coffin king', and second cousin of Ch'ŏlchong.
8 Kim Pyŏnggi of the Andong Kim (1818–1875).
9 Kim Pyŏngguk of the Andong Kim, nephew of Kim Mun'gŭn and kinsman of Kim Pyŏnggi (1825–1904.)
10 Unhyŏn-gung was the private residence of the Hŭngsŏn Taewŏn'gun. It stood a little west of the Ch'angdŏk palace, on the south side of the road. The last traces of it disappeared in 1970.
11 During the minority of a boy-king, if his mother or grandmother were acting as regent she took counsel with the ministers in a throne-room with a screen hung between the throne and the ministers, because propriety forbad them from sitting face to face with her. This was called *suryŏm ch'ŏngjŏng*. Very often the child-king sat beside her. Cf table p 304.
12 *Manse* strictly means *ad multos annos*.

13 Gale exaggerates the problem. There was precedent for the situation. See notes 4 and 7 above.
14 The Kyŏngbok Palace had originally been intended to serve as the regular royal residence, but it was burnt during the Hideyoshi war and had never been rebuilt. The king had lived in the Ch'angdŏk-gung, the 'East' or 'summer palace'. The Taewŏn'gun's extravagant project, carried out between 1865 and 1869, was a symbol of his ambition. The Kŭnjŏng-jŏn is the main throne-room and the Kyŏnghoe-ru is the 'Hall of Happy Meetings', a huge pavilion in the lotus pond at the back.
15 Kim Chwagŭn(1797–1869)and Kim Hŭnggŭn(1796–1870)werecousins of Kim Mun'gŭn. Both were prime minister at different times. If the story is true it must pertain to the years 1865–68.
16 Chŏngjo was really the brother of the king's great-grandfather.
17 Nodŭl was the colloquial name for the ferry at Noryang-jin on the Han river south of Seoul.
18 Son'ga-jŏng is a village near Tosŏn-sa, the temple where the Gale family often went during the hot summer season, in the area now generally called Ui-dong.
19 It is difficult to convey the value of 100,000 *yang* in 1865, the more so since the Taewŏn'gun's experiments in currency at this period made the value of money extremely unstable. In theory a *yang* was one *tael* of silver. The *tael* was not constant, but was heavier than the avoirdupois ounce. Even the buying power of silver at the time is hard to gauge. The total amount spent on the rebuilding of the palace is estimated to have been something rather more than 7,700,000 *yang*. The country was despoiled to raise the money. Anyone who gave 10,000 *yang* was given official rank, and anyone who gave 100,000 was appointed to rank equivalent to mayor of a city or magistrate of a county.

Chapter 37

1 By western counting it was little more than two years. Ch'ŏlchong died in January 1864 and the wedding took place in the summer of 1866. Cf genealogical table p 304.
2 By western computation she was little more than one year older than the king.
3 Cf *Documents rélatifs aux martyrs de Corée de,1866* Hong Kong 1925 pp 10 and 126.
4 It is odd that Gale does not here mention that the Welsh missionary Robert Jermain Thomas was one of those killed in the *General Sherman* incident. He has been venerated as the 'first protestant martyr of Korea'. See note 5 below.
  'The old-time hermit' presumably means 'the then member of the Hermit Kingdom'. Pak Kyusu (1807–1876) was a distinguished statesman and diplomat who later played a leading role in the negotiations with the Japanese for the Kanghwa treaty of 1876.
5 The *General Sherman* was an American vessel and had some Americans aboard, but Ch'oe Nanhŏn seems to have been Thomas. The Korean records are clear and correct in saying that he was British. In China he used the name T'o Ma-szŭ (Korean: T'ak Masa)
6 The Treaty of Kanghwa.
7 The treaties of 1882 were with America, Britain and Germany. For Li Hung-chang see below chapter 38 note 2.
8 This took place in 1881. Cf TSYP 422
9 Sixty students led by Kim Yunsik (see below chapter 38 note 24) went in 1881 to study the modern arsenal.
10 A dozen men went on this delegation to Japan in 1881. Cf TSYP loc. cit.
11 TSYP loc. cit
12 Min Kyŏmho (1838–1882) was paymaster-general and Kim Pohyŏn (1826–1882) was governor of Kyŏnggi province. Min Yŏnghwan (1861–1905) was a distinguished and enlightened statesman who committed suicide in 1905 when Korea became virtually a vassal of Japan. A bamboo grew through the floor of the room in Seoul where his bloody clothes had been put. It eventually withered, but since the bamboo is a symbol of loyalty and does not grow easily as far north as Seoul, it was considered miraculous. It is known as *hyŏlchuk*, 'the blood bamboo'.
13 The house was in fact at Changho-wŏn, on the border of Kyŏnggi and Ch'ungch'ŏng province, nearly twenty miles from Ch'ungju.
14 It had been declared that the queen was dead and appropriate mourning started.
15 Paul Georg von Möllendorff (1848–1901), known in Chinese as Mu Lin-te (Korean Mok

Lindök) was a Saxon, educated at Halle, who went to work in the German consular service in China. In 1882 Li Hung-chang arranged for him to go to Korea as adviser on diplomatic affairs and customs administration. He remained in Korean government service till the summer of 1885. He died at Ningpo. The *Manual of Chinese bibliography*, written in collaboration with Otto Franz von Möllendorff, was published in Shanghai in 1876.

16 Thomas Edward Hallifax (1842–1908), known in Korean records as Haeraebaeksa, began his career as a telegraph engineer in India, and went on to do the same work in Japan 1871–77. In 1883, after a period of sea-roving, he came to Korea to construct a telegraph system. The project was premature and Möllendorff gave him a job in the new English Language School in Seoul. During 1886 and 1887 he installed the Seoul-Pusan overland cable and ran a school for telegraphists. He then returned to Japan, where he taught English till he returned to Seoul as an assistant teacher in the Government School for Foreign Languages. He retired in 1908 and died shortly afterwards in Seoul.

17 Percival Lowell 1855–1916, American astronomer and statesman. His book was published in Boston in 1885 and in London the following year. For the translation of Chosŏn as 'land of the morning calm' see *Chosŏn* page 209. See also above chapter 1 note 1.

18 This paragraph is based on information from Allen's *Chronological index*.

Jardine Matheson of Hong Kong opened a branch at Chemulp'o in 1883 and ran a steamship service from Shanghai via Nagasaki and Pusan to Chemulp'o.

J. R. Morse, Townsend and Company was the name used for a short time by the American Trading Company after it was founded by Walter D. Townsend (1856–1918) at Chemulp'o in 1884. Townsend had worked in the company's Yokohama office since 1878, but spent the rest of his life in Korea. James R. Morse, president of the firm, lived in Yokohama. Until the 1930's the firm was called Townsend and Company. Its present name is the American Trading Company Korea Ltd.

Edward D. Meyer of Hamburg started a branch in Korea (Sech'ang Yanghaeng) when Carl Wolter arrived at Chemulp'o in 1884. It was a finance company, later involved in gold-mining.

The first consul to arrive in Seoul was the American Lucius H. Foote (May 1883). The British came in March 1884, and the Russian (Waeber), Italian and German consuls in June 1884. The French arrived in 1888, the Japanese and Chinese had representatives from an earlier date. There was a British consul in Chemulp'o (1884), and Japanese consuls at Pusan (1880), Wŏnsan (1880), and Chemulp'o (1883).

A mint started by German technicians in 1887 ceased operation after the Sino-Japanese war (1895).

A glass works started by the German-American Joseph Rosenbaum planned to make glass from Han River sand, but was early abandoned.

A model farm with American seed and livestock was started in 1884, but the experiment was virtually extinct by 1896. 'Paper mill' was a misprint for 'powder mill'. Townsend built one in 1886, but it burned down in 1888. Jardine Matheson started alluvial gold-mining in 1884, but the scheme was soon abandoned. An electric light plant for the palace was ordered in 1884, but the Seoul Electric Company was not founded until 1897.

19 Horace Newton Allen (1858–1932) failed as a presbyterian missionary to China and came to Korea, ostensibly as physician to the US legation. As a result of the incident described in this paragraph he was allowed to open a hospital, with which J. W. Heron was soon associated. In 1890 he transferred to the US foreign service, and was highly influential in diplomatic and business affairs till he left Korea on the closing of the legations in 1905. See above pp 16, 22.

20 The banquet was in the Post Office buildings, part of which still stands a little south of the An'guk-dong intersection.

21 TDKN V 86

22 Pak Yŏnghyo (1861–1939) was one of the ringleaders of the 1884 'Post Office *émeute*'. See chapter 36 note 5. The title marquis is the second of five honorary feudal titles, attributed to Yao and Shun, used at times in China and during the Koryŏ dynasty in Korea. In Yi times they were replaced by *kun, taegun, puwŏn'gun* and other titles of similar kind. After the annexation of 1910 the Japanese gave feudal styles to Korean nobility. The five titles and usual

translations are: *kung* (duke), *hu* (marquis), *paek* (earl), *cha* (viscount), *nam* (baron).
23 TDKN, ibid.

Chapter 38

1 Yüan Shih-k'ai (1859–1916) was Chinese 'resident' in Korea from 1882 until the end of the Sino-Japanese war. He later became a favourite of the Empress Dowager, and in 1913 the first President of the Republic of China. Gale met him at the Herons' house and elsewhere.
2 Li Hung-chang (1823–1901) controlled the foreign policy of China from 1870 until his death.
3 Cf Allen *Fact and Fancy* 187
4 Allen op cit 178. Cf John vi 53.
5 TDKN V 97, An Hyoje's petition for her execution in 1893. Chillyŏng-gun was a Yi who claimed to be possessed by the spirit of Kuan Yü, the god of war. She was a favourite of Queen Min and persuaded her to build a shrine for Kuan Yü in Sung-dong, Seoul (the Kwan-wang-myo). She survived An Hyoje's petition for her execution in 1893, and for a time attended Gale's church in Yŏnji-dong. Another similar *mudang* was a Yun called Hyŏllyŏng-gun. She was the Lady Ŏm's favourite, and had the west temple of Kuan Yü built in 1902. Chillyŏng-gun's was the north temple; for the other two temples see above chapter 9 note 16. Cf *Kyemyŏng* XIX 14.
6 Cf TDKN V 98 The account is muddled. Ch'oe Poksul and Ch'oe Cheu were the same man, executed in 1864. The petition of 1893 was made by his followers for his rehabilitation. His teaching was the famous Ch'ŏndo-gyo.
7 Ibid
9 The Tonghak movement had become a popular peasant revolt against injustice and economic oppression.
9 At the mouth of the Yalu.
10 The present Masan, Kyŏngsang South province.
11 *Varyak* means 'Varangian' (the name of the Scandinavian people who ruled a principality in southern Russia from the 9th to 12th centuries), *Koryeets* means 'Korean', and *Sungari* is the name of the great river of Manchuria. The *Varyak* was a cruiser, the *Koryeets* a gunboat, and the *Sungari* a transport.
12 See Chinese characters, p 324.
13 Yi Sangjae (1850–1921). See Gale's biography, p 34.
14 Ito was assassinated at Harbin railway station on 26 October 1909. He was shot by the Korean patriot An Chunggŭn.
15 *Chronological index* page 197.
16 Heinrich Albert Wilhelm (1862–1929), son of Frederick III, brother of Wilhelm II, visited Korea in the summer of 1899. See the biography of Gale, and Allen's *Chronological index*.
17 George Nathaniel Curzon, Marquess of Kedleston (1859–1925). An outstanding viceroy of India (1899–1905) and British foreign secretary (1919–23). Visited Korea 1892.
18 William Jennings Bryan (1860–1925). American politician, leader of the Democratic party 1894–1922. As Nebraska delegate to the Democratic national nomination congress of 1896 he took up the 'free silver' theory (an ill-thought-out economic theory that was seen as a crusade for economic justice) in a famous speech whose key sentence was 'You shall not press down upon the brow of labour this crown of thorns, you shall not crucify mankind upon a cross of gold.' He died at Dayton, Tennessee, shortly after taking the side of fundamentalism in the Scopes trial. His visit to Korea, 14–17 November 1905, was part of a world tour. He spoke at the Seoul YMCA on the 16th.
19 John Griffith London (1876–1916), the American writer, traveller and socialist, visited Korea as a correspondent for the Hearst newspapers during the Russo-Japanese war of 1904. Chapter xv of his *The jacket* (called *The star rover* in the USA) 1914, is a fantasy loosely based on the story of Hamel, tricked out with details from Hulbert's *Passing of Korea*.
20 Horatio Herbert, Field-Marshal Earl Kitchener of Khartoum (1850–1916), British general who gained distinction in Egyptian and South African wars, was war minister of Britain during World War I. He visited Korea in October 1909 while travelling from Port Arthur to Japan on his way to Australia to advise on military defences.

21 James Viscount Bryce (1838–1922) British jurist, politician and historian, was HBM ambassador to Washington 1907–13. On the way home from that appointment he visited Seoul for two days in late June 1913. His books never mentioned Korea, but he wrote to Gale after the 1919 demonstrations. See biography of Gale above, pp 65–6.

22 Chün-tzŭ-kuo is a phrase from the *Shan-hai-ching,* a geography written about the 2nd century BC. The name refers to Confucius's reference to a superior man living among the eastern barbarians (Analects IX 13) and is doubtless a euphemism.

23 See above chapter 8 note 16

24 *Unyang chip* I 1. A photograph and a holograph letter are reproduced in the first volume of this set. For Kim Yunsik (1835–1922) see bibliography at *Unyang chip*, below page 368.

BIBLIOGRAPHIES

I BOOKS USED BY GALE IN COMPILING THE HISTORY OF THE KOREAN PEOPLE

A collection of all the books which Gale used in his writings would make an enviable library for the student of Korea. The volumes he handled were apparently from his own private collection; from the Landis Collection owned by his friend, Bishop Trollope; or from the Chosen Christian College library. Most of his own books are now in the Library of Congress at Washington, and what remains of the other two collections forms the nucleus of the Yonsei University Library section of old books.

If an historian of today attempted a work of the same scope as Gale's, he would certainly use the early Chinese dynastic histories which refer to Korea and the *Yijo sillok* (Authentic records of the Yi dynasty). Gale knew the extracts from Chinese dynastic histories in Korean compendia; he did not use the *Yijo sillok* because they had not been released for publication by the Japanese government-general of Chosen before he left Korea.

Gale did not read Japanese works; he refers to Japanese sources only for their illustrations. In the later chapters of his history he appears to have relied heavily on the oral tradition.

a The Chosen Kosho Kanko-kai and Chosŏn Kwangmun-hoe editions

The publications of the Chosen Kosho Kanko-kai (Society for the publication of old Korean books) formed a series of 79 volumes published at approximately monthly intervals from November 1909 to June 1916 by a group of Japanese bibliophiles living in Seoul. The project was initially under the patronage of Prince Ito Hirobumi (1841–1909), one of the makers of modern Japan, who was Japanese resident-general in Korea from 1905 to July 1909. He resigned to become president of the Japanese Privy Council and on 26 October of the same year was shot dead on Harbin railway station by the Korean patriot An Chunggŭn. He was therefore dead by the time the first volume was published. Other members of the society included Asami Rintaro, Maema Kyosaku, Imanishi Ryu, the scholar-banker Ayukai Fusanomosuke, and some Korean statesmen, among whom were Yi Wanyong and Kim Yunsik. All the books were set in modern metal type and published in western-style volumes. Some were sketchily edited and contain misprints. They have mostly been superseded by subsequent publications. See also above pp 49–50.

In 1910 the young Korean scholar Ch'oe Namsŏn (1890–1957) founded the Chosŏn Kwangmun-hoe (Society for promoting Korean books), a rival to the Kosho Kanko-kai. Some of the Kwangmun-hoe titles duplicated the Kosho Kanko-kai work. The books were inexpensively produced, but some of them had variant texts, better edited than the Kosho Kanko-kai editions. Gale sent a complete set to the Library of Congress in Washington.

No complete lists of these two series have been published. The lists given here are as complete as I can make them. The books used by Gale in the *History* are listed again and described in the bibliography below. No explanatory notes are added to titles that occur elsewhere in these bibliographies.

Chosen Kosho Kanko-kai editions

First series *(Chosen kunsho taikei)*
November 1909–October 1911. 24 volumes.
1909 1 *Samguk sagi*

2 *Taedong yasŭng I*
1910 3 *Chosen bijutsu taikan* (Survey of Korean art, 1910)
4-12 *Taedong yasŭng II–X*
13 *P'aryŏk chi* (also known as *T'aengni chi*); *Tongguk kunhyŏn yŏnhyŏk p'yo* (Table of the counties and districts of Korea, 18th century); *Sa kun chi* (Account of the four Han prefectures and *Kyŏngdo chapchi* (Notes about Seoul) Yu Tŭkkong, 18th century); *Pukhan chi* (Account of Pukhan fortress, Sŏngnŭng, 1745); *Tonggyŏng chapki* (Miscellaneous records of Kyŏngju, Min Chumyŏn 1669).
14 *Taedong yasŭng XI*
1911 15 *Parhae ko* (Study of Pohai Yu Tŭkkong 1784); *Koryŏ kodo ching* (Description of the old capital of Koryŏ Han Chaeryŏm 1847); *Pugyŏ yosŏn* (Decuments on northern boundaries, Kim Nogyu 1903); *Hsüan-ho feng-shih Kao-li t'u-ching (Koryŏ togyŏng,* An imperial envoy's description of Korea, by Hsü Ching, 1123); *Puksae kiryak* (Brief account of the northern borders by Hong Yangho, 18th century).
16 *Taedong yasŭng XII*
17 *Chunggyŏng chi* (Account of Kaesŏng Kim Ijae 1830); *Kanghwa-bu chi* (Account of Kanghwa, Chŏn Nojin, 18th century)
18 *Taedong yasŭng XIII*
19 *P'ahan chip* (Collected anecdotes of Yi Inno, 1152–1220); *Pohan chip* (Collected stories of Ch'oe Cha, 1187–1260); *Ikchae chip* (Collected writings of Yi Chehyŏn, 1287–1367); *Aŏn kakpi* (The misuse of some Chinese expressions, by Chŏng Yagyong, 1762–1836); *Tongin sihwa* (Stories of Korean poets, by Sŏ Kŏjŏng, 1420–1489)
20–23 *Haedong yŏksa* I-III and supplement
24 *Yong-bi-ŏ-ch'ŏn ka* (Song of the ascending dragons, 15th century. An encomium of the founders of the Yi dynasty)

Second series (*Chosen kunsho taikei zoku*)
November 1911–September 1913. 24 volumes.
1911 1 *Kinyŏn aram* (Chronology for children, Yi Manun 1777)
2 *Munhŏn ch'waryo* (Bibliographical digest, by Chŏng Wŏnyong 1783–1873)
1912 3–5 *Tongguk t'onggam I-III*
6–10 *Sinjŭng Tongguk yŏji sŭngnam*
11–13 *Yŏllyŏ-sil kisul I-III*
1913 14–16 *Yŏllyŏ-sil kisul IV-VI*
17 *T'ongmun-gwan chi*
18 *Taejŏn hoet'ong* (Collection of statutes 1865)
19–21 *Yŏllyŏ-sil kisul, Appendices I-III*
22–23 *Tongguk Yi sangguk chip I-II*
24 *Shin Chosen oyobi shin Manshu (*New Korea and Manchuria*)*

Third series (*Chosen kunsho taikei zoku-zoku*)
November 1913–November 1915. 24 volumes.
1913 1 *Chingbi-rok*
1914 2 *Haedong myŏngin nok* (List of distinguished Korean persons, by Kim Yuk 1580–1648)
3–6 *Haehaeng ch'ongjae I-IV* (Collection of accounts of travels to Japan, originally compiled by Sŏ Myŏngung 1733–4, and used by Cho Ŏm on later voyages):
I Extracts from the works of Chŏng Mongju and Sin Sukchu, *Haeyu-rok* by Sin Yuhan (1719) and two late sixteenth-century works.
II Accounts of embassies in 1607, 1617, 1624 and 1636; also *P'yoju-rok*, account of a shipwreck by Yi Chihang (1636).
III Accounts of missions in 1636, 1643, and 1655.
IV Two accounts of the mission of 1682, the diary of Cho Ŏm's mission of 1774, and *Cheju p'yo hanin ch'ŏmunjŏng subon* (Report of the investigation of fifteen Fukienese survivors from a shipwreck off Cheju 1701)
7 *Kajae Yŏnhaeng nok*

 8–13 *Tongmun-sŏn*
1915 14–17 *Tongsa kangmok I-IV*
 18–20 *Sŏngho saesŏl yuson I-III*
 21–22 *Chibong yusŏl I-II* (Encyclopaedia of Yi Sugwang 1614)
 23 *Tonghwan nok* (Historical geography of Korea by Yun Chŏnggi c 1859)
 24 *Samŭn chip* (entitled *Saŭn chip* inside. Incomplete collections of the works of the 'three (or four) hermits'; Toŭn (Yi Sungin 1349–1392), Yaŭn (Kil Chae 1353–1419), Mogŭn (Yi Saek 1328–1396), and P'oŭn (Chŏng Mongju 1337–1392).

Additional volumes (*Chosen kunsho besshu*)
December 1915–June 1916. 7 volumes.
1915 1 *T'oegye chip I*
1916 2–4 *T'oegye chip II-IV*
 5 *Sambong chip*
 6 *Chungjŏng Namhan chi*
 7 *Ch'in-ting Man-chou yüan-liu k'ao* ((Imperial study of Manchurian origins 1777)

Chosŏn Kwangmun-hoe editions
(The numbers in this list are not those of the original publications, which were unnumbered.)

 1 *Yŏrha ilgi* 'Diary of a journey to Jehol' by Pak Chiwŏn, describing his visit to the 70th birthday celebrations of the Ch'ien-lung emperor in 1780. (1911)
 2 *Tongguk pyŏnggam* 'Military history of Korea' compiled by order of Munjong and published 1608. (1911)
 3 *Tongguk sesi ki* 'Account of Korean seasonal customs' by Hong Sŏngmo (1849), bound with two other similar works. (1911)
 4 *Tongguk t'onggam* (6 vols 1911)
 5 *T'aengni chi* (1912)
 6 *Haedong yŏksa* (6 vols 1912)
 7 *Yŏllyŏ-sil kisul* (11 vols 1912)
 8 *Sŭnggyŏng-do* The chart of an indoor game, similar in principle to the western 'Monopoly' where the players throw a special form of dice (*sŭnggyŏng-do-al*) to decide their moves. The chart sends them through good and bad fortune in government rank and political service. (1912)
 9 *Tori p'yo* A table of mileages (1912)
 10 *Haedong sok sohak* 'Korean addenda to the *Hsiao-hsüeh*', a collection of sayings by Korean sages, compiled by Pak Chaehyŏng (1912)
 11 *Tangŭi t'ongnyak* A history of Korean factions compiled by the nineteenth-century author Yi Kŏnch'ang. (1912)
 12 *Kibo* An account of the game *padŭk* ('the pebble game') (1912)
 13 *Tonggyŏng chapki* (1913)
 14 *Hunmong chahoe* A Chinese character primer by Ch'oe Sejin 1527. (1913)
 15 *Taedong unbu kunok* A Korean encyclopaedia arranged according to word-rhymes. It was printed in 1798, but the text was written by Kwŏn Munhae in the 16th century. (3 vols 1913)
 16 *Sangsŏ pojŏn* Additional commentaries on the *Shu ching*, by Hong Sŏkchu, early nineteenth century. (1913)
 17 *San'gyŏng p'yo* A systematic list of Korean mountains. (1913)
 18 *Haedong yŏksa sok* (1913)
 19 *Im Ch'ungmin Kong silgi* Accounts of Im Kyŏngŏp (1594–1646) a famous Korean martyr for the Ming. Compiled 1791. (1913)
 20 *Chunggyŏng chi* (2 vols 1914)
 21 *Kyŏngse yup'yo* A work on political and economic reform written about 1816–17 by Chŏng Yagyong (1914)
 22 *Samguk sagi* (2 vols 1914)
 23 *Moha-dang munjip* The works of Kim Ch'ungsŏn, (1571–1642) a Japanese who was natural-

ized as a Korean after the Imjin wars (1915)
24 *Sin chajŏn* 'A new dictionary of Chinese characters', compiled by Ch'oe Namsŏn. (1915)
25 *Tongsa kangmok* (6 vols)

b Korean compendia

1 *Chŭngbo munhŏn pigo* (Revised encyclopaedia)
An encyclopaedia of Korean affairs, consisting mainly of quotations and extracts, prepared with the purposes of the government in view, printed in Seoul in 1907. Edited by Yi Wanyong (1858-1926) and others.

The book was originally called the *Tongguk munhŏn pigo* (Korean encyclopaedia), and was compiled by order of King Yŏngjo on the model of Ma Tsuan-lin's 13th century *Wen-hsien t'ung-kao*. It was published in 1770 as a royal edition of about 100 copies.

In 1782 King Chŏngjo ordered an enlargement and revision by Yi Manun. This was delivered to the king in 1796, but never published. In 1807 Yi Manun's son, Yujun, further revised and slightly shortened the work. The manuscript became badly worn, so in 1813 another copy was made, and at the same time a few unofficial copies were taken.

The commission of the Hongmun-gwan which prepared the 1907 edition used both the 1770 edition and the 1807 menuscript, but rearranged the material and brought it up to date. At the same time all the terminology was altered so that Korea appeared as an empire on an equal footing with China.

A convenient photographic reprint was issued by Tonghwa Munhwa-sa, Seoul, in 1956.

The contents are arranged under scientific and administrative categories. Historical and critical material is placed within these categories.

The categories of the 1907 edition are: (1) astronomy and meteorology; (2) geography of Korea; (3) royal genealogy; (4) rites; (5) music; (6) military affairs; (7) justice; (8) land revenues; (9) other financial matters; (10) census; (11) liens and doles; (12) foreign relations; (13) selection of officials; (14) educational institutions; (15) government departments; (16) literature.

2 *Haedong yŏksa* (Compendium of Korean chronicles)
A compendium of information about Korea, edited by Han Ch'iyun (b1765) and completed by his nephew Han Chinsŏ, based on about 550 earlier books, including Chinese and Japanese sources. It is characterized by the critical and empirical attitude of the *sirhak* school. The first printed edition was that of the Chosen Kosho Kanko-kai(1911). Chosŏn Kwangmun-hoe published an edition in 1912-1913.

The 85 books are divided as follow: 1–16 Annals of the various Korean states from Tan'gun to Koryŏ; 17 astronomy; 18–21 rites; 22 music; 23 military matters; 24 justice; 25 revenues; 26–27 products; 28 customs; 29 housing; 30–41 foreign relations; 42–59 literature; 60 the Suksin (Su-shen) peoples; 61–66 national defence; 67–70 personalities. Supplementary 15 books contain geography, written by Han Chinsŏ.

3 *Sinjŭng Tongguk yŏji sŭngnam* (Revised survey of Korean geography)
This annotated gazetteer of Korea was begun in 1445 by Yang Sŏngji, and finished in 1481 by No Sasin and others under the direction of King Sŏngjong, based on the material in the *Sinch'an p'alto chiri chi* (New geography of the eight provinces) prepared by order of Sejong in 1432, but modelled on the *Ta-Ming-i-t'ung chih* recently received from China (1461). It was first printed in 1487, with the title *Tongguk yŏji sŭngnam,* and several times revised before the revision of 1530 with the present title, which is the only text now surviving. The Chosen Kosho Kanko-kai edition was 1912. There is a photographic reprint of the 1530 edition published by Tongguk munhwa-sa in 1958.

The work begins with a description of Seoul, followed by Kaesŏng, Kyŏnggi, Ch'ungch'ŏng, Kyŏngsang, Chŏlla, Hwanghae, Kangwŏn, Hamgyŏng and P'yŏngan, in that order. There is a map of each province showing the counties and chief mountains, and a map of the whole country showing the provinces and most important mountains. Each provincial section is divided by counties, and the information given under each county is subdivided into: brief history;

rank and number of magistrates; variant names of the area; main surnames; local customs; outstanding landscape features; mountains and rivers; fortresses; military stations; beacons; pavilions; schools; post-stations; bridges; storehouses; buddhist temples; shrines; royal tombs; antiquities; famous officials of the past; other celebrities (including filial sons and faithful women); poems about the area.

The arrangement for the cities of Seoul and Kaesŏng is slightly different, but follows the same principles. At the beginning of the Seoul section is the *Ch'ao-hsien fu,* a description of Korea written by the Ming envoy Tung Yüeh in 1488.

In addition to the verses in the poetry section for each county, the other subheadings contain generous excerpts from earlier writers, including many poems.

c Korean official histories

1 *Samguk sagi* (Records of the Three Kingdoms)
The earliest extant source for Korean history. It was compiled by Kim Pusik and others by order of Injong of Koryŏ, 1145. The oldest known edition dates from 1393-4, another from 1512-13. The chief editions available to Gale were Chosen Kosho Kanko-kai 1909; Tokyo Imperial University 1913; Chosen Kenkyu-kai 1914. Several editions and translations into Korean have been published in Seoul since 1950.

The work is modelled on the traditional Chinese historiography of Szŭ-ma Ch'ien. Volumes 1–12 are annals of Silla; 13–22 annals of Koguryo; 23–28 annals of Paekche; 29–31 chronological tables; 32–40 monographs on sacrifices, music, dress, vehicles and harness, utensils, housing, geography, and officials; 41–50 biographies.

2 *Koryŏ-sa* (Records of Koryŏ)
According to the custom whereby each dynasty edited the official history of the preceding dynasty, the annals of Koryŏ were edited about 1395 under the supivision of Chŏng Tojŏn. A second draft was completed by 1442, and printed in 1448, but Sejong had criticisms. The edition was suppressed and a new editorial board, headed by Chŏng Inji, set to work, remaking it in traditional Chinese annalistic form. The writing was finished in 1451, and the publication was achieved in 1454. This is the book we now have. It has some unique records of Mongol China, and used many contemporary records of the Koryŏ period, but there is reason to believe that the later parts are less reliable, because Yi historians needed to justify the change of dynasty and therefore exaggerated the failures of Koryŏ. The Japanese Kokusho Kanko-kai produced a modern typeset edition in Tokyo in 1909. In 1955 Yonsei University published a photographic reprint of a woodblock print which is the edition referred to in this book.

The *Koryŏ-sa* contains 2 books of lists of contents; 46 books of annals; 39 books of monographs on astronomy, calendar, the elements, geography, rites, music, dress, selection of officials, official posts, revenues, military affairs, and justice; 2 books of chronological tables; and 50 books of biographies.

3 *Kukcho pogam* (Mirror of the dynasty)
In Gale's day this was the only official account of the Yi dynasty that had been published. It was a record of the noteworthy sayings and doings of Yi kings, collected together with important memorials submitted by notable subjects, as a manual of examples for subsequent kings. Therefore anything of distress or shame to the royal house was either not mentioned or glossed over. It is no longer regarded as a text of major importance.

The first plan for its compilation was Sejong's order for a volume commemorating the deeds of his father and grandfather, but he died before it was completed. Sejo had the work carried out by Sin Sukchu and others, stopping short of the reign of Tanjong (whom he had had murdered), and printed it in 1458. Supplements and reprints were made, till the third complete re-edition was issued in 1848 in 92 books. The final edition of 90 books in 26 volumes was published in 1908, a partially redone version of the 1848 book. Among the editors were Yi Wanyong and Kim Yunsik. The editing of the 1908 version consisted partly in bringing the material up to the reign of Ch'ŏlchong (1863), partly in treating T'aejo, Changjo, Chŏngjo, Sunjo and Munjo as emperors (a title they had been accorded in 1899) and partly in removing other references to dependence on China. Gale had access to both the later versions and to the Chosen Kenkyu-kai's *kanamajiri* edition (5 volumes) of 1917.

4 *Tongguk t'onggam* (Complete mirror of Korea)
56 books in 28 fascicules compiled by a royal commission led by Sŏ Kŏjŏng and completed in 1484. It is based on earlier official histories (*Samguk sagi, Koryŏ-sa,* and Chinese sources) and the *Samguk yusa,* covering the Three Kingdoms and Koryŏ in chronological order. It includes many comments by Kwŏn Kŭn (1352–1409), which are freely quoted by Gale. A sixteenth-century woodblock print exists, but Gale also had access to the Chosŏn Kwangmun-hoe edition of 1911, the Chosen Kosho Kanko-kai edition of 1912, and the Chosen Kenkyu-kai edition of 1915. It was a popular work during the centuries, but is now regarded as being of secondary importance, although it was the first history of Korea written by a Korean.

The first twelve volumes deal with the Three Kingdoms, and the remaining 44 volumes with the history of Koryŏ. At the head of the work is an extra volume (*oegi*) dealing with Tan'gun, other legendary history, and history before the founding of Silla. The model for the compilation was Szŭ-ma Kuang's *Tzŭ-chih t'ung-chien* (1084). The standpoint is strongly confucian.

d Chronologies, unofficial general histories and collectanea

1 *Tongsa kangmok* (Outline history of Korea)
A general history from Ch'i Tzŭ (Kija) to the end of Koryŏ compiled by An Chŏngbok (1712–1786) from Korean and Chinese sources and evidently intended as a textbook. It was modelled on the *T'ung-chien kang-mu* of Chu Hsi (12th century). At the beginning are maps and tables, and at the end a collection of early legends including Tan'gun. It uses the *Tongguk t'onggam,* but is influenced by Chu Hsi's philosophy and attempts greater systematization than earlier works. Gale probably used the Chosen Kosho Kanko-kai edition of 1915 in 4 volumes. This edition was photographically reprinted by Kyŏngin munhwa-sa in 1970.

2 *Yŏllyŏ-sil kisul* (Lighted Bramble Records)
'Lighted Bramble' was the pen-name of the compiler, who collected extracts from some 400 sources of various kinds to make a history of the Yi dynasty. His regular name was Yi Kŭngik (1736–1806). He drew on memorials, biographies, diaries, letters, and collections of anecdotes. It was not printed before the first decade of the 20th century, when a mimeographed version of part of it was made. Both the Kwangmun-hoe and the Chosen Kosho Kanko-kai produced typeset editions, the former more accurate, but shorter (34 books only), and the latter a fuller recension published between 1912 and 1914. Gale apparently used the latter. Various other editions now exist.

Books 1–33 contain a chronological account of the Yi dynasty from 1392 to 1674 arranged in sections according to the reigns of successive kings. The account of each reign has a biographical account of the king himself, followed by accounts of the chief events of the reign and groups of biographies of notable statesmen, scholars, writers, and soldiers. A supplement of 7 books deals with the reign of Sukchong (1675–1720). There is an encyclopaedic appendix of 19 books; dealing with the royal family and rites; relations with China; official organization; revenues; produce; doles; census; military affairs; justice; music; customs; dress; housing; slaves, entertainers, and buddhism; literature; astronomy; geography; defence; and pre-Koryŏ history.

3 *Taedong yasŭng* (Unofficial records of Korea)
This large compilation of 57 collections of anecdotes, diaries, and lists of personalities was published in 13 volumes by the Chosen Kosho Kanko-kai between December 1909 and April 1911. The first volume contains a preface written in Japanese by Asami Rintaro. A photographic reprint in four volumes was published by Kyŏnghŭi University, Seoul, in 1968.

Some of the contents are chatty collections of trivia, some are weightier works. A number of the pieces were also printed elsewhere. The earliest pieces date from the second half of the fifteenth century, though they include stories going back to the founding of the Yi dynasty.

The latest piece was written about 1650.
The original manuscript was divided into 72 *kwŏn*.
The principal contents are:

    I   *Yongjae ch'onghwa*, a miscellany by Sŏng Hyŏn (1439–1504). Similar shorter works by Sŏ Kŏjŏng, Nam Hyoon, and Ch'a Ch'ŏllo. A fragment of *Haedong akpu*, by Sim Kwangse (1577–1624).

    II *Ch'ŏngp'a kŭktam* (Yi Yuk 1438–1498). *Haedong yaŏn* (Hŏ Pong 1551–1588).

    III Materials about purges of scholars before 1589. *Sŏktam ilgi* (otherwise *Kyŏngyŏn ilgi*) by Yi I.

    IV Materials on the political trials of 1589. *Haedong chamnok*, a collection of biographical notes.

  V-VII Materials relating to the Imjin War, its preparations and aftermath.

 VIII-X Materials on the reign of Kwanghae-gun.

XI-XIII Diaries and miscellanies of the sixteenth and seventeenth centuries.

4 *Taedong kinyŏn* (Korean annals)
Printed in Shanghai and published 1903. Usually attributed to Homer B Hulbert, though his name is not mentioned in it. It was vigorously promoted by the advertising pages of Hulbert's *Korea Review*, and he probably inspired the compilation of the work, though he cannot have written it. It is a history of the Yi dynasty, written in strictly annalistic form, with materials taken from a number of unofficial collections (including the *Yŏllyŏ-sil kisul*), and the *Kukcho pogam*. For the latter years the *Hansŏng sinbo*, a newspaper, was also used. The five volumes bring the story of the dynasty down to 1896.

5 *Tongsa yŏnp'yo* (Korean chronological tables)
The first modern attempt to compile a chronology of the whole of Korean history, from earliest times to the present day, edited by Ŏ Yunjŏk, and published in 1915. The basic dateline is given according to the legendary Tan'gun era, but western, Japanese and Chinese dates are shown parallel. Many sources were drawn on, some of them of very little value—such as legends of prehistoric times written into family genealogies. A second edition of the book in 1929 pruned away some of the worthless material. The original chronology ended at 1910.

6 *A chronological index*
Edited by Horace N Allen, American Minister to Korea, and published by him in Seoul in 1901. Reprinted in *Korea: fact and fancy* in 1904. Part I is a chronology in English of Korean affairs from 97 BC to AD 1877. It is brief and, except for the latter part, of little value. Part II is a chronology from 1875 to 1903, detailed and of great interest; the Appendix extends the chronology very briefly for a further two years. Part III has a list of Korean treaties and agreements. Part IV is a list of foreign diplomatic representatives to Korea from 1877 to 1904. Part V Korean Foreign Office chiefs and diplomatic staff overseas. Part VI chief officers of Korean Customs; foreign decorations conferred on Koreans; a brief bibliography. There is a good index.

7 *Kukcho inmul chi* (Prominent people of the dynasty)
Brief accounts of worthies of the Yi dynasty, drawn from 117 sources by An Chonghwa (1860–1924) and published in Seoul in 1909. The names are arranged in groups under reigns, and end with the reign of Ch'ŏlchong. Three volumes.

8 *Pan'gye surok* (Pan'gye's scheme)
A plan for the reformation of Korean administration and finance by Yu Hyŏngwŏn (1622–1673). It was partly unworkable, partly insufficiently radical. King Yŏngjo ordered three copies of it in 1769, printed with movable type. A woodblock edition was printed by local initiative at Kyŏngju in 1770. There is a photographic reprint by Tongguk munhwa-sa 1959, and a reprint with Korean translation by Ch'ungnam University, Taejŏn, 1962–68 (4 volumes).

    The book is an early example of the *sirhak* or practical learning school. There are 26 books: 1–8 a reformed land system; 9–12 training of leadership; 13–14 selection of officials; 15–18 organization of government officials; 17–20 revenues and doles; 21–24 military matters; 25–26 miscellaneous; addenda on local administration.

9 *T'aengni chi* (Selection of habitats)
A human geography dating from 1714. It has several names, including *P'aryŏk chi* (Account of the eight provinces), *P'aryŏk pokkŏ chi* or *P'aryŏk kagŏ chi* (Suitable habitats of the eight provinces), and *Pakchong chi sansu-rok* (General account of topography). It was compiled by Yi Chunghwan (1690–c1750) and provides a cultural guide to the areas of Korea by location, means of livelihood, landscape, cultural and historical characteristics. There was an edition by the Chosen Kosho Kanko-kai in 1910, and another by the Kwangmun-hoe in 1912. A Japanese translation *(Chosen hachiiki shi)* by Kondo Masuki, was published in Tokyo in 1881.

10 *Sŏnghŏ saesŏl* (Collectanea of Yi Ik)
A vast collection of information on Chinese and Korean affairs from Han times onwards by Yi Ik (1671–1763), another early *sirhak* writer. He was a poor man who declined public office, but had a splendid library collected by his ancestors on embassies to Peking, including much Ch'ing dynasty material. The work is in 30 volumes, divided into five *mun* (sections), containing notes made by Yi Ik on various occasions during nearly forty years, often as answers to pupils' queries. It was re-edited and condensed with Yi Ik's permission by his disciple An Chŏngbok, and the resultant text, *Sŏngho saesŏl yusŏn* (Digest of Yi Ik's collectanea), filled only 10 volumes. An's recension is much better-organized and easier to refer to. The original five *mun* he renamed *p'yŏn*, dividing each *p'yŏn* into smaller *mun*, as follows: I Astronomy and Geography (astronomy, geography, spirits) II Mankind (humanity, learning, rites, family matters, state matters, morality, food and clothing, utensils, arts); III Natural history (zoology, botany); IV Literature (prose, poetry).

The Chosen Kosho Kanko-kai edition appeared in 1915. There is a Kyŏngin munhwa-sa photographic reprint of Yi Ik's text in 2 volumes (1970) and a similar reprint of the *yusŏn* by Kyŏnghui University, Seoul, 1968.

11 *Taedong kimun* (Intriguing Korean tales)
A modern collection of stories by Kang Hyosŏk published in Seoul in 1926. It contains anecdotes of the Yi dynasty, arranged chronologically. It seems to contain the only printed source for the story of Chu Chi-fan, Wŏlsa, Sŏkpong and Ch'a Ch'ŏllo, retailed by Gale in chapter 30 of his *History*, from which it was copied by Bishop Trollope and Joan Grigsby.

12 *Kimun ch'onghwa* (Collection of anecdotes)
Four volumes of manuscript stories, attributed by the colophon to one Unsŭngja ('Rider of the clouds'), and dated *chŏngch'uk* (year of the red ox, ie 1757, 1871, or 1877—the earlier dates are possible). Gale used the copy now in Yonsei University library, and described it in his 'Short list of Korean books' (TKBRAS XXI 1931 page 88 No 42). The stories are copied from a dozen or more earlier collections, of which the best known is the *Ŏu yadam* of Yu Mongin (1559–1623). The stories date from the seventeenth and early eighteenth centuries, although the subject matter describes events as early as the reign of Sŏnjo (1568–1608). The stories frequently deal with spirits and preternatural wonders.

13 *Kajae Yŏnhaeng nok* (Diary of a journey to Peking)
The diary of a journey to Peking in the winter of 1712–1713 when Kim Ch'angŏp accompanied his elder brother Kim Ch'angjip, who was the official envoy for that year. Gale used the Chosen Kosho Kanko-kai edition of 1914. Kajae or Nogajae ('Old farmer') was Kim Ch'angŏp's literary pseudonym. See above pp 56, 280–83.

14 *Chŭngjŏng Namhan chi chŏnjip* (Complete records of Namhan fortress, revised).
Written by Hong Kyŏngmo (1774–1851) and dated 1846. Hong revised the original *Namhan chi* of Sŏ Myŏngŭng written in 1779. Gale made this work the basis of his account of the Namhan siege of 1637, using the Chosen Kosho Kanko-kai edition of 1916, which contains material

bringing the story up to 1858.

15 *T'ongmun-gwan chi bu Haeyu-rok* (Journals of the T'ongmun-gwan and Sin Yuhan's account of his journey to Japan). Chinsŏ edition.
T'ongmun-gwan chi the journal of the Office of Interpreters in the Seoul government was edited in 1720 and 1778, and re-edited by Kim Kyŏngmun and others about 1881. Gale undoubtedly had this Chinsŏ edition, which has records as far as 1888 (also published by the Chosen shiryo sokan No 21, Tokyo 1944). The Chosen Kosho Kanko-kai edition (1913) ends the record at 1862. This edition, published in Tokyo and Seoul in 1905 by the Kankoku Chinsho Kanko-kai, is a Japanese publication and has as an appendix Sin Yuhan's account of the embassy to Japan 1791–1720. This was the first printed version of Sin's *Haeyu-rok*. There is another edition in *Haehaeng ch'ongjae* I (Chosen Kosho Kanko-kai 1914). Gale's typescript shows that he translated the whole of Part I, finishing at the 'Song of Sodomy'.

16 *Chingbi-rok* (Warnings of adversity)
Notes and documents on the Hideyoshi invasions of 1592–1598, compiled by Yu Sŏngnyong (1542–1607), first printed 1647. Two versions exist. One consists of the first two books only, the other adds books 3–5 memorials *(Kunp'o chip)*, 6–14 memorials *(Chinsa-rok)*, 15–16 *Kunmun tŭngnok* and supplementary *Nokhu chapki*.
The Chosen Kosho Kanko-kai edition of 1913 is the full 16-book version.

17 *Suno chi* (Fifteen days' writings)
A rare work of miscellaneous jottings, written in 1678, by Hong Manjong. There are several manuscripts and mimeographed editions. Hong was a voluminous writer on Korean and literary subjects, but most of his output remains in manuscript. He flourished c 1637–1707. *Suno chi* shows his interest in taoism.

e   Literary anthologies

1 *Tongmun-sŏn* (Anthology of Korean writings)
The major anthology of Korean writings, prepared by Sŏ Kŏjŏng and others at the command of King Sŏngjong and completed in 1478. It was enlarged by the addition of a supplement during the reign of Chungjong (1506–1545) and again during the reign of Sukchong (1675–1720). Gale used the Chosen Kosho Kanko-kai edition of 1914. The authors represented begin with Ch'oe Ch'iwŏn (857–910) and continue up to the date of compilation. The first draft was modelled on the famous *Wen hsüan* (Anthology) made by Hsiao T'ung, ruler of Liang 501–531, while he was still the Prince Chao-ming. The classification of the pieces contained in it is complex, but the general outline is the traditional arrangement of verse, followed by prose of various kinds (letters, prefaces, notes, decrees, memorials, essays, biographies), inscriptions, and ritual compositions, both confucian and buddhist. All the texts are in Chinese.

2 *Myŏngsim pogam* (Precious mirror of the enlightened heart)
A collection of Chinese sayings and quotations, some of them from spurious works, which attained great popularity in Korea, and has frequently been reprinted, even in modern times. It is often attributed, though with little justification, to Ch'u Ch'ŏk (late 13th century), and a spurious preface and postface attributed to Yi I (Yulgok, 1536–1584) are printed in some editions.
The extracts are drawn from about 35 Chinese authors from Confucius to Chu Hsi. They include non-confucians such as Chuang-tzŭ, but no buddhist writers. The divisions of the anthology are perseverance, providence, obedience, filial piety, uprightness, study, education of children, self-examination, government, rites, speech, friendship, wifely behaviour, and so on.

3 *Komun chinbo* (Treasures of ancient literature)
A Korean edition of the *Hsiang-shuo ku-wen chen-pao ta-ch'üan*. It was first printed in Korea in 1472, copying a 15th-century Chinese edition. Other editions were issued in Korea in 1612,

1676, and 1803. Both the Chinese text and the Korean version have been through several recensions. The version most printed in Korea in popular editions is abbreviated. The fuller version is in two parts: Part I consists of poetry, from Ch'ü Yüan to Chu Hsi, and Part II of *fu* and prose from the same periods. The selection was based on moral as well as stylistic criteria.

The latest popular edition of the complete version is that from Sech'ang-sa, Seoul, 1964.

4 *Namhun t'aep'yŏng ka* (Songs of peace and prosperity)
Gale published 36 translations of *sijo*, and all but two came from this anthology. It was probably edited and published in 1863. The book is a collection of texts for singers, and includes 224 *sijo* as well as some longer pieces. The name (literally 'Songs of peace on the Southern breeze') is derived from the name of the golden age of the mythical emperor Shun.

Gale's copy was described by him in the *Korea Bookman* III 2 (June 1922), page 13. The woodblocks were in the possession of a friend of Yang Kit'aek's father, and Yang had a set of sheets struck for Gale. Gale discusses only the *nak sijo*, a musical classification mistranslated by him as 'songs of happy days'. See above pp 29–30. The 1920 reprint is common.

5 *Yŏlsŏng ŏje* (The writings of the kings)
There are several collections of kings' writings under this or similar titles. The first was compiled by Yi U about 1691, representing the work of kings from T'aejo to Hyŏnjong. The special edition for Chŏngjo's reign (*Chŏngmyo ŏje*) contains some passages quoted by Gale. The last edition was edited by Chŏng Wŏnyong, bringing the contents up to Ch'ŏlchong.

A modern version published by the Yŏlsong-ŏje Ch'ulp'an-sa in Seoul in 1924 has convenient texts of some passages quoted by Gale, and may well have been his source for them.

6 *Tongsi chŏngsŏn* (Selected Korean poems)
2 books and supplement in 1 volume edited by O Sŏgyŏng and printed in Seoul with modern metal type under the imprint of Yehyang Sŏru in 1917. It contains a discriminating selection of poems, all written in Chinese and arranged according to metre. Gale certainly used this book.

7 *Taedong sisŏn* (Selected Korean poems)
5 volumes published by Kwanghak Sŏp'o, Seoul, in 1918. The poems range from earliest times to 1918, save that no kings or living poets are represented. Poems by buddhist monks, *kisaeng* and other women are included. Edited by Chang Chiyŏn and Kwŏn Sun'gu. All the poems are five- or seven-syllable Chinese verses.

f Individual collections (*chip*)

Since Liu Hsieh first made the classification in *Wen-hsin tiao-lung* ('The literary mind and the carving of dragons') in the sixth century, the traditional classification of books written in Chinese has been into *ching* (*kyŏng*) or classics, *shih* (*sa*) or history and geography, *tzŭ* (*cha*) or arts and sciences (including fiction), and *chi* (*chip*) or the collected works of individual authors. *Chi* or *chip* used to be translated as '*belles lettres*', but a better rendering would be 'literary remains'. When a man of any importance died his family would collect his remaining manuscripts and arrange for them to be printed. The collection thus produced might fill anything from two volumes to several hundred. The title was usually *chip* (collection), *yugo* (relict manuscripts) or some word of similar import, prefixed by the author's literary style or *ho*. Reissues of a collection and different issues of the same edition sometimes have slight differences in the title. In Korea the practice of publishing *chip* became common from late Koryŏ times onward, and several thousand Korean *chip* are now listed.

The arrangement of material within a *chip* varies considerably, but the following is a typical pattern: 1 tabular matter, including chronologies and lists of contents; 2 verse, usually with the longer forms (*pu* and *sa*) before the shorter forms (*si*); 3 prose works, including (a) records of places and events (*ki, nok, chi*, etc); (b) literary criticism in the form of prefaces and postfaces to other men's works as well as the author's own (*sŏ, pal, p'yŏngsul, so, po,* etc); (c) dissertations, essays, treatises and notes (*non, pyŏn, ŭi, sŏl, ch'aek, ko, kyŏl,* etc); (d) memorials to superiors (*chin, ch'aengmun, so, p'yo, tapcha, kyeiŏn, chang*); (e) letters to equals (*sŏ, tok, kan, ch'al, ch'ŏp*); (f) instructions to inferiors (*cho, yŏng, pi, tap, kyo,* often drafted for the monarch); (g) biographies, both critical accounts (*chŏn*) and memoirs (*haengjang*); (h) miscellaneous compositions (*chapchŏ*), including admonitions and epigrams (*cham, myŏng*) often in metrical form, and encomia or eulogies, of things and animals as well as men (*song, ch'an, p'umbo*); 4 ritual compositions, including funerary inscriptions for stones (*myobi, myogal, myop'yo*), for stones on the way to the tomb (*sindobi*), and writings to be buried with the body (*myoji, myomyŏng,* etc); laments and sacrificial prayers (*aesa, chemun, chesa, ch'uk, ch'ŏngsa*); and buddhist and taoist compositions (*sŏktoso, pultoso, toryangiae, ch'oso chemun,* etc).

The brief list of *chip* given here includes those that Gale certainly used. He had access to many more, and often quoted material which was available to him both in *chip* and anthologized in such compendia as *Yŏji sŭngnam* and *Tongmun-sŏn*.

1 *Ch'unjŏng chip* Pyŏn Kyeryang 1369–1430
First printed in 1433, and last in 1825. Pyŏn was the greatest writer and editor of the last years of Koryŏ and the first of the Yi dynasty.

2 *Haeŭn chip* Kang P'irhyo 1764–1848.
Kang was a noted scholar and writer who occupied several minor administrative posts in the government in various places. He was an enthusiast for Chu Hsi's philosophy.

3 *Igye chip* Hong Yangho 1724–1802
Printed in metal type 1843. The *oejip* (classical and historical studies) has preface and postface by Chi Yün (1724–1805), a Chinese scholar with whom Hong corresponded. Hong was employed largely in diplomatic relations with China and in literary work (he edited the *Kukcho pogam* among other things). He promoted interest in Ch'ing 'empirical research' (*k'ao-cheng*) principles of historiography. He was one of Gale's favourite authors.

4 *Ikchae chip* Yi Chehyŏn 1287–1367
First printed in 1363. Subsequent editions include 1432, 1601, 1693, 1814 and 1911. The 1814 edition is photographically reproduced in *Yŏgye myŏnghyŏn chip* (Sŏnggyun-gwan, 1959). Yi lived for many years in China, and helped introduce the neo-confucianism of Ch'eng Hao and Chu Hsi into Korea. He is also the chief Korean to have written longer Chinese poems in the *tz'ŭ* form. The work is divided into *Ikchae nan'go* and *Nŭgong p'aesŏl*.

5 *Kŭmnŭng kŏsa munjip* Nam Kongch'ŏl 1760–1840
Printed in 1815. Nam was a great literary stylist, and once prime minister. His *chip* is unusual in that he edited one version himself before his death.

6 *Kyewŏn p'ilgyŏng* Ch'oe Ch'iwŏn 857–910
Not strictly a *chip*, but a collection of Ch'oe's writings while he was at the T'ang court 874–885. The edition now current was printed in 1834. A modern reprint was issued by the Ch'oe family of Poryŏng-gun, Ch'ungch'ŏng Namdo, in 1967, reprinted in 1968. The title means 'Brush-pen ploughings in gardens of cinnamon'.

7 *P'oŭn chip* Chŏng Mongju 1337–1392
There have been many printings, some of them by royal order, The Sŏnggyun-gwan *Yŏgye myŏnghyŏn chip* (Seoul 1959) contains a reprint and a historical note about the various editions. Gale had, among others, the Chosen Kosho Kanko-kai edition of 1914.

8 *Sambong chip* Chŏng Tojŏn c1345–1398
First printed 1397, redone in 1474, enlarged in 1497. Completely new edition 1791. Gale had also the Chosen Kosho Kanko-kai edition of 1916.

9 *T'oegye sŏnsaeng chip* Yi Hwang 1501–1570
Early seventeenth century woodblock editions photographically reprinted by Tongguk Munhwa-sa 1958. Chosen Kosho Kanko-kai edition (1915) is less complete.

10 *Tonggo yugo* Yi Chun'gyŏng 1499–1572
Printed about 1715. Yi was prime minister for five years.

11 *Tongguk Yi sangguk chip* Yi Kyubo 1168–1241
The first edition of 1251 was many times reprinted and revised. The Chosen Kosho Kanko-kai edition of 1913 was printed from a seventeenth-century edition. There is a modern reprint by Tongguk munhwa-sa 1958.

12 *Ubok chip* Chŏng Kyŏngse 1563–1633
The 1844 woodblock is a standard edition. Chŏng was a highly esteemed writer who fought against the Japanese invaders but fell from favour in the reign of Kwanghae. He favoured Yi Yulgok's philosophy.

13 *Unyang chip* Kim Yunsik 1835–1922
Lithographed 1913; reissued 1917. *Sokchip* (addenda) 1930. Kim was a diplomat of the closing years of the Yi dynasty, embroiled in the struggle of the progressives with Queen Min, whom he opposed. After 1910 the Japanese made him a viscount and chairman of their Korean advisory board, but after 1919 he was working as a Korean patriot, and his viscountcy was forfeited. He was personally known to Gale. See also page 355.

14 *Wŏlsa chip* Yi Chŏnggu 1564–1635
68 books were issued in 1636 and again in 1688. 7 more books were added in the edition of 1720. Wŏlsa was often sent on missions to China, and was once deputy prime minister.

15 *Yangch'on chip* Kwŏn Kŭn 1352–1409
The 1674 edition is standard. There is a modern photographic print by the Kwŏn family (1969). Much of Kwŏn's writing was quoted in Yi dynasty compendia, but Gale quotes verses from the *chip*, to which he had access in Chosen Christian College Library.

16 *Yulgok chŏnsŏ* Yi I 1536–1584
Engraved in 1611, and supplements added in 1675 and 1681. A nearly complete collection was produced in 1749 in 44 books. A woodblock edition of this was printed in 1814, and photographically reprinted by Sŏnggyun-gwan University, Seoul, 1958.

g Buddhist works

1 *P'alsang-nok* (The eight phases of the life of the buddha) Life of Sakyamuni, divided into eight scenes or aspects. It was a popular work in Korean script, and several texts exist. No serious study has yet been made of them. Gale appears to have used a cheap printed edition, no longer traceable.
    The eight scenes are: 1 Reincarnation in the womb of Maya; 2 Birth in the Lumbini Gardens; 3 Conversion by the four distressing sights; 4 Escape from his father's palace; 5 Ascesis in the Himalayas; 6 Enlightenment under a pipal ('the *bodhi* tree') at Bodh Gaya; 7 Preaching in the Deer Park at Sarnath; 8 Entry into Nirvana.

2 *Chosŏn pulgyo t'ongsa* (Comprehensive history of Korean buddhism)
Two thick volumes published in 1918 by Yi Nŭnghwa, son of Gale's friend Yi Wŏn'gŭng. Yi Nŭnghwa was a pioneer in modern studies of Korean religion and folklore. The book was photographically reprinted in 1968 by Kyŏnghŭi Ch'ulp'an-sa, Seoul. It is divided into three sections: I Chronologically arranged themes from Korean buddhist history, centred on individuals and buildings. (This part consists chiefly of extracts from other works, with

comments by the editor. At the end of it is a list of the temples and their organization in 1918); II An account of the various sects of buddhism in Korea, their doctrines and development; III About 200 essays on many subjects relating to Korean buddhism. This book remains a basic source on the subject, a quarry for materials. Gale used it for a number of details.

3 *Samguk yusa* (Reliques of the Three Kingdoms)
This book is usually classed as a history, but is really a collection of buddhist lore. It was written by the monk Iryŏn of Koryŏ (1206–1289) but not printed until 1512, at Kyŏngju. Gale may have used the 1904 edition from Tokyo Imperial University, or the 1915 edition from the Chosen Kenkyu-kai, Seoul.

The outline of the book keeps some of the traditional scheme of Chinese annals by beginning with two sections of chronological tables. Section III retails 62 marvels and 37 stories of the establishment of buddhism (mostly of Silla); IV tells of 13 great monks; V has 3 tales of esoteric buddhism, 10 buddhist miracles, 10 stories of hermits, and 5 tales of filial piety. It is surprising that Gale made so little use of it, because its many tales of the occult would have suited his taste.

4 *Kŭmgang-banya-baramil-gyŏng* (Diamond sutra)
Kumarajiva's translation (AD 402) of the fourth-century *Vajra-prajna-paramita-sutra*, Korea's most popular buddhist scripture. It is one of the Mahayana 'wisdom sutras', teaching the 'transcendental wisdom' of the void. The earliest known of many Korean editions dates from 1387. There were Korean translations and a nineteenth-century English one by Max Müller.

h Chinese books

To Koreans 'Chinese classics' meant the books of the confucian canon, usually in the editions prepared and commented by the Sung scholar Chu Hsi (1130–1200). Many editions were printed in Korea, and translations into the Korean language were sometimes added, either section by section or in supplementary volumes.

Koreans followed a Chinese tradition in grouping the confucian texts into 'four books and three classics', sometimes adding two more titles to the latter category to make 'four books and five classics'. The 'classics' were the pre-confucian writings which the sage was supposed to have edited, and the 'books' were accounts of Confucius and writings of his followers. Another Chinese enumeration listed these nine titles together with four others as the 'thirteen classics', but although all thirteen were known in Korea, this enumeration has never been popular here.

The three classics were the *Book of Changes,* the *Book of Songs* (or *Poetry*), and the *Book of Documents* (or *History*). The two extra titles to make up five classics were the *Record of Rites* and the *Spring and Autumn Annals.* The four books were the *Analects,* the *Great Learning,* the *Doctrine of the Mean* and the *Mencius.* The status of this group of four was defined by Chu Hsi, following Ch'eng I, in the twelfth century AD, for use in elementary education.

In the following notes Korean pronunciation of book-titles is given after the Chinese.

1 *The book of changes* (*I ching; Yŏkkyŏng;* or *Chou-i; Chuyŏk*)
The history of this book is complex and obscure. Its earliest element is a series of 64 hexagrams, providing all the possible permutations of whole and bisected lines combined in groups of six. In their original 'natural' order, traditionally ascribed to the mythical Fu Hsi, they were recognised by Leibnitz as a method of writing the numbers from 0 to 63 in binary notation. They may date from the second millenium before Christ. The philosophic principle by which the permutations of the hexagrams are used in the book is variously explained, but they were undoubtedly first used in divination by shuffling milfoil stalks.

The natural order of the hexagrams was later changed into a different and purely symbolic order. Tradition ascribes this rearrangement to Wen Wang (1231–1135), founder of Chou, who is also supposed to have added the verses, usually referred to as 'text', which now accompany each hexagram. (The natural mathematical order of the hexagrams is usually still recorded at the beginning of the book).

Each text now has several appended paragraphs. The Duke of Chou, son of Wen Wang, is supposed to have added those called *t'uan* (judgment). At least two others (*hsiang* and *yao*) are traditionally ascribed to Confucius. These paragraphs and some supplementary essays printed with the book are called the 'ten wings' (*shih i*). Korean editions usually also print the commentaries of Chu Hsi and Ch'eng Hao (1032-1085). Thus the primitive strata have gradually been augmented with a variety of confucian materials.

The developed form of the *Book of changes* has been of fundamental importance in the formation of Korean symbolism and philosophy.

2 *The book of songs* (*Shih ching; Sigyŏng* or *Sijŏn*)
This is a collection of songs, dating perhaps from the second millenium BC, and was much esteemed by Confucius, who is supposed to have edited them into their present form. The 305 songs are arranged under *feng* (or *kuo-feng*) (regional folksongs), *ya* (songs for court banquets and receptions), and *sung* (hymns for ancestral rites). The *ya* are divided into two groups: *hsiao-ya* and *ta-ya*. There is much diversity of opinion about the significance of this division. It may be a merely arbitrary grouping. Some scholars believe that the *hsiao-ya* were for festivities given by the prince, *ta-ya* for occasions when the vassal lords gathered by themselves; others think the grouping is chronological. The *ya* are aristocratic, the *feng* are presumed to be proletarian. Korean tradition, attracted by the moral interpretation of the songs, has always paid most attention to the *feng*. Moral allegorization was the orthodox confucian interpretation during most of the book's history, but is now recognized as having little or nothing to do with the original meaning of the songs.

The book is also often called *Mao shih* (*Mo-si*) because the present redaction was the work of Mao Heng in the second century BC.

3 *The book of documents* (*Shu ching* or *Shang-shu; Sŏgyŏng, Sŏjŏn,* or *Sangsŏ*)
A collection of speeches and declarations attributed to rulers from legendary times till Chou. It may date from the first half of the millennium before Christ, and is the oldest Chinese prose extant. Two texts exist, a 58–chapter *ku-wen* (old script) and a 33–chapter *chin-wen* (modern script). Gale quotes from the *ku-wen*, but it is now agreed that only the 33 chapters of the *chin-wen* belong to the original compilation.

4 *The Record of Rites* (*Li chi; Yegi*)
A collection of various materials, including some stories and sayings of Confucius and the *Book of Rites* which he is presumed to have used. It is a Han collection, (circa second century BC) of which some parts may be ancient, but some are late confucian traditions. The lengthy and elaborate descriptions of funeral rites have had a fatal fascination for Koreans, and many of the internecine struggles of the Korean court centred on disagreements about their interpretation.

5 *The Spring and Autumn Annals* (*Ch'un ch'iu; Ch'unch'u*)
The only book said to have been compiled by Confucius himself. It is a bald record of events, especially matters of ritual importance, in his native state of Lu from 772 to 481 BC, and is a seminal work in Chinese historiography, because the choice of vocabulary was supposed to indicate the apportioning of praise and blame. Since Han times it has usually been produced together with a commentary. The earliest of these was the *Kung-yang chuan* accepted by the end of the second century BC. It was followed by the *Ku-liang chuan* rather less than a century later. These were moralising annotations, defining the praise and blame to be accorded to each event of the annals. The third 'commentary', *Tso 'chuan* (*Chwajŏn*, the *Tradition of Tso*), was accepted about the time of Christ. It is not a true commentary, but an independent work which has been assimilated to the *Spring and autumn annals,* an elaborate and imaginative reconstruction of the period, written by Tso Ch'iu-ming, probably between the late fourth and second centuries BC. It came to set a standard for narrative style.

6 *The analects* (*Lun yŭ; Nonŏ*)
A collection of reminiscences of Confucius's teachings, mostly answers to questions put to him by his disciples. Chapter x is usually understood to describe his own manners and style of living, but is sometimes interpreted as a series of injunctions for the ideal gentleman. Confucius lived c 551–479 BC, but the *Analects* (the English title was devised by Legge) were composed after his death.

7 *The great learning* (*Ta hsüeh: Taehak*)
A treatise on ethics and government, traditionally attributed to Confucius's disciple Tseng Ts'an, but undoubtedly written much later. It is chapter xlii of the *Li chi* (above, 4).

8 *The doctrine of the mean* (*Chung yung; Chungyong*)
A commentary and elaboration of Confucius's ethical teaching, traditionally ascribed to Tzŭ-szŭ, grandson of Confucius and disciple of Tseng Ts'an; but really chapter xxxi of the *Li chi* (above, 4).

9 *The Mencius* (*Meng-tzŭ; Maengja*)
Mencius lived c372–289 BC. His teachings are recorded in this long book, probably compiled soon after his death.

To complete the reckoning of thirteen classics the *Great learning* and the *Doctrine of the mean* are not counted as separate books, but the three commentaries on the *Spring and Autumn annals* rate as separate works, and the following four titles are added:

10 *The ceremonies and rituals* (*I li; Ŭirye*)   11 *The rituals of Chou* (*Chou li; Churye*)
Two works of similar character and date to the *Li chi*.

12 *The filial piety classic* (*Hsiao ching: Hyogyŏng*)
Attributed to Tseng Ts'an, but really an essay on themes from the *Li chi* dating from the thi rd or second century BC.

13 *Erh ya* (*Ia*)
A thesaurus of literary glosses, arranged topically, dating from the third century BC.

Another confucian text much used in Korea was:

14 *The lesser learning* (*Hsiao hsüeh; Sohak*)
A chrestomathy of quotations from earliest times to Sung, made by Liu Tzŭ-ch'eng under Chu Hsi's supervision in 1187.

Non-confucian works of great importance are:

15 *Lao-tzŭ* (*Noja*)
The famous taoist scripture 'The way and power' (*Tao te ching; Todŏk-kyŏng*), so named from the first words of the two parts of the book (*tao* and *te*). It is a composite work of the third century BC, attributed to a mythical *lao-tzŭ* ('old philosopher'), and rarely printed in Korea, where its mystical philosophy of nature, as opposed to confucian ethical humanism, was considered heterodox. Gale used H A Giles's translation (Hong Kong 1886).

16 *Chuang tzŭ* (*Changja*)
The other important taoist florilegium, probably written mostly in the third century BC. An attractive book full of poems and parables which early gained Gale's attention, it was well known in Korea, where it was thought heretical.

17 *Ch'ien-tzŭ wen* (*Ch'ŏnja-mun*, '*The thousand-character classic*')
A poem in rhymed four-syllable couplets, containing exactly 1,000 different and unrepeated logograms, written by Chou Hsing-szŭ some time between 507 and 521. It is also known as

Pai-shu-wen (*Paeksu-mun*) from the legend that it was composed during a single night and the effort turned the author's hair white. It is divided into four unequal sections: I cosmology and human civiliszation; II confucian ethical principles; III the magnificence of the empire; IV the ideal simplicity of domestic life.

In Korea this book became the standard primer and the text was also used as a series for numbering from 1 to 1,000. There are a modern edition with translations by Francis W Paar(Frederick Ungar, New York, 1963), and an account of its use in Korea together with a translation by Richard Rutt and George Rainer (TKBRAS XXXVI pp 33–35 and 68–75).

18 *T'ao Ching-chieh chi* (*To Chŏngjŏl chip*)
The collected poems of the Chinese Six-Dynasties poet T'ao Ch'ien, better known in Korea as T'ao Yüan-ming (To Yŏnmyŏng) (365–427). He was one of the Chinese poets most influential in forming the Korean tradition. His *Kuei-ch'ü-lai tz'ŭ* (*Kwigŏrae-sa*, 'The return') has been described as the best-known piece of poetry in the Orient, and its theme of rustic peace and simplicity became a major concern of Korean poets. Ching-chieh was the poet's posthumous honorific name. He is well represented in *Komun chinbo*.

The chief Korean edition was engraved on wood in 1583, after the Chinese edition of Ho Meng-ch'un (otherwise Ho Yen-ch'üan, in Korean: Ha Yŏnch'ŏn) and was often reprinted from the same blocks. There are two books in two fasciscules. Book I contains *fu*, and poems in four- and five-syllable verses; book II contains the *Kuei-ch'ü-lai tz'ŭ* and prose pieces, including the famous *T'ao-hua-yüan chi*, the account of the 'Peach-blossom Spring'.

19 *Hsüan-ho feng-shih Kao-li t'u-ching* (*Koryŏ togyŏng*)
In 1123 Hsü Ching came with an embassy of the Sung emperor Hsüan-ho to Kaesŏng, and stayed there for a month. On his return he wrote an account of his visit in 40 short books, originally illustrated with pictures, but the pictures were lost in the Jürched invasions. The Chosen Kosho Kanko-kai edition was published in 1911.

20 *Shih-lüeh* (*Saryak*, Historical outline)
A short account of Chinese history from the mythical emperors onwards, compiled by Ts'eng Hsien-chih in Yüan times, and used by Koreans as a standard text-book under the title *Saryak*. There were many Korean editions and it was used until very recently in rural *kŭlpang* (cottage schools). Gale does not quote the work directly, but some of his Chinese history derives from it, either through his own reading or from his Korean acquaintances.

21 *K'ang-hsi tzŭ-tien* (K'ang-hsi dictionary)
The great dictionary of Chinese characters edited by order of the K'ang-hsi emperor and published in 1716. It settled the method of classifying Chinese characters by 'radicals' and is the norm for all subsequent dictionaries of Chinese characters produced in Korea. It contains 40,545 characters, and has lengthy quotations from earlier works.

22 *The Chinese reader's manual*
'A handbook of biographical, historical, mythological and general literary reference' by William Frederick Mayers, published by the Presbyterian Mission Press, Shanghai 1874.

Mayers (1839–1878) was born in Tasmania, son of an English anglican priest, and educated in England. At the age of 21 he went to China as a student-interpreter and became Chinese secretary at the British legation in Peking. He was closely associated with General Gordon in the Soochow area during the T'ai-p'ing rebellion. He also wrote *The Chinese government* (1877). He died in Shanghai at the age of 39.

The Chinese reader's manual was reprinted by Probsthain of London in 1910. It is in three parts: I Index of proper names; II Numerical categories; III Chronological tables. The flyleaf of Gale's copy is inscribed: 'Jas. S. Gale, June 12th 1895, Gensan, Korea'.

23 *San-kuo-chih yen-i* (The romance of the three kingdoms)
The earliest printed edition of this book dates from 1494, but it was written by Lo Kuan-

chung (1260–1341) at the end of the Yüan dynasty. He is supposed to have based the story on the history of the Three Kingdoms by Chen Shou of Tsin. It covered the period from 184 to 280 during which the three kingdoms of Wu, Wei and Shu were established. The work was considerably revised by Mao Tsung-kang during the K'ang-hsi period (1662–1722) and it is Mao's version which has been read ever since. The most popular prose work in the Far East. Gale probably referred to the English translation by C H Brewitt-Taylor (Kelly and Walsh, Shanghai, 1925, reprinted Tokyo 1959 and Taipei 1967)

i Korean vernacular literature

1 *Sinmi-rok* (Record of the year of the white sheep, 1811)
Large numbers of vernacular Korean story (*kodae sosŏl*) books were printed, especially during the nineteenth century. The only one to which Gale refers is *Sinmi-rok*. This was printed in Seoul in 1861. It is the story of the rebellion of Hong Kyŏngnae in P'yŏngan province in 1811 and 1812. By the solar calendar the event took place entirely during 1812, and another version of the story is called *Imsin-nok*, 'Record of the year of the black monkey'—i.e. 1812.

j Japanese archaeological collections

1 *Chosen koseki zufu* (Albums of Korean antiquities)
Fifteen volumes of photographs of Korean archaeological material, including architecture and stone memorials, published between 1915 and 1935. There is no explanatory text, but the presentation of the photographs is sumptuous. Before Gale left Korea in 1927 seven volumes had been published. The chief editor was Sekino Tadashi, for whom Gale had great reverence. The first seven volumes were I Han colonies and Koguryŏ; II Koguryŏ (both 1915); III Mahan, Paekche, Imna, Okchŏ, Ye, Old Silla, and Three Kingdoms buddhist images; IV Unified Silla (pagodas, temple sites, stone tablets, flag-mast bases, stone lanterns, fortifications and bells) (both 1916); V United Silla (royal tombs, buddhist images, stele and tiles) 1917; VI Koryŏ (palace sites, city walls, fortress sites, temples, stone pagoda, memorials, flag-mast bases) 1918; VII Koryŏ (stone lanterns, bells, buddhist images, buddhist utensils, pictures, royal tombs, funerary inscriptions, stone coffins, pagodas) 1920.
   Published by the Japanese Government-general of Chosen.

2 *Chosen kinseki soran* (Complete survey of Korean inscriptions).
A two-volume collection published by the Government-general of Chosen in 1919, containing a chronologically-arranged selection of inscriptions on stone and metal. Nearly all extant inscriptions of United Silla and earlier are included, and a selection of Koryŏ and Yi examples. The inscriptions date from 85 to 1910. Gale drew on this work continually in making his translations of inscriptions.

II WORKS WRITTEN WHOLLY OR IN PART BY JAMES SCARTH GALE

a Books in English

1 *A CONCISE DICTIONARY OF THE KOREAN LANGUAGE Vol I Korean-English (Han-yŏng chajŏn)* Kelly and Walsh, Yokohama 1891. By H G Underwood, assisted by Homer B Hulbert and James S Gale. 239 pages. See above p 15.

2 *A KOREAN-ENGLISH DICTIONARY (Han-yŏng chajŏn)*
   (a) First edition, published by Kelly and Walsh, Yokohama 1897. 1,168 pages.
       Part I: Korean-English dictionary of about 35,000 entries, arranged in the alphabetical order devised by the missionaries of the Paris Foreign Missions Society in the *Dictionnaire Coréen-Français* (Yokohama 1880). Based on that work and dictionaries of

Underwood (1890) and Scott (English Church Mission Press, Seoul 1891).

Part II: Chinese-English dictionary containing all the Chinese characters in the eighteenth-century Korean dictionary of Chinese characters *Chŏnun okp'yŏn*; with traditional Korean identifying definitions (*saegim*), and meanings copied from Giles's *Chinese-English dictionary* (1892). Arranged in the alphabetical order of the French fathers. There is an index by radicals.

Appended tables: Japan from 660 BC to the present (a table of dynasties and emperors); Chinese rulers from 2953 BC to the present; Korean rulers from 2317 BC to the present; the twenty-four solar terms; the twelve branches; the ten celestial stems; the decimal system; concordance of western years with the Chinese sixty-year cycles.

Part II was also bound separately as a single volume. See above p 28.

(b) Second edition, printed by Fukuin Printing Company, Yokohama, but published by the Yesu-gyo Sŏhoe (Korean Religious Tract Society) in Seoul. Part I 1911; Part II 1914. The two parts issued and bound separately. See above p 51.

Part I: 1,168 pages. Korean-English dictionary of about 50,000 entries, including many new entries of historical and geographical proper names. The order is that of the Korean alphabet. The tables of rulers from the first edition are combined into one comprehensive table with corresponding western names in an additional column. The table of concordances of era years from the first edition of Part II is added, and also a table of the correspondences between years, months and days in the western and Chinese calendars from 1835 to 1934.

Part II: *A Korean-English dictionary (the Chinese character)* printed and issued separately from Part I. 252 pages. The order of the characters changed to accord with the order of the Korean alphabet, and about 50 characters added. A few new definitions inserted. Index by radicals, but no tables. (The tables were now in Part I.)

(c) Third edition. *The unabridged Korean-English dictionary (Han-yŏng tae chajŏn)* printed by Korean YMCA Press, Seoul, and published by the Christian Literature Society of Korea, Seoul 1931. Edited by Alexander A Pieters. 1,800 pages. Contains about 75,000 entries, 35,000 of which were taken from *Chosengo jiten* (Chosen Government-general, Seoul 1920). About 10,000 of the place and person entries of the second edition are deleted. Introductions of previous editions reprinted, partly corrected. See above p 74.

Appended tables: dynasties and kings of Korea; names of Korean kings in alphabetical order; names of years 1850–1951; the twelve horary characters; concordance of western year-numbers with sixty-year cycles; concordance of years, months and days in western and Chinese calendars from 1851 to 1950.

There was no third edition of the Chinese character dictionary.

3 *KOREAN GRAMMATICAL FORMS* (*Sagwa chinam*)

(a) First edition, published by the Trilingual Press, Seoul 1894. 249 pages. Contains 164 grammatical word-endings, with illustrative examples distinguishing written and spoken idioms; 1,098 model sentences, including some lines from *sijo* and much information about Korean customs and beliefs. Pages 2–60 have the *kugyŏl* (abbreviated Chinese script) forms of word-endings in the margin, unexplained. See above pp 21–22.

(b) Second edition. Methodist Publishing House, Seoul 1903. 229 pages. Printed with smaller type; paper covers, smaller format. Material slightly re-arranged and most mistakes corrected. See above p 33.

(c) Third (revised) edition. Korean Religious Tract Society (Yesu-gyo Sŏhoe), Seoul 1916. 270 pages. Printed by Fukuin Company, Yokohama.

Virtually a new book, better arranged, greatly expanded, with better examples and updated vocabulary. Contains: 240 word endings; 100 model sentences; 200 colloquial proverbs; 550 miscellaneous sentences; and 321 'colloquial *muncha* sentences' (Chinese phrases). See above pp 51–52.

4 *PRESENT-DAY ENGLISH-KOREAN (THREE THOUSAND WORDS)* Christian Literature Society, Seoul, 1924. Korean title: *Samch'ŏn chajŏn*. 77 pages. See above p 74.

5 *KOREAN SKETCHES* Fleming H Revell, New York 1898. Also issued under the imprints of William Briggs, Toronto; and Oliphant, London and Edinburgh. 256 pages.
A collection of short essays on Korean life and personalities. The chapter titles are: I First impressions (an account of his three months at Sorae in 1889); II The coolie (reprinted from the *Korean Repository*); III The Yalu and beyond (from the *Korean Repository*); IV From poverty to riches (the story of one Nam of Kapsan); V The Korean pony (from the *Korean Repository*); VI Across Korea (written for the Yokohama Literary Society); VII The Korean boy (i.e. houseboy or servant); VIII Korean New Year; IX The Korean mind; X The Korean gentleman (from the *Korean Repository*); XI Korea's present condition (a conversation with Yi Pŏmjin, Korean Minister to the USA, recommending, among other things, the exclusive use of the Korean alphabet and the abolition of Chinese characters in Korea); XII Some special friends (vignettes of several Korean types, including Prince Ŭihwa); XIII A missionary chapter. See above p 31.

6 *THE VANGUARD* Fleming H Revell, New York 1904. 320 pages. A fictionalized account of the early stages of presbyterian mission work in Korea, centred on P'yŏngyang and Wŏnsan, and suggested by the autobiography of Ko Ch'anik, an elder of the church. See biography above pp 24 and 44. There is a vivid description, based on an eye-witness account, of the *General Sherman* incident of 1866 in Chapter xiv, pp 106–109.
Danish translation: *Fra Forpostkampen* en skildring af den aandelige brydningstid i Korea autoriseret oversaettelse for Danmark og Norge ved M. Wolff. Hovedkommission for Danmark det Schønbergske Forlag — København 1910. 278 pp.

7 *KOREA IN TRANSITION* Board of Foreign Missions, Presbyterian Church in the USA, New York 1909. A series of essays intended as study outlines for young people's organizations in the Presbyterian Church. 194 pages.
Danish translation: *Korea I forvandilingens tegn* autoriseret oversaettlese for Danmark og Norge ved M. Wolff. Hovedkommission for Norge, Lutherstiftelsens Boghandel, Kristiania 1911. 164 pp.

8 *KOREAN FOLK TALES - Imps, ghosts and fairies*, translated from the Korean of Im Pang and Yi Yuk. Dent, London (Dutton, New York) 1913. Reprinted by Charles Tuttle, Tokyo and Rutland, Vermont, 1963 and 1971. 245 pages. See above pp 50–51.
53 stories from the Chinese of: 'an old manuscript copy' of stories by Im Pang (1640–1724); *Ch'ŏngp'a kŭktam* by Yi Yuk (1438–1498); and three tales from unidentified sources. Biographical notes from *Kukcho inmul chi* by An Chonghwa, Seoul 1909.
Four of the stories are quoted in HKP: xxiv 'The home of the fairies' (HKP chapter 2); xxvii 'The fortunes of Yu' (HKP chapter 25); xlii 'The perfect priest' (HKP chapter 24 Namnu or Chabi *sujwa*); xlvi 'Faithful *Mo*' (HKP chapter 24)
xxii 'The man who lost his legs', an anonymous tale, described by Gale as 'Korea's Sindbad', is a variant of the Polyphemus story.

9 *THE CLOUD DREAM OF THE NINE* Daniel O'Connor, London, 1922. Introduction by E K Robertson Scott. 347 pages.
Gale's translation of *Kuun-mong*, a novel written in Chinese by Kim Manjung about 1689 and translated several times into Korean. Gale's translation was made at the suggestion of Kim Tohŭi. The text used was the Chinese two-volume woodblock edition printed in Naju in 1725, or a text closely resembling it. See biography, above pp 58–60.

10 *THE HISTORY OF THE KOREAN PEOPLE* Christian Literature Society, Seoul. No date (1927?)
A volume of bound offprints from the original printing of the work as articles in the *Korea*

Mission Field, July 1924 to September 1927, monthly except for February 1927 (because that issue was written entirely by Koreans). See above pp 77–78, 91–92.

b   Articles in English

1   *Transactions of the Korea Branch of the Royal Asiatic Society*, Seoul
Volume I (1900) pp 1–24: 'The influence of China upon Korea'.
A paper describing the depth of Korea's indebtedness to China in all cultural fields. It contains a reference to the *Ch'ŏnggu akchang* (apparently a copy of the nineteenth-century anthology of *sijo* and other Korean-language songs now usually known as *Kagok wŏllyu*) and lengthy translations from *Ahŭi wŏllam*, a children's primer by Chang Hon, 1803.
Hulbert's answer is printed on pages 25–42, and Gale's response to that answer on pages 42–47. See biography, above p 40.

Volume II ii (1901) pp 2 – 43: 'Han-yang (Seoul)' See above pp 38–40.
A description of the city, drawing on the *Yŏji sŭngnam, Tongguk t'onggam, Samguk sagi, Yŏllyŏ-sil kisul, Kukcho pogam,* and *T'aengni chi.* It includes a translation of most of the *Ch'ao-hsien fu*, an account of Seoul by the Ming envoy Tung Yüeh in 1488, taken from the text in *Yŏji sŭngnam* I 5b iv – 9b ii, and 10a viii to 12b iii. The list of place-names is interesting.

Volume IV i (1912) pp 13–61 'The Korean alphabet'
A study of the origin and qualities of the Korean alphabet (*ŏnmun* or *han'gŭl*), emphasizing the neo-confucian inspiration of its creators. The chief sources used by Gale were the *Munhŏn pigo*, the 1911 edition of *Yong-bi-ŏ-ch'ŏn ka* issued by the Chosen Kosho Kanko-kai, and publications of Chu Sigyŏng's pioneering Kungmun Yŏn'gu-hoe (Korean Language Research Society), with which Gale was associated. See above p 52.

Volume IV iii 1913 pp 18–22: 'Selection and divorce'
The whole article was revised and reprinted with the same pagination, because the first printing had misprints in the Chinese characters. A very brief treatment of the subject. The section on the selection of spouses depends on the popular manual *Ch'ŏn'gi taeyo* (Digest of divine providence), and the section on divorce is merely a short quotation from the *Sohak (Hsiao hsüeh)*. See above p 52.

Volume VI ii 1915 pp 1–22: 'The pagoda of Seoul'
A description of the Wŏn'gak-sa pagoda in Pagoda Park, Seoul, with a translation of the inscription on the memorial tablet beside it. Gale correctly unravelled the previously obscure history of the pagoda. See also above pp 61,

Volume XIII (1922) pp 1–67 and i-vi: 'The Diamond Mountains'
A collection of quotations about the Diamond Mountains, together with a diary of Gale's own trip there 21 September to 22 October 1922. The Diamond Mountains in Kangwŏn province had been famous for many centuries as one of the most beautiful areas in the Far East. This paper contains: two brief unidentified passages: a note from Kwŏn Kŭn (YJSN XLVII 4a7, also in *Yangch'on chip* XVII 9); preface to a travel diary by Hong Ŭnggil, written by Yi Hwang (*T'oegye chip* XLII 1a 11); a preface to the same book by Yi I (YC XIII 29); the inscription on the stele of Changan-sa by Yi Kok (YJSN XLVII 10 a 6); passages from Yi Wŏn *Kŭmgang nok* (1489); Yi Chŏnggu (*Wŏlsa chip* XXXVIII 1a 1 – 9b 1 *Yu Kŭmgangsan ki*) (1603) (quoted HKP chapter 30); Cho Sŏngha (*Kŭmgang-san ki* 7b 5 – 9b 3) 1865. See above pp 61, 77, 269. The mountains are named after the Diamond Sutra.

Volume XV (1924) pp 3–22: 'A shipwreck (Korean) in 1636 AD'
A translation of the text entitled *P'yohae-rok* in the Kishigawa collection at Tokyo University Library, printed in Chosen Kosho Kanko-kai *Haehaeng ch'ongjae* III (1914), as *P'yoju-rok* though Gale does not identify his original. It was written by Yi Chihang of Tong-

nae, who was shipwrecked off the east coast and blown to Sakhalin, where he met Ainu. He was eventually repatriated through Tokyo and Tsushima, after almost a year's absence from Korea. See above p 77.

Volume XXI (1932) pp 59–104: 'A short list of Korean books – (A catalogue of some Korean books in the Chosen Christian College Library)'
Brief descriptions of 73 titles of old Korean books in the library of Chosen Christian College, now Yonsei University, Seoul. The notes are sketchy and ill-organized. They were never prepared for publication, but were printed without editing, in order to save them from being lost. The list has been wrongly attributed to Bishop Mark Trollope because it follows a paper on 'Korean books and their authors' written by the bishop. H H Underwood's note on page 108 of the same volume states clearly that the list is Gale's work.

2 *The Korean Repository*, Seoul
Gale published 24 articles in this review (1892 and 1895–8). The translations of *sijo* are II 121–122, 228; III 1, 303; and V 443. 'Korean history – translations from native writers' was a series of four translated selections from *Tongguk t'onggam* (*Oegi* and books I–V). Most of the remaining articles are essays on his experiences in Korea. See above pp 26, 29–30.

3 *The Korea Review*, Seoul
Three translations by Gale appear in Volume I (1901): two from Chuang-tzǔ and two from Courant's *Bibliographie Coréenne* (1891).

4 *The Korea Magazine*, Seoul. See above pp 53–58.
Printed at the Seoul YMCA Press and published from January 1917 to April 1919. The editorial board consisted of S A Beck (American Bible Society), W G Cram and W A Noble (methodists), and Gale. The object of the magazine was to give missionaries information about Korean culture and affairs. The majority of the articles were written by Gale.
Articles signed by Gale include regular monthly essays on aspects of the Korean language, and two other pieces.
Articles signed 'E.T.' (Esson Third) appeared during 1917; the most interesting is a symposium of quotations from Korean authors about tobacco.
Articles signed 'Spectator' appeared during 1917. They include a catena of translations about flies: a description of the *sŏkchŏn* ceremony at the Sŏnggyun-gwan; and an essay entitled 'Grind', discussing the Korean method of learning by sheer memory work, and suggesting that the Church will not succeed in imposing the western concept of learning-by-thinking.
Articles signed 'A student of the Orient' form a series of eight entitled 'Korea's noted women'. All the women are Chinese.
'Yung Oon' is the signature on translations from Ch'oe Ch'iwŏn (mostly reprinted in HKP chapter 15), Sŏng Hyŏn (six anecdotes from *Yongjae ch'onghwa*), Yi Chesin and Kwŏn Ŭngin (the latter wrongly attributed to Yi Chesin) in the first two issues of the magazine.
Unsigned translations of eighty poems and stories are selected from twenty-nine authors. Eleven of the pieces are reprinted in HKP. Apart from pieces mentioned in the biography of Gale, the following points are of special interest: three passages from Hong Manjong *Suno chi* (seventeenth century) III 12–13, 55–9, 154–6; a letter of Hong Yangho (1724–1802) to Chi Yün, about christianity II 507–8; Im Ŏngnyŏng 'From Naksan monastery' (*Sŏkch'ŏn chip* VI 15–16) III 5–6; five stories from *Kimun ch'onghwa*, II 14, 22, 24, 27, 70; thirteen pieces from Sŏng Hyŏn *Yongjae ch'onghwa;* twenty pieces from Yi Kyubo; and three from Yi Talch'ung (d 1395).
Ten extracts from Kim Ch'angŏp *Kajae Yŏnhaeng nok* appeared monthly from July 1918 to April 1919. Parts were reprinted in HKP chapter 32. See above pp 280–3.
'Choon Yang' is a translation of the modern prose version of *Ch'unhyang ka*, written by Yi Haejo (1869–1972) and published as *Okchunghwa — Ch'unhyang ka* in 1911.
The first five issues of KM contain ten unsigned 'Questions and answers' on such matters

as Korea's oldest monument, oldest poem, and the date of the introduction of the abacus. The latter mentions the older *sugaji* (*sc. san'gaji* counting-sticks).

An article entitled 'Odds and ends' explains why Koreans eat boiled grain with a spoon by saying that Confucius is recorded in Analects x as eating millet with a spoon. (The quotation is wrong: the phrase *fan-shu-wu-i-chu*, 'do not eat millet with chopsticks', is in *Li-chi* I 29.)

Six articles during 1918 deal with 'Places of interest about Seoul'.

Six more deal with ancient remains from T'ung-kou and P'yŏngyang to Iksan, Puyŏ, and Kaya (Koryŏng).

Thirty-seven more articles deal with history, archaeology, religion, customs, and literature. The most interesting are: 'Hong Pongju', telling of Thomas Hong, a Roman catholic martyr of 1866 (Gale possessed his copy of the poems of Hong Kan (d 1304). It is now in Yonsei Library), I 306-7; a group of extracts about 'Tan'gun', chosen from some twenty sources, I 404-414; 'Village government in old Korea', a description of the old-style village headman, I 455-60; 'Christianity in Korea', an account of articles published in the Seoul daily *Maeil sinbo* 11-17 October 1918 by Ch'unwŏn (Yi Kwangsu); 'Korean playing-cards' (*t'ujŏn*), III 108-11; three articles on Korean literature, I 297-300, 354-56, II 293-302; 'The kisaeng', II 198-202.

5 *American church magazines*
Gale published articles in *The outlook, World outlook. The missionary, The missionary review of the world, Over sea and land, The church at home and abroad, The evangelist, Field despatches* (all of New York), *The Assembly herald* and *Women's work for women* (Philadelphia), and *The presbyterian witness* (Toronto). Twenty-one such articles have been traced. They date from 1893 onwards.

6 *Other missionary literature*
There are two articles in *The bible in the world* (London); one each in *The student missionary appeal* (New York 1898), and *The Presbyterian Year Book of Prayer for Missions* (1935).

7 *Non-church publications*
Articles in *Overseas travel magazine* (1927); *Folklore* (London 1900); *The Globe* (Toronto); *Japan Daily Mail* (1896); *Seoul Press* (on Korean printing types 1913); *The open court* (Chicago, 1918: XXXII 79-103 'Korean literature', containing twenty translated passages and poems, about half of them not published elsewhere): an essay in the report of the Australasian Association for the Advancement of Science (Brisbane 1895).

8 *Periodicals published in Japan and Korea*
The christian movement in the Japanese empire and its successors (Tokyo) contain interesting articles on Korean literature and culture, especially 1923 pp 465-71 and 1926 pp 375-382.

The Korea field and *The Korea mission field* contain forty-one articles by Gale, varying in subject-matter from obituaries and book reviews to essays on literature and translation. There are a few translations of poetry.

The Korea bookman (CLS 1922-25) has seven articles by Gale.

Gale wrote the *General Report* of the Seoul station of his mission 1899-1900; one of the *Quarto-centennial papers* of his mission (1909), a paper in the *Report of the Korea Mission* of his church (1914); two obituaries in *The Korea Methodist* (1905).

9 *The North China Daily News*
The only complete files of this paper, it appears, are in Peking. Some of the articles which Gale wrote for it were reprinted in *The North China Herald and Supreme Court and Consular Gazette* (also published in Shanghai). The earliest article discovered is dated October 1899; the latest August 1905. During this period the *North China Herald* printed twenty-four articles by Gale. Another thirty-six survive in manuscript which were apparently contributed to the *North China Daily News*. The last one appeared 13 October 1923. See above pp 35,74.

c Books in Korean

1 *Ch'ŏllo yŏkchŏng*
A translation of John Bunyan's *Pilgrim's Progress*, Part I. (Part II was done by Mrs H. G. Underwood in 1920). See above p 27.
The 1895 woodblock edition on Korean paper was printed at the Paejae Haktang in Seoul. It has 202 pages, originally bound in two fascicules. There are 21 pictures. The same pictures appear in a metal type edition on Chinese paper with 67 pages, printed in Shanghai.
2nd edition, 1910. Presbyterian Mission, Seoul, 210 pages. Metal type. Illustrations as in the first edition.
3rd edition, 1919. Korean Religious Book and Tract Society, Seoul. A reprint of the second edition, 210 pages.
4th edition, 1926. Christian Literature Society of Korea, Seoul. In this edition word-divisions have been indicated to some extent; in previous editions they were not.

2–5 *Yumong ch'ŏnja* (Korean readers). See above pp 36–38.
A series of four books designed for use in mission schools. The title, literally 'The enlightened thousand characters', indicated that this series was intended to replace the old Thousand Character Classic (*Ch'ŏnja-mun*), the traditional primer of Korean children (see above p 371), by readers with material better suited to the needs of the twentieth century. Each of the first three volumes introduces the pupil to a thousand Chinese characters. The fourth volume was entitled *Yumong sokp'yŏn* ('continuation volume') because it was published three years later than the other volumes and differs from them markedly in content. All four volumes were still offered for sale in the catalogue of the Literature Society in 1911. The third edition is much inferior to the others in typography and in accuracy. Yi Ch'angjik was co-author.

Volume I. Fukuin Printing Company, 1901. 2nd edition, 61 pages, Taehan Sŏnggyo Sŏhoe, (printed by Fukuin) Seoul, 1903. 3rd edition, 70 pages. Published by Korean Religious Tract Society and Kwanghak Sŏp'o, Chong-no, Seoul, as Hulbert Educational Series, No 3, 1909.
Each of the 25 lessons introduces Chinese characters in compound words of two or three characters, giving the sound in Korean script, but not the meaning. The preface is in plain Korean script. There is a glossary of the Chinese characters used in the book, printed at the end in Korean alphabetical order.
The subject matter of the lessons is: 1 the earth; 2 races: 3 customs; 4 dress; 5 head-dress; 6 animals; 7 birds; 8 fish; 9 astronomy; 10 clouds; 11 rain; 12 snow; 13 thunder and lightning; 14 earthquakes; 15 volcanoes; 16 fruits; 17 arithmetic; 18 trade; 19 money; 20 time and time-pieces; 21 exercise; 22 sickness; 23 iron and steel; 24 lead; 25 work.

Volume II. Fukuin Printing Company, 1901. 70 pages. 2nd edition? 3rd edition, 1909, Korean Religious Tract Society and Kwanghak Sŏp'o, Seoul. 80 pages.
The preface is in pure Korean, but the lessons are slightly longer and the style is more difficult. The Chinese characters are used in phrase-groups of up to four characters. The new characters in each lesson are given singly, with the traditional meaning of each individual character as well as its sound. The glossary is like that in volume I. The lessons introduce narrative and make their moral points obliquely.
Subject matter: 1–3 the vision of Mirza (from Addison); 4–6 the skater and the wolves; 7 the *aurora borealis*; 8 the atmosphere; 9–16 Columbus discovers America; 17–19 the five senses; 20–21 the planets; 22–24 Leonidas and the three hundred Spartans; 25–27 the death of Little Paul ('What the waves were always saying', Chapter XVI of Dickens's *Dombey and son*); 28–31 Vesuvius (the death of the elder Pliny); 32–33 coal.

Volume III Fukuin Printing Company 1901, 82 pages. 2nd edition? 3rd edition, Korean Religious Tract Society and Kwanghak Sop'o 1909. 86 pages.
The preface is in plain Chinese, and the lessons are written in a heavily Chinese style which amounts to Chinese prose with Korean grammatical insertions (*t'o*). Otherwise modelled on

volume II.

Subject matter: 1–2 the Boston tea-party; 3–4 the battle of the Nile; 5 the pyramids; 6–7 the story of the diffident man; 8–9 Beethoven's *Moonlight Sonata*; 10–11 Alfred the Great; 12–13 the pearl elephant (a condensed translation of Rudyard Kipling's *Moti Guj— Mutineer* from *Life's Handicap*, 1891); 15 Grace Darling; 16 the North American Indian; 17–18 Crusoe's Man Friday; 19–21 the taking of the Bastille; 22–23 the assassination of Julius Caesar; 24–26 King Richard I; 27–30 Thomas à Becket; 31 Cincinnatus.

Volume IV *Yumong sokp'yŏn*. 1st edition 1904. 2nd edition, Korean Religious Tract Society (Hulbert Educational Series No 4) Seoul, 1907. 92 pages. 3rd edition, Korean Religious Tract Society and Kwanghak Sŏp'o, Seoul, 1909. (Hulbert Educational Series No 4) 110 pages.

Contains selections from twenty-seven Korean writers, printed in plain Chinese, drawn from a dozen Korean books. 756 new characters are introduced. Vocabularies and glossary modelled on those in volumes II and III.

The passages used are;

1–2 Ch'i Tzŭ (Kija) Extracts from the *Hung-fan*. (*Shu ching* ku wen text XXIV 1–16 and 17–34).

3 King Sejong; *Kyeju p'yŏn* (A warning against drink, KCPG VI Sejong, 15th year)

4 King Sukchong: *Ch'angp'a-p'yŏnju-do chi* ('The little boat'—a colophon on a painting. KCPG Sukchong 11th year 11th moon)

5 Sŏl Ch'ong: *Hwaju kye* (The warning of the Flower King, SGSG XLVI yŏlchŏn 6)

6 Ch'oe Ch'iwŏn: *Sang taesa sijung chang* ('To the grand preceptor'—an outline of Korean history. SGSG XLVI)

7–9 Yi Saek: *Chip'yŏng-hyŏn Miji-san Yunp'ir-am ki*. (Yunp'il Hermitage. TMS LXXIV 19.); *Namyang-bu Manghae-ru ki* (The Manghae Pavilion, TMS LXXVI 5,); *Un'gŭm-nu ki* otherwise called *Suwŏn-bu kaeksa chijŏng ki*. (The Cloud Silk Pavilion. TMS LXXIV 14)

10 Chŏng Mongju: *Kimhae sansŏng ki* (The walled city of Kimhae YJSN XXXII 5.)

11 Ha Yun: *P'oŭn sŏnsaeng chip sŏ* (Preface to the works of Chŏng Mongju. TMS XCIII 8)

12 Pyŏn Kyeryang: *P'oŭn sŏnsaeng sigo sŏ* (Preface to the poems of Chŏng Mongju. *P'oŭn munjip*, preface)

13 Chŏng Tojŏn: *Kŭnjŏng-jŏn sŏ* (The Audience Hall—a treatise on diligence. YJSN II 17)

14 Kwŏn Kŭn: *Sikp'a-jŏng ki* (The Sikp'a Pavilion. TMS LXXIX 18)

15 Yi Kyubo: *Kyeyang manghae chi* (A sea view. TMS CV 29)

16 Sŏ Kŏjŏng: *Sau-dang ki* (The hall of the Four Friends—ploughman, herdsman, fisherman and woodcutter. YJSN VII 19)

17 Sin Sukchu: *Un'gŭm-nu chungsu ki* (Repairing of the Un'gŭm Pavilion. Otherwise called *Suwŏn-bu tong-nu ki*. YJSN IX 4.

18–20 Ŏ Hyoch'ŏm: *P'ungsu-sŏl sangso* (A protest against geomancy. KCPG VII Sejong 26th year. TMS LVI 7, 8b8; 10b5)

21–22 Chŏng Inji: *Nakch'ŏn-jŏn sŏ* (The Nakch'on Pavilion. YJSN III 13 'Choja-do'.) *Hunmin chŏngŭm sŏ* (The native script. Postface to Sejong's *Hunmin chŏngŭm*. Text in MHPG CVIII 1a)

23 Kim Chongjik: *Hwanch'wi-jŏng ki* (The pavilion in the green. YJSN L 30)

24 Cho Wi: *Toksŏ-dang ki* (The hall of learning. YJSN III 23)

25–29 Yi I: *Sip'ye so* (Present day evils. *Yulgok chŏnsŏ* VII 27b4; 29a1; 33a1; 34b8)

30–31 Pak Hongmi: *Ch'ŏnggang pu* (The Blue River *fu*. Kwanp'o chip I 44); *Mongp'o sŏl* (The dream feast. *Kwanp'o chip* II 29)

32 Song Siyŏl: *P'oŭn sŏnsaeng chip chunggan sŏ* (Preface to collected works of Chŏng Mongju. *P'oŭn chip* preface)

33–34 Cho Kŭksŏn: *Anjŏng-dong yugo ki* (Life of Anjŏng) *Yagok chip* V 9)

35 Chŏng Kyŏngse: *Kukp'o ki* (The chrysanthemum garden. *Ubok chip* XV 17.)

36–45 Hong Yangho: *Pangan sa* (Freeing the wild goose IGC VIII 10) *Ch'ŏngp'a-ru ki* (The pavilion that listens to the waves IGC XIII 9) *Yoya ilch'ul ki* (Sunrise in Liaotung IGC XIII 35) *Niwa ki* (The hut in Chinkogae. IGC XIII 1) *Kyego-dang ki* (The schoolhouse IGC XIII 3) *Kyemun yŏnsu pu* (The gossamer mists of Kyemun IGC I 12) *Chŭng Hong*

sangsa Sŏnggi (Sangch'ŏl) kwi Namyang sŏ (A letter to Hong Chinsa IGC XI 18) *Soyŏng kŏsa Hong Sangch'ŏl chugap sŏ.* (Hong Chinsa's sixtieth birthday IGC XI 21) *Ssangch'ŏng-jŏng* ki (The Ssangch'ŏng Pavilion IGC XII 7) *Yŏngp'a-ru chungsu ki* (Reparing the Yŏngp'a Pavilion IGC XII 11).
46 Kang P'irho: *Puji-hŏn ki* (The house of ignorance. *Haeŭn yugo* XVI 11. Wrongly attributed by Gale to Hong Yangho)
47–48 Nam Kongch'ŏl: *Sŏgyang-nu* (The sunset pavilion. *Kwiŭn-dang chip* V 1. *Kŭmnŭng chip* XII 8) *Imsil hak ki* (Imsil studies. *Kwiŭn-dang chip* V 3)
49 Kang P'irho: *Siu-dang ki* (The house of care. *Haeŭn yugo* XVI 7)

6 *Sŏnggyŏng yori mundap*
Translation of the *Shorter catechism* of the presbyterian church. The first edition seems to have been in 1906. The 4th edition of 1916 had 52 pages.

7 *Rut'ŏ kaegyo kiryak*
A life of Martin Luther. Published in the name of Min Chunho, a teacher of Kyŏngsin School, by Kwanghak Sŏp'o, Seoul, 1908. 196 pages. Sometimes referred to as *Rodŭk kaegyo kiryak*. Yi Ch'angsik is named as copyreader. The back of the book contains an interesting list of educational books published by Kwanghak Sŏp'o, including titles by Yun Ch'iho, Chang Chiyŏn, Yu Kilchun.

8 *Yesu haengjŏk kinyŏm si*
'The Life of Christ in verse, with notes explanatory'. Christian Literature Society, Seoul 1911. 14 pages. A curious mnemonic, consisting of eight quatrains of eight-syllable verses, intended for children. The verses take up 3 pages and the rest of the pamphlet is explanations of Chinese Bible phrases and bible references. Yi Ch'angjik assisted.

9 *Yŏnghon p'yŏn*
The spirit of man. A popular presentation of the facts of the human mind, with chart, advertised in the CLS catalogue of 1911. 17 pages.

10 *Yesu-ŭi chaerim.*   See also above p 64.
A translation of *Jesus is coming* by William E Blackstone (Re-revised edition Chicago: Fleming H Revell Co 1908; Chicago Moody Bible Institute n.d.) CLS Seoul 1913. 267 pages.

11 *Yesu-ŭi in'gyŏk*
Translation of the *The manhood of the Master* by Henry Emerson Fosdick (1913), translated under the direction of J S Gale and F M Brockman (of Seoul YMCA) CLS Seoul 1921. 273pp.

12 *Ŭihoe t'ongyong kyuch'ik*
Robert's *Rules of Order*, prepared by J S Gale from T H Yun (Yun Ch'iho)'s translation. CLS 1916. 38 pages.

13 *Kuyak yep'yo*
Old Testament types and shadows. Written by J S Gale. CLS Seoul, 1923. 172 pages. Essays on biblical typology.

14 *Yŏn'gyŏng chwadam*
'The gospel as sung' by J S Gale and C C Yi (Yi Ch'angjik). CLS Seoul 1923. 203 pages. The gospel story told in a style suitable for old-fashioned chanting (arranged in phrases of 7 or 8 syllables). See above p 68.

15 *Sŏnyŏng taejo Taehak* ('Korean and English parallel text of *Ta-hsüeh*')
The title is usually translated as 'Great Learning', but Gale calls it the 'Higher Students'

Course', and attributes the work to 'Cheng-ja', by whom he means Tseng Ts'an, the disciple of Confucius traditionally regarded as author of the book. The Korean translation is the traditional *ŏnhae*. The Chinese text is given. CLS Seoul 1924. 33 pages.

16 *Yuryak hwangdo ki*
Translation of *The Swiss Family Robinson or Adventures on a desert island* by Johann Rudolf Wyss, Bern, 1813. Translated by J S Gale and Yi Wŏnmo. CLS Seoul 1924. 165 pages. (Previously serialized in *Kidok sinbo*)

17 *Yanggŭk t'amhŏm ki*
Polar exploration, by the Scottish explorer William Spiers Bruce (1911), translated from the Chinese of Loo Heng-seng by Yi Ch'angjik, Yi Wŏnmo, and James S Gale. CLS Seoul 1924. 232 pages. A text obtained from the Shanghai CLS.

18 *Yŏngmi sini-rok*
Strange stories from England and America translated by J S Gale and Yi Wŏnmo. CLS Seoul 1925. The stories included are: Washington Irving, *Rip van Winkle;* Walter Scott, *The tapestried chamber*; F P Humphrey, *Lucia Richmond* (Century Magazine, November 1890); *The missing bills (An unsolved mystery)* (Blackwood's Magazine, January 1874); Charles Nibbs, *Asman Bolta Hai* (Chambers' Journal, February 1924)

19 *So yŏngung* ('The little hero')
Little Lord Fauntleroy by Frances Hodgson Burnett (1849–1924) translated by J S Gale and Yi Wŏnmo. CLS Seoul 1925. 60 pages.

20 *Kŭruso p'yoryu ki*
Defoe's *Robinson Crusoe*, translated by J S Gale and Yi Wŏnmo. CLS Seoul, 1925. 88 pages.

21 *Kidok sŏngbŏm*
De Imitatione Christi by Thomas à Kempis (1380–1471) translated by Yi Wŏnmo. CLS Seoul 1925. 286 pages. Although his name does not appear in connection with the publication, Gale states in a letter that he worked on this translation. The translation was probably not complete. The original consists of four books: two of general counsel on the spiritual life, one on the interior dispositions of the soul, and a fourth on the Blessed Sacrament.

22 *Wap'yo chŏn*
Walter Scott's *The Talisman,* translated by J S Gale and Yi Wŏnmo. CLS Seoul, 1925. 101 pages.

23 *Sinyŏk sin'guyak chŏnso*
The bible translated by J S Gale, assisted by Yi Wŏnmo, Yi Kyosŭng, and Yi Ch'angjik. Published by Kidokkyo Ch'angmun-sa. Seoul, 1925. Old Testament 796 pages, New Testament 310 pages. (The testaments were also bound separately.)
   The preface is signed by Gale and Yi Wŏnmo, and says that help was also given by Pak Sŭngbong, Kim Tohŭi, Nam Chuwŏn and Cho Chongman. The translators made reference to the Hebrew Old Testament, the Septuagint, the Greek New Testament, the English Authorized and Revised versions, and the versions of Moffat and Luther, among others.
   This was the first translation of the bible into Korean published independently of the Bible Societies. See also above pp 72–74.

24 *Moja sŏnggyŏng mundap*
By J S Gale with Yi Ch'angjik. Twenty-five talks on bible characters between a mother and son. 87 pages. Mentioned in CLS catalogue 1933.

25 *Tokhye immun*
   The gate of virtue and wisdom by Griffith John, translated by J S Gale with H G Underwood.

122 pages. CLS catalogue 1933. John (1831–1912) was a pioneer Welsh congregationalist missionary to China who did much literary work there.

26 *Yesu haengjŏk yŏnp'yo*
A chronology of the life of Christ. A chart. 4th edition, CLS catalogue 1933.

27 *Nasaret moksu Yesu*
Jesus the carpenter of Nazareth by a layman (Robert Bird). 2nd edition revised, New York, 1891. Translated by Gale and Yi Wŏnmo. 288 pages. CLS catalogue 1933.

28 *Sado haengjŏn* The Acts of the Apostles, translated. See above p 26.
(1) 81 pages, metal type on Chinese paper, 1892
(2) 2nd edition, 63 pages. 1895
     (in these two editions God is called *Teusŭ* (Deus))
(3) 3rd edition, 63 pages. (*Teusŭ* changed to *Ch'ŏnju*) 1895
(4) 4th edition, 25 pages, western paper. (*Ch'ŏnju* changed to *Hananim*) 1896.
(5) 5th edition (*Hananim* changed to *Ch'ŏnju*) 1896

29 *Yohan pogŭm* St John's Gospel, translated. See above p 26.
(1) 56 pages, metal type on Chinese paper. 1895 (*Teusŭ*)
(2) 2nd edition. (*Ch'ŏnju*) 1895
(3) 3rd edition. 22 pages, western paper. (*Hananim*) 1896
(4) 4th edition. 22 pages. (*Ch'ŏnju*) 1896.

d Articles in Korean

It is impossible to do more than guess at what Gale wrote as contributions to Korean papers and magazines. Korean ephemera published before 1950 are difficult to trace. There are, however, three interesting articles in *Sinhak chinam*, the P'yŏngyang seminary magazine, for 1921: 'Yesuŭi moch'in Maria' is the Korean version of the essay on Mary mentioned at the end of the biography, page 87; and two other articles contain a translation of the Westminster confession.

e Unpublished writings and drafts

A number of diaries and notebooks are in the possession of Dr Gale's son and daughter, as well as two brief autobiographical statements. The family also preserves some reports to the CLS in typescript, a number of letters, and the index to the Bath library.

The Library of Congress, Washington DC, has five bibliographical manuscripts, one describing the 150 early christian Korean publications which Gale gave to the library.

A large number of unpublished draft translations are kept by Mr George Gale in Montreal. *P'alsang-nok* is complete. Sin Yuhan's *Trip to Japan 1718* completes part I only, and Kim Ch'angŏp's Peking diary is also incomplete. More or less complete versions of *Hŭngbu chŏn, Kŭmsu chŏn, Kŭm-pangul chŏn, Hong Kiltong chŏn,* and *Ongnu mong. Unyŏng chŏn* was typed out in September 1917.

Sixteen unpublished essays include nine written in Bath. 'Charles Dickens and oriental writers' for the Bath Dickens Fellowship, quotes the story of Dickens visiting a Chinese junk in London docks, taken from John Forster's *The life of Charles Dickens* (1872–4) II iii.

III A NOTE ON MATERIALS USED IN WRITING THE BIOGRAPHY AND BIBLIOGRAPHIES

Apart from the works mentioned in the bibliographies above and referred to directly in the course of the biography and notes, I have used a wide range of standard reference works in

English and Korean. On the Canadian background I also used Margaret Brown *MacGillivray of Shanghai* (Toronto 1968), J R Connon *The early history of Elora* (Elora 1930), *The historical atlas of the county of Wellington* (Toronto 1906), William Scott *Canadians in Korea* (Toronto 1970), *Alma through the years* (Anon. n.d.—John Mortimer, Elora, 1967), and *Knox College Monthly* 1888-90.

There is an account of the McAll Mission in P & C L Buhlmann *The joy of active service* (New York 1939).

Articles by Harriet Heron Gale appeared in *Children's work for children, Women's work for women,* and *The children's missionary.* John McNab wrote an attractive account of Gale in *In other tongues* (Toronto 1939).

Reports of the Bible Committee of Korea (1905-7), the British and Foreign Bible Society Korean Agency (1908-27), CLS (1911-31), the Librarian of Congress, Washington (1919, 1927, 1928), and the Chosen Mission of the Presbyterian Church USA contain much relevant matter. So do the periodicals published in Korea to which Gale himself contributed.

Ch'oe Chun wrote an account of Gale in *Sint'aeyang* magazine (October 1957 Seoul), 'Han'gugŭi uin chŏn I'. Most other Korean references to him add nothing not found elsewhere.

Some details have been checked from photographs, the inscriptions on the Gale graves at Yanghwa-jin, copies of Gale's degree certificates, his original YMCA missionary commission, Heron's royal patent granting the rank of *kasŏn taebu* (kept in Sungjŏn University Christian Museum, Seoul), and missionary letters in the possession of Dr S H Moffett.

Index